A QUICK
& DIRTY
GUIDE TO
WAR

A
QUICK & DIRTY GUIDE TO
WAR

BRIEFINGS ON PRESENT AND POTENTIAL WARS

REVISED EDITION

JAMES F. DUNNIGAN
& AUSTIN BAY

Quill
William Morrow
NEW YORK

It is the policy of William Morrow and Company, Inc., and its imprints and affiliates, recognizing the importance of preserving what has been written, to print the books we publish on acid-free paper, and we exert our best efforts to that end.

Library of Congress Cataloging-in-Publication Data

Dunnigan, James F.
　　A quick and dirty guide to war : revised edition: briefings on present and potential wars / by James F. Dunnigan and Austin Bay. — Rev.
　　　　p.　　cm.
　　Includes bibliographical references (p.　　) and index.
　　ISBN 0-688-10033-3
　　1. War.　2. World politics—1985–1995.　I. Bay, Austin.
II. Title.
U21.2.D83　1990
355′.033′0048—dc20　　　　　　　　　　　　　　　　　　　　　　　　91-4387
　　　　　　　　　　　　　　　　　　　　　　　　　　　　　　　　　　　　CIP

Printed in the United States of America

First Quill Edition

1 2 3 4 5 6 7 8 9 10

BOOK DESIGN BY PATRICE FODERO

To peace

PREFACE

The simulations and analyses for the original edition of *A Quick & Dirty Guide to War* were formulated in 1984, a year before its publication. Long lead time is unavoidable in the book business which makes writing about ongoing conflicts a dicey proposition.

Yet seven years later the analyses supporting those chapters have had "legs"—they have proven to be sound, solid, and accurate. Such success does not scientifically verify the book's methodology, but it does give the book a remarkable track record.

The journalistic explanation and historical sections provided readers with a colorful and fast summary of many complicated and complex political situations. There was little debate on that score; even a few nit-picking academic types admitted the book's broad scope and thrust packed a lot of accurate and useful information into a small and available package.

But critics unfamiliar with "war-gaming" or simulations methodology had trouble with "all the numbers" and the "Potential Outcome" projections of the various conflicts. One reviewer, a young woman writing for a major economic journal, dismissed the book as the work of "fantasists." She was particularly amused that we mentioned "Indian" and Native American conflicts and violence by animal rights activists as small "wars." In 1990 the Canadian Army attacked Mohawk "warriors" in a dispute in Quebec. The nominal subject was a golf course and a bridge, the real subject was Native American rights. Since 1985, violence by animal rights activists has, in a macabre fashion, emulated that of a number of European guerrilla groups. The animal rights fanatics, at least in their propaganda, speak of being at war with "science." Fantasy becomes reality, which most historians will admit is all too common.

Okay, Native Americans have real gripes and some of the animal rights activists are decidedly extreme in their protestations, but we were looking at the seeds of conflict, the seeds that grow into greater tragedies, and our analyses, which were accurate, challenged the young critic's notion of the world too strongly. Gloat?—not really, for that reviewer's reaction was expected and the book received far less of that light-caliber flak than anticipated. We admitted at the outset that we were experimenting and that what we were doing was risky, but unlike the Establishment academics, we're not "risk averse"—that's the pompous euphemism for intellectual cowardice.

In statistical terms, what was the "success" record of the original edition? Remember Twain's admonition about lies, damned lies, and statistics. But using a "power-weighted" basis for analyzing the "Potential Outcomes" accuracy, where the "most likely" outcome received "x" points for occurrence, other "mentioned outcomes" received points on a sliding scale if they occurred within the time frame projected, and a penalty was incurred if "what happened in reality" was not mentioned (or modeled) at all, the first edition scored a notch above 80 percent. Not a bad hit rate. Better than anything else around, except perhaps for the major national intelligence agencies. But then you can't pick up a copy of their forecasts in your local bookstore.

The biggest success was the Philippines. The biggest mistake was Nicaragua—at least so far. The Sandinistas are down but not out. But most of the other outcomes, like real life, were somewhere in between raving success and dismal failure. Take the projections in the "Central Front" chapter of the first edition—a chapter devoted to looking at the East-West bloc Cold War confrontation in Central Europe. In January 1984 we had already picked up on the downward trend in the Soviet economy. Of course, like almost everyone else in the world, we didn't know how deep the Soviet Union's economic failure was. Still, we had a good feel for the historical elements shaping the conflict, and armed with the limited economic data, knowledge of the Russians' recent political failure in the 1983 "Euromissile" crisis, and an appreciation of the cracks emerging in the Soviet Union's imperial edifice (Afghanistan, Poland, etc.), we came out with these as the third and fourth projections (of five) in our "political gaming":

"3. 10 percent chance before 1999: The Great Uprising. Local rebellions in Russia's East European 'ally' nations spread into a general uprising, and the fighting in Hungary, Czechoslovakia, and East Germany spills across the border. These allies have rebelled or been restive ever since they were liberated in 1945. In 1945 Yugoslavia successfully moved the Russian Army out of the country at gunpoint. In the 1950s East Germany and Hungary fought Russian tanks in the streets. In the 1960s Czechoslovakia was reoccupied, and the 1970s saw Poland get uppity. Rumania has been constantly uncooperative. Only little Bulgaria remains faithful. Russia has made concessions, but a permanent fix appears impossible. The East European allies are too corrupted by Western thought to have anything but contempt for their Russian overlords. Through the centuries, such testy allies eventually came to blows. If the Russians become too heavy-handed and the situation gets out of control, several allied states could rebel at once. The Hungarian Army resisted in 1956. The Russians feared the Czech Army would resist. The Russians hesitated to invade Poland in 1980 because of the volatile reputation of the Polish armed forces.

"4. 5 percent chance: The Empire Crumbles. There are plenty of internal and external threats to the empire that is Russia. Should an explosive combination of these problems occur, the resulting civil and/ or imperial conflict could spill over into Europe. This would not be a Russian invasion of Europe, but a European invasion of (or 'intervention in') Russia. This is the Russians' greatest fear and it lies behind their desire for security through strength . . ."

Maybe these projections wouldn't play in the State Department, but as some smart alecks might say, close enough for *non*government work—and certainly close enough to cue readers on what to look for on the historical horizon. The European "invasion" of Russia was political rather than military—thank God. The events occurred in the fifth year (1989) rather than the fifteenth (1999). In the 1986 paperback update of the book we also made the statement that Gorbachev would continue to pursue an "irrational version of security" based on keeping a massive military. (Though as of early 1991 the Soviet Army has only now begun to shrink, it looks as if the Russians mean it about downsizing their forces.) This pursuit of an irrational version of security—the squandering of billions of rubles on the military, as well as the failure of that strategy to frighten the West—began to bring the Russian Empire to its knees.

When the hardcover edition was published, one interviewer asked coauthor Austin Bay if all of *A Quick & Dirty Guide*'s numbers and quantitative analyses indicated that political science had become a "true science." Well, first off, "political science" is a misnomer. Both the term and the question mask several unfortunate attitudes, not the least of which is the inferiority complex of many scholars who aren't scientists and fear they should be. The answer is no, *A Quick & Dirty Guide* isn't the harbinger of any such baloney. Human beings don't reduce to mathematical thingamajigs, not yet anyway. Free will is a hellacious statistical variable. Quantitative analyses are tools, like an understanding of a nation's language, culture, art, literature, ethnic groups, geography, history, energy resources, and architecture. We'd like to propose a better moniker for studies like this one: Applied Humanities—bringing together good research, common sense, and an open, inquisitive mind.

ACKNOWLEDGMENTS

We wish to thank the following people for their help and advice in the research and preparation of this book: Frank Bay, Kathleen Ford Bay, Margaret Boeth, Alison Brown Cerier, Jack Dunnigan, Diane Goon, Larry Graham, James M. Hardesty, Sterling H. Hart, Paul Henze, Ken Hoffman, Bonnie Hoskins, Joseph Jacobson, John Koham, Lionel Leventhal, Jim Llamas, Doug MacCaskill, Ray Macedonia, Jay Maloney, Bill Martel, Howard Miller (for the University of Texas Library card) Sylvia Morrison, Bill Murphy, Steven Patrick, Christina Pogoloff, Allen Rehm, Jim Simon, John Stewart, Dave Tschanz, Dick Weary, Bob Wood, and Kathy Antrim, Bonnie Crisalli, and Susan Leon.

The maps were prepared by Marie Frederick of Washington, D.C., with the assistance of Marcia Scott.

We would like especially to thank A. A. Nofi for his invaluable research assistance, counsel, constructive criticism, energy, sense of humor, professionalism, erudition, and particularly his advice on the charts.

CONTENTS

INTRODUCTION

Wars don't just happen. Organized violence, like the weather, is never a complete surprise. There are signs and long-term trends. You cannot predict the exact outcome of a war or battle any more than you can predict exactly what the weather will be at noon tomorrow. You can, however, analyze past and ongoing conflicts and use the results to project the major trends shaping similar current and future events.

No one can predict an outbreak of war by psychic magic or mathematical hocus-pocus. Intelligence analysts, however, can estimate the likelihood of war or armed conflict in the same way meteorologists predict a hurricane's path. Weather forecasters collect current weather data, compare the most reliable information with evidence gained from past experience, add a large dose of intuition and probability, then stick their necks out and put a storm track on the weather map. This track is not as much a prediction as it is a projection of what could occur. Still, this projection may have extraordinary utility and is useful for activating flood control procedures, warning local populations, formulating plans of evacuation, and analyzing the vulnerability of coastal lowlands.

The daily press tends to play down the predictability of wars. This is understandable as sameness does not sell newspapers or induce one to view TV news. Wars are easier to sort out than the news suggests. This does not imply that all journalists indulge in sensationalism; that is simply not the case, though TV reporting has yet to resolve successfully the conflict between the camera's need for drama and the journalist's commitment to accurate reporting. Actually, the problem with the daily press is often that it does its job too well in recording and reporting the events of the last twenty-four hours. But such reports tend to be nearsighted—a sound historical and contextual focus is lost in the magnifications of immediate headlines.

While newspapers come to conclusions too quickly, the prediction professionals in think tanks have the opposite problem: They seem never to come to a conclusion, which puts military leaders and citizens in a predicament. The press often screams out sensational predictions and conclusions while government officials are served by think tank advisers who essentially say that definitive conclusions are impossible to reach.

It's very true that no one can predict the future with any precision. At the same time, government leaders, and the citizens who elect them, must plan for and make decisions about the probable future. Military and diplomatic analyses must be made, and defense and state department budgets must be planned. Even deciding to do nothing is a decision, and often the least favorable one. How then do decisions usually get made?

The two primary sources of decision-influencing information, the press and the experts, are used quite differently. The free press, while often suspect because of the political leanings of reporters and editors, is highly regarded for its immediacy and the range of conclusions it provides. Moreover, press conclusions are in the open and subject to useful criticism and debate. At least this gives the government decision maker and the citizen a variety of analyses from which to choose and adapt.

Then we have the experts. There exists within the U.S. government a multibillion-dollar-a-year intelligence and analysis community. These are the experts who, with a worldwide network of agents, analysts, and electronic wizardry, are charged with creating an official analysis of events and future prospects. This group is responsible only to the decision makers they support, and this creates a curious relationship. These experts, given their enormous resources and professional pride, strive for an academic perfectionism. This often leads to an extensive, expensive, and complex analysis of every topic under study—whether the subject is Russian wheat production, bee excrement, or toenail growth rates of nineteen-year-old corporals testing a new jungle boot. The employers of the experts usually have neither the time nor the experience to grasp all the data they are given. The usual result is unfortunate. The decision makers reach their conclusions based on press information, gossip, and very brief summaries of the massive research done for them (2,532 pages of analysis and research can shrink to a single three- by five-inch briefing card). Expert information often becomes an after-the-act justification for conclusions the decision makers have already reached. Thus the tail (decision makers' conclusions) wags the dog (research done by the appointed experts).

This absurd situation is caused in part by the security requirements under which the experts operate. One must have a security clearance to work on or review all of the research. Much of this work is thus subject to very little criticism and informed debate. In addition, massive amounts of raw information often tend to blur the situation rather than illuminate it. Common sense gets lost in the metric shuffle of increasingly arcane forms of analysis.

Bureaucratic analyses also suffer from the committee problem. As in any large organization, there are more chiefs than Indians in the intelligence community. All these chiefs must justify their existence and often do so during uninformed debates on the validity of the research done and preliminary conclusions reached.

The research gatherers and analysts (the Indians) are often quite competent and dedicated. So are their superiors (the chiefs). But many potential futures are created with no easy way of choosing the "official" one. Sharp analysis dulls, and clarity becomes bureaucratic murkiness.

Remember that we are attempting to project the outcome of wars that have not yet been fought (and may never, one hopes, be fought) or, if the conflicts are in progress, have not concluded. The potential outcomes have varying implications for the size and compositions of defense budgets and armed forces. The size of these budgets also has serious effects on the economies that produce the funds through taxation. Thus the decision makers' most immediate problem is not how correct their experts are, but how well any decisions can be "sold" to other interest groups within the government and nation. Accurate analysis and projection become secondary to the more immediate problem of getting enough people to agree on a course of action and move forward to a conclusion. The defense intelligence and analysis community fails so often not because of a lack of skill or resources, but because there are so few people with the ability, power, or sheer nerve to choose from the often unpleasant conclusions presented. Ugly realities are often swept aside in favor of more palatable political pictures. The officials' version is generally the more expedient, not the most accurate, product of billions of dollars of research and analysis.

Our approach in presenting a lot of data is to be open, straightforward, even simple. We try to explain, but we leave a lot of interpretation to you. Most of you are citizens, taxpayers (probably), and voters (we hope). What you have here in this book is often no more than many military and political decision makers have available when crucial decisions must be made. As several readers of the manuscript pointed out, we have given a complex body of knowledge manageable form. Observe and reach your own conclusions.

This book covers several current major wars and violent political conflicts, ongoing and potential. It explores the geographical factors and historical trends affecting these conflicts, takes a look at the human beings involved, then focuses on the present and possible future conflicts.

The key to understanding current wars, and their likely development, is knowledge of the fundamentals. We look at the political, ethnic, and economic makeups of the participating societies, the local geography, the societies' essential history, and the capabilities of their armed forces. This is the foundation for a conflict assessment.

If you can "predict" the past with such tools (and historians have been "predicting" the past and present for centuries), you can expect to have a better understanding of the present and future.

While this book is nonfiction, it makes many potentially, and one hopes ultimately, fictitious projections. Portraying the future is a popular spectator sport, but the spectators' wrath will fall on those who fail too often to divine events that have not yet happened.

Our primary technique in projecting the future is first to predict the past, with the idea that the future is an extension of the past. Details may differ, but patterns remain remarkably consistent: Human nature hasn't changed; time is doing its thing; some groups are winning, some losing; most people continue to suffer and reproduce.

World wars I and II could be seen incubating in the Balkans, Central Europe, and northern China. Today the Middle East is a primary source of potential world conflict. How do we know this? We compile data, turn the data into lists employing commonly used geopolitical factors like population and gross domestic product (GDP, or the total value of domestic goods and services produced yearly by a country), sort through the lists, then take a qualitative and quantitative look at the new arrangements of information. In some cases we applied simple statistical mathematical analyses to the information to create the conflict models that lie behind this book. Other analyses relied more heavily on geographical, historical, or political "gaming" to produce potential outcomes. The war chart at the end of the book, which was prepared through this method, clearly shows that the Middle East in general and the Persian Gulf in particular are steady producers of little wars. Out of such conflicts, world wars grow.

There is nothing mysterious or particularly difficult about this technique. Common sense, intuition, and recent headlines might tell you that the Middle East is the world's most dangerous trouble spot. However, when all the trends are laid out in a comparative manner, you begin to get a better picture of why this is true, where trouble comes from, and where the trouble might lead.

Data about armed conflict are relatively easy to find. Enterprising journalists and opposition politicians spend a great deal of energy collecting and reporting this information. An armed confrontation's causes, however, are often more obscure. History and geography give the best clues. Geopolitical interests rarely change, though sometimes the actors do. People have to eat and find shelter. Nations have to feed their people and maintain some degree of order. Our analysis of the available evidence relies on such primary human concerns. When one gets fancy and tries to guess the specific reasons for specific actions or policies, one generally walks where the ground is not. Experience teaches the analyst to guess where the ground might be.

There may be a large number of tactical options, but there are relatively few strategies. Strategy usually takes place on such a grand scale that one can guess with reasonable accuracy what strategic path a group has chosen to take. We assume that survival is the basic human strategy. A group of people can become a community of farmers—that's one strategic option for survival. Another group can become a gang of thieves. Although a couple of bad crops may turn the farmers into thieves, trends begin to emerge. The thieves, if they are to survive as thieves, must sharpen their wilier skills. Farmers forced to become thieves have to learn the trade from point zero, or hire some thieves to do their dirty work— yet another strategy. Farmers harassed by thieves can buy them off, which may work if the thieves are just hungry, or they can fight the crooks. Or perhaps the farmers can hire a few samurai to protect them from theft. (The movie *The Seven Samurai* is a detailed look at this strategy.) One can substitute oil for crops, nations for farmers and thieves, fighter-bombers for samurai.

This book focuses on basic strategies. Just as opposing armies keep track of each other by building up data over time, we kept track of a number of conflicts. Patterns begin to emerge. An analyst would call it a picture of the situation. A few good guesses about "state secrets" enhance the picture. Governments attempt to keep military secrets, but over time most details leak out. People can't keep their mouths shut, reporters have to write stories.

As we mentioned earlier, weather forecasting is a good analogy for this method of analysis. A computer powerful enough to model all the essential elements of a weather system has not yet been developed, and given the chaos of reality, trying to define with certainty what those essential elements are might be a fruitless pursuit. However, we can and do generate useful weather forecasts, most of which rely on analyses of past weather events. Farming has long been dependent on such crude but useful predictions. It would be helpful, but not essential, for a farmer to know exactly how much rain there would be in a given growing season. Knowledge of when the first and last frosts will occur would also be useful but isn't absolutely necessary. Farmers get by with a weather almanac of past events and an ability to judge the present situation.

Judging contemporary warfare and the potential for future wars is somewhat more complex than judging weather patterns. Herein we provide you with an almanac of past and current events. Add your judgment and you have as good a means as any for analyzing the course of present and future armed conflicts.

HOW TO USE THIS BOOK

Each intelligence briefing or chapter consists of ten or eleven complementary sections, plus appropriate appendixes. The authors designed the book so that the reader, usually a taxpayer financing the departments of state and defense, has a chance to play the role of highfalutin politico or military officer. In a very real sense the book is an adult role-playing game, with the reader as decision maker and the authors as briefers.

These briefings are not designed to be exhaustive. A briefing without some brevity isn't very functional. The challenge to both authors and reader is to do justice to the complexities of the issues—which entails including a certain amount of detail—while making the information readily available to someone who has to be at work on time. Most people don't have the time to become "experts." This book takes that into account. There is some repetition from section to section (or chapter to chapter)—in most cases just a phrase or sentence—because rather than refer you to another page for an item, we duplicate it where needed. We found that readers appreciated this, so don't let it bother you (if you tend to dislike such things). Most people use this book as a reference, not something to be read straight through.

Reading each chapter from start to finish will provide a more thorough description of each conflict. We know, however, that many of you will require only certain kinds of information, such as who are the regional powers interested in a specific situation. If that's what you want to know, then go straight to the Regional Powers and Power Interest Indicator

Chart(s) in the chapter. If you understand the organization of each chapter and its sections you can then locate the information you want.

INTRODUCTION

Gives a summary of what is covered in the chapter. The section also includes a brief description of who is fighting over what.

SOURCE OF CONFLICT

Contains a brief description of how the situation became a conflict. Often outlines the major causes of the conflict and provides preparatory information that will be expanded upon in the "Geography" and "History" sections.

WHO'S INVOLVED

Describes the important players in the conflict.

GEOGRAPHY

Analyzes the fundamental geographic considerations involved. Geographic considerations are of vital importance and, in geographically ignorant nations such as the United States (at least according to recent academic surveys), will, one hopes, open a few minds.

HISTORY

Describes some of the more important historical events still affecting the region and attempts to take the situation up to fall 1990. In some chapters ("Lebanon," for example) in which there is a lot of history, this portion will be more expansive.

LOCAL POLITICS

Gives an in-depth look at some of the area's more peculiar political participants.

Often this section deals with personalities and the organizations they inspire. In certain large nations like China, organizations totally predominate. In smaller nations like Burma, for example, organizations dominate but personalities get more ink. Americans in general lose sight of just how divided a population can be politically. This section demonstrates how fractured many nations are.

POLITICAL TREND CHARTS

Provide a quick and quantitative assessment at a particular nation's prospects for the 1990s. The charts are not meant to be anything more than "good guesses" drawn from the authors' research into the region. In several cases we "create" a theoretical nation that could split from existing nation-states. (For example, a "Kurdistan" forming at the expense of Turkey and Iraq.) The charts examine the government type in 1990 and rate that government's effectiveness and stability on a comparative scale. A guess is made at the kind of government you might find in the nation in 1996, based on political trends. (In many cases we hope we are dead wrong.) The nation's "political cohesion" (a rough estimate of its ability to remain a nation) is rated. The comparative level of government repression is estimated for 1990 and another estimate is made for 1996. (Is this nation's government more or less likely to allow free speech and free expression?) Economic development trends and an "education status" are also projected. These short charts have already stirred debate, which is good. Readers and critics are encouraged to construct their own.

Sample Political Trend Chart

(This is a chart of a "created" theoretical nation that could split from surrounding existing states. It contains only a 1996 column since, of course, it didn't exist in 1990. Of course, it may not exist in 1996 either.)

"Kurdistan" (Carved from Turkey and Iraq)

Not much here except bare mountains, tough people, and oil in Kirkuk. That's the plus in all the poverty.

	1996 (Authoritarian Coalition)
Government Effectiveness	3
Government Stability	2
Political Cohesion	6
Repression Level	7
Economic Development	1+
Education Status	1−

NOTE: 0 = minimum; 9 = maximum.

Government effectiveness—How effective will this government be in achieving order and imposing its will? The lower the number, the less effective are its capabilities.

Government stability—How stable is this government? Can it be overthrown? The lower the number the more likely it will collapse, either by vote or by gun.

Political cohesion—A lower level indicates a tendency toward civil disorder and civil war.

Repression level—The higher the level the more oppressive the conditions. At some point repression demands revolution.

Economic development—A very rough gauge that combines current economic output with estimates of current and future economic development. It is an attempt to answer the question: Will this nation get wealthier over the next few years? Poverty breeds conflict.

Education status—This is drawn from level of literacy and quality of education resources in the country. Poorly educated populaces are a drag on economic development.

REGIONAL POWERS AND POWER INTEREST INDICATOR CHARTS

Attempt to provide a "comparative quantitative rating" of the major national (and sometimes subnational) players' economic, historical, political, and military interests in various aspects of the conflict under discussion. They also provide an analysis of the participants' "comparative Force Generation Potential" (FGP). The FGP shown on the chart is relative to the specific conflict only. A rating of "9+" means a particular player can bring overwhelming power to bear in that conflict. (There are no 9+ ratings in this book.) A "0−" would indicate that the player can't even mount a decent street demonstration.

Each player's ability to intervene diplomatically and politically is also rated. In several instances a nation's ability to contribute to regional economic development is rated as well.

PARTICIPANT STRATEGIES AND GOALS

Takes a practical view of the political-military strategies and options of the players. It draws on information in the entire chapter to synthesize a view of participant aims.

This section attempts to dispense with volumes of superfluous detail that usually surround a current conflict. While not slighting the numerous undertones of a situation, a clear description of who wants what from whom goes a long way to putting each conflict into better perspective.

POTENTIAL OUTCOMES

Gives the reader a look at possible futures, depending on certain events. Consider this to be the authors' betting line, and the most controversial aspect of the book.

COST OF WAR

Provides (in some chapters) estimates of the fiscal and human costs of the conflict. The cost of any war is expressed in two currencies: lives and material wealth. Wealthy nations generally fight a war of matériel. Life is precious, so they can afford to throw wealth into the battle instead of lives. Poor nations have nothing to commit but lives. Wars between nations with material resources are more likely to escalate. Warfare between less wealthy nations tends to be bloodier, assuming the combatants can afford sufficient weapons to fight more than one or two battles.

Even without a lot of weaponry, warfare in poor nations can cause numerous nonbattle deaths. Civilians flee the areas where fighting occurs. Deprived of their normal shelter and sources of food and other support, the refugees are more prone to disease and death. War is hardest on the youngest and the oldest refugees.

When large populations are forced to flee for extended periods, ugly situations often arise in the areas they flee to. Their new neighbors are rarely pleased with the descending horde of strangers, and frictions usually develop which frequently lead to another war.

The purely wealth-destroying aspects of warfare often have a curious effect. If the population is not seriously depleted and is given some means to rebuild, the result will often be a reconstruction superior to prewar conditions. Losing a war, however, is a very expensive way to revive one's industrial infrastructure.

Still, few people really consider what the differences might be if the destruction of war had not taken place. The afflicted populations usually move forward, carrying their hatred with them. They are guided not by visions of what the future might have been without war, but by the primordial urge for revenge. Turning that urge into a reality is, over time, the highest cost of any war, for it provides the psychological framework for the next bloodletting.

What Kind of War

Describes what kind of fighting is likely to take place in the conflicts described in the chapter.

Appendices

Provides more background information or additional analyses for the reader who is interested in more specific information and the sidelights involved in each conflict. In some cases, exotic items are tossed in so the reader can spice up a dragging cocktail party conversation.

Quick Looks

Gives short descriptions of either interesting local situations that we felt should be highlighted or of conflicts that are analogues of wars more exhaustively discussed in other chapters.

Data Bank on Wars Present and Potential

Combines all the conflicts discussed in the preceding chapters, plus several dozen other wars, into several truly "quick and dirty" charts. The introductions to these chapters tell how they can enhance the information found in the other chapters.

PART ONE
THE MIDDLE EAST

In an arc of death and destruction stretching from Afghanistan through the Persian Gulf to the back alleys of Beirut, the Middle East has become the most volatile region of the late twentieth century. A combination of recent oil wealth and ancient antagonisms have combined to produce an ever-expanding list of grievances and the means to attempt resolving them by force of arms.

CHAPTER 1

LEBANON:
THE CRUSADERS' CHILDREN

*. . . let fire come out of the bramble
and devour the cedars of Lebanon.*

Judges 9:15

INTRODUCTION

Since 1975 civil war has raged in Lebanon. Israel and Syria have taken sides, sometimes with the same factions. Iranian-sponsored religious radicals, refugee Palestinians, terrorist clans, and superpower and regional power intrigue feed the violence.

For the last thousand years Lebanon has been an uneasy collection of Christians and outcast Muslim sects. Until independence in 1943, the peace was kept by outside rulers. Independence, and the influx of a million Palestinians since the creation of Israel in 1948, has upset the fragile balance between Christian and Muslim. A dozen or so religious warlords with crosses or scimitars supplemented by high explosives defend their fiefs' millennium of ethnic and religious identity against (1) an imperial vision of a "Greater Syria," (2) displaced Palestinians, (3) Israeli intrigue, (4) the warlord next door. Involved are armed religious factions, Syria, Israel, a down-but-not-out PLO, Iranian agents, come-and-go peacekeepers, and the innocent and not-so-innocent caught in between. The chaos and conflict in Lebanon refuse to abate.

SOURCE OF CONFLICT

Lebanon is filled with simplistic historical and psychological analogies. It is also filled with armed men who believe in them. U.S. Marines bivouacked around Beirut International Airport were pacifiers and liberators to some, and another form of Crusader to others, this time wearing camouflage fatigues instead of armor.

Lebanon in the 1940s, 1950s, and 1960s seemed like an oasis of tolerance, where Maronites, Greek Orthodox, Sunni Muslims, and Shiites lived together in a sort of Middle Eastern Switzerland. Arab princes and businessmen from orthodox Muslim countries ogled the girls, drank, and did their banking. The underground trade with Israel flourished—after all, many Lebanese said, this is Phoenicia, we'll sell to anybody. But displaced Palestinians living in refugee camps weren't part of the consensus, nor were the Syrians who envisioned Lebanon as an integral part of "Greater Syria." Those who saw Lebanon in the late 1970s got a quick view of the eleventh and twelfth centuries; with no outside power in total control, the uneasy consensus returned to its armed fragments.

The current conflict in Lebanon is technologically and politically complex. Combat ranges from sniping and unorganized street fights to sophisticated electronic warfare and the use of surface-to-surface missiles. The weapons and tactics reflect the spectrum of battle from stone-throwing neighbor against stone-throwing neighbor to nuclear power against nuclear power; in some cases, however, the local neighborhoods have weapons almost as sophisticated as those of the superpower troops, and the local soldiers have more opportunity and a greater willingness to use them.

The various Lebanese factions have displayed a political savvy that Washington and other world capitals have not matched. But then the constant struggle for political survival has honed their skills. Jerusalem and Damascus understand them somewhat better.

Three problems lie at the core of the conflict:

1. What should be done with the Arab Christians, including a substantial minority of the Palestinian Christians?
2. Where should the Palestinians go since the creation of Israel?
3. How will the imperial ambitions of Syria be stopped or accommodated?

Obviously, the local trouble in Lebanon intertwines with the regional troubles of Israel and Syria (see chapters 2 and 3).

The agreement of 1932 that gave the then-majority of Christian Lebanese guaranteed control of the major governmental functions has been outdated by demographics: Because of birthrates and immigration, the

Muslims now outnumber the Christians three to two. Several hundred thousand of the more well-off Christians have left the country, if only because they could afford to. The Palestinian problem is code-named "the overall Middle East settlement." Diplomatic rhetoric, Arab-Israeli wars, the Israeli invasion of Lebanon in 1982, Israeli and Palestinian conflict in the West Bank area, and continuing international negotiations have not resolved it. Arabs who openly settle with Israel get killed: Anwar Sadat was shot and Bashir Gemayel was blown to bits. Political intrigue in Damascus and "peacekeeping" Syrian Army units at the border and in the Bekaa Valley reinforce questionable Syrian historical claims.

The role of other outside peacekeepers in Lebanon is not news. When Turkish invaders took control in 1517, the local fighting diminished. Turkish political control in Lebanon was not absolute and the area still experienced the occasional factional dispute, one in 1860 being particularly bloody. After the Ottoman (Turkish) Empire collapsed in 1918, the British and French, under a League of Nations mandate, kept an imperial pressure on the local instability. In 1958 American Marines intervened and took the role of strong outsider ready to keep the peace. Vietnam changed the Middle East's perception of the Marines and produced a United States that was politically reluctant to take unilateral military action.

Today, the French and Americans hope for a stable eastern Mediterranean. The Syrians, no longer certain of Russian political and military support, still seek to reconstruct a "Greater Syria" from the ashes of Lebanon's internecine fighting. The Russians still demand "a say in the Middle East." Covert terror organizations representing the bloody splinters of the political edge seek to overturn any negotiations that don't conform to their precise view of the world. Iraq's Kuwait debacle has its effects. In Iran, its Shiite Islamic revolutionaries, and a violent cohort of local ideologues still pursue former ayatollah Ruhollah Khomeini's vision: Like decadent Saladins they seek to throw the West back across the Bosporous, or perhaps the English Channel.

Historical note: The ayatollah's vision is a historical slight to Saladin, who was quite chivalrous to his enemies. Khomeini was not.

WHO'S INVOLVED

Syria—President Hafez al-Assad must keep his state militarized in order to maintain control of the populace. But almost all of the Syrian internal political factions have visions of a "Greater Syria," which encompasses Lebanon, Jordan, and Israel. Since the late 1970s, Syria has stationed approximately 30,000 troops in the Bekaa Valley—25,000 of which were officially mandated by the Arab League to "keep the peace"—with another 10,000 to 12,000 in areas in and around Beirut. Syrian involvement in Lebanon limits Syria's capabilities against Iraq.

Israel—Operation Peace in Galilee in 1982 brought the Israel Defense Forces (IDF) to Beirut, and consolidation of pro-Israeli Lebanese in the south and subsequent Israeli withdrawal effectively partitioned the country. Israel regularly bombs terrorist facilities in Lebanon and launches airmobile infantry and armor raids into southern Lebanon.

Israeli-Arab allies—These are Christian and Shiite militias near the southern border, mostly in "Haddad-land." The pro-Israeli militia has some 3,000 men under arms.

Shiites—At 1.1 million people, Shiites are the single most populous group in Lebanon. The same Islamic sect as Iran, they live in Beirut's southern suburbs, south Lebanon, and Baalbek region.

Iranian-controlled Shiites—A small but most explosive group, this sect takes credit for blowing up the U.S. embassy and attacking the French and American peacekeepers. It may number as few as three hundred.

Maronite Christians—Being 700,000 strong, they control a large portion of Lebanon's wealth and inhabit east Beirut and north-central Lebanon. They are the most powerful of all Christian groups in the Arab world, though by no means the most numerous. (According to the most accurate data, the Greek Orthodox are the most numerous.) At first a schismatic sect named for the fifth-century hermit Saint Maron, the Maronites trace their origin to the Orontes River valley area in Syria (near Hama, one of the sites of anti-Assad Syrian rebellions and massacre of civilians by Syrian government troops). Then they fled from the Orontes region to escape the seventh-century Muslim onslaught and settled in the isolated Mount Lebanon area. Some claim ancestors among original first-century Christian converts in Lebanon.

Druze—An Islamic sect with 300,000 living in Lebanon, they inhabit the Shuf Mountains, Aleih, and Hasbeya (over 50,000 live in Israel, 100,000 in Syria, and 13,000 in the occupied Golan Heights). The Druze have served with distinction in the IDF and the Israeli Druze have provided support for the Lebanese Druze.

The Druze sect dates from the tenth century. Founded in Egypt by Caliph Hakim of the Shia dynasty of the Fatimids, the sect came to the

Lebanese Mountains in order to escape persecution. The Druze have, like the Christians, been severely persecuted by larger and more powerful Muslim groups. They have a mystical tradition and believe in emanations of Allah and the transmigration of the soul. They also believe Caliph Hakim isn't dead and that he will reappear to lead them to victory and salvation. Only a small minority of Druze are ever initiated into the deeper mysteries of the sect. They conceal their beliefs from outside groups, a practice called *taqiyya*, which gives them a strong internal identity and extreme distrust for outside interference. Other Muslims consider the Druze to be heretics. (In the Middle East, heresy is punishable by death.) Nevertheless, the Druze have a long tradition of tolerance for other religious faiths, provided the others leave them alone.

Sunnis—These are "Mainline" Muslims, 600,000 strong, who live in West Beirut, Sidon, Tripoli, and Akkar.

PLO—The Palestine Liberation Organization may still have 5,000 to 7,000 loyalist troops in Lebanon.

PLO Factions—These are various groups, most controlled by Syria, with a total of about 15,000 troops.

Palestinians—Depending on whose story you hear, these Palestinians either left Israel on their own initiative or were expelled. They are victimized by fellow Arabs, the Israelis, and the PLO; they wait, hunger, and die in the refugee camps. There are approximately 450,000 in Lebanon.

Greek Orthodox—Christian but not always allied with the Maronites, 400,000 strong, they live in Al Koura, and East and West Beirut. Many claim, with perhaps more legitimacy than the Maronites, to be the descendants of first-century Christian converts.

Armenians—Both Orthodox and Catholic, they are 250,000 strong and live in East and West Beirut and Anjar.

Melchites—This Christian sect, 250,000 strong, lives in Christian districts.

Protestants—This group, 100,000 strong, includes other Christian minorities, who live in West Beirut (near the American University) and Tripoli.

United Nations and various multinational peacekeeping forces—Italians, Americans, Fijians, Senegalese, Irish, etc., and the Secretary General all come and go. The purpose of their being in Lebanon is to avoid superpower confrontation and another Arab-Israeli war.

France—France deserves special recognition as a result of its long historical interest and political involvement in Lebanon. In 1536 the Turks recognized the French as protectors of all European and Asian Christians in the Turkish empire. The Maronites have a phrase *"inna faransa immana hanuna,"* which translates as "truly France is our benevolent mother." In a surprisingly consistent manner, though under a different political guise, France continues its historical role.

United States—Strong support for a political settlement and a strong Sixth Fleet mark U.S. involvement in Lebanon.

Russia—As of 1990, Russia still maintained antiaircraft troops in Syria (manning SA-5 long-range antiaircraft sites and radars). Russia's taste for confrontation is on the wane.

Iraq—Iraq has supplied arms to the Maronites. After the crushing defeat in Kuwait, all that's left is the terror card.

GEOGRAPHY

Mountains provide safety for their inhabitants by isolating them from outside aggressors. Isolation can also lead to factionalization. Foreigners usually fail to appreciate the mountainous character of Lebanon.

Still, the country's 10,450 square kilometers are remarkably diverse. There are sandy beaches along the coast, fertile valleys, and 3,000-meter-high snowcapped peaks. Tourist brochures usually focus on the old Phoenician ports of Sidon and Tyre (or what was downtown Beirut), not on the two mountain ranges that enclose the Bekaa Valley. In fact, the narrow coastal strip is rarely more than 3 kilometers wide.

The Lebanon Mountains rise from the rocky Mediterranean coast. The Anti-Lebanon Mountains, with snowcapped Mount Hermon by the Israeli border, slope eastward from the Bekaa to Syria. The Bekaa Valley is barely more than 10 kilometers wide.

Lebanon at its broadest part is almost 60 kilometers. Its length is approximately 225 kilometers. South and east of Beirut lie the Shuf Mountains, part of the first rugged coastal range, which many Druze inhabit. North, between Beirut and Tripoli in the Lebanon Mountains, runs a series of rugged east-west valleys (Marounistan), the traditional home of the Maronites. Between the northern port of Tripoli and the Syrian border lies the Akkar, a fertile agricultural plain. The Litani River drains both the Lebanon and the Anti-Lebanon mountains via the Bekaa Valley, then bends west to empty into the Mediterranean, drawing a significant political and tactical line across southern Lebanon just north

of Tyre. The major east-west route is the Beirut-Damascus highway, a traffic artery easily severed in either mountain range.

The isolation that made the Lebanese mountains attractive to dissidents has been somewhat overcome by civil engineers and military technology. Although the road network is primitive by European standards, armored forces backed by infantry can move rapidly through the region. Roadnets are extensive enough that truck-borne terrorist attacks, like that on the U.S. Marine compound at the Beirut International Airport in October 1983, are relatively easy to execute. Helicopters can rapidly move Israeli paratroopers (or other raiders) in and out of the region. Finally, strong-points and fortifications that could slow down or resist Crusader or Muslim sieges cannot stand up to intense air strikes.

HISTORY

Lebanon's once numerous cedars provided the resins required for Egyptian mummification. They also provided the planks for Phoenician ships sailing throughout the Mediterranean and beyond the Pillars of Hercules (Gibraltar). Their backs protected by the mountains, the early Phoenicians, from about 1500 B.C. on, used the sea for communication and trade. Carthage, Rome's ancient enemy, was a Phoenician colony.

The mountain backlanders were very similar to their Canaanite neighbors to the south; shepherds and subsistence farmers, they worshipped Baal, one of the Old Testament's false gods. For centuries to come, no matter who was the current imperial ruler (Hittite, Assyrian, Roman, Byzantine, Arab, and, later, French and British), the mountaineers were generally left alone as they paid taxes and didn't interfere with trade and communications.

The collapse of Byzantine control in the face of the seventh-century Muslim invasion framed the present-day set of affairs. Initially the Muslims were tolerant of Christians and Jews, whom Muhammad called "people of the book." But this attitude changed. How it changed depends on the religion and ethnic identity of who tells the story, but conflicts erupted, exacerbated by Byzantium's attempts to retake the region.

Though by no means the only Christian sect in the area, the Maronites began to rise in prominence. They saw the Greek Orthodox as direct beneficiaries of Constantinople and the Muslims as the imperialist masters. In the eleventh century the Druze, fleeing persecution, began to enter Lebanon in significant numbers. When the Crusaders arrived in the eleventh and twelfth centuries, the Maronites viewed the westerners as their protectors. The West at the time meant the Western church. In 1180 the Maronites recognized the pope in Rome as the leader of all Chris- tendom. It was a purely political kind of recognition—the Maronite lit- urgy remained written in Syriac. Later papal decisions were ignored as irrelevant, since communication with Rome often lapsed for years. But the Maronites didn't find bliss with the Crusaders and their subsequent Latin states, so they, along with the Druze, engaged in several rebellions against Crusader knights and mercenary forces.

In 1289 the Sunni Muslim Mamluks of Egypt took Tripoli. After years of fighting the Byzantines and Crusaders, the Mamluks began per- secuting the Greek Orthodox and went after the Druze. The Maronites seemed to have cut a deal—leave us alone in the mountains and we will pay your taxes. Whether the Mamluks played divide and conquer or the Maronites survived by guile is unclear.

In 1517 the Turks toppled the Mamluks. The Druze became the nominal lords of Lebanon—nominal since the Maronites maintained a strong political and theocratic mini-state—with the Christians as vassals. Lebanon prospered.

In 1860, responding to a Druze massacre of Christians, the European powers moved to establish a Christian ruler in Lebanon, though one still under nominal Turkish control. Years of relative calm resulted. After World War I, the French were given Syria under a League of Nations mandate and they immediately made Lebanon a separate state. In 1920 the French added to Lebanon some traditionally Syrian lands in the Bekaa Valley.

In 1932 a census was taken that showed the Christians were in the majority. Based on this census, a system of allocating parliamentary seats and executive positions was established.

In World War II, Lebanon rejected the Vichy government of France and chose to support the Free French and the Allies (many other Arabs backed the Germans). As a result, Lebanon became independent in 1943.

In 1957, with the threat of outside intervention from Syria and the then extant United Arab Republic, U.S. Marines entered the country. *Life* magazine published pictures of Marines being greeted on the beaches by bikini-clad sunbathers.

In the early 1970s, after being kicked out of Jordan by King Hussein's Bedouin forces during the Black September War, the PLO entered Lebanon en masse. The fragile political situation once again tipped toward sectarian violence. In several Lebanese villages, the PLO became a de facto government.

Since the PLO *Völkerwanderung*, Lebanon has become a mosaic of religious and political fiefdoms bristling with weapons. The region looks more like a Roman arena than a country, with factional gladiators slaying one another for survival. Regional and superpower Caesars sit in the stands—Israeli, Syrian, French, American, Russian, Iranian, and Iraqi Caesars who put thumbs up or thumbs down. UN observers wring their hands, the international press wails but reports on the sport. Vague alliances are made, then broken with the thrust of a knife in the back. The Syrians' armor-clad Goliath stakes out one end of the arena; an Israeli David controls the other end. This late twentieth-century David is about five times as big as Goliath.

Too much tongue in cheek? Perhaps, but the arena analogy conjures up an image that recounting four-thousand years of savagery, intrigue, and manipulation could only begin to suggest. Recent emigration figures tell it better: Over 800,000 Lebanese have left the country since the civil war began April 13, 1975. Over $20 billion in Lebanese assets have been moved to banks outside the country. Still, emigration from Lebanon has been a fact of life since the trouble in the 1860s: According to Lebanese sources, 13 million Lebanese now live outside of Lebanon in twenty-five different countries. Two million live in the United States and 5 million in Brazil.

Here's a look at the arena as of summer 1990. The Israelis maintain large armored "reaction" task forces just inside Israel's Lebanese border. Pro-Israeli Shiite and Christian militia units (South Lebanon Army), paid for and supported by Israel, provide a buffer south of the Litani. UNIFIL (UN) troops occupy porous outposts south of Sidon and east toward Beaufort Castle. Occasionally, PLO and Shia guerrillas cross the UN zone to strike the pro-Israeli forces.

The various Palestinian clans take some heart in the intifada on the West Bank, but internecine struggles afflict the PLO in Lebanon.

Multinational occupation in and around Beirut has proved to be ineffective, but then international peacekeeping in the Middle East has always been a failure. The Syrians still occupy the Bekaa and the Baalbek region, areas they believe belong to "Greater Syria." Some Syrian forces are deployed near Beirut. The Syrians protect several pro-Iranian terrorist groups in the Bekaa and the Israelis regularly bomb these bases. The

Druze have largely emptied the Shuf of Christian villages. Amal (a Shiite militia group) and factions supporting the Party of God have squared off in the Shiite villages southeast of Sidon. Amal members fought PLO guerrillas from 1985 to 1987 in order to stop PLO reinfiltration into areas the Israelis drove them from in 1982. South Lebanese Shiite civilians remember their bitter years under PLO control. Still, the PLO and various Palestinian splinter groups maintain power bases in the refugee camps and in the Bekaa. They are, however, no longer a de facto government in southern Lebanon.

The summer of 1990 found Beirut a near wasteland. West Beirut, the Muslim sector, experiences continual strife between various Shia organizations. The Green Line separating East and West Beirut continues to be a sniper's arcade game played with real bullets. In many areas, public services have collapsed—but don't underestimate "Phoenician" resourcefulness or business acumen. Corner stores arrange international phone calls via Cypriot satellite hookups, hustling entrepreneurs haul water in tanker trucks, private courier services move mail—though the telling fact is that it is often easier to get a (nonexplosive) package delivered to Boston than it is to the other side of Beirut. The currency of choice is the American dollar. Still, the destruction is bleak and the living grim.

The Maronites, who in 1976 purged large numbers of Muslims from East Beirut and the suburbs, eventually turned a large measure of their ferocity upon themselves. In late January 1990, Christian Lebanese Army troops loyal to dissident Gen. Michel Aoun began fighting with Samir Geagea's Christian Lebanese Forces militia. By fall, the intermittent struggle had killed at least 1,200 and wounded another 4,000; the fighting included artillery duels, tank battles, and house-to-house infantry warfare. The intra-Christian fighting took place in the Christian's 800-kilometer-square central Lebanese enclave, where 900,000 Christians live. Several outside groups, including France and the Vatican, attempted to negotiate a cease-fire.

Aoun's forces were also the frequent target of Syrian shelling and attack by Islamic factions. General Aoun refused to recognize the so-called Taif Peace Accord, signed by most Lebanese factions in late 1989. Subsequent to the accord, Elias Hrawi was named president of Lebanon and Selim al-Hoss prime minister. Aoun refused to acknowledge this "new Lebanese government." Aoun claimed that (1) the fragile coalition was a tool of the Syrians, (2) the Syrians first had to leave Lebanon (or be "driven out") before the Lebanese could begin to settle their own affairs, and (3) he considered himself to be the legitimate government of Lebanon (basing this claim on the fact he was the last commander of the Lebanese Army under the government of Amin Gemayel and was directed by Gemayel to form a "caretaker government" after Gemayel left office in September 1988). The politics of the situation are not only complex but they are also chaotic. Curiously, Aoun had some Sunni support, at least for his demand that the Syrians exit Lebanon (a third of Aoun's troops were Muslim). In the arena of contemporary Lebanon, today's friends are tomorrow's enemies, and the enemy today may be tomorrow's cherished comrade.

In September 1990, President Elias Hrawi's government declared the "birth of the Lebanese Second Republic." This new "republic" was founded on a political power-sharing formula based on equality between Muslims and Christians. General Aoun remained adamantly opposed to any Lebanese government backed by Syrian troops. Finally, in mid-October the Syrians made their move and Aoun capitulated. The bombed-out presidential palace (and the adjacent military HQ) was taken over by Hrawi and Aoun sought safety in the French embassy. While all of this had great symbolic significance, it did not usher in any great reconciliation. Although Aoun ordered his troops to surrender, many refused the order and fought on. Aoun may be considered another casualty of the Iraqi invasion of Kuwait. In true Middle Eastern style, Iraq supported Aoun from the beginning because he defied their enemy Syria. With most of the world arrayed against Iraq, Aoun found himself in an untenable situation, while Syria came one step closer to disarming the militias and taking over Lebanon. Saddam Hussein was a lousy ally. The militias pulled out of Beirut into new "military zones." The problem of "pacification" is as immense at it is long-term.

The terror continues to be the political thread that binds the disparate factions. Shooting diplomats, hijacking airliners, and killing opponents hiding out in Western Europe send an angry message to the world. Blowing up an explosives-laden Mercedes in the village market carries a message to more local powers. It also adds to the hopelessness.

Local Politics

Lebanese Army—As of fall 1990, split into at least three factions. The major Christian faction, with 25,000 troops, includes those previously under the command of General Michel Aoun. It may have up to 4,000 militia reserves on call. Aoun's faction has received weapons from Iraq, including FROG-7 artillery rockets. Maj. Gen. Sami Khatib was commanding Muslim units.

Gen. Michel Aoun—Former Maronite "renegade commander" who claimed the presidency of Lebanon and opposed the Syrians and the "reconstructed" Lebanese government. His forces were defeated in 1990.

Radio Lebanon—Propaganda voice of Aoun's forces.

Lebanese Arab Army—Muslim breakaway faction of the Lebanese Army, which at one time numbered 2,000.

Taif Agreement (also Taif Accord)—Agreement signed in Taif, Saudi Arabia, in October 1989. Brokered by Syria, it proposed reuniting Lebanon wherein Muslims would dominate the local political system of the Syrian hegemony. This was favored by some Maronite leaders. Implementing the agreement would leave Syrian troops in Lebanon for at least two years. The first president was Rene Moawad, a Maronite, who was assassinated in November 1989 and replaced by Elias Hrawi, who is also a Maronite.

National Liberal party (NLP)—Chamille Chamoun's Christian-dominated party which controls the Tiger Militia.

Phalange party—Party that controls the Lebanese Forces militia (15,000 troops). The Gemayel clan once dominated the party. The militia now is under the command of Dr. Samir Geagea and headquartered in Karantina, the port district of East Beirut.

Voice of Free Lebanon (also Voice of Lebanon)—Pirate radio station of the Phalange and Lebanese Forces militia.

Patriarch Nasrallah Butros Sfair—Spiritual leader of Maronite Catholic communion, who was under Syrian protection for a while.

Guardians of the Cedars—Radical Christian sect, also known as gifted terrorists.

Patriotic Christians—Group of Christians (many Greek Orthodox) from Muslim West Beirut who see themselves as a political alternative to the Maronites.

Socialist party—In the main a Greek Orthodox militia outfit hostile to the Maronites.

Druze factions—Major group of which is the National Movement (formerly run by the now dead Kamal Jumblatt). Other splinter and left-oriented groups exist, among them the Progressive Socialist party. They have a total of perhaps 15,000 troops and have made pacts with local Syrian commanders.

Walid Jumblatt—Son of Kamal Jumblatt who was allegedly assassinated by the Syrians. He used to have a reputation as a sophisticated Lebanese playboy but with his father's death he assumed the leadership of the Druze.

Syrian Army—Up to 40,000 troops deployed in Lebanon. The Forty-first Brigade is the main-force unit.

Syrian National Socialist party—Syrian ally in Lebanon that controls a small militia force and is suspected by many of being a front for Syrian absorption of Lebanon.

Saiqa—Pro-Syrian Palestinian commando group whose strength estimates vary from 1,000 to 5,000, with the lower figure more probable.

Palestine Liberation Front (PLF)—Splinter Palestinian group which remained neutral during Syrian–PLO rift.

Popular Front for the Liberation of Palestine (PFLP)—Ahmad Jibril's radical Palestinian group.

Fatah Revolutionary Council (FRC)—Terrorist band headed by Abu Nidal (Sabry al-Banna). Now fractured by the defection of Nidal's top aide, Atef Abu Bakr, to the PLO, the FRC has several bases in Lebanon, including Rashidiye refugee camp. (Abu Bakr formed the Fatah Revolutionary Council Emergency Leadership organization.)

Marxist Democratic Front for the Liberation of Palestine (DF)—Marxist Palestinian faction founded by George Habash that at one time boasted of intimate KGB connections.

Socialist Arab Labor party—Lebanese group once allied with Habash and suspected in several assassinations of foreign diplomats.

Muslim Brothers (also Muslim Brotherhood)—Radical Sunni group active in Syria, Jordan, and Lebanon; also increasingly active in Egypt and North Africa. Ten thousand supporters were slaughtered by Assad in Syrian town of Hama in 1981.

Al-Murabitoun—Sunni Muslim militia unit allegedly supported by Libya. The group, originally formed by Nasserite Arab nationalists, during 1982 was largely dismantled by the Israelis, but after the Israeli withdrawal, Al-Murabitoun returned. The militia unit has fought street battles with its Druze allies—and lost to them.

Voice of Arab Lebanon—Pirate radio station of Al-Murabitoun.

Saeb Salam—Former Lebanese prime minister, Sunni Muslim leader, opposed to Al-Murabitoun.

Mufti Hassan Khaled—Lebanese Sunni Muslim religious leader.

Amal—Well-organized and well-armed Shiite militia group headed by Nabih Berri. It may have 20,000 troops.

Nabih Berri—Shiite Muslim leader and Western-educated lawyer with strong American connections who is viewed as a moderate acceptable to Christians and moderate Muslims.

Sheik Abdel Amir Qabalan—The Grand Mufti (or Supreme Justice) of Shiite areas in parts of south Lebanon.

Zokak al-Blat—Heavily populated Shiite section of West Beirut.

Hizbullah (also in English, Hazbullah or Hezbollah)—"Party of God" terrorist group at one time allied with Iraq's Al-Dawa clique. It is one of several amorphous but dangerous Iranian-backed terrorist groups capable of dramatic and suicidal action. Others are Islamic Jihad (Islamic Holy War), Islamic Unity, and a half dozen more. Predominantly Shiite, many of these groups are temporary organizations and alliances of convenience—the names change from terrorist operation to operation. Islamic Jihad claims responsibility for the attacks on the French and U.S. Marine compounds, on the U.S. embassy, and on the U.S. embassy annex (see "The Suitcase from Allah" in Chapter 3). Hizbullah, whose spiritual leader is Sheik Mohammed Hussein Fadallah, has over 2,000 militia fighters in southern areas of West Beirut.

Followers of God—South Lebanon Muslim guerrilla organization and probably an avatar of Hizbullah.

Arab Red Knights—Splinter radical group of Islamic terrorists who wore light red uniforms, hence their nickname "Pink Panthers." They seem to have disappeared as an organization in late 1989 but may exist as a different one now.

Marada (also the "Giants Brigade")—Group run by the Franjiehs and located in Zghorta area.

Squad 16—Lebanese security police.

Suk al-Gharb ("Market of the West")—Hilltop Maronite fortification besieged by Syrians since 1983 that controls the main transportation routes into the Christian enclave.

Green Line—Line dividing East and West Beirut into essentially Christian and Muslim zones.

Hamra Street—Beirut drag once lined with lots of pricey French boutiques.

Summerland and Coral hotels—Former resort hotels in West Beirut which became home for many wealthy Maronite Christians fleeing the battles of East Beirut.

Kesrouan Mountains—Mountainous, Christian-dominated area northeast of Beirut.

Al-Matan—Major Christian district.

The Gemayels—Maronite Christian family clan. Amin Gemayel became president of Lebanon, replacing his assassinated brother, Bashir. Amin broke an Israeli withdrawal agreement under pressure from Syria and factional opponents. He left power in 1988. Bashir Gemayel, younger brother of Amin and a bright, articulate, and an utterly ruthless warlord, was made chief executive of Lebanon and then assassinated by terrorist bombing on September 14, 1982.

National Salvation Council—Group, now dissolved, formed by Bashir Gemayel to try to bring about a national government under his leadership.

The Franjiehs—Major northern Maronite family that often rivals the Gemayel and Douaihis clans and is alleged to have excellent contacts with the Syrian regime. (It maintains that its family name comes from "Franks," as in French Crusaders.)

Red Line Agreements—U.S. proposals once tacitly accepted by Syria and Israel whereby Syria could maintain forces in Lebanon but not install ground-to-air missiles or use aircraft to support troops. These were an attempt to stop factional fighting and effectively divided Lebanon into Israeli and Syrian zones before war in 1982.

Maj. Saad Haddad—Founding commander of "The Republic of Free Lebanon" in the border strip north of Israel. His militia became the South Lebanon Army. Haddad died in 1984 but his creation lives on.

Gen. Antonine Lahd—Replacement of Haddad as commander of the South Lebanon Army.

South Lebanon Army—Israeli-backed Christian and Shiite militia of about 3,000 troops operating in the border zone. Viewed by many as essentially a part of the Israeli border guards, it is immediately backed up by 1,000 Israeli troops and ultimately by the entire IDF. It is kept on a short leash by the Israelis, if only because the South Lebanon Army could drag Israel into a major conflict in Lebanon.

Voice of Hope—Radio station, originally operated by born-again Christians from California under the aegis of Israel; now the radio of the South Lebanon Army.

United Nations Interim Force in Lebanon (UNIFIL)—Troops drawn from various UN nations (Ireland, Fiji, France, Finland, etc.) that are deployed in the south.

Armenians—People armed, neutral, and left alone.

POLITICAL TREND CHART

LEBANON

The chart for Lebanon should be read as a "region"—it certainly isn't a country. The chaos subsides, the warlords become an oligarchy.

	1990 (Disputed)	1996 (Authoritarian Oligarchy*)
Government Effectiveness	1	4
Government Stability	1	3
Political Cohesion	0	2
Repression Level	5	6
Economic Development	4	5
Education Status†	5	6

NOTE: 0 = minimum; 9 = maximum.
*In this case, still backed by Syrian troops in the Bekaa Valley.
†Urban population only.

PARTICIPANT STRATEGIES AND GOALS

Maronite Christians (many formerly backed General Aoun)—This faction relies on a tough and brutal private army to maintain local control while maintaining strong Western ties, to France in particular, and wants either: (1) the Impossible—a return to the situation in Lebanon as it was before 1975, when they were in control of the parliament, the Army, and the major government executive posts; or (2) a Syrian withdrawal and Lebanese negotiations resulting in either de facto or de jure partition. This is not likely—even the U.S.-sponsored security plans require the Maronites to share power, and to the Maronite extremists, sharing means losing. With strong economic backing, they might outlast their neighbors should the factional fighting continue. The radical Maronites know this, and so do their Swiss bankers. An Israeli attack that drives the Syrians out of Lebanon would boost Maronite fortunes.

Hrawi government—Basically, the political factions gathered in this hardly unified group want a cessation of hostilities and the maintenance

REGIONAL POWERS AND POWER INTEREST INDICATOR CHART

LEBANON

Israel and Syria contend with distant powers France and United States for influence.

	Economic Interests	Historical Interests	Political Interest	Military Interest	Force Generation Potential	Ability to Intervene Politically	Ability to Promote Economic Development
U.S.	5	5	7	6	6+	2	3
Israel	6	8	8	9	8+	5	4
Syria	7	9	8	9	6	7	3
Iraq	2	3	5	5	2+	3	2
Turkey	2	4	3	3	2	1	1
France	5	8	6	3	2	3	4
Iran	1	2	5	2	1	3	1
Russia	0	1	3+	1	2+	2	1

NOTE: 0 = minimum; 9 = maximum.

of some kind of central Lebanese state. They are willing to accept Syrian assurances that Syria will ''act benevolently''—and ultimately withdraw after Lebanon stabilizes.

Druze—Maintenance of autonomy, which means remaining armed no matter what the political settlement may say, is what the Druze want. At one time or another they have fought against or cooperated with everyone in the Middle East. They have shown they can survive with the Israelis and the Syrians as long as they are allowed to maintain their own communities and religion. They will not submit to a political solution that denies them either. Strange as it may seem, given the intense fighting with the Maronites, the Druze still have more politically in common with the Christians than with either the Israelis or the Syrians.

Moderate Lebanese Sunnis—The Sunnis want to avoid coming under the yoke of Syria's Alawite-ruled government. They also want a cessation of hostilities and a chance to get back to the business of business. For the most part, the Sunnis have a major stake in a stable self-governing Lebanon, but they have been torn by the demands of the PLO and the Israeli invasion. They have tried to stay out of the cross fire and, with Saudi help, might try to pick up the pieces.

Syria—Maintaining an active presence in Lebanon does several things for Syria:

1. It keeps Syria militarized and makes it easier for Assad's Alawite Muslim minority to stay in control (dictators need external enemies).

2. It perpetrates Syria's image as the key front-line state in the confrontation with Israel, and deflects extremists' criticism from the agreement that has made the Golan border with Israel as quiet as the border between Vermont and New Hampshire.

3. It keeps open the possibility of absorbing the Bekaa and Baalbek regions into the ''Greater Syria'' which Syrian President Assad believes is his imperial right. A side benefit has been the opportunity to turn parts of the PLO into an arm of the Syrian Army.

Iran—Lebanon's a wonderful place to throw bombs at the United States' embassy and Marines. Holding hostages gave Iran some political leverage with the West and a lot of press attention. But that wanes.

Israel—Security is the name of the game, which means keeping the northern border out of 130-mm artillery range (about forty kilometers). Israeli founding father David Ben-Gurion dreamed of having a Christian state as an Israeli neighbor, but the Israelis are painfully aware that a Christian state would be small and not economically viable.

The Israelis want:

1. Recognition of Israel's existence as a state by the Lebanese government—whatever form it may take. (This was something Bashir Gemayel was prepared to do.)

2. A comprehensive security arrangement that will weaken the PLO and help lead to a solution of the West Bank troubles. Occupation of southern Lebanon costs lives and shekels; Israel can waste neither. Israeli-backed Arab militias, such as the South Lebanon Army, may be the next best bet.

Russia—Syria lost Russian-supplied aircraft at the rate of eighty-five to one during the 1982 Israeli invasion. Eighty-five Migs biting the dust was terrible PR for Russia's most important export, weapons. From the arms-sales perspective, another round of Syrian-Israeli fighting might help the Russians—if the Syrians were to improve upon their sorry record. But the Russians have turned to solving their own problems, and they haven't quite cut Syria off or (as of 1991) reneged on the mutual defense pact between Syria and Moscow. Russia retains major interests in the Middle East. Having Islamic allies is a means of somewhat deflecting its troubles in the Islamic republics. Continuing to sell arms to Syria and Iraq brings in export earnings and, to a degree, deflects Arab criticism of Russian-Jewish immigration to Israel.

United States—Ultimately the United States wants the Arabs to recognize Israel's existence as a state. This means solving the Palestinian problem. Former President Ronald Reagan's plan involving Jordan had a great deal of merit; unfortunately, diplomatic and economic leverage do not work on fanatics. Now Jordan has its own problems with fundamentalist revival on the one hand and renewed demands for parliamentary democracy on the other. The so-called Baker Plan (named after Bush administration Secretary of State James Baker), while directed at resolving the West Bank crisis, would ease troubles in Lebanon vis-à-vis the Palestinian Diaspora. But its implementation is speculative (see chapter 2). The United States learned the hard way that one Marine amphibious unit dug in around the international airport doesn't convince fanatics of much, either. The U.S. strategy of arming Israel to the teeth, arming Egypt to the dentures, protecting the Persian Gulf states, and then jawboning Arab moderates is about the best that can be managed, but there are policy enhancements that entail possible benefits and certain risks. There is always the lingering possibility of armed U.S. intervention. No matter how bitter the partisan rhetoric in the United States regarding whether or not to use American troops, the United States acts when acting is in its interests. The Kuwait War demonstrated this. No responsible political Middle Eastern leader—especially a calculating leader like Assad—can ever rule out U.S. military action. The U.S. Navy makes a big impression. Libya's Colonel Qaddafi calls the U.S. Navy the world's number one terrorist force. It frightens him. It reminds others that the American giant, though often fumbling and frequently kicked, has in the final analysis a very long and powerful arm. The United States, like Israel, won't allow a radical anti-American government in Lebanon. And in a card game like Lebanon, the threat of trump is a valuable political card.

POTENTIAL OUTCOMES

1. 35 percent chance before 1996: Lebanon is partitioned. South Lebanon below the Litani becomes a quasi-military state run by Israeli-backed Christians and Shiites. The Bekaa, Baalbek, and northern Lebanon, including Tripoli, become a province of Syria. Sidon, the Shuf, and West Beirut become at least one Muslim state, perhaps three. (There will at least be an autonomous Druze region.) The area from East Beirut to Tripoli becomes a separate Maronite Christian state. Diplomatic terms for this include "cantonization into confessor states."

2. 35 percent chance before 1996: Factional fighting continues and after more bloodletting a political accommodation similar to the Taif Accord is finally accepted by rejectionist Maronites: The Maronites lose parliamentary power but retain some autonomy in their central enclave. Syria remains as a more-or-less permanent occupation force in Bekaa and Baalbek—at least as long as the Alawite minority remains in power in Damascus. (The Lebanese might assist the Syrian Sunni resistance.)

3. 10 percent chance before 1996: Same situation as outcome 1 vis-à-vis Israel and Syria, except the Christian state and Muslim states do not formally divide and form a "rump" Lebanon. If

Sunnis in Syria rebel against the Alawites, or if threat of rebellion is very serious and the Syrian Army is forced to withdraw from all but Bekaa, the odds go up to 40 percent.

4. 10 percent chance before 1996: U.S. peace plan accepted by the Lebanese and withdrawal of Syrian troops arranged. A new Lebanon accord is reached.

5. 5 percent chance before 1996: Western powers, led by France, intervene to establish an Arab-Christian state. Syria retains Bekaa, Baalbek, and northern areas as a payoff. The remainder of Lebanon north of the Litani unites in a loose Muslim state.

6. 4 percent chance: Syria attacks and absorbs all of Lebanon north of the Litani. It stops Israeli counterattack (politically more than militarily) and gives Israel assurances it will close the border to terrorists as it has along the Golan. (If this happens, there will be a long guerrilla war.)

7. 1 percent chance: Maronite/Phalange (.5 percent) or Druze/Muslim (.5 percent) victory without outside intervention.

COST OF WAR

Over a hundred thousand dead, several hundred thousand injured. Several hundred thousand have fled the country. Life expectancy is cut substantially due to breakdown of government services. Over $50 billion in infrastructure destroyed, along with other losses. The nation of Lebanon has been ravaged by over fifteen years of continuous warfare. Between Syria and Israel, over $100 million a year goes into maintaining their "clients" in Lebanon. One of the great tragedies of the twentieth century.

WHAT KIND OF WAR

While not the only example of widespread civil disorder, this is most widely known and most frequently viewed on television. Basically light-infantry combat in largely urban areas, frequently backed by artillery and less frequently by armored vehicles. Most of the militia troops are paid salaries (some even have pension plans). While some of these troops have formal training, many more have learned on the job and have thus become quite good at urban infantry warfare.

CHAPTER 2

ISRAEL AND THE MIDDLE EAST: BABIES, SHEKELS, AND BULLETS

INTRODUCTION

Israel's many wars with its Arab neighbors have failed to create a permanent peace. The military situation remains distinctly unsettled, and the armed conflict ranges from stones thrown by eleven-year-old West Bank Palestinians as part of the intifada (in Arab eyes, a Palestinian David challenging the Goliath of the Israeli Army) to large-scale conventional combat. The horror of a regional nuclear war with Israeli involvement is no longer such an extreme possibility.

In 1947 Israel fought Saudis, Jordanians, Egyptians, Syrians, Palestinians, and a few Iraqis. In 1956 Israel once again fought the Egyptians, who deployed Palestinian units in their army. In 1967 Israel fought Egypt, Jordan, Syria, and a host of Arab combat contingents supplied by Iraq, Libya, and Algeria. In 1973 the Israelis took on the Egyptians and the Syrians, both once again supported by a smattering of Arab contingents. The Israeli terrorist war involves the Palestinians and contingents of guerrillas from across the globe, including Japanese Red Army fanatics and a few leftover German "revolutionaries." In the 1982 Lebanon War, Israel tangled with the Palestinians, the Syrians, and practically every armed faction in the entire Middle East. In late 1987 simmering Arab discontent on the occupied West Bank boiled over and the intifada began—the Palestinian uprising against the Israeli occupation of and Israeli settlement in the West Bank. In some ways

the intifada has become the cruelest and bitterest of Israel's wars.
Iraq's ability to mask its naked invasion and annexation of Kuwait
behind the Palestinian issue, and to use violence in the West Bank to
its advantage, illustrates the depth of the trouble. Iraq's crude attempts
to draw Israel into the Kuwait War, most noticeably with Scud missile
attacks and terrorist incidents, preyed on this issue.

Put simply, as time passes, Israel grows stronger militarily and weaker
economically. (The increase in military strength in comparison to its
immediate Arab neighbors may be even more dramatic since Russian
military support for its Arab clients has become more tentative.) There
is still an internal Israeli economic war waged between the needs of the
economy and the accelerated demands of defense. The Arab population
grows faster than the Jewish, though the arrival of settlers from Eastern
Europe and the devolving Soviet Union complicates ethnic and religious
arithmetic. Long-standing differences between different Jewish ethnic and
religious groups cause more political divisions within Israel. In terms of
producing a wider war—a war involving major regional powers and
nuclear arms—any full-scale war involving Israel remains the most dangerous in the Middle East.

SOURCE OF CONFLICT

The basic source of conflict is the very existence of Israel and the
dispersal of its former Palestinian inhabitants. The Middle East is an area
of long memories and tenaciously held grudges. Three major (and several
minor) wars have been fought over this issue since 1948. Israel has been
victorious every time. Yet the basic antagonisms remain and get worse
as new hatreds arise.

Any Middle Eastern war involving the State of Israel has the potential
of escalating into a regionwide and possibly worldwide conflict. U.S.
commitment to Israel's survival means any local war could expand into
a larger confrontation. So far Israel has more than held its own in the
political arena and has mastered its opponents on the battlefield.

But there are subtler kinds of combat, the demographic and economic
wars that Israel and dozens of other countries have yet to master. Ultimately motherhood is mightier than either the pen or the sword. Demographic combat—the battle of human population statistics—begets
several problems. Here are a few examples.

A population boom brings more mouths to feed, as in India. There can be more workers or more dissidents, as with Russia and its Muslims. If a nation is being built out of a struggle, population growth can bring either more soldiers or more guerrillas, as in Zimbabwe with the Matabele tribe. A slowdown in population growth can mean there may not be enough soldiers, which is what West Germany, before the events of November 1989, feared would happen in the 1990s. The *Kinderlos* society was not producing enough *Kinder* to fill the Bundeswehr's *Garten*. The absorption of East Germany and the relaxation of tensions in Central Europe mitigate the problem. But prospects for a crack in the Israel-Palestine wall of hate are slim, though Iraqi defeat in Kuwait offers hope.

The welcome relaxation of tensions in Eastern Europe has opened up a new source of people (or, cynics might say, cannon fodder) for Israel—Russian Jews bailing out from the chaos of the devolving Soviet Union, and Arabs perceive this influx as a demographic attack.

In democracies a population increase can mean there are more voters to appease—and these new potential voters may be culturally and/or ethnically different from those groups currently in power. But the problem isn't unique to democracies. Totalitarian societies fear rapid increases in nondominant ethnic groups. One of the causes for turmoil in the Soviet Union was the struggle between Russia and its majority of non-Russian ethnic groups. Either traditions change or revolutions erupt.

Israel, with a Jewish population of 3.7 million, faces two kinds of potential population problems. The most obvious is Arab population increase. Arabs number 15 percent (approximately 600,000) of the population in the State of Israel proper. Some of these Arabs are pro-Israeli Druze. But in the occupied West Bank, 50,000 Israeli settlers mix with at least 800,000 and perhaps as many as 1.15 million Arabs. Extreme Zionists talk of annexing the West Bank, calling it biblical "Judea and Samaria." To do so would create a huge demographic shift unless the Israelis completely displace the Palestinians. Palestinians average 5 children per family, while the Israeli average is 2.7, though this may be trending upward. (Note: Several credible 1989 figures give the total Arab population of the occupied zones of Gaza and the West Bank as 1.4 million.)

Some Israelis dispute the notion of the demographic time bomb, citing figures of Arab emigration from the West Bank of some 20,000 per year, but these people seem to have been the wealthier Palestinians, and the number appears to be dropping. Likewise, the arrival of Russian and East

European Jews adds another element of uncertainty. Some Israelis anticipate the arrival of 750,000 Russian and Eastern European Jews by 1995; over 20,000 arrived from the Soviet Union during the first three months of 1990. In 1989, 12,900 Russian Jews arrived in Israel, but 15,000 Israelis left Israel for other nations. Indeed, since the establishment of the State of Israel, an estimated 370,000 Jews have left the nation. The fact is, large-scale emigration has been a fact of life in ''Greater Palestine'' for thousands of years.

The other political population problem Israel faces is even subtler. The Ashkenazim Jews of Europe, who are currently in political and cultural power, are slowly being outnumbered by the Asiatic and African Sephardim. The addition of Ashkenazim Russian Jews ameliorates this only a little—they do not come from a land familiar with democratic solutions to problems. Election laws, which allow for representation of even the most extreme splinter groups, exacerbate the political effects of this Israeli fractiousness.

Then there's the economic war. The horrendous inflation rate in Israel shows that this is one fight Israel is losing.

Overwhelming military superiority vis-à-vis one's neighbors, such as that enjoyed by Israel, can be an expensive kind of staying ahead of the Joneses—just ask the Russians. Tanks and fighter-bombers—even those paid for in large measure by the United States—exact not only a huge initial capital cost, but they also generate high fuel and maintenance bills. Do you buy tanks, build roads, buy butter, or support a government bureaucracy? War costs money. You can continue to print shekels, but unless the amount of ''work and value'' in the country reflects the number of shekels circulating, inflation results. Losing an economic war may be slower and less dramatic than losing a shooting war, but the effect can be almost as devastating.

And finally there is that shooting war. At present Israel has an overwhelming military advantage. But new and more sophisticated weapons are coming into Arab hands. Examples are SA-5s and SS-22s in Syria, U.S. M1A1 tanks and AWACs in Saudi Arabia, and a once large armed force equipped with chemical weapons and ballistic missiles in Iraq.

What does this mean and where does it lead?

Josiah, king of Judah, fought the forces of Necho, king of Egypt, on the plain of Megiddo. Josiah took a couple of arrows and died. This story is covered in the Old Testament (II Chronicles). Megiddo is better known by its New Testament name, Armageddon. The battle of Armageddon, according to some interpretations of the prophecy, will lead to the destruction of the earth.

Various "plains of Megiddo" have been identified in the nexus region of Israel, Lebanon, and Syria. Identification of the specific piece of dirt really doesn't matter. What does matter is that this is one of those regional conflicts that could lead to nuclear war and devastation—in other words, World War III. It doesn't take a revelation to realize how dangerous that is.

WHO'S INVOLVED

Israel—Is Israel a democracy under siege or a European colony of Jewish Crusaders? The democracy continues to work.

Egypt—Cairo signed a peace treaty with Jerusalem, then the peace went "cold." The intifada put the moderate Egyptian government in a political vise which Iraq and Libya exploited.

Jordan—King Hussein is caught between Arab radicals, Arab money, and Israeli military might.

Syria—Visions of Greater Syria (see chapter 1), a threatened dictatorship, and militant pan-Arabism lead Syria into constant struggle with Israel. But the Golan border remains quiet and free of terrorists.

United States—The U.S. moral commitment to Israel is real. American arms and dollars support Jerusalem. Or is it Tel Aviv? The U.S. embassy remains in Tel Aviv because the United States doesn't want to offend the Saudis. The United States and PLO can't seem to come to terms on a common definition of terror. Basically, the United States wants to have Israel and it wants to have peace. The United States wants to buy Arab oil. The United States wants Arab allies. The United States wants a lot.

Russia—Moscow supported the creation of Israel, but Arab disenchantment gave Russia the opportunity to win friends by supplying arms. Then the Arabs started paying for the arms, which was even better to the cash-strapped Kremlin. During the height of the Cold War, the Middle East was the fecund ground of the KGB as it played the terror game. But with rumblings in the Muslim republics of the Soviet Union and with Russian Jews moving to Israel, Moscow could turn into a PLO terror target.

Palestinians—Dispersed around the Middle East, some throw bombs, most just suffer. They suffer at the hands of Israelis and at the feet of other Arabs.

Wild Cards

Iraq—Saddam Hussein threatened to "burn half of Israel," then invaded Kuwait. The post–Gulf War Iraqi—literally a military powerhouse—went into Kuwait brandishing tanks, combat-trained divisions, chemical and nuclear weapons, and fancy medium-range ballistic missiles. Though the Kuwait War and Iraq's defeat changed the strategic picture, the Iraqis still don't like Israel, but they are distracted by Saudis, Turks, Kurds, and, yes, even the Iranians. Even with their armed forces destroyed in 1991, Iraq will still be a factor.

Saudi Arabia—Money can't buy happiness, or peace, but it can act as a prod. The Saudis have been paying everybody off because they're scared of everybody.

Lebanese factions—Lebanese conflict could topple everyone's house of cards (see chapter 1).

Super Wild Cards

Iran—Successful spread of Islamic revolution could topple moderate regimes.

Libya—Libyan-backed PLO terrorists spiked the U.S.–PLO rapprochement. Libyan crazies always have a move up their sleeve—and perhaps a nuke as well.

GEOGRAPHY

Israel is surrounded. That's the Israeli point of view.
Israel is (choose any or all):

1. A Zionist dagger in the side of Arab political unity.
2. A European-Zionist-Crusader dagger in the side of Arab unity.
3. An American-Zionist dagger in the side of Arab unity.
4. A necessary enemy; otherwise Arabs would be fighting only one another.

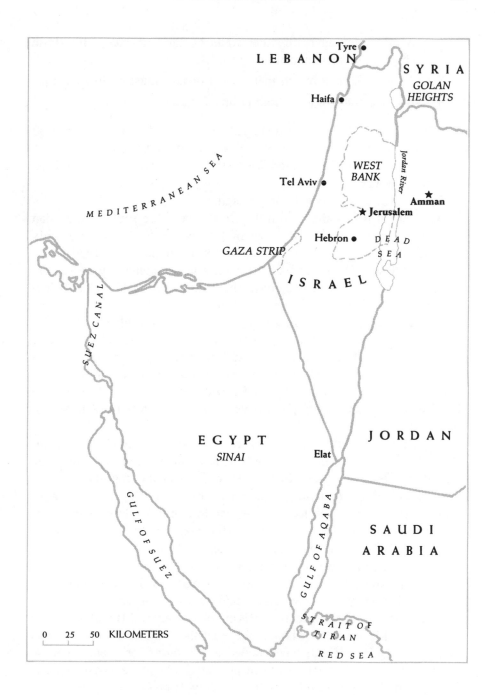

5. A disheartening reality that could be ignored except for those obnoxious Palestinians.

6. A tough Zionist bunch that, like it or not, must be lived with.

7. All of the above (the Arab point of view).

The map shows that Israel is shaped something like a dagger, 20,000 square kilometers' worth—the Red Sea port of Elath at the point, the Negev desert as a double-edged wasteland, Jordan to the east, and the Sinai to the west.

Up north it begins to get complicated.

The Jordan Rift Valley, with the Dead Sea to the south, the Jordan River, and Lake Tiberias (the Sea of Galilee) to the north, not only separates the West Bank from Jordan but also provides a militarily significant division. Operations in the valley are hindered by extremely broken terrain, a veritable badlands. The Dead Sea, at 396 meters below sea level, is the lowest point on the planet.

The central hills of Israel and the West Bank are also broken and rugged. Agriculture is an iffy proposition, given the scarcity of water and the area's rockiness. On the coastal plain region, north to south on the Mediterranean, are the major transportation arteries, the Tel Aviv metropolitan area—and the occupied Gaza Strip. The coastal plain, like the Negev, is agriculturally productive if sufficient water is available for irrigation.

Jordan, on the other side of the river, lies on the Arabian plateau. Most of its present territory, 91,000 square kilometers, not including the West Bank, is open desert. In fact, 88 percent of the country is desert waste which Bedouin nomads inhabit. Amman, however, is a large, modern, urban area. The western area of Jordan has a large number of Palestinians and a substantial Arab Christian community. Over 90 percent of Jordan's 2.3 million inhabitants are Sunni Muslim.

Jordan has few natural resources. Several oil companies have explored the eastern provinces, but unlike Iraq to the east and Saudi Arabia to the south, Jordan has yet to show significant petroleum reserves.

The Golan Heights border region is characterized by difficult, buckling mountains which rise from Israel and meet the Damascus plain. Syrian guns on the Golan Heights have shelled Israeli farms for twenty years— 130-mm guns sited in the hills can almost reach the seacoast. This is why the Israelis are very reluctant to withdraw from Golan, even if Syria were interested in negotiating.

The Israeli-Egyptian border (from the Negev to the Sinai) is characterized by large sand plains and uneven rocky terrain. The interior of the Sinai Peninsula is broken by mountains and a number of rocky mesas. The southern tip of the Sinai juts into the Red Sea, where the Strait of Tiran, between the Sinai and Saudi Arabia, controls sea traffic into the Gulf of Aqaba. Egyptian threats to close the straits to Israeli shipping or actually to close down the strait entirely, as in 1967, have figured in all three major Arab-Israeli wars.

HISTORY

Contemporary Zionism, the political movement dedicated to the creation of a Jewish state in the old biblical homelands, was given its framework in the nineteenth century by Theodore Herzl. Jews settled the Ottoman-controlled Palestinian region, always with the ultimate intention of establishing their own state. The Palestinians didn't like the Ottomans either, but they wanted a Palestinian state, as well as a Bedouin state (somewhere across the Jordan River and then south into the Arabian Peninsula) free of Turkish control. World War I, British and French defeat of the Turks, Lawrence of Arabia, and the conquest of Syria by Arab tribes allied to the West created a political situation characterized by several mutually exclusive goals (just like the current situation in Israel). Britain's 1917 Balfour Declaration promised the Jews a "Jewish home." But the British had also promised the Arabs their own states and the way Britain's League of Nations mandate was drawn created further problems. Under the Turks, the East and West banks of the Jordan had been the same administrative district. Under the mandate, the west zone came under a British administrator while the east became the semi-autonomous state of Transjordan, an emirate that included large portions of present-day Syria.

Essentially, the defeat of the Ottomans left the Arabian Peninsula and the Holy Land vulnerable to any politician with an itch to draw new maps. Significant numbers of Palestinians ended up in Jordan, Israel, Lebanon, and Syria, and several riots and armed exchanges between Jews and Arabs occurred during the 1920s. Jewish leaders demanded that the Balfour Declaration be carried out, asserting that the Emirate of Transjordan was effectively an Arab state, so where was the land for the Jews? The British and French put off a response to that demand until Hitler's Holocaust made any Western opposition to a Zionist state impossible. Jewish rebel activities, like Irgun terrorism, also had an effect. But the

Arab League didn't agree. Palestine had been Arab since the prophet's imperialist forces overran the Jordan Valley, with the exception of Latin Crusader states that hung around for a couple of centuries. Israel looked like the work of Jewish Crusaders backed by the West.

With postwar Britain and France retreating from colonies, "backed by the West" came to mean "backed by the United States." America gave Israel weapons, money, and strong moral support; Arabs needed weapons and Russia was ready. Russian willingness to send weapons has proved to be the basis of a working relationship, though almost all Arab countries have no love, and less trust, for Moscow.

These armed client states, Jewish and Arab, cannot be controlled by their superpower suppliers. The presence of radicals willing to engage in worldwide terror campaigns further complicates the situation. American troops in the eastern Mediterranean (whether currently on ships or shore) raise the political and military antes.

The 1982 Israeli invasion of Lebanon left everybody in disarray, including Israel. The PLO was already divided into several factions, but the invasion of Lebanon left the strong anti-Arafat rebel sects effectively under the control of Syria. Until the intifada erupted, Arafat became the "Wandering Jew" of Middle Eastern diplomacy, but a waif with an international reputation and a strong influence among West Bank Palestinians. And the PLO, like the Palestinians, continues to thrash and twist between its moderate and radical factions.

Jordan looks at Syria and Iraq and winces. The country's large Palestinian population creates a dangerous situation, especially as the intifada progresses on the West Bank. Moderate factions press King Hussein for help in setting up the West Bank as an autonomous region, but radicals could turn any agreement Hussein makes into a call for his assassination and a civil war in Jordan. Domestic pressures in Jordan, both from the radical Muslim Brotherhood (see p. 74) and from Arab democrats desiring more independence, increase instability. The economic situation remains tenuous: Assistance from oil-rich Arab states (Saudi Arabia and UAE) has dropped from $1.2 billion in 1981 to $400 million in 1989. In 1988 and 1989 Jordan spent nearly $600 million on defense (over 15 percent of GDP) and Jordan's economy cannot sustain such expenditures. The Kuwait War demonstrated how financially dependent Jordan is on the "Iraqi trade." The highway linking Jordan's port of Aqaba to Baghdad is a modern-day caravan route, except Mercedeses and Mack trucks haul the load instead of camels, with 40 to 50 percent of Jordan's economy linked to trade with Iraq.

During the Iran-Iraq War, Jordan was a solid Iraqi ally, supplying Iraq through its port at Aqaba (when Iraq's Persian Gulf ports were closed) and allowing Iraqi warplanes to use Jordanian air bases. Jordan also "lent" Iraq an armored brigade as a signal of its political support. As a thank-you, Iraq gave Jordan over 120 British-made Chieftain tanks captured from the Iranians and at least 30 American-made M60A1 tanks.

Syria and Israel are at loggerheads in Lebanon and the Golani border. (Lebanon is at loggerheads with Lebanon; see chapter 1.) The Golan Heights border is as quiet as the Swiss border—real stability and respect exist there; no terrorists cross that zone.

Egyptian criticism of the 1982 Israeli invasion of Lebanon finally provided a diplomatic opening for Cairo at the Islamic Conference, and Egyptian readmission was inevitable. Egypt's size, power, and prestige could not be ignored, and Egypt did not deny the Camp David accords. Egypt is using the peace to improve its agriculture, to modernize its army, and to sidestep Islamic fundamentalists. Camp David did a lot for Egypt—the nation regained the Sinai. The squabble with Israel over the Taba beach resort (near the Israeli port of Eliat), which was resolved in Cairo's favor, was a political plus. It also illustrated, once again, the Egyptian government's contention that the best way to deal with Israel is negotiation.

The Iran-Iraq War slowly exhausted itself with the battle lines roughly where the borders were in 1980. But the militarized Iraqi state that emerged became an open threat to Israel: Iraq had a battle-experienced army, an improved air force, and a developing chemical and nuclear weapons capability. During the Kuwait War, the Iraqi Baath regime's greatest political dream was to link, by any means, its aggression against Kuwait to the Israeli-Palestinian issue. The linkage failed, weakening Arafat's PLO leadership.

Meanwhile, on the money front, inflation in Israel continues. Defense is gobbling up from 30 to 35 percent of the Israeli GNP. Radical politics feeds on failing economies—and this applies to Israelis and Arabs. U.S. anger at perceived Israeli intransigence over the West Bank settlements and human rights violations in the intifada conflict is matched only by U.S. disgust at PLO unwillingness to quit the terror war.

Significant Dates

May 14, 1948—Israel declares its independence, and the simmering conflict between Israel and its neighbors breaks into total war—the Palestine War. Four armistice agreements are reached between Israel and Egypt, Jordan, Lebanon, and Syria. But no general peace agreement, or recognition of the Jewish state, is made.

October 1956—Provoked by a huge Egyptian arms buildup and Nasserite threats, Israel invades the Sinai and occupies the Gaza Strip, as Britain and France invade the Suez region after Egyptian President Gamal Abdel Nasser "nationalizes" the Suez Canal. The 1956 Sinai War.

June 1967—Egyptian President Gamal Abdel Nasser sends nearly 100,000 troops and 200-plus tanks into the Sinai; he asks the UN to withdraw its UNEF peacekeepers and they depart. The Strait of Tiran is closed to Israeli shipping, and Israel launches an "anticipatory counteroffensive" against Egypt and its war-ready allies, Jordan and Syria. Israel takes Sinai, the Golan Heights, and the West Bank. The Six-Day War.

October 1973—Egypt and Syria attack Israel during Yom Kippur. Egyptians cross the Suez Canal and inflict a surprise defeat on Israeli counterattackers. Light Israeli forces on the Golan are almost overrun by Syrian armor. Israelis counterattack and cross the canal into Africa, while still punishing Syrian forces. War ends with the Egyptian Army in the Sinai surrounded. Russia threatens to intervene and the United States responds with a worldwide general alert, including nuclear retaliatory forces. The October War.

November 1977—Sadat visits Jerusalem. The Camp David agreement, brokered by President Jimmy Carter, ends the state of war between Egypt and Israel. Israel ultimately withdraws from the Sinai Peninsula.

May-June 1982—Israel launches Operation Peace in Galilee into Lebanon; at first a small series of moves on the northern border, it eventually breaks out into a full-scale two-day war between Israel and Syria. Israelis shoot down eighty-five-plus Syrian aircraft with the loss of only one Israeli plane.

December 1987—The Palestinian uprising, the intifada, erupts on the West Bank. By late 1990 nearly a thousand Palestinians have been killed in a series of demonstrations and civil resistance to Israeli occupation of the West Bank. At times such major West Bank towns as Nablus, Tulkarm, and Bethlehem have been closed to Western journalists by Israeli authorities.

July 1988—Jordan's King Hussein renounces his kingdom's historic claim to the West Bank. According to Hussein, from now on Jordan will support the West Bank Palestinians' desire to secede and set up their own nation.

December 14, 1988—The United States and the Palestine Liberation Organization agree to open direct talks, as the PLO "officially" rejects terror, and hope for a negotiated and moderate settlement arises. The talks, however, are suspended in June 1990 after the PLO refuses to rebuke and disassociate itself from an attempted sea-launched Palestine Liberation Front terrorist attack on Israeli beaches. (Israel stops the May 1990 attack.)

August 2, 1990—Iraq invades Kuwait, announcing that this move is to support the Palestinian cause against Israel. Most Arab states unite against Iraq, ignoring Israel for the moment. Jordan backs Iraq.

October 8, 1990—Twenty-one Palestinians are killed near Muslim holy places in Jerusalem. Arabs turn their attention to Israel once more.

January 1991—Iraq attacks Israel with Scud missiles. Israel waits.

March 1991—Iraq defeated in Kuwait.

General Assemblages

UN Security Council Resolution 242—Calls for an end to warfare by all states in the Middle East, and to territorial integrity and political independence. It sets guidelines for Israeli withdrawal from the areas seized in the 1967 War (which dates from November 22, 1967).

UN Resolution 338—Calls for a lasting peace based on negotiations; this is followed by the October War (1973).

The two-state solution—A separate, autonomous Palestinian state is formed on the West Bank, which "recognizes" Israel (the "second state in Palestine"). This is referred to by some as "the three-state solution," since Jordan is also directly affected and since large numbers of Palestinians live in Jordan.

LOCAL POLITICS

Israel

Likud party (also Likud bloc)—Right-of-center Israeli party composed of liberal, Herut, and La'am factions. Never holding power until 1977 when Likud's Menachem Begin became prime minister, its militant policies have a broad appeal among Sephardic Jews who have been oppressed under Arab or pro-Arab regimes. Its emphasis on Jewish identity and power may appeal to Russian Jews who have experienced anti-

Semitism in Russia. The right-wing elements demand that Jerusalem be made the capital of Israel.

Moledet party—far right Israeli party favoring the expulsion of the Arabs from the West Bank and the incorporation of the occupied territories into Israel.

Constraint ministers—Most hard-line members of the Likud. In 1990 the members were Gen. Ariel Sharon, Yitzak Modai, and David Levy.

Labor party (also Labor Alignment)—Left-of-center party containing the Labor and Mapam factions. This is regarded as the Israeli party most likely to achieve a settlement based on granting a Palestinian homeland. It is made up primarily of Ashkenazim and its major leaders are Shimon Peres and Yitzak Rabin.

Religious splinter parties—Extreme Orthodox parties who almost always support the Likud bloc in coalition governments.

Other splinter parties—Parties including the Communist party and socialist factions.

Ashkenazim—Jews of European origin.

Sephardim—Jews of Asian and African origin.

Histadrut—General Federation of Labor, Israel's all-encompassing labor, economic, and industrial organization. Over 65 percent of Israel's workers belong to the Histadrut.

Mossad—Israeli intelligence service. This is the top intelligence operation in the Middle East—perhaps the best in the world.

Shin Bet—Domestic intelligence and security agency.

Aman—Israeli military intelligence service.

The Irgun—Underground Jewish resistance and terrorist group, who fought against the British and Arabs from 1945 to 1948.

The Stern Gang—Formally called Lohamei Herut Israel (Fighters for the Freedom of Israel), the most radical of Israeli underground organizations in the late 1940s. In September 1948, in Jerusalem, the Stern Gang assassinated UN envoy Count Folke Bernadotte, a Swedish diplomat sent by the Security Council in May 1948 to attempt to establish a cease-fire between the Israeli and Arab armies. The Stern Gang was a splinter group of the Irgun and named for its first leader, Avram Stern. At one time Likud leader Yitzak Shamir was a member of the Stern Gang. Arab terrorists justify their attack on moderates and those interested in truces by pointing to the action of early Israeli terrorist groups such as the Stern Gang.

Israel Defense Force (IDF)—Now the holy of holies, soldier for soldier the best tactical army in the world. Only Jews and Druze Arabs are subject to the Israeli draft—the Druze decided to willingly submit to conscription (see chapter 1) since they are considered to be heretics by the other Muslims.

Israeli Arabs—Officially 650,000 strong, with perhaps as many as 800,000, residents who have Israeli passports but Palestinian origins. They are generally put at 18 percent of the population, but account for only 5 percent of the university students. Of the 650,000 Israelis classified as living below the poverty level, half are Arabs. Seven Israeli Arab deputies sit on the 120-member Israeli parliament. The Israeli Arabs have recently formed several splinter groups, including the left-wing Sons of the Village, and are being increasingly influenced by the Muslim Brotherhood.

Sabras—Native Israeli Jews.

Aliya—"Ascendancy," the movement of Jews from Diaspora to Israel. The latest *aliya* is that of Russian Jews.

Kibbutzim—Voluntary socialist "organizations," many of which began as farms but are now involved in various industrial enterprises.

"Judea and Samaria"—Likud code words for the West Bank. They are used as a pretext for asserting historical Israeli control over the West Bank, part of what Likud leader Yitzak Shamir once referred to as a "big Israel" where Russian Jews might settle. Judea and Samaria are traditionally part of "Eretz Yisrael"—the Land of Israel.

Kiryat Arba and Ariel—Government-subsidized Israeli settlements in the West Bank.

The Israeli political system—Israeli parliamentary system built upon a system of representation whereby parties representing bare fractions of electoral opinion can win seats. Seats in the Knesset (the parliament) are divided according to the proportion of votes the party receives since voters vote for parties, not individual candidates. This makes individual politicians directly accountable only to other party members. This system is blamed for immobilizing coalition governments—look for electoral reform to be a major issue in Israel.

Military Order Number 158, Order Amending the Water Supervision Law of October 1, 1967—Order stating that "it shall not be permissible for any person to set up or to assemble or to possess or to operate a water installation unless he has obtained a license from the Area Commander" (the occupied West Bank is "governed" by Israeli military authorities). Carried to an extreme, this order effectively gave the Israeli Army control over local agriculture by allowing them to control irrigation development.

Syria

Arab Baath party (Socialist Resurrection party)—Dominant Syrian party whose upper echelons are controlled by the Alawites (see chapter 1).

Other parties—Syrian Arab Socialist party, Arab Socialist Union, Unionist Socialist party, Communist party.

Jordan

Arab National Union—Sole party allowed in Jordan's constitutional monarchy until political agitation forced the monarchy to liberalize the system.

The Arab Legion—Jordanian Army. Largely Bedouin, it was the best in the Arab world and personally loyal to Jordan's king. It was regarded by some as the real army of Saudi Arabia, since the Jordanians have been the Arabs' best soldiers and they have close ties to the Saudi throne. This was one reason the Saudis continued to subsidize their brethren to the north until Jordan backed Iraq in August 1990.

September 1970—"Black September," when Palestinian radicals tried to take over Jordan. A Syrian unit participated, disguised as a Palestinian force, but the Jordanians defeated the Palestinians and later expelled all PLO guerrillas. Both the PLO and the Jordanians remember this date.

Egypt

Arab Socialist Union—Official government party. Egypt has banned or suppressed all opposition parties—Leftist Progressive Unionist party (the remnants of Egyptian Nasserism), Communist party, and Party of Communist Labor.

Muslim Brotherhood (Egyptian branch)—Armed Sunni fundamentalist movement that is dangerous and devout and has no sense of humor when it comes to religion. The Brotherhood was encouraged by the success of the religious fundamentalists in the 1990 Arab elections in Tunisia.

Palestine

Palestine Liberation Organization (PLO)—Most visible Palestinian political organization. The PLO is racked by factionalism and fratricide.

Yassir Arafat is the head of the main faction, Al Fatah. The PLO maintains that Saudi Arabia has given the organization $1 billion since 1979. The Saudis also provided nearly $75 million to support the intifada on the West Bank and in the Gaza Strip between December 1987 and March 1990. The PLO also collected a 5 percent tax on income of Palestinians working in Gulf states. It amounted to $100 million a year. That's gone now. The PLO's decision to back Iraq after its invasion of Kuwait also dried up the Saudi bank roll.

Palestinian National Council (also Palestine National Council)— PLO's "government of Palestine in exile." Members of this "parliament" are scattered throughout the world.

Non-PLO activists—Certain West Bank mayors who have tried to carve out a separate, non-PLO international position. Several of them have been accused by other Palestinians of being "collaborators with Israel."

Islamic Jihad—Radical Palestinian-dominated terrorist sect which is also active in Lebanon and Egypt. It has issued communiqués threatening Russian Jews arriving in Israel and claimed "credit" for attacks on Israelis visiting Egypt. Its subunits include the "Al-Suri Martyr Unit" and the "Martyrdom Lovers' Battalion."

Fatah Revolutionary Council (FRC)—terrorist band headed by Abu Nidal (literally, "soldier of nothing") whose real name is Sabry al-Banna). Now fractured by the defection of Nidal's top aide, Atef Abu Bakr, to the PLO, the FRC has several bases in Lebanon, including Rashidiye refugee camp. (Abu Bakr formed the Fatah Revolutionary Council Emergency Leadership organization.)

Palestine Army in South Lebanon (also Palestine National Army [PNA])—3,500-man force formed by Arafat in mid-1989 that the PLO hopes will be the building block of a future Palestinian army. A rough breakdown of late 1989 Palestinian combat strength shows that there are 10,000 troops and militiamen under the PLO command (in Lebanon and "elsewhere") and the anti-Arafat Popular Front for the Liberation of Palestine-General Command (PFLP–GC), Ahmed Jibril's organization, and the Fatah Revolutionary Council (FRC), Abu Nidal's group, control approximately 3,500 troops and militia.

Fellahin—Arab peasant farmer.

Fedayeen—PLO guerrilla fighters.

POLITICAL TREND CHARTS

ISRAEL

The Israeli democracy becomes increasingly authoritarian and economically threadbare.

	1990 (Representative Democracy)	1996 (Authoritarian Democracy)
Government Effectiveness	7	7
Government Stability	7	6
Political Cohesion	7	7
Repression Level	5	7
Economic Development	6	4
Education Status*	8	7

NOTE: 0 = minimum; 9 = maximum.
*Urban population only.

Now, for purposes of further argument . . .

ISRAEL 1996

(with separate Palestinian state achieved by "peaceable" means; see outcomes 3 and 5 in "Potential Outcomes")
What the State of Israel was meant to be.

	1996 (Representative Democracy)
Government Effectiveness	8
Government Stability	8
Political Cohesion	8+
Repression Level	3
Economic Development	6
Education Status	8

NOTES: 0 = minimum; 9 = maximum.

ISRAEL 1996 (*continued*)

The demographic time bomb is defused—and this indicates a negotiated solution is in the interests of Israelis interested in maintaining both a democracy and a "Jewish homeland." In this Israel, Jews make up over 85 percent of the population—possibly 90 percent. For this particular series of projections we "averaged" several sources and decided to use the following figures for breaking down the 1990, 4.4 million Israeli population (a figure excluding the West Bank and Gaza Strip). Native born "sabra" Jews—17.5 percent; Soviet Jews—7.1 percent; other Jews of European origin—17.5 percent; North and South American Jews—5 percent; African Jews—18 percent; Asian Jews—16.5 percent; Muslim Arabs—14.2 percent; Christian Arabs—2.5 percent; Druze and other Arabs—1.7 percent. We used a baseline Palestinian population of the West Bank as 750,000.

"NEW STATE OF FREE PALESTINE"*

	1996 (Authoritarian Democracy)
Government Effectiveness	5
Government Stability	4
Political Cohesion	7
Repression Level†	8
Economic Development	3
Education Status	5

NOTE: 0 = minimum; 9 = maximum.

*This state becomes more likely since Iraq's defeat in the Kuwait War. It would have no military forces. Aging PLO radicals (Arafat, etc.) must be pushed aside if free Palestine is to come into existence.

†High repression index due to the repression of radicals.

JORDAN

Fallout from the Iraqi invasion of Kuwait and Palestinian unrest weaken the Jordanian state.

	1990	1996
	(Authoritarian Constitutional Monarchy)	
Government Effectiveness	6	4
Government Stability	6	4
Political Cohesion	6	4
Repression Level	5	6
Economic Development	4+	3*
Education Status	6	5

NOTE: 0 = minimum; 9 = maximum.
*The Kuwait War harmed Jordan's economy.

EGYPT

A stability of sorts, as long as the jails have room for Islamic militants.

	1990	1996
	(Authoritarian Democracy)	
Government Effectiveness	6	6
Government Stability	7	7
Political Cohesion	6	7
Repression Level	6	6
Economic Development	4	5*
Education Status	5	3

NOTE: 0 = minimum; 9 = maximum.
*Post–Kuwait War Saudi investment improves Egyptian economy; otherwise it would degrade to a 3.

PARTICIPANT STRATEGIES AND GOALS

Israel—Israel continues to hang tough against Arab terrorist groups by continuing reprisal tactics. It seeks to extend political ties to Egypt, including increasing trade and technical assistance for agriculture and industry, and will punish Syria when it gets too militant in Lebanon.

REGIONAL POWERS AND POWER INTEREST INDICATOR CHARTS

ISRAEL

Syria, Jordan, and the PLO contend with Israel for control of the many parts of "Palestine."

	Economic Interests	Historical Interests	Political Interest	Military Interest	Force Generation Potential*	Ability to Intervene Politically	Ability to Promote Economic Development
U.S.	5	8	8	7	5	6	7
Jordan	8	9	9	9	4	5	4
Syria	3	8	9	9	7†	4	1
Egypt	6	7	9	7	7†	6	5
Iraq	1	6	7	4	0+(‡)	1	0
"PLO"	8	9	9	9	1	6	5
Iran	3	5	5	5	0+(‡)	1	1

NOTE: 0 = minimum; 9 = maximum.

*Israeli force generation potential up to 100 kilometers from its borders is a "9."

†Given time for mobilization—Syria needs three weeks, Egypt ten weeks.

‡A plus for Iraq due to chemical weapons and terror; an Iranian plus for terror.

WEST BANK

The West Bank is a particularly sore point between Jordan and Israel.

	Economic Interests	Historical Interests	Political Interest	Military Interest	Force Generation Potential	Ability to Intervene Politically	Ability to Promote Economic Development
Israel	7	8	9	9	9	7	8
Jordan	7	8	9	8	4	6	7
Syria	3	4	7	7	5	4	2

NOTE: 0 = minimum; 9 = maximum.

JORDAN

Jordan, and its Bedouin rulers, bring Saudi Arabia into the fray.

	Economic Interests	Historical Interests	Political Interest	Military Interest	Force Generation Potential	Ability to Intervene Politically	Ability to Promote Economic Development
Israel	5	8	8	8	8+	5	7
Syria	3	7	7	7	8	6	5
Iraq	5	7	7	7	3	5	4
Saudi Arabia	5	9	8	8	1	7	8
U.S.	4	7	8	7	4	5	7
"PLO"	5	8	8	8	2	6	4
Iran	1	2	5	6	1−	1	2
Britain	4	7	5	3	1	2	3

NOTE: 0 = minimum; 9 = maximum.

EGYPT

Egypt is more concerned with Libya and Islamic radicals than with the concerns of the Palestinians on the other side of the Sinai desert.

	Economic Interests	Historical Interests	Political Interest	Military Interest	Force Generation Potential	Ability to Intervene Politically	Ability to Promote Economic Development
U.S.	5	7	8	8	4	4	7
Israel	6	8	9	9	7	3	4
Libya	3	7	8	9	3	5	2
Russia	1	5	6	6	1	2	1
Islamic Radicals	2	9	9	8	4	5	1
"EEC"	6	6	7	6	2	3	7

NOTE: 0 = minimum; 9 = maximum.

One of the problems that Israel is not currently handling very well is the steady stream of immigrants. Only 40 percent of the 60,000 immigrants who arrived in 1989 obtained jobs there within the first six months. In fact, over 10 percent of the Israeli work force is jobless. The potential influx of 750,000 Eastern European Jews, while bringing more soldiers, will also sorely test the economy. The economy may crack, making Israel vulnerable to radical politicians at home. (It may also increase U.S. and European political leverage as Israel applies for economic handouts.) The Israeli economy, in fact, the State of Israel itself, with a Jewish population of 3.7 million and an area of 20,000 square kilometers (80 percent of which is desert), will be hard-pressed to absorb 750,000 or more immigrants between 1990 and 1994. Some think it is impossible.

Israel must find an accommodation on the West Bank. The two options are stark and harsh: either an accommodation and some sort of autonomous Palestine, or "transference"—an Israeli euphemism for the removal of Arabs from the West Bank.

Other long-term goals include such basics as Arab recognition of Israel's right to exist as a state and destruction of radical terrorist factions who launch attacks upon Israelis.

The Israeli strategy of counting on the United States may become less viable. The United States may be less willing to provide Israel with all-out support in a regional conflict (especially if the Israelis opt for "transference" on the West Bank) if that support might harm its rapprochement with Russia. Look for the Israelis to increase political and propaganda activity in the United States.

Egypt—Egypt continues to improve its economy and flex its growing political clout in the Arab world (because of its size and power it was never truly "isolated" from the other Arab nations due to its support of the Camp David accord). It needs to develop a stronger moderate base which might include Jordan and some PLO faction in an accord on the West Bank. Its primary goal is the recovery of its position as a dominant Arab country, which it gained by successfully defeating Iraq in the dispute over Kuwait. Egypt must control Islamic fundamentalist strength inside its own borders and continue to develop Sinai oil fields. It must also keep a wary eye on its western desert frontier with Libya, as well as on events in the Sudan. Events in "Upper Egypt" (of which part of the Sudan may be considered) have always affected dwellers in the Nile valley.

Palestine—Palestinian moderates seek a Palestinian state independent of Israel. They will try to use world opinion to improve conditions under

Israeli occupation and, ultimately, leverage some form of autonomous (if not independent) Palestinian state. Radicals seek a Palestinian state and the destruction of Israel—they will continue terror war.

Jordan—Jordan continues to pursue a moderate line that fends off attacks by Arab radicals and Israeli annexation of the West Bank. Its primary goals are to resolve the Palestinian question in a way that does not entail the total dismemberment of Jordan, and to control and suppress Islamic fundamentalist groups within Jordan. And, if Jordan doesn't have enough problems, if Israel and Iraq go to war, Jordan will be caught in between and must also fend off potential Syrian aggression, which is why the "moderate" Jordanians go in for a military relationship with Iraq. That relationship could prove fatal, as Jordan's support of Iraq over the Kuwait issue diminished vital economic support from the Persian Gulf states.

Syria—Syria will continue to walk the militant line against Israel, which ensures radical Arab support and keeps the Syrian people militarized and easier to control. Its primary goals are the resolution of the situation in Lebanon with the incorporation of the Bekaa Valley into "Greater Syria" (see chapter 1); the return to Syria of the Golan Heights; and the recognition of Syrian leadership of the Arab world. The ultimate Syrian goal is the annexation of Jordan and Palestine into a "complete Greater Syria." In addition, Syria seeks some rapprochement with Egypt as a hedge against Iraqi power. The Assad government may no longer feel that it can take extreme measures against the Muslim Brotherhood as it did in 1982 when at least 10,000 Muslim Brotherhood sympathizers were killed at Hama. There may be some internal changes, but all factions will insist on militancy toward Israel, which shows that they are all "true Arabs" and Syrian patriots.

Iraq—The Kuwait War devastated Iraq. Still, stirring the pot in Palestine always curries favor among the radicals, which is why Iraq garnered instant and overwhelming Palestinian support for its invasion of Kuwait. The aftereffects of the Kuwait invasion may result in the dismemberment of Iraq; Iraqi military power has been neutralized for the next few years. This will diminish the overall threat against Israel, as the Arab states still have to watch out for Iranian aggression.

United States—American strategy and goals revolve around efforts to guarantee Israel's existence and resolve the question of a Palestinian homeland. The United States wants to see stable (and moderate) Arab regimes in power throughout the area. The relative end of the Cold War leaves the United States as the superpower, which to some degree increases U.S. leverage.

POTENTIAL OUTCOMES

For "future watchers," we offer these possibilities. However, the Middle East is a difficult subject for probability equations. A radical with a weapon and the will to use it is an ultimate variable. Here are the projections:

1. 20 percent chance through 1996: There is what might be called "the status quo but worse." The Israeli economy suffers further damage from its war burden and influx of over 500,000 new immigrants; "border" areas of the West Bank are incorporated into Israel under the aegis of "necessary for defense"; the intifada continues; terror war continues; and repression of Arabs in Israel increases. (This might be called the "Middle Easternization of Israel." Israel would be behaving like every other country in the Middle East, i.e., favoring a particular ethnic group, waging war on its neighbors, and casting off ethnic groups it didn't want.)

2. 20 percent chance: The intifada expands into an armed Palestinian revolt on the West Bank. If this occurs, there is an 80 percent chance of a Palestinian bloodbath at the hands of the Israeli Army, a 19 percent chance of "minor" massacres and a return to low-grade intifada, and less than a 1 percent chance of the Palestinians pulling it off. If there is a bloodbath, there is a 75 percent chance of mass Palestinian expulsions (forced into Syria or Jordan) in the aftermath and a 25 percent chance of an internal settlement between Palestinians and Israelis, giving Palestinians autonomy with security guarantees to Israel. Note 1: This is an outcome that extreme right-wingers in Israel would like to see happen, since the odds are 3 to 1 in favor of expulsions ("transference") of West Bank Palestinians. This gives extremists in Israel a reason to provoke Palestinians to even more extreme action. The 25 percent outcome would be predicated on an Israeli electorate so repulsed by the bloodbath that they toss their extremists out of power. Note 2: A surprise variable that could kick off this chain of events is the mounting competition for water resources on the

West Bank between Israeli settlers and Palestinians, and between Israel and Jordan. Israeli settlers have dug deep wells that the West Bank Arabs claim sap their shallower wells. Depletion of water resources and the prospect of starvation could be the final push to total armed rebellion.

3. 20 percent chance: Saudi, Egypt, and PLO moderates succeed in forging a "non-Arafat, nonradical" negotiating team that opens direct channels to the United States. If this happens, there's a 60 percent chance that a Palestinian entity will be created on the West Bank. Israel retains its "defensive settlements." Palestine has no army. The "police force" is limited to 3,500 men. Jordan is in charge of day-to-day Palestinian foreign affairs. (This increases to 50 percent if a Labor party government comes to power and holds a clear majority in the Israeli Knesset.)

4. 10 percent chance: There is another Israeli-Syrian War. If this occurs there is a 15 percent chance of the war escalating into a major all-front war including Egypt and Jordan. There is a 95 percent chance of Israeli victory if the war is contained to one front, an 80 percent chance if it expands to all fronts. There is a 65 percent likelihood of Assad's Alawite minority being toppled from power as a result of Syrian loss—the likely replacement government is a Syrian Sunni–majority government. If there's a Syrian "victory" and Israel is not destroyed, look for no negotiations of any kind. The Israelis would give up nothing and the Arabs wouldn't budge since they could anticipate Israel's defeat in the next round of fighting.

5. 10 percent chance: Israeli economy comes to a screaming halt and the United States, Japan, and the EEC demand a West Bank Palestinian state as the price for aid. Saudi Arabia is coerced into bankrolling Palestinian moderates. (This is the "poverty talks" scenario.) There is a 20 percent chance if there's a Labor government with strong majority in the Knesset. Note: The covert side of this event might be free rein given to Mossad assassination teams to kill Palestinian radicals.

6. 8 percent chance: Jordan and Syria go to war, either against each other or as part of a Syrian-Iraqi conflict. If this occurs, and Iraq is not already a participant or does not intervene on Jordan's behalf, there is a 50 percent chance that the Israelis will provide

Jordan with defensive air cover—and stall the 'Syrian offensive.
The intifada goes on hold as the Arabs sort things out.

7. 2 percent chance: Political changes inside Egypt lead Cairo to
    renounce Camp David, which results in a 50 percent chance of
    a major war. All Israeli-held land becomes "nonnegotiable,"
    with probably no significant negotiations on anything for over a
    decade.

The Mushroom Beyond the 100th Percentile

We're not into predicting the millennium or Armageddon (that's for
theologians, prophets, and religious salesmen); however, there are two
not-so-distinct possibilities here.

Case one is an Arab-Israeli nuclear war. The initial warheads could
fly from either direction. These would be small-yield, aircraft-delivered
A-bombs or small warheads on Scud-type battlefield missiles. This rates
a 5 percent chance if a major war occurs. As long as the Arab-Israeli
conflict stays conventional, there's less than a 1 percent chance of a
superpower conflict. If the Arab-Israeli war goes nuclear, the chance of
superpower participation jumps to 85 percent. Patriot antitactical ballistic
missiles make such attacks less of a threat, but a Scud with a working
nuke is a great danger.

Case two is the chance of a terrorist-delivered nuke. This would be
the Suitcase from Allah (see p. 126). We offer no percentage on this
event; suffice it to say that there are many people in the Middle East who
would use a nuclear weapon if they could get one. Mossad, the CIA,
etc. are on the watch for this event.

COST OF WAR

The human toll of over 120,000 dead and injured to date in the Arab-
Israeli wars is dreadful. The economic toll can be considered equally
grim. Most nations can get away with spending only 5 percent or less of
their GNPs on defense. Israel and its fractious neighbors spend two to
three times that rate. Since the 1948 creation of Israel, the Israelis have
spent over $200 billion in war-related defense expenditures. The damage
to crippled economies has undoubtably been even higher. We estimate

that the total economic cost of the Arab-Israeli conflicts has been over half a trillion dollars.

WHAT KIND OF WAR

This is one of the few areas in the world where every type of conventional warfare is possible and has actually occurred on more than one occasion. The intifada is very low-level guerrilla warfare, often waged by teenagers throwing rocks. Combat in this area moves up the scale to terrorist actions by individuals and small groups and, ultimately, to massed tank armies slugging it out with the assistance of artillery and air power. For an armored type of war, military analysts from all over the world keep a close eye on Israel in order to divine what might happen if other nations had to fight a major battle with modern weapons. Out of all this has emerged the Israeli Defense Forces, which no longer has as many combat veterans as it once did but which is still one of the best-trained forces in the world. The IDF has every incentive to train and prepare effectively as, almost alone among the world's armies, it knows that it is quite likely to have to fight again.

IF PEACE CAME, WHAT WOULD BE FOUGHT OVER?

Many commentators focus on the Arab-Israeli conflict in the Middle East without realizing that this dispute is only one of many in the region. The recent Iraq-Iran and Iraq-Kuwait wars makes this point more forcefully, as well as the lingering troubles between Turkey and Syria and Iraq, and the constant strife in Lebanon. What would the patterns of conflict be like should the Arab-Israeli dispute be solved?

The first thing to consider are those differences that divide peoples in the Middle East: ethnicity, politics, religion, history, and wealth. The divisions are abysmally deep.

- The major ethnic groups are Arabs, Egyptians, Europeans, Africans, and Aryans (Persians).
- Political differences range from orthodox Marxism to unfettered capitalism.

- The major religious groups are Muslims (of various kinds), Catholics (Orthodox and Roman), and Jewish (Orthodox and non-Orthodox).

- A plethora of ancient territorial claims exists in the region, claims driven by ideas like "Greater Syria," the Persian Empire, the "leader" of the Arabs, and "Greater Egypt."

- Then there is the division between the very wealthy and the poor, exploited by the Iraqis after their invasion of Kuwait. Put simply, poor Arabs resent the wealthy Arabs with petrodollars.

Each of these differences has, in recent memory, been the cause of armed conflict. The Arab-Israeli conflict stems from a combination of many of them. The primary ones are ethnicity (European Jews moving in on Palestinian Arabs), politics (socialist Jewish settlers displacing basically capitalist Palestinians), religion (Jews dominating Muslim and Christian Arabs), and wealth (the rich Arabs generally having fled Palestine in 1948, leaving the poor Arabs and Middle Eastern Jews to resent the wealthier Arabs and European and American Jews).

Even while the Arab-Israeli conflict continues, all these other differences increase in intensity. Internally, Israel has increasingly visible antagonisms between poor Middle Eastern Jews and wealthier European Jews.

The wealthier Palestinians have dispersed throughout the Middle East, where they become unpopular with the economically less successful locals. These Palestinians are also politically suspect in the wealthy Persian Gulf kingdoms, which have become dependent on these skilled exiles.

The disparities of wealth are a fundamental cause of conflict throughout the Middle East. When combined with religious and ethnic differences, a volatile mixture is created. The Iran-Iraq conflict springs from this combination. The presence of oil wealth in Iran created class, religious, and political differences that destroyed the shah's government and produced the radical religious government of Ayatollah Khomeini. Similar differences produce potential conflicts in the Arabian Peninsula, between Libya and Egypt, and elsewhere.

When two parties have a dispute, they will go to war only if one feels that it has a chance of success. No one feels there is a reasonable chance of success against the Israelis. This was a significant factor in producing peace between Egypt and Israel. Warfare, then, is much more likely in disputes that do not involve the Israelis.

The Israelis themselves are most threatened by internal conflicts, particularly those created by the fiscal havoc their military spending is causing their economy and internal social relationships.

WHY ISRAEL'S RELATIVE MILITARY POWER INCREASES

Many Israeli soldiers, particularly the younger ones, consider themselves to be the professional heirs of Heinz Guderian and the *Panzertruppen* of World War II. This appears to be ironic only superficially, since the troops hold Guderian's military professionalism, not Nazi politics, in high regard, and the proud and successful Israelis feel two critical differences between themselves and their German models: They will not persecute Jews and they will not ultimately lose their war.

Religion and ethnic heritage have much less to do with military competence than do education, technical skill, and leadership. The Israelis have all these three. As individual fighters, the Arabs are not outclassed by the Israelis. However, when it comes to creating technically competent, well-led, and resourceful combat units, the Israelis have the edge.

Events like those in the 1973 October War have honed the Israeli edge. After the 1967 War, many Israelis thought that they had an innate military superiority over the Arabs. In 1973, this overconfidence and contempt cost them many lives. The Egyptians trained hard, planned carefully, and at least in the early stages of the war, were well led. Nowadays, any Israeli soldier who wants to rest on past accomplishments is brought up sharply with a reminder about 1973.

It is difficult to maintain a superior military capability during peacetime, which is true for the Arabs as well as for the Israelis. The Arab nations are torn between training scarce technicians to prepare for war or to build the peacetime economy. The usual solution is to attempt both and accomplish neither. However, having a large pool of highly educated, technically skilled manpower gives Israel an advantage. And as the weapons become more complex, the Israeli advantage widens.

The leadership gap also continues to widen. The Israeli armed forces, while not entirely neutral politically, are not nearly as involved with running the government as are their Arab counterparts. The battlefield performance of political soldiers is usually dismal when compared to that of purely military officers.

The Arabs are catching up in one area: They are piling up more equipment. This, however, is the least significant aspect of battlefield power, so new Arab military equipment just gives the superb Israeli Army something new to capture.

The West Bank is a different story. Israel cannot occupy and incorporate the West Bank and keep an Israeli demographic superiority. To incorporate the West Bank would mean to abandon democracy. But since Arabs refuse to recognize Israel's right to exist, there appears to be little hope for a long-term solution. The post–Kuwait War, Middle Eastern political climate, however, may be ripe with welcome surprises.

QUICK LOOK: THIRD WORLD BALLISTIC MISSILES

So-called Third World ICBMs pose a serious threat to the entire globe. Though at present few of the missiles in the hands of Third World nations possess truly intercontinental range and are more correctly classified as medium-range "theater" weapons, their ability to carry high-explosives, poison gas, or nuclear warheads throws a new and extremely dangerous twist into world politics.

The ICBM-terrorist potential is obvious. These missiles could give Third World leaders or terrorists an opportunity to push a button and send a nuclear warhead toward Moscow or Washington. The Russians are not taking this lightly. Kremlin military planners are painfully aware that the southern Soviet Union is already threatened, given the ranges of missiles already available to Iran and Iraq.

Israel is another target. The Israelis are particularly concerned with the Russian-made SS-12s employed by Iraq and the Iraqi "Al Husayn" and Al Abbas derivatives of the old Scud-B. These weapons made Saddam Hussein's June 1990 threat to "burn half of Israel" a credible threat. Iraq's conventional warhead Scud attacks during the Kuwait War, however, were little more than terrorist strikes. The Chinese-made CSS-2 with a 1,600-mile range has been sold to Saudi Arabia, and Israel—and Iraq—are both potential Saudi targets. Syria also possesses several medium-range missiles. The stunning performance of U.S.-made Patriot "PAC-2" missiles blunted the Iraqi Scud threat to both Israel and Saudi Arabia.

Currently Israel is pressing development of its "Arrow" antitactical missile system as a means of countering the threat of Arab missiles. The Arrow, a high-speed antimissile missile, is in fact a "mini-SDI" weapons system. Israel is also developing the Jericho IIb, a ballistic missile (almost certainly nuclear-capable) that has a range of over 900 miles and puts the Russian cities of Sevastopol and Odessa within Israeli missile range.

There are other dangers beyond the "terror" missile. Ballistic missiles are a means of quickly and radically expanding a border squabble into a much hotter regional or international conflict. For example, during the Gulf War, Jordan let Iraq park combat aircraft on Jordanian air bases beyond the range of Iranian bombers. Iran didn't have a weapon that would reach Jordan, so Jordan and Iran remained, nominally, at peace. However, a "neutral" air base filled with enemy aircraft is a tempting target for an ayatollah with a long-range missile. Fire it, and you've got a bigger international mess.

Easily manufactured chemical weapons ("primitive" nerve gases and the like) give these ballistic missiles "cheap" warheads capable of mass destruction. First of all, during their "war of the cities," Iran and Iraq bombarded each other's civilian neighborhoods with upgraded Scud-B missiles. Second, the Iraqis used chemical weapons on Iranian infantry. And finally, it's a frighteningly narrow step, in the mind of a dictatorial clique, to put a nerve gas warhead on a missile and fire on civilian targets (although tricky technical problems exist, as Iraqi failure to use gas warheads in the Kuwait War showed). The warheads can burst over the targets, showering a city with a deadly rain. Casualties, among an unprepared population, from one missile could reach the tens of thousands, making the Bhopal chemical plant disaster in India look like a minor problem.

These weapons can't be wished away, and it's very unrealistic and naïve to expect international negotiations and agreements to control their availability. There are just too many foreign-exchange hungry and amoral missile makers willing to supply a demanding market. Brazil has three short- to medium-range surface-to-surface missiles under development. India's Space Launch Vehicle 3 has a range of up to 1,500 miles and can be topped with a warhead. And Argentina is developing the Alcaran, which with its 500-mile range turns the Falkland Islands into a bull's-eye.

Obviously, the United States is also a potential target—which leads to an ongoing debate over "thin-shield" strategic defense systems. Even a relatively simple ABM interceptor system would help stop a "terrorist" missile as well as provide a means of intercepting an accidental ICBM launch—*if*, however, the "thin-shield" system were properly sited and intelligence was timely. These are huge *if's*.

The debate over scaled-down SDI systems will continue. Full-scale "Astrodome" SDI systems are expensive, of questionable effectiveness, and with the end of the Cold War probably obsolete—although many sound analysts differ on the "probably." Still, the threat presented by the proliferation of Third World ballistic missiles and the success of Patriot missiles in protecting Israel and Saudi Arabia may make "thin shield" SDI a bipartisan U.S. defense program. Terrorists haven't disappeared. In the wake of the Kuwait War, an LSPS (Limited Strike Protection System) could prove to be a smart defense investment. Terrorists haven't disappeared.

CHAPTER 3

MESOPOTAMIA— SABERS IN THE SAND: IRAN, IRAQ, AND SYRIA

INTRODUCTION

The "Fertile Crescent" of ancient Mesopotamia, that extended sweep of land between the Tigris and Euphrates rivers, has played a critical role in human history: as an incubator of some of the world's earliest urban centers; as a nexus of religious, trade, and agricultural development; and as the crossroad of continents and empires. Babylon and Nineveh, Assyrians and Hittites, spread their power from this central region. In subsequent centuries, the nearby state of Persia (modern Iran), or the city of Baghdad (Iraq), or the city of Damascus (Syria) was the focal point of Eurasian trade and political affairs.

In the large lens of history, the economic and social development of Western European civilization, along with the advent of long-distance merchant shipping (sea routes around Africa) and, to some extent, the intricacies and depredations of Ottoman Turkish rule in the region after the collapse of the Omayyad (Damascus) and Abbasid (Baghdad) caliphates, removed the Mesopotamian states from the center stage of trade and influence. The long caravans from the east slowly became superfluous. Internal struggles among Arabs and between Arabs and Persians flared. The region turned into a colonial eddy.

In the twentieth century, the destruction of the Ottoman Empire, Arab tribalism evolving into a kind of nationalism, the discovery of the world's largest oil fields, the intrigues of the Cold War, and the creation of the

State of Israel have made "Mesopotamia" and the entire Middle East a crescent of conflict, introducing new strategic instabilities in the area, which has led to intense international concern. Iraq's tragic August 1990 invasion of Kuwait brought this fact home to the entire world. Advanced weapons systems, chemical and nuclear warheads in the hands of unstable regimes, and the fallout of Iraq's attack on Kuwait make the regional situation extraordinarily fragile and dangerous. The Iraqi assault proved to be more than just another border war.

This chapter, focusing on Iran, Iraq, and Syria, and the following chapter on the rest of the Arabian Peninsula, provide an overview of recent and portending troubles in the region. They both elaborate on issues raised in the chapters on Israel and Lebanon.

SOURCE OF CONFLICT

The Kuwait War (provoked by Iraq's invasion of Kuwait) was not a culmination but rather a continuation of a long-term and bloody regional struggle. Likewise, in many significant ways the Iran-Iraq Gulf War of 1980 to 1988 was simply the latest flare-up of an old conflict between the Persians and their neighbors to the west over control of the mouth of the Tigris and Euphrates rivers, the Shatt-al-Arab. This fight has raged, lapsed, then recurred with some regularity since at least 500 B.C. (and even earlier with a different cast of characters). In the Iran-Iraq War, supersonic aircraft, Exocet antiship missiles, and modern tanks were mixed with "human-wave" infantry attacks led by religious zealots. These high- and low-tech forces, tied to inadequate logistics systems that were incapable of supporting sustained offensives, produced high-casualty attrition combat along a static front. The international press often called it World War I in the salt marsh and sand.

The revolutionary appeal of Islam exacerbated the Iran-Iraq War. The Shiite revival, led by the Persians, still sends religious shock waves throughout the region. In twenty years, Sunni purists could stage their own uprising. Iraq, whose secular leadership is predominantly Sunni Muslim, has a population that is, by a narrow majority, Shiite. The Iranians tried (unsuccessfully) to co-opt the Iraqi Shiite (Arab) community.

Iran, with its "Islamic revolution," remains both a major regional power and a very troubled nation. Though it is war-weary, intrigues in Teheran, dicey politics with a troubled Soviet Union, potential involvement with unraveling Soviet "Islamic SSRs," and old scores with the Arabs assure anything but peace.

Iraq, at the geographic center, is on the fringe politically. The Iraqis distrust all their neighbors. Even as Baghdad attacked and sacked Kuwait and became the target of international military action, the Iraqi Baath regime continued to pursue a war against its Kurdish minority. With a prewar arsenal of ballistic missiles and chemical weapons, and attempts to acquire nuclear warheads, Iraq proved to be dangerous to all of its neighbors. Its 1991 defeat cut it down to size militarily. Still, newly discovered oil fields make Iraq an even more potent force in world oil markets—once it pays off its war debts.

Syria, confronting Israel to the west and deeply involved in Lebanon, nests in a region of troubles. As a counterpoint to Israel, Syria is like a political gear, engaging in a multitude of conflicts. Before August 1990, Syria's conflicts with Lebanon and Israel made headlines in the West. In Damascus, however, the "back door" to Iraq was a growing worry. Iraq and Syria have a centuries-old rivalry; in fact, the Syrian Alawite (and Syrian Baath) regime regarded Iraq as its second most important regional enemy after Israel.

Syria "turned its back on its fellow Arabs," as the Iraqis say, and supported Iran during the Gulf War. On one hand, Syria was glad to see Iraq threatening Israel. At the same time, though, Syria resented Iraq's increased regional influence and feared Baghdad's growing military power. Divisions between the Syrian and Iraqi branches of the Baath party (Arab Resurrection party, sometimes translated as Arab Renaissance party) run violent and deep. Syria sits astride the Euphrates River, and Syrian dams back up water that Iraqis believe belongs to them. Yet, if access to Euphrates River water becomes an issue of national survival, Syria and Iraq could become strange allies, tangling with an old and common enemy, Turkey (see chapter 5), which, being even farther upriver, controls Syrian access to the Euphrates. Stranger things have occurred.

The next round of fighting between or among Iraq, Iran, Syria, nations on the Arabian Peninsula, and others in the region, however, may not be another World War I or another Kuwait War. With the addition of chemical and nuclear warheads and ballistic missiles and precision-guided conventional weapons, the next round might be more along the lines of what World War III is expected to be like: a few thermonuclear warheads blistering desolate battlefields already laced with nerve agent and other chemical weapons. Just because the Kuwait War didn't take this shape doesn't mean the next one won't. And don't think Iraq won't reacquire advanced weaponry.

Who's Involved

Iran—Perceived as "the loser" in the Gulf War, Iran, while in the midst of the chaos of its antishah Islamic revolution, threw back the Iraqi invasion and recovered all of the territory Iraq had initially seized. Iraq's defeat by the U.S.- and Saudi-led UN coalition "remade" Iran as a major regional power. Iran played both sides against each other, regaining territory from Iraq, making money from embargo breaking and smuggling, and (subtly) reestablishing ties with the United States. Iran also gained a "new" air force when over 140 Iraqi planes flew into Iran to avoid destruction by the USAF.

Iraq—Saddam Hussein's Baath regime invaded Kuwait and ignited the first post–Cold War crisis. Iraq was the leading Third World arms buyer. Iraq is one of the world's top five nations in proven oil reserves. It lost forty-two divisions to the allied air and ground assault and half of its six hundred or so hardened aircraft bunkers were destroyed. Preliminary estimates are that Iraq lost four hundred aircraft in the war (besides the 140 that flew to Iran). Iraq is militarily weakened, but the brutal Iraqi attack on the southern Shiite rebels and the Kurds in the north kept the Sunnis (and Baathists) in Baghdad in control of the region. By mid-1993 Iraq will field twenty to twenty-five divisions, but they will be an infantry army. Still, the old problems of internal troubles and rivalry with the neighbors remain. Now Iraq owes even more money to both them and the world, which will cause trouble for any Iraqi ruler.

Syria—still friendly with Iran and pursuing a vision of "Greater Syria" in Lebanon, Syria has old dominions lying to the east. Its political rivalry with Iraq is ages old and embedded. Backing Saudi Arabia and serving in the coalition reestablished Syrian standing and brings in a new source of cash. But Syria's internal troubles remain.

Wild Cards

Jordan—Geographically positioned between Iraq and Israel, Jordan has no great love for Syria. The Jordanians were Iraq's most reliable ally during the Gulf War, providing "safe haven" air bases for Iraqi aircraft and making the Jordanian port of Aqaba a primary source of Iraqi resupply. During the Kuwait War, Jordan backed Iraq. From 40 to 50 percent of Jordan's economy is tied to trade with Iraq. Now Jordan suffers economically and politically for that support.

The Kurds—This Iranian-related (linguistically, etc.) group of over fifty different clans and tribes has been waging war against Baghdad, Persia, and Turkey for over two thousand years. The Saddam Hussein Iraqi regime has conducted a brutal war against the Kurds and has killed thousands of them with chemical weapons. After the Kuwait War the Kurd War continued—bloodily.

Saudi Arabia—During one six-month stretch of the Iran-Iraq War, Saudi Arabia gave Iraq $1 billion a month to keep the Iranians and "Islamic Revolution" away. But the Iraqi debt load was too big for the Saudis (and the rest of the Gulf Arab states) to forgive. Saudi Arabia emerges from the UN coalition victory with great political prestige to go with economic power. In the past the House of Saud paid off enemies and friends. That failed. It now has an open relationship with the West and the United States in particular (but ARAMCO always meant Arabian-American Oil Company). While still not desirous of a permanent U.S. ground presence in the region, the Saudis have always tolerated "advisers" and "technical assistance." The Saudis relied on their Bedouin-dominated National Guard to help push the Iraqis out of Khafji in the early phases of the war; this National Guard will be enlarged, as will the Army. The Saudi Air Force is a crack outfit. Saudi cash and U.S. support go a long way.

Qatar—Hey, their tankers know how to fight. Qataris, Saudi National Guardsmen, and allied air power defeated the Iraqi attack on Khafji.

Bahrain—The U.S. Middle East Task Force (U.S. Navy) was based there before the war. Will a "permanent" U.S. air base follow?

Turkey—The Ataturk Dam is perceived as a threat to Syria's and Iraq's share of water drawn from the Euphrates River. Friction over the Kurds remains a problem. The Iranian radicals think Turkey's secular (and Sunni) state is heretical. Finally, none of the Arab nations likes the Turks. The Turks don't particularly care for the Arabs either and have a saying "Do not meddle with the affairs of the Arabs." For seventy years the Turks have subscribed to and benefited from this policy.

Russia—Moscow tried to sit on the fence during the Iran-Iraq War. The Russians are very sensitive about the Iranian border, abutting troubled Azerbaijan. Russia was a traditional supplier of Iraq during the Cold War, although Russian arms show up in both Iran and Iraq, and Moscow likes the fact that Iraq pays cash. Russia, despite its problems and still a military superpower, fears nuclear weapons in the hands of Islamic radicals. If ideology no longer runs Moscow, be assured that self-interest, in the advent of a nuclear war in Mesopotamia, would.

Israel—In 1981 the Israelis attacked the Iraqi reactor at Ozirak, suspecting that it was producing plutonium (to make nuclear weapons). By 1990 Iraq possessed a large army, ballistic missiles, chemical weapons, and—quite possibly—dreaded nukes. Although the Israelis supplied Iran with spare parts during the Gulf War, they are the hated target of Islamic revolutionaries in Teheran and the Iranian's Lebanese allies, the Shiite "Hizbullah" radicals. Israel and Syria square off in Lebanon and along the Golan. But the Israelis remain powerful, and the Israeli intelligence agency, Mossad, knows what is happening in the Middle East—or at least it knows more than anyone else.

United States—The Carter administration's Rapid Deployment Force (RDF), the cavalry designed to rush to the Persian Gulf and the Middle East, was renamed the Central Command. (CENTCOM's troops now wear the patch of the U.S. Third Army, Gen. George Patton's World War II command.) The United States maintains the Sixth Fleet in the Mediterranean and carrier forces in the Indian Ocean. The United States's primary allies are Israel, Egypt, and Saudi Arabia. The U.S. "rescue" of Saudi Arabia in the Kuwait War was not entirely unexpected. With the end of the Cold War and the defeat of Iraq, U.S. military and political prestige are at their highest point since the end of World War II. But problems between the West and conservative and radical Islamic nations persist.

Egypt—Egypt emerged from the Kuwait War as the major Arab military power. Egypt may rotate as many as two ground divisions between Egypt and Saudi Arabia, just to keep the Iraqis thinking—and to earn Egypt some Saudi petrodollars.

Kuwait—The wealthy emirate, though stripped of its assets, still wields influence. Rebuilding costs bucks, but Kuwait's got them to spend. A "tougher" Kuwait has emerged from the war.

GEOGRAPHY

Syria covers 185,000 square kilometers and has a population of 11.5 million people. Ninety percent of the people are ethnically Arab, while other important groups include Kurds, Armenians, and Turks. Seventy percent of the people are Sunni Muslim, 6 percent are Shiite and Druze, 13 percent are Christian, and around 10 percent are Alawite Muslim.

Syria is cut by two mountain ranges that rim the Mediterranean coast, the Anti-Lebanon and Ansariya ranges. The Euphrates River runs from the northern Turkish border and turns to the southeast, where it enters Iraq. The Jebel al-Druze Mountains are in the south. The land bordering Iraq is desert and semidesert plateau.

Iran has an area of almost 1.65 million square kilometers and a population of some 50 million, well over 75 percent of whom are Shiites. The Baluchis in eastern Iran make up a large and potentially anti-Teheran minority. Before the revolution the capital city of Teheran had a population of about 4 million; now accurate current population estimates are unavailable. A substantial Arab minority lives in the province of Arabistan (also called Kuzistan), where near the Shatt-al-Arab were the Gulf War battle sites of Abadan and Khorramshahr.

Iran borders Turkey, several Soviet republics, Afghanistan, Pakistan, and the Persian Gulf, and it features some of the world's driest and most rugged terrain. Mountains cover half the nation with the Zagros range running from the Turkish and Azerbaijani SSR border region south and east. The city of Teheran sits on a high plateau, and while open to ground attack from the north (i.e., from the Soviet Union), it is relatively immune from attack by Iraqi land forces, although certainly well within range of Iraqi missile and air attacks. Baghdad, on the other hand, is much more exposed.

Iraq has an area of 438,000 square kilometers and a population estimated at 17.5 million, slightly more than half of whom are Shiite Muslims. The two most significant ethnic groups in Iraq are the Arabs and the Kurds, while Iraqi Arab Christians make up around 4 percent of the population.

Iraq is, geostrategically, a nation surrounded. Ironically, the attack on Kuwait, to seize the oil fields and obtain the best deep-water port in the Gulf, left it even more isolated. Iraq found itself boxed in from four sides, trapped within an "Iron Quadrangle" of its own making: Iran to the east, Turkey to the north, Saudi Arabia and its allies to the south, Syria and—behind pusillanimous Jordan—Israel to the west. This political trap, and the military units reinforcing it, gave the allied strategy of embargo and economic strangulation great potential bite.

The region west of Baghdad, toward the Syrian border and on into Syria, turns increasingly dry and harsh—a desert wasteland. If a war broke out between Iraq and Syria, the highway linking the Syrian town of Dayr-az-Zawr and Iraq's Al Qa'im would be a major battleground. Both cities are on the Euphrates River. A major Syrian target would be the Iraqi-Turkish oil pipeline, which crosses from Iraq into Turkey west of the northern Iraqi town of Zakhu.

The key terrain at the northern end of the Persian Gulf region includes the Shatt-al-Arab, the intertwined and muddied delta area of the Tigris and Euphrates rivers, which divides Iraq and Iran. Control of the Shatt-al-Arab has been one of the most basic reasons for Arab-Persian wars. The Shatt-al-Arab controls access to Iraq's chief port, Basra.

Seventy-five percent of Iraq's population inhabits the alluvial plain running north from Basra to Baghdad, the ancient sites of Babylon and Ur. One major Iranian military objective during the Gulf War was to break through into these populated areas.

Upriver, the Iran-Iraq border area turns increasingly rugged and dry. The northern border region is raked with tough mountains and hills. The "Kurdistan" area features this kind of rugged terrain and the mountains continue into Turkey and Iran.

The terrain around the mouth of the Shatt-al-Arab, in the Basra-Abadan-Khorramshahr area, consists of mud flats, marsh, salt flats, and salt marsh. Kuwait, tucked between Iraq and Saudi Arabia and near the Shatt-al-Arab's delta region, is 18,000 square kilometers of oil-soaked desert. Its location made it the victim of spillover artillery and missile attacks during the recent Iran-Iraq War. Though the emirate had been ruled for over 250 years by the al-Sabah family, under Turkish administration part of Kuwait had been assigned to the "millet of Basra." It was under this pretext that Iraq invaded Kuwait, also claiming Kuwait was taking more than its allotment of oil out of the shared Rumalia oil field. In addition, Iraq wanted to control the Khawr Abd-Allah, a brine channel situated between the Iraqi coast and Kuwait's Bubiyan Island. The Khawr Abd-Allah circumvents the Shatt-al-Arab and allows access to the Iraqi port of Um Qasr.

HISTORY

Iraq and Iran: Background to the Iran-Iraq War (1980–88)

The peoples east of the Shatt-al-Arab have been raiding (or invading) west of that waterway for thousands of years. Alexander the Great fought in the area, as did the Romans and their successors, the Byzantines. Persia (renamed Iran in the 1930s) has occupied Iraq three times since 1500: 1508–14, 1529–43, and 1623–38. Boundary disputes, specifically over the Shatt-al-Arab, and old enmities caused the wars. In 1639 Arabs and Persians signed the Treaty of Peace and Frontiers, a peace ensured by tribute money paid by Baghdad to the Persian shah. But that failed to resolve the border problem.

In 1818 war broke out again, also over the Shatt-al-Arab. The first Treaty of Erzerum (1823) failed to solve the dispute. In 1847, Britain and Russia tried to stop an impending Persian-Ottoman war over the river mouth and imposed the second Treaty of Erzerum. Abadan, Khorramshahr, and the east bank of the Shatt became Persian, and the Ottomans received sole control of Zuhab Province, an area that for almost two centuries had been under Persian military occupation. But these efforts also failed to resolve the border problem.

The failure of the 1911 Teheran Protocols, the collapse of the Ottomans after World War I, conditional Iraqi independence, and Persian refusal to acknowledge the new Arab state all combined to produce a chaotic boundary situation. The Kurds, who didn't acknowledge a border anyway, exacerbated things by conducting "bandit actions" against both Arabs and Persians. In 1936 the Iraqis made several concessions that set the boundary in midchannel. The Persians guaranteed the Shatt would be open to Iraqi shipping.

This agreement held up until Iraqi nationalists came to power in 1958. They regarded the agreement, with some justification, as a sellout of Arab interests. When the radical Baath party took control in 1968, its nationalist program included a demand for the return of Iraq of the Arab-populated areas of Kuzistan and called for Arab resistance to Iranian authority in Kuzistan.

The Iranians returned the favor by sponsoring anti-Iraqi activity by the Kurds. By 1976 a full-scale Kurdish rebellion against Baghdad was under way wherein the Kurds received the backing of the United States. Iraq also harbored a fugitive whom the shah of Iran didn't like—the Ayatollah Khomeini. The Iraqis wanted the Iranian border closed to Kurdish rebels, and the shah wanted the ayatollah out of the region in order to keep him from stirring up Shiite activists. A deal was cut—but Khomeini turned out to be a razor. Khomeini returned to overthrow the shah in 1979.

The regime of Saddam Hussein in Baghdad saw the chaos following the fall of the shah and the establishment of the extremist Islamic revolution as an opportunity to settle the border problem in Iraq's favor. Successful flexing of Iraqi military might would also forestall any attempts by the Iranians to promote Islamic revolution among Iraq's Shiite community.

The Gulf War began in August 1980 with a direct Iraqi tank and motorized-infantry assault into Arabistan. While the Iraqis made initial progress, their logistical (supply) deficiencies and a rigid command structure stopped them from taking advantage of initial Iranian weakness. No "Arab rebellion," however, came to pass in Kuzistan. The Iraqis halted their already stalling invasion and called for negotiations. Ayatollah Khomeini's regime in Teheran refused, and Iran counterattacked. The campaign escalated into full-scale conventional warfare, with the two forces locked in attrition combat within a 30-kilometer sector on either side of the Tigris River branch of the Shatt-al-Arab. Iran conducted lurching, foot-infantry offensives, with "human wave" attacks led by zealot Revolutionary Guard regiments. Iraq, suddenly realizing it was outmanned, got smart and responded with layers of trenches and fortifications and carefully laid traps. Iranians would break through a trench and bunker line and suddenly find themselves in a pocket of fire, enfiladed by dug-in artillery, tanks, and infantry on their flanks. On several occasions the Iraqis violated international law and used chemical weapons against Iranian infantry concentrations. In general, both sides used air and armor forces piecemeal, and as a result, tank and fighter-bomber forces were very ineffective.

In February 1986 the Iranians launched an offensive and took the Fao (or Faw) Peninsula. This put Persian troops next door to Kuwait. Iraq counterattacked in April 1988 and retook the Fao area. In July 1988 Iran bitterly accepted UN Security Council Resolution 598 (passed in July 1987) that called for an Iran-Iraq cease-fire. In effect, both sides lost the war (as many of their neighbors had hoped). Iraq's invasion of Iran in 1980 failed miserably, and Iran's subsequent invasion of Iraq from 1982 to 1988 failed even more tragically. Iraq lost fewer troops but spent more (largely borrowed) money. These debts, and Iraq's ruined economy, in part led Saddam to invade Kuwait in order to refill his depleted coffers. Iran saw its religious revolution weakened by a failed jihad against Iraq, but it did get back some inconsequential lost territories when Iraq pulled out of Iran after the invasion of Kuwait. Several sources suggest Iraq owed as much as $80 billion before its invasion of Kuwait. Of course Iraq's basic economic infrastructure was devastated by "coalition" air attacks. Iran also has large debts ($15–$20 billion in one estimate), and parts of Abadan and Teheran remain in ruins.

The "sideshows" to the Iran-Iraq War were also serious: the Tanker War, which brought the United States into the fray; the War of the Cities (the Missile War); and the endless war against the Kurds. The Tanker War was begun by Iraq in 1982 when Syria closed down the Iraqi Mediterranean oil pipeline that crosses Syrian territory, which the Iraqis saw, correctly, as an attempt to strangle Iraq economically. It consisted of Iraq's shooting at Iranian tankers, an attempt to curtail Iranian oil shipments, and the Iranians responding by attacking tankers belonging to nations Iran regarded as supportive of Iraq. The United States reflagged several Kuwaiti tankers and conducted naval-escort missions into the

Persian Gulf. Iran used mines for most of its antitanker attacks, with occasional surface attacks launched by the Revolutionary Guards in Swedish "Boghammer" speedboats. The Iranians also acquired Chinese-built "Silkworm" antiship missiles, and the most notable Silkworm strike was launched against a stationary target, a Kuwaiti offshore oil port. U.S. and Iranian forces fought on a number of occasions; for example, in April 1987 U.S. forces sank an Iranian frigate and the United States became a de facto "ally" of Iraq. The most serious attack against U.S. forces, however, was accidentally launched by Iraq in May 1987. An Iraqi fighter-bomber fired two missiles at a "naval target" which happened to be the U.S. Navy frigate *Stark*, and thirty-seven sailors were killed. One of the largest losses of life occurred in July 1988 when the U.S. Aegis' guided-missile cruiser "Vincennes" accidentally shot down an Iranian passenger plane (Iranair Flight 655) flying from Bandar al Abbas across the Strait of Hormuz and 290 civilians died. The "Vincennes" weapons officers mistook the Iranian airbus for an Iranian F-14 Tomcat fighter.

The War of the Cities consisted of Iraqi bombardments of Teheran and other Iranian cities with Soviet-supplied but Iraqi-modified Scud tactical ballistic missiles. The Iranians replied in kind. In it, at least one Iranian missile landed in Kuwait. The Iraqis maintain that this Scud war was actually started by Iranian fighter-bomber attacks on civilian areas in Baghdad. Several thousand civilians were killed or injured in these counterattacks on cities.

After the Iran-Iraq War the war against the Kurds continued to grind on. In the north the Kurds became active against the Iraqis, with support from Iran and bases inside Iran. After the 1988 cease-fire, the Iraqis struck back, burning and gassing several Kurdish villages. They struck the Kurds again after the Kuwait War.

Iraq and Syria

In 1975 Iraq and Syria mobilized their armies along the frontier. Water resources, a touchy subject in the Middle East long before oil became the economically dominant liquid, was the question. The immediate cause of the dispute was Syrian construction of a dam complex on the Euphrates River. Saudi Arabian intervention defused that crisis.

But other tensions fire the Iraqi-Syrian troubles. Historically, one can look back to the replacement of the Syrian-based Umayyad Caliphate

(A.D. 661–750) by the Baghdad Abbasid Caliphate. The Syrians also hated Iraq's former Hashemite monarchy, which tried to incorporate most of Syria into a "Greater Iraq." Today, the battle continues between the Syrian and Iraqi wings of the Baathist party.

Baathism was founded in 1940 by Michel Aflaq, a Syrian Greek Orthodox Christian Arab, and Salah al-Din al-Bitar, a Syrian Sunni Muslim. The Baath party (Arab Resurrection or Renaissance) is a secular pan-Arab party. Its motto and political creed, "Unity, Freedom, Socialism," has been a rallying cry for Arabs seeking a non-Islamic or modern basis for Arab unity and nationalism. Its pan-Arabism is based on language and ethnicity, not religion, and as a result it has attracted a number of Arab minorities (such as the Alawites in Syria).

The Baath, as part of its historical "anticolonial" crusade, contends that all Arab states created after the collapse of the Ottoman Empire in 1918 are illegitimate, since the borders were drawn by Great Britain and France. The Baath wants to create a pan-Arab state running from the Persian Gulf across North Africa to Morocco. Initially the Baath party maintained "regional commands" in each Arab country.

The Baath party began to splinter in 1966 when young members of the party tossed out the "old guard" and formed what some call "the neo-Baath party." In 1968 Iraq decided to give old-guard Syrian Baathist exiles a safe haven. The old guard had been toppled by a young, Alawite-based Baathist cadre and was a threat to the new group's hold on power. Syrian President Hafez al-Assad, an Alawite who took power in 1970 in a bloodless coup, was particularly angered by the Iraqi Baathists.

Iraq tried to ignore Syria while it was tied up with Iran in the Iran-Iraq War. Iraq provided military and economic support to several Lebanese factions (most notably the Maronite Christians) in an attempt to keep Syria distracted in Lebanon. The fact that the Syrians cooperated with Iran, and even cut off Iraq's oil pipeline to the Mediterranean at Iran's behest, is not forgotten or forgiven. Syrian cooperation with Saudi Arabia, and the United States, following the invasion of Kuwait surprised everyone except the Iraqis. The coalition victory puts Syria in a better position to settle the old scores with Baghdad, but not without running internal risks.

It is a geographical and historical fact—or fate—that Syria faces both east and west, bringing the eastern Mediterranean in contact with Mesopotamia. Once more Syria is in a geographical straddle. Iraq has ambitions of replacing Egypt as the leader of the Arab world and controlling the central Syrian position is a geostrategic key to realizing this political ambition.

Syria Versus Syria Versus Lebanon

Syria itself is a potential Lebanon. Power there is held by the Alawite religious minority, which dominates the Syrian Army's officer corps, the secret police, and the intelligence services. Every fifth Muslim in Syria belongs to a schismatic sect. The Alawites and Druze form local majorities in certain regions of the country, the Alawites in the Latakia region and the Druze in the Jebel al-Druze. Alawite conflicts with the Muslim Brotherhood resulted in the 1982 Syrian Army assault on Hama that left 10,000 dead. Some sources suggest there were a total of 120,000 casualties and parts of the city were razed as a lesson to would-be rebels. Syria's internal mosaic is ripe for continuing troubles, a weakness that in the past Iraqi leaders have attempted to exploit.

Iraq Versus Kuwait Versus the World

Iraqi Background

When the nation of Iraq was established in 1931, it consisted of the three ancient provinces of Baghdad, Mosul, and Basra. There was some dispute with the new Turkish republic, as the Mosul province, and the Kirkuk oil fields, were more Turk than Arab (and possibly more Kurd than anything else). The British gave the northern area to Iraq, partially to reward their Arab allies for their services in World War I and partially to ensure that the Turkish republic did not have future oil wealth with which to entertain ideas of reestablishing another Turkish empire. In hindsight, this proved a big mistake, as the forward-looking Turks turned westward in their thinking and have been a staunch ally of the Western democracies ever since.

Britain imported a prince to rule Iraq from the (then and now) ruling Hashemite family in Jordan; they had been another of Britain's local allies during World War I. The British kept a hand in Iraqi politics and actually took over Iraq again during World War II when a large number of Iraqi Army officers sought an alliance with the Nazi Germans. Iraqi and Nazi officers apparently had a lot in common, at least in terms of politics and attitudes toward Jews. After World War II, the British left, leaving Iraq's Hashemite royalty to their fate.

Baghdad's imported aristocrats were lined up against a wall and shot when the Iraqi Army took over in 1958. With the Hashemite royal family dead and the Army in control, a civil war of sorts began. While the Army was a potent political power, it was overshadowed by the Arab nationalist Baath (Renaissance) party, the Iraqi branch of which was founded in 1949, partially as a reaction to the creation of Israel. Initially the Baath party wanted to overthrow the monarchies and unite all Arabs from Iraq to Morocco into one powerful state. This lofty ideal soon fell apart under nationalist pressures inside both Iraq and Syria.

Iraq initially sought a Baath-controlled unification, largely with Sunni Arab Syria, as a way to solve its minorities problem. There was one catch, the Baghdad Arabs of Iraq would then be an even smaller minority in the united nation and the more numerous (and nearly as bloody-minded) Syrian Sunni Arabs would run the whole show. Syrian Sunnis also had a minorities problem, but not as severe as that in Iraq. The Syrian Baath party members were not gentle people and dealt harshly with real or imagined opposition. Thus began the ongoing, bloody feud between Baath factions in Iraq and Syria over, essentially, which wing of Baath would control the other.

Saddam Hussein, the author of Iraq's ill-fated invasions of Iran and Kuwait, first appeared on the Iraqi political scene in 1958, when, after the fall of the monarchy, he tried to assassinate the (non-Baath) general ruling Iraq. Saddam failed, was wounded in the incident, and found refuge in Syria. He returned to Iraq and joined in the eventual Baath takeover in Iraq. Saddam was one of many from the "Tikrit clan" to rise in Iraqi politics. Tikrit is a region of a few hundred thousand people a hundred miles north of Baghdad. While Baghdad contains several warring clans, the Tikrit group has remained fairly united, which can in no small way be attributed to the skill and ruthlessness of Saddam.

In 1968 the non-Baath Iraqi Army officers were purged and the Baaths had sole control of the Army—and Iraq. At the time, the second in command of the Iraqi Baath party, and the real power in the country, was thirty-one-year-old Saddam Hussein, who waited in the shadows until he could take complete control of the country.

The Attack on Kuwait

Kuwait never wanted anything to do with joining Iraq. Because of its long-standing tradition of local rule under the Al-Sabah dynasty and its ongoing good relations with the British, in the 1930s Britain guaranteed Kuwait's independence. Though many Baghdad Arabs protested that Kuwait should be part of Iraq, it was not considered worth the trouble to press the issue with the British. The new nation of Iraq had enough problems with other Iraqi minorities without taking in some traditionally hostile Bedouins. And no one knew at the time just how much oil wealth there was in Kuwait.

When he invaded Kuwait, Hussein gambled that the Saudis and the rest of the world would tremble and then ignore Kuwait, just as the world had essentially ignored Mussolini's invasion of Ethiopia in the 1930s. Unfortunately, he overlooked a critical point: Ethiopia hadn't been in the oil business. When Saddam invaded Kuwait, he raised a dagger—an economic, political, and military dagger—to the world's petroleum artery. After seizing Kuwait, Iraq controlled a billion barrels of production a year. And if the Iraqis had taken Saudi Arabia's oil (or damaged those oil fields), another 1.3 billion barrels a year would have been lost. The smaller Gulf states produce a further 600 million barrels a year. Loss, or prolonged interruption, of this oil shuts down the industrialized economies, causing an economic depression until adjustments are made.

But the problem is worse than economic disruption and recession in the industrialized countries. The Third World nations that depend on the industrial nations for trade and aid (particularly food) and those that are industrializing are injured much more severely by price increases in the oil process, with millions in danger of starvation. This was the case twenty years ago when the majority of oil-producing countries got together and increased the price of oil. In the summer of 1990, oil cost about twice what it should have if only market conditions had been setting the price. With the price of oil nearly doubling again because of Iraq's invasion of Kuwait, citizens of industrialized nations suffered, but citizens of Third World nations suffered more.

The Kuwait War was another tragic outcome of a string of strategic political miscalculations. Certainly Baghdad miscalculated. But there is plenty of blame to go around. The truth astonishes as well as hurts: Western powers and the Soviet Union supplied the Iraqi war machine with its more lethal weapons systems. Already the United States media has slapped the State Department for taking a placating diplomatic tone toward Iraq in the weeks immediately before the invasion—a soft approach, considering the United States was dealing with Saddam Hussein, one of the world's most aggressive and yet curiously isolated gangsters.

In the historical sense, Hussein's greatest misstep will prove to be his serious underestimation of Saudi political abilities. The Saudis were fast, astute, and decisive in the face of Iraqi armed might. Saddam also sorely misjudged U.S. willingness to act and may have misjudged U.S. military capabilities. Relatively isolated in his Baathist regime—having left Iraq only a couple of times in the last decade, his most extensive foreign experience, outside of countries on his border, being several trips to the Soviet Union—he may have thought B-52s were an American propaganda tool.

They were not. U.S. air power was decisive in Iraq's defeat, but the air power would never have had a chance if the political coalition had not formed and held together. (U.S. President George Bush did an outstanding job of public and personal diplomacy. He and his administration reacted quickly and decisively to the crisis.) U.S., Egyptian, and Saudi diplomacy (as well as Israeli cool in response to Iraqi Scud missile strikes) held the coalition together.

The world was astounded at the display of U.S. military prowess, in particular U.S. technical prowess. Though cruise missiles didn't function as well as their initial touts, the fact remains that U.S. hardware functioned well. Smart weapons took out targets with great precision. Once the Iraqi Air Force was neutralized, the Iraqi ground forces were bombed and bombed some more. Iraqi units quit the battle en masse. When the "ground war" began in late February 1991 the Iraqi Army in Kuwait began to surrender. French and U.S. units covered the "deep flank" in Iraq. U.S. and British armor swung west of Kuwait and destroyed the Republican Guard Corps near Basra. The Iraqi army was destroyed in one hundred hours.

LOCAL POLITICS

Iran

Islamic Republican party—Political front constructed by now-deceased Ayatollah Ruhollah Khomeini, completely dominated by the priests (mullahs).

Revolutionary Guards (also Pasadaran)—Iranian youths forming the Islamic revolutionary Army. They were used to purge the remnants of the old imperial Army and now operate as political and military shock troops.

Tudeh party—Iranian Communist party.

National Front—Ill-defined, anti-Islamic, republic-opposition group composed of a few remaining shah supporters, who supported the interim Baktiar regime after the shah's fall. The National Front operates out of France.

National Council of Resistance—Anti-Islamic republican group composed of liberals and leftists, a large number of whom once supported Khomeini. Former President Bani-Sadr, the only man in the entire 3,500-year history of Persia who was ever democratically elected to any national office, is involved with some of the individuals in the National Council of Resistance. Most members of any consequence are in exile in France.

Kuzistan (also Arabistan)—Iranian province with a large Arab minority (over 30 percent) and enormous oil-producing fields.

National Liberation Army (NLA)—Anti-Khomeini Iranian opposition group made up of 15,000 troops under arms and supported by Iraq.

Great Satan—The United States. Lesser Satans have included France, Iraq's Saddam Hussein, Israel, etc.

Savak—The shah's former secret police force and intelligence service.

Iraq

Arab Baath party—Iraqi branch of the Arab Resurrection (Baath) party, which first took power briefly in 1958. The current Baath regime assumed power in a bloodless coup in July 1968 and is bitterly at odds with Syrian Baathists.

Republican Guard Forces Corps—Elite corps of politically reliable troops within the Iraqi Army who are recruited (especially the officers) from Saddam Hussein's native Tikrit region.

Iraqi Special Forces—Well-armed and -trained paramilitary "secret police." They are organized into Army-type units tasked with monitoring the Iraqi Army and the Republican Guard.

Kurds—Border-area ethnic group between Iran and Iraq (see the map) whose major political organization is the Kurdish Democratic party (KDP).

Al Dawa—Iraqi Shiite opposition group loyal to the Iranian revolutionary regime, whose full name is Al Dawa Al Islamiyah—Islamic Call.

They are involved in numerous terrorist incidents in the Persian Gulf area and in Lebanon.

The National Progressive and Democratic Front in Iraq—Coalition group of almost every flavor of anti-Iraqi Baathist opposition. Based in Damascus, it includes Nasserites, the Shiite Socialist party, Communists, etc.

Tikrit—Iraqi hometown of many of the current Baathist regime's highest-ranking members (the ''Tikritis''). It is a province that provides a large base of loyal, and favored, supporters for Saddam.

''Marsh Arabs''—Arabs living in Shatt-al-Arab marshlands. Their area, especially around Majnoon Island, was the scene of some of the war's most bitter fighting.

''The Big Gun''—131-foot-long, 39-inch-bore ''supergun'' designed by rogue ballistics genius Gerald Bull (who was assassinated in Brussels in March 1990—his killer used a silenced 7.65-mm automatic pistol). Italy, Turkey, and Great Britain intercepted parts of this huge weapon. Some sources estimate that the gun would have had a potential range of 600 kilometers and could have fired chemical, nuclear, or conventional ''booster-assisted'' shells or placed a small satellite into orbit. Mr. Bull also designed the long-range G5 155-mm howitzers for South Africa's Armscor Company, which then exported them to Iraq and anyone else willing to buy.

Syria

Arab Baath party (Arab Resurrection party)—Syrian branch of the Baath; the dominant Syrian party, whose upper echelons are controlled by Alawites.

After the collapse of the Nasserite United Arab Republic (the UAR, the short-lived, 1958–61 ''unification'' of Syria and Egypt), the Baath party divided into two contentious factions: the ''civilian'' faction, with founders Aflaq and Bitar, and the ''nationalist'' or ''military'' wing. In February 1966 the military wing purged the civilian wing and Aflaq and Bitar fled to Iraq. Bitar was assassinated by unknown agents in London in 1980; Aflaq died in Baghdad in 1989.

Other parties—Syrian Arab Socialist party, Arab Socialist Union, Unionist Socialist party, Communist party. (Several of these are banned or repressed.)

Alawites—Religious sect. ''Alawi'' translates to ''the followers of Ali,'' and as such, Alawites consider themselves to be Shia Muslims. Other Muslims, including most Shiites, regard Alawites as heretics. Alawites are quite secretive about their beliefs and practices, and their doctrine includes several non-Islamic concepts, such as the transmigration of souls and the divinity of Ali. True believers are initiated into the sect through a series of mystic rites. The Alawi faith has been influenced by Christianity—allegedly an initiated|Alawi|also |believes|in a "mystical trinity." One commentator believes, first of all, that the Alawite community is in fact a remnant of an ancient Canaanite pagan sect that succeeded in isolating itself in the Syrian mountains, and, second, that the Alawis continue to practice an ancient paganism, which is now garbed in Islam just as it was once cloaked by Christianity. This view argues that only in the eleventh or twelfth centuries did the Alawites actually begin to identify with the regionally dominant Muslim faith. Sunni Muslims have a long track record of persecuting the Alawites.

Syrian Army—Traditionally "leftist" Army whose officer corps is controlled by Alawites.

Muslim Brotherhood—Radical Sunni group active in Syria and opposed to the Alawite dictatorship.

Mezze Prison—Main prison for political prisoners in Damascus.

"Mukhabarat"—Special Syrian secret police network that stifles dissent within Syria.

POLITICAL TREND CHARTS

IRAQ

Fallout from the strike on Kuwait weakens the military dictatorship.

	1990	1996
		(One-Party Military Dictatorship)
Government Effectiveness	8	4
Government Stability	4	3
Political Cohesion	6	5
Repression Level	8	7
Economic Development	4	3
Education Status*	3	3

NOTE: 0 = minimum; 9 = maximum.
*Urban population only.

IRAN

The Islamic revolution continues to fade as Iran looks more toward its own internal problems.

	1990 (Theological Dictatorship*)	1996 Coalition Dictatorship†)
Government Effectiveness	3	4
Government Stability	3	4
Political Cohesion	6	5
Repression Level	8	7
Economic Development	2	3
Education Status	5	6‡

NOTE: 0 = minimum; 9 = maximum.
*Actually a coalition of religious radicals.
†Incorporates both religious and secular wings.
‡As revolutionary fervor wanes, look for Iran to once more make gains in education.

SYRIA

Syria creeps toward Lebanization as long-suppressed tensions assert themselves.

	1990	1996
	(One-Party Dictatorship*)	
Government Effectiveness	7	6
Government Stability	6	4
Political Cohesion	5	4
Repression Level	8	7
Economic Development	4	3
Education Status†	5	5

NOTE: 0 = minimum; 9 = maximum.
*Actually, a ruling minority group, the Alawites.
†Urban population only.

REGIONAL POWERS AND POWER INTEREST INDICATOR CHARTS

IRAN AND IRAQ (GULF WAR III)

This war is less likely since Iraq's defeat.

	Economic Interests	Historical Interests	Political Interest	Military Interest	Force Generation Potential	Ability to Intervene Politically	Iraq/Iran Ability to Promote Economic Development
Syria	7	8	8	8	3+	5+	4/1
Russia	5	7	7	7	7−	5	3/3
Turkey	6	8	8	8	5	3	5/2
U.S.	7	4	7	6	3	3	4/4
Jordan	6	8	8	7	2	4	2/1
Egypt	3	7	7	5	2	5	1/1
Pakistan	2	4	6	6	2	4	1/3
Israel	2	7	7	8	2	1	1/2

NOTE: 0 = minimum; 9 = maximum.
 FGPs: Iran, 9; Iraq, 6.

Iraq Versus Saudi Arabia and Allies (Kuwait War II)

1996? Would the Saudis strike north?

	Economic Interests	Historical Interests	Political Interest	Military Interest	Force Generation Potential	Ability to Intervene Politically
Syria	4	8	8	8	4+	6
Russia	4	7	7	7	6−	4
Turkey	6	7	8	8	6	3
U.S.	7	4	7	6	8	6
Jordan	9	8	8	7	2−	4
Egypt	6	7	8	5	4+	7
Pakistan	4	4	6	6	1	1
Israel	2	7	7	8	2	1

NOTE: 0 = minimum; 9 = maximum.
  Iraqi FGP, 4+; Saudi, GCC FGP, 3+.

IRAQ AND SYRIA

For a thousand years, these two nations contended with Egypt for leadership of the Arab world.

	Economic Interests	Historical Interests	Political Interest	Military Interest	Force Generation Potential	Ability to Intervene Politically	Iraq/Syria Ability to Promote Economic Development
Iran	4	7	8	8	7	6	1/1
Russia	5	7	8	6	5	5	3/4
Turkey	6	8	8	8	5	3	5/5
U.S.	6	6	7	7	3	1	4/2
Jordan	7	8	9	9	4	5	2/3
Egypt	3	7	8	5	2	5	1/3
Israel	2	8	9	9	5	2	1/4

NOTES: 0 = minimum; 9 = maximum.

FGPs: Iraq, 4+ ; Syria, 4+ .

PARTICIPANT STRATEGIES AND GOALS

Iran—Radicalizing Shiites in Iraq, and in the Arabian Peninsula countries, will further weaken Iraqi and Arab power. Revolutionary Iran's goal is to spread the gospel of Islamic "Koranic" government—or at least its xenophobic version of the Koran—and drive Western influences out of the Islamic world. There is also no toleration of Communist atheism and little toleration for Baathist secularism. Iran wants to be the dominant power in the Persian Gulf and in the Islamic world. It also has another motive: The war is a populist diversion from the revolutionary excesses by the Islamic republican revolutionaries and the resulting failing economy. The Iranian mullahs see the creation of an Islamic republic in Iran as move number one in the establishment of a pan-Islamic federation. Iran is still stinging from the Gulf War and having to accept a cease-fire. Baghdad was the aggressor, as the Iranians see it, and the Iraqis got away with it. Fomenting trouble between Iraq and Syria, or even Iraq and Israel, gives Teheran a chance to get even.

Iraq—Until they attacked Kuwait, the Iraqis were the military leaders of the Arab Middle East. The desire for political and economic leadership (oil pricing in OPEC) was too much of a temptation, and the firestorm and destruction that the invasion provoked leaves Iraq in a questionable circumstance. Yet anti-Israeli saber rattling embellishes prestige, and from the Iraqi perspective also protects vulnerable West Bank Palestinians as they conduct the intifada. But the old troubles with its Kurds, and with Iran and Syria (and potentially with Turkey), have not gone away. Genocide against the Kurds is an obscene possibility. Iran is still in existence and the Iraqi port of Basra can be closed by a new war. Iraq is rushing new oil fields on line and may be able to produce up to 6.5 million barrels of oil a day (2.4 billion a year). There is still the indigenous arms industry developed by Saddam Hussein that is only marginally affected by embargo. The hard-currency-hungry Chinese are once again an important weapons supplier.

Syria—Hafez al-Assad's Syria will continue to walk the militant line against Israel, which ensures radical Arab support and keeps the Syrian people (the non-Alawites) militarized and easier to control. Syria's primary goals are the resolution of the situation in Lebanon, with the incorporation of the Bekaa Valley into "Greater Syria" (see chapter 1); the return to Syria of the Golan Heights; and the recognition of Syrian leadership of the Arab world. The ultimate Syrian goal is the annexation of Jordan and Palestine into a "complete Greater Syria." The Israelis and Lebanese are not as much a threat to the continuance of Syrian Baathist power as are the Iraqis—and there's the rub. A strong Iraq presents the Arab world, and the Syrians, with a choice of Arab (and Baathist) leadership, and that's the root of a potential war. A mitigating factor against continued Syrian hostility toward Iraq, though, is the loss of Soviet support as the Cold War ends. Nevertheless, Syria may seek some rapprochement with Egypt, as a hedge against Iraqi power. The growth of Iraqi power may also mean that the Assad government may no longer feel that it can take extreme measures against the Muslim Brotherhood as it did in 1982 when at least 10,000 Muslim Brotherhood sympathizers were killed at Hama. There may be some internal changes, but all the factions will insist on militancy toward Israel which shows that they are all "true Arabs" and Syrian patriots.

Saudi Arabia—The Saudis continue to rely on U.S. and Egyptian support as a counterweight to Iraqi and Iranian power. The invasion and pillaging of Kuwait by Iraqi troops will not be forgotten or forgiven.

Russia—Despite its internal problems, Russia maintains considerable influence in Iran and, as its primary weapons supplier, has continued influence in Iraq. The Russians also have a supply "tether" on the Syrians—most Syrian equipment is of Soviet manufacture. The Russians' biggest objective is to try and put a damper on the turmoil in the "Islamic SSRs." Russia wants to keep the Islamic revolution in Teheran from spilling over into Russia. Long-range Russian strategy in the Mesopotamian and Gulf region is to guarantee Russian access to oil supplies if their own fields peter out. The Russians also fear proliferation of chemical and nuclear weapons. As for tactical ballistic missiles, they have only themselves to blame—they initially supplied both the Iranians and Iraqis with the weapons. Now they may become a target.

United States—Trying to maintain some third-party contacts within Iran and hoping that if moderates come to power they will be pragmatic enough to see that, at some point, even Teheran must deal with the world's superpower is the United States' tack. Ultimately, the United States is the only counterbalance to Russian influence. The United States wants to ensure stable Gulf governments so that the oil flow isn't interrupted, having demonstrated already that it is willing to make a military commitment to the area. Operation Desert Storm showed how U.S. military might could be used to deflect a threat to the Arabian oil fields.

As for Iraq, the United States still wants to curb Iraqi military power.

Washington is particularly concerned about chemical and nuclear weapons and the potential for renewed troublemaking.

Washington's focus on Syria is primarily through the Israeli lens, but trouble between Syria and Iraq is turmoil just south of Turkey, a U.S. ally. The United States is also concerned that Iraq may try to develop even more sophisticated long-range missiles. The American nightmare is a nation, such as Iraq, with an ICBM capability. Iraq is reported to have asked the poverty-stricken West African nation of Mauritania for permission to build a missile-test-firing facility there in exchange for hard cash. In April 1990 the Mauritanian embassy in Washington denied this report.

Turkey—Ankara is seeking a solution to its own Kurdish insurgency. The Turks would like to see peace in the region so they can concentrate on internal development and the potential development of "Turkic nations" in the Soviet Union's Islamic republics. Turkey sees a future market in the old Soviet south.

The Kuwait War gave Turkey a chance to be the "European Army" in the field. Turkish operations on the northern Iraqi front were, and are, critical. Ankara, however, is still concerned about Iraq's ability to renew conflict. All of Turkey is a potential target for Iraqi nuclear-tipped missiles.

France—Despite French military opposition to the Kuwait invasion, Iraq remains a major French market. The Syrian market (potentially for arms) also looms in the picture.

POTENTIAL OUTCOMES

Iraq's Kuwait debacle focused the world's attention on the weakness of Saudi Arabia and the Gulf states. Only massive Western (i.e., U.S.) intervention, and remarkable politics by the Saudis and Egyptians, thwarted Iraq's aggression. The Iraqis are smarting and looking at what they missed. The Iraqi regime wishes to solidify its internal control and plays upon this dissatisfaction. That's the local political key to a 10 percent chance of a major war erupting before 1996. If a major war occurs there's a 98 percent chance of a repeat of the allied and United Nations' return to the Persian Gulf region. (A repeat of August through October 1990, but with less concern for political delicacies.) With those as starting points, here are the projections:

The Iraq War of 199?

1. 85 percent chance: There will be an allied victory over Iraq (though oil production in the region is disrupted for a year).
2. 14 percent chance: A renewed political stalemate will occur, but with Iraqi forces inside their pre-August 2, 1990, borders. Iraqi regime solidifies its domestic political control by standing up to "the Saudis and the West." Some Arab debts are forgiven.
3. 1 percent chance: Iraq has military success as the United States is distracted by a disintegrating USSR.

Gulf War II: Iran Versus Iraq, or the "Stab in the Back": Iran and Syria Versus Iraq

There's an overall 8 percent chance (rather high, actually) through 1996 of this major conflict resurfacing for another dreadful round. If it occurs, and Syria does not join the battle, look for the same result as the last war, though the conflict would be of a much shorter duration. What would set it off? The Iraqis attacked once and, if they perceive Iranian weakness, might do so again—especially if they can rebuild a potent army. On the reverse side, another toppling of the Iraqi Baath dictatorship leads to a power vacuum in Baghdad—and, also, an opportunity for Persian revenge. A fresh outbreak of Islamic revolution might also anger the Baathist Iraqis. If it starts, there's a 40 percent chance of the "Stab in the Back," where Iran and Iraq square off and this time Syria decides to take Iraq down several pegs by annexing western Iraq. This could involve Saudi encouragement, as well as old scores between the Baathist divisions.

1. 50 percent chance: An attrition stalemate results between Iran and Iraq along their border, just like during the Gulf War. The Syrian offensive in the west is blunted. War stops due to mutual exhaustion, followed by convenient diplomatic cover that allows all sides to look like victors. Iraq loses prestige gained in first Gulf War.
2. 20 percent chance: There is an Iraqi "victory." Baghdad hits Teheran with missiles and douses Iranian troops with chemicals. Iraqis threaten Damascus but don't really want to fire on fellow Arabs. The Syrian offensive bogs down in the desert, and the

Iraqis toss them back. The Iraqis assume leadership of the Arab world, excluding Egypt.

3. 20 percent chance: Syria will have political victory. Iraq submits to Syrian demands in exchange for peace on the Syrian front. Iraq turns on Iran. War sputters and turns into a new attrition conflict.

4. 10 percent chance: Syro-Iranian victory occurs. The remnant Iraqi Baathist party is toppled from power.

Syria Versus Iraq

Only a 15 percent chance of a minor skirmish and a less than 8 percent chance of a major war between Syria and Iraq exclusively through 1996. What might kick it off? Trouble between Syria and Jordan, with Iraq coming to Jordan's aid is one scenario. The other would be Syrian jealousy of Iraqi power and renewed Iraqi swordplay with the Saudis over oil policy leading to a Syrian show of force on the Iraqi border. The Saudis pay cash for it, of course. If a minor conflict occurs, there is a 95 percent chance of no change. If a major war results? Look for Iraqi tanks to charge up the Euphrates valley, then withdraw. A 65 percent chance of Iraqi victory.

WHAT KIND OF WAR

Iraq and Iran are traditional enemies and have been fighting each other for thousands of years. Syria is also a traditional antagonist of Iraq (and all of its other neighbors). These nations have traditionally fought each other with whatever weapons they have at hand. Terrorism is another traditional weapon and continues to this day. Although the Iran-Iraq War of 1980–88 is typical of combat that can be expected between those two nations, Syria and Iraq are a different story. Both nations possess large mechanized forces—even after Iraq recovers from the Kuwait War, it will still have mechanized forces. Iraq, though, will be weaker, which will continue to tempt Iran and Syria to settle disputes with their relatively larger forces.

Israel and Turkey are also potential combatants. Israel is one of the premier mechanized armies in the world and for that reason is unlikely to be attacked by Syria (much less by Iraq or Iran). If Israel were involved, the war would likely follow the pattern of previous Arab-Israeli conflicts. Turkey is another matter, with most of its forces being infantry. War between Turkey, Iraq, and Syria over water rights is a possibility and the mountainous nature of the areas in dispute would tend to favor an infantry war.

Israel has nuclear weapons and most other nations in the region are trying to obtain them. Eventually, some of these other nations will get nukes, and at that point, the chances of a nuclear war will be very high—any nuclear war is likely to be in this region.

COST OF WAR

The Iran-Iraq War of 1980–88 killed over half a million people and injured several times that amount. It cost over $50 billion in economic damages, which would be the high end of the scale for wars in the region. The low end would be about 10 percent of the high end. If nuclear weapons are used, losses will exceed the normal high-end figures.

SUNNIS AND SHIITES: ARAB VERSUS PERSIAN, ARAB VERSUS ARAB

Iraqi and Iranian enmity can be traced back to local Arab-Persian ethnic confrontations, as well as political conflicts over control of river valleys (the Tigris and Euphrates, for example) and trade routes. Some Iranian militants also resent Arabs because historically Arab elites have exercised an often very arbitrary political and economic hegemony in Persia. As the Persians saw it, the liberality of Islam—equality before God—didn't translate into political equality in the Arab empire. This is an old anger. Other angers also affected the Gulf War, such as disputes between Sunni and Shiite Muslims and the lingering Persian, Arab, and Ottoman disputes over the Shatt-al-Arab.

A quick history of the Sunni-Shiite schism provides some background. After Muhammad's death, his earthly successors had difficulty consolidating the new Islamic political empire. Abu-Bakr, the first caliph, died after only two years in office. A period of confrontation followed between the new Arab political and military elite and the tribes of their empire. Taxes imposed by the government in Medina were one issue, but the fundamental problem was political and judicial inequality. Abu-Bakr's replacement, Umar, was killed by an angry Persian slave. The Islamic movement plunged into a political contest between Muhammad's followers, Ali and Uthman. Uthman was the choice of the Meccan power elite; Ali ibn Abi Talib, Muhammad's son-in-law, was the favorite of the Arab tribes. Uthman was murdered. Another power struggle between Mu'awiya and Ali's followers erupted into an intra-Islamic war. Ali became caliph and was murdered, and Mu'awiya took control of the movement. Mu'awiya's followers centered Islam on a Meccan elite. The Shiites, "the followers of Ali" (*Shia* means "the partisans of Ali"), rejected this as secular and also objected to the "citification" desired by Meccan merchants. The Shia saw in Hussein, Ali's son, killed by yet another rival for the caliphate, a heroic martyr who sacrificed his life for true Islam. Hussein, in fact, was assassinated near the present-day Iraqi city of Karbala, hence the frequent use of "Karbala" as a code name for Iranian offensives during the Gulf War. The name was a direct appeal to martyrdom.

Generalizing about Sunni and Shia differences is an invitation to trouble. It is accurate to say, however, that among Arabs, Shiism still retains an antiestablishment appeal, both politically and religiously. But it's different with the Iranians. In the 1500s the Safavid rulers of Persia adopted Shiism as one more way to distinguish their empire from that of the Sunni Ottomans and the Turks' Arab fiefs. An early Persian literary movement know as Shuubiya is regarded by some as a Persian reaction to Arab dominance. Iranian Shiism blends Shiism's resentment of the Meccan secularists with the old Persian monarchical tradition. Iranian Shiism became in part a way of drawing ethnic and cultural distinctions. It also made the Persian Shiites a bit more attractive to Arab Shiites, who often chafed under the rule of Arab Sunnis. During the Gulf War, Iran's Islamic revolutionaries hoped to use this appeal to topple the governments in Bahrain and Iraq. The Shiite Arab minorities, however, seemed to prefer Sunni Arab leaders to a leadership controlled by Persians.

Many Shiites, in Iran and elsewhere, believe in a line of twelve descendants of Muhammad through Ali which are the twelve Imams, or spiritual guides. The twelfth Imam, it is said, never died but became hidden somewhere in the world. Until the twelfth Imam returns, Shiite priests are directed to lead the Shiite faithful and make decisions "according to Allah's will." This belief in the hidden Imam and the priests' specified role as interpreters and guides in the Imam's absence often puts Shiite priests in direct conflict with temporal and secular (non-Shiite) authorities. The Shia clergy's logic is clear: God's will overrides human laws. Shiite priests tend to have more direct political and social sway with their flocks than to their Sunni counterparts. Several Middle Eastern scholars have suggested that this fact accounts for the often surprising strength and depth of Iran's Islamic revolution. The argument is simple and direct: Shiite priests already enjoyed a great deal of structured political power among the people before the revolution; the rebellion against the shah merely removed the competition. The late shah's father understood this power and let the mullahs know they opposed him at their own great personal risk. Less concern for priestly authority among the Sunnis may also explain why Iranian Shiite radicals have a hard time attracting significant support in predominantly Sunni lands.

But there are even more personal and fundamental divisions. Shiism, according to some Sunnis (from *Sunna*, "the path or code of proper or customary Islam"), is also highly tainted with elements of animist religions, Manichaeism, and Persian astrological notions. In other words, in the eyes of Sunni critics, modern Shiism is a heresy, a mixed-bag "people's religion." The Shiites, in turn, deeply resent this Sunni snobbery.

THE SUITCASE FROM ALLAH: NUCLEAR KAMIKAZES

The Western world has been shocked by Arab and Iranian terrorists who willingly blow themselves to paradise while taking a few infidels in the same dreadful blast. The 1983 truck bomb attack on the U.S. Marine compound in Beirut may be the most famous suicidal terrorist assault, although it is by no means unique. There exists a tradition, especially among Shiite Muslims, of such suicidal action "in the cause of Allah." They identify with Husayn, although in the twentieth century, TNT has replaced daggers. A high-explosive blast, however, is an inconsequential firecracker when compared to "the suitcase from Allah"—a terrorist-borne nuclear weapon.

U.S. security analysts dread the thought of Islamic terrorists acquiring a nuclear weapon either by theft or underground purchase. A nuke acquired by theft, from a U.S. nuclear weapons "igloo" in West Germany for example, is actually the least worrisome prospect. While the terrorists could grab a small tactical nuclear warhead (say, on a 100-pound 155-mm howitzer shell), they would be hard-pressed to detonate the device unless they also stole the weapon's activation codes. These codes, which activate and control supersecret Permissive Action Links (PALs) on the weapon, are held in U.S. command channels. So unless a terrorist can simultaneously break into a half dozen U.S. headquarters, and then know which of several million potential codes go with the precise warhead he's stolen, the nuclear weapon is just a hunk of uranium and high explosive. But it's a hunk that's good for lots of headlines.

A weapon acquired by purchase or codevelopment, with the Pakistanis or Iraqis for example, presents another kind of problem. It is indeed possible to make a crude atomic weapon and carry it around in a steamer trunk. Even if it failed to make "the big bang," the target area could still be contaminated with low-level radiation.

Where would Islamic terrorists employ such a weapon? Getting one into the United States (to drop out of the Goodyear blimp as one movie suggested) would be quite a feat, but it's not impossible. Penetrating Israeli security takes work, but Mossad could slip up and nuclear terrorists could slip in. A major candidate for a terrorist-delivered nuke is Russia, especially in Moscow's Muslim republics, and the Russians are well aware of this. During the Cold War the terrorists' scenario went something like this: (1) the terror team detonates a nuclear weapon inside a Soviet city or near a Soviet military installation; (2) the Russians think the United States did the dirty deed; (3) the two military superpowers eradicate themselves with a strategic nuclear exchange and Islamic radicals pick up the pieces. This maximum result was never all that probable and is less probable now—the United States and Russia would most likely contain any further escalation. But the damage done and chaos spread by such a terror strike would be immense. The terrorists' point, however, would have been more than made.

Given Russia's political troubles, all kinds of other political improbabilities could occur in the wake of such a strike. Conceivably, hard-line military forces could assume control of frightened Soviet republics and border nations as the populace screams for protection. In fact, it wouldn't be beneath the ability (or philosophical inclination) of neo-Stalinists to help Islamic terrorists stage such a strike.

There has been no shortage of volunteers for past suicide missions, and there won't be a shortage of volunteers for the job of nuclear triggerman. As one Shiite terrorist leader told *The Washington Post* (February 3, 1984), "In one week I can assemble 500 loyalists ready to throw themselves into suicide operations. No border can stop me. We are coming to the end of the world. Presidents and ministers are eating each other up. Military men are traitors. Society is corrupt. The privileged, the notables are not worried about the poor. Only Islam can give us hope.'' Such millennial thinking justifies the use of any kind of weapon—and any degree of destruction.

POISON GAS: THE EVIL GENIE IN THE BOTTLE

The huge trench systems and enormous attrition battles of World War I forced tacticians to look for ways to break the deadlock. In April 1915 at Ypres, Belgium, the Germans experimented with a new mass-casualty weapon—chlorine gas. A special engineer regiment dispersed along the front trenches. When the wind began to blow toward the British and French forces, the engineers opened the chlorine cylinders. This experiment, with its resulting greenish-yellow chlorine cloud, opened a two-division-wide hole in the Allied lines. The Germans were as little prepared for their success as the Allies were to defend themselves against gas. After-action reports speculated that if the Germans had followed up the gas attack with a prepared infantry assault, they could have broken through to the English Channel.

Poison gas offers the would-be user a cheap mass-casualty weapon. Chemical agents like liquid mustard are relatively easy to make. College chemistry students with access to a lab can synthesize even more exotic weapons. Many Third World countries can produce potential chemical agents and use them, whether in aerial sprays (like crop dusting from aircraft), mines or fire pots on the ground, bombs, or artillery shells. Several regional powers in the Middle East—Iraq, Iran, Syria, and Israel as noted examples—can top off a medium-range ballistic missile with a chemical-agent-filled warhead with the likely targets being population centers or air bases. The warhead detonates in an "airburst" high over the target, and the chemical agent falls as a deadly drizzle on troops and equipment. Iraq's failure to do this in the Kuwait War does not mean it cannot be done.

Chemical weapons may be of dubious value, however, when used on well-trained and well-equipped soldiers like NATO troops or front-line Russian forces. British and U.S. forces estimate that trained troops, with equipment available, would have fewer than 5 percent casualties, even from a surprise nerve gas attack. The Israelis put a great deal of emphasis on chemical-defense training—their units can be ready for a gas attack in seconds. But Third World forces, like Afghan guerrillas or Iranian Revolutionary Guards or Kurdish insurgents, have no protection; they don't even carry gas masks. And poison gas not only kills, it also terrifies.

Mustard gas (H, HD, or HN in chemical agent symbols) isn't a gas but a liquid. It is a delayed-action and persistent chemical agent which produces large and painful blisters eight to twelve hours after contact. Apparently the Iraqis sprayed Iranian lines with the mustard agent while the Iranian infantry was amassing for "human wave" attacks. Iraq may have also used GA, a nerve agent. It has used a nerve agent on Kurdish insurgents and villages and may have used mustard gas as an "area-denial agent" in Kurdish territory. Iraq's threats against Saudi and allied forces in the wake of the Kuwait War are well documented.

GB, a nonpersistent nerve agent capable of being delivered by artillery shell, and GD "Soman," a semipersistent nerve agent developed by the Russians, may also be available in the Middle East. Iraq still has GB stocks. Syria may have stocks of GD.

Chemical weapons, however, are dangerous to the user as well. During the Gulf War, Iraqi troops were little better prepared to face Iranian chemical attacks. And no nation's civilians, including Israel's, are prepared for a surprise nerve gas attack.

Persistent chemical agents, like mustard gas, remain on the battlefield, and civilians continue to suffer after the shooting and spraying stop. Farmers in France, over seventy years after World War I, still occasionally develop mustard blisters after plowing old battlefields.

SOLDIERS OF THE QUEEN

Most nations are understandably nervous about trusting foreigners to run their armed forces. Yet mercenary troops have long been a logical way for rulers to control their subjects while avoiding revolution spawned in the local military barracks. The only trick is to obtain reliable mercenaries. A ruler has to make sure he is buying troops who will stay bought once they sign their contracts.

The British are familiar and at ease with mercenary arrangements; the Gurkhas from northern India and Nepal still serve in the British and Indian armies. In the "merc world," the British participate by supplying officers and NCOs to many nations. In the 1970s and 1980s, this old tradition was very much alive in the Persian Gulf, particularly in Oman.

And in the 1990s, the Soldiers of the Queen, though less overtly active, continue to press on.

The rulers of the Persian Gulf states are generally local strongmen whose power the population prefers to recognize rather than to resist with arms. So, raising troops from among the locals is not a good way to sustain a strongman's power. An obvious solution is to use mercenaries, which are easy to obtain—many groups in the area have traditionally served as mercenaries for whoever could afford it. Baluchi tribesmen of Iran, Afghanistan, and Pakistan, who tend to be outstanding soldiers, bear arms for the highest bidder.

Other forces from the region, particularly from Pakistan, are available, officially or otherwise, to serve appropriate (meaning non-Israeli) foreign rulers. The Pakistani government has made several defense arrangements with Persian Gulf potentates, lending brigades and fighter-bomber squadrons for local defense. The deal is that the lendee pays for maintenance and expenses, and Pakistan gets the troops and equipment when it needs them (for example, before a war with India).

One problem with using local, homegrown armed forces is the danger of their being lured into local political intrigues. But of course mercenary leaders can also become involved. In December 1989, Col. Robert Denard, a French mercenary commanding the five-hundred-man Comoro Islands' presidential guard, organized the assassination of the Comoro Islands' president, Ahmed Abdallah. Denard, however, while allegedly connected to French intelligence services, was something of a classic mercenary lone wolf. The British Army, though, retains direct links to its officers and NCOs "seconded" to foreign service, and they remain Soldiers of the Queen. For this reason, Gulf rulers have always looked favorably on obtaining British officers and NCOs to lead mercenary troops, or even the local armed forces.

As with any army, the officers and senior NCOs are the keys to effectiveness and reliability. The British Army has had several hundred years of experience in leading mercenary forces and has acquitted itself well in this capacity. While the British government has not been averse to interfering in the affairs of the Gulf states, it has generally done so with diplomacy and tact. (The United States, Russia, Cuba, and Iran rarely display such tact.) With regard to the recent Kuwait conflict, the British have, once again, shown themselves to be militarily reliable as well as discreet.

British officers and NCOs serving in foreign armies often resign from the home forces for the duration of their foreign service, then often rejoin the British Army afterward—with their foreign service time conveniently counting toward retirement. What is even more striking about this foreign service is that the British mercenaries actually command foreign troops in the service of a non-British ruler. This arrangement serves all concerned and demonstrates why some mercenary forces survive and will most likely continue to do so.

INSIDE THE IRAQI ARMED FORCES

The Iraqi Baath regime relies on constant surveillance of both the populace and itself. This is reflected in the "multiple structure" of the Iraqi military. There are several intelligence and security agencies in Iraq, all led by Saddam's personal allies and all having him as their titular leader. Commanders are transferred at the least hint of disloyalty, or often for no reason at all, just to keep everyone off balance. A long-standing Russian practice of having hundreds of thousands of paid and unpaid informers is widely used and provides an up-to-date picture of who is for or against Saddam and to what degree. He trusts no one and sees to it that everyone else in Iraq feels the same way.

Special Forces (SF) brigades are assigned to watch the People's Army and civilian population areas. Critical facilities—including dams, oil fields, pumping stations, and power generation sites—are watched by the local police, the secret police, and elements of the SF. SF units are located near chemical weapons production plants and nuclear facilities and an SF division is assigned to keep what remains of the Republican Guard Forces Corps (RGFC) stable. The SF brigades have been organized into large divisions for "special assignments" such as attacking Kurdish villages with chemical weapons. Iraqi SF units are not special operations forces like U.S. Special Forces, U.S. Rangers, or British SAS; they are political police units capable of conducting extended military missions.

The Republican Guard Forces Corps consists of politically approved troops with its divisions getting the pick of new equipment and support services. Some journalists have compared RGFC units to Hitler's Waffen SS. That comparison is a bit ambitious, but just as the Waffen SS acted as a check on the Army, the RGFC provides the regime with backup in case of a showdown with the People's Army—it has superior firepower and mobility. The U.S. forces in the Kuwait War therefore gave the RGFC particular attention and destroyed six of the eight divisions. Still, the RGFC put down the Shiite rebellion in the aftermath of the war.

The Kuwait War devastated the People's Army. Before the Kuwaiti conflict, the Iraqis had the ability to motorize—for short periods of time and for short distances—anywhere from five to fifteen People's Army infantry divisions.

The Iraqi Air Force was, and is, a mixed bag. Flying the cream of its aircraft to Iran during the Kuwait War did nothing for its reputation. Still, post–Kuwait War Iraq has over 250 aircraft, including Mig-29s and Mirage F1s. These are effective against Kurds and Iranians. The effectiveness of these planes, however, is far more susceptible to economic embargo than Army infantry units, as avionics and parts must be replaced. At the start of the war, Iraq deployed a squadron of Mig-29s when the war began and two wings of Mirage F1s. Quality in second-line Iraqi aircraft, though, falls dramatically. Mig-23s and Mig-21s are still quite capable planes, but before the Kuwait War Iraq was short on qualified pilots and now that shortage is even more dramatic. Chinese J6 and J7 aircraft proved to be in even poorer condition than the Russian aircraft. Iraq still has Sukhoi 7s, Sukhoi 20s, and even older Mig models in its aircraft inventory. However, the Sukhoi-25, the Soviet version of the A-10A attack fighter-bomber, while proving to be a capable aircraft in Afghanistan, is of questionable value in the hands of Iraqi pilots.

CHAPTER 4

THE ARABIAN PENINSULA: RING OF FIRE AROUND ARABIA

INTRODUCTION

The Gulf War posed a severe threat to Arabs living on the Arabian Peninsula. Kuwait received missile and artillery attacks. Iran threatened Saudi Arabia and still tries to spread "Islamic Revolution" (a Shiite variety) to this fragile region, but in the "peace" that followed, Iraq, the victor, proved to be a far larger threat. Demanding control of oil pricing, Iraq, with a combat-proven army, invaded Kuwait, sparking the first post–Cold War crisis.

SOURCE OF CONFLICT

The Kuwait War and the Gulf War are but two of several ongoing wars that border the Arabian Peninsula and circle the Persian Gulf. The tiny nation of Oman sits at Saudi Arabia's back door. It also covers the south side of the Strait of Hormuz, the delicate neck of the Persian Gulf. Just west of Oman lies Yemen. Oman and Yemen have waged a quiet little "camel war" since the early 1980s, with Yemen receiving boatloads of Russian equipment and a large number of Eastern European combat advisers. The Omani Army got a better deal—it obtained a brigade of the late shah of Iran's imperial army and a small but very effective group of British Army instructors.

As the Cold War lapses and Russian support wanes, the Marxist ideology of Yemen is dissipated. In 1990 South Yemen and the royalist northern Republic of Yemen attempted a tentative reunification but their antagonisms go beyond the ideological divide of communism and monarchism.

The troubles of monarchism, geostrategic change, the problems of an Islamic society in the modern world, and the impact of wealth brought by oil—all these factors combine to plague Saudi Arabia, the United Arab Emirates (UAE), a couple of oil-soaked sand pits named Bahrain and Qatar, and a Saudi offspring named ARAMCO. All these brought tragedy to Kuwait in the shape of Iraq's invasion in August 1990 and the subsequent looting of that emirate.

Theology was kind to Saudi Arabia, for it was the original home of Allah's prophet Muhammad. Geology was also kind to Saudi Arabia, leaving it with some 150-plus billion barrels of crude oil. But Saudi Arabia treated the nearly one million Yemenis, expelled during the Kuwait War, for whom it was a temporary home like second-class citizens. This makes the Yemenis, along with a restive Shiite minority in Saudi Arabia and Bahrain, receptive to the Islamic Revolutionary gospel being spread by the ayatollah's heirs in Teheran.

Who's Involved

Saudi Arabia
Gulf nations (Kuwait, Bahrain, UAE, Qatar)
Yemen (North)
Oman
Iraq

Wild Cards

Iran—The shah sent troops to help Oman—and to spread his influence. If an Iranian regime, revolutionary or otherwise, wants to completely control the Strait of Hormuz, it must either politically co-opt or militarily control Oman.

Pakistan—A large number of Pakistani technicians and soldiers assigned as mercenaries by the Pakistani government serve throughout the Arabian Peninsula.

Jordan and Egypt—Jordan could again become a vassal of the Gulf states; Jordan needs the money. The Egyptians, as the largest Arab nation, could see the need to act should Saudi Arabia be threatened.

Other Regional Players

Egypt
Jordan
Israel

Wild Cards

United States
Russia
Turkey
Japan
Islamic republics of the Soviet Union

GEOGRAPHY

Let's start below the ground with a little oil geography. On the Arabian Peninsula, immense structural traps of Mesozoic Age carbonates (like limestone) hold the world's biggest deposits of oil. Saudi Arabia's Khawahr field holds over 80 billion barrels of crude oil. Down south in the Oman mountains the fields are in the comparatively puny 1.5-billion range. However, when compared to the less than 10 billion barrels that were in Alaska's Prudhoe Bay, this puny amount is huge by any other standard.

In Iraq, Iran, and Kuwait, the subsurface is a little different. Kuwait's oil is held in sandstone deposits instead of carbonates; and in Iran, faulting makes locating new oil fields more difficult. But in an era of fossil-fuel-powered economies, the presence of lots of oil increases the strategic significance of the sand and mountains aboveground, where the oil pump sits.

The Strait of Hormuz, the narrow channel between the tip of Oman and Iran, is the throat of the Persian Gulf. The deepest part of the channel lies on the Omani side and is trafficked by outgoing oil tankers. The strait narrows to fifty kilometers in width and much less if the various Iranian and Omani islands are taken into account. Antiship missile batteries, firing Exocet-type missiles, or long-range guns sited on these islands can easily close down the Gulf to merchant ship traffic, but mines are the weapon of choice, as Iran illustrated during the "Tanker War" phase of the Gulf War. (The Iranians seeded the area and Persian Gulf shallows with mines; some moored mines dating from pre–World War I tsarist Russia!)

At the northwestern end of the Persian Gulf near the Shatt-al-Arab lies the tragic emirate of Kuwait wedged between Iraq and Saudi Arabia. ("Kuwait" in Arabic means "small fort.") Iraq and Kuwait signed a border agreement in 1932, but in 1961 Iraq reneged and claimed Kuwait as Iraqi real estate, asserting that Kuwait had once been part of the Ottoman Empire and under Iraqi control. This claim was one pretext for the Iraqi invasion of 1990.

On a per capita basis, before the 1990–91 war, Kuwait was one of the wealthiest nations in the world. (An estimate of the amount of cash and the value of Kuwaiti investments outside of Kuwait is $120–$200 billion.) Of the 1.9 million people living in Kuwait, only 700,000 of them were Kuwaitis. (Of the native Kuwaitis, 70 percent are Sunni Muslim and 30 percent are Shiite Muslim.) The other "expatriates" either worked in the oil industry or "waited" on the Kuwaitis. The Iraqi invaders counted on dissatisfaction among Kuwait's many "servants."

Bahrain Island, the largest of the six islands that make up the tiny nation of Bahrain (600 square kilometers), lies near Saudi Arabia midway between the Strait of Hormuz and the Shatt-al-Arab. Five hundred thousand people live in Bahrain, which essentially serves as a "'pleasure island" for the region. Any government in Bahrain unfriendly to the Saudi monarchy would seriously threaten Saudi Arabia and the UAE.

Qatar (11,000 square kilometers) consists of flat, barren desert. Slightly less than 50 percent of the 320,000 people living in Qatar are Arab—20 percent are Pakistani, 20 percent Indian, and 10 percent Iranian. The United Arab Emirates are a federation of seven Arab states: Abu Dhabi, Dubia, Sharjah, Ajman, Umm al-Qaiwan, Ras al-Khaimah, and Fujairah. Less than 20 percent of the 1.8 million people living in the UAE are UAE citizens; nearly 50 percent of them are Indian or South Asian. The southern boundary of the UAE runs into the Rub al-Khali (the Empty Quarter) of Saudi Arabia. The boundary is undefined; in fact, almost all of the borders on the southern end of the Arabian Peninsula are undefined. The Rub al-Khali borders of Oman, South Yemen, and Yemen are not drawn and Oman and South Yemen are separated by an "administrative line"—no one is quite sure where the boundary is. Yemen, formerly called North Yemen or the Republic of Yemen and South Yemen, share an indefinite desert boundary. Since they opted for confederation, the boundary matters less than it did.

Oman, the elbow of the peninsula, is approximately 300,000 square kilometers in size (everything is approximate since no one is sure of the borders). Part of Oman, the Musandam Peninsula is separated from the rest of the country, as it juts into the Strait of Hormuz. A third of the world's daily oil production sails through this passage aboard tankers. A long coastal plain stretches northwest of Muscat, mountains lie within the interior, and foothills and dry desert extend to the south and west. Oman, bordering the Arabian Sea, benefits from the summer monsoons. Of the 1.3 million people living in Oman, almost 70 percent are of the Ibadhi ("community of the just") Muslim sect, a Shiite offshoot, and the rest are either Sunnis or Shiites. Sizable Indian and Baluchi Pakistani communities live in Muscat and Matrah.

South Yemen has a population of almost 2.4 million. Covering 330,000 square kilometers, the terrain consists of a flat and sandy coastal zone with a mountainous interior. The administrative line dividing South Yemen and Oman moves from the low coastal zone through rocky, dry country, into the mountains and desert. Aden, the capital of Yemen and its major city, is unusual when compared to the rest of the Arabian Peninsula and the Yemeni hinterland in that it has a large African and Indian population and a strong labor union movement. This ethnic mix and the international orientation of Yemen have been one of the causes of trouble with the more tribal Yemen to the north. Recent oil discoveries suggest Yemen may have a billion barrels in reserves, a puddle by Arabian Peninsula standards.

Northern Yemen has a population of nearly 7 million people, with 25 percent of its people working outside of the country as emigrant labor. Most of them are in Saudi Arabia, though many Yemenis also worked in prewar Kuwait. Most of Yemen's 195,000-plus square kilometers are very mountainous, with the tallest mountains being over 3,600 meters high. There is a 64-kilometer-wide coastal strip along the Red Sea, and the mountainous interior is well-watered and supports intensive agriculture. Sana, at an altitude of 2,130 meters, was the capital. Yemen was once the largest part of the ancient Kingdom of Sheba. Recent oil discoveries suggest modest reserves of two to three billion barrels. As of

1990 these fields are beginning to produce and are injecting much-needed hard currency into the country. Still, Yemen resents the Saudi and Kuwaiti oil wealth. Yemen and Saudi Arabia also have some minor border disputes, which explained, to some degree, a Yemeni "tilt" toward Iraq immediately following Iraq's invasion of Kuwait.

Saudi Arabia is approximately one third the size of the continental United States (over 2,330,000 square kilometers). Exact population figures are hard to find, but over 10 million people live in the country, some 7 million of which are Saudis. Riyadh, with a population of over 1.8 million, is the capital. Desert of one form or another—sand, plain, rocky waste—covers the land, and there are no permanent rivers. There are five principal regions: the northern region near Jordan, which is desert populated by Bedouin nomads; the al-Hasa (Eastern Province), which borders the Persian Gulf; the Najd region, where Riyadh is situated; the Asir, a mountainous area on the southern Red Sea coastline; and the al-Hijaz (Western Province) region, which borders the Red Sea. Mecca, Islam's most holy city, is located in the al-Hijaz.

HISTORY

The Persian Gulf area is the site of both strategic and regional conflict. First, but fading, there is the strategic tug-of-war between the West (the United States, Japan, and Western Europe) and Russia over control of oil-supply lines. Though the end of the Cold War makes "the big battle" between the United States and the Soviet Union highly unlikely, the Arabs know that in the long run the Russians may yet have an interest in their oil—a military interest. Second, there are a number of petty but lethal intertribal and ethnic squabbles that have existed for centuries. In the past these squabbles weren't all that deadly; now, however, everyone is armed with automatic weapons and tanks. Some of the participants have first-rate jet fighter-bombers and tactical missiles capable of carrying chemical and nuclear warheads. Some of the participants have used chemical warheads.

The South Arabian states have a history of antagonism between the more worldly coastal dwellers and the nomads in the hinterland. During World War I, T. E. Lawrence ("Lawrence of Arabia") made shrewd use of this fact when orchestrating an Arab "tribal rebellion" against the Ottoman Turks. Even before this time religion was often the nominal reason for these city-dweller-versus-nomad squabbles. These bandit-level set-tos tended to flare suddenly, then die a negotiated death after a half dozen or so of the principals were beheaded. Negotiated settlements usually involved promises of obedience to the sultan and some yearly tribute. Political sides didn't really exist with any more definition than borders drawn in blowing sand. The sand hasn't changed, but the situation has. South Arabia possesses a decidedly strategic position, with easy air-and-sea access to East Africa, the Indian Ocean, the Red Sea, and the Persian Gulf.

World War I, the collapse of the Ottoman Empire, and British-French colonial intrigues in the Middle East introduced nationalism as another religious cause for combat. Pan-Arabist nationalists and "tribal nationalists" (tribes with flags, as some commentators refer to the Middle East) entered the potent brew. Politics remained personal, fragile, and feudal, and compromise on the complex and heterogeneous issues that plague the modern world was often impossible as eleventh-century methods met the twentieth-century. Colonialism made things worse.

South Yemen (or Aden, as it was known under British hegemony) is not the typical case, but it is a case in point. Fighting among leftist groups (1965–68) left the British protectorate of Aden in chaos as Britain withdrew from the colony. The National Liberation Front (NLF), a coalition of socialists and Communists, succeeded in winning the street battles and established a new government in November 1967, then in June 1969 the radical Communist wing of the NLF took control. With certain internationalist additions, such as South Yemeni support for the Palestinian attack on an Israeli tanker in the nearby Mandeb Strait in 1971, the old coastal-versus-nomad antagonisms continued—though in this day and age many of the nomads had replaced camels with Mercedeses. The Southerners have fought pitched battles with Saudi forces inside Saudi Arabia in 1969 and 1973. (In the early 1970s there were a number of PLO and the more radical Popular Front for the Liberation of Palestine (PFLP) guerrilla and terrorist training camps set up in South Yemen, which were supported by the KGB.)

South Yemen's longest sustained combat was with Oman. Beginning with political sponsorship of dissident residents of Dhofar, the South Yemenis began to supply arms and troops to the Dhofar Rebellion along with East German and Cuban military advice. They also set up an Omani "government in exile," indicating they had a bigger goal than Dhofar. The Dhofar War began in the early 1970s, with full-scale guerrilla battles in 1972 and 1973.

In 1973 the shah of Iran offered his paratroops to the sultan of Oman. In September 1973 nearly 1,000 of the 3,000 active Dhofari rebels defected to the Omani government, just as the Iranian-led offensive began to hit back. In December 1973 and early 1974, offensive operations by the shah's paratroopers laid the groundwork for the rebels' defeat, though the fighting dragged on into 1975. Omani units in Dhofar operated with British advisers, and Jordan also sent military support units. Some Iranian Army advisers remained in Oman until the fall of the shah.

In 1979 South Yemen signed a treaty of friendship with Russia. Oman accused Russia of providing renewed support to the would-be rebels. During that year there were reported to be between 800 and 1,000 East bloc military advisers in South Yemen.

Sporadic fighting erupted in Dhofar in 1979 and 1980. In late 1980 and early 1981, South Yemeni troops made several raids across the administrative line.

South Yemen also has an on-again, off-again border war going with Yemen. In February 1979 South Yemeni mechanized forces, allegedly accompanied by East German and Cuban advisers, attacked Yemen and took the villages of Qatabah and Harib. Fighting took place as deep as sixty kilometers inside Yemen. The United States responded by sending aid and equipment to the Yemeni government in Sana. The fighting was renewed in October and December 1980.

Yemen and South Yemen, despite the fighting, have discussed unification on several occasions. The problem, according to most Yemenis, is South Yemen's professed communism: Muslims regard communism as incompatible with their religion. This could well become a problem for South Yemen if the urban Communist elites fail to stem the Islamic revolution that the Iranian Islamic revolutionaries plan on exporting to South Arabia. The two Yemens did unite in 1990.

LOCAL POLITICS

Saudi Arabia

Wahabi sect of Sunni Islam—Highly puritanical Saudi and Gulf state sect of Islam. By tradition, Wahabi law and conduct are modeled on those of the first Islamic communities in Medina and Mecca. The sect is named for the eighteenth-century Islamic religious scholar Abdel Wahab, who became a political ally of the Saud tribe.

House of Saud—Royal family of Saudi Arabia, who spring from the tribe of Saud. Saudi Arabia is run by the royal family in conjunction with several other aristocratic families and the tribal sheiks (*ulama* and *umara*). The House of Saud follows the Golden Rule of Consultation (*shura*) and Consensus (*ijma'*). The king, princes, and aristocrats always try to hammer out a common position that will not alienate the sheiks or the tribes. The regime's legitimacy relies on a careful personal alliance between the House of Saud and the sheiks.

Abd al-Aziz ibn Saud (also Ibn Saud)—Founder of the nation of Saudi Arabia. Born in 1881, he was an ally of the British during World War I. He died in 1953.

The Bridge over the Strait of Tiran—Possible fifteen-mile-long system of bridges and causeways, being discussed by Saudi Arabia and Egypt, that will connect the tip of the Sinai Peninsula to Saudi Arabia. This will be a land route that bypasses Israel and Jordan. Ostensibly for tourists and to help pilgrims on their way to Mecca, the bridge would be actually a wedge against Iraq and Iran—a way of quickly moving Egyptian troops into Saudi Arabia. The bridge, however, faces international environmentalist opposition, as it must cross some of the world's most beautiful reefs.

Kuwait

Pre-1991 Kuwait was ruled by an emir. Until 1986, Kuwait had a parliament—a noisy and free-wheeling forum that was dissolved by royal decree. The parliament had fifty elected members and twenty-five government appointees. In 1989 and 1990 agitation began among Kuwait's many well-educated, well-heeled, and bucks-up citizens. The Iraqi invasion put an end to the democratic agitation.

Diwaniya—Tradition of "open discussion" begun by Kuwaiti sailors and merchants who, in the preoil "Ali Baba" days of Gulf life, gathered to share information ranging from the price of fish and marine rope to the quality of pearls being found offshore. Kuwait is the only Gulf state with anything resembling a democratic tradition—*diwaniya* is the basis of that tradition. *Diwaniya* can also refer to a special room, separated from the house, where these "discussions" take place. Kuwaiti nationalists exiled by the Iraqi invasion strongly favor a democratic government in "restored Kuwait."

Bahrain

The government of tiny Bahrain is a "constitutional emirate" whose ruling clan is the Al-Khalifa family. The Emir dissolved the National Assembly in 1975.

Offshore banking units (OBUs)—Banks based in Bahrain that do not handle local deposits but only deposits for the region's many troubled nations.

United Arab Emirates (UAE)

Federation of seven mini-kingdoms, each run by a prince (emir) and a cohort of sheiks. All were British protectorates until 1971, and because of their size, Abu Dhabi, which constitutes 85 percent of the UAE's area, and Dubai, with its harbor, dominate. The rivalry between all the emirs is rampant.

Trucial Coast—Former name of the UAE area derived from the 1853 "Perpetual Maritime Truce" between the British and tribal leaders. The "truce" was designed to curb local pirates from preying on British shipping between England and India.

Qatar

Qatar is a traditional emirate wherein Wahabi Islam shapes the policy. Its ruling clan is the Al T'hani family but their power is somewhat curbed by the Consultative Council, whose elected members advise the ruling sheik and his council of ministers. The Qatari tank battalion knows how to soldier.

Oman

The government of Oman is an absolute monarchy run by the Al Bu Said dynasty with no political parties. The current ruler, Sultan Qaboos, is a benevolent, educated autocrat, who received his education at the British military academy at Sandhurst. Sultan Said ibn Taimur, his father and the preceding ruler, was a medieval, and rather murderous, autocrat whom Qaboos deposed by a coup in 1970.

Dhofar Province—Site of the low-grade war between Oman and South

Yemen and sometime home of the Popular Front for the Liberation of Oman and the Arabian Gulf (PFLOAG), which later became the Popular Front for the Liberation of Oman (PFLO). The PFLO was a Marxist group supported by South Yemen.

Omani Army—Force of 21,000 strong, with nearly 1,000 British officers and NCOs. Dhofar Province has a 3,500-troop home guard now composed of many of the former rebels sponsored by South Yemen.

Kanjar—Traditional Omani curved dagger.

South Yemen

As of 1990 the government merged South Yemen with Yemen to form a united Yemen.

National Democratic Front—South Yemeni–sponsored leftist political organization that until 1989 was an "exile opposition" to the Yemeni government. Basically it's an organ of the South Yemen government.

Yemen

The Republic of Yemen has an elected general assembly with 159 seats—the Shura Council. Political parties are not allowed, though Baathist, Nasserite, and Islamic fundamentalist groups operate in the open. Its politics are essentially tribal and the government rules by granting fiefs to local tribal rulers. Its courts are basically Islamic and/or tribal. Outside Sana, Yemen is remniscent of the fourteenth century.

Qat—Mildly narcotic leaf chewed in Yemen; men hang out in *qat* dens.

Jambiyas—Traditional, highly ornamented Yemeni daggers. The most precious of these have handles made from rhinocerous horn which makes Yemeni daggers an ecological taboo, and Sana a market for East African poachers.

General

Emir—Title indicating a patriarchal ruler in the Arabian Peninsular nations. It is also an archaic term for a military leader or a provincial governor.

Gulf Cooperation Council (GCC)—Body originally organized in 1981 as a fledgling defense group for the UAE, Saudi Arabia, Qatar, Kuwait, and Oman. Now it is a sort of regional political sounding board.

Mecca—Holiest city in Islam, regarded as a protectorate of the Saudi monarchy. True Muslims must make at least one pilgrimage to the House of God in Mecca during their lifetime. Hizbullah, the Iranian-backed Shiite-Muslim terrorist sect operating out of Lebanon, has called for the removal of the Saudi royal family as the guardian of Islam's holiest shrines located in Mecca and Medina.

The Mahdi (the "Expected One")—The restored leader of Islam who will lead Muslims to final worldly victory. There have been several dozen false Mahdis in the last century.

Caliph (khalifa)—Agent or successor acting on Muhammad's behalf.

Sunna—Islamic code of correct faith and conduct. Sunna is derived from the root of the Arabic word for "custom," suggesting the customary or "the beaten path."

Sunnis and Shiites (Shia Muslims)—Two main sects of Islam.

The Koran—Book of Muhammad's revelations through the Angel Gabriel, the holy writ of Islam, which is augmented by accepted "say-

POLITICAL TREND CHARTS

SAUDI ARABIA

The Gulf War, the Kuwait War, and UN Coalition begin to force changes in the Saudis' "high-tech feudal state."

	1990	1996
		(Absolute Monarchy)
Government Effectiveness	7	6
Government Stability	7	6
Political Cohesion	6	6 −
Repression Level	5	4
Economic Development	7	7 +
Education Status*	6	6

NOTES: 0 = minimum; 9 = maximum.

　All figures apply to Saudi Arabians, not guest workers.

*Urban population only.

KUWAIT

The recovery from Saddam's invasion is quick but not complete.

	1990 (Parliamentary Monarchy)	1996 (Representative Democracy)
Government Effectiveness	5	7
Government Stability	4	6+
Political Cohesion	7	7
Repression Level	3	3
Economic Development	7+	5
Education Status	7	7

NOTE: 0 = minimum; 9 = maximum.

OMAN

Still the Arabian Knights, successfully clinging to a centuries-old life-style.

	1990	1996
	(Absolute Monarchy)	
Government Effectiveness	7	7
Government Stability	7	7
Political Cohesion	6	6
Repression Level	6	5
Economic Development	6	6
Education Status	3	4*

NOTE: 0 = minimum; 9 = maximum.
*Sultan Qaboos is spending a greal deal of money on education; local schools are being built.

ings'' (*hadith*) attributed to the prophet. The Koran is the revealed word for "Islam," submission to the will of God.

Organization of Petroleum Exporting Countries (OPEC)—Arab oil cartel headquartered in Vienna and modeled after the Texas Railroad Commission. It was established in 1960 to coordinate member oil production policies.

United Yemen

United Yemen continues to struggle. Compare this to the charts of the "separate" Yemens.

	1996 (Authoritarian Coalition*)
Government Effectiveness	3
Government Stability	5
Political Cohesion	3
Repression Level	5
Economic Development	3
Education Status	3

NOTES: 0 = minimum; 9 = maximum.

Union appears to be an overall bad deal for North Yemen, until one considers the fact that South Yemen won't be a military threat. But the political union would still be unstable. Getting along with North Yemen will help South Yemen shed its totalitarian image and ease its reentry into the world economy.

*An authoritarian coalition of some type, probably an authoritarian oligarchy with democratic trappings and "autonomy" for locals in Aden.

North Yemen (Yemen Arab Republic)

	1990 (Authoritarian Oligarchy*)
Government Effectiveness	6
Government Stability	5
Political Cohesion	6
Repression Level	4
Economic Development	2
Education Status	2

NOTE: 0 = minimum; 9 = maximum.

*An authoritarian oligarchy with some democratic trappings, and tribally based.

SOUTH YEMEN (PEOPLE'S DEMOCRATIC REPUBLIC OF YEMEN)

	1990 ("Socialist" Dictatorship)
Government Effectiveness	5
Government Stability	2
Political Cohesion	4
Repression Level	7
Economic Development	2
Education Status	3

NOTE: 0 = minimum; 9 = maximum.

PARTICIPANT STRATEGIES AND GOALS

Arabian Peninsula

Saudi Arabia—The Saudis rely on the United States as the guarantor of their existence, though Saudi Arabs dislike the West and the presence of non-Islamic foreigners in their nation. Because of its economic clout, Saudi Arabia is wooed by the rest of the world and other Arabs. As a comparatively defenseless nation, however, the Saudis know they are subject to intimidation by Iraq and Iran, so theirs is a balancing game. Farsighted members of the ruling Saudi aristocracy also know that Russian oil production may peak in the 1990s, and unless Siberia's Arctic reserves pan out, Moscow could once again look south. That means, like it or not, a relationship with the world's superpower, the United States.

Oman—Oman is receiving new U.S. and French equipment, along with U.S., European, and British training groups, of which the British have been by far the most effective. It continues to improve its armed forces and buy more modern weapons. Oman relies on "backdoor" U.S. support to counteract Iranian intrigue. To openly embrace the United States would make Oman vulnerable to Islamic reaction, which could easily spread into Islamic revolution.

Yemen and South Yemen—These countries are exploring unification. The driving factor behind South Yemen's interest isn't simply the end

Regional Powers and Power Interest Indicator Charts

Saudi Arabia and the Arabian Peninsula

Japan is the biggest player that has not shown up to play.

	Economic Interests	Historical Interests	Political Interest	Military Interest	D + 5* Force Generation Potential	Ability to Intervene Politically	Ability to Promote Economic Development
U.S.	7	5	6	7	4	5	5
UK	6	7	5	5+	1	5−	3
France	6	6	5	5	1	4	3
Russia	3	4	4	4	2+	4†	0
Iraq	8	9	8	8	8	7+(§)	4

Iran	7	8	8	7	1‡	7	2
Jordan	8	9	8	8	3+	5	1
Israel	1	7	8	8	4	1	4
Egypt	7	8	8	7	2	7	1
Saudi Arabia	9	9	9	9	2	8	9
Japan	9	1	2	1	2	1	4

NOTE: 0 = minimum; 9 = maximum.

*FGPs as of D-Day plus 5. Except for local armies and militias (e.g., Saudi Arabia itself), virtually all military forces require "lift" or "march time" to bring significant forces into target areas of the peninsula.

FGPs inside their own borders: Oman, 2; Kuwait, 1; UAE, 1–; Qatar, 1–; South Yemen, 2; Yemen, 1+; Bahrain, 0.

†Russian political influence is perhaps higher in South Yemen–Aden region.

‡If the Iranian Air Force and Army are rebuilt into a pre-1979 "shah-sized" force, give Iran an FGP of "3–" for Saudi Arabia and the Persian Gulf coastal area, except the Straits of Hormuz (for that area, see the next chart.)

§Iraq will increasingly use its political sway and military might to influence regional politics (i.e., oil production, oil prices, and curbing Egyptian and Iranian influence).

of the Cold War. Hunt Oil Company has found large oil deposits in Yemen, and South Yemen, which now has some limited petroleum reserves of its own, wants to share in the bounty.

Iraq—Iraq wants to stay together and still compete with Iran and Syria for power in the region.

Iran—Though the desire to spread "Islamic revolution" throughout the region has waned, especially in light of the Kuwait crisis, Iran benefits by keeping other regimes as unstable as Teheran is, which lessens the threat to the Iran "revolution" and also gives Iran a card to trade. Hiz-

STRAIT OF HORMUZ

The Strait of Hormuz is a specific geographic area rather than a nation, but one that is strategically vital. This chart focuses primarily on military capabilities. Remember, force generation potential reflects comparative capabilities in the specific region or country.

Whatever happens in the Gulf states, the ship traffic still has to pass through the Strait of Hormuz.

	Economic Interests	Historical Interests	Political Interest	Military Interest	D + 5* Force Generation Potential
U.S.	6	4	7	7	5†
Japan	8	4	7	5	0
"EEC"	7	6	7	5	2−
Russia	2‡	5	5	6	4+
Iran	9	9	8	9	6§
Oman	8	9	8	8	1−
Saudi Arabia	8	8	9	8	1−

NOTE: 0 = minimum; 9 = maximum.
*For D-Day plus 5.
†D + 15 days' strength is 7.
‡Russia's economic interests could increase if Moscow needs new oil sources.
§FGP of 6 applicative on the Iranian side of the Strait; give "revolutionary Iran" an FGP of 2 for operations in Oman. Shah forces would have had a 4+. Oman's FGP of 1− is for the Iranian side. FGP of 2 in Oman.

bullah's call for stripping the Saudi royal clan of its role as guardian of Islamic shrines is an example of this strategy at work. Ayatollah-inspired assassinations and bombings due to "Islamic revolution" have severely disrupted the rich Arab states of Kuwait, Bahrain, and the UAE. Propaganda directed at Gulf state Shiites has so far failed to ignite a revolution, probably because the Shiite Arabs don't care too much for the Persians and the chaos in Teheran isn't as appealing as domestic peace.

United States—The United States is reconfiguring the U.S. Central Command along the lines of high-tech light infantry and maintaining stocks of heavy tanks within the region. It is trying to get Oman to agree to a permanent U.S. military presence, say, on the island of Masirah, an old British base, which is off the coast and not so cozy as to disturb the local population. The United States and the Saudi monarchy are in this together: The Saudis want to stay rich, which means being able to sell their oil, and the United States, for the sake of its own economy as well as those of its allies', must blunt both left-wing and Islamic revolutionary destabilizations, as well as Russian and Russian-client penetrations. This takes long-range planning, careful politics, domestic political will, and a Central Command that can actually get to the Persian Gulf in time and in force. Selling AWACS aircraft to Saudi Arabia has limited the effectiveness of surprise air raids on Saudi oil fields and military installations.

POTENTIAL OUTCOMES

Events in the Arabian Peninsula will be greatly affected by those in Iraq, Iran, and Syria (see chapter 4) and events affecting the Israeli-Palestinian question. Still, the following events, because of the geostrategic interest in the oil-rich region, will make headlines if and when they occur:

1. 25 percent chance through 1996: Jordanian monarchy toppled.

2. 10 percent chance through 1996: "Successful" "Islamic revolution" sponsored by Iran in Bahrain. Elsewhere in the region (Oman, UAE, Saudi Arabia, Kuwait) there is a 1 percent chance of this.

3. 20 percent chance through 1996: Iraqi "spillover" violence from internal conflict involves Saudi Arabia and Kuwait in a new border war with Iraq. (See p. 121. This could kick off the new "major war.")

WHAT IS SAUDI ARABIA?

The very name of Saudi Arabia denotes the nation's historical origins: Saudi Arabia was initially organized as the personal fiefdom of the Saud family, one of the many Bedouin clans that have long wandered across Arabia trading and warring with one another. In the last two hundred years, three clans have dominated the Arabian Peninsula: the Saudis, the Rashids, and the Hashemites. There were also the Ottoman Turks and various European nations, but until oil was discovered in the area, these external powers did not evince great interest in the affairs of the desert tribes and the only areas of any interest were along the Persian Gulf coast (for fishing, trading, and commerce) and in the (relatively) densely populated Yemen area to the south, where there was more rain and thus more intensive grazing and agriculture.

In the 1700s, the Saudi clan supported a religious revival among local Muslims (Wahabism, still a factor in puritanical Saudi Arabia) and gained control of most of the Arabian Peninsula except for the Muslim holy cities of Mecca and Medina—the Hejaz area. Control of the Hejaz brought with it economic benefits, since Muslim pilgrims had plenty of money to spend. The dozens of tribes that made up the Saudi coalition were difficult to control, and the Saudis lost a lot of their power to internecine tribal fighting in the 1800s. But by exploiting the religious fervor of the tribal warriors, the Saudis regained control of central Arabia, and then parts of western Arabia (controlled by the Rashid clan) in the two decades before World War I. Taking support from the British from 1915 on, the Saudis eliminated the Rashids as a major power by the early 1920s (without making any efforts to assist T. E. Lawrence's "Arab uprising" against the Ottoman Turks). But Lawrence's main Arab ally was the Hashemite Arabs (of Jordan and, until 1925, the Hejaz). In 1925 the Saudis gained control of the holy cities of Mecca and Medina and the Red Sea coast. To keep the peace, the British guaranteed the Hashemite kingdom of Jordan and installed a Hashemite prince as the king of the new nation of Iraq in 1931. The Saudis renamed their larger territory Saudi Arabia in 1932.

British diplomats had not spent all their time with the Saudi clan. Treaties were also made with the ancient (and numerous) Arab emirates on the Persian Gulf coast as well as in Yemen (which was largely hostile to any Bedouin unity). Through the 1920s and 1930s the Saudis had their hands full reining in the Bedouin warriors, who had gotten into the habit of raiding into neighboring Syria, Jordan, Yemen, the Gulf emirates, and

Iraq. This was their sport, and it took a succession of strong Saudi kings to bring these nasty habits under control.

While the Saudi princes struggled hard to tame the tribal warriors, they were also dependent on these same men of the desert for support. What changed this ancient relationship was the first oil wells that began operating in the 1930s. The trickle of oil income began to sharply rise after World War II and became a flood when the oil cartel was formed and prices sharply increased in the early 1970s.

After World War II, Saudi rulers realized that they needed a modern army and air force. But this required educated men to fill the ranks of officers and technicians. The most likely candidates were available from the townspeople, particularly from the Hejaz region. The Hejaz had been conquered by the Saudi-led Bedouin tribes of central and eastern Arabia early in this century. The House of Saud did not feel quite safe with so much of the military being run by Hejaz officers. This problem was solved by recruiting the Hejaz for the Army and Air Force and setting up a separate army, the National Guard, staffed entirely by tribesmen traditionally loyal to the Saudi clan. Thus, the Saudi Arabian Army watches foreign enemies and the National Guard watches the Army. In wartime, of course, both forces would be equally fervent in defending their holy (and oil-soaked) homeland. What the Saudi princes worried most about was a military coup in peacetime.

The Bedouin House of Saud and their personal fiefdom (Saudi Arabia) are unique in other ways. The Saudis are the guardians of the holiest shrines in all of Islam. Every Muslim is obliged to attempt at least one pilgrimage to Mecca, and with increasing wealth and cheaper air travel, many more do so. It is a great honor for the Saudis to guard and maintain the holy places, but they do so largely through enforcing a very orthodox, and puritanical, form of Islam in their nation. The House of Saud came to rule the holy places partially because they were more devout than their rivals and largely because they were more astute militarily and politically. For example, they became allied with the United States because, as they put it, ''America is far away and has no designs on Saudi Arabia.'' This may be less true as the United States becomes ever more dependent on Persian Gulf oil. But the move toward a U.S. alliance is another example of Saudi pragmatism. The Saudis manage to be one of the loudest opponents of Israel (largely because of the Muslim holy places in Jerusalem) while remaining close to Israel's most powerful ally.

The Saudis (and the more worldly Kuwaitis) have managed to live well with their ''gift of oil.'' Although Saudi Arabia is a monarchy, the standard of living of all Saudis has made spectacular gains in the last two generations. Each year, thousands of Saudis pour forth from universities around the world. Few university graduates are taught that monarchy is the best form of government. Yet the Saudi monarchy is also based on ancient tribal practices: The monarchs lead only if the people follow. Three generations ago, a bad king would have to face the rifles of unhappy subjects. Today, unhappy subjects can still shoot a king they are dissatisfied with (as happened in 1975, while the king was giving one of his regular audiences where any subject could petition him), but they can also clamor for democracy or any other new idea that catches their imagination. The House of Saud has so far made a successful effort to merge ancient tradition with twentieth-century wealth and aspirations.

Two other aspects of Saudi wealth capture wide attention. The Saudis maintain the traditional Bedouin (and Islamic) precepts of charity and hospitality. Hundreds of thousands of Palestinians and other Muslims in need are direct recipients of Saudi aid. Within Saudi Arabia, no one is allowed to want for anything. Although millions of foreign workers live in the country, they are well paid and send billions of dollars home each year. But Saudi Arabia is a very puritanical nation (at least by Western standards). Alcohol and public socializing with women are forbidden, and diligently enforced. Lawbreakers are whipped, mutilated, or publicly beheaded or stoned to death. The practice of any religion but Islam is not allowed, nor are Jews allowed in the country. The Saudis, however, are also human and many of the (largely male) aristocrats (up to 1 percent of the population) spend a lot of time outside the country sinning in Western fashion. Saudi princes were always prone to living it up and now they can afford to do it away from the scrutiny of the religious authorities, and this helps keep the peace at home. But it does not keep the peace in other Arab nations. For thousands of years the Bedouin Arab nomads in the area were considered less civilized than the better-educated Arabs living in the urban areas in other parts of the Arab world. The enormous wealth that has fallen upon these ''camel herders'' seems somewhat unfair to many less fortunate Arabs. There is a lot of resentment, and perhaps even more envy, in the rest of the Arab world. It was for this reason that Iraq had some popular support for its takeover of Kuwait. But the Saudis have had to live with the envy and resentment for a long time. They have made their alliances carefully and, being what they are, put their trust in God and keep their weapons and allies handy.

PART TWO

EUROPE

This section starts off, appropriately enough, with Turkey, which has increasingly become the bridge between the Middle East (and Asia) and Europe. Although the Cold War is over and the superpowers and their allies are standing down from over forty years of confrontation, the potential for war still remains in Europe and in many of the usual places.

CHAPTER 5

TURKEY: AS THE SOUTH FLANK BEGINS TO FRAY...

INTRODUCTION

In 1918 the Ottoman Empire collapsed into miserable chaos. But by the mid-1920s, after a bloody war with Greece (in Anatolia, Thrace, and Ionia) and an extended military and political confrontation with French, British, and Italian occupiers, a new republic of Turkey under the remarkable leadership of Kemal Atatürk (Gen. Mustafa Kemal) regained control of the Turkish heartland. The Kemalist republic, using the armed forces as a source of stability, focused on internal Turkish development. The 1910 Turkish "Sick Man of Europe" became the 1990 "Quiet Man of Europe." What was once one of the most powerful and successfully imperialist of nations disengaged from "empire," even from its Arabian fiefs. Under the direction of Atatürk, the Islamic superpower of four and a half centuries embarked on a mission into modernity—a secular government, use of the Latin alphabet, women's rights, public education, and a careful program of industrial modernization. A cornerstone of the Turkish republic was nonrecidivism: Turkey made no claims on lost provinces. What was over would be over. This brought Turkey its longest period of peace, nearly seventy years' worth to date.

As the last decade of the twentieth century began, Turkey maintained the second largest army directly committed to NATO. Ankara's fleet and ground forces guarded the critical Turkish straits (the Bosporus and the Dardanelles), facing off Soviet units committed to Bulgaria and, along the eastern border, inside the Soviet Union itself. But Turkey, ''the flank of NATO,'' also faces other long-standing troubles that will not disappear: armed conflict with Iraq's bloody Baathist regime; lurking conflict with Syria and Iraq—old Arab-Turk hatreds renewed by hostility over water resources; a bleeding Kurdish insurgency in the southeast; Islamic fundamentalist revivals and opposition to the Kemalist secular state; disagreement with the European Economic Community (EEC) which Turkey would love to join; continual strain with Greece over Cyprus and other issues; resentment and suspicion in the Balkans, particularly in Bulgaria; lingering claims of Ottoman-directed genocide by the Armenians; and, last but not least, the prospect of extraordinary change in the old Soviet Union, especially roiling and bloody change in Russia's Turkish provinces.

Now the flank begins to fray . . .

SOURCE OF CONFLICT

Turkey is involved in several active, simmering, or latent armed conflicts. The Kurdish insurgency has flared on and off for *years*. The current insurgency springs from several sources: **(1)** genuine Kurdish nationalism stemming from Kurdish dreams of an independent Kurdistan which was supposed to be established after World War I; **(2)** Russian/ USSR Cold War intrigue, using Kurdish radicals to destabilize an important NATO nation; and **(3)** Kurdish activism in Iran, Iraq, and Syria, spilling over the border. Turkey has also taken in a growing number of Kurdish refugees fleeing Iraq. During the Iran-Iraq Gulf War both combatants made use of Kurdish insurgents. After Iraq launched a series of brutal attacks against the Kurds in 1988, including dousing Kurdish villages with poison gas, the number of Kurdish refugees inside Turkey increased. In the wake of the Kuwait War, Kurds fled Iraq for Turkey, exacerbating the crisis.

The external troubles also have deep historical roots. During Ottoman times, Syria and Iraq were both Turkish fiefs. Arab tribes and urban peoples chafed ''under the Ottoman heel.'' As the Arabs remember it, Ottoman troops and ''high sheriffs'' (''beys of the Sublime Porte'') placed hard taxes and harsher laws on Arab locals. Moreover, the Central Asian Turks were ethnically different from the Arabs. The Turks were also united, tough, and successful, and they did not hide their disdain for the Arabs. In the Middle East, memories of past cruelty, and success, are, unfortunately, long and abiding.

Many Arabs also resent Turkey's comparative success at modernization. Another group, the religious fundamentalists, truly abhor the modernization and Ankara's secular state.

The current border between Turkey and Syria is little more than a line drawn in the sand based roughly on the line Turkish forces withdrew to at the end of World War I. Syria still claims the region around Iskenderun (Alexandretta) and the town of Antakya (Antioch) as part of "Greater Syria."

Iraqi Baathists dream of leading the Arab world and becoming the most powerful state in the Middle East. In part, the Iraqi assault on Kuwait was an attempt to actualize this dream. While Turkey has spent the last seventy years looking toward Europe, the end of the Cold War and changes in the entire southern tier of "Soviet" Turkish republics provide a temptation for renewed and intimate Turkish involvement in the region. Iraq's attack on Kuwait, and Turkey's role as a NATO nation bordering on Iraq, once more pulls Turkey into the Middle Eastern turmoil, where it could once again become the region's powerhouse. But a deeper problem lurks. Iraq's and Syria's thirst for recognition and power might take a backseat to the more immediate question of water. Turkey has a system of dams on the upper Euphrates and also controls the sources of the Tigris. Iraq has railed at Syria over its Euphrates water projects and in the last three years has focused even more concern on the Turks. Iraqi access to chemical and nuclear weapons makes this problem even more significant. On the flip side, in the aftermath of Iraq's attack on Kuwait, Turkey has demonstrated that the back door to Iraq is the northern Turkey-Iraq border.

Europe is another realm of contest. Turks and Europeans have contested the Balkans for nearly eight hundred years. The Bulgarian Communist government, prior to its fall, conducted a vigorous pogrom against Bulgarian Turks, causing 300,000 or more to flee to Turkey. Though some Bulgarian Turks returned to Bulgaria after the revolution of late 1989 and early 1990, the fact remains that the Bulgars despise the Turks, and vice versa, and ethnic suspicions are heightened by memories of Ottoman cruelties both real and imagined.

Greeks still rankle at the years of Ottoman domination. The fact that Constantinople *is* Istanbul has never been forgiven. Many Greeks talk about their successful revolt against the Ottomans—dating from the 1820s—as if it were recent history. Some Greeks covet the Ionian coast, at least from Troy to Bodrum (Halicarnasus). The Greco-Turk War from 1919 to 1922 stirs both Turks and Greeks. All those double names—

Smyrna for Izmir, Adrianople for Edirne, Nicaea for Iznik—are a linguistic clue. Add to this the troubles of Cyprus and its still bleeding
conflict between a Greek majority and a Turkish minority—a Turkish
minority protected since 1974 by an invading and occupying Turkish
army. Add the trouble over exploration for and exploitation of mineral
resources on the Aegean shelf. Add the oftentimes-vicious squabble over
air rights above the Aegean. Add Turkey's desire to join the EEC and
Greece's petulant frustration of that desire. Still adding? How is it (or
how was it) that these two mutually antagonistic nations were ever called
allies in NATO? American money and diplomacy, and indeed the genuine
threat of Russian attack, kept the Turks and Greeks from tangling. And,
to give credit where it is due, the Turks demonstrated great forbearance
in the face of constant Greek provocation.

Islamic fundamentalists inside Turkey have increased their vocal opposition to the heretical Turkish secular state. Likewise, pan-Turkish
extremists, many with ultraright and near-fascist programs, see the potential reorganization (or collapse) of the Soviet Turkish republics as an
opportunity for establishing a new Turkish empire. At the very least, it
is an opportunity to settle old scores with the Russians, whom some Turks
refer to as a "Western" power.

Finally, there is yet another "old war" that won't disappear: the
Armenian situation. Armenian radicals scattered throughout the world
have turned to terrorism to dramatize their call for recognition of the
"Armenian Genocide." The Armenians allege that Ottoman troops killed
over 600,000 Armenian civilians during World War I. The Turkish government, besides disputing the genocide on facts, claims it isn't responsible for what the Ottoman caliphate did or did not do. That only further
angers the Armenians, especially those who dream of establishing a new
Armenian state.

WHO'S INVOLVED

The Kurdish Insurgency/Struggle for Kurdistan

Turkey—This comprises the government in Ankara and the "Euro-
Turks" of western Turkey.

Kurds—Labeled by Ankara as "mountain Turks," the Kurds are a
unique ethnic group related to the Iranians, although they have been a

separate group for over two thousand years. Some Kurds believe they are the descendants of the ancient Assyrians, while others say they are the "Carduchi," the tribesmen who harassed Xenophon and the Ten Thousand as they retreated from Persia in the fourth century B.C. (see p. 74).

Iran and Syria—These two nations have Kurd minorities, and Kurd troubles. Iran has about five million and Syria has several hundred thousand.

Iraq—Iraq has about four million Kurds, some loyal to the Iraqi Baath regime, some influenced by the Turks, and some at odds with all non-Kurd regimes.

The Greco-Turk "Balkan" War

Turkey—Turkey is satisfied with the status quo.

Greece—In the Greeks' eyes, Istanbul is Constantinople and Izmir is Smyrna and so on.

Bulgaria—Hatred for Turkey and Turks runs deep in Bulgaria, as does a desire for western Thrace, now held by Greece.

Wild Cards

Russia, Yugoslavia (or perhaps as Macedonia and Serbia-Montenegro), the United States, Germany, and other NATO and EEC nations allied with both Greece and Turkey.

The Cyprus Conflict

Turkey—The Turkish Army invaded Cyprus in 1974 and at least 25,000 troops remain.

Greece—In 1974 the "Colonels regime," the military dictatorship in Athens gave Greek Cypriot radicals the go-ahead for enosis (the unification of Cyprus with Greece). But the unification failed: The Turks invaded and the "colonels" fell from power.

Greek and Turkish Cypriots—These people inhabit the same island but are divided by language, religion, and tradition.

UN Forces Cyprus—UNFCYP.

Wild Cards

Great Britain—A remnant of the empire, Britain maintains two sovereign base areas on Cyprus, an old protectorate.
EEC—It could see its interests threatened.

The Great Mesopotamian Water War

Turkey
Syria—The Euphrates River is vulnerable to Turkish dams.
Iraq—The Iraqi leg of the Euphrates is vulnerable to both Turkish and Syrian dams; the Tigris River faces increasing Turkish water demands as well.

Wild Cards

Russia, Israel, the United States

Super Wild Cards

Greece, Bulgaria, the Kurds, Germany

The Back Door to Baghdad

Turkey—Until 1918 Mosul and Kirkuk were Turkish, or at least Kurdish cities.
Iraq—In August 1990 Iraq invaded and looted Kuwait.
Saudi Arabia and Arab allies
NATO nations
United States

Wild Card

The UN

The "Pan-Turkic" Conflicts

1990 Nation-states involved:
Turkey
Russia—Moscow dances as its southern empire dissolves.
Iran

National Wild Cards

Bulgaria, Greece

"Turkic Tribes" Involved and/or 1990 "Islamic" Soviet Socialist Republics (SSRs)

Approximately 50 million Turkic peoples live in the Soviet Union (by 1989 census); 11 million in Iran; 7 million in China; 2 million in Afghanistan; 900,000 in Bulgaria; 400,000 in Iraq; 200,000 each in Romania, Mongolia, and parts of Yugoslavia; 140,000 in Cyprus; 130,000 in Greece; and 100,000 in Syria. Here are a few of the tribes:

Kirghiz—Islamic, Turkic-speaking, with a Mongol background, the Kirghiz number 2.2 million in Kirghizia SSR (about 50 percent of population). A significant minority are still described as "pastoral herders" (a few may indeed be seminomadic), though many Kirghiz work in cotton-related industries and mining. Having been Siberian nomads in the Yenisei River region, most of the Kirghiz migrated to Kirghizia in the late 1600s.

Turkomen—There are 4 million Central Asian Turks, over 80 percent of them living in Russia. A small minority still live as nomads, relying on camels for transport.

Azeris—Found in substantial numbers in Azerbaijan SSR, Armenia SSR, and northern Iran. Azeris consider themselves to be Turks. They concluded a trade and broadcast treaty with Turkey in September 1990.

Khazaks—Related to the Kirghiz, most Khazaks are sedentary now, producing a third of Russia's grain in an area as large as the United States east of the Mississippi. Nearly 1 million live in China.

Tadziks—These Muslim people are not a Turkic tribe but a mingling of Caucasian (as in the Caucasus) and other peoples. Their language is related to Persian (Iranian). There are over 7 million, mostly in mountainous border areas of Russia, where they care for herds of sheep and other animals. They are often counted with other Turkic groups in Russia and, because of their proximity, are certainly a part of the Turkish bloc in the area.

Tatars—Crimean Tatars were expelled from the Crimea by Stalin in 1944 but have been drifting back there in the last ten years; 18 million in the USSR.

Uzbeks—This major ethnic group's new nationalist organization, Unity, has 500,000 members. There are 6 million.

Meskhetian Turks—A small Turkish group exiled from Caucasus. Many died at the hands of Uzbek Turks during riots in 1989.

Ethnic/SSR Wild Card

Armenians living in both Armenia SSR and in the Nagorno-Karabakh region of Azerbaijan, and elsewhere in the USSR.

The Armenian genocide—This remains a point of contention. Was it genocide, forced emigration, or a tragedy of war? Did it occur in 1915 or continue until 1923?

Turkey—Is the "Republic of Turkey" responsible for what the Ottoman regime did or did not do to Armenia?

Armenian "diaspora"—Armenians live all around the world, scattered by a history of invasion, forced resettlement, and poverty. Armenia was freed from Persian domination by Alexander the Great (331 B.C.), but history can be cruel to a border state that's between Greece and Persia, then between Rome/Byzantium and Persia, then between Byzantium and Islamic Arabia, then between Byzantium and Turkish tribes, then between Ottoman Turkey and tsarist Russia, then between Turkey and the Soviet Union, then between . . . But the Armenians have never been assimilated; they retain a strong sense of identity and a creative culture. An influential and wealthy Armenian community lives in the United States.

Armenian terrorists—These terrorists have conducted numerous attacks on Turkish citizens and Turkish diplomats around the world.

U.S. Congress—Is Turkey guilty of genocide? Are the U.S. House of Representatives and the Senate capable of making a judgment? Two or three bills suggest some legislators think so.

"International opinion"—This title is given to views expressed on CNN's *World News Report*, ABC's *Nightline*, WNET's the *MacNeil/Lehrer NewsHour*, and on the *New York Times'* and *Wall Street Journal*'s editorial pages.

The Struggle for Turkey's Soul

Kemalists—Will the secular institutions of Kemal Atatürk survive into the twenty-first century?

Islamic fundamentalists—Sunni Muslim clergy believe modern Turkey has lost its Islamic identity and therefore its soul.

Right- and left-wing extremist organizations—These are groups ready to pick up on the chaos (see p. 173).

Turkish Army—Will the Army continue to be the Kemalists' "tool of modernity" or will fundamentalists change its outlook?

GEOGRAPHY

The peninsula of Asia Minor is a geographic bridge between Eastern Europe and the Middle East. Turkey either contains or borders on some of the world's most sensitive geostrategic terrain: eastern Thrace, the Turkish straits (the Dardanelles, the Sea of Marmara, and the Bosporus), the Aegean Sea, the Black Sea, and the southern tier of the Soviet Union. As well Turkey borders on the volatile nations of Syria, Iraq, and Iran. The entire country covers almost 767,000 square kilometers, an area slightly bigger than Texas or roughly double the size of California.

Turkey has a population of 55 million. Turks make up 80 percent of this figure. Kurds account for another 15-plus percent (over 8 million), which makes them a significant ethnic minority, with some sources estimating that as of mid-1990 there were 10 million Kurds in Turkey. Turkey is overwhelmingly Muslim (98 percent). Of that 98 percent, at least 80 percent are Sunnis, with the remaining being Alevi Muslims, a Shia sect. Though making up only 2 percent of the population, important Jewish and Christian communities exist in Turkey, most notably in Istanbul, where Jews have thrived for five hundred years—a world record.

Anatolia (central Turkey) consists of an elevated, fertile plateau ringed by hills and mountains with a comparatively moderate climate. Anatolia was the heart of the Ottoman Empire and remains the center of contemporary Turkey. The ancient kingdom of Galatia occupied eastern Anatolia. (The Galatians of St. Paul's Epistle were Jewish converts to Christianity living in what is now the Ankara area.) The Aegean coastal region, Ionia in particular, is also a fertile area dotted with numerous small harbors. Narrow straits separate the Turkish from the Greek islands close to the coast.

Eastern Turkey is crisscrossed by rugged mountains and badlands and harsh winters characterize its climate. Lake Van, a 130-kilometer-long inland sea in eastern Turkey, was once a major Armenian area. In general, the Kurds occupy the southeastern corner of the nation. Turkey's most famous mountain is Mount Ararat (5,165 meters high) where the Book of Genesis says Noah's Ark docked (permanently). In the northeast the mountains rise sharply from the Black Sea coast and then drop down to the Iraqi frontier. The glacier-fed Tigris River rises in the eastern regions of the Cilo and Sat mountains and twists east then south. The Euphrates River rises to the west and flows through Syria and into Iraq. These rivers share a delta, the Shatt-al-Arab, the strategic waterway that was the hub of the Iran-Iraq Gulf War.

The border with Syria does not follow a natural boundary—except for the city of Antakya and its immediate environs, the border is more or less the World War I cease-fire line drawn along an old railroad bed then extended into the sand. The city of Antakya (ancient Antioch) lies in the southernmost niche of modern Turkey, the Hatay (formerly the Sanjak of Alexandretta or Iskenderun) between Syria and the Mediterranean. It still has a substantial Arab population, which voted to stay with the Turks in a 1920s referendum.

HISTORY

The peninsula of Asia Minor has been so central to European and Middle Eastern history—indeed, human history—that even a ten-thousand-page account would scarcely do it justice. Troy, on the south side of the Dardanelles, flowered and died at least seven times before the birth of Christ. The New Testament, especially the letters of Paul, is like a gazetteer of Asia Minor. And the Council of Nicaea (fourth century A.D., hence Christianity's major statement of faith, the Nicene Creed) took place in what is modern Turkey's town of Iznik.

In A.D. 330, the Roman emperor Constantine moved his capital to Asia Minor, to his new city of Constantinople. The "eastern empire" evolved into Byzantium and more or less held out—through invasion from the east and the Crusades from the west—until A.D. 1453 when Mehmet II and his Turkish army breached the walls.

The Ottoman Empire traces its roots to the Osman Turks. Originally an Oghuz tribe, the original Ottoman, Osman (ruling from 1299 to 1326), was a tribal leader from the border region between Seljuk Anatolia and Byzantium. The Ottomans were successful "ghazis," followers of Islam living on the border with "the infidels," who spread the faith as they extended their power into the heathens' territories. The Ottomans knew how to extend their power over the faithful as well, so other Turkish tribes and eventually many Arab lands fell under their sway.

Mehmet II (1451–81), Selim I (1512–20), known as Selim the Grim, and Suleiman the Magnificent (1520–66) were the Turkish conquerors who brought the empire to its height. For centuries the Ottoman Empire either ruled or contested southeastern Europe, controlled the Arabian Peninsula, either held suzerainty or exercised strong influence over Persia, and dominated North Africa from Egypt to Morocco. The "Sublime Porte" (the Ottoman court and center of the empire) struggled bitterly with the Russians over control of the Black Sea and domination of Central Asia.

The Ottoman Empire began its slow decline in 1683 with the defeat of the invading Turkish forces under the command of Kara Mustafa Pasha at the gates of Hapsburg Vienna. The Austrians and their allies counterattacked, reaching into Hungary, Greece, and the Black Sea coast. The Treaty of Karlowitz (1699) marked the first time the Ottoman Empire signed a peace treaty as the defeated party in a major conflict. Hungary, Transylvania, and parts of Croatia were ceded to Austria, and Podolia was ceded to Poland. From the Treaty of Passarowitz (1718), which ceded the Banat to Austria, to the Treaty of Sèvres (1920), the cease-fire peace treaty concluding World War I, the Ottoman Empire slowly and bloodily shrank. The Treaty of Lausanne (1923), which ended the Greco-Turk War of 1920–22 (called the War for Independence by the Turks), restored some territories.

The Turks refer to the nineteenth century as "our longest century," as it was a period of retreat and failure. There were several attempts to "Westernize," most notably in 1839 when *tanzemat* ("restructuring") a Turkish perestroika was attempted, and largely failed. The rot continued.

The First Balkan War (1912–13) and the Second Balkan War (1913) spelled the end of Turkish power in Europe. These conflicts were kicked off by Austria's grabbing Bosnia (1908) and a series of revolts in Albania (1910–12). The linchpin of the Serbian, Montenegrin, Bulgarian, and Greek alliance was hatred for the Turks. In the First Balkan War, the Greeks took several Aegean islands and the Greek Navy bottled up Ottoman reinforcements. Bulgars besieged Istanbul. The Second Balkan War broke out when the Bulgars attacked Greece and Serbia, feeling they had done most of the fighting but hadn't received their share of the spoils. So as the rest of the Balkans ganged up on Bulgaria, the Turks retook eastern Thrace. Their halcyon days in Europe, however, were finished.

Though the Young Turks (1908–18) of the Committee of Union and Progress (CUP) had tried to revitalize and modernize the Ottoman Empire and Ottoman Army, it was too little too late. The Ottoman Empire was a medieval creature that had blundered into modernity, but with its sheer size and remnant armies, it remained a force to be reckoned with long after its economy, diplomatic creativity, and human energies had fossilized. World War I, and Turkey's decision to side with the Central Powers, finished the Ottomans.

The Treaty of Sèvres (August 1920) carved Turkey into several interesting pieces. Turkey's Arab provinces left the empire and became mandates run by Britain or France. Greece, after acquiring western Thrace from Bulgaria, gained eastern Thrace to a point forty kilometers from Istanbul (the Catalca Line). Greece also gained control of the area around Smyrna (Izmir), where after a five-year period, the people could choose by plebiscite to join the Greek state, and Greece received the Aegean Islands. Italy got Rhodes and the rest of the Dodecanese Islands. The Turkish straits, while under nominal Ottoman control, would actually be administered by an international force which put France and Britain in de facto control of the straits. The Treaty of Sèvres also contained two other promises. An autonomous Kurdistan was to be organized in eastern Turkey, with the Kurds having the right, after a year, to opt for total independence. Likewise, an independent Armenia was to be created. U.S. President Woodrow Wilson would help draw the new Armenian borders. The Ottoman Army was limited to 50,000 troops.

Greek government under King Constantine wasn't satisfied with its slice of Thrace and Izmir behind the Milne Line. Constantinople had to be retaken and, if possible, western Anatolia as well. The Greeks had launched an offensive in June 1920 and had made major gains in central Turkey and eastern Thrace. Mustafa Kemal, the hero of the Turkish defense against the British and Commonwealth assault on Gallipoli in 1915, became the center of Turkish political and military resistance. (He refused to accept Sèvres.) At the First Battle of Inonu (January 1921), along the Inonu River just north of Kutahya, Turkish forces under the command of Ismet Bey stopped the Greek attack. During 1921 each side failed to budge the other. In August 1922, the Turks launched the "Great Offensive" that retook Izmir, with some supplies and arms provided by the new Soviet regime in Moscow, ignoring British and French demands to halt their advance. The Turkish Army reoccupied the straits.

The Greek defeat in Asia Minor was near total. The Turks eventually reoccupied Edirne (Adrianople) and claimed eastern Thrace to the Maritsa River.

The Treaty of Lausanne (July 1923) resulted in forced emigrations of Greeks from Asia Minor and of Turks from most of the Aegean Islands (Turkey received Tenedos and Imbros since they controlled access to the Dardanelles). The Turkish minority in western Thrace was allowed to remain in Greece, and the ancient Greek community in Istanbul was allowed to remain in Turkey. Britain retained its mandate over the oil-rich province of Mosul (Iraq) despite its Turkish and Kurdish populations. No provisions were made for creating an independent Armenia or Kurdistan.

Mustafa Kemal changed his name to Atatürk ("Father of Turks"). He also wrought, organized, and led one of the most far-reaching—and comparatively successful—social and political engineering feats in human history. The Ottoman Empire was toppled in favor of the new republic of Turkey on October 29, 1923. Polygamy was outlawed. The fez was banned. Women were given the vote (1930). The Islamic caliphate (religious primate) was abolished (1924), and Turkey became a secular state. The Latin alphabet was adopted to replace "Arabo-Turkic" script.

Atatürk died on November 10, 1938. He was succeeded by Ismet Inonu (Ismet Bey, the victor of the Battle of Inonu in the 1922 Greco-Turk War). Meanwhile, the abolition of the caliphate and disestablishment of state Islam has made Turkey the bitter target of Muslim fundamentalists and extremist groups.

In 1939 France, holding the postwar mandate to Syria, ceded the disputed Iskenderun region (the Hatay, where Antakya lies) back to Turkey, much to the dismay of the Syrians. While viewed by some as an opportunistic return to squabbling over borders (despite Atatürkists' claims to renounce "irredentism and recidivism"), the Hatay issue had been left dangling in 1920. France and Britain saw giving the Hatay back to Turkey as a means of assuring Turkish neutrality in the approaching war with Germany (World War II).

Atatürk's Republican People's party (RPP) ruled Turkey as a rather unique single-party state, although at the same time encouraging the development of the opposing Democratic party. Though created in 1946, the Democrats won the election of 1950 and assumed power. The Turkish military has acted as arbiter of Turkish politics and has taken, and released, governmental power three times in the last forty years.

The Kurds rebelled in 1925, protesting the Kemalists' disestablishment of the Islamic caliphate. In 1930 a Kurdish insurgency broke out in the Lake Van and Ararat region (the town of Dogubeyazit was destroyed in the fighting). In 1937 Kurds and Turks clashed in the Tunceli area. Turkey was pursuing anti-Kurd policies, referring to Kurds as "mountain

Turks," thus playing down the nationalist angle in favor of unruly mountaineers, and many of the eastern provinces were under permanent martial law. Ankara moved thousands of Kurds from the east and settled them in western Turkey. Kurdish nationalists were deeply involved in the leftist agitation of the late 1970s, the political activity that led to the Turkish Army takeover in 1980.

In 1984 the latest round of Kurdish attacks inside Turkey began. The Kurds had been involved in guerrilla activities inside Iran and Iraq, both before and during the recent Iran-Iraq War. Ironically, Turkey has been a haven for many Kurdish refugees fleeing the Iraq War and Iraqi attacks on Kurdish villages in Iraq. In 1989 and 1990 the Turkish Army and Kurdish guerrillas regularly clashed in the southeastern mountains.

Cyprus has been a constant sore in Greek-Turkish relations. The alleged birthplace of Aphrodite, the goddess of love, Cyprus has historically been a Greek island, though one ruled by a series of foreign invaders. The Turks took the island in 1570. In 1878 Great Britain took over, and by that time a large Turkish minority lived on the island.

During the 1950s, the Greek Cypriots began to press for enosis, union with Greece. The Greek Cypriot terrorist organization EOKA (directed by Colonel George Grivas) waged an ugly insurgent war against the British, whose stupidity prolonged the conflict. In 1960 an independent Cyprus emerged, with a Greek president, Archbishop Makarios III, Greek Orthodox Primate of Cyprus, and a Turkish vice president, Rauf Denktash. Britain retained two military bases "in perpetuity." It and Turkey were to guarantee Cypriot sovereignty and Turkey was allowed to post a small contingent of troops on the island; enosis with Greece was denied.

In 1963 the Cypriot government collapsed. EOKA terrorists attacked Turkish villagers and battles broke out between Greek and Turkish Cypriots. Turkey threatened an invasion. British troops failed to bring calm, as did UN forces (UNFICYP). In 1967 Colonel Grivas, supported by the militaristic "Colonels regime" in Athens which had taken power in Greece, formed a new force, EOKA-B, also dedicated to enosis.

In 1974 EOKA-B attempted a coup in Cyprus. The Turkish Army, invading to protect the Turkish Cypriot minority, eventually took nearly 40 percent of the island. As of 1990, Turkey still occupies the northern third of Cyprus, with a rump "Turkish-Cypriot republic" (Republic of North Kibris)—recognized only by Ankara—governing in the Turkish-occupied zone.

Turkey and Greece have also clashed over air control and air corridor rights over the Aegean, as well as over exploration for and exploitation of Aegean shelf resources. The Greek community in Turkey has dwindled, which the Greeks claim is due to Turkish interference. In 1955 there were a series of anti-Greek riots in Istanbul in which over fifteen hundred people died. The Turks claim that Turks living inside Greece (western Thrace) have had their land stolen and that Turks on the island of Rhodes have been forcefully "Hellenized."

Turkey and Bulgaria have been at bitter odds over Bulgaria's treatment of its Turkish minority. In 1989 over 300,000 Bulgarian Turks fled across the border into Turkey but the collapse of the Bulgarian Communist regime has somewhat mitigated this current round of Bulgar-Turk ethnic friction. In January 1990, at a mass anti-Turk rally in Bulgaria, demonstrators chanted, "Bulgaria is not Cyprus," referring to the division of Cyprus into Greek and Turkish zones after the intervention of the Turkish Army.

Turkey's often troubled relations with Iraq and Syria have several rotten historical roots. The Iraqi province of Mosul and the area around the town of Kirkuk, both oil-producing regions, were once a Turkish province with a Turkish majority. Syria was not at all happy about the loss of the Hatay (Iskenderun/Antakya). All three nations have trouble with the Kurds, and all three have played the "Kurdish card" on one another. During the Iran-Iraq War articles appeared in the Turkish press discussing what Turkey might do if Iraq lost and were dismembered; speculation included recovering the "lost Turks" of the Mosul area. The Iraqi invasion of Kuwait, which used a latent Iraqi claim to Kuwait as justification for Baghdad's annexation of the emirate (based on control of Kuwait via the Turkish fief of Basra), raised eyebrows—Turkey's claim to northern Iraq had a better basis in fact than Iraq's claim to Kuwait.

The Southeast Anatolia Project (SAP), a huge water control and dam project on both the Tigris and Euphrates rivers, has become particularly troublesome. Filling the immense reservoir behind the Ataturk Dam (one of twenty-one dams and seventeen hydroelectric projects in the SAP) will require four times the annual flow of the Euphrates. When the SAP is completed (around 2005), Syria's water flow in the Euphrates could shrink from 32 billion cubic meters a year to 20 billion; Iraq's from 30 billion to less than 11 billion. In 1990 the Syrian government blamed Turkey for a series of electrical outages allegedly caused by loss of flow in the Euphrates River. The Iraqi invasion of Kuwait and Iraqi threats to use chemical weapons on Israel and Saudi Arabia was also a message for the Turks. The Turks reacted.

Relations with Iraq went from bad to terrible. The Turks pinned down ten Iraqi divisions during the Kuwait War and allowed coalition air attacks from Turk bases. Iraq's pillage of the Kurds lays the groundwork for more trouble.

Finally, there's the Armenian problem. In 1915 at least 600,000 Armenians died—which is a rough figure the Turks accept. Armenians claim nearly 1 million were killed in a genocide conducted by the Ottoman armed forces. However, 600,000 seems to be the consistent figure. The source of all this mayhem was World War I. In 1915 the Russians attacked through eastern Armenia and many Armenians supported the invaders. There is no question that a number of Armenian leaders in Istanbul were rounded up and executed. The historical issue is the deaths of Armenians displaced by the fighting. Were they massacred by Turkish troops in a calculated act of genocide or did Armenian civilians die from starvation, exposure, and "incidental" fighting? The Turks point out that 2 million Muslims (i.e., Turks) died at roughly the same time, and they call it a reprehensible tragedy all the way around—but not a genocide. The Armenians don't believe it. They point to evidence that the Ottomans gave permission to the Kurds to destroy Armenian communities. The Armenians contend that the atrocities continued until 1923 and that the Turk-Armenian conflict of 1920 was part of the genocide. They also note that in 1926 Atatürk himself deplored the killings in a press interview.

The political battle continues, as does a terrorist conflict. Armenian extremists began assassinating Turkish diplomats in 1973. Since 1975 the Armenian Secret Army for the Liberation of Armenia (ASALA) has been the primary Armenian terrorist organization and is allegedly connected to several Lebanon-based Arab terrorist organizations. A substantial Armenian community lives in Lebanon and Syria.

Armenia has existed as a separate state on several occasions, most notably in the first century B.C. when "Greater Armenia" stretched from the Caspian Sea to the Mediterranean (the empire of Tigranes the Great). For the greater part of recorded history, however, it has been a country "in between"—wedged between major regional and/or world powers. Armenia was the first state to accept Christianity as its official religion (A.D. 301). The Armenians' "Christianity in a Muslim sea" helped them keep their identity in conflicts with various Turkish peoples, the Arabs, and the Persians, but the Armenians didn't get along with fellow Christian Georgians and Russians either. An Armenian state (Eviran) existed briefly in 1920, but was overrun by the Red Army and incorporated into the Soviet Union. At the present time there are at least 4.5 million Armenians in the Soviet

Union, and in fact, the Armenian SSR is the most ethnically homogeneous Soviet republic—nearly 95 percent of the population is Armenian.

LOCAL POLITICS
Turkey

The Meclis—Grand National Assembly with 450 elected members.

"7–10"—Formula for U.S. military assistance for Turkey. For every ten dollars Turkey receives, Greece gets seven.

Motherland party (Anap)—Kemalist party dominated by Turgut Ozal. This is the major party in Turkey.

Social Democrat Populist party (SHP)—Left-wing party led by Erdal Inonu (the son of Ismet Inonu), a faculty member of the elite Robert College (University of the Bosporus) in Istanbul.

True Path party (Dogru Yol—DYP)—Right-wing party headed by Suleiman Demirel. This is sometimes translated as the "Correct Way party."

Democratic Left (DLP)—Led by ex-premier Bulent Ecevit.

Green party—Nascent Turkish environmentalist party.

Welfare party (WP)—Formerly the National Salvation party (NSP), a party openly espousing an Islamic political philosophy.

Nationalist Labor party—Formerly the Nationalist Movement party, a neo-fascist party and political home of the Gray Wolves.

Gray Wolves ("Boz Kurt," literally, "ashen wolves")—Fascist Turkish underground terrorist movement led by Col. Alpasla Turkes. The Gray Wolves may now be involved in the drug trade and are allegedly tied to the Bulgarian Communist secret police. They take their name from Turkish mythology: Out on the steppes of Central Asia the "first Turk" was supposedly suckled by a wolf. The Gray Wolves could become a potent force.

Turkish Socialist party—Party of Maoist-oriented socialists.

Irtica—Turkish word of Arab origin meaning "religious reaction" —in Turkey's case, Islamic fundamentalist religious reaction.

Pro-Iranian "Islamic" political parties or pressure groups—Hizb al-Islam (People of Allah), Islamic Jihad, and Hizb al-Tahrir (Freedom party).

Tarikats—Militant religious orders with a long history in Turkish culture and politics. The basic unit is a *dergah*—a small group of the faithful united around a specific teacher (a *seyh* or *halife*). The orders include the Nurcu, the Suleimanci, and the Naksibendi. The Naksibendi dates back to the fourteenth century. The Isikcilar is a Naksibendi splinter group that supports the Motherland party.

Dev Sol ("Revolutionary Left")—Radical Marxist terrorist group nominally supportive of the Kurds and involved in assassination of several members of the Turkish government.

Turkish Army of the Aegean—Turkish armed forces not committed to NATO.

Incirlik—Site of the major U.S. Air Force base in south central Turkey. F111s attacked Iraq from this base.

Kurdistan

Workers party of Kurdistan (Parti-ye Karkaran-i Kurdistan—PKK) —Main Kurdish resistance group active in Turkey. Organized by Abdullah "Apo" Ocalan, it is drawn primarily from the poorest Kurdish area. The followers of Ocalan are also called Apocus. The PKK units are called HRKs (an acronym for Kurdish Liberation Brigades). It did have troops trained in Lebanon, but its support bases have now shifted to Iraq. The PKK receives significant support from Syria. Ocalan is alleged to be living in Syria.

Pesh Merga ("Those Who Face Death")—General term for Kurdish resistance, but usually applied to Kurdish resistance inside Iraq.

Fatsis—Kurdish "people-free" zones, areas "liberated" in Turkey where the PKK can operate relatively free of Turkish or Iraqi interference.

Turkish Gendarmerie—120,000-man-strong internal police force whose primary task (along with Turkish National Police Commando units) is confronting the PKK guerrillas.

Kurdistan Democratic party (KDP)—Kurdish party inside Iraq.

Kurdish Republican party—Kurdish party inside Iraq.

Illegal Iraqi Kurd parties—Democratic party of Kurdistan, Socialist party of Kurdistan, and Patriotic Union of Kurdistan.

National Liberationists of Kurdistan (KUK)—Kurd organization often at odds with the PKK.

Massoud Barzani—Kurdish leader seeking total Kurdish autonomy from Iraq.

Saladin—Most famous Kurd who is remembered for his successes against the Crusaders—he retook Jerusalem for Islam in 1187.

Yazidi (or Yezidi, "Peacock Worshippers")—Yazidi Kurds numbering 80,000–100,000, who worship the sun and hold water sacred as well. They are said to believe that God may ordain what happens on earth but He lets the devil execute His orders. They may be direct descendants of Assyrians and are viewed by Sunni Turks (and most Sunni Kurds) as extreme heretics.

Treaty of Sèvres—Document that in 1920 divided the Ottoman Empire and promised the Kurds autonomy with "fixed frontiers," i.e., their own homeland, Kurdistan. This treaty was replaced by the Treaty of Lausanne (1923).

Cyprus

Political parties—Cypriot Democratic party (DIKO), Democratic Rally party (DISY), Cypriot Socialist party (EDEK), and Communist party of Cyprus (AKEL).

Cypriot National Guard—Greek Cypriot Army which consists of 10,800 troops with another 2,000 "regulars."

"Turkish Republic of Northern Cyprus"

National Unity party—Rauf Denktash and Dervis Eroglu Republican Turkish party and Communal Liberation party—Mustafa Akinci; leftist opposition parties.

New Cyprus party—Alpay Durduran

Turkish Army—Of approximately 30,000 soldiers, the two infantry divisions and armored regiment inside Cyprus.

Armenia

Armenian Secret Army for the Liberation of Armenia (ASALA)—Terrorist organization founded by Hagop Hagopian.

Armenian Revolutionary Federation—International revolutionary and socialist party that wants to establish a "United Armenia." This would consist of Armenia SSR, plus the rest of the region demarcated for an Armenian state by the Sèvres Treaty, plus Nakhichevan and Nagorno-Karabakh, which are autonomous regions of Azerbaijan SSR.

Armenian Apostolic Church—Central Armenian Christian church. Because Mount Ararat was the center of Armenia, many Armenians believe that God chose Armenia as the place to begin humanity anew after the biblical Flood.

Treaty of Turkmanchai (1828)—Document that ceded the province of Erivan (Armenia) from Persia to Russia.

Greece and Bulgaria (See p. 161.)

POLITICAL TREND CHARTS

TURKEY

Turkey makes significant social and economic strides in the 1990s. It took eighty years for the "Sick Man of Europe" to begin to get well. Political chits earned during the Kuwait War will also pay off.

| | 1990 | 1996 |
		(Authoritarian Democracy)
Government Effectiveness	6	7
Government Stability	6	7
Political Cohesion*	6	6+
Repression Level	5+	4
Economic Development	4+	5+
Education Status	4	5−

NOTE: 0 = minimum; 9 = maximum.
*Excluding Kurdish problem = 7.

GREECE

The corruption of the recent Papandreou government harmed Greece. But Greek business savvy and enterprise should push economy on an upward trend. A stable oil price is critical to Greek economic performance.

| | 1990 | 1996 |
		(Representative Democracy*)
Government Effectiveness	3	6
Government Stability	4	7
Political Cohesion	7−	8−
Repression Level	4	3−
Economic Development	5−	6(6+ ?)
Education Status	5+	6

NOTE: 0 = minimum; 9 = maximum.
*A representative democracy, but with very authoritarian aspects, especially if the Greek Socialist party (PASOK) is in power.

And, for an argument's sake:

"Independent Cyprus" (combining Greek and Turk halves of the island of Cyprus)

This theoretical country is ripe for another split.

	1996 (Representative Democracy*)
Government Effectiveness	4
Government Stability	3
Political Cohesion	2
Repression Level	4
Economic Development	4 −
Education Status	4

NOTE: 0 = minimum; 9 = maximum.
*A representative democracy, but a curious one; the Turks would have to have extensive political guarantees to keep them from being politically victimized by the Greek majority.

"Turkish Republic of Cyprus"

It's theoretical, it's Turk, and it's poor.

	1996 (Foreign Military*)
Government Effectiveness	6
Government Stability	6
Political Cohesion	6
Repression Level	6
Economic Development	2
Education Status	2

NOTE: 0 = minimum; 9 = maximum.
*In this case, Turkish.

"Kurdistan" (carved from Turkey and Iraq)

Not much here except bare mountains, tough people, and oil in Kirkuk. That's the plus in all the poverty.

	1996 (Authoritarian Coalition)
Government Effectiveness	3
Government Stability	2
Political Cohesion	6
Repression Level	7
Economic Development	1+
Education Status	1−

NOTE: 0 = minimum; 9 = maximum.

"Armenia" (carved from Turkey and former Armenia SSR in the USSR)

Actually, this theoretical country might make it, The Armenians have economic drive and a supportive (and rich) "exile network."

	1996 (Authoritarian Democracy)
Government Effectiveness	5
Government Stability	6
Political Cohesion	7
Repression Level	4
Economic Development	3−
Education Status	4

NOTE: 0 = minimum; 9 = maximum.

REGIONAL POWERS AND POWER INTEREST INDICATOR CHARTS

TURKEY AND ITS TROUBLES

Germany has a long-standing interest in, and ties with, Turkey. This could become significant in the future as a united Germany grows economically stronger.

	Economic Interests	Historical Interests	Political Interest	Military Interest	Force Generation Potential	Ability to Intervene Politically	Ability to Promote Economic Development
Russia	4	9	7	8	9−(*)	5	1
Greece	3	9	9	9	3	4	3
Syria	2	8	7	8	4	2	2
Iraq	3	6	6	7	1+(†)	2	0+
Iran	2	4	5	2	1	3	1
Israel	3	3	3	3	1+	1	2
U.S.	5	4	7	7	4	7	5
Germany	7	6	7	6	1−	5+	6+
Bulgaria	4	8	7	6	1−	2	4
Kurds	6	9	9	8	2	3−	1
"Armenia"	7	9	8	8	1−	1	0

NOTE: 0 = minimum; 9 = maximum.

*"All-out" Russian effort in Thrace, the Black Sea, and eastern Turkey; highly unlikely but Moscow can do it, even with conventional forces.

†An Iraqi "+" for "future" oil pipeline payments.

GRECO-TURK "BALKAN WAR"

Choosing up sides for the next chapter of a three-thousand-year-old war.

	Economic Interests	Historical Interests	Political Interest	Military Interest	Force Generation Potential*
Greece	8	9	9	9	6+
Turkey	9	9	9	9	8
Bulgaria	7	9	8	8	3
U.S. †	5	5	8	8	5
Russia †	5	8	8	7	8‡
Yugoslavia †	6	7	7	7	2‡
Romania †	6	6	7	7	1‡
Germany †	6	6	9–	7	1

NOTE: 0 = minimum; 9 = maximum.

*FGPs for Thrace; southern Bulgaria, and the Aegean regions of Turkey and Greece.

†Actual combat participation unlikely, but forces must be considered.

‡Russia FGP for D+20 in Bulgaria and European Thrace; Yugoslavian and Romanian figures for Bulgaria and Grecian (western) Thrace.

CYPRUS

Centuries-old battleground between Turkish and Greek partisans.

	Economic Interests	Historical Interests	Political Interest	Military Interest	Force Generation Potential	Ability to Intervene Politically	Ability to Promote Economic Development
Turkey	3	8	9	8	9	8	7
Greece	2	8	9	6	3	8	7
UK	1	7	7	6	3	4	6
U.S.	1	5	7	6	6	7	5
Israel	2	6	6	7	2	1	2
Syria	2	7	3	6	1	2	0
"UN"	—	7	8	8	1	7	—
Greek Cyprus	9	9	9	9	2	6	9
Turkish Cyprus	9	9	9	9	1–	5	9

NOTE: 0 = minimum; 9 = maximum.

KURDISH INSURGENCY

Many nations have an interest in preventing Kurdish unity, few gain by a united Kurdistan.

	Economic Interests	Historical Interests	Political Interest	Military Interest	Force Generation Potential	Ability to Intervene Politically	Ability to Promote Economic Development
Turkey	7	9	9	8	8	8	6
Iran	6	8	7	6	3+	7	6
Iraq	8	8	8	8	8	7	7
Russia	2	6	6	5	3	5	1
U.S.	1	5	2	2	1–	6*	4
Syria	2	6	6	6	1	5	1

NOTE: 0 = minimum; 9 = maximum.
*The United States may gain leverage after the Kuwait War victory.

MESOPOTAMIAN WATER WAR

Turkey is where the great Tigris and Euphrates rivers start, and Turkey is willing to defend its right to do what it wants with that water. (The chart assumes Turkey, Syria, and Iraq are combatants.)

	Economic Interests	Historical Interests	Political Interest	Military Interest	Force Generation Potential*	Ability to Intervene Politically
Turkey	8	8	9	9	8	—
Syria	9	9	9	9	7+	—
Iraq	9	9	9	9	5–	—
Iran	2	8	7	7	1+	6
Israel	2	7	7	8	3	2
U.S.	5	6	7	6	2	7
Russia	4	6	7	7	3	7
Greece	1	4	8+	8	—	2
Bulgaria	1	2	7	6	—	1

NOTE: 0 = minimum; 9 = maximum.

*FGPs for southeastern and southern Turkey, Iraq north of Baghdad, and all of Syria. Greece and Bulgaria could exert pressure on Turkey along Aegean and Thracian fronts. U.S. FGP could hit a "7" in an emergency.

Participant Strategies and Goals

Turkey—Ankara's first order of business is to improve its economic performance. The Turkish government is engaged in a massive attempt to improve public schools and raise education standards. The Turks perceive the devolution of the Soviet Union as a potential economic boon. For the first time in five hundred years Turkey could be an exporter of technology—to Russia and to the Turkic SSRs.

But the Kurdish problem remains. The strategy of detribalization of the Kurds hasn't worked—they've been moved into the cities where they stay poor. The most likely move is to continue to try to destroy PKK guerrillas in the field and hope an expanding economy will buy off Kurdish moderates. The Turks have been more successful in pacifying their Kurds than has Iraq or Iran, but that's not saying much.

Ankara would accept an independent Armenia, if it were made up of the old Soviet Armenian SSR; but troubles would continue if the new Armenia began to agitate for "old Armenian lands." Ankara might (quietly) encourage the Russians to keep a lid on the Armenians.

Turkey is still wary of Iraq's armed forces and advanced weapons. Ankara thinks Syria and Iraq should trust it not to turn off the water spigot on the Tigris and the Euphrates and has so far let it go at that. The Turks have never had a high opinion of Arab military prowess, and the Iraqis' army and chemical weapons are respected, but not feared. The Turks' response to the Iraqi Kuwait invasion illustrates this point.

The Turks are confident that relations with Greece and Bulgaria will remain stable—perhaps rhetorically nasty at times but no more than that. Turkey wants desperately to join the EEC and resentment of Greek blockage of Turkish admission to the EEC could grow. Turkey's long-range aim in Cyprus since the late 1970s is partition—Ankara believes nothing else is practical.

Syria—Damascus has played and will continue to play the "Kurdish card" against Turkey. Right now the issue is control of water. It could once again become Alexandretta and Antioch. Syria is wrapped up in Lebanon and still faces down Israel. It cannot really afford to become militarily involved with Turkey, but if Turkey gets into a scrape with the Greeks and Bulgars, and if Syria's share of the Euphrates River water is threatened . . .

Iraq—Iraq wants its own Kurds to know their place—as second-class citizens. Iraq's brutal treatment of the Kurds after the Kuwait War showed how afraid Baghdad remains of the Kurds and of fracturing into a "big

Iraqi Lebanon.'' Iraq never wanted trouble with Turkey—Baghdad's Baath regime was shocked by Turkey's shutdown of its oil pipeline and military alliance with Saudi Arabia. The Kurd conflict, the damming of the Euphrates River, and control of the Mosul-Kirkuk region remain live issues between Ankara and Baghdad.

Armenian nationalists—The Armenians continue to court world opinion and hope the devolution of the Soviet Union will give them hope for establishing an independent Armenia. After that, they'll start working to regain the Lake Van area from Turkey. Whatever happens, Armenian radicals will continue to be active—with bombs and bullets.

Pan-Turkic radicals—Though it's small in number, pan-Turkism, the unity of all Turkic peoples, has a grand romantic appeal. The devolution of the Soviet Union gives these groups what they perceive as a unique historical opportunity to return Turkey to its glory.

Muslim fundamentalists inside Turkey—This group keeps bemoaning "the loss of Turkey's soul" to Western materialism and hoping that economic failure will lead to an increase in their political power.

Greece and Bulgaria—This opposition to Turkey will continue to forge an anti-Turkey alliance in the Balkans and wait for an opportunity to settle scores. If they can get Turkey caught up with Iraq and Syria, they might (mistakenly) perceive an opportunity to act militarily.

Greek Cypriots—Though the prospect of enosis grows remoter, there is still some hope for withdrawal of the Turkish Army and a reunification of the island.

Turkish Cypriots—Turkish Cypriots continue to demand equal status at negotiations with Greek Cypriots. If enough time passes, an independent Turkish Cyprus may be a de facto reality.

POTENTIAL OUTCOMES

Kurdistan

1. 35 percent chance through 1996: Kurdish resistance, post–Kuwait War publicity, and Turkish political concerns vis-à-vis EEC integration and world opinion lead to an autonomous Kurdish region within Turkey and Iraq. Kurds emigrate into Turkey from Iraq and Iran, exacerbating regional tensions.

2. 25 percent chance through 1996: The Turkish Army wins this round of Kurdish conflict inside Turkey and suppresses revolt for a decade or more. Turkey pays an initial political price in Europe; but, alas, Europe soon forgets about the Kurds.

3. 25 percent chance through 1996: Insurgency continues at late 1980 levels with no resolution. Turkey pays the political price in Europe but accepts it.

4. 8 percent chance before 1996: The Mesopotamian Water War or another regional war erupts (Iran invades Iraq?) and the Kurds ally themselves with Turkey in hopes of backing a winner and gaining Kurdistan. (The Kurds don't forget that Iraq gassed them.)

5. 7 percent chance before 1996: Iraq, Iran, Turkey, and Syria cooperate to defeat the Kurds. (Iraq, in particular, and Iran commit genocide; the Kurds accept Turk conditions in preference to the hell of Iran and Iraq. The "Kurdish problem" disappears in Turkey for fifty years.)

Greco-Turk Balkan War

There is a minimal 4 percent chance of outright war erupting through 1996. The United States still has a great deal of political sway in Athens and Ankara. As for armed friction occurring (ships pointing weapons at one another, airplanes buzzing one another), it's a 99.9 percent sure thing if the Greek Socialists (PASOK) are in power. Otherwise, it's a near certain 85 percent.

Who wins if this stupid conflict occurs? The biggest likelihood is a massive and expensive stalemate.

1. 80 percent chance: There is a stalemate with border shifts of ten kilometers or less, and one or two islands lost or taken. Still, look for several thousand casualties.

2. 12 percent chance: There is a Turkish victory whereby Turks gain three or four islands, smash several Greek and Bulgarian regiments, and maim the Greek Navy.

3. 8 percent chance: There is a Greco-Bulgarian victory whereby the Greeks gain a slice of the Turkish coastline and/or take a Turkish island, hold a couple of medium-sized Turkish towns, sink a pair of Turkish destroyers, and bottle up the rest of the Turkish Navy in the straits and Black Sea. The Bulgars shell Turkish Thrace and feel like they've accomplished something.

Cyprus

1. 75 percent chance through 1996: The Turkish Army continues its occupation and the current (1990) Greek and Turkish zones remain split. (There is a great deal of stability in this situation. The Turkish Cypriot community fears any Turkish Army pullout.)

2. 20 percent chance through 1996: A UN-brokered treaty leads to a Turkish Army pullout and UN forces guarantee the protection of a Turkish minority. Cyprus is reconstituted, but Turkish Cypriots retain a great deal of autonomy in their canton (which will be about 35 percent of the island). Call this the ''Swiss solution.''

3. 5 percent chance through 1996: The Turkish sector completely separates and forms a new nation. Greek Cypriots finally say, ''What the hell,'' and agree to accept it if most of the Turkish Army pulls out. Intermittent violence occurs.

Kuwait War Redux

There is a 5 percent chance of this conflict recurring through 1996, with Turkey and NATO forces invading Iraq. The call on this is straightforward: a resurgent, militant, and heavily armed Iraqi Baath regime acquiring nuclear munitions.

Great Mesopotamian Water War

There is a 2 percent chance of this conflict occurring in any form through 1996. Not very likely, thank goodness, for this is one of those conflicts that could lead to all kinds of unforeseen sorrow. Here is how one scenario develops: Iraq, believing it is being cheated of its water rights, fails to receive political satisfaction (and more water) from Turkey and/or Syria. Iraq turns to saber rattling or actual use of its potent armed forces with air strikes or missle attacks on the dams. Iraq could also stir up the Kurds inside Turkey, promising them a Kurdistan at Turkey's expense—unless Turkey limits its water draw from the Euphrates. How would the United States respond if one of its longtime allies like Turkey is threatened by a rogue nuclear power like Iraq? Ankara and Istanbul are already within range of Iraqi missiles.

Still, the Turkish Army is a force to be reckoned with. If the Balkan, Aegean, and Cypriot fronts don't erupt simultaneously, and especially if the United States (or Israel, for Jews have lived in comparative peace in Turkey for five hundred years) helps the Turks take out Iraqi nuclear and chemical weapon delivery systems, there's a 70 percent chance of a Turkish victory if Turkey and Iraq fight alone, and a 60 percent chance of Turkey's prevailing against Syria and Iraq. A Turkish-Syrian alliance against Iraq, while unlikely, would best Iraq 75 percent to 25 percent.

Armenian Conflicts

The likelihood of an independent (or at least autonomous) Armenia made from the Armenian SSR before 1996 is 5 percent. The likelihood of a "Greater Armenia" coming into existence, as proposed by Armenian radicals, is near zero. Turkey is too strong and Armenia remains surrounded by Muslims. But trouble and bloodshed on this issue are a sure bet, not only between the Armenians and Azeris inside the Soviet Union (as in 1988 and 1989) but between the Turks and Armenians as well.

Wildest Card

An Iraqi, Greek, and Bulgarian alliance. Near zero chance, but interesting.

COST OF WAR

Wars in this part of the world tend to be pretty bloody, especially if Russians or Turks get involved. The Ottoman Turks kept the peace among their restive Arab subjects by sending in the troops with orders to shoot to kill, and kept doing it until the malcontents were cured of their bad habits. The Arabs still remember Turkish military prowess and would only go up against the Turks if they were prepared for some serious fighting. Deaths would likely run into the hundreds of thousands even for a short war. Aircraft enable the Turks to go after valuable national assets like Iraqi oil fields. Except for the dam project in western Turkey, most Turkish assets are spread around or concentrated far away near Istanbul. Still, none of the nations in the area is very wealthy and a war of any length would cost tens of billions of dollars in resources.

WHAT KIND OF WAR

Turkey is an ideal region for war: mountains for some rough infantry combat; several key flatlands in which to exercise mechanized forces; and large campaigning areas and relative paucity of aircraft to make it easier for aircraft to sneak around and actually bomb thinly guarded enemy installations.

CHAPTER 6

THE BALKANS

PART 1: BACK TO THE BALKANS

INTRODUCTION

Trouble between Albania and Yugoslavia, frictions between the polyglot ethnic and nationalist groups that (for now) make up Yugoslavia, squabbling between desocializing Hungary and Romania over the sad (and strange) case of Transylvania, and the Balkan region's traditional trouble of relentless irredentism have the potential for turning the area into a mountainous bloodbath. One more time.

Contrary to the fashion of certain intellectual circles (those trapped by Hegel), history has not ended. With the demise of the frozen state of communism, history in Eastern Europe has begun again—in Russia, Poland, Hungary, Czechoslovakia, and especially in the Balkans. The Balkans (the name is derived from a Turkish word for mountain) have had a lot of history—if one simply totals obnoxious and bloody political events. The region has been a locus of conflict and war. To the *ghazis* of Turkey, the Balkans were the door into the realm of war, the land of the infidel. But the inhabitants of the Balkans were at it—and each other—long before the arrival of the Turks.

The Albania and Yugoslavia chapter in the first edition of *A Quick and Dirty Guide to War*, written during the 1984 Winter Olympics at Sarajevo (Bosnia), didn't go over well with some readers. One critic argued that projecting a Yugoslav breakup over the Kosovo issue was farfetched, given the superpower bloc division of Europe, and that the legacy of Tito and East-West "pressure" would keep the state together. Within the context of the Cold War, the Yugoslav trouble (Serbian, actually) with Albanian natives in Kosovo Province would be resolved as an "internal" matter. Yugoslavia was modernizing, heading for a Swedish-model socioparadise.

The Swedish model hasn't served Sweden so well, and Yugoslavia is becoming the six to eight countries it always was—a basket of angry basket cases.

But nowhere has history restarted as it has in Romania. Perhaps the most devilish and clever of the East bloc dictators, Nicolai Ceausescu, took Albania's evil Enver Hoxha three or four steps worse—and in so doing beggared a productive nation.

The Communists haven't disappeared in Romania, and given the peculiar conditions in that nation, it's a safe bet to say that like Transylvania's most famous resident, Count Dracula, old members of Ceausescu's Securitate secret police will be rising from the totalitarian tomb for the next three or four decades. Immediate legend has it that the December 1989 Romanian revolt may have been planned by dissident Securitate elements and that the events in Timisoara merely kicked off the Communist-versus-Communist coup a little early. Witness Elena Ceausescu's pleas on videotape, scolding her "children" for their revolt, just before she and Nicolai were killed.

No matter what type of government finally takes roots in Romania, the new regime will face the "old histories" of the Balkans, including a looming scrap with Russia over Moravia, a tug with Yugoslavia (or Serbia) over border regions, sniffs with the Bulgars over other border adjustments, and then, worse yet, a war with Hungary over the big prize: Transylvania.

Balkan politics demand attention. World War I began in the Balkans, and throughout history the region has sparked many other major wars. Over a dozen major ethnic groups live in the Balkans and each group suffers from internal political and social divisions. In Yugoslavia these factions, large and small, are torn between the possible advantages of unity and the desire for ethnic independence. On the rest of the peninsula, the ghosts of geographic irredentism and lost populations lurk behind fragile borders.

As always, the Balkans are a major crisis waiting to happen.

Geography

Three significant geographic features characterize the Balkan Peninsula and have directly affected the region's political history:

1. Most Balkan rivers follow erratic, rocky courses and are not
    navigable.
2. Rugged mountains are the dominant terrain.
3. There is a dramatic absence of geographical centers, one or two
    central areas with good surface routes to the rest of the country,
    around which a national state can coalesce.

These three geographic ingredients are perfect for strategic isolation.
Even in the latter days of the twentieth century, the absence of a significant, navigable river system makes large-scale trade expensive; before
railroads and highway systems, the lack of navigable streams cut off the
more easily developed coastline from the backcountry. The presence of
mountains exacerbates the situation. Without one or two geographic centers, which even in mountain countries can exist in the form of fertile
transverse valleys, every valley or hill mass becomes its own ethnic,
cultural, and, usually, political center. The creation of Yugoslavia did
not solve the great Balkan problem of who rules whom and what constitutes a Balkan nation-state.

Grating against Central Europe, extending into the Eastern Mediterranean, and in too-close proximity to the Middle East, the Balkans occupy
a strategic and sensitive position, where any potential conflict in the
peninsula dramatically affects the European power balance. Before the
Warsaw Pact–NATO division, there existed Axis versus Allies, Grand
Alliance versus Triple Entente, and Ottoman Turkey versus everyone.
At that time, everyone worried about the Balkans.

Yet geopolitical control is only one aspect of the problem. The end
of the Cold War, while lessening the likelihood of thermonuclear war,
actually increases the chance for the small, ugly conflicts so typical of
the Balkans. Local ethnic groups, some quite small, violently object to
the cartographer's status quo. They see themselves as belonging to a
nation-state other than the lousy one the last war stuck them in. Agitation
and instability begin at the local level. When Turkey, "the Sick Man of
Europe," finally lost control of its European provinces, a power vacuum

appeared. The end of the Cold War, and the power vacuum left by Russia's retreat, allows the festering, old Balkan hatred to surface.

PART 2: ALBANIA AND YUGOSLAVIA CONTINUE THE BALKAN TRADITION

SOURCE OF CONFLICT

The current problem of ethnic Albanians in Yugoslavia is but one example of several dozen such Balkan conflicts that continue to simmer and occasionally erupt into combat. This unrest cannot be taken lightly. A Serbian explosion under the Austro-Hungarian Empire led to World War I. The next Serbian trigger (or will it be Croatian?) could spell the end of a united Yugoslavia.

As of early 1991, Yugoslavia and Albania are nominally Communist states. For socialist brothers they have radically different genes; with communism oozing out of fashion, the old ethnic struggles, boundary disputes, and political rivalries inside Yugoslavia and between the Yugoslav republics and Albania have received new energy. Locals replace the lost faith of communism with ethnic and historical identifications. In the Balkans, ethnic and historical identification doesn't mean eating Italian food on Columbus Day or drinking green beer on St. Patrick's—it means fighting thy neighbor's tribe.

Yugoslavia is a fragile ethnic composite, while, with the exception of a significant Greek community in its south, Albania is largely Albanian. The Albanians maintain that Yugoslavia's Kosovo Province with its 1.3 million Albanians belongs to "Greater Albania." They feel that the Serbo-Croatian variety of Slavic imperialism keeps Kosovo separated from its legitimate rulers in Tiranë.

Yugoslavia, however, is on the verge of falling apart. If one province slips from the fold then what's to keep the entire flock from scattering? If Yugoslavia divides into several countries, they become a weak collection of petty republics, each with lingering claims against one another. The internal troubles of Big Brother Slav (Russia) have removed the immediate threat of Russian domination, but what happens after, say, 2010, if the Russian house is recemented in some sort of "tsarist" order? And who knows, the Italians (and before them, Venetians, Genoans, and

Romans) might return from across the Adriatic. The Italian invasion might be economic: In the Balkans, the Italian lira is hard currency. Italy is poised to be "the Japan of the Balkans," and behind the Italians are Austrians with schillings and Germans with D-marks. While hard cash and good times might roll for a while, economic resentments and the perception, if not reality, of economic domination have led to Balkan bloodshed in the past.

If Albanians in Kosovo were the only issue, the problem wouldn't be insurmountable. But Macedonians, Serbs, Croats, Montenegrins, Slovenes, Bosnians (Bosniaks), Greek minorities, Turkish minorities, Bulgar, Magyar, and even a few displaced Austro-Germans, all with their own national and strong ethnic aspirations, are all part of the Yugoslav powder keg. In many ways, Yugoslavia is a smaller version of the entire Balkan problem.

WHO'S INVOLVED

Albania—The xenophobic regime of deceased Albanian maverick Communist leader Enver Hoxha (pronounced Hod-yah) kept a heavy lid on Albania. The revolutions of 1989 finally began to put some pressure on Ramiz Alia, the Hoxha lieutenant who took over power in 1985. In late 1990, the Stalinist regime began to unravel and the nation remains mired in poverty. Of the 4.1 million Albanians in the world, 2.5 million live in Albania. A "semi-democratic" election took place in 1991.

Albanian minority in Yugoslavia—1.8 million (some sources give the figure as 2 million) Albanians live in Yugoslavia, which is about 9 percent of the total Yugoslav population. Over 1.4 million Albanians live in Kosovo Province (85 to 90 percent of the provincial populations), which is the poorest region in Yugoslavia.

Greek minorities in Albania—With 280,000 to 300,000 Greeks in Albania, an Albanian grab for Kosovo might shake the Greeks into reaching for Northern Epirus, which is what Athens calls southern Albania. Albania officially claims there are only 58,682 Greeks in Albania.

Yugoslavian government—The federation's executive oligarchy, which is made up of members from each ethnic state, annually rotates the position of chief of state.

Major Yugoslavian ethnic groups—The federation experiment may not work now that Tito's gone. There are between 23 and 24 million

Yugoslavs. (Population figures for Yugoslavia are highly politicized. Our best figures indicate a 1990 population of 23 million is more accurate.) The mix includes:

Serbs—"Serbia proper" (the republic minus the autonomous provinces) has a total population of 5.8 million, 3.5 million of whom are Serbs—the entire republic has a population of 9.4 million, with 6.2 million Serbs. The total Serb population in Yugoslavia is around 8.1 million; the total population of Vojvodina is 1.95 million; and the total population of Kosovo is around 1.6 million. The Serbs complain of Yugoslav economic discrimination against Serbia. Their third of Yugoslavia's population garners them only a one-eighth share of governmental power. The Serbs claim that Tito (a Croat) and Edvard Kardelj (a Slovene) engineered the 1974 Yugoslav constitution so that Serbia was divided (i.e., Vojvodina and Kosovo were made autonomous provinces, bypassing Serb authority, and in effect making them minirepublics). Serbs write the Serbo-Croatian language in the Cyrillic alphabet.

Montenegrin Slavs—670,000 Montenegrins live in Yugoslavia (about 3 percent of the population). The Montenegrins divide into the *Zelenasi* (Greens) who favor Montegrin separatism and the *Bjelasi* (Whites) who favor union with Serbia.

Slovenes—1.8 million Slovenes live in Yugoslavia. The Republic of Slovenia's total population is near 2 million. Located adjacent to Austria and Italy, Slovenia is the most economically and socially progressive of the Yugoslav republics; its per capita personal income is nearly two and a half times higher than Macedonia's. The people are predominantly Roman Catholic, and a strong nationalist party is active.

Macedonians—1.5 million Macedonians live in Yugoslavia, and the republic's total population is right at 2 million, 20 percent of which is Albanian. The Macedonians have been caught between Bulgarian and Serbian domination, but right now they fear the emergence of a "Greater Albania" that will incorporate part of western Macedonia.

Croats—4.5 million Croats live in Yugoslavia. The population of the Republic of Croatia is around 4.6 million. There is a strong nationalist movement inside Croatia. If Yugoslavia comes apart, however, the Croats fear that the 600,000 Serbs living in Croatia would demand some form of association with a separate Serbia. Many Croats are Catholics. They argue that historically Bosnia is closely linked to Croatia, and that Bosnia's Muslim Slavs are ethnically Croats. Croatia has a long history of political association with Hungary. Croats write the Serbo-Croatian language in the Latin alphabet.

Bosnians and Bosnian Muslims ("Bosniaks")—There are 2 million
Bosnian Muslims, or 9 percent of the total Yugoslav population. The
Republic of Bosnia and Herzegovina, with a population of 4.4 million,
include substantial Croat and Serb communities. Bosnia has been tugged
back and forth by Serbia and Croatia for centuries. Bosnian Muslims tend
to favor preserving Yugoslavia, since they see their religious rights better
protected by a national government.

Hungarian minority in Yugoslavia—About 600,000 Hungarian (Magyar) ethnics live in Yugoslavia, most of them in the Vojvodina autonomous province of Serbia.

Greece—Its border claims against Albania remain unresolved.

Bulgaria—De-Stalinizing Bulgaria covets Macedonia.

Wild Cards

"Alpen-Adria"—This is an informal collection of Central European
states and parts of states which formed in 1978 to explore cooperation
in sporting, cultural, environmental, and energy issues. Its members include Croatia, Slovenia, the German state of Bavaria, Hungary's two
western regions, five Austrian "Lander" (states), and parts of Italy.

Italy—Italy is increasingly willing to involve itself financially, politically, and militarily in foreign disputes.

Hungary—There are lots of Magyars (Hungarians) in Serbia's Vojvodina autonomous province, and after all, the Balkans are old Austro-
Hungarian (Hapsburg) stomping grounds.

Turkey—Geographic proximity in eastern Thrace, bitter historical
memories of Ottoman action in the Balkans, and its current antagonisms
with Greece and Bulgaria put Turkey close to the trouble if Yugoslavia
and Albania go to war or if Yugoslavia disintegrates in civil conflict.

Romania—Lingering internal troubles, ethnic problems, irredentism,
and proximity put Romania close to the fuse.

Germany—The role of peacemaker may fall on a resurgent, reunified
Germany. Look for Germany's involvement in NATO or EEC garb.

Austria—Perhaps Ljubljana should still be named Laibach. These are
old Hapsburg stomping grounds, but as for an insight into the Austrian
"attitude," recall Prince Metternich's line, "Asia begins with the Landstrasse." The Landstrasse (the "Provincial Road") leaves Vienna and
heads toward Hungary and the Balkans.

Super Wild Cards

Russia—Pan-Slavism was an old Russian ploy before the Comintern. Imperial communism is over, but imperialism isn't. South (Yugo) Slavs, however, have bought into Pan-Slavism only at gunpoint.

Libya—In the early 1980s, Libya was reportedly taking young Muslims from Albania and Yugoslavia and bankrolling an ''Islamic'' education.

GEOGRAPHY

Yugoslavia occupies 256,410 square kilometers, an area about two thirds the size of California, and has a population of 23–24 million (see p. 194 for a finer population breakdown). As of early 1991, the Socialist Federal Republic of Yugoslavia consists of six republics: Croatia (capital, Zagreb), Slovenia (Ljubljana), Montenegro (Titograd), Bosnia and Herzegovina (Sarajevo), Macedonia (Skopje), and Serbia (Belgrade). Serbia nominally controls two autonomous provinces, Vojvodina and fractious Kosovo, and Belgrade also serves as the federal capital. Serbs make up 54 percent of the population of Vojvodina, which contains parts of the old kingdom of the Hungarian county (*megye*) of Bachka and half of the Banat region. (The other slice of the Banat is in Romania.)

The most important land routes between the Aegean Sea/Bosporus and Central Europe run through Yugoslavian territory. The Adriatic coastline is rocky but has good harbors. The Danube River, central and southeastern Europe's most important waterway, flows through northeastern Yugoslavia and past Belgrade.

The populous and agriculturally developed lowlands, running north and northwest from Nis and Paracin in the east to the Zagreb region in Croatia, have river plains, some swamps, and a few minor mountain ranges. Tito and his partisans visited this area to either recruit or shoot Axis soldiers. For permanent guerrilla campsites, partisans preferred the other two thirds of the country—the rough and rugged mountains, especially the Dinaric Alps which parallel the Aegean coastline (in some ways a micro-Afghanistan). The Julian Alps cover the northwest corner. Kosovo Province also contains some of those rough and rugged mountains—tough country capable of protecting insurgent guerrilla groups.

Albania is significantly smaller than Yugoslavia, approximately 28,500 square kilometers, or about the size of Maryland. Tiranë, the capital, is the only city of any size. About 180,000 people live in Tiranë. Durrës (the ancient Illyrian city of Epidamnos and the Roman Dyrrachium) is the only significant port, though Vlorë can handle shipping. Durrës, being one of the few places in the nation open to the rest of the world, has been the scene of severe anti-Stalinist rioting. For the most part, Albania is rural and undeveloped, despite Hoxha's insistent propaganda to the contrary. The Gheg Albanians live to the north of the Shkumbi River; the Tosk to the south.

Mountains, many with conifer forests, dominate Albania. The northern mountains are an extension of the Montenegrin Dinaric Alps. The 20 percent or so of the country that is coastal plain is infertile and often swampy; malaria once scourged visitors, and for all the World Health Organization knows, it may still.

Armies have always been able to move through Albania. The great Roman road that crossed ancient Illyria, the Via Egnatia, attests to that. The difficulty lies in controlling the mountainous backcountry and digging out the armed clans that inhabit it. Falling back into the mountains and cutting themselves off from the invader or landlord is the classic Albanian tactic; it is how the Montenegrins escaped Turkish domination.

HISTORY

As a political entity, Yugoslavia is relatively new. To some cynical minds Yugoslavia isn't as much a "new" political entity as it is a phony political entity. Yugoslavia attempts to bring together as one nation six republics and two autonomous regions with a population of 24 million people drawn from five major ethnic groups using two alphabets, practicing three major religions, and speaking four different languages. Yugoslavia came into existence at the end of World War I with the defeat of the Austro-Hungarian Empire. The Great Powers wanted to solve the perennial Balkan problem of what to do with the small, fragile, yet strategic southern Slavic states, so they established a kingdom of the Serbs, Croats, and Slovenes with Serbian King Peter I as ruler. Yugoslavia combined the former Austro-Hungarian provinces of Croatia, Slovenia, Bosnia and Herzegovina with the previously independent states of Montenegro and Serbia. Macedonia, the other present-day Yugoslav republic, was originally part of Serbia. Bulgars claim Macedonians are Bulgars and Serbs claim Macedonians are Serbs.

It is impossible within the constraints of this book to attempt to do justice to the rich, violent, and intriguing histories of Yugoslavia's republics before World War I. But to be pithy—the history is one of short periods of stability punctuating long sentences of petty internecine conflict over land claims and ethnic rights, and paragraph-length episodes of outside imperial powers dividing the squabbling Balkan countries. In the main, Serbia got the best of the others, but the Croats, Slovenes, and Macedonians have all had their turns in the driver's seat. The Montenegrins have for the most part held out in their mountainous niche against the influx of Turks, Serbs, and Germans. The Montenegrins pride themselves on being the only Balkan Christians who never succumbed to Muslim Turkish rule. From an ethnic standpoint, Serbs regard Montenegrins as fellow Serbs, and many Montenegrins concur that, yes, they are of Serbian stock, with the caveat that as Montenegrins they are a little bit more independent, wilier, tougher, braver, and so on. Serbs and Montenegrins tend to cooperate ethnically and politically. One ethnic rule of thumb, which verges on cynicism, says a "South Slav" is a Croat if he's Catholic and uses the Latin alphabet, a Serb if he's Orthodox and uses the Cyrillic alphabet, and a Bosnian if he's Muslim.

Between the two world wars, Yugoslavia tried to find a common political ground; still, there was much infighting. Yugoslavia frequently accused Hungary of intending to pry back its lost Banat and Bachka regions. Old League of Nations documents are filled with Yugoslav and Hungarian charges and countercharges. In 1934 the Yugoslavian government accused Hungary of covertly supporting the radical Croat Ustase terrorist organization.

In April 1941, Nazi Germany invaded Yugoslavia as part of Hitler's plan to shore up his Italian allies. Mussolini's army, based in occupied Albania, was bogged down in its war with Greece. (In fact, the Greek forces had launched several successful attacks against the fascists.) Yugoslavia's ruler, King Peter II, established a London-based government in exile. Within Yugoslavia two rival partisan armies emerged: the Communist National Liberation Army under Marshal Tito, a multiethnic group, and the Yugoslav Army of the Fatherland, or Chetniks, of Drazha Mikhailovich, also multiethnic but with strong Croatian support. The Chetniks fought the Germans and the Communists, and made the mistake of noticeably cutting deals with the Nazis. Tito waged a consistently anti-Nazi, nationalist campaign—no mean feat considering that there was no such thing as a Yugoslavian national. This is the key to Tito—his communism was very secondary to his nationalist mission. During World War II, over 2 million Yugoslavs lost their lives, more than half of them slain by fellow Yugoslavs. With the defeat of both the Germans and his Chetnik adversaries, Tito became premier in 1945. He severed his close relationship with Moscow in 1948 and closed the Macedonian border to Russian-backed Greek Communists who sought to topple the Athens government. As Tito saw it, the most imminent imperial threat came from the east. Western governments, the United States in particular, were slow to recognize the truly nationalist aims of Tito. Since Tito's death the ethnic and factional divisions in Yugoslavia have grown. Political squabbles have become miniarms races (that old trouble in the Balkans). While Serbian and Montenegrin officers largely control the Yugoslav Army, Croatia and Slovenia have "allowed" the formation of "republic gendarmeries" from local militia forces. The Serbs fear these forces could form "local" Croat and Slovene armies.

Albania is similar in many respects to the other petty Balkan states, Montenegro in particular, in that it has a long history of clans retreating into the wilderness and maintaining some degree of self-determination and a definite identity. Albania claims to be the descendant of the ancient kingdom of Illyria, a contemporary of the early Greek city-states. It is a reasonably valid claim; certainly it is an important element of the Albanian national myth and Albanian pride.

Albania is one of history's greatest losers. With the brief exception of 1443–78, when Albania's national hero, Skanderbeg, drove the superior Turkish forces from the country, from Roman times to 1912 Albania was occupied by some foreign power. An independent state of sorts did exist in the interior as Roman power waned, but the Byzantines soon appeared, then the Venetians, the Turks, and more Turks.

The Ottoman policy of passing out fiefs to soldiers and civil servants gave many countries under their reign a legacy of rapacious feudalism. There was little interest in long-term development of a country since, in all but a few rare cases, the fief could not be passed on to an heir. Albania was no exception. Already poor and backward, Albania was further impoverished by Turkish rule.

During the Balkan Wars (1912–13) and World War I, Albania was a battleground for Greek, Bulgarian, Serbian, Austrian, Italian, and other forces. After World War I, a civil war among various mountain clans sputtered. When one battle stopped, the mountain clans' vendetta tradition would kick off a new round of fighting. In 1925 Ahmed Zogu declared Albania to be an independent republic and by 1928 Zogu had made himself king. Renewed Italian intrigue, sparked by Mussolini's quest for a New Rome as well as Albania's oil deposits, culminated in an invasion in 1939. Albania was the springboard for Italy's bungled attack on Greece. Germany's attack on Yugoslavia was precipitated by Italy's impending loss in the Balkans.

By 1944 Hoxha's Albanian resistance group had driven out the Axis armies. The Albanians won without the benefit of an invading Russian or Allied army. In 1946 Albania declared itself a Communist republic with Hoxha as premier. A strict Stalinist, Hoxha broke with Yugoslavia when Tito broke with Russia. When Stalin died, Hoxha became an even more virulent Stalinist—Khrushchev and his revisionist gang had destroyed the old wartime Communist camaraderie, or so it appeared to Hoxha. In 1961 Albania withdrew from the Warsaw Pact and became Communist China's European ally. Hoxha admired Mao's revolutionary fervor and extremism. Since Mao's death the Chinese relationship has gone sour. Hoxha died in 1985. In late 1990 Albania finally felt some of the changes taking place in Eastern Europe. In December 1990 the ruling Communist party reacted to riots in Durrës and Tiranë and allowed open political opposition. Elections were planned for early 1991. The Communists won amid cries of "Fraud." Due to the nation's extreme poverty, many young and well-educated Albanians have tried to leave Albania through the suddenly less-restrictive borders. Their destinations have been Italy, Greece, Germany, and, yes, neighboring Kosovo Province.

Kosovo Province is particularly dear to the Serbs, though they make up only 10 percent of the population. In 1389 Christian forces under Serbian Prince Lazar were defeated by the legions of Turkish Sultan Murad I in the Battle of Kosovo. You know you have begun to comprehend the Balkans when you accept the fact that these nations venerate defeats. Serbs regard Kosovo as the cradle of Serbian civilization. Kosovo was the core of Serbia's medieval empire.

The ethnic Albanians, however, who make up the vast majority of Kosovo's population, demand to be "liberated from the tutelage of Serbia" despite huge Yugoslavian investments in the province made in the early 1980s. The Kosovian Albanians are very wealthy compared to the Albanians in Albania, but strong demands for ethnic identification don't seem to be mitigated by economic development. Belgrade believes there must be outside agitation from Albania and Russia, with possible aid from Bulgaria. However, discontent has long been a phenomenon in Kosovo. There were student disturbances in 1968, demonstrations in the provincial capital of Pristina in 1976, and a number of riots, some of the worst occurring in 1981. In the last decade an estimated 100,000 or more Serbians have left Kosovo because of harassment by Albanians. The Albanians claim they cannot get jobs. The Albanikos, at first an ill-defined resistance group in Kosovo which began a series of public demonstrations in 1984, have evolved into several aboveground resistance groups which Belgrade fears are the vanguard of a revolution.

Finally, there is the Greek view. The Greeks refer to southern Albania as Northern Epirus. Up to 400,000 people of Greek descent live in Albania. In 1981 a number of Greek groups estimated that Hoxha held nearly 20,000 Greeks in Albanian jails or labor camps, which Albania denied. Greece has never formally relinquished its claim to Northern Epirus, though it seems to want to leave well enough alone. It is no secret that the Greeks fear trouble in Kosovo could turn the Balkans into a madhouse. As communism wanes, the split between Greek Orthodox Christians and "revivalist" Islam among formerly "atheist" Albanians could lead to further trouble.

LOCAL POLITICS

Albania

Albanian Workers party (Party of Labor)—Communist party of Albania.

Ghegs—Northern group of Albanians who speak the Gheg dialect of Albanian.

Tosks—Dominant southern group of Albanians who speak the Tosk dialect.

Enver Hoxha—Former Albanian Communist leader. He survived all of Khrushchev's and Tito's alleged attempts to remove him. Of Albanian Muslim background, Hoxha was violently anticlerical, opposed to all religions, and the alleged "founder of the world's first atheist state." He fancied himself a philosopher. His widow serves in current government.

Ramiz Alia—Current Albanian national leader who replaced Hoxha in 1985. Of Muslim background, he served with Yugoslav partisans in World War II.

Nexhmije Hoxha—Enver Hoxha's widow and a former ally of Alia. She is regarded as "old guard" Stalinist and still has a strong base of support in the secret police.

Mehmet Shehu—Hoxha's supposed ordained replacement but died in 1981 from "mysterious causes," purportedly associated with a coup attempt.

Sigurimi—Albanian Communist secret police.

Decree #4337 of the Presidium of the People's Assembly ("On the Abrogation of Certain Decrees")—Decree passed on November 22, 1967, finalizing the creation of "the first atheist state in the world"—Hoxha's death knell for religion in Albania. In 1967 the Albanian government closed nearly 2,200 churches, mosques, and shrines; the country was supposedly 70 percent Muslim, 20 percent Orthodox, and 10 percent Catholic.

"Law of Blood Vengeance"—Holdover feature of Albania's mountain clan past, one that has survived Christianity, Islam, and communism. Yugoslav sources estimate that "blood revenge" accounts for the deaths of one hundred Albanian men a year in Kosovo Province. There are no current figures for Albania, other than admission from refugees that the ancient ritual continues. The "law" requires the family of a victim of a slaying (or fatal accident) to either kill an adult male from the family of the person who caused the death, or make the offender's family pay handsomely for the loss. Some Montenegrin hill clans allegedly still carry on this practice.

Albanian Democratic party—Largest legalized opposition party which publishes the *Democratic Revival* newspaper. Other parties include Republican party, Forum for Human Rights, and Ecological party.

Arnauts—Albanian Muslim troops serving with the Turkish Army. Arnauts often did the Sublime Porte's dirty work in the Balkan fiefs—a fact that is remembered by Albania's neighbors.

Shqiperia—Albanian name for Albania which translates as "the Land of Eagles." Hence, Albanians are *Shqiptars*, or "Eaglemen."

Yugoslavia

League of Communists of Yugoslavia—Yugoslavian Communist party. The voters elect delegates to the bicameral assembly. The Federal Executive Council is the executive branch with a rotating premier—it is essentially a nine-member collective presidency. By the fall of 1990 this Yugoslav "federal" institution was in shambles.

1974 Yugoslavian constitution—Legislation that says that the federal state is composed of "voluntarily united nations" and implies that these nations have the right to pull out of the federation, but autonomous regions, such as Kosovo, do not have such a right. Here lies the rub.

Tito—Josip Broz (1892–1980), the godfather of all Yugoslavs, whose legacy even after his death still plays an enormous role in Yugoslavian politics. He was an anti-Nazi resistance hero who led the partisan movement from 1941 to 1945, a true Third World leader, a pain in the side of Russian Imperialism. He stressed that the only Balkan Slav state that could survive was a federation and believed infighting would bring in strong outsiders (i.e., Russia) to divide and conquer the Balkan Peninsula.

The Yugoslav Army—Army primarily officered by Serbs and Montenegrins.

The Blue Train—Tito's private luxury train.

Goli Otok and Sveti Grgur—Islands holding, respectively, torture prisons for men and for women. They are run by Tito's secret police.

"Illyrism"—Nineteenth-century literary, linguistic, cultural, and philosophical movement which evolved into the concept of "Yugo-Slavism." It sought to bridge South Slav divisions and set the stage for the formation of a united Yugoslav state. Its major figures included the Serb Vuk Karadzic and the Slovene poet Jernei Kopitar.

Battle of Mohacs—Turkish victory in 1656 that led to the division of Croatia between Turkey and Hapsburg Austria. Strategically, the Turkish victory over the Hungarian and Balkan forces assured the Ottomans long-term control of the Balkans.

Serbia

Slobodan Milosevic—President and nationalist leader of the Serbian republic.

Serbian Orthodox Church—Religious institution that is also central to Serbian "cultural identity."

Revived pre-1941 Serbian parties—Radical party and Democratic party.

Serbian Nationalist Revival (Srpska Narodna Obnova)—Ultranationalist Serbian group led by the Serbian writer Vuk Draskovic and banned by the Communists in 1990. It advocates the establishment of a "Greater Serbia," which includes Macedonia, Montenegro, Bosnia, and large parts of Croatia.

Vojvodina Province—Province in which Serbs make up 54 percent of population but in which is still a substantial Hungarian ethnic minority.

Kosovo Province

Albanikos—Albanian ethnic irredentists (in Yugoslavian political jargon roughly meaning "people we don't like") living in Kosovo Province in Yugoslavia.

League of Democrats of Kosovo (also Albanian Democratic Alliance of Kosovo)—Albanian ethnic party in Kosovo.

Croatia

Croatian Democratic Union—Coalition of Croatian nationalist parties which has attracted many former Communists.

Coalition of National Understanding—Croatian centrist party, some members of which still favor some kind of Yugoslav federation.

Croatian Peasant party—Revived pre-1941 Croat party.

The Ustase—Ultranationalist Croatian movement formed as a political party by Hitler and Mussolini. The core group was made up of members of the Ustase radical group active in Croatia after World War I, and they participated in several terrorist incidents. The Ustase ruled the puppet state of "Greater Croatia" during World War II. It was responsible for atrocities committed against Jews, Serbs, and Gypsies.

Hungary—The "Catholic" friend up north.

Slovenia

Party for Democratic Renewal—New name of old League of Communists of Slovenia.

Demos—Coalition of opposition parties who favor an independent Slovenia with its own currency and own military forces.

Liberal party—New opposition party in Slovenia.

Windisch—Slovenes favoring "Germanization." Many are found in Carinthia.

Bosnia

Bogomilians—Twelfth-century Manichaean heresy which continued to find followers in Bosnia, and believers in Bosnia and Herzegovina were numerous. Some historians believe this heritage of Bosnian religious schism paved the way for Islam's ready acceptance in Bosnia. The persecution of Bogomilians by Catholics made Islam look good.

October 7, 1908—Day of infamy. Austria annexed Bosnia and Herzegovina.

Sarajevo—Site of the first shot of World War I: Gavrilo Princip, a Serb, assassinated Austrian Archduke Francis Ferdinand on June 28, 1914. Also, the site of the 1984 Winter Olympics.

Macedonia

"Autocephalous" Macedonian Orthodox Church—Splinter sect of Serbian Orthodox Church not recognized by Serbian Church.

POLITICAL TREND CHARTS

ALBANIA

Poverty. Poverty. Poverty. And a bit of instability also.

	1990 (Socialist Totalitarian)	1996 (Military Authoritarian)
Government Effectiveness	7	6
Government Stability	4	5
Political Cohesion	4	5
Repression Level	9	7
Economic Development	1	1+
Education Status*	1+	1+

NOTE: 0 = minimum; 9 = maximum.
*Urban population only.

"GREATER ALBANIA" (ALBANIA PLUS KOSOVO)

Greater Albania: a land of poverty and war.

	1996 (Military Authoritarian)
Government Effectiveness	5
Government Stability	3
Political Cohesion	4
Repression Level	7
Economic Development*	2
Education Status	3

NOTE: 0 = minimum; 9 = maximum.
*On the average, the people of Kosovo are wealthier and better educated than other Albanians.

"Yugoslavia"

If it's still together as anything more than a trading confederation, the Yugoslavia of 1996 will be the least cohesive state on the globe.

	1990 (Socialist Authoritarian)	1996 (Authoritarian Democracy)
Government Effectiveness	2	1
Government Stability	2	2
Political Cohesion	2	1
Repression Level	6	5
Economic Development	3 − (*)	4
Education Status	4	3 +

Note: 0 = minimum; 9 = maximum.

*The annual inflation at the end of the 1980s reached over 1,000 percent. The output of goods fell each year during 1981–88.

"Greater Serbia and Montenegro" (a fantasy state including Montenegro, Serbia, Vojvodina, and the northern part of Kosovo to the city of Pristina)

A genuine nation, and a genuine threat to its neighbors.

	1996 (Authoritarian Democracy)
Government Effectiveness	5
Government Stability	4
Political Cohesion	5
Repression Level	6
Economic Development	4
Education Status	5

Note: 0 = minimum; 9 = maximum.

"INDEPENDENT KOSOVO" (FROM THE CAPITAL OF PRISTINA SOUTH)

More war and poverty.

	1996 (Military Authoritarian)
Government Effectiveness	4
Government Stability	2
Political Cohesion	5
Repression Level	8
Economic Development	1
Education Status	3

NOTE: 0 = minimum; 9 = maximum.

"INDEPENDENT CROATIA"

Another genuine nation-state.

	1996 (Representative Democracy)
Government Effectiveness	5
Government Stability	5
Political Cohesion	4
Repression Level	5
Economic Development	5
Education Status	5

NOTE: 0 = minimum; 9 = maximum.

"INDEPENDENT SLOVENIA"

An economically viable proposition if Slovenia gains access to the EEC.

	1996 (Representative Democracy)
Government Effectiveness	6
Government Stability	7
Political Cohesion	7
Repression Level	2
Economic Development	7 −
Education Status	6

NOTE: 0 = minimum; 9 = maximum.

"BOSNIA"

This fantasyland might not last too long if Croatia and Serbia have their way.

	1996 (Representative Democracy)
Government Effectiveness	5
Government Stability	5
Political Cohesion	4
Repression Level	5
Economic Development	4 −
Education Status	5

NOTE: 0 = minimum; 9 = maximum.

"MACEDONIA"

Drawing the borders of this state could lead to lots of trouble, sort of like a Kurdistan in Europe (although the Macedonians have not been as agitated as the Kurds).

	1996 (Authoritarian Oligarchy)
Government Effectiveness	4
Government Stability	4
Political Cohesion	5
Repression Level	6
Economic Development	3
Education Status	3

NOTE: 0 = minimum; 9 = maximum.

PARTICIPANT STRATEGIES AND GOALS

Kosovo Problem

Albanikos and other Albanian ethnics in Kosovo—With strikes, sabotage, and threats to the Serbs, they are keeping up the pressure on Belgrade to make Kosovo a republic. Their goal is a separate republic that would then unite with a "free" "Greater Albania."

Albania—Albania is continuing to provide political, propaganda, monetary, and perhaps armed support to the Albanikos.

Yugoslavia—Yugoslavia wants to stop the development of Albanian ethnic terrorist cells while stressing the comparative wealth of the Albanians in Kosovo vis-à-vis the Albanians in Albania. Direct Serbian military and political control of the province brings on repression, but from the Serb point of view it is justified. A quick war with Albania (the punch in the nose that will give the Albanians in Kosovo an "object lesson") is a long-range option. Serbia wants to retain Kosovo, and especially the Pristina area. A division of Kosovo, with Serbia retaining Pristina and the northern half, remains a distant but distinct possibility, but that still would not satisfy the Albanian population. But then "forced emigration" isn't a new concept in the Balkans.

REGIONAL POWERS AND POWER INTEREST INDICATOR CHARTS

ALBANIA AND "YUGOSLAV" WAR

Albania can't win, but Yugoslavia will certainly come out of it weaker.

	Economic Interests	Historical Interests	Political Interest	Military Interest	Force Generation Potential	Ability to Intervene Politically
Albania	9	9	9	9	2/5*	6
Yugoslavia	8	9	9	8	5/7	8
Romania	2	5	6	3	1	2
Bulgaria	2	7	7	7	1+	4
Hungary	1	6	6	4	1	5
Turkey	1	6	3	3	1+	1
Russia	3	5	6	4	7	6
U.S.	1	2	5	4	5	7
Germany	3	5	7	5	2	7
Austria	4	6	7	6	1	6
Italy	4	6	7	7	4+	7

NOTE: 0 = minimum; 9 = maximum.
*Regional offense/defense.

"YUGOSLAV" CIVIL WAR

Another all-around loser. No winners here at all.

	Economic Interests	Historical Interests	Political Interest	Military Interest	Force Generation Potential	Ability to Intervene Politically
Serbia/Montenegro	9	9	9	9	5/7+(*)	8
Slovenia	9	9	9	9	1−/3	5
Croatia	9	9	9	9	3/5	7
Bosnia	9	9	9	9	1/2	4
Macedonia	9	9	9	9	1/3	5
Albania	7	8	9	9	2	2
Romania	6	7	8	9	1	4−
Bulgaria	6	8	8	9	1+	4−
Hungary	4	8	8	8	1	5
Turkey	2	5	6	5	1+	0
Russia	3	5	7	6	7	4
U.S.	2	4	5	6	5	6
Germany	5	6	7+	7	2	6−
Austria	7	8	8	7	1†	5
Italy	7	8	8	7	4+	6

NOTE: 0 = minimum; 9 = maximum.

*Combat power is offense/defense; offensive FGP is inside 1990 boundaries of Yugoslavia, defensive FGP is inside home republic.

†Austrian rating inside Slovenia is 3+.

Yugoslav Devolution

Nationalists in constituent republics—Be they Serb, Croat, Slovene, etc., the object is to plug for separatism and "local" government, either with or without economic confederation (i.e., a free trade zone inside "old" Yugoslavia). Their goal is to have internal relations in Yugoslavia evolve (or devolve) into international relations—among separate states.

Bulgaria—Bulgaria continues to demand that Macedonia become a province of "Greater Bulgaria." Peace and quiet are, however, in Bulgaria's long-term economic interest.

Russia—Both tsarist and Communist Kremlinites once coveted Yugoslav and Albanian air and naval bases on the Adriatic. The Balkans have been a graveyard for failed Russian foreign policies, and there are a lot of bones to prove it. The current Kremlin wants change in the Balkans, and wants someone else to pay for it, but definitely demands a say in the management of that change. Moldavia may ultimately be allowed to join Romania, but the Kremlin will demand solid military guarantees and (perhaps) "economic adjustments" (i.e., ransom). Any Balkan bloodshed will raise Russian concerns about spillover into the Soviet Union, but when it comes to military might, Russia is and will remain the military powerhouse.

Greece—Greece continues to support Belgrade diplomatically to ensure Balkan stability. If a Yugo-Albanian war erupts and Albania gets the worst of it, Athens may attempt to "recover" Northern Epirus (southern Albania). If Yugoslavia falls apart, Greek eyes will be on Macedonia: Athens may either blunt a Bulgarian grab for Macedonia or make "an arrangement" with Bulgaria to divide it. (That deal may also be made with the Serbs, but Greece now finds it has more in common with Bulgaria, i.e., suspicion of Turkey.) Greece's short-term goal is to ensure protection of Greek minority in Albania.

Italy—Italy is willing to support the "concept of Yugoslavia" but prepared to help make the transition to a multistate "confederation" as bloodless as possible. It aids Albanian dissidents by providing a haven and low-profile support. Italy sees the Dalmatian coast, Croatia, and Albania as its logical "sphere of influence" in rebuilding Communist-devastated Eastern Europe.

Hungary—Budapest needs a peaceful southern border but spending on defense would beggar Hungary's economic recovery. Hungarians, however, will keep a place open for the return of the Hungarian borderlands in Vojvodina.

POTENTIAL OUTCOMES

Chance through 1996 of the "Third Balkan War" (with all its nations involved) is 3 percent—but it is a very dangerous 3 percent. This outcome could be ignited by any of the potential political and military crises discussed on pp. 203–207. How does this "super outcome" work in our game projections? None of these postulated chains of events is discrete. When reading through the potential outcomes, understand that "spillover conflict" is implicit in our analyses of the potential for war in each individual case. Political conflicts may be individually identified but conflicts are rarely isolated. In the Balkans, one neighbor's fire is the next guy's fuse.

For example, the 5 percent chance of a Russian invasion of Romania might strike some as high—until one considers the "architecture of instability" in the region. A general Balkan war would drive up Russian blood pressure. The situation in Moldavia becomes a context (or pretext) for action.

Kosovo, Albania, and Yugoslavia

1. 40 percent chance through 1996: Occasional riots and sporadic terrorism continue, with Albanian ethnic resentment exacerbated by the Albanian government in Tiranë. Yugoslavia (and/or Serbia) continues to deny the ethnic Albanian demand that Kosovo be an Albanian republic within Yugoslavia. Belgrade buys off resentment by increasing local autonomy and granting a larger Albanian voice in Belgrade, and the Albanian minority in Kosovo accepts the payoff.

2. 40 percent chance through 1996: The same situation described in outcome 1 continues except that rioting leads to a military crackdown by Yugoslavia (Serbia) and the Albanian revolt is crushed. Should this tiny civil war occur, Yugoslavs (Serbs) have an 80 percent chance of victory with a 10 percent chance of stalemate and a 10 percent chance of Albanian rebel success. If Albanian rebels begin to win, look for intervention by the Albanian Army and a Yugoslav counterattack on Albania with a 60 percent chance of support from Greece. (This is a variant of Yugo-Albanian war in outcome 2 of the "Yugoslav Breakdown" section.)

3. 20 percent chance through 1996: Yugoslavia (Serbia) capitulates to the ethnic Albanian demand for a separate Albanian republic. Albanians in Montenegro and Macedonia request that they be included in this new republic. (Look for forced emigrations.) If an Albanian republic is created, there's a 10 percent chance that it will remain part of Yugoslavia, a 90 percent chance that it will withdraw from the federation. It obviously isn't in Serbia's interests to make Kosovo an Albanian republic. The odds go to 50 percent if either Albania gains military or political victory per outcome 2 in this section and outcome 2 of the "Yugoslav Breakdown" section, or if Serbia is weakened by the "gang war" of outcome 3 of the "Yugoslav Breakdown" section.

Yugoslav Breakdown

1. 55 percent chance through 2000: Yugoslavia acrimoniously (riots, civil demonstrations, occasional terrorism) but peacefully (no outright war) devolves into five (if Serbia and Montenegro unite) or six separate republics linked as a free-trade zone. (Call it a Yugoslav "EEC.") All the republics maintain independent paramilitary and military forces, but a "national defense pact" remains and a rump Yugoslav government continues to operate in Belgrade. Serbia continues to control Vojvodina and Kosovo.

2. 15 percent chance through 2000: Yugoslavia (or, in the case of a breakdown, Serbia, Montenegro, and Macedonia) attacks Albania because of Albanian "troublemaking" in Kosovo and Macedonia. If this occurs, there's a 50 percent chance of a stalemate as the offensive bogs down in Albania, a 35 percent chance of Yugoslav victory, and a 15 percent chance of Albanian "political" military victory.

3. 15 percent chance through 2000: Yugoslav devolution sparks a Serb-Croat, Serb-Albanian, Bulgar-Serb, Greek-Albanian, Greek-Bulgar, Greek-Turk, Romanian-Serb, Bulgar-Romanian, Bulgar-Turk, or you-name-the-combination armed conflict. A general Balkans war erupts with a 99 percent chance of bloodbath. No winners. If everyone gangs up on Serbia and Serbia loses, there's a 50 percent chance of Serbian loss of Kosovo Province.

4. 15 percent chance through 1996: The "center holds" and Yugoslavia stays together.

COST OF WAR

In the struggle pitting the Albanikos against Belgrade, there have been several hundred dead and wounded, a few thousand imprisoned, and less than $100 million of economic disruption. However, the potential for enormous loss exists should another Balkan war break out. The Balkan peoples have historically pursued their warfare vigorously. Given the historical trends in Balkan warfare, the cost of a war would be several million dead and many millions more injured. The economic cost would be over $200 billion for property destruction and lost earnings.

PART 3: DRACULA'S WAR

SOURCE OF CONFLICT

There are three lingering conflicts centering on Romania:

1. The Romania-Hungary tussle over the province of Transylvania, where a large Hungarian (Magyar) population lives. Though as of 1990 a province of Romania, Transylvania has been part of Hungary.
2. The brewing trouble between Romania and Russia over Moldavia SSR. Moldavia was part of pre–World War II Romania (Bessarabia) until it was incorporated by Stalin into the Soviet Union.
3. Renewed civil war in Romania between democratic forces and "new guard" members of former dictator Nicolai Ceausescu's Securitate secret police and paramilitary forces.

WHO'S INVOLVED

The "Transylvanian War"

Participants—Hungary, Romania, and the Hungarian minority in Transylvania.

Wild Cards

Austria—The other "half" of the Austro-Hungarian empire.

Russia—Even though there are troubles at home, this fight is on Russia's front porch.

Serbia—Hungarian absorption of Transylvania might cause Budapest to look south at Vojvodina, the autonomous province with a large Hungarian minority.

Germany—A reunited Germany returns to the geopolitics of Mitteleuropa.

Moldavia SSR—Romanians in-waiting.

The "Moldavian Crisis"

Participants—Romania, Russian and "Soviet" reformists, Russian Stalinists and imperialists.

The Kremlin—Who's in charge and how the Kremlin manages (or denies) devolution is a big key.

Wild Cards

Hungary—If Romania can "recover" Moldavia, why can't Hungary have Transylvania back?

Germany—A reunified Germany returns to the old political crises of Mitteleuropa.

"NATO"—Any military action involving Russia could raise the Cold War shield.

The "Second Romanian Civil War"

Participants—"Securitate" factions, democratic dissidents, and Hungarian minorities in Transylvania.

Wild Cards

Romanian fascist factions.

The neighborhood—Hungary, Bulgaria, Serbia, Russia, "Moldavians."

Super Wild Card

France—The French considered sending troops to aid democratic rebels during the fighting in December 1989.

GEOGRAPHY

Hungary is a horseman's land of rolling plains and valleys edged by low mountains in the northeast and northwest. The total area is 93,000 square kilometers, or about the size of Indiana. The Danube River is a major geographic feature, describing a stretch of the Czech-Hungarian border, then hooking south past Budapest and continuing on into Yugoslavia. Lake Balaton, in the middle of western Hungary, is large enough to be considered an inland sea—it is the largest landlocked stretch of water in Europe.

In 1990 Hungary had a population of around 11 million, with 93 percent being ethnic "Magyar" (Hungarian—a combination of the original central Asian Magyars, plus Slav and anyone else who wandered by). Gypsies and German ethnics account for about 3 percent each. Nearly 70 percent of the people are nominal Roman Catholics. The capital, Budapest (actually two cities, Buda and Pest), with a population of nearly 2.2 million, is the economic and cultural center of the nation. The classic political schism in Hungary pits Budapest (intellectual, cosmopolitan, influential Jewish minority, before communism regarded as wealthy) against "the countryside" (nationalistic, stolid, hardworking, commonsensical, salt of the earth, etc.). An anti-Semitic bias has often cloaked itself in rural opposition to Budapest elites.

Romania covers nearly 238,000 square kilometers. The country divides into the "Old Kingdom" (the land south of the Transylvanian Alps and east of the Carpathians), the northern region of Transylvania (the disputed province), and Romanian Moldavia in the northeast. The Soviet Socialist Republic of Moldavia, carved by Stalin from Romania, lies to the east. The Carpathian Mountains form a rugged, often wild and beautiful scythe cutting through Romania.

The Danube River describes the southern section of the Romanian-Yugoslav border then continues east, separating Romania and Bulgaria. Southeast of the capital of Bucharest (near Calarasi) the Danube begins to turn north and enter its expansive delta, finally wandering into the

Black Sea. The central area of Romania (around Bucharest) is the heart of the old Kingdom of Walachia. The Dobruja is the area between the Danube, as it swings north to its delta, and the Black Sea. In its delta the Danube divides into three arms: the Kiliya, Sulina, and Saint George.

In 1990 Romania had a population of 24 million, 86 percent Romanian and slightly under 10 percent (around 2.3 million) Hungarian. Most of the Hungarians live in Transylvania. A close-knit community of 200,000 ethnic Germans also live in Romania, as well as 60,000 Serbs, most of whom live in Serbian villages along the Yugoslav (Serbian) border. After World War II, some 600,000 Romanian Germans emigrated to West Germany; essentially, the Bonn government paid Ceausescu ransom in order to gain permission for the Germans to leave. There are also an estimated 700,000 Gypsies living in Romania. Bucharest, the capital, has around two million inhabitants.

The border region between Hungary and Romania—the likely scene of any armed confrontation—is predominantly rolling plain. Transylvania possesses three types of countryside: the mountain ranges, a central plateau, and the plains around the river valleys. The Banat region has plains in the west, as it dips toward the Danube, and mountains in the east (the Szemenik and Orsova extensions of the Transylvanian Alps).

Moldavia SSR is one of the Soviet Union's least urbanized republics. The best estimates give a population of 3.8 million. Sixty-six percent are "Moldavian" (Romanian), 14 percent Ukrainian, and 11 percent Russian. The Turkic Gaugaue people make up under 3 percent of the population. The Moldavian language is a dialect of Romanian.

HISTORY

Transylvania and the Banat

In 1920, 192,000 square kilometers of the Kingdom of Hungary (part of the Austro-Hungarian empire, the big loser in World War I), which began the war with 293,000 square kilometers, was parceled out to Hungary's neighbors. The most grievous losses were Transylvania (or Erdely, as the Hungarians call it) and the Banat, which were ceded to Romania in the Treaty of Trianon (1921).

The Transylvanian region was conquered by the Romans under Trajan in A.D. 106. Between A.D. 274 (when the Romans pulled back south of the Danube) and A.D. 975, the area was overrun by numerous "barbarians"—Goths, Avars, and Huns. Magyar (Hungarian) horsemen and the rest of the tribe arrived on the nearby Hungarian plains around A.D. 890. Hungarians maintain they first occupied Transylvania in A.D. 1009. From 1526 (the Battle of Mohacs) to 1699, Transylvania was under Turkish suzerainty (and at times Romanian control, through the Principality of Walachia, a Turkish fief). In 1699 the Treaty of Karlowitz ceded Transylvania to Hungary. During the Hungarian revolution of 1848, the Vlachs (Romanians) of Transylvania failed to support Louis Kossuth and his liberals in their rebellion against the Hapsburgs. The Austrian crown took direct control of Transylvania.

The Banat region, of which Timişoara (Temesvár) is a part, is another "lost" Hungarian territory. One third of the old Banat lies in Vojvodina (in Yugoslavia, running from the present Romanian border to the Danube), the other two thirds in Romania (from the border back to the Transylvanian Alps). The Banat, which has a large ethnic Hungarian population, has never been an independent political unit. The Magyar tribe colonized the Banat in the late eleventh century and in 1552 the Turks conquered it. Since 1718 (the Treaty of Passarowitz), the Banat has bounced between Austrian, Hungarian, Romanian, and Serbian control.

When World War I broke out, Romania remained neutral (though it was secretly a member of the Central Powers alliance.) In August 1916, Romania entered the war on the side of the Entente (France, England, and Russia) and promptly invaded Transylvania. At first the Romanians made progress, but the German Balkan Army (under Erich von Flakenhayn) struck Romania from Bulgaria. The Germans rolled through Walachia and pushed the Romanian Army back into Moldavia. Despite French efforts to reconstitute the Romanian Army, by late 1917 Romania was thoroughly demoralized and signed a peace treaty with Germany in May 1918. The peace treaty allowed for occupation of Bessarabia. Romania bided its time. In November 1918 Romania reentered the war, just in time to enjoy the collapse of the Austro-Hungarian Dual Monarchy and retake Transylvania.

Border complaints between Hungary and Romania during the years between World War I and World War II were frequent.

The Hungarian community in Transylvania has always feared Romanian assimilation, and their cousins across the border support them in their struggle. Ceausescu's "systemization plan" was perceived as a

direct attack on their identity—to "Romanianize" the Hungarian minority. The legacy of Ceausescu is particularly bitter for the Hungarians.
After the 1956 Hungarian revolt against Russia, Communist leader
Gheorghiu-Dej (and later Ceausescu) saw an opportunity. Hungarians
could be singled out as both class and national enemies. In Romanian
minds, the Hungarian aristocracy had played a brutal, dominating role
in Transylvania over the landless Romanian peasants. The Hungarians'
1956 revolt against socialism paved the way for "communization in
Romanian garb." The Magyar autonomous region of Romania, established in 1950, was reformed and "de-Magyarized" in 1960. After Ceausescu came to power, "anti-Magyar" policies reinforced his own peculiar
brand of hard-line socialism and Romanian nationalism, and he denounced
"Hungarian revanchism" as a constant threat to both Romania and international socialism.

In 1987, Romanian repression of Transylvania's Hungarian community got so bad that there were even rumors of a war between the then
still Communist Hungarians and the Romanians.

One continuing trouble for Hungarians in the post-Ceausescu world
is education. The Hungarians want their own language and culture. They
believe even a post-Ceausescu Romania is "too primitive" to become a
multinational European state. At best, minorities in Romania will receive
token concessions, but their rights will be trampled. The establishment
of a democratic government in Hungary, formalized in 1990 but really
the result of a nearly-twenty-year-long Hungarian economic and social
exodus from communism, makes unification with Hungary attractive.

For their part, Romanians complain that the Hungarians are arro-
gant and see themselves as being culturally superior—when, of course,
they aren't. There is also a long historical legacy of Hungarian oppression of Romanians when Hungary possessed Transylvania. The Romanians point out Hungarian edicts promoting "Magyarization of the
Vlachs" living in Hungarian-ruled Transylvania. Romania also makes
extensive historical claims to Transylvania, tracing its occupation there
back to the pre–Roman Empire Dacians and Daco-Roman-mixed populations of intermarried Dacians and Roman legionaries and settlers.
The Romanians claim that the descendants of these people were in
Transylvania when the barbarian Magyars arrived on horseback. The
Hungarians, however, maintain that "the Vlachs" didn't reach Tran-
sylvania until 1175, when they were pushed out of Bulgaria. The
Romanians point out the ancient Russian chronicle (Nestor's chronicle)

that states that after the Hungarians crossed the Carpathians "they began to fight with the Walachs and Slavs who lived there" (in Transylvania). Romanian histories also point out the existence of an anonymous Hungarian chronicle written in the twelfth century that mentions the Hungarians' hearing of a Romanian leader named Gelou who ruled over Romanians and Slavs in a "land renowned for its goodness"— Transylvania. Many historical events dear to Romanian memory occurred in Transylvania.

As a nation, Romania traces its more recent roots to the late medieval principalities of Moldavia and Walachia. In 1456 the Turks took control of Walachia, beginning a long period of Turkish domination of the Romanian princes (*voivodes*). The greatest Walachian prince was Michael the Brave of Walachia, who ruled from 1593 to 1601. He twice defeated the Turks, gaining more autonomy for Walachia, and also took control of all of Transylvania. The most famous prince of Walachia was Vlad Tepes (1456–62), better known as Count Dracula, who impaled his enemies on stakes. Tradition has it that Bran Castle in Transylvania was his home. The Moldavian prince Stephen the Great (1457–1504) stopped three Turk invasions during his reign and at one time tried to organize an alliance of "the Christian nations and Persia" against Turkey. After Stephen's death, however, the Turks forced the Moldavians to submit. From 1714 to 1822 (the Phanariote period), Turkey administered Walachia and Moldavia through the Greeks of the Phanar (lighthouse) Quarter of Constantinople. This Greek "nobility" acted as a tax collector for the Turks.

France became diplomatically active in Romania in the late eighteenth century. In the nineteenth century, Napoleon III favored a "free Romania" as a Latin state in the Balkans. In 1859 Alexander Cuza was elected prince by the Moldavian and Walachian assemblies and formed the new nation of Romania which didn't gain formal independence from Turkey until May 1877.

The Romanian Civil War

Romania was something of a maverick in the old Warsaw Pact camp. Soviet troops pulled out in 1958 and Ceausescu removed Romania from some of the Warsaw Pact's military commitments. This gave him a political card to play in the West.

Ceausescu also pursued a radical, go-it-alone economic program. While he and his cohorts lived in luxury (and hid gold in Switzerland) Ceausescu kept the countryside impoverished by exporting everything of value. Ironically, in the post–Cold War ecopolitical environment, Ceausescu's ruthless program has left Romania with one slight economic advantage—there is little foreign debt. However, there is also little of anything.

In December 1989 Romania caught the revolutionary tide sweeping Eastern Europe. Between December 12 and 17, protests broke out in Timişoara and seemed to spontaneously spread across the country. Coverage on Yugoslav and Hungarian television of the troubles in Timişoara appears to have given many Romanians hope that a rebellion could succeed. Ceausescu reacted and sent the Romanian Army and the Securitate military units into action. Elements in the Army balked. Soon combat broke out in all of the major cities. For what are still obscure reasons, the Ceausescus decided to leave Bucharest. They were captured and on Christmas Day, 1989, they were tried by a tribunal and executed.

Power in Romania fell into the hands of what appeared to be a broad popular coalition, the National Salvation Front (NSF). The NSF included many dissidents, anti-Ceausescu Communists, and a smattering of religious leaders.

Since the fall of Ceausescu, many Romanian democrats (and many sympathizers in the West) have come to believe that the revolutionary momentum created by those first haphazard protests—and those were genuine, democratic protests—was used as an opportunity to execute a long-planned anti-Ceausescu coup orchestrated by anti-Ceausescu members of the Securitate. The protests in Timişoara moved up the timetable for the coup and gave the anti-Ceausescu elements of the secret police a convenient democratic cover.

Many dissident and democratic elements of the NSF either left or were forced out of the coalition in the first months of 1990. The hardline members of the NSF bused in counterdemonstrators to break up dissident rallies. When democrats asked for laws banning members of the Securitate from running for office for at least ten years, NSF hardliners (many of them suspected Securitate agents) shelved the requests. The 1990 Romanian elections, while nominally open and free, put the NSF in firm control of the Romanian government, a government that is afflicted by continued protests and work stoppages. In October 1990 President Ion Iliescu confirmed that a number of former Securitate agents were still running "technical operations" in his government.

The Moldavian Problem

Moldavia SSR was formerly the fruit-growing Romanian region of Bessarabia. Bessarabia, part of the Romanian principality of Moldavia, was taken by Russia in 1812. Parts of it were returned to Moldavia in 1856 but were given back to Moscow in 1878 at the Congress of Berlin. Out of the chaos of World War I and the collapse of the Russian tsar, a democratic Moldavian republic was founded in 1917 by democratic, anti-Bolshevik Romanians. This led to voluntary union with Romania in April 1918 (though some historians and many Russians question the degree of "volunteerism," given the presence of Romanian Army units in Bessarabia). In 1924 the Bolsheviks established the "Autonomous Moldavian Soviet Socialist Republic" as part of the Ukraine SSR—in part as an objection to incorporating Bessarabia into post–World War I Romania. The "puppet province" was used as a base for propaganda operations and covert activities inside Romania. Russia invaded and annexed the whole of Bessarabia in 1940 and began a process of "Russification." Romania briefly retook the region after the Nazi invasion of the Soviet Union in 1941, but the Red Army returned in 1944 and eventually took the whole of Romania.

As the Soviet Union goes through its wrenching processes of change, Moldavia is just one of many potential break-off nations. Yet 35 percent of the population of Moldavia is not Moldavian Romanian.

In the fall of 1990, the name of the main boulevard in Kishinev, the Moldavian capital, was changed from Lenin Street to Stephen the Great, memorializing that great Romanian (Moldavian?) leader.

LOCAL POLITICS

Hungary

Hungarian Democratic Forum (HDF)—Center-right party in Hungary regarded as the largest party there. Its nationalist platform plays well outside of Budapest even though the party describes itself as a "European center party" eschewing rabid nationalism. HDF's leader is the longtime Hungarian anti-Communist dissident and participant in the 1956 revolt Jozsef Antall.

Alliance of Free Democrats—Pro-Western party whose core is the old Budapest-based dissident movement.

Federation of Young Democrats—Small party allied with Alliance of Free Democrats.

Independent Smallholders party—Hungarian agrarian reform party. This is a revival of the old Smallholders party, which won 58 percent of the vote in the 1945 election, then was suppressed by the Communists. The party advocates returning to the former owners all property confiscated by the Communists.

Christian Democrat party—Center-right party generally supportive of democratic forum.

Hungarian Socialist Workers party (HSWP)—Debunked Hungarian Communist party. It reorganized as the Hungarian Socialist party (Magyar Szocialista party) and took 10 percent of the vote in 1990 elections.

Louis Kossuth—Nineteenth-century Hungarian liberal nationalist (of Slovakian origin), who led the failed 1848 revolt against Hapsburgs.

Szentkorona orszagai—Lands of the Holy Crown of Saint Stephen. This refers to "historic Hungary" (Hungary minus Croatia and Slavonia) as it existed before 1918. He who wears "the Holy Crown of Saint Stephen" is the king of Hungary. That crown was worn by the Hapsburgs from 1527 to 1918.

Green Shirts—Storm troopers of Hungarian fascism during the 1930s and 1940s, who wore crossed arrows (the Arrow Cross) instead of a swastika. The Arrow Cross became a leading fascist party.

Romania

National Salvation Front (NSF)—Group behind the Council of National Salvation. At first seemingly a broad coalition, one month after the revolt, NSF leaders decided to participate in "elections" as a party rather than as a transition government. Now, led by Ion Iliescu, a "former" Communist, they are accused of being "neo-Communists" and "children of Ceausescu."

Opposition parties—Civic Alliance (led by Mihai Sora), National Peasants party (Ion Ratiu), National Liberal party (Radu Campeneau), Democratic party of Romania. The Peasants party and the National Liberal party advocate privatization and a free-market economy.

Romanian Workers party—Romanian Communist party. Its Political Executive Committee was the equivalent of the Politburo.

Nicolai and Elena Ceausescu—Old bosses. Nick was one of the worst dictators in the world, but when it came to sheer totalitarian cunning, Elena may have had it up on him. She served as deputy prime minister and was in charge of party personnel assignments. In the "trial video" made by their executioners, Elena scolds her "children" (the Securitate) for trying them. This leads critics of the National Salvation Front to conclude that the "revolution" really was an inside job. The genetic Ceausescu kids are still around: son Nicu, a playboy and former Communist chief in Sibiu; daughter, Zoya, a mathematician; and son Valentin, a physicist.

"Systemization plan"—Ceausescu's plan for eliminating thousands of Romanian villages and moving their inhabitants to large apartments —his version of modernization and indoctrination. Hungarians in Transylvania felt the plan was primarily aimed at eradicating their culture. Ceausescu targeted eight thousand villages and several villages with buildings dating from the thirteenth century were razed before the December 1989 revolt halted the program.

King Michael—Romanian monarch toppled by Communists in 1947. He was exiled in Switzerland, and in 1990 wanted to make a comeback.

The Iron Guard—Fascist movement active in Romania before and during World War II. Its headquarters was the notorious "Green House" in Bucharest.

Dealul Spirei—Hill in Bucharest where the old national parliament buildings stand.

Transylvania

Hungarian Democratic Union—Party representing Hungarians in Romania. In 1990 it claimed 650,000 members.

Vatra Romaneascea (Romanian Hearth)—Political group that seeks to defend and protect Romanian culture in Transylvania.

Rev. Lazlo Tokes—Timişoaran Reform Church minister who organized protests against the Ceausescu regime. His courage was instrumental in starting the popular revolt. Tokes is an ethnic Hungarian.

Moldavia SSR

Moldavian Popular Front—Coalition front from Moldavian dissident and nationalist groups, who took control of the Moldavian parliament in

1989. Its extremist members advocate separation from the Soviet Union, and many support reunification with Romania. One of the chief party aims is to reestablish the Latin alphabet. By the fall of 1990, most of the street and road signs in the major cities were "dual language"—the names were found in both Cyrillic and Latin.

Moldavian Social Democratic party—Small centrist "pro-glasnost" party which opposes extreme nationalists.

Moldavian Language Laws—Laws passed in 1989 that require that Moldavian be written in the Latin alphabet (like Romanian) not in Cyrillic letters. They say that by 1994 Russian speakers holding leading governmental positions must learn Moldavian or lose their jobs.

"Moldova"—Name for Moldavia SSR preferred by Moldavian (or is it Moldovian?) dissidents.

Gagauze—Turkic-language-speaking Christian minority of 150,000 living in Moldavia who have "revolted" against Moldavia.

Dniester Republic—Republic proclaimed by "anti-Moldavian" Russians in Moldavia.

PARTICIPANT STRATEGIES AND GOALS

Hungary—Hungary's chief strategy is to build a strong economy and shake off the rust and ruin of communism. Hungary has already begun to shrink its army and free up its economy. But its ties to Transylvania loom large—Transylvania is a "lost half" of Hungary—and the travails of the Hungarian community in Romania are felt as well as heard— Hungary has reoriented its army to face Romania. A peaceful solution, freedom and democracy in Romania for Romanians as well as Hungarians, is much preferable. In the long term, a plebiscite in Transylvania regarding minority rights and even border adjustments is a Hungarian goal. Would Hungary go to war over Hungarian ethnic rights in Transylvania? Hungarians point out that they were the only nation that openly revolted against the Russians (1956). During the Cold War, Hungary's elite mountain infantry units have trained with Austrian commandos. (In turn, the Austrians conducted exercises with U.S. Special Forces units in order to demonstrate their neutrality.) The Hungarians assured the Austrians that if the Russians ever attacked, Hungarian forces would hit the Russians from the rear. The Austrians' assessment of the Hungarian mountain

POLITICAL TREND CHARTS

HUNGARY

Given peace, Hungary will make significant economic strides.

	1990 (Evolving Democracy)	1996 (Representative Democracy)
Government Effectiveness	5	6
Government Stability	6	7
Political Cohesion	7	7+
Repression Level	4	3
Economic Development	4−	6−
Education Status*	6	6

NOTE: 0 = minimum; 9 = maximum.
*Urban population only.

"GREATER HUNGARY" (HUNGARY PLUS TRANSYLVANIA)

Likely only over a lot of Romanian (and Hungarian) dead bodies.

	1996 (Authoritarian Democracy)
Government Effectiveness	5
Government Stability	4
Political Cohesion	5
Repression Level	4
Economic Development	5
Education Status	5

NOTE: 0 = minimum; 9 = maximum.

ROMANIA

The transition from totalitarianism will be a struggle.

	1990 (Authoritarian Coalition)	1996 (Authoritarian Oligarchy)
Government Effectiveness	3	4
Government Stability	2	5
Political Cohesion	2	3
Repression Level	7	6
Economic Development	2	2+
Education Status	4	4

NOTE: 0 = minimum; 9 = maximum.

infantry is that they are tough, resourceful, and highly trained troops. For this reason, the Russians stationed several divisions in Hungary and kept the Hungarian Army on a short leash, and short rations.

Hungarian community in Transylvania—A new "Magyar Autonomous Region" still politically attached to Romania might work out, *if* Romania becomes a democracy

Romania—Even in a democratic Romania the debate over "who lost Transylvania" would be traumatizing; the "guilty" party or leaders would be politically (or literally) dead. A totalitarian or authoritarian regime would fan the flames of nationalism by making Transylvania a constant issue. It helps keep the starving populace thinking about something besides their stomachs. Still, under a stable and democratic government some compromise is possible, including a plebiscite.

Romanian dissidents—They don't want to be portrayed as the people responsible for "losing Transylvania," but the core leadership sees "Euro-freedom" as the wave of the future—if the future can only penetrate Romania's borders. The trick is to keep political pressure on the NSF by appealing to international opinion and acquiring the support of the West.

Kremlin reformists—Cutting Moldavia loose would rid Russia of one more problem; but the thing is, Moldavia is right beside the Ukraine,

REGIONAL POWERS AND POWER INTEREST INDICATOR CHARTS

TRANSYLVANIA WAR

A very volatile, and ancient, situation that could very well develop into a war that no one, except perhaps Russia, would pay much attention to.

	Economic Interests	Historical Interests	Political Interest	Military Interest	Force Generation Potential	Ability to Intervene Politically
Hungary	8	9	9	9	5	9
Romania	9	9	9	9	6	9
Russia	3	8	8	9	9	5
U.S.	3	5	8	7	4	6
Germany	6	8	8	7	2	6
"Yugoslavia"	3	6	8	6	2	2
Serbia	3	8	9	8	2	2

NOTE: 0 = minimum; 9 = maximum.

MOLDAVIAN WAR

More likely to be part of a larger Russian civil war than a conflict between Russia and Romania.

	Economic Interests	Historical Interests	Political Interest	Military Interest	Force Generation Potential	Ability to Intervene Politically
Russia	8	8	9	9	9	9
Romania	9	9	9	9	5	8
Hungary	5	8	8	8	2	5
U.S.	2	3	8	7	4	6
Germany	6	8	9	8	2	7
Poland	4	8	9	7	0	3

NOTE: 0 = minimum; 9 = maximum.

ROMANIAN CIVIL WAR

Of all the 1989 Eastern European revolutions, this one is most likely to go into a second, and more violent, round.

	Economic Interests	Historical Interests	Political Interest	Military Interest	Force Generation Potential	Ability to Intervene Politically	Ability to Promote Economic Development
Hungary	7	9	8	8	2	6	3
"Yugoslavia"	5	7	8	7	3	2	1
Serbia	5	8	8	8	2	2	1
Bulgaria	4	8	9	8	2	3	1
Russia	6	7	8	8	9	6	2
U.S.	2	3	5	4	4	4	4
Germany	4	6	7	6	2	5	7
France	3	6	6	3	2	5	6

NOTE: 0 = minimum; 9 = maximum.

which all Russians view as key to economic survival. A Russian-Ukrainian trade and defense association might suffice, then Moldavia can leave.

Russian Stalinists and imperialists—Losing Moldavia is just one more sign of Russian weakness. If there's trouble, send the tanks.

NATO (Germany and the West)—Economic redevelopment in Eastern Europe requires stability. Irredentism in a key Eastern European nation like Hungary would negatively affect economic recovery and investment.

POTENTIAL OUTCOMES

Transylvania

1. 40 percent chance through 1996: The conditions of 1990 continue. The bad years of Ceausescu are over, but ethnic frictions continue. Still, the situation is tolerable in comparison to the past.

2. 25 percent chance through 1996: A new "Magyar autonomous region" inside Romania is established. All but the most radical elements of Hungarian ethnics are politically satisfied and turn to economic restructuring.

3. 15 percent chance through 1996: A democratic plebiscite is conducted in Transylvania and some border adjustments occur. The odds increase to 25 percent if the Hungarian economy prospers and Hungary can provide economic aid to Romania. The incorporation of parts of Moldavia SSR into Romania also positively affects this outcome.

4. 15 percent chance through 1996: Hard-line elements in the Romanian regime crack down on dissidents and democrats, Russian attack on Romania, or chaos caused by civil war sparks Hungarian occupation of Transylvania to "protect" the ethnic Hungarians. Hungary takes Timişoara and the border regions and holds them. Negotiations stop war. Border readjustments occur.

5. 5 percent chance through 1996: Romanian civil war occurs and Hungary does not occupy Transylvania. Ethnic tensions in the region increase.

Second Romanian Civil War

1. 45 percent chance through 1996: The National Salvation Front (NSF) maintains power and becomes increasingly authoritarian; dissident activity is repressed but not eliminated. The elections are "controlled" so that the NSF holds majority power.

2. 20 percent chance through 1996: "Soft-line" leadership in NSF moves Romania toward democracy, repression level drops, and the economy improves. Successful negotiations with Russia over Moldavian "autonomy" improve the popularity of regime.

3. 15 percent chance through 1996: The Transylvanian War kicks off and the "hard-line" element of the NSF assumes control. Martial law is established inside Romania, which conveniently continues after the fighting in Transylvania stops.

4. 10 percent chance through 1996: Fighting between NSF supporters and dissidents kicks off a new civil war. The Romanian Army splits; old Securitate elements reemerge. If this event occurs and there is no outside intervention, there's a 60 percent chance of a "hard-liner" (totalitarian) victory, and a 40 percent chance of a dissidents' victory. If outside intervention (in order of likelihood: France, the UN, Germany/NATO, Russia) occurs that places foreign troop units in Bucharest, the chance of a dissidents' victory jumps to 85 percent.

5. 5 percent chance through 1996: Democratic parties assume power through a free election and the NSF accepts the results. The hard-line NSF and hidden Securitate, however, attempt the Sandinista tactic of "rule from below." The democratic government is highly unstable. The possible trade-off: no prosecutions of old Communists and Securitate forces for past crimes.

6. 5 percent chance through 1996: War or "war tension" with Russia over Moldavia leads to the collapse of the Romanian government. Civil war erupts. Same odds on civil war as outcome 4.

Moldavia

1. 75 percent chance through 1996: Moldavia SSR becomes an "autonomous republic" within the Soviet political and economic

confederation. Cultural exchange and trade pacts are signed with Romania.

2. 10 percent chance through 1996: Kremlin hard-liners impose direct rule in Moldavia. The Kremlin acts under the pretext of preserving Russian and Ukrainian rights in Moldavia. The Russian Army rules the republic.

3. 10 percent chance through 1996: Moldavia SSR "splits," with the "Russified" area of Moldavia (east of Kishinev and along the Dniester River) remaining in the Soviet Union and the western half joining Romania.

4. 5 percent chance through 1996: War (or a dead-serious threat of war) breaks out with Romania over Romanian support of the extreme Moldavian nationalists. As with outcome 2, the Kremlin acts under the pretext of preserving Russian and Ukrainian rights in Moldavia, but decides that the dissidents' supporters in Bucharest need to be set straight.

COST OF WAR

The Romanian revolution of 1989 was partially propelled by lurid stories of thousands of protesters shot dead in the streets. The reality was hundreds dead. Still a grim number, but at least demonstrating that people have enough sense to leave the area when someone starts shooting. Neither Hungary nor Romania has particularly large or lethal armed forces. Poverty and Russian paranoia have kept the local arms holdings modest. Both nations are letting their armed forces waste away so the funds saved can be spent on economic revival. Still, a war between Hungary and Romania would be an ugly affair, no matter how ill-trained, ill-armed, or plain inept most of the troops would be. The death toll, including civilians caught in the cross fire, could easily go into the hundreds of thousands before one side prevailed. Intervention by other European nations to stop the fighting is possible, which would add to the losses. The economic losses would be even more devastating, and worst of all, an attempt at a military solution, no matter what the outcome, would not solve the problem. Only a genocide (not unknown in this part of the world) or a mass population transfer (also a familiar sight) would settle the issue, more or less, in the long term. A war would probably be proceeded by some terrorism, and repression, in Transylvania. The losses here would be in the thousands, but that would only get everyone's blood up for a larger war.

WHAT KIND OF WAR

Transylvania is not great tank country, as there is much broken terrain and forests. It would be largely a nasty infantry-shoving match. The area is better suited for terrorists and guerrillas—there are plenty of places to hide.

QUICK LOOK AT BALKAN IRREDENTISM: THE THIRD BALKAN WAR

How far does the pie go? Better to ask, how many ways can you cut a peninsula and parts of Central Europe. Here are some of the claims and counterclaims on land in the Balkan region. We've tried to be thorough without becoming trivial.

Bulgaria: Claims parts of Grecian (western) Thrace, Turkish (eastern) Thrace, Grecian Macedonia, and Yugoslavian Macedonia. Bulgaria also believes parts of the southern Romanian coast are more properly placed in Bulgaria.

Greece: Claims parts of southern Albania and some islands in the Adriatic near Albania. Also there are latent claims to Yugoslav Macedonia as well as to a slice of Bulgaria going toward the Black Sea. Greece covets eastern Thrace, and its stifled claims against Turkey outside of the Balkans (but close at hand) are numerous.

Romania: Claims slices of the Serbian border area as well as the whole of Moldavia and part of Black Sea coastline south of Moldavia. In 1913 Romania and Bulgaria fought over Silistra regarding the Dobruja frontier.

Austria: After a visit to the irredentist dentist, old Hapsburgians look fondly at Slovenia (they call Ljubljana "Laibach") and Austria's missing seaport, Trieste.

Italy: Latently claims the Dalmatian (Yugoslav) coast based on Venetian control.

Albania: Has claims against Kosovo Province in Yugoslavia (Serbia),

Montenegro—region around Lake Scutari (Skadarsko), and the old port of Ulcinj, which Albanians believe was swiped from them by British and Montenegrin intrigue in the early 1880s.

Hungary: Wants to protect Hungarians in Transylvania and the Banat. Perhaps the best protection is making Transylvania part of a democratic Hungary? Also, there are latent troubles with Serbia (Yugoslavia) over the Vojvodina (Bachka and that half of the Banat).

Turkey: Kemal Atatürk forswore irredentism, but . . . well, the Balkans were Ottoman lands . . . Bulgaria, Greece, Albania, the squabbling Yugoslav provinces, and Hungary.

Yugoslavia: As a federation still has claims on "parts of Macedonia now in Bulgaria." Yugoslavia believes Italy's control of Trieste is not quite proper. U.S. forces had to keep the Yugoslavs and Italians apart after World War II in this area.

Yugoslav Claims Broken Down

Serbia: Kosovo Province is the "old core" of Serbia and must remain so. The Vojvodina belongs to Serbia and possibly the old "Baranya" county around the city of Pecs in Hungary (an area of heterogenous population occupied by Serbia at the end of World War I). Slices of Romania are inhabited by the Serbs—border readjustments there. Bosnia, because of "geopolitical realities," is Serbian. Montenegrins are Serbs. If pressed, Serbian nationalists believe all of Macedonia (including the part currently "occupied" by Bulgaria) should be Yugoslavian (and later, Serbian). Finally, those troublesome Croats tend to oppress the Serbs. Parts of Croatia are more properly Serbian (as to which parts . . .).

Slovenia: Segments of the Istrian coast (including Trieste?) should belong to Slovenia. If pushed, there's always the subject of Carinthia, the region around Klagenfurt in Austria. That was a big issue at the Paris Peace Conference in 1919.

Croatia: Bosnia is Croatian. The Montenegrin coastline more properly belongs to Croatia, but we might let them have it for "future considerations." And the Slovenes are wrong, actually, Trieste belongs to Croatia.

Macedonia: Many Macedonians on all sides of the Balkan borders think Macedonia should exist as a separate state and maybe even have an empire like the one of Alexander the Great, who was Macedonian.

EXTENDED LOOK AT GREECE AND BULGARIA

The rather extensive chapter detailing Turkey and its problems includes much of the information dealing with a potential "Greco-Bulgarian alliance." This "extended look" provides further background for the material covered in the chapters on Turkey and the Balkans.

GEOGRAPHY

Greece

Greece, at the bottom of the Balkans, is a land of mountains tumbling into the sea. Eighty percent of the nation's 133,000 square kilometer surface is covered by mountains and rugged hills. Greece also has nearly 2,000 islands, though fewer than 180 of them are inhabited year round. Greece has no navigable rivers, but does boast this interesting bit of geographic trivia: No point in Greece is more than 100 kilometers from the sea. With little arable land, no wonder Greeks go to sea. Greece has one of the world's largest merchant navies.

Greece has nine geographic regions. In the north, running from west to east, Epirus, Macedonia, and (western) Thrace are the Balkan borderlands. Mainland Greece consists of Thessaly, Central Greece (Attica), and the Peloponnesian peninsula. Insular Greece consists of the Ionian Islands in the Adriatic (along the west coast from Albania to the Peloponnesus), the Aegean Islands between Greece and Turkey, and Crete.

Greece has a population of around 10 million. Over 95 percent of the people are ethnic Greeks. Greeks overwhelmingly belong to the Greek Orthodox Church.

Bulgaria

Bulgaria covers 110,000 square kilometers, about 75 percent of which are covered by mountains and rugged hills. There are three comparatively distinct regions: the Danube River "tablelands" in the north along the Romanian border, the Stara Planina Mountains in the middle, and the Thracian plain, the Rhodope, and Pirin mountains along the frontier with Turkey and Greece.

Bulgaria has a population of 9 million—85 percent Bulgars, 9 percent ethnic Turks. Most Bulgars belong to the Bulgarian Orthodox Church.

HISTORY

Greece

Greece, the "cradle of Western civilization," managed to escape the "Ottoman yoke" in 1824 and reestablish itself as an independent nation. Greek memories of Turkish domination are bitter. Turkish control of Constantinople, the seat of the Patriarch of the Greek (Eastern) Orthodox Church, is, to many Greeks, a fresh wound. Greek city-states flowered in the fifth and fourth centuries B.C., spotting Greek trading colonies from the Black Sea to the Pillars of Hercules. The height of Greek power, however, was "Hellenized" Byzantium. The Eastern Roman Empire, with its capital in Constantinople, evolved into a Greek-speaking, Greek-dominated state.

Recent Greek history centers on the trauma of the army coup (in cahoots with the National Union of Young Officers [EENA]) in April 1967 that put in power the notorious "Colonels regime," led by George Papadopoulos. The "colonels" fell in 1974 after Turkey's invasion of Cyprus. To some extent the rampant scandal and theft of the PASOK government during the 1980s was tolerated because the socialists were viewed as heroes who had stood up to the "colonels."

Bulgaria

Bulgars first appeared in the Balkans around A.D. 650. In 809 the Bulgarian Prince Krum besieged Constantinople and ravaged the Grecian lands. In 893 Tsar Simeon established the first Bulgarian Empire. Simeon was "Tsar of the Bulgarians and Autocrat of the Greeks," and his empire included much of Serbia. After his death the empire began to unravel. In 1014 the Byzantine "Basil the Bulgar Slayer" (Boulgaroktonos) overthrew Tsar Samuel. Byzantium made Bulgaria a Greek dependency. In 1186 the Bulgars rebelled and established a second empire. In 1330 they were defeated by the Serbs (Battle of Kustendil) and became a Serbian principality. Then the Turks started to arrive. In 1393 the Turks took Trnovo and five centuries of Turkish domination began.

Unlike Russia's other neighbors, Bulgaria looks upon the Muscovites as longtime allies and friends. That's because in 1878 (as a result of the Russo-Turkish War of 1877) the Russians liberated Bulgaria (the "Principality of Bulgaria" and "Eastern Rumelia") from their bitterest of enemies, Turkey. Though to be technically accurate, Bulgaria remained under nominal Turkish suzerainty until October 6, 1908. Like Russian, written Bulgarian uses the Cyrillic alphabet.

During the twentieth century, Turkey has continued to be a focal point of Bulgarian thinking. The Bulgarians remember the Turks' harsh rule. Many Bulgarian nationalists believe Thrace (western and eastern) is more properly Bulgarian territory, and for short periods during this century (the Balkan War, World War II) Bulgaria has held parts of Thrace with an outlet to the Aegean Sea. During the headier days of the Warsaw Pact, Bulgaria was supposed to be the Soviet Union's "jumping off point" for the invasion of Turkey. Forget ideology and pap about "defending socialism," an invasion of Turkey fit well with Bulgarian historical politics. From 1977 to 1987 Bulgaria spent nearly 7 percent of its meager GNP on defense. The Bulgarian Navy was built to provide amphibious lift for Warsaw Pact forces on assaulting the Turkish straits. The Black Sea ports of Burgas and Varna were expanded to facilitate rapid "through put" of Soviet troops heading south. Though the Warsaw Pact is militarily bankrupt, these facilities are still in place.

In 1984 Bulgarian Communist leader Tidor Zhikov began an anti-Turkish policy of enforced "Bulgarization": He banned the Turkish language and Turkish names were Slavicized (Mehmet became Mikhail).

Greek and Yugoslav (Serbian) Macedonia also looms large in the minds and memories of those who dream of a "Greater Bulgaria."

In the revolutions of 1989, the Bulgarian Communist government of Zhikov collapsed. In December 1989 the anti-Turk policies were renounced by the new government. Still, in January 1990 some 10,000 Bulgars in the city of Kurdjali protested the decision to reverse the discriminatory policies. Bulgarian Communists, unlike those in Hungary, Poland, Czechoslovakia, and East Germany, haven't received as much blame for Bulgaria's economic and political failure. They retained power during free elections in mid-1990.

In 1986 Greece and Bulgaria signed a "declaration of friendship" which has since been expanded. In early 1990, Greece and Bulgaria began to discuss a mutual defense pact. The mutual threat? Turkey. Other contingencies? Devolution in Yugoslavia leading to "mutual opportunities" in Macedonia.

LOCAL POLITICS

Greece

New Democracy party (Nea Demokratia)—Greek center-right party led by Konstantin Mitsotakis.

Panhellenic Socialist Movement (Panhellinon Socialistiko Kinima—PASOK)—Greek socialist party led by Andreas Papandreou.

Democratic Initiative party—Party formed by ex-PASOK members that advocates a decentralized, mixed economy.

Democratic Center Union—Democratic socialist party.

Democratic Renewal party—Center-right party.

Communist party of Greece.

Greek National Political Society (EPEN)—Ultraright-wing organization promoted by George Papadopoulos.

Plaka—Nightclub district of Athens where (allegedly) the real governmental decisions are made.

Bulgaria

Socialist party—New name for old (and disgraced) Bulgarian Communist party.

Union of Democratic Forces—Coalition group of anti-Stalinist forces. They were active in toppling the Zhikov regime and are now the main opposition "party" to the Socialist party.

Agrarian party—Small party, formerly a member of the Communist coalition.

"Pre-Revolution" dissident groups—Eco-Glasnost, Independent Discussion Club for the Support of Glasnost and Perestroika, and Independent Society for Human Rights in Bulgaria.

Podkrepa—"Support," a pre-1989 revolution group of trade unionists loosely modeled after Poland's Solidarity.

Tidor Zhivkov—Stalinist leader who ruled Bulgaria for thirty-five years. He was overthrown in 1989.

Bulgarian Turks—Turks numbering approximately 1 million; 330,000 went to Turkey during the anti-Turk repressions.

Saints Cyril and Methodius—Missionaries (and brothers) who converted the Bulgars to Christianity around A.D. 860. Saint Cyril is reputed to have invented the Cyrillic alphabet.

POLITICAL TREND CHARTS

GREECE

After two decades of political, diplomatic, and economic turmoil, Greece appears ready to settle down.

	1990	1996 (Representative Democracy)
Government Effectiveness	3	5
Government Stability	2	6
Political Cohesion	7 –	8
Repression Level	4	3 –
Economic Development	5 –	6*
Education Status	5 +	6

NOTE: 0 = minimum; 9 = maximum.
*This assumes the government pursues competition-oriented policies and gets control of inflation. Inflation rate in Greece in 1989 was 15 percent. If inflation continues at that rate, the 1996 economic rating would be 3. Greece would be a near basket case.

"GREATER GREECE"

"Hellenic Greece"—this is your ultra-Greek nationalist fantasy state. It includes all of Thrace, including Constantinople; parts of Ionia around Smyrna and north to the Dardanelles; Cyprus and all of the Aegean islands. The likelihood of this state existing in 1996 is virtually nil. The dream, however, exists and the dream is not a joke.

	1996 (Authoritarian Democracy*)
Government Effectiveness	4
Government Stability	3
Political Cohesion	4
Repression Level	6†
Economic Development‡	2
Education Status	6

NOTE: 0 = minimum; 9 = maximum.
*Democracy for Greeks, authoritarian for Turks.
†The repression inside the former Turkish mainland territory would be an 8 +.
‡The economy would be beggared by war and military expenditures.

BULGARIA

Economic and social progress in Bulgaria, through 1996, will be slow. The second half of the decade, however, may be brighter, but communism savaged this society and polluted the land.

	1990	1996
	(Authoritarian Democracy)	
Government Effectiveness	3	4
Government Stability	4	4
Political Cohesion	5	6
Repression Level	6	5
Economic Development	2+	3
Education Status	4−	4

NOTE: 0 = minimum; 9 = maximum.

"GREATER BULGARIA" (BULGARIA PLUS MACEDONIA)

Achieving this status would probably be via a ruinous war.

	1996
	(Authoritarian Oligarchy*)
Government Effectiveness	4
Government Stability	3
Political Cohesion	3
Repression Level	7
Economic Development	3+
Education Status	4

NOTE: 0 = minimum; 9 = maximum.
*A Bulgarian grab of Macedonia would lead to militarization and probable martial law in Bulgaria.

QUICK LOOK AT EUROPEAN TRIBES: THE MOSAIC OF THE EEC AND OF EUROPE

As this book is written, 1992 and the economic and political unification of the European Economic Community (EEC) are a year away. The trend in Western Europe has been toward increasing political, economic, social, and cultural cooperation. Military cooperation within NATO and the now increasingly active Western European Union (WEU), political and economic cooperation within the EEC, and five decades of comparative Western political and economic success have led to a relaxation (and perhaps erasure) of old antagonisms and made for a climate of integration and peace. Mikhail Gorbachev, president of the Soviet Union, even speaks of a "common European house" where the integrative trend (and political and economic success) of the EEC ultimately moves east.

But Europe is a quilt of history—the cultural and tribal pieces are many, and the tribal flags still dot the landscape. They may fly over old and rotting castles, but they remain.

There are numerous examples of unresolved and historical rivalries in virtually all of the current European states, east and west, north and south. Ethnic and historical realities still have the ability to create a war of words which radicals can turn into a war of bombs, bullets, and civil conflict.

The map of Europe shows central states, but certain populations beg—and sometimes shoot—to differ. This is a dispute that is over two thousand years old and 1992 will not be an end point.

Local European issues can ignite large European wars, World War I being an ideal example. Ethnic nationalism in the Balkans put the fuse to a Europe primed for armed conflict. Often the local issues that set fire to a region appear to be petty grievances, like demands for use of a language or local autonomy for an ethnic group no one has heard of since the Middle Ages. It leads one to conclude that the Middle Ages are still with us.

They are. Europe, like the rest of the world, is inhabited by tribes—lots of them—some very large (for example, perhaps 150 million Russian Slavs) and some very small (for example, 25,000-plus Slavic Wends outside Berlin).

What is a "tribe"? One definition is an ethnic group. And who is a member of an ethnic group? Almost anybody who says he or she is. Ethnic groups identify themselves by

1. A relationship (usually involving oppression) with another ethnic group that says, "You are different from us."
2. Shared religious beliefs.
3. Shared linguistic heritages (sometimes the same language but different dialects).
4. Historical identification, often involving a "golden age." Almost without exception, each of Europe's unassimilated groups can look back into history and find a gilded era when it was in control of the countryside. History somehow went wrong.

Today throughout the world, some tribes form "nation-states" by reaching a consensus based on geographic, economic, historic, or ethnic considerations. Generally, these tribes finished fighting in so distant a past that everyone has forgotten who killed whose cousin. There is also a second group: those recently at war in which the bloodshed was so bitterly exhausting that the tribal councils are resigned to cooperation. Other tribes form their states—and keep them—with armed force (until 1990, Russia and South Africa were good examples). If the dominant tribe slips up, rebellion results.

Europe's tribes are still trying to sort themselves into nations. This is a dangerous business, especially when Germans get involved. German political reunification, completed in October 1990 when West Germany essentially absorbed East Germany into a new federal republic, is certainly an example of the consolidating and integrative political trend. Many, however, even people delighted at the relative end of the Cold War, are still not overcome with joy at the reunification of Germany. Poland, France, the United Kingdom, the Netherlands, and Russia all harbor deep reservations. The so-called "German problem" may finally be on the road to some resolution, but don't bet on it—it has been with us for many centuries. German politics—in large measure, the Germans attempt to sort their various states into a German nation—have directly or indirectly been the cause of most European wars since the first century A.D. The Slavs, principally the Russians, have lost over fifty million lives to the various German reichs. The Russian antipathy toward Germany has nothing to do with Communist ideology and everything to do with a long-standing fear of another German *Drang nach Osten* ("movement to the east"). A lot of folks (and *volks*) are betting that West Germany's association with the West (i.e., longtime occupation by the United States) has given the Germans a solidifying dose of democracy.

Is it a good bet? Western humanists would like to think that democracies are immune to the various tribal diseases. The idea is that democracies stage planned rebellions called elections, which seek to reestablish the consensus. This works to some extent, but the demands of ethnic groups are sometimes very difficult to accommodate. The new Germany may succeed, but other European nations, Russia as the extreme example, face stupefying odds.

Sometimes accommodation is possible. Take the United Kingdom for example. The Celtic tribe of Wales has historic, linguistic, and religious roots that differ from those of the dominant Anglo-Saxons (Germans). Wales today is an occupied country with significant social and economic grievances, but it is pacified by parliamentary representation—no armies. England failed to use that form of pacification with a former colony now called the United States. Remember "taxation without representation"?

Not all European tribal demands are so well met. Northern Ireland is an ugly sore; Corsicans throw bombs; Basques assassinate all kinds of Spaniards; Flemings and Walloons square off in bitter brick-throwing street demonstrations. Then there are the problems waiting in the wings: Celtic Bretons angry with the central Frankish state in Paris; Tirolers who, never quite happy with Vienna, look at the Sud Tirol and wonder if Italy will turn their southern brethren into pasta lovers.

This doesn't begin to address the tribal problems long hidden under the Cold War and occupation by the Russian Army. (See this chapter on the Balkans for a taste of real tribal trouble.) The Russian tsars' Slavic state was always an ethnic hodgepodge. Now that the Bolshevik Revolution is over and the Germans have been fended off for a while, the ethnic and nationalistic desires of the Ukrainians (who did have a little revolt going until 1954), Latvians, and Lithuanians are boiling (see chapter 7).

Not only do European tribal conflicts debilitate their own provinces and destabilize the nation-states the tribes currently inhabit, but in a nuclear-armed Europe a local tribal demand can demolish everything. Gone are the days when folks rebel by simply burning the other guy's castle and salting his wheat fields.

Yet there are remarkable examples of successful accommodation— even accommodation in places rent by recent and terrible civil wars. Spain provides an example. The Catalans and their relationship with Madrid serve as a striking illustration of the dynamics of European tribal politics leading to a moderating situation. Unlike the Basques, the Catalans have controlled their terrorists and struck a working economic and cultural bargain with Spain. But no astute Spanish politician should take the Catalonian stability for granted. Catalans do not have the size and power (yet) to create their own nation. However, forming 17 percent of Spain's population, and having 25 percent of the GNP, gives the Catalans the size and power to do a great deal of damage to someone should they elect to do so.

As tribes go, the Catalans haven't been one of Europe's big winners (at least not for four hundred years), but they certainly cannot be counted among Europe's losers. Catalans have a large measure of wealth and power to complement their sense of ethnic identity.

The Catalans' twentieth-century intrastate quarrel with Madrid doesn't have the same geopolitical implication for Europe that it did five hundred years ago. Geographically, Catalonia isn't situated so that a disturbance in Barcelona could become the Sarajevo of World War III, although the Spanish Civil War (1936–39) did serve as a diplomatic and military test bed for World War II.

Catalonia versus Madrid, when compared with other ongoing European intrastate conflicts, is remarkably restrained. Unlike the Basques, the Corsicans, or the IRA in Ulster, the Catalans have avoided bombing and assassination. While anarchist members of the now fractious National Confederation of Labor (NCL) as well as other radical separatists occasionally extort "revolutionary taxes" from businesses afraid of being bombed, in Catalonia they get sent to prison.

The Catalans do spill across an existing border (France), but unlike the Tirolese or Albanians, most of the Catalan population lives in one political region, with the Balearics as an island offshoot. Such cohesiveness reduces the degree of nationalistic grief and raises the group's power vis-à-vis the central state government.

Economically, the Catalans seem to have struck a reasonable bargain with Madrid. Politically they have a great deal of autonomy. So, what is the problem? Maybe that Catalonia was never meant to be part of Spain?

Stated simply, the problem is unresolved nationalism. In the larger lens, unresolved nationalism will be the wolf stalking the EEC.

European Ethnic Minorities Chart

All nations in Europe are not covered here, but those nations shown will give you the general idea. The first column represents the ethnic group, the next column represents the percentage of the nation's population (Britain, France, etc.) the ethnic group constitutes.

EUROPEAN ETHNIC MINORITIES

Group	Percentage of Population
Britain	
English	83.00
Scots	9.10
Welsh	4.50
Irish	1.80
France	
French	73.80
Occitans	17.70
Bretons	2.10
Germans	1.90
Catalans	0.90

European Ethnic Minorities (Continued)

Group	Percentage of Population
France (continued)	
Corsicans	0.70
Basques	0.15
Flemings	<.01
Italians	<.01
Greece	
Greeks	96.40
Turks	1.80
Macedonians	1.10
Romanians	0.50
Albanians	0.20
Bulgarians	0.20
Italy	
Italians	96.50
Sardinians	1.80
Friulians	0.70
Germans	0.50
French	0.40
Romanians	<.01
Albanians	<.01
Rhaetians	<.01
Catalans	<.01
Croats	<.01
Greeks	<.01
Slovenes	<.01
The Netherlands	
Dutch	97.90
Surinamese	1.30
Frisians	0.70
Indonesians	0.70

European Ethnic Minorities (Continued)

Group	Percentage of Population
Romania	
Romanians	83.90
Hungarians	7.70
Germans	2.70
Bulgarians	<.01
Spain	
Spanish	71.40
Catalans	16.20
Galicians	7.00
Valencians	4.00
Basques	1.90
Switzerland	
Germans	68.80
French	22.10
Italians	10.30
Rhaetians	0.80
Turkey	
Turks	90.90
Kurds	3.40
Arabs	0.70
Circassians	0.20
Armenians	0.10
Greeks	0.10
Georgians	0.10
Bulgarians	<.01
Yugoslavia	
Serbians	40.10
Croats	22.10
Bosniak Muslims	8.10

EUROPEAN ETHNIC MINORITIES (CONTINUED)

Group	Percentage of Population
Yugoslavia (continued)	
Slovenes	8.10
Albanians	6.10
Macedonians	5.90
Montenegrins	2.30
Hungarians	2.20
Italians	1.10
Romanians	0.50
Bulgarians	0.40

CHAPTER 7

RUSSIA:
THE PRISON HOUSE OF NATIONS

INTRODUCTION

Russia has reached a watershed in its history. The 1917 revolution destroyed the ancient aristocracy and rejected democracy and Western techniques for industrializing. But the 1917 revolution didn't work. The overbearing and inept tsarist aristocracy eventually returned in the form of overbearing and inept Communist party officials and state-appointed industrial managers.

SOURCE OF CONFLICT

Russia is one of the world's last genuine military empires. The Russian military empire is named the USSR—the Union of Soviet Socialist Republics. It is an empire in deep and agonizing trouble. The Soviet Union contains over a hundred distinct ethnic groups (and eighteen languages, each spoken by at least 1 million people). The "real" Russians make up only about half the population of 290 million. During the 1990s, Russians will become a steadily shrinking minority in their own nation.

Russia's problems are converging; given the Soviets' still potent military might, internal Russian problems become world problems. Economic decline throughout the empire has reached critical proportions and key segments of the population have lost faith in communism. A lack of democracy, plus inefficient economic policies, ruined the economy.

After two world wars, one civil war, one revolution, and several rebellions and border wars, Russia is worse off now, relative to the rest of the industrialized world, than it was before the 1917 revolution. And the Russian people know it.

The Soviet Union's non-Russian minorities have begun to assert demands for autonomy or independence. Russian military forces possess over twenty thousand nuclear weapons, scattered in over a hundred storage depots throughout Russia. Should the situation degenerate into civil war or one or more fanatical factions seeking a desperate solution for their grievances, some of these nuclear weapons could be used. The winds of change are blowing in Russia, and one can only hope that the breeze doesn't turn into a nuclear typhoon.

WHO'S INVOLVED

With the loosening of political restraints, over three dozen identifiable political parties have emerged in Russia—about as many as existed in the chaos during World War I that set the stage for the 1917 revolution and Communist takeover. Rather than plow through a list of political parties, many of which have constantly shifting agendas and goals, we will describe the major interest groups, those collections of like-minded people who will pursue their own goals despite party labels.

The Communist party "reformist liberals"—This post–World War II generation of Communist party officials has a significantly different outlook than the earlier generation. The liberals are not liberal in the Western sense. Rather, the Russian Communist party liberals see the need to reform the party, economy, and society in order for Russia to survive. Such reforms will require a substantial change in the way Russia is run. This "liberal" group generally lacks the searing personal experience of World War II and all the horrors that preceded it, thus it is more willing to risk change and the potential disorder that goes with change. Most liberals were born of parents who were already Communists and have known nothing else. They then are liberal relative only to Communist doctrine, not Western concepts of personal liberty and economic enterprise. Many of these "liberals" still see the Communist party surviving in one form or another, although an increasing number accept the complete demise of the Communist party.

The Communist party "conservatives"—Few members of the Communist party believe that Russia can be run in the future as it has been in the past. But a large part, perhaps a majority, of the Communist party is not keen on any radical changes in the way the party dominates all aspects of Russian life. This is where the liberals and conservatives part company. The conservatives want gradual, controlled change; they are more fanatical about maintaining order (a traditional Russian obsession). Given a solution that has a fifty-fifty chance of success, the conservatives would turn it down because of the 50 percent chance of failure. They are also out of touch with how bad the situation is. Having spent several decades establishing themselves and creating their privileged and isolated life-style, the conservatives are neither motivated nor willing to move far or quickly to reform the system that has served them so well.

Urban proletariat—Over half the population lives and works in urban areas. These are the people for whom the revolution was launched. Yet living standards are low. Housing is in chronic short supply, and what exists is poorly built and maintained. Working conditions are often dangerous, management is usually lax, and pay is low. Basic necessities such as housing, staple foods, and clothing are inexpensive but in chronic short supply. In addition to money, it takes influence or some special talent to gain access to scarce items or services. Most urban workers have little access to special goods because they have nothing particularly valuable to trade. Managers and Communist party officials do have things to trade, and the urban workers resent these privileges and the manner in which the system is supposed to work versus how it actually functions. The urban proletariat have lost faith in the Communist party. Revolution is in the air among these people, the traditional foot soldiers of Russian revolutions.

Rural proletariat—One notable, although hardly praiseworthy, accomplishment of Russian communism was to turn the normally resourceful Russian farmer into a rural version of the lackadaisical urban worker. Russian farmers had largely been serfs or tenant farmers until the nineteenth century. When the 1917 revolution came along, most Russian farmers had had only a few years of economic freedom: Reforms after the 1905 revolution had enabled enterprising farmers to break away from the centuries-old collective ownership of land by all village workers. Many farmers had done much with this freedom, turning Imperial Russia into a major exporter of food. But the Communists soon changed that. Russia cannot be a great economic power until it can once more energize its farmers. This is a daunting prospect, not so much for political or economic reasons, but for cultural ones.

The generals—The Russian armed forces are a very elitist organization. Through a combination of custom, culture, and design, the senior officers in the armed forces are largely a well-educated, highly intelligent, and lavishly cared for group of older men. While those officers who do not make it to the senior ranks in their fifties find themselves pensioned off, the ones who do become generals can soldier on into their sixties and seventies. This peculiar habit arises out of ancient (and pre-Communist) Russian custom, wherein a general's power, privileges, and wealth disappear upon retirement. One problem with having a meritocracy in the military is that the senior officials will be quite adept at holding on to their positions. These aging senior officials not only clog up promotion to the senior ranks but often provide feeble leadership. When faced with demands for solving urgent military problems, or indulging in some organizational conflict to retain one's position, guess which gets the most attention? The generals became aware during the 1980s that the economy was in trouble, and the government discovered via Afghanistan—and a large number of lesser military disasters—that the generals were not taking care of business as diligently as they were supposed to. From 1905 to 1945 Russia was under constant military threat and the armed forces became accustomed to getting first pick of Russia's resources. But after 1945 the likely enemies disappeared. By the 1980s this truth sunk in, and more important, the enormous expense of modern weaponry outstripped Russia's crumbling economy's capabilities. The generals had lost their unquestioned claim on the Russian economy—their claim was not completely gone, but it was no longer unquestioned.

Nomenklatura—This ''list'' of senior officials is an institution that predates the Communist revolution by several centuries. The prerevolution system worked rather well, and it is still debated whether the ancient Nomenklatura could have reformed Russia and avoided the Communist revolution. That is historical speculation, while the current Nomenklatura's prospects are the future of Russia. The future is bleak. The older Nomenklatura had competition in the form of private enterprises and foreign investments. The Communist Nomenklatura has no such competition to keep it somewhat honest and occasionally on its toes. This lack of inspiration and encouragement has created a Communist Nomenklatura that is more the problem than the solution. The several hundred thousand Nomenklatura officials, their families, and key associates are a potent power bloc. Little can be done to reform Russia, short of a revolution, unless the Nomenklatura goes along.

Technocrats—While the Nomenklatura makes decisions, there is another class of professionals who are well-educated, dedicated, and often effective in spite of all the obstacles thrown in their way. These are the technical and scientific workers. Most have university educations, and most of the remainder have an exceptional talent for getting things done. Many of the more capable Nomenklatura officials come from the ranks of these technocrats. Yet what most distinguishes this class is its aversion to politics and administration. It has in it scholars, engineers, scientists, and artists. This one group is widely recognized as possessing world-class talents. Despite their misgivings and discomfort about getting involved with politics, the technocrats are being drawn into political affairs and their inexperience and discomfort show. The technocrats will never replace the Nomenklatura, but they are, and will be, a valuable resource in redefining the political, cultural, and economic landscape in Russia.

The KGB—The secret police and intelligence services is another centuries-old Russian institution. Many of the tsar's operatives joined the Communist secret police after the 1917 revolution without any qualms. The KGB is a curious combination of the best and worst elements of Russian society. The top KGB staff (fewer than 100,000 officers and such) contains some of the most competent people to be found in the country. The lower ranks (over 500,000 staff and operatives) have a goodly share of thugs and bullies. Well, it's a dirty business, but someone has to do it. It was the KGB that started the current liberalization process. It has always been the KGB's job to peer into the future and warn the Russian leadership of impending disasters or opportunities. In this case, it pointed out the economic and social problems coming to a head in the 1980s. It was the KGB that played a key role in getting Gorbachev into power. Gorbachev is, in effect, their man as was his predecessor Andropov (a former head of the KGB). The KGB is a very privileged outfit, both in terms of power and access to the good life. It has much to lose if the system breaks down or changes to the extent that the KGB's existence is threatened. The KGB is the most efficient and capable organization in the country—unfortunately, it is not organized to run the country, or even reorganize it. The KGB watches events and analyzes their import for its masters. It is a tool, not normally a solution. After all, the tsar's secret service was not able to save the old regime.

Russian nationalists—These are the Russian ultrapatriots, largely rightist and often extremist. It was Russian nationalism that got Russia into the empire business in the first place. Not content to just mind their own affairs, a significant portion of the Russian population has always enthusiastically supported making Russia stronger and larger and more Russian. The primary motive was the idea that Russians were destined to rule everything in sight, by any means fair or foul. This is the driving force behind every empire. Communism played down the "Russian" aspect of this nationalism in the name of socialist internationalism. Although the old Russian empire was to be run for the benefit of all, the Russians always seemed to do a bit better. When socialism in its many forms failed, the Russian nationalists popped out of the woodwork again. They want Russia, and Russians, first in any post–Soviet Union setup, by any means, at any cost. The radical (and sometimes anti-Semitic) Pamyat movement draws support from many Russian nationalists.

Slav nationalists—Russian Slavs amount to only 145 million people, most of them living in an area bounded by the Ural Mountains, the Black Sea, and the Baltic. There are also 50 million Ukrainians (some in Eastern Europe) and another 10 million Byelorussians north of the Ukraine. Although they both have been part of the Russian empire for over three hundred years, the merger never took completely. The Ukrainians in particular have never accommodated themselves to Russian domination and stubbornly maintain their own language and customs. Ukrainian nationalism is so strong that many Ukrainians fought for the Germans during World War II, and bands of Ukrainian nationalist partisans were still operating in the Ukraine until the early 1950s. The Byelorussians still hold themselves apart from the Russians, but are not as intent on independence. With a population of only 10 million, and being surrounded by groups equally as intent on domination as the Russians are, the Byelorussians have traditionally been content to make do. They do not have as strong a tradition of independence as the Ukrainians have. How serious a move the Ukrainians can make for independence is hard to say. Much traditionally Ukrainian territory has large non-Ukrainian minorities, and many Ukrainians have integrated themselves with the national Russian culture or with cultures of neighboring areas. Moreover, the Ukrainians themselves have many different groups that don't agree on a lot of things, including the form and shape of independence.

Non-Russian nationalists—While the Slavic Ukrainians and Byelorussians have been part of the Russian empire for centuries, most non-Slavic peoples were acquired only in the nineteenth century. Chief among these are nearly 60 million Muslims, most of which are in Central Asia, with 6 million Azeris (Turks) in the Caucasus, where there are also 9 million Georgians and Armenians. Bordering Romania there are 4 million Moldavians, who are actually Romanians and would like to rejoin their motherland. Up on the Baltic coast there are 8 million people in the Baltic states (some are Slav and definitely not Russian; others are Finnish). Most of these groups would be rather enthusiastic about no longer taking orders from Moscow. To further complicate matters, there are millions of Russians living in these non-Russian areas, as well as millions more non-Russians living in ethnic Russian areas or other regions populated largely by a different ethnic group.

Eastern Europe—Russia and Eastern Europe need each other, at least for the moment. Historically Eastern Europe has been a buffer—militarily, politically, economically, and culturally—between Russia and the West. Since World War II, this relationship has been changed to one where the Eastern European nations were forcibly linked in all ways with Russia. After 1989 all but some of the economic links were severed. Russia is still a viable market for Eastern European products that cannot yet compete on Western markets. And most Eastern European nations obtain much of their energy supplies and some raw materials from Russia. These last economic ties will continue to wither away as Eastern European nations turn increasingly to the West. Eastern Europe has demonstrated the ability to convert its economies to a Western standard faster than Russia. This does not do much for Russia, which will as a consequence find itself increasingly cut off from its best source of many consumer and industrial items that it cannot produce itself. Yet the four decades of Russian domination did produce many links that are worth keeping, and goodwill from Eastern European nations will go a long way toward easing the transition of Russia from its Communist past to whatever the future holds.

Western Europe—Historically, Russia has yearned to be accepted as part of Western Europe instead of being viewed as the unstable (and slightly unsavory) giant to the east. Western Europe, with the exception of Germany, has been allied, or at peace, with Russia for over a century. With Communist dogmatism becoming less of an issue, there is a willingness to do some serious business with Russia. Whether this can become a mutually beneficial relationship depends on how well Russia reforms itself politically and economically. Avoiding war with Communist Russia is proving to be easier than doing business with the New Russia.

United States—Russia is far more affected by its neighbors than by the distant United States (despite the common border between far-off

Alaska and Siberia). The biggest impact of the United States on Russia is through U.S. allies and trading partners. But even this influence is diminishing as Russia becomes less of a common enemy and more of a trading partner. In this respect, America's military allies become economic competitors chasing after the same business opportunities within Russia. While many Russians would prefer to do business primarily with the United States (for a complex mélange of reasons), other closer, more eager, and equally capable trading partners seem likely to diminish opportunities for trade with the United States.

Japan—A demilitarized Japan is seen as a potentially big help to Russia economically (and diplomatically as an ally against any problems with the Chinese). Should Japan substantially rearm, then it's a different story, as Japan could make as much of a case as Russia (or China) for owning Russia's far eastern provinces. The potential for either trade or conflict remains. With Russia possibly slipping into civil disorder, Japan would be faced with opportunities and dangers in dealing with such a situation. There is also the matter of several islands to the north of present-day Japan that were taken by Russia after World War II. The Japanese would like them back, peacefully, if possible. In the fall of 1990 the Kremlin announced that two of the Kuril Islands might be ceded to Japan for certain considerations. Is the bidding on?

China—Communism is also going through some changes in China, and although the changes are not quite the same as those occurring in Russia, the potential for civil war or disorder is on the same scale. Russia and China cannot do a lot for each other economically, but they can do great damage to each other militarily. There is also little love lost between the populations of both countries, particularly because of the Russian territories on China's northern border whose historical ownership is in dispute.

Other neighbors—Every one of Russia's other neighbors has some grievance with it. The ones we just listed are the ones most likely to be meaningful in the future.

Third World clients—For thirty years Russia did what Russia had never done before: played the game of international diplomacy and economic subsidization well beyond the borders of its immediate neighbors and traditional adversaries. This was a process that was also beyond Russia's financial, technical, and diplomatic resources. Too often the lack of sufficient money, resources, and trained people led to embarrassment. But the winds of postcolonial revolutionary change blew in Russia's direction and the Russians were keen to play the role of world leader of the revolution. It turned out that what these desperately poor countries really needed was a social and economic system that worked. Russian-style communism wasn't it, but one of Western-style democracy and market-driven economy was. Through the late 1980s more Third World people began to notice this, and Russian prestige and influence suffered accordingly.

GEOGRAPHY

Russia is the world's largest nation with 8.6 million square miles (versus the United States' 3.5 million). Most of Russia is generally flat, often frozen, and largely unpopulated. Two thirds of the population lives on 20 percent of the land west of the Ural Mountains, the traditional border between Asia and Europe. Almost all of the country lies as far north as Canada. The climate is varied but generally harsh. Overall, it's a dry and chilly country with relatively little arable land. All the major ports are blocked by ice for part of the year. While the bulk of the country is uninhabited, and uninhabitable because of bad climate, there are ample natural resources located in the wilderness areas. Getting these goodies out is a major obstacle, as the rivers generally run north to south and moving raw materials to where they are needed requires east-west movement. Geography, like history, has not been kind to Russia.

HISTORY

At least 3,500 years ago, Indo-European tribes began moving north from the Caucasus Mountains into the largely uninhabited Eurasian plains. Some of these tribes spread north and west and became the "root stock" of all Slavic peoples. Life was tough. Population increase—or its flip side, death from starvation—often forced Central Asian tribes to move west. These mounted nomads came wandering—and marauding—across the plains into the lands of the early Slavs. Sometimes the horsemen stayed on and joined the peasantry. Almost always—like all armies—they left babies.

The Slavic people living in the proto-Russian "core region" were also hit from the north by Vikings (A.D. 800–1000), many of whom took over as local aristocracy, organizing their lands on a primitive, feudal basis.

These waves of mounted attack from the east went on for centuries, culminating with the attack of the Golden Horde (the Mongols) in the thirtccnth century. Though Christianity (which arrived in A.D. 988) was a centering and profound influence on Russia's development, and the tentative contact with the west and Byzantium also left important legacies, the Oriental invasions had made a permanent mark. Russia was neither wholly Western nor Eastern. It would become a cultural, political, and military battleground of West and East.

Modern Russian history begins with the conquests of the principality of Muscovy (Moscow). As early as the twelfth century, Moscow was an important river town and the center of what eventually became the Duchy of Muscovy. One of a handful of Russian provinces not conquered by the Mongols, Muscovy led the counterattack against the Mongols, and it was Prince Dimitri of Moscow who finally defeated the Mongols in the fourteenth century. After that, Moscow proceeded to conquer its Slavic neighbors. By the eighteenth century, Muscovy had become Russia, at least west of the Urals. In the process, Russia had made war on all its neighbors (who, at times, attacked first) and laid the foundation for the modern fear of Russia shared by all of Russia's neighbors. Throughout this period, Russian explorers had also been pushing east into the frozen forests and plains of northern Asia. These largely uninhabited areas were systematically spotted with Russian settlements (200,000 Russians by 1700, 500,000 by 1800, 8 million by 1900) and this region became known as Siberia. In the seventeenth century, Russian adventurers reached the Pacific Ocean and in the eighteenth century settled Alaska. In the nineteenth century, Russians began moving from Siberia into the warmer (with fewer than 150 days a year of snow) and more populated regions to the south. This is where Russia acquired all its Muslims, as well as its disputed borders with Turkey, Iran, and China. As Russia entered the twentieth century, it was even larger than it is today. In 1900 Russia also occupied Finland, Poland, and portions of China.

Then came the wars of the twentieth century. In 1905 Japan defeated Russia and threw the Russians out of China. In 1914 Russia entered World War I and, although technically on the winning side, ended the war minus Finland, the Baltic States, and its Polish territories. Several other bits were lost, but these were largely regained in the subsequent civil war. By 1925 Russia was the world's first Communist state. The next twenty years were filled with death on a scale never before experienced by a large nation. Over 30 million Russians were killed, nearly half of them by the paranoid Communist party and the rest by the invading Germans.

The end of 1945 saw the Russian economy in ruins. The memories of the bloody previous forty years had a searing effect on the survivors. Terrorized and/or in shock, the Russian population hunkered down to rebuild their nation and do whatever was needed to avoid another invasion or civil war.

While the Russians were fearful of what other nations might do to them, their neighbors were equally afraid of them. The nations of Eastern Europe, occupied by Russian troops after World War II and forcibly turned into Communist states, showed their distaste for this arrangement early on. The Russians dismissed this boorish behavior as ingratitude and the machinations of agents from the capitalist West (especially the United States).

Until the 1960s, there was a goodly amount of idealism among many Russians and Communist party members. The rapid rebuilding of shattered farms and factories masked the flaws of the centrally planned and run Communist economy. Rebuilding the economy was one thing, running it efficiently was beyond the capabilities of a centralized system, which began to show in the 1970s. But by this time, the senior leadership believed its own press releases and decided to get into an arms race with the United States. Big mistake, as weapons were becoming more dependent on high technology and it was in the area of advanced technology that Russia was falling further behind. Russian scientists could design equipment similar to that found in the West. The problem was that Russian industry was too inefficient to manufacture the equipment in quantity. The full import of this was not accepted until the 1980s.

Overstepping its capabilities in technology was not the only error of ambition that Russia made in the 1960s and 1970s. The Western nations abandoned their colonies in the 1950s and 1960s, creating scores of new nations. Most of these newly minted countries were initially run by people strongly influenced by Communist ideas. The concepts of "scientific" management and "benevolent" dictatorship had strong appeal to the leaders of these new states. Russia found its support in demand by numerous new nations. These countries were scattered all over the world, and for the first time in its history, Russian diplomacy went far beyond neighboring states. This was a novel and heady experience for Russian leaders and diplomats. But these new client states adopted the same inefficient economic policies as their patron's and by the 1980s both clients and patron were suffering severe economic problems. Russia could no longer afford to subsidize the growing demands of its faltering clients. Aside from the economic angle, international politics was vastly changed by this economic collapse. The former socialist colonies had played the United States and Western nations off against Russia in order to obtain aid from both superpowers—or one and then the other. With Russia out of the foreign aid and, to a lesser extent, the foreign affairs game, there is a dramatic shift in how international diplomacy is conducted.

Going into the 1990s, Russia finds itself at another watershed in its history. It is a shrinking superpower that is in danger of disintegrating as a nation. While Russia may simply shrink a bit, there is a significant danger of a disastrous civil war, particularly if nuclear weapons are used by one or more of the factions.

Local Politics

The problem with local politics in Russia is that, officially, there are no politics. The Communist party takes care of everything and no other political parties are allowed. That is, until glasnost (openness) and perestroika (restructuring) appeared in the 1980s.

Mikhail Gorbachev became leader of the Soviet Union in 1985. He represented a new generation and immediately began to install others of his generation (or way of thinking) into positions of power. He soon proclaimed a new policy of glasnost so that the problems of Russian society could be uncovered and discussed. Along with that he pushed perestroika in order to reform those aspects of current Russian society he found wanting.

People outside Russia were surprised at how quickly, and apparently easily, Gorbachev was able to propose and implement one change after another. There was no mystery to it, as dissatisfaction with the older generation of leaders had been growing for over a decade. Many within the Communist party, the Nomenklatura, and the military were simply waiting for someone to get the ball (and the heads) rolling. Apparently the economic crisis, the "old guard"'s glaring political failures in Afghanistan, and the 1983 political battle with NATO over the deployment of intermediate-range missiles gave the "new thinkers" an opportunity to move.

Gorbachev's personality was a political asset: Russia has a long tradition of respect for the strong, forceful leader. Young taxi drivers have pictures of Stalin, a bloody-minded dictator who died before many of them were born, posted in their cabs. Russians are willing to overlook many character flaws in a strong and successful leader. But the leader must be successful as well as strong. And a lack of success in many areas may be what will bring Gorbachev down.

The major problem in Russia is that nothing seems to work very well, and increasingly the standard of living in Russia compares unfavorably with those of many non-European nations. Economic statistics are as unreliable as many other things in Russia. The "official" GNP is somewhere around 1.5–2 trillion rubles. For years the ruble was declared to be worth $1.50–$1.60, but gradually this fiction came apart and rubles can be had for anywhere between five and fifteen *cents*. This places the GNP at about $200 billion and the per capita GNP at around $700. It's not quite as bad as that, as Russia's command economy is so distorted that exact comparisons with market economies are inexact. If Russia's economy were suddenly made into a market economy (and the nation survived the experience), per capita GNP as of 1990 would probably be $1,000–$1,500—still quite low by Western standards. Don't let the relatively flush city folks fool you, the countryside is awash in abject poverty and there are vast slums in all the major urban areas. About 2 percent of the population lives comfortably, another 10 percent lives at a threadbare Western-style level, and many of the rest live as their ancestors did a century ago. There's not a lot of indoor plumbing in Russia and there are few telephones, cars, or any of the multitude of consumer goods people in the West take for granted.

A major factor crippling Russian economic reform is a widespread distaste for enterprising individuals. Even before the Communists came along, there was an ancient collective attitude toward economic activity. Even the nobility was little more than a well-paid group of senior civil servants who were more interested in maintaining their privileges than in becoming top dog. Competition was looked down on at all levels of society. Those capitalists who did thrive before the revolution were members of minority religious communities, foreigners, or the occasional eccentric (and capable) aristocrat. The Communists purged all these groups and preached collectivism as the highest form of social organization. Most of the population took naturally to this attitude and, even now, are not eager to abandon it. "Entrepreneur," "hustler," and "thief" are all interchangeable terms to most Russians. Their idea of a businessman is an efficient and honest government official running a factory for a modest salary. This does not work if you want to create a Western-style economy. Even socialist Sweden, often touted as a model for the future Russia, derives its economic power from a large number of unabashably market-driven enterprises owned and run by enterprising Swedish businessmen.

Russians have long had an inferiority complex regarding their European neighbors. The other nations of Europe were always wealthier, better-educated, or, as many Russians would put it, "more cultured." Through the 1970s, Russians became aware that "backward" areas like Taiwan, Japan, Hong Kong, and South Korea were surpassing Russia economically. This was a double blow to Russian pride, as not only were these nations Oriental (the Russians have a thing about Orientals) but in most cases they were in worse shape than Russia was after World War II. The post–World War II generation of Russians was also less likely to explain away these disparities by the need for Russia to make sacrifices to support "international socialism." Decades of exposure to details of life in the West (via print and movie versions) and a growing number of Russians traveling overseas (and bringing back Western consumer goods) have created a "why not here?" attitude. When the standard of living actually started to decline in the 1980s, the nation was ripe for change.

Glasnost and perestroika were tentative at first. After seven decades of repression, many people were not eager to be first to demand answers to embarrassing questions or propose radical change. But the few who had always been willing to speak up, no matter what the price, found that they were no longer harassed, jailed, or persecuted—no matter how outrageous their statements. The murmur quickly turned into a roar. Gorbachev had unleashed more than he bargained for and soon he had to accept, at least in principle, the full range of Western-style democratic institutions. This eventually included the heresy that there could be other political parties besides the Communist party. This, he had originally pledged, would never be allowed. Ironically, what was being played out was similar to what had happened in the 1860s and before World War I. In both cases, reform came. Or at least reform came close before there was a lapse back into anarchy and repression. The 1905 reforms and the 1917 revolution spawned dozens of political factions that were unable to unite and run the country. The Communists took over with firepower, not ballots. Russians are mindful of their past and take little comfort in it while contemplating their future.

POLITICAL TREND CHARTS

"USSR"

The "X" rating should say it all. The prospects are not good. The USSR is an idea whose time has come and gone. The USSR could be divided into four or five "groups."

	1990 (Socialist Authoritarian*)	1996 (X†)
Government Effectiveness	4	X†
Government Stability	4	X†
Political Cohesion	4	0
Repression Level	7+	—
Economic Development	3	3+
Education Status	5	—

NOTE: 0 = minimum; 9 = maximum.
*Although with increasing democratic trappings.
†Nonexistent, except as a possible "economic" or "confederal" shell.

"RUSSIA" (RUSSIAN SSR)

The second half of the decade, if Russia achieves its economic goals, could be a Russian renaissance.

	1990	1996
	(Authoritarian Democracy)	
Government Effectiveness	4	5
Government Stability	2	4
Political Cohesion	4	5
Repression Level	6	5
Economic Development	3+	4−
Education Status	7+	7+

NOTE: 0 = minimum; 9 = maximum.

REGIONAL POWERS AND POWER INTEREST INDICATOR CHART

CIVIL WAR IN THE USSR

The nervous neighbors (and the United States) would prefer to sit this one out, but may not be able to avoid involvement.

	Economic Interests	Historical Interests	Political Interest	Military Interest	Force Generation Potential	Ability to Intervene Politically	Ability to Promote Economic Development
Russia*	9	9	9	9	9	8	9
U.S.	5	8	8	9	6	6	4
Germany	8	9	9	9	5	5	5
Poland	8	9	9	9	2	3	3
Czechoslovakia	7	8	9	9	1−	2	2
Hungary	7	8	9	9	1	2	2
China	3	5	8	9	6	4	1−
Japan	6	6	7	8	3	3	5
"EEC"	6	8	8	9	2	5	4
Turkey	7	9	8	9	3+	2	1
Iran	3	5	6	7	1+	1+	0

NOTE: 0 = minimum; 9 = maximum.
*The current Russian Soviet Republic as a separate state.

PARTICIPANT STRATEGIES AND GOALS

The Communist party liberals—This faction has transformed itself into a pragmatic political party that is Communist in name only. Its attitude is that only its pragmatism can save the Communist party—and Russia. Gorbachev is the founder and, as long as he lasts, the leader. The liberals can go on without Gorbachev, but without one of their number leading the country, their program of pragmatism and reform is in big trouble. Others are jockeying for control, particularly Boris Yeltsin and other Russian nationalists. Russian politics in the 1990s will not be as dull as it used to be.

The Communist party conservatives—This group covers a wide range of attitudes, beliefs, and solutions. These range from those who are doctrinaire Leninists, who want to do it by the book no matter what, to factions that agree in many respects with the party liberals but want to go slower, and more carefully, into an uncertain future. The more opportunistic members of this faction (a large minority) will wax liberal or conservative depending on which way the political winds are blowing.

Urban proletariat—This bunch is not very political. Life is such a struggle for them, and a way out so obscured by their dismal surroundings, that they will support anyone who can get results. So far, no one has. Gorbachev and the party liberals talk a good talk, but there is less food in the stores and less of everything else that was never abundant to begin with. This group would rebel if that presented any hope of change, but it fears disorder more than most urban proletariats around the world. (Not very good mob material here.) The urban proletariat is also likely to stall many reform measures in an attempt to keep whatever material privileges it has through its workplace "collectives." A striking feature of Russian life is for factories and other large commercial organizations ("collectives") to develop their own social services. The collectives will often control housing, food stores, clinics, and access to many other goods and services. The managers of the collective use whatever goods their enterprise produces (or controls, if it's a government agency) to barter with other organizations. In many cases, the resources of the collective substantially increase the living standards of its members. Economic reform would make these collectives less capable to provide these goods and services, and the collective members would not react kindly to this loss. The "collective" approach to things preceded communism as a fixture of rural Russian life for many centuries, thus the "collective" is not seen as Communist but Russian. For this reason, the urban population of non-Russian areas (the Baltics, the Caucasus) are quite happy to dispense with the "foreign" collective approach and get on with a market economy and Western-style democracy.

Rural proletariat—The farmers have been given opportunities to go into business for themselves, but few have done this. Cynicism about the government's programs along with memories of their sufferings during the 1920s and 1930s have the rural population waiting for some more tangible evidence of true change in government agricultural policy and some material evidence of the same. It is not forgotten that those farmers who went into independent farming before the revolution were exterminated during the collectivization drives of the 1920s and 1930s. Moreover, the Russian (as opposed to the non-Russian) farmers have a pre-1917 tradition of collective ownership of farmland. Unlike China, and most other countries, Russia does not have an untapped pool of potential agricultural entrepreneurs.

The generals—The senior military officers were among the first to notice the economic problems. So, as much as they dislike seeing their budgets cut, there is little prospect of a better alternative. There is much talk outside Russia of the danger of a military coup. There is less fear of this within Russia, as the military has traditionally avoided politics (before and after 1917). The KGB and the Communist party also keep a close watch on the officers, disciplining any that show signs of disloyalty. Moreover, as leaders of a largely conscript army, the officers cannot be sure of their troops following them into a government takeover. It is partially for this reason that many Russians resist calls for a professional, volunteer (Western-style) military. But the military professionals are, well, largely concerned with building a professional combat force. The officers have just enough exposure to the dreadful economic conditions (while monitoring military production) to realize that they would do no better (and probably worse) trying to run the country. One bright spot in the military situation is that in reducing the size of the military a large number (perhaps several hundred thousand) of skilled technicians and managers will be released to the civilian economy. If these people can be placed in the right jobs, they can make a difference.

Nomenklatura—As a modern version of feudalism, the Communist party, through its monopoly on state power, owns (or controls) nearly everything. But all these goods and property are actually administered by several million "civil servants," who are a combination of Communist party officials and managers of service and manufacturing enterprises. Those who are capable, enterprising, and willing to change are willing to try a market economy. This group of civil servants is probably a minority (although a large one, perhaps more than a third of the No-menklatura). The remainder are eager to hang on to their jobs, as they are unlikely to get anything better under a new system. But how to get these people out of the way is the primary problem of the reformers and those members of the Nomenklatura who do want to change things. The inept portion of the Nomenklatura are likely to dig in their heels and resist anything that threatens them. The reformers find it easier to go after the Communist party, which can be voted out. The government bureau-crats are another matter. One Polish academic suggested (half seriously) that the Nomenklatura be the subject of a leveraged buyout. The idea is that the economy would be much more productive without the Nomen-klatura and this increased productivity would make it worthwhile to buy off the old officials. What this professor did not address was the problem of power. The Nomenklatura has it, and no amount of money can replace it as the ultimate luxury. As reform is unlikely to occur with most of the Nomenklatura in place, we have the makings of either a stalemate or civil disorder. It's happened many times before, in many nations (in-cluding Russia).

Technocrats—This talented group, made up of fewer than 100,000 people, is one of the most crucial in reforming the economy. The ability of the technocrats to face a situation, develop a solution, and implement it without being sidetracked by tradition or custom is precisely what's needed. Few of these people have been trained as managers, although many of them are in management positions. As experience has shown in the West, technocrats can make excellent managers, particularly if they are given sufficient incentive to give up their technical vocation. Many technocrats have been at the forefront of the reform movement, despite their misgivings about taking on the Nomenklatura officials. It's up to many of them to take the final step and play a very personal role in the new economy and government. It remains to be seen if enough of them will do that.

The KGB—The security services are both feared and respected. One of the few efficient organizations in the country, it has not backed reform for wholly altruistic reasons. Seeing what happens in nations (particularly Communist ones) that suffer economic collapse and subsequent civil disorder, the KGB wants to solve the problem without its organization suffering any more than it has to. The KGB gives encouragement (and a little muscle) to reform efforts it believes in. No peaceful reform is possible without KGB cooperation. KGB leaders are a highly intelligent and powerful group, although many have become hacks and leeches over the years. But they are traditionally advisers and followers. They need a leader, and when they have one they will follow him. They had Andropov, and then Gorbachev, and they will probably have others until Russia emerges from its current crises or goes up in flames.

Russian nationalists—While the nationalists all have Russian nationalism in common, they diverge widely in terms of other goals and how to achieve them. The nationalists range from various fascist groups to liberals who want to be rid of non-Russian territories in order to concentrate resources at home. Many of the Russian nationalists also want to keep all the non-Russian territories, by force of arms if necessary. Apartheid on the steppes has also been mentioned. But because of their diversity, one cannot expect to obtain any coherent support from these groups.

Slav nationalists—Only the Ukrainians are a real danger here, as their large population of 50 million and ample resources provide them with a reasonable means of maintaining themselves as an independent nation. However, the Ukrainians have severe problems to deal with. First, there is the lack of natural barriers on the flat Eurasian plain they share with the Russians which led to the subjugation of the Ukrainians in the first place. The flat terrain is still there and the Russians still have superior military forces to move across it. Another problem is the divisions with the Ukraine. Like any nation of 50 million people, there are many differences. Indeed, the primary unifying force is the Ukrainian language, but a large minority within the Ukraine (some estimates go as high as a third) does not speak Ukrainian and many of these are Russians or other nationalities. The regional, ethnic, religious, and other divisions within the Ukraine may not be overcome by any strong urge for an independent Ukraine. There may be agitation, unrest, and a lot of noise; but effective moves toward independence are unlikely.

Non-Russian nationalists—These groups are most likely to get away with some kind of separation from the Soviet Union. The more economically advanced (the Baltic States, the Georgians) are more eager for independence and will use their economic prowess as a bargaining chip. The Armenians and Muslims are a different story. The Armenians were originally taken in by tsarist Russia to protect the Christian Armenians from the Muslims (Persians and Turks). The Armenians still live near and among a lot of hostile Muslims. To Armenians, independence is a desire, and security from the Muslims is a necessity. The 60 million Muslims within Russia are also a complex situation. There are dozens of different ethnic groups that share only their Muslim religion. Despite this shared faith, many of these groups are constantly at one another's throats. Without the Russian security forces and army to keep the peace, there would be a lot more armed conflict within the Muslim community of Russia. Russians show increasing willingness to let the Muslims go their own way. Quite a bit of wealth is regularly transferred from non-Muslim to Muslim areas, and the Central Asian Muslims are no longer the military threat as the Golden Horde of six hundred years ago. Azerbaijan is another matter, as this province still contains some (rapidly depleting) oil reserves and related industrial facilities. A large Azeri population is also found in Iran, and the Azeris (and Iranians) think it would be a splendid idea if all Azeris were reunited within Iran (or even an independent state—but let's be realistic).

Eastern Europe—The Eastern Europeans understand, perhaps better than many Russians, what the Russians are going through and what must be done to reform Russia without triggering a catastrophe. Having been forced to endure a Russian-style economic and political system since the late 1940s, yet being basically Western European in outlook, the Eastern Europeans may appear uncommonly accommodating to Russia now that Eastern Europe is free. What the Eastern Europeans are trying to do is ensure that Russia doesn't turn toward despotism again and take Eastern Europe back into Russian bondage. Eastern European nations, except those that get waylaid by their own internal problems, will assist Russia diplomatically, encourage the liberals, and act as a bridge between the West and Russia as a means of discouraging the Russians from once more turning Eastern Europe into satellite nations.

Western Europe—The changes in Eastern Europe and Russia are seen as a great boon for Western Europe. The threat of Russian invasion has greatly diminished and with it opportunities to reduce defense spending. Moreover, Eastern Europe and Russia are now open to Western companies. The potential benefits are great, but only if Russia avoids slipping into disorder, or worse. More so than the United States, Western Europe is eager to do whatever it can to ease Russia's transition from communism to whatever else works and doesn't threaten the security or economic stability of Europe.

United States—Being much farther away from Russia, both historically and geographically, than Russia's numerous neighbors, the United
States is more circumspect in dealing with the rapidly changing situation
in Russia. For decades the primary role of the United States in world
affairs was to "contain" Russian expansion and to block any Russian
attempt at nuclear (or other kinds of) blackmail. This task remains, but
its role as leader of the Western nations against Russia's attempt to spread
communism has disappeared. The United States doesn't know quite what
to do with itself. Russia would prefer economic assistance, free trade,
and cooperation in dealing with lesser world troublemakers. The post-
1989 situation has Russia becoming the leader in the new superpower
relationship, if only because Russia has more neighbors who are both
concerned about Russia's future and how to influence it.

Japan—Eager to develop new markets, Japan also wants to recover
the Kuril Islands (and several other minor ones), lost to Russia after
World War II. While these islands are of no great economic value, their
recovery is an emotional (and political) issue in Japan. A deal could be
struck, as the Russians had, in the last century, traded the Kuril Islands
to Japan in return for Sakhalin. Russia needs Japanese technology more
than it needs another chilly island off its coasts.

China—There is some opportunity for trade between China and Russia
which has been steadily increasing, even though the long distance between
each nation's major industrial and population centers limits economic
exchanges. There are still disputes, such as China's claim on Russia's
Pacific provinces. But the Chinese, who take the long view in these
matters, see the recovery of these territories as an eventuality. Of more
immediate import is the political turmoil caused by Russia's abandoning
dictatorship while China tries to hang on to it. Both nations are working
hard to not inflame matters in the other country. If either nation fell into
civil disorder, it would probably have an effect, possibly grave, on the
other.

Other neighbors—Russia's numerous other neighbors nervously
watch events unfold. To the north, Finland sees its decades of subser-
vience to Russia paying off. Finland now stands to reap large economic
rewards when, and if, the Russian economy recovers. To the south,
Turkey and Iran see Russia as less of a threat, for the moment. Russia's
other Muslim neighbors, Afghanistan and Pakistan, go about their own
affairs with less potential for Russian intervention.

Third World clients—This group is hit the hardest by the changes in

Russia and has few options. One remaining tie these nations have with Russia is debt. Russia has sold (on very generous credit terms) over $100 billion worth of goods to its various Third World clients. Most of this debt is unlikely to be recovered, especially now that an economically strapped Russia can no longer threaten to withhold future shipments. Russia's fall from diplomatic power has also caused unrest in many Third World client states that had copied Russia's Communist government and economic policies. Without Russia to play off against the United States, the foreign aid game just became a much less renumerative undertaking. Many poor nations will continue to depend on Russia, if they can find hard currency to pay for the cheaper Russian goods.

POTENTIAL OUTCOMES

1. 35 percent chance through 1996: The USSR divides into five "groups": the Baltics, a Russia-Byelorussian-Ukraine and Kazakh federation, "Southeastern Muslim," "South Muslim," and "Christian" fragments (Georgia, Armenia).

2. 30 percent chance through 1996: The same old USSR exists—mediocrity has a certain stability to it. Even with all the different groups up in arms, there is a lot of pressure to maintain order.

3. 15 percent chance through 1996: Russia slims down. Many economic and political problems are solved by allowing many of the non-Russian parts of the Soviet Union to go their own way and fragment. Perhaps a customs union or "common market" remains, but basically Russia becomes Russia again, with 150–200 million people.

4. 10 percent chance through 1996: Russia turns around its economy and most of the USSR holds together. Politics and the economy survive a transition so Russia becomes something resembling the countries in Western Europe. This is what most Russians would like, if they could figure out exactly what "being European" is.

5. 10 percent chance through 1996: Russia loses it—there is civil disorder, economic collapse, perhaps even civil war—the worst case that everyone will strive to avoid the closer it gets. There have been several civil wars in Russian history, and yet another

Russia and Its Neighbors

	Population (in millions)	Population (per sq. mile)	Percent Muslim Population	Percent of Arable Land	Per Capita GNP	Average Life Expectancy
Russia	290	34	11	11	1,400	68
Finland	5	38	0	8	17,000	75
Poland	39	322	0	48	5,000	70
Romania	24	260	0	43	5,000	70
Turkey	56	186	98	30	1,200	65
Afghanistan	15	60	89	12	200	42
Mongolia	2	3	0	1	400	63
China	1,100	297	1	11	300	69
No. Korea	22	472	0	19	500	68
Japan	124	850	0	13	22,000	79
France*	56	252	2	34	14,000	75

*Included for comparison.

one is not out of the question. There's perhaps a one-third chance that nuclear weapons would be used. But it's hard to say, as there has not yet been a civil war in a nation armed with nukes.

COST OF WAR

The last round of civil disorder and reform (1917–38) killed off nearly 20 percent of the population. Russia has a strong incentive to manage change with less bloodshed this time. Even so, the casualty list has grown through the late 1980s. While the losses are only in the thousands, the excess deaths due to the failing economy are even greater. Poor medical care and low living standards have led to an acknowledged decline in life expectancy during the 1980s. This pushes the losses to over a hundred thousand dead and fuels the discontent that causes the armed conflict. A major civil war could easily kill millions, even without someone using a nuclear weapon. Large-scale civil unrest could push the death rate way into the tens of thousands. Along with any of these disorder situations would come economic damage that would cost billions of dollars to repair.

WHAT KIND OF WAR

The irregulars—Lebanon and Russia have one thing in common: lots of free-lance fighters running around with AK-47s. Sloppy administration and endemic pilferage have allowed hundreds of thousands of Red Army weapons to reach civilians since World War II. During periods of civil disorder, as in the Caucasus and Central Asia in the late 1980s, even more weapons were taken (or sold by the ill-paid troops) and used in ethnic clashes. Millions of small arms, and hundreds of thousands of heavier weapons, are stored in hundreds of poorly guarded warehouses, belonging to over a hundred reserve divisions, throughout the country. Most of the troops assigned to these divisions (as little as 10 percent of the divisions' full personnel strength) are young conscripts who are paid only a few dollars a month. Slipping an AK-47 or some other weapon out the back door for a few bottles of vodka is so common that officers spend more time on paperwork recording the thefts than on trying to stop them. As a result of this leakage of weapons, several of the non-Russians already have private militias operating, some of which consist of thousands of armed and organized fighters. In many areas of the Caucasus, the central government had lost control by 1990 and was reluctant to press the issue by force lest such action escalate to a full-blown local civil war.

The riot police—The Ministry of the Interior (MVD) controls the national police force which in turn contains, in theory, over 100,000 paramilitary troops (out of 300,000 MVD personnel) for putting down large-scale disturbances. These MVD troops are mostly conscripts and are specially selected from the nearly 2 million young men inducted each year. Nearly all are Slavs and are chosen for their political reliability. The job is something of a choice assignment, as the MVD are more police than infantry and the work is easier. However, the training and discipline are halfhearted—the duty consists largely of endless guard duty. This is a fetish with the Russians—even transportation facilities are heavily guarded in peacetime. When facing an angry mob, many of the young troops remember that they would really rather be civilians. This attitude results in uneven riot control, which often results in the Army getting called in. The army troops are even more inept at riot control. The MVD does have an extensive intelligence operation, including millions of paid (but mostly unpaid) informers. But over the decades since Stalin's death in 1953, the operatives have become lackadaisical and the population less intimidated. The result has been urban firefights in many areas, which resemble those going on in Lebanon since 1975.

The secret (security) police—The Russians recognize that teenage riot police are just a temporary solution and fight to win these urban disputes on another level. The MVD and KGB both have agents and extensive files on nearly all citizens. After, and often before, riots break out, the secret police go around with lists of actual or suspected troublemakers and arrest or intimidate as many as possible. Now that the prison camps are largely gone and Stalin's massive slaughters forgotten, the midnight knock on the door doesn't have the effect it used to. In the non-Russian areas, the KGB/MVD secret police's control is often tenuous. This breakdown in control has enabled the non-Russian ethnics to organize military units and fight pitched battles with the MVD and the Army.

The elite combat units (Vozdushno Desantnye Voiska—VDV)—This airborne landing force is the elite force of the Red Army. Its six currently combat-ready divisions are deployed throughout the most populated areas of the Soviet Union:

7th Guards, Kaunus (Baltic States)

76th Guards, Pskov (Leningrad)

98th Guards, Kishinev (the Ukraine)

103rd Guards, Vitebsk (Byelorussia)

104th Guards, Kirovabad (the Caucasus)

106th Guards, Tula (Moscow) (This is a training division and not considered a combat-ready unit. In wartime it would be needed to train replacements; in peacetime it could be turned out for riot duty.)

There are two other divisions that were recently disbanded:

44th Guards, Jonava (Baltic States) (An NCO training unit, this was disbanded in the late 1980s but it could be reconstituted.)

105th Guards, Fergana (Turkestan) (This was sent to Afghanistan and there disbanded to form two air assault brigades which still exist but are no longer controlled by the VDV.)

Each division has about 7,000 troops organized into three regiments, an artillery regiment, and some support units. Unlike Western airborne units, the Russian divisions have several hundred (lightly) armored BMD infantry combat vehicles. These proved useful in 1989 when the parachute forces were sent into the Baltic States and the Caucasus to put down unrest. The reductions in the armed forces (the disbanding of the 105th and 44th Guards) have brought forth suggestions that one or two airborne divisions be disbanded. Increasing unrest may stall this proposal; indeed, one or both of the already disbanded divisions may be revived.

The Big One—One of the bloodiest wars of this century was the little-known (in the West) Russian civil war. This took place from the end of World War I to the early 1920s and saw the armed forces of Russia split along ethnic and class lines. It could happen again, except that this time each faction would at least have some nuclear weapons.

QUICK LOOK AT THE INTRINSIC PROBLEMS OF ETHNICITY AND EMPIRE

The widespread formation of nation-states in the last century has blinded many people to the persistence of empires and the problems these artificial entities bring with them. Russia, Iran, China, and India are a few of the empires still with us and their inherent instability is a continuing threat to world peace.

Nation building is a relatively recent process which involves more than a central government and well-defined, and defended, borders. For a group of people to consider themselves citizens of a nation rather than simply members of some tribe or ethnic group, the nation must share some of the same characteristics as a tribe. Tribes are groups of people, perhaps several million, who are held together by a common language and customs. The earliest nations achieved the transition from tribe to nation by taking a large number of people with the same (or very similar) language and customs and governing them with a centralized bureaucracy, a national army, and well-defined borders. These nations could grow in three ways. Natural population increase was one. Another was absorption of adjacent peoples, either as immigrants (or slaves) or by forcibly imposing the nation's language and customs on its neighbors. This second method has worked, but not always. When it doesn't work—when you don't absorb the new people but simply annex them—you don't have a larger nation, you have an empire. That's the third way to make your nation larger.

In the past, empires were more common than larger nations. Because of the unstable nature of empires—the annexed people were always eager to be independent again—they came and went with great frequency. More widespread literacy and better communications made nation building easier in the last century. No longer isolated, annexed ethnic peoples could travel freely to the nation that conquered them, which made it easier for the conqueror to educate new generations of annexed peoples in the conqueror's language and customs. In this way England absorbed the Gaelic Scots and Welsh to form Great Britain—though they were less successful with the Irish. France went through a similar consolidation process, and quite recently, as early as in the nineteenth century, most of the people in France didn't even speak French. The United States, and Australia, Canada, and many Latin American nations, are examples of nations built from migrants speaking many different languages. The price of admission was accepting a new mother tongue, and millions were quite willing to do so.

This brings us to the empires that still exist and why they must be carefully watched. Empires always break up, if only temporarily. And when they do, they do so violently. Several of the current major empires have nuclear weapons, so there is real danger of their breaking up in a spate of nuclear explosions.

Russia is the most troublesome empire. The Russian empire began forming over four hundred years ago. The first major acquisitions were kindred peoples who spoke similar languages and shared many customs (those in Byelorussia and the Ukraine). Much of Russia's expansion until the nineteenth century was eastward through the thinly populated Siberian wilderness. Russia put many of its own people into these lands and made the territory indisputably Russian. But during the nineteenth century, Russia gobbled up many of the alien peoples who are now clamoring for freedom.

The Russian empire has already broken up once in this century—in the aftermath of World War I. It wasn't until the mid-1920s that the new Communist government gathered most of the pieces back together. The cost was over ten million dead, and some of the pieces (Finland, Poland) were never recovered. The Baltic States (Lithuania, Latvia, and Estonia) were retrieved only in 1940 with the connivance of Nazi Germany. This shows you what lengths an empire will go to in order to keep it all together.

For decades Russia kept the empire together with a succession of real or contrived emergencies. After the 1920s civil war, there was the "unity" needed for reconstruction and recovery. Then came World War II (when many non-Russians saw the Nazis as liberators), followed by more reconstruction and recovery. But in the 1970s, the Communists ran out of emergencies and the ethnic minorities began to stir. Through the 1990s, the minorities will not only be agitating for independence on the usual ethnic grounds, but also attempting to get free from the failing socialist economy.

Those few multiethnic nations that have survived, of which Switzerland is the shining example, have done so by keeping everyone fat and happy. Most people in the Soviet Union are lean and unhappy. However, even in Switzerland the ethnic differences still exist, but they are smoothed over with a heavy slaver of prosperity and a desire not to risk losing it all.

The Soviet disUnion

Imagine, for a moment, that the Soviet Union broke up into its component parts. There are many configurations of a busted-up Russian empire. This is just one of them.

The data for each item in the chart on p. 284 is based on each region's current share of the economic wealth. Because the Soviet Union's economy is so centralized, with a few huge plants producing key items in many sectors, the economies of many of these parts of it would quickly fall apart. There would have to be tight economic cooperation and coordination for up to a decade before the new national economies could attain any semblance of independence.

Russia—Of all the regions of the Soviet Union, Russia has the highest standard of living. This is not saying much, and the majority of Russians live in what Westerners would call poverty. While the Russian area is well-endowed with raw materials and an educated population, it also benefits from the tendency of the Soviet Union to put many of the economic goodies in "the center"—that is, Russia. Because Russia is the original core of the Soviet Union (and the preceding tsarist empire), prudence dictated that many essential facilities be placed away from the border areas (which also happened to contain conquered non-Russian people). In this way, invaders would trash the non-Russian Russians before they got to the real Russians. Now that these non-Russians manning the frontiers want independence, the Russians noted that without these less-well-off folks there would be more wealth for the Russians. All of a sudden it became an attractive proposition to make Russia independent.

Population of the Soviet Union

	Population (in millions)	Population (per sq. mile)	Percent Muslim Population	Percent of Arable Land	Per Capita GNP	Average Life Expectancy
Russia	145	22	1	3	1,600	67
Byelorussia	11	125	0	22	1,400	68
Ukraine	57	223	0	30	1,500	68
Baltic States	9	118	0	32	2,100	70
Caucasus	16	225	35	10	1,600	72
Central Asian Republics	52	34	80	2	700	66
France*	56	252	2	34	14,000	75

*Included for comparison.

The Russians never cared much for the non-Russian members of the Soviet Union, so cutting off Russian subsidies for these wretches appears perfectly reasonable to many Russians. That such an action would also tend to increase the Russian standard of living has not gone unnoticed either.

Byelorussia—The Byelo("White")Russians are not that different from the "Great Russians." At least not as different as the Ukrainians. With a little effort, this region could remain a part of Russia.

The Ukraine—A rich agricultural area with substantial natural resources, the Ukraine could easily become a viable economic entity. Three hundred years of subjugation by the Russians have made it difficult to bring this off. Possible, but not easy. Moldavia is included in the Ukraine for the sake of this chart. It is somewhat less wealthy than the rest of the Ukraine, and the people want to rejoin Romania, as they are Romanians. A deal could be worked out and the Ukraine would be none the worse for it.

Baltic States—The three Baltic states are already talking about some kind of union, which is likely in order for them to have any economically viable size. Sort of a Switzerland on the Baltic.

The Caucasus—This would be more of a shotgun marriage. Georgia would like to be all by itself, but with all those Muslims to the south and an Armenia which is even more fearful of the Muslims, some kind of arrangement is likely. Azerbaijan would like to go back to Iran, but there's still valuable oil left that can't be lost. If Azerbaijan were separated out, the Caucasus would have seven million fewer people and would be somewhat wealthier.

Central Asian republics (CAR)—The CAR could be anything, including a patchwork of warring states. Whatever the case, the Russians are not unhappy about stopping the massive subsidies that go to this region. Per capita income would drop a bit more if this area were not a part of the Soviet Union.

The "Mingle" Factor and the Cost of "Unmingling"

While the numerous different ethnic groups in Russia prefer to live among their own kind, there is a fair amount of intermingling. In particular, many Russians live outside of the Russian area of the Soviet Union. The Baltic States' population is over a quarter Russian and even the central Asian republics are about 20 percent Russian. Because of geography and similarities in culture, there is a lot of population mingling between Russia, the Ukraine, and Byelorussia. If there were to be a breakup of the empire, there would be a lot of pressure on people (gentler in some areas than in others) to ''go back where they came from.'' This already happened in the Caucasus during the late 1980s and there are now several hundred thousand Russian refugees wandering about Russia. A major reorganization of the Soviet Union would see over ten million people being displaced. Russia has already gotten a taste of this by the removal of some of its troops (and the officers' families) from Eastern Europe. There is no housing for these people in the Soviet Union and many are living in tents. This movement of populations in a nation notoriously short of housing is a major problem that would reach catastrophic proportions if large numbers were involved.

Well, What About the Nuclear Weapons?

Russia has over 20,000 nuclear weapons, most of which have always been stored within the Russian part of the Soviet Union. After the ethnic disturbances of the late 1980s, those few thousand that were outside Russia were removed from the other Soviet regions and brought ''home.'' Even so, there are over a hundred locations where these weapons are stored, and even though they are guarded (and controlled until released for use) by the KGB, it doesn't take much imagination to see how easily the wrong people could get their hands on some nukes if civil disorder broke out in the Soviet Union. Plans are probably in place to disable any weapons that come in danger of being seized by unauthorized personnel. But the way things work in Russia, such plans are rarely (let's say never) perfect.

Just having a nuke is not enough—you have to know how to use it. So it's more than just having a mob liberate a few nuclear weapons. You have to have someone with experience in operating them. Usually only officers are entrusted with the details of getting a nuclear weapon into action, and there are plenty of active and retired officers with nuclear weapons experience (probably nearly 100,000). Of course, there are many different types of nuclear weapons, so an officer who was in charge of naval nuclear weapons might have a difficult, if not impossible, time working with a nuclear artillery shell.

The possibility of uncontrolled use of nuclear weapons is real in Russia, but it is not as likely as it might appear on the surface.

PART THREE

AFRICA

Africa est omnis divisa in partes tres.

All Africa is divided into three parts. In the north lies the Saharan, Arab-dominated slice, the Sahel. In the south sits South Africa, the apartheid state of the white Boer tribe. In between exist very tentative states in various stages of anarchy, chaos, economic disorder, and warfare—the results of powerful tribalism and the recent release from colonialism. The few exceptions manage to maintain their sovereignty by difficult political and economic trade-offs, though some of the genuine middle African success stories, such as the Ivory Coast, still suffer from graft, a high-debt load, and lack of transportation.

If any single continent deserves its own dedicated *Quick and Dirty Guide*, Africa is the nominee. The continent's mix of colonialism, neocolonialism, potent tribalism, religious conflicts, foreign troops, modern weapons, economic decline, political aspirations, mounting international debts, racism, nationalism, and pan-nationalism creates extreme volatility. And Africa's human resources and relatively untapped natural resources make it an inevitable ground for geopolitical competition. This section will look at three African conflicts: the Sahel wars, a series of conflicts in this dry region that share many common characteristics; South Africa versus its neighbors and itself; and Zaire and the battle against disintegration, including Zaire's many neighbors that share the same problems.

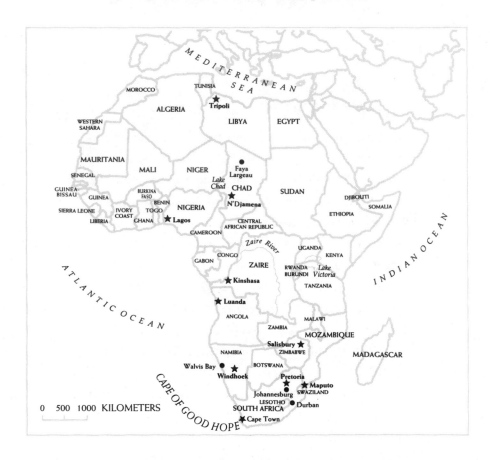

CHAPTER 8

THE GRAND SAHEL: BAD ECOLOGY, BAD POLITICS, BAD TIMES

INTRODUCTION

The Sahel is a semidesert "weather zone" cutting across Africa's north, just south of the Sahara Desert. Technically, the Sahel proper, a savanna land, exists only in the western reach of the continent, but the ecological and, sadly, political conditions characteristic of this "desertifying" region now extend as a band ("the Grand Sahel") straight across the continent, from Mauritania on the Atlantic coast through Chad in central Africa to Somalia and the Red Sea in the east.

This huge belt land serves as the rough and rugged border between Arab Africa in the north and black Africa in the south. In the last century the entire region has been increasingly plagued by severe, periodic droughts which, because of growing human populations and the destruction of vegetation, have led to "desertification," the encroachment of the Sahara and the transformation of pastoral and sparse cropland into so much dust.

In the popular, Western imagination, mention of the Sahel conjours up TV pictures of emaciated refugees, bankrupt countries, and rock musicians raising money for international food drives. The nations in the sub-Saharan strip, Mauritania, Senegal and Gambia (erstwhile Senegambia), Niger, Mali, Chad, Sudan, Ethiopia, Somalia, and Djibouti, are desperate and struggling by any definition. The dire economic conditions in these nations—exacerbated by ancient animosities between tribes, races, and religions, by the legacy of European and Arab colonialism, and, in the case of Ethiopia, by the final breakdown of an ancient empire—have produced a relentless cycle of armed conflict and death wrought by combat and starvation. In the Sahel starvation has become both a weapon in and a cause of war.

SOURCE OF CONFLICT

Rapid population growth in the first half of this century, plus the departure of colonial governments and establishment of local regimes in the 1960s, has led to political and economic collapse in the area. Intermittent warfare, cyclic famine, millions of refugees, and other woes now characterize the region.

The periodic famines and endemic ethnic conflicts have intensified the traditional rivalries and plunged the region into a constant state of conflict. The warfare is basically fought with small arms; although occasionally heavier weapons and aircraft are used when any of these poor nations can beg, borrow, or steal them from wealthier benefactors or opponents. Nearly all the warfare is internal, between different ethnic, political, and/or religious groups within the same nation. The ugly little wars of the Sahel are driven by hate and a desire to survive. The individual suffering is new, but at times the form of warfare is almost ancient— camels and horses are used for supply and troop transport almost as often as Toyota Land Cruisers, heavy trucks, and armored personnel carriers. Sometimes prisoners are literally enslaved.

Aiding and often encouraging the strife are several major outside groups. Many Arab nations give support to their Arab kinsmen and fellow Muslims in these nations. On occasion, Col. Muammar Qaddafi of Libya sends in troops. In particular, Chad and the Sudan have been Libyan stomping grounds, though Libya has allegedly armed and politically supported "rebels" in Mauritania and Senegal as well. During the Cold War, Russia got heavily involved in the weapons and covert aid business. These fragile nations were the perfect spot to "wage war on the periphery," and by exploiting old colonial antagonisms, the Kremlin figured to gain allies and victories quite cheaply. But current internal problems in the Soviet Union seem to be causing a cutback in this support. Victories were few, losses added up, and nothing was cheap.

Western nations have also supported various groups and governments in the Sahel, partially to counterbalance Russian interference and partially to maintain influence in their former colonies. The United States and many other Western nations have provided considerable food and economic assistance to these nations. France in particular is a major player in the region. Djibouti, while nominally sovereign, is still essentially a French Foreign Legion post and navy base covering the critical Horn of Africa.

Ethiopia with its long-running wars is, in some ways, an intensified example of all of these troubles. Essentially, Ethiopia as it exists today is the remnant of an empire at least twenty-five hundred years old. Overrun by specifically Italy in the 1930s and by the twentieth century in general, and with the fall of Emperor Haile Selassie (the Lion of Judah) in 1974, the Ethiopian empire centered in Addis Ababa has finally shattered. The long subjected Tigre and Omoroan peoples now fight in league with rebellious Eritrea Province (formerly Italian Somalia).

WHO'S INVOLVED

General note: Many Arab states provide aid and assistance to their fellow Arabs and Muslims in the northern portions of most Sahel states.

Ethiopia

"Marxist" Central Ethiopian government.

"Cuban Foreign Legion"—Allied with the Ethiopian Marxists, this is a mechanized infantry brigade made up of Cuban troops. A Cold War holdover, it was still active as of 1990.

Eritrean People's Liberation Front—This is a group primarily centered in the old Italian colony of Eritrea.

Tigre People's Liberation Front (Tigre)—A loosely organized coalition of rebels, this group is centered in Tigre province.

"Ogaden secessionists"—Located in Ethiopia's bite of the Ogaden desert, this loose coalition of tribes was formerly propped up by the Somali government.

Somalia—Claims the Ogaden region.

Wild Cards

Israel—The "return" of Ethiopian "black Hebrews" to Israel has been dependent on the flow of Israeli advice and Israeli arms.

Russia—At times Russia has propped up both the Somali and Ethiopian governments.

United States—The United States has port facilities and air base rights in Berbera and Mogadishu, the capital of Somalia.

France—France maintains a garrison in Djibouti (on the northern border of Somalia).

The Sudan

Muslim and Arab north—This part of the region maintains traditional dominance over black Africans.

Black tribal groups, Christian and animist, all in the south, fighting for independence.

Wild Cards

Egypt—Egypt is interested in "stability" along the upper Nile.

Libya—Libya supports several rebel groups.

Ethiopia—Support for Ethiopian secessionists has been funneled through the Sudan.

United States—The United States wants peace and stability. With the Cold War over, there's nothing much else to aspire to.

Chad

Anti-Libyan political and tribal groups.

Pro-Libyan political and tribal groups.

Libya—Extend its power, and perhaps pick up valuable territory.

France—French troops and arms back up N'Djamena. Paris has remained involved in its former colonies in the area from Senegal to Chad.

Wild Cards

Nigeria—Nigeria has a large army next door.
United States—The United States, trying to keep a low profile about it, has provided some military aid to Chad in an effort to counter Libyan invasion.

Mauritania and Senegal Emigration War

Mauritania—Representing the Arab north.
Senegal—Representing the black south.
Gambia—Essentially a part of Senegal.

Wild Card

Nigeria—The "Brazil" of Africa.

GEOGRAPHY

The Sahel is the semiarid fringe of the Sahara Desert. For thousands of years, its grassy plains and slender rainfall (marginally heavier than the under ten inches a year on the Sahara) kept the desert at bay. Every ten years or so, drought hits the Sahel, population growth stops, or reverses, and then the rains come again for a few years. Sometimes the droughts last two or more years, and large population deaths, and movements, occur.

The Sahel begins near the Senegal River as coastal grassland. (Ecologically, Gambia, located along the Gambia River in the middle of Senegal, is not in the Sahel, but political events in Senegal resonate in Gambia.) Four hundred miles from the coast the land rises several thousand feet to an equally semiarid plateau that extends nearly three thousand miles eastward (broken only by some hills in southwestern Sudan) to the Ethiopian highlands (over six thousand feet higher). Nearly five hundred miles farther east, the land drops again to the Somali Plateau and then to the Red Sea coast.

The Sahel, then, was a natural buffer zone between the arid wastes of the Sahara and the tropical rain forests of central Africa. The people living in the Sahel live largely off their herds of cattle, goats, or sheep.

Nearly five thousand years ago, this flat corridor provided a well-marked path for the spread of the dark-skinned Nilo-Saharan and Cushite people of the west coast to the east, which they did until they bumped up against the Negro peoples in the Niger River area three thousand years ago. Eleven hundred years ago, the camel was introduced on a large scale, making it practical to trade regularly with the Arab states to the north (along the Mediterranean coast). Three hundred years ago, the population of the area stood at about ten million, largely at the east and west extremes. The twenty-five-hundred-mile region in the middle was largely for nomadic grazing and travel. Currently the population of the Sahel region is over seventy million. The agricultural infrastructure has not kept pace with the growth.

Life was always hard in the Sahel, with the population increasing during years of good rainfall and declining as periodic droughts ravaged the region, while famine and disease killed off children and the elderly.

Colonial government in the nineteenth and twentieth centuries brought improved medical care, sanitation, and better organization in general. This allowed the population to increase dramatically. Better able to survive the regular droughts, the population then began to overgraze the land. Resources were gobbled up by enlarged herds which led to a steady spreading of the Sahara Desert and a reduction in grazing land.

The biggest factors affecting the population, however, were not the overgrazing and expansion of the desert (though these are, of course, significant), but the periodic breakdown in government administration which prevented food movements from reaching famine areas. Man's actions, not nature's, were the biggest cause of death. Politics increased the impact of ecological damage.

Senegal and Mauritania both contain the western extremity of the Sahel. The most severely desertified portion of the Sahel in this area lies in Mauritania, most of whose territory is now taken up by the Sahara Desert.

Mali, Niger, and Chad form the core of the region. The northern portion of Mali is Saharan desert and Sahel; the lower portion is better-watered and more suitable for farming or more intensive grazing. Niger is much the same as Mali, desert in the north and moister land in the south (particularly along the Niger River). Chad is the inland "keystone" to central Africa. It borders Libya to the north, Sudan to the east, the Central African Republic to the south, Cameroon and Nigeria to the southwest, and Niger to the west. Mountains cover the northwestern

POPULATION OF THE NATIONS OF THE SAHEL

	Population (in millions)	Sq. Kilometers (in thousands)	Population (per sq. kilometer)	Percent Muslim Population	Percent of Arable Land	Per Capita GNP	Average Life Expectancy
Senegal	7.8*	208*	38	92	27	380	47
Mauritania	2.0	1,031	2	99	2	450	45
Mali	8.7	1,240	7	90	2	190	42
Niger	7.0	1,267	6	97	3	200	44
Chad	5.8	1,271	5	44	2	150	44
Sudan	26.0	2,506	10	70	5	360	49
Ethiopia	48.0	1,221	39	40	13	120	43
Somalia	8.6	638	13	99	2	300	44
France†	56.0	550	99	2	34	14,000	75

*Includes Gambia.
†Included for comparison.

corner of the country and the area south of Abéché. Lake Chad divides Chad from Nigeria and is a vital water source since most of the country is desert or arid pasture land.

Sudan is also mainly desert or savanna. But Sudan also has the Nile River, along whose banks agriculture is possible. Southern Sudan is also capable of some farming and intensive grazing.

Ethiopia is largely better-watered highlands. The country has always supported a larger population than its surrounding areas, which are largely desert or semiarid.

Somalia is chiefly a coastal desert, receiving about as much rainfall as the Sahara gets, and is, in effect, a southeastern wing of the Sahara Desert. If the Ethiopian highlands were not in the way, the Sahara would stretch unimpeded from the Somali coast to Mauritania on the Atlantic. As it is, the Sahara Desert climate skips across the Nile River valley right to the Red Sea coast and then down around the "Horn" of Africa.

HISTORY

In the beginning, over five thousand years ago, there were five major ethnic groups in sub-Saharan Africa. Along the west coast from Senegal to Nigeria were the ancestors of the Negro peoples. Near the center, below Egypt, were the Nilo-Saharans, a dark-skinned but non-Negro group. On the east coast there were the Cushites, also dark-skinned, the ancestors of the Ethiopians, Somalis, and other related peoples. In central Africa were the Pygmies and to the south the Bushmen (or Click-language speakers). North of the Sahara was a subgroup of the Middle Eastern Semites.

The Bantu peoples split off from the original Negro group some two thousand years ago and moved east and south, overwhelming the Pygmies and Bushmen with greater numbers, better organization (formal military units), and superior technology (metal weapons). The Nilo-Saharans went west along the Sahel corridor, as did some of the Cushites. In the east, a 500 B.C. invasion of Semitic tribes into Eritrea, the heart of Ethiopia, transformed the local Cushite tribes into what we now consider Ethiopians and Somalis (dark-skinned people with non-Negro features).

With the exception of Christian Ethiopia, most of the Sahel peoples became (officially, at least) Muslim about a thousand years ago. Pockets of paganism (animism) persist to the present day, and many pagan religious practices continue to coexist with Muslim customs.

The savanna lands have never been peaceful, but they are too poor and thinly populated to support many major wars, or attract big-time conquerors. Most of the population is nomadic, so raiding (for horses, livestock, slaves) is the predominant form of conflict. The Negro Bantu peoples to the south were not eager to advance out of their familiar forests toward the dry north. The North African Semites, confronted with the vastness of the Sahara Desert, were slow to move down into the Sahel; but gradually groups of them did move there when the camel was introduced on a wide scale in the eighth century A.D. Eventually, the more numerous, better-organized, and more warlike Arabs to the north overcame the difficulty of getting across the Sahara Desert in large numbers. Thus, most of the Sahel became populated with a mixture of Negro and North African peoples, who all adopted a pastoral life-style, moving their herds toward what little water fell on this semiarid area.

On the west coast, the Sahel savanna was dominated as early as the eighth century by the kingdom of Ghana, which controlled Arab access to large gold mines to the south. But eventually, as the Arabs worked their way down the west coast of Africa and began converting blacks to Islam, Ghana declined in the eleventh century, only to make a comeback a century later as blacks reacted violently against Arabs and Islam (a pattern that continues to reappear). In the thirteenth century, one of Ghana's vassal states, Mali, grew enormously, forming the largest black kingdom in history. Greater Mali controlled a large tract between Chad and the Atlantic (although not the coast itself). The Mali kingdom eventually shrank and was replaced by the even larger, Arab-dominated Songhai empire, which eventually succumbed to Arab conquerors from Morocco to the north and became the fabled kingdom of Timbuktu.

From the ninth to the sixteenth centuries the Sao tribes controlled most of Chad, Niger, and parts of the Sudan. Their black, central African kingdom was under constant pressure from Arabs and black Islamic converts to the north. By the seventeenth century the Arabs were in nominal control of Chad.

Adjacent to Chad is the Sudan, a desert centered on the upper portion of the Nile. The Sudan has long been populated by the dark-skinned Nilo-Saharans, many of whom migrated across the Sahel thousands of years ago. The Sudanese have traditionally been caught between the advance of Egyptians from downriver and the Cushite people pressing out from the Ethiopian highlands, with lesser incursions coming from the thinly populated Sahel.

Egyptians have always been concerned with the Sudan. The threat of direct attack on Egypt from the south was somewhat mitigated by the fact that portions of the upper Nile are long rapids and unnavigable. The geography also works the other way. Water flowed down the Nile to Egypt, but the Egyptians could not sail up the Nile to the Sudan. Marching upriver to Sudan was a long and expensive process.

The Sudan always contained a multiplicity of ethnic groups, most of whom did not get along very well. Even today there are over 150 languages spoken there.

While the threat from Egypt was infrequent, the threat posed by Sudanese tribes against one another was constant. The herding Sudanese tribes were nomadic—their cattle following the availability of grassland—and raiding the more settled groups along the Nile for food, gold, slaves, and cattle became an accepted part of their everyday lives.

There were a number of cities that grew up along the Sudanese tributaries of the Nile, and these became centers for a succession of kingdoms and empires which were usually feudal and quite loose in organization. Their primary purpose was mutual protection in order to keep the Egyptians and other strangers out of the Sudan.

Arab tribes began to predominate in the more arid north, while black farmers predominated in the south. The Arabs eventually became Muslim; the blacks became, and tended to remain, Christian or pagan.

Except for a short period during the fourteenth century, the Egyptians (and Arabs) were kept from controlling the Sudan. That, though, did not keep a lot of individual Egyptians and Arabs from coming into the country to settle or trade, which was tolerated. It wasn't until 1811 that Egypt, using European weapons, training, and tactics, again conquered the Sudan. However, this turned out to be a disastrous undertaking—the expense eventually bankrupted the Egyptian government, and was one of the reasons the British managed to take control of Egypt.

Egyptian control gave the disparate Sudanese tribes and factions a common enemy and warfare sputtered in the hinterland for nearly seven decades. In 1881 an all-out rebellion, linked to religious revivalism, broke out. Zealous religious warriors supporting "the Mahdi" went on a rampage that sent the Egyptians back down the river. In 1896 the new rulers of Egypt, the British, marched up the Nile and exorcised the Mahdists with machine-gun fire. This put the Sudan under foreign (British) control until 1956. In the east, the Abyssinians (as the Ethiopians were called up until recently) held forth in the relatively well-watered mountain highlands. This area possessed the only good farmland in the Sahel region;

surrounding it were deserts and arid grasslands. Converted to Christianity in the fourth century and until driven from the Eritrean coast by Muslim Arabs in the eighth century, the Abyssinians had one of the more potent kingdoms in the region.

The eighteenth and nineteenth centuries witnessed the arrival of European colonialism. While the Arabs had been mixing genes, religion, and dynasties in the western Sahel, the Europeans had been building big ships, big guns, and big ideas about an empire.

The Portuguese had been trading down the west African coast since the 1400s. For several hundred years all that Portugal, or other European powers, wanted was gold or slaves (the same commodities that had attracted the Arabs, who had gotten there earlier). The Europeans would control a port area and barter with the coastal and interior tribes. Some trading posts were spotted in the interior, but their direct colonial administration was for the most part nonexistent. For example, the French had established trading forts on the Senegal River in the seventeenth century, but during this period the area was governed by a number of Fulani (Negro Muslim) city-states, which would occasionally be united under one strong ruler or another. Disease, and lack of enthusiasm in Paris, kept the Senegal adventure small.

But in the mid-1800s actual colonies became practical—with a colony structure, all the goodies fell under direct control. In 1830 France took over the administration of part of Senegal. Once the French decided to get heavily into the colony business in the 1870s, the Senegal River area was already covered by a number of French forts and trading posts. By 1890 French control had crept several hundred miles inland along the Sahel corridor. By 1900 nearly all of west Africa between the Senegal River and modern Nigeria had become the colony of French West Africa. Senegal was the first French colony in Africa, as well as one of the first European colonies in tropical Africa. Senegal was also the first of the many colonial ventures that, between 1860 and 1880, saw European nations carve up all of Africa into colonies or "spheres of influence." Only Ethiopia, the old Abyssinian empire, and Liberia (under American protection) avoided colonization.

Two events propelled colonial extension further. First there was the discovery, in the 1840s, that a daily dose of quinine would keep malaria from killing off most Europeans trying to live in the tropical areas of Africa. Next came the French defeat by Germany in the 1871 Franco-Prussian War. This led to an uncharacteristically long forty-three-year period of peace in Europe. Without one another to fight, Europeans looked for something else to conquer. America was off limits, Asia was already taken, but Africa had been overlooked till now because of the disease problem. So, with machine guns, quinine, and bureaucrats in tow, Europeans began a mad scramble to stake out real or imagined claims to African territory.

All of this came as a bit of a surprise to the Africans. While much of interior Africa was not governed in the traditional sense (except by thousands of independent tribal organizations), the coastal areas and the Sahel corridor were largely covered by a changing mosaic of feudal-type kingdoms and principalities. However, these local entities were several centuries behind the Europeans in technology, and the European bureaucrats, industrialists, and soldiers proved an overwhelming combination.

By the late 1880s, the French also had nominal control of the area to the north of the Senegal River (Mauritania). But this was largely desert area populated by Arab rather than black tribes. There was little immediate exploitative worth in this portion of the Sahel, and the nomadic tribes saw any French interlopers as just another source of loot and pillage. This attitude of the Arab tribes toward blacks and Europeans south of the Senegal River continues. After the area became independent, the Senegal River provided a clear boundary between the Arab north and the Negro lands south of the river.

By 1914 France had nominal control of all the western Sahel as far as modern Sudan. The British controlled the rest, except independent Ethiopia and the Eritrean coast, which was controlled by Italy.

The major impact of colonialism was an uncharacteristic spell of law and order, imposed with the help of machine guns and a European-style civil service. Most of the population was left to pursue their customary life-styles, although a small minority of the urban population was exposed to European-style education and European ideas. Thus when colonial rule ended in the 1950s and 1960s, the Sahel people were left with a new set of borders and an upper class of people who were often more European than African in their manners and ideas.

While African leaders often complain of the "artificial" borders forced on them during the creation of the colonies, those borders, the first system of national frontiers to be established throughout the entire continent, have since been regarded as inviolate by their inhabitants. While these borders, now serving as the frontiers of the current African states, were imposed by outsiders, and Africans constantly complain about it, everyone is scared of the increased conflict border changes would surely bring.

Historical Impact of Ethnicity and Religion

One thing that the colonial period did not change was the historical enmity between Muslim and non-Muslim and between Arab and Negro. The hundreds of languages still spoken in the Sahel saw to it that the newly declared national borders meant little to the "citizens" of these nations who had little in common with their fellow citizens. Not that this was anything new. The numerous empires and kingdoms that had preceded the colonial states also had had to contend with the multiplicity of ethnic groups to be ruled. The colonial powers simply did it in a more systematic fashion, thanks to modern technology (telegraph, radio, railroad, trucks, aircraft, etc.).

Ethnicity has always been a key factor in the Sahel. Chad alone has over a hundred different languages spoken within its borders, as does the Sudan. Beyond that, there are over two hundred different ethnic groups in Chad and nearly as many in the Sudan. Most other Sahel nations have fewer than ten distinct ethnic groups, but that's more than enough to keep domestic politics on the wild side. Before the Europeans came along with their colonial governments, local strongmen would cobble together kingdoms at sword point, several of which lasted far longer than any of the European colonies. What the Europeans left behind was the technology for a local politician or soldier to gather together sundry ethnic groups into a tightly controlled entity. Power was maintained by using the weapons and communications technology the Europeans left behind.

Even without European technology, the Sahel had traditionally contained the bulk of sub-Saharan empires. This was largely due to the ease with which soldiers on horseback could quickly get around and keep the locals in line. The threat of a few hundred, or few thousand, armed horsemen descending on your pastures did wonders to maintain your loyalty to some far-off king who may not have even spoken your language.

Formation of many of the Sahel empires was prompted by the need to protect the local population from Arab raiders coming across the Saharan wastelands looking for loot and adventure. The Sahara was not entirely a sandy wilderness; much of it contained some vegetation, and there were numerous well-known waterholes. Some of these were large enough to form an oasis capable of supporting a small settlement. There were three major corridors from the north along which raiders would travel against an undefended Sahel. But strong Sahel kingdoms would force the Arabs to come as traders and merchants instead of soldiers.

The Sahel economy had herds of animals and some agriculture, plus gold and slaves from the south. The Arabs brought cloth and technology. It was from the north that the Sahel and the rest of Africa obtained the technology to work iron. From the Arabs, the Sahel also received Islam, although the Muslim religion met more opposition than the techniques for making iron weapons. And though many blacks became Muslims, there was still a great deal of animosity between the lighter-skinned Arabs and the darker-skinned Sahel natives.

Chad became a particularly striking example of ethnic animosity. In the sixteenth century a major movement of Negro nomads from the Niger River area collided with a similar Arab nomad movement from the east in what is now Chad. The result: over two hundred ethnic groups speaking over a hundred distinct languages, all within a population of six million.

The Arab-Negro animosity was more than just the Arabs' thinking themselves more "civilized." There was also the slavery issue. Slavery was an ancient custom in the area. Slavery is less an enduring problem when people of the same appearance enslave one another. Europeans enslaving other Europeans died out only some four hundred years ago and was quickly forgotten by the slaves and the owners. The former slaves easily slipped into the culture that had enslaved them. But for centuries Arabs would take several thousand blacks north each year, where dark skin became another sign of a people considered inferior. That many of the slaves were captured by black Saheleans from Negro tribes farther south did nothing to ameliorate the feelings. Blacks enslaved other blacks. But the way the Arabs carried on was much more bothersome. Moreover, as of 1990, some Arab slaving allegedly continues (with markets in the UAE and Oman).

All of the Sahel's wars have, at their root, vicious animosities between Arabs and blacks that continually fuel the area's conflicts.

In the west, Arab Mauritanian merchants dominate retail trade in Senegal and treat the Negro Senegalese with disdain. In Chad, Libyan Arabs set one group of black Chadians against another to further Libyan attempts to annex portions of Chad. In the Sudan, Arabs from the north of the country raid and enslave blacks from the south. Ethiopian blacks battle Arab-supported Somalis.

Local Histories After Independence

Senegal and Mauritania

Mauritania and Senegal were both French colonies that achieved independence in 1960. Both nations are largely Muslim. Mauritania aligns itself with the Arabs, although only a third of the population is Arab (another 40 percent is mixed Arab/Negro while the remainder are Negro, largely from Senegal tribes). Senegal has a much stabler government, which as of mid-1990 was one of the few functioning democracies in Africa.

Mauritania has gone through the usual string of coups and military takeovers associated with single-party rule. Mauritania had a rough time of it in the 1970s, when it was caught in the middle of the war between Morocco and Algeria over the disputed territory of Western Sahara. A small portion of this territory was claimed by Mauritania, so part of the irregular warfare was directed at Mauritania. This wrecked much of its fragile export economy.

Islamic fundamentalism does not play as well among Negro Muslims as it does among Arabs and this is the chief political dispute between the two nations. Despite decades of relative peace since World War II, war between Senegal and Mauritania seems to be more probable after a small incident in April 1989 rekindled old animosities. This was followed by some armed skirmishes on the border. Ancient resentments in Senegal increased to the point that mobs attacked the resident Mauritanian Arab minority, most of whom were merchants who dominated the retail trade. This forced the emergency evacuation of over sixty thousand Arabs, the majority of whom were Mauritanians. Both countries expelled each other's ambassador. Additional troops were sent to the border.

The ill will between the two nations also has economic and ethnic origins. Mauritanian farmers want access to pasture in Senegal, particularly the rich "bottomland" in dispute along the Senegal River valley. A four-hundred-mile stretch of the Senegal River forms the border. Only one major road crosses this border near the coast. The river is fordable in many places and there are a few small bridges, and there is a lot of traffic across the river/border, as it is the most productive part of Mauritania and one of the more fertile parts of Senegal.

In the event of war, due to the length of the border and the small number of combat units available to each side, there would be no front line in the conventional sense. Infantry or mechanized units could rampage into each other's territory and do little else. While both sides have what amounts to a mechanized brigade, neither side can afford to concentrate this force in one area (nor could either supply such a concentration over the primitive road network). Senegal is largely inhabited cropland and pasture; Mauritania is largely uninhabited desert.

During the crisis of 1989, Iraq flew over thirty tons of weapons into Mauritania (Iraq wants to set up a long-range-missile test site there). Both nations have inadequate stocks of ammunition and cannot afford to purchase more in a hurry. Both use mostly French equipment. France would likely supply Senegal, and various Arab states would supply Mauritania. Both states have paratroops and the aircraft to deliver them up to company strength. Neither has enough combat aircraft to intercept an airdrop, nor enough antiaircraft weapons to establish a barrier network. Airborne raids would probably precede any attack. Both have a limited amphibious capability, but the presence of radar-equipped maritime patrol planes would make it hard to use. Actual territorial conquest is highly unlikely. France would not allow Mauritania to hold any significant Senegalese territory for very long, and Senegal has no interest in acquiring Mauritanian desert property. Even so, there are some minor border disagreements caused by periodic changes in the course of the river, causing considerable tension.

Conceivably, Mauritania might attempt to "punish" Senegal for perceived injustices, and either side could use force to resolve the small border disputes. Any war is likely to be short, violent, and expensive.

Niger

Niger achieved independence in 1960. A constitutional democratic government existed until 1974, when Lt. Col. Seyni Kountche took power in a bloodless coup. Kountche later promoted himself to general, but his ruling cabinet included many civilians. He died in 1987. The new government under Ali Saibou promotes policies encouraging private enterprise and public education.

Libya claims the northeastern corner of Niger and has backed Tuareg desert tribesmen in attacks on several towns in Niger. France keeps a small military garrison near the capital, Niamey.

Chad

Chad was a part of French Equatorial Africa (FEA) until the FEA was disbanded in 1959. In 1975 a military coup toppled the fifteen-year-old regime of Ngarta Tombalbaye. Fighting broke out between the new junta and various rebel groups, the strongest one led by Muslim rebel leader Hissen Habre. A coalition government with former junta leader Felix Malloum and Habre sharing power proved to be unstable.

Nigerian mediation arranged a new truce in 1979, and Goukouni Oueddei was installed as a compromise leader. Religious rioting and the massacre of southern Muslims shook Oueddei's government. Nigeria once again tried to mediate but in 1980 the cease-fire broke down again. Habre finally overthrew Goukouni in 1980.

One of the major reasons for the overthrow of Goukouni's regime was the Libyan report of January 6, 1981, that Goukouni and Col. Muammar Qaddafi, the Libyan dictator, had decided to merge the countries of Libya and Chad. This, combined with Libya's interest in the potentially mineral-rich (uranium) Aozou Strip, added to a series of internal disagreements that ended in the overthrow of Goukouni by Habre and a coalition of southern tribes. Sudan and Egypt supported Habre during the final stages of the civil war.

What followed in the next few years was complex and almost a comic opera in its execution. Let's take these events one step at a time:

1981 (October)—Bowing to pressure from other African states, Libya withdraws its forces from Chad.

1982 (June)—After several months of fighting, anti-Libyan Chadian forces under Habre occupy the capital and send the pro-Libya Chadian leader, Goukouni, into exile in Cameroon. Other factions are brought into line and a peace of sorts is achieved.

1983 (June)—The pro-Libyan faction (Goukouni) leads several of the northern (Borku, Ennedi, and Tibesti regions) tribes into rebellion. The anti-Libyan faction resists successfully.

1983 (August)—Libyan forces cross the border and put the anti-Libyan faction (Habre) on the defensive. French Army and Air Forces, with the aid of U.S. air transport and supply, intervene to stabilize the situation. A cease-fire is declared which partitions the country.

1984 (November)—Libya announces that it has withdrawn the forces it continues to maintain were never inside Chad in the first place. The French withdraw troops except for a training cadre. Satellite photos show that the Libyans are still in Chad, so the French send their troops back in. Two years of relative peace ensue.

1986 (February)—Libyans and their Chadian allies (Goukouni) attack across the "Red Line" that divides the country. French aircraft bomb and successfully disrupt this advance.

1986 (October)—From Tripoli, Libya, the leader of the pro-Libyan faction (Goukouni) proposes peace with the anti-Libyan faction (Habre). Goukouni is reported shot and wounded while "resisting arrest." Some of Goukouni's Chadian forces promptly switch sides.

1987 (December 1986–September 1987)—The "Toyota War" begins as French aircraft sweep Libyan planes from the air. In January, anti-Libyan Chadian forces (Habre) move north. Their fast-moving columns contain a large number of Toyota Land Cruisers and pickup trucks. In the back of the trucks are Chadian soldiers armed with machine guns and antitank weapons (MILAN antitank missiles, recoilless rifles, RPGs). The tactics are reminiscent of the ancient attacks by nomadic horsemen: rapid movement to the battlefield, a quick jab at the Libyan column or fortified position, a rapid breakthrough and attack from the rear. The "Toyota tactics" prove hugely successful. By March, several battles with Libyan forces leave Chadian forces in control of most of their country. In August, the Libyans are driven from the disputed Aozou Strip on the Libyan desert. This small sliver of desert has been the main cause of the Libyan-Chad conflict in the first place. The Libyans counterattack and retake one of their Aozou bases. The Chadians respond by crossing the Libyan border and destroying a large Libyan air base. A cease-fire is then declared. Libya has lost over seven thousand troops and nearly $2 billion worth of equipment. The Chadians have lost less than a tenth of that.

1988—All quiet on the Libya-Chad front. The United States gives Chad a number of Stinger antiaircraft missiles to counter any future Libyan use of aircraft. Libya proceeds to build a chemical weapons plant.

1989—The war isn't over yet. Libya and Chad agree in August to end their state of war. Then several tribal factions switch sides once more, and military activity starts up again on Chad's northern borders.

1990—Chad announces free elections. Meanwhile the Libyan-backed "Islamic Legion," led by Idriss Deby, captures towns in Eastern Chad, then seizes power. (Deby does N'Djamena.)

Chad's conflicts are typical of the long struggle between the Arabs in the north and the blacks in the south. In Chad, however, Arabs and blacks not only collided from the north and south, but also when Arabs moving in from the east meet blacks from the west.

Colonel Qaddafi's and Libya's direct meddling, in the name of Arab/Muslim interests, stirred up an already volatile situation. The political situation in France seems to favor a continued military involvement in Chad, especially as long as Libya remains an antagonist. Even if the Libyans are completely shut out of Chad, the locals will continue to struggle with each other for supremacy.

Unfortunately, Chad can be expected to experience low-level warfare well into the next century.

Sudan

Formal independence from colonial rule came in 1956. This also meant an end to Egyptian influence, as the British considered their administration a joint enterprise with the Egyptians. One could send the Arabic (Egyptian) bureaucrats back down the Nile River, but one couldn't dispense with the fact that most of the population in northern Sudan was Arab and Muslim, while most of the population in southern Sudan was not.

The year before independence witnessed serious riots in the south and a major Army mutiny of black troops which took some difficulty to put down. In 1958, the worst fears of the southern blacks were realized when the Arab-dominated armed forces staged a coup against the civilian politicians the British had installed. The new junta immediately began to persecute the (largely black) Christians in the south.

By the early 1960s, a black rebel movement sprang up and for the next ten years waged incessant war against the better-trained and -armed Arab northerners. Nearly half a million people, largely civilians caught in the cross fire, perished.

In 1969 there was another coup, and the new military man in charge, Jaafar Nimeiri, turned out to be surprisingly statesmanlike. In 1972 he made considerable concessions to the southerners in order to stop the rebellion. The more numerous minor tribal players in the civil war were not as willing to settle down, but most parties accepted the need for peace.

This "peace" did not solve Sudan's problems. The economy was mismanaged, Libya encouraged Muslim fundamentalists, and the non-

Muslim blacks in the south still felt put upon by the Arabs in the north. In 1983 the civil war began again. This renewed revolt was led by John Garang, a college-educated (in the United States) Christian from the large Dinka tribe. Immediate survival of Dinka populations was at issue: One of the Sahel's periodic droughts had created famine. The Arab-dominated Sudanese government had not done much to save the drought victims, so the blacks saw it as a struggle for survival.

In 1985 Nimeiri was overthrown by a great-grandson of the nineteenth-century Mahdi (military-religious leader who forced the Egyptians out). Sadig el-Mahdi, the new ruler, came to power preaching more Arab and Muslim privilege in the country as well as an even harder line on the black rebels. Thus, as the drought got worse, food (or lack of it) was used against the rebels and the civilians that could, or did, support them.

El-Mahdi was overthrown by an impatient military in 1989, with no end in sight for Sudan's internal disorder.

Sudan's liberation from British colonial rule in 1956 has still left it at risk to its traditional enemies, Egypt and internal rancor between the Arab and black inhabitants of Sudan (yes, inhabitants, not citizens, as Sudan has always had a fragile concept of unity). What now constitutes Sudan was historically a constantly changing mosaic of large and small "nations" held together by the successful conqueror of the moment. Modern technology and the concept of nation-states (as opposed to feudal entities) have provided a larger entity (Sudan) for the hundred-plus ethnic groups to fight over. The only likely change in this is a split-up of Sudan into two states—a predominantly Arab one in the north and a largely black (and Christian) one in the south.

Ethiopia

Aside from the brief Italian occupation during the 1930s and World War II, Ethiopia has not known any prolonged colonization. Alone among the many nations covered in this chapter, Ethiopia does not have a recent independence from colonial rule to mark its current period.

Since the 1960s, Ethiopia has experienced four wars. Over half the population of forty-four million is in rebellion (four million Eritreans, five million Tigreans, and fifteen million Oromoans). The recently annexed country of Eritrea wants independence. The provinces of Tigre and Oromo both want independence or a larger degree of self-rule.

Somalia, the nation at the tip of the Horn, wants the Ethiopian province of Ogaden, a desert area largely populated by Somalis. However, Somalia has its own internal problems (dictatorship and rebellion).

Eritrea is the coastal area closest to the traditional highland of the Christian Amhara (Ethiopian) people. But ever since the upsurge of Islam in the seventh century, Eritrea has been increasingly populated by Arabs and Arabic-speaking peoples. These Arabs had strong ties with other Arabs in the Red Sea area, and thus Muslim Eritrea was strong enough to dominate adjacent Christian populations.

Although occasionally a strong Ethiopian leader could occupy Eritrea, the Arabs would quickly take it back. Eritrea became an Ethiopian province only after World War II. This was done unilaterally by the Western Allies as a form of guilt payment for having abandoned Ethiopia to Italian aggression in the 1930s.

When the Ethiopian government in Addis Ababa made this annexation permanent in 1962, the halting Eritrean rebellion went forward in earnest. At first the Ethiopians simply marshaled their forces and marched into Eritrea to smash the rebels and reestablish central government control at any cost. This tactic failed, as the rebels were backed by other Arab nations and Russia. But in 1974 a military coup in Ethiopia brought a Marxist government to power. The Russians did a little arithmetic and promptly switched their support to the Ethiopian Communists. Backed by generous Russian arms shipments, Red Army advisers, and finally Cuban troops, the Ethiopians reversed the situation in Eritrea. They were, however, unable to completely suppress the rebellion.

Meanwhile, a Christian Eritrean rebel movement usurped the Arab movement and continued the rebellion from the interior hill country. The Eritreans were determined to maintain their independence. The military-age population headed for the bush to take up guerrilla warfare.

Many Ethiopian conscripts were not keen on a war of conquest among these alien Eritreans and had no stomach for the fighting. The Eritreans gradually built up a string of battlefield successes, and piles of captured Ethiopian weapons.

In 1989 Russia, increasingly wound up in its own internal problems, tired of the apparently futile exercise and began cutting back support. The Eritreans began "main-force" attacks on Ethiopian positions and cities. By mid-1990 they controlled almost all of Eritrea and had troops pressing south toward Addis Ababa.

Adjacent to Eritrea is the province of Tigre. Ethnically close to the

Amharic people of the Ethiopian heartland, Tigre has been (with a few breaks) part of Ethiopia for centuries. About a third of the Tigreans are Muslim and several Ethiopian emperors have come from Tigre.

From a famine in 1972–73 over a hundred thousand Tigreans starved to death, largely through the incompetence of the Ethiopian government. While the military took over in Ethiopia, the Tigreans rebelled for greater self-determination and an end to the central government incompetence that had caused so much Tigrean grief in the past. With Russian and Cuban help, Ethiopia has held on to the major towns and ravaged the countryside.

Oromo (also known as Galla) is the largest and most fertile of Ethiopia's provinces. While ethnically related to the traditional Ethiopian Amharic people, the Oromo people are not Christian and speak a different language. From time to time, a strong Ethiopian emperor would conquer and hold Oromo for a time; Ethiopia has held on to Oromo for the last century. The current revolution began in the wake of the 1974 coup and is largely supported by the small urban, and educated, population. The 90 percent of the people living in the countryside are less involved and as a consequence this rebellion is less intense than the others. However, the Ethiopians are not inclined to make any concessions. For one thing, the current Ethiopian leader, Mengistu, is from Oromo.

Somalia

Somalia juts out from Africa like a finger pointing toward the Arabian Sea. Oil tanker traffic to and from the Persian Gulf, as well as access to the Red Sea and the Suez Canal, make Somalia, the French protectorate of Djibouti, and Ethiopia the flip side of Yemen. Air and naval bases in the African Horn can be used to support forces in the Arabian Peninsula—or to close the entire region to merchant traffic.

In 1964 and 1977–78 Ethiopia and Somalia fought over Ogaden and in both 1964 and 1978 the Somalis were defeated by superior Ethiopian forces. (Cuban troops fighting in a mechanized brigade group were used by the Ethiopians in 1978.) Through the 1980s, constant military pressure by the Somalis has kept the Ethiopians (who are distracted by their other rebellions) on the defensive. (Somalia also has similar disputes with Kenya and Djibouti.)

The current government of Somalia is a rather nasty dictatorship that maintains power through terror just like the one that was overthrown in early 1991, and the fact that Somalia has a rather homogeneous population compared to most other nations in the area. There are differences based on affiliation to different Somali tribes, and Ethiopia has supported members of the Issak tribe against the Marehan tribe.

LOCAL POLITICS

Senegal

Senegal is one of the few functioning democracies in Africa, largely because there are two strong major parties.

The Socialist party (PS)—Party in power since the early 1980s, led by Abdou Diouf.

Senegalese Democratic party (PDS)—Principal opposition party to the PS.

Minor parties—African Independence Movement and National Democratic Alliance.

"Brotherhoods"—Islamic sects also active in economic development in Senegal. The various brotherhoods are led by *marabouts* ("spiritual guides"). The Mouride Brotherhood has over 650,000 members.

Senegambia Confederation—Confederation of Senegal and Gambia dating from February 1982. Senegal has promoted a unification of Senegal and Gambia; Gambia isn't so sure. But the two neighbors do cooperate politically and economically.

Gambian parties—Progressive People's party, Gambia People's party, and National Convention party

Kunte Kinte—Ancestor of Alex Haley (*Roots*) who hailed from Juffure in Gambia. The eighteenth-century slavers worked this area over rather well.

Mauritania

Mauritania has no political parties, officially or unofficially. It is an Islamic republic run by the Army. The first coup was in 1978, with another group in the Army taking over in a bloodless coup in 1984.

Niger

Political parties are banned in Niger.

Supreme Military Council—Governing body in land. This council directs "national development councils" throughout the country.

Mali

Democratic Union of Malian People—Major party in Mali.

Timbuktu—Located in Mali, the heart of one of the many Arab desert kingdoms.

Chad

National Union for Independence and Revolution (UNIR)—President Hissein Habre's faction. General Debi formed a new antigovernment coalition in Sudan and launched an attack which drove Habre from power in N'Djamena.

GUNT—Formerly pro-Libyan party, several of its units switched sides in 1987.

Sudan

Like everything else in Sudan, the political parties in the north are largely Arab and Muslim, while those in the south are Negro and animist or Christian.

Sudanese Army—Controlling group in the Sudan. There is a large number of political parties in Sudan, but the Army, which doesn't see itself as one, is the only one that counts. Even when the Army is not directly running things, its influence hangs heavily on those civilians who think they are. Two years after independence in 1956 there was a military coup. In 1964 a civilian rebellion installed a civilian government, but in 1969 the Army took over again. In 1985 another uprising installed a civilian government, which was overthrown by yet another Army coup in 1989.

Government Revolutionary Command Council—Political front of the Army. Chairman and Prime Minister Brig. Gen. Umar Hasan Ahmad al-Bashir is in charge in 1990.

Major "northern" parties—Umma party (Ansar Muslim sect), Democratic Unionist party (Khatmiyyah Muslim sect), National Islamic Front (Muslim Brotherhood, actually right-wing and Islamic fundamentalist), Sudanese Communist party, and the Sudanese Baath party. The Umma party is the largest.

Sharia Law—Islamic law that the Sudanese Muslim radicals want established throughout Sudan.

Major southern parties—Sudan African Congress and Southern Sudanese Political Association.

Southern rebel movements—Sudan People's Liberation Army (SPLA), largely from the Dinka tribe, and Anya Nya (literally, "snake poison," from the Nuer tribe). The SPLA is headed by Col. John Garang, an American-educated Christian Dinka with a Ph.D. in economics. The SPLA is well-organized and disciplined.

Ethiopia

Ethiopian Workers party (WPE)—Only officially recognized party in Ethiopia. Headed by Mengistu Haile-Mariam, who is also the chief of state, its form of government is Communist dictatorship, which means that all the opposition groups take the form of armed revolutionary groups.

The Amhara—People who have historically formed the core of the Ethiopian empire. They number 11 million and are largely Christian.

Eritrean People's Liberation Front (EPLF)—Rebel group of four million and largely Muslim, seeking independence for the normally independent coastal portion of Ethiopia.

Tigre People's Liberation Front (TPLF)—Rebel group of five million and largely Christian.

Oromo Liberation Front (OLF)—Rebel group of eighteen million, Christian and animist. The OLF, based in Ethiopia's largest province and potentially the most dangerous, has not spread much beyond the tenth of the local population that is educated and lives in urban areas.

POLITICAL TREND CHARTS

MAURITANIA

While poor and thinly populated, this is considered an Arab country and thus receives moral and material support from stronger Arab states in disputes with black African nations on its border.

	1990	1996 (Military Authoritarian)
Government Effectiveness	6	6
Government Stability	6	6
Political Cohesion	6	6
Repression Level	4	4
Economic Development	1	1+
Education Status	1	2

NOTE: 0 = minimum; 9 = maximum.

SENEGAL

In African terms, Senegal is a powerhouse.

	1990	1996 (Representative Democracy)
Government Effectiveness	3	4
Government Stability	3	3
Political Cohesion	4	4
Repression Level	8	7
Economic Development	3	4−
Education Status	2+	3

NOTE: 0 = minimum; 9 = maximum.

NIGER

Once the most powerful and prosperous black African state, now a backwater in the crumbling Sahel.

	1990	1996
	(Military Authoritarian*)	
Government Effectiveness	4	5
Government Stability	5	5
Political Cohesion	4	5
Repression Level	5	4
Economic Development	2	2
Education Status	2 −	2

NOTE: 0 = minimum; 9 = maximum.
*A curious military government, however. The legacy of Seyni Kountche lives on.

CHAD

No real change, even if the civil war ends and the Libyans stay out.

	1990	1996
	(Military Authoritarian)	
Government Effectiveness	3	3
Government Stability	3	4
Political Cohesion	3	5
Repression Level	4	4
Economic Development	2 −	2 −
Education Status	2	1

NOTE: 0 = minimum; 9 = maximum.

SUDAN

A land of misery and more misery. Little chance of improvement as long as the Arab (north)/black (south) civil war continues.

	1990	1996 (Military Authoritarian)
Government Effectiveness	3	4
Government Stability	8	7
Political Cohesion	2	3
Repression Level	8	7
Economic Development	1	1 +
Education Status	2 −	2 −

NOTE: 0 = minimum; 9 = maximum.

"INDEPENDENT SOUTH SUDAN"

A viable entity, especially once free of Arab domination.

	1996 (Military Authoritarian)
Government Effectiveness	3
Government Stability	5
Political Cohesion	6
Repression Level	5
Economic Development	1 −
Education Status	2

NOTE: 0 = minimum; 9 = maximum.

ETHIOPIA

Ethiopia needs peace in order to have any chance of even minimal economic rebuilding.

	1990	1996 (Military Authoritarian)
Government Effectiveness	3	4
Government Stability	2	3
Political Cohesion	3	4
Repression Level	8	7
Economic Development	1	2 −
Education Status	2	3

NOTE: 0 = minimum; 9 = maximum.

"ERITREA"

This could be an economically viable country, as it has been in the past.

	1996 (Military Authoritarian)
Government Effectiveness	6
Government Stability	5
Political Cohesion	6
Repression Level	6
Economic Development	3 −
Education Status	4

NOTE: 0 = minimum; 9 = maximum.

"Tigre"

This would be another land of suffering, just as it was in the past when the area was momentarily free of Ethiopian domination.

	1996 (Military Authoritarian)
Government Effectiveness	4
Government Stability	5
Political Cohesion	4
Repression Level	7
Economic Development	1 −
Education Status	1

NOTE: 0 = minimum; 9 = maximum.

Somalia

No matter which military's in charge, it won't seem to matter.

	1990	1996
	(Military Authoritarian)	
Government Effectiveness	4	5
Government Stability	5	5
Political Cohesion	5	5
Repression Level	7	7
Economic Development	2	2 −
Education Status	2	2

NOTE: 0 = minimum; 9 = maximum.

"GREATER SOMALIA" (SOMALIA PLUS OGADEN AND DJIBOUTI)

A somewhat more viable entity, in part because there would be fewer Somalis across the border and under foreign domination.

	1996 (Military Authoritarian)
Government Effectiveness	4
Government Stability	4
Political Cohesion	3
Repression Level	7+
Economic Development	2+
Education Status	3

NOTE: 0 = minimum; 9 = maximum.

DJIBOUTI

Has successfully existed in the past as an independent state and can continue to do so. Particularly with ongoing French support and Saudi investment.

	1990	1996 (Authoritarian Democracy)
Government Effectiveness	6	6
Government Stability*	7	7
Political Cohesion	6	6 −
Repression Level	4	4
Economic Development	3 −	4 −
Education Status	3 −	3

NOTE: 0 = minimum; 9 = maximum.
*The French Foreign Legion keeps it stable, and also keeps out Somalia.

REGIONAL POWERS AND POWER INTEREST INDICATOR CHARTS

CHAD

Libya gets involved in the Chad civil war.

	Economic Interests	Historical Interests	Political Interest	Military Interest	Force Generation Potential	Ability to Intervene Politically	Ability to Promote Economic Development
Libya	7	8	9	8	2+/5*	7	1
Chad Government	9	9	9	9	3+	7	—
Chad Rebels	7	8	9	9	2	7	—
France	4	6	6	6	4	7	6
U.S.	2	2	5	6†	4–	5	3
Nigeria	2	3	5	6	3–	1	1
Japan	1‡	0	1	0	0	1–	4

NOTES: 0 = minimum; 9 = maximum.

French, U.S., and Nigerian FGPs are based on a 180-day buildup; French 1990 force power in Chad is 1.

*Inside Chad/inside Aozou Strip and Libya—a logistically weak and poorly led army, but 5 FGP is there.

†The United States is always concerned when Qaddafi's Libya is involved.

‡Advertisement for Toyotas.

MAURITANIA-SENEGAL

Another chapter in the ancient conflict between Arab and black in the Sahel region.

	Economic Interests	Historical Interests	Political Interest	Military Interest	Force Generation Potential	Ability to Intervene Politically	Ability to Promote Economic Development
Mauritania	9	9	9	9	1	6	—
Senegal	8	8	9	9	2+	7	—
France	4	5	5	4	4	8	5
U.S.	2	2	3	3	4	5	3
Libya	0	1	2	1	1–	2	1
Iraq	1	2	2	1	1–	5*	1

NOTE: 0 = minimum; 9 = maximum.

*In Mauritania.

SUDAN

Sudan area Arabs and blacks have been fighting each other for thousands of years, often with the assistance of foreign powers. Egypt has been the traditional outside force—now it is Egypt and Libya, plus Saudi Arabian money (although less so because of Sudan's support for Iraq in 1990).

	Economic Interests	Historical Interests	Political Interest	Military Interest	Force Generation Potential	Ability to Intervene Politically	Ability to Promote Economic Development
Egypt	7	8	7	7	6	6	3
U.S.	2	3	4	3	2	4	2
Libya	1	2	6	6	1	3	1
Saudi Arabia	2	4	6	4	0	5	4
Chad*	1	4	6	7	1+	1	0

NOTE: 0 = minimum; 9 = maximum.
*Rebels in Chad use bases in Sudan. The Chadian government, with its abundant supply of captured Libyan weapons, could prop up anti-Sudanese government rebels.

ETHIOPIA "INTERNAL WARS" (ERITREA, TIGRE, OROMO)

Despite the poverty and relatively small size, Ethiopia is just another empire coming apart.

	Economic Interests	Historical Interests	Political Interest	Military Interest	Force Generation Potential	Ability to Intervene Politically	Ability to Promote Economic Development
Ethiopian Govt.	9	9	9	9	7	7	—
Eritrea	9	9	9	9	5−	6	—
Tigre	9	9	9	9	2−	5	—
Oromo	9	9	9	9	2−	5	—
"Cuba"*	0	1	2	3	2	1	0
U.S.	3	4	5	4	3	4	3+
Israel	2	6	6	3	1	1−	3
Egypt	4	5	5	4	2	2	1

NOTE: 0 = minimum; 9 = maximum.
*Signifies old Cold War support from old "East bloc" and USSR.

ETHIOPIA-SOMALIA "OGADEN WAR"

Another ancient conflict between Arab (Somali) and black (Ethiopian).

	Economic Interests	Historical Interests	Political Interest	Military Interest	Force Generation Potential	Ability to Intervene Politically	Ability to Promote Economic Development
Ethiopia	6	8	8	8	4	8	—
Somalia	7	9	8	8	3	8	—
Kenya	3	5	7	8	1	2	—
Saudi Arabia	2	6	6	5	0+	4–	5
U.S.	2	2	5	6+	4	4	4
"Cuba"	0	1	2	4	2	1	0
France	1	3	5	6	4	4	2

NOTE: 0 = minimum; 9 = maximum.

PARTICIPANT STRATEGIES AND GOALS

The four principal conflicts in this area each have fundamentally different situations and, consequently, different strategies.

Mauritania-Senegal

Mauritania—Even after Mauritania extracted itself from the western Sahara conflict in 1980, economic conditions did not appreciably improve. The droughts that periodically punish the Sahel were particularly hard in the early 1980s. Mauritania needs more than peace, it needs a new climate. Large-scale birth control will help, but the population pressures loom large. That's why the Senegal expulsions are a large problem.

Senegal—Senegal's primary aim is to maintain its stable democracy and keep the economy growing. As with most black African nations, there are always nervous glances northward at the historically dominant Arabs. Senegal wants to maintain "the French connection," which assures French aid in its confrontation with Mauritania.

Chad

Central government—With over a hundred distinct (different customs and language) ethnic groups in a nation of five million, it's a major goal just to maintain some form of national unity. Chad continues to rely on French and Western support as a prop against Libya and Libyan-backed rebels.

Libya—Libya wants the Aozou Strip. It will continue to back guerrilla groups in Chad until a government to its liking takes power and cedes the Aozou.

Colonel Qaddafi—This strong Libyan militant thinks he's a great leader and that continuing to fight his many "enemies" shows his prowess. His defeats in Chad still haven't sunk in.

Sudan

The basic political dispute is between the Arab-dominated north (only 40 percent of the population is Arab, while 70 percent is Muslim) and the largely Negro south. The south wants some autonomy, and while many Arabs and Muslims would just as soon grant it, there is a strong Islamic faction (made up of Islamic fundamentalists and Arab supremacists) that would prefer that all Sudanese were Muslims and that the nation conformed to Islamic law. Without the religious issue, Negroes and Arabs would probably get along. But religion is present in a big way and the strife continues.

The fighting and economic disruption have killed nearly half a million people to date, and have created over two million refugees. This is in addition to nearly half a million dead from the earlier civil war that ended in the early 1970s. The Arab northerners have also grown weary of the fighting and have largely withdrawn their army from the south. Instead, Arab tribesmen have been given automatic weapons and the freedom to raid the south as they have done for centuries. These raids result in most of the male victims being killed and most of the women being taken into slavery.

With half the population in the south, even after over 5 percent of the population has been killed in the last twenty-five years, the Arabs still cannot realistically hope to prevail. But as long as the Arabs and Islamic fundamentalists persist in their traditional domination of south Sudan, the fighting will continue. Eventually the south will, in effect, either break away or else autonomy will be achieved.

Ethiopia

The attempt to hold on to Eritrea, and institute Stalinist communism on an essentially feudal culture at the same time, has brought the Ethiopian nation to the brink of dismemberment. The Communist government has been in a survival mode since 1988 and will eventually bend (quite a bit) or be driven from power.

POTENTIAL OUTCOMES

No one has any burning interest in making a substantial effort in settling these Sahel wars.

Chad

France is already backing away from her long involvement with Chad and expends little more than soothing words regarding the Mauritanian-Senegal conflict. Libya is seen as a threat, not in the Sahel but in North Africa and the Middle East (not to mention as a base for worldwide terrorism). Chad will continue to lurch along with rival factions challenging one another and occasionally taking power from one another. The rest of the world will ignore the changes in power as long as the rival Chadian factions do not embrace the Libyans or other radicals.

Mauritania-Senegal

Mauritania-Senegal will be largely ignored by the rest of the world and a war there will probably never amount to much because the Mauritanians are too weak to get what they want from the Senegalese, and there is nothing in Mauritania that the Senegalese want.

Sudan

Sudan is a similar situation. There is nothing there that grabs the world's attention, except the millions of starving refugees and victims of the fighting—and even then only on a very slow news day.

Ethiopia

Ethiopia gets marginally more attention because the fighting occurs close to major shipping lanes for Western oil.

QUICK LOOK AT THE WESTERN SAHARA

Immediately to the north of Mauritania lies the coastal desert strip formerly called the Spanish Sahara. Here, until 1975, the Spanish Foreign Legion fought a low-level insurgency sponsored by Marxist Libya and radical Algeria and looked upon favorably by Morocco. After the Spanish left, Morocco moved in, conducting a peaceful invasion by marching civilians (and troops) across the border. The Moroccans then became the Polasario's enemy.

This war has sputtered on. Combat has ranged from sniping and terrorism to jet-aircraft-fighting tanks and mobile surface-to-air missiles. The oddest wrinkle has been ''the Wall''—a long rock, concrete, sand, and miscellaneous defensive system thrown up along the border by the Moroccans to keep Polasario guerrillas from infiltrating from the desert into the few towns and population areas.

Who's Involved

Morocco—Morocco wanted to retain the part of Spanish Sahara that Spain abandoned.

Polasario—These are local rebels who want to turn Western Sahara into an independent nation.

Algeria—In order to limit the potential power of its traditional enemy, Morocco, Algeria supports the Polasario.

Wild Cards

Libya—Libya has it in for Morocco.

Spain—Spain wants to maintain good relations with Morocco.

United States—The United States supports Spain and Morocco, both traditional allies.

CHAPTER 9

SOUTH AFRICA

INTRODUCTION

The economic dominance of white South Africans and their state's noxious apartheid laws are under intense political and military fire. Though politically defunct, the legacy of apartheid remains. Under apartheid law, only Caucasians (14 percent of the population) are allowed to vote and fully participate in government. This approach to running the country has brought down on the South African whites a worldwide maelstrom of criticism, sanctions, and deserved ill will.

Still, the ideological and racial issues all too often mask an underlying trouble of tribalism and sustained historical rivalries. South Africa, for all of its many troubles, is the best-run, most prosperous, and safest African nation in which to live. How can this be? Despite political turmoil, continued strife, and economic sanctions, South Africa has a higher standard of living than any other African nation for its disenfranchised black citizens. Of course, this South African black "standard of living" pales in comparison to the good life enjoyed by the local whites. The key issue: South African blacks don't compare themselves to other black Africans, but to South African whites—as well they should, since their sweat contributes to the economic success.

Propelled by economic and democratic desires, the winds of change have grown to hurricane proportions on the southern tip of Africa.

SOURCE OF CONFLICT

The desperate problems that beset southern Africa are all too often perceived solely as a confrontation between white and black faces. British colonialism, Zulu imperialism, and the refugee Boers' quest for independence all set the stage for a twentieth-century economic and political "coup" that put the white Afrikaaner tribe in charge of the Republic of South Africa (RSA). From the beginning, in the seventeenth century, and into the eighteenth and nineteenth centuries, the Boers curled up inside their laagers to fend off attacks by African tribesmen or British colonial intrusions. Having been harried and oppressed for so long, the Afrikaaners developed blatantly racist but remarkably effective "apartness" (*apartheid* in Afrikaans) laws to control the other tribes in South Africa, black and nonblack alike.

At the turn of the century the Boers were brutally uprooted from their farms by British troops and placed into detention camps. Now they uproot other tribes and transport them to poverty-pocket "homelands" which are little more than large detention camps. The black tribes are kept out of the political and economic structure, and this political and economic exclusion forms the basis of apartheid, which is, in reality, little more than a system remarkably similar to medieval serfdom. "Nonwhites"— a category that includes blacks as well as "coloreds and Asians"—get few educational opportunities. Nonwhite literacy is less than 50 percent; white literacy is over 90 percent.

The Boer and white South African defenses put in place military, economic, and political defenses to become the modern equivalent of the Boers' laager. The Afrikaaners have made their land into one big laager, and to them the laager means survival—it is the Boer tribal totem. And besides, as Boer reasoning goes, we're not doing anything different from what goes on in other African countries. Look how the black tribes mistreat one another in South Africa and throughout the continent. And where were the Western liberals when the British were destroying us? No one looks out for Boer interests except the Boers. Their reasoning is, "We're criticized simply because we're white and economically successful."

The Boers are right about one thing—black Africa is notoriously undemocratic, at least on the national level, and its tribes are mutually exploitative when one monopolizes a government (as is often the case). Black African tribes murder one another with little remorse because, ironically enough, the bonds of tribal kinship are so strong. Tribal strife in South Africa has killed many more blacks than apartheid has. Until recently the white African tribe couldn't, or wouldn't, change this. White, and nonwhite, South Africans have much to be fearful of if their future holds in store the dictatorial rule so common in the rest of Africa. In the thirty years of independence from colonial rule, less than 2 percent of the 150-plus African rulers left office voluntarily. Most were killed, driven into exile, or simply supplanted by someone who controlled more fire-power. The Boers practice democracy among themselves, as do many of the other African tribes. Pointing to the Boer system's superior economic results, they proclaim this a marvelous state of affairs.

The Boers, however, are caught in a bind. They want to be accepted by the West as a Western nation and they want economic integration with the West. But they want to be "African" as well, which to them means absolute tribal dominance over the local competition. The Boers' version of tribal dominance is apartheid, state-sanctioned and -supported serfdom. South Africa's economic success is fueled by cheap black labor which does the dirt work for its white employers but has no voice in the nation's government and very little say about its wages. Supported by the peculiar theology of their Dutch Reformed Church, many Boers believe this is the way God planned it. But then so did medieval monarchs whose feudalism worked in a similar fashion. Western nations no longer accept feudalism, and therein lies the source of the Boers' ostracism.

But Boer theologians, like economists, have been forced to adapt. When the United States went off the gold standard in 1971, one of South Africa's major exports began increasing in value. Gold prices peaked in 1980 at twelve times their 1971 value. The price of gold has since de-clined, but it is still over three times the 1971 price (adjusted for inflation). This gave South Africa one of the highest economic growth rates in the world and enabled the country to survive all manner of Western economic sanctions. The gold boom also increased the number of jobs, far in excess of what the white population could supply labor for. The result was an inexorable influx of black workers into white areas. The Boer dream of keeping the blacks "in Africa" while the whites lived it up in a Western-style industrial economy became untenable.

Other industrialized countries have learned that worker demands can-not be ignored forever. The nationalist aspirations, economic interests, and the human rights demands of the other South African tribes were intensified by this unexpected economic boom. Black radicals were able to get weapons and international support. The physical isolation the Boers once had no longer existed in a world of instantaneous communication. South Africa is no longer a forgotten end of the earth. Apartheid can't be hidden, and the Western world doesn't approve of serfdom—at least not when practiced by white folks aspiring to be treated as equals by the other industrialized nations. Serfdom and even slavery still exist in other parts of the world, particularly in Africa; but one is supposed to do such things in the shadows, not in a nation that puts itself forward as a modern society.

South Africa has also engaged in regional multistate guerrilla struggles involving the nationalist ambitions of several tribal groups located in the Republic of South Africa, Angola, Namibia (Southwest Africa), Zimbabwe, and Mozambique. Neighboring Botswana and Swaziland were also indirectly involved. Most of these operations have since been discontinued or cut back as South Africa directs more of its efforts toward putting its own house in order.

Then there are the geopolitical considerations. Southern Africa occupies a strategic position. Naval units based near the Cape of Good Hope can sweep into the South Atlantic or into the Indian Ocean. The very large crude carriers (VLCCs), which cannot squeeze through the Suez Canal, must circle the cape on their way to European oil refineries. Southern Africa is rich in strategic mineral deposits. In effect, South Africa sits atop some of the most ancient (nearly two billion years old) rock formations in the world. Unlike similar rich mineral formations elsewhere, these lie close to the surface, making extraction easy and cheap. South Africa mines nearly 70 percent of the non-Communist world's gold plus major portions of other valuable minerals. Neighboring Zimbabwe possesses some of the world's highest-grade chromium deposits. Most important, and often overlooked, is South Africa's position as the strongest economic power on the continent and, oddly enough, the most stable politically—which doesn't say much for the state of governance in the rest of Africa.

WHO'S INVOLVED

Republic of South Africa (RSA)—The RSA has three capitals, a legacy of the British incorporation of the Boer republics into South Africa: Pretoria is the administrative capital, Cape Town the legislative, and Bloemfontein the judicial.

African National Congress (ANC)—This is the umbrella organization for most black political reformers in South Africa. Some of the organization's leadership and trained members still reside in neighboring countries, even though the ANC is now a legal organization, going through a transition from a clandestine revolutionary movement to a democratic party operating in the open.

Inkatha—This Zulu organization led by Zulu chief Mangosuthu Buthelezi was set up as a more conservative and traditional alternative to the left-leaning ANC. Inkatha wants to make sure that historically dominant Zulus are not subordinated to other more numerous Bantu tribes.

Boers—These are a minority within the white minority. Depending on how you count Boers (and their non-Boer supporters), they are several million people who can put several hundred thousand armed fighters into action on short notice.

The dozens of other parties—ethnic and special-interest groups—which, while not quite the crazy quilt found in the rest of Africa, account for a lot of minor players.

Regional Confrontations

Namibia—This former German colony in southwest Africa was placed under South African control after World War I by a League of Nations mandate. It finally split from RSA control in 1989.

Angola—A former Portuguese colony, as of early 1991 Angola was still engaged in a civil war pitting the Marxist governing Movimento Popular de Libertação de Angola (MPLA) (Popular Movement for the Liberation of Angola) against the National Union for the Total Independence of Angola (UNITA).

Mozambique—There is chaotic civil war in Mozambique pitting the governing and semi-Marxist Front for the Liberation of Mozambique (FRELIMO) against the renegade and often anarchic Mozambican Resistance Movement (RENAMO).

GEOGRAPHY

The Republic of South Africa, encompassing over 1.2 million square kilometers, borders on Namibia, Botswana, Zimbabwe, Mozambique, and Swaziland, and completely surrounds the independent Kingdom of Lesotho. The South African government, as part of its apartheid policies, has organized several "independent tribal homelands" which include Transkei, Bophuthatswana, Venda, and Ciskei. These countries are supposed to be totally separate political entities but, in fact, are dumping grounds of black South Africans and vassal states of Pretoria. Few countries recognize the independence of these states.

The whole of southern Africa consists of a huge plateau dropping from eastern Angola and Zambia down through Zimbabwe and Botswana and looping around Namibia and South Africa. The plateau parallels the coastline, with the distance to the sea ranging from 40 to 200 kilometers. The edge of the plateau is called the Great Escarpment. Elevation on the plateau varies from just under 1,000 to about 2,000 meters. Rainfall varies widely. The climate is mostly semiarid. It's subtropical along the coast with sunny days and cool nights. The vast interior plateau is dry. Some two thirds of the land is meadows and pastures, with only 3 percent forest and woodland. General lack of rain and large rivers require extensive water conservation and control measures. The Kalahari Desert in Botswana and Namibia receives very little precipitation. Parts of the eastern plateau receive a great deal of rain—from 75 to over 120 centimeters (the well-watered parts of the United States receive 100 centimeters or more a year). The Natal coast is exceptionally fertile, but the topsoil of the plateau is thin and more suitable for cattle grazing and herding than agriculture.

Southern Africa holds vast mineral reserves. The world's largest gold ore vein runs from the Orange Free State into the Transvaal. Zimbabwe has large deposits of chromium and South Africa and Namibia have huge deposits of diamonds. Other minerals found in abundance include copper, manganese, iron, platinum, silver, nickel, tungsten, and uranium. Coal reserves are in the range of 75 to 80 billion tons, a bonanza on a par with the vast Saudi Arabian oil fields.

Major rivers in the southern African loop are the Orange River, running west through South Africa's Cape Province then defining the RSA's southern border with Namibia, and the Limpopo River, which runs northeast and east, separating Transvaal Province from Botswana and Zimbabwe. The Limpopo cuts across southern Mozambique and empties into the Indian Ocean. Kruger National Park, a huge game preserve and conservation zone, separates the RSA and Mozambique along their border north of Swaziland. Kruger National Park has been the scene of a number of guerrilla actions. Mozambique claimed South African-sponsored dissidents used base camps in the Kruger. South African security forces have fought African National Congress forces trying to infiltrate through the Kruger from Mozambique. Stopping guerrilla infiltration through the Kruger was, for both sides, a major part of the 1984 RSA-Mozambique disengagement agreement. The South African Defense Force's (SADF) anti-guerrilla operations have made it even more difficult for ANC infiltrations across the border.

The southern oil tanker routes from the Persian Gulf parallel the coastline of southern Africa. Naval units wishing to interdict this oil traffic could be based in Mozambique's port of Maputo or the South African ports of Durban, Port Elizabeth, or Cape Town. Walvis Bay, the Atlantic port claimed by South Africa which is surrounded by Namibia, could also support naval units. Angolan ports have been regular anchorages for Russian blue-water naval forces.

HISTORY

Click-language speakers are the earliest known inhabitants of southern Africa. The Bushmen and Hottentots were hunter-gatherers and primitive herders. Bantu speakers entered the Transvaal region sometime before A.D. 1000, pushing Bushmen and Hottentots south and west into the Cape and the Kalahari Desert. In the fifteenth and sixteenth centuries, Zulus and Xhosas settled the eastern portion of the RSA and Mozambique from the Limpopo and Zimbabwean border to the coast. The Portuguese explorer Bartholomeu Dias rounded the Cape of Good Hope in 1488. In 1652, under the sponsorship of the Dutch East India Company, the ancestors of the Afrikaaners, or Boers, arrived from the Netherlands. The Boers and the Xhosas didn't clash until a hundred years later, when Boer farmers began to meet Xhosa parties in the vicinity of the Great Fish River between present-day Port Elizabeth and East London. This was a clash of migrations—the Boers going north and east and the Xhosas heading south to get away from the Zulus. Other tribes went north to get away from the Zulus and settled in Zimbabwe.

Initially, neither side could get the best of each other. Both groups depended on herding and agriculture for existence, and they both needed the land. But the Boer firearms (muzzle-loading muskets) and the Xhosas' greater numbers (although without firearms) led to an uneasy stalemate.

The British destroyed the stalemate in 1795 when they grabbed the Dutch cape colony in the name of Holland's Prince of Orange, an exile in Britain hiding from the French Revolution. The Boers, many of them from families already 150 years out of Europe's mainstream, chafed under British rule. But it took the British twenty-five years to get down to the colonial business of a policy called "Anglicization" which meant the elimination of the Afrikaans' language, schools, and churches. Britain also decreed the end of slavery in 1833, endangering one form of Boer relationship with blacks. The Boers began to leave. The largest migration took place in 1836 when ten thousand Boers left the cape en masse— this was the "Great Trek" of the "Voortrekkers."

Moving farther north on the great plateau, they found an empty plain marked by piles of skulls and burned-out kraals (Bantu communal homes). The Zulus had been busy.

In the second and third decades of the nineteenth century the Zulu Army was the Southern Hemisphere's most formidable war machine. Formed by the raw military genius of the Zulu chieftain Shaka (also spelled Chaka), who ruled from 1787 to 1828, the Zulu impis (the rough equivalent of regiments) ran roughshod over the whole of southeast Africa. Shaka was one of the world's most brilliant military leaders, ranking with Alexander, Hannibal, and Napoleon. He seems to have been that kind of most unusual person, the "first thinker," someone who creates a tradition rather than creating out of a tradition. He invented Zulu tactics, developed a grand strategy of conquest, created the Zulu army organization, and designed weaponry. A brilliant and efficient leader, he took a small Nguni clan of less than a thousand Bantu people (the original Zulus) and absorbed hundreds of thousands of other Bantu clans into the growing Zulu empire. Those that were not absorbed, for one reason or another, were slaughtered, enslaved, or forced to flee. Soon the Zulu reputation for ferocity became almost as effective as the Zulu army in overcoming resistance. The current distribution of Bantu peoples across southern Africa is largely a result of Zulu military activities in the early 1800s.

Shaka was also a megalomaniac. Human sacrifice was already a Zulu tradition, as it was in many other parts of Africa, but Shaka is said to have set the Zulu record when one day he had twelve thousand captives and slaves slaughtered at his whim.

The Voortrekkers, and their black slaves, skirmished with the Zulus for a few years, then finally, at the Battle of Blood River in 1838, the Boers decisively defeated a Zulu attack. The Zulus withdrew to their northern tribal kingdom and left the plateau to the Boers. Each side respected the other's power, and an uneasy peace ensued, bloodied by occasional raids.

The Boers formed two independent republics, the Transvaal (1852) and the Orange Free State (1854). But British demands, and the discovery of diamonds at Kimberly in 1870, once again put the Boers under the English thumb. The Zulus didn't like the British intrusions either. The British decided to hit the Zulus first. In December 1878 they invaded KwaZulu, Zululand. On January 22, 1879, the impis dealt the British Empire its most severe defeat in a colonial battle. At the Battle of Is-andhlwana, Zulu forces under Cetewayo smashed the British imperial troops and opened a path for the invasion of Durban. Unfortunately the Zulus proceeded to fritter away their opportunity by attacking the small British outpost at Rourke's Drift, the famous "Alamo with survivors." The British reorganized, stopped the Zulu assault, and by July 1879 had destroyed the Zulu army in the Battle of Ulundi. This was the death knell of Zulu military power.

Now the British turned to the Boers. The first Anglo-Boer War (1880–81) gained London economic rights in the Boer republics. The second round, the Boer War (1899–1902), gained Britain all of South Africa—at an ugly cost. The Boer commandos, operating as horse-mounted guerrillas, fought a bitter partisan war. The British defeated the Boers by starving them. Unable to beat the Boers on the battlefield, the English burned the Boers' farms and herded over 120,000 Boer women and children into "detention camps." The camp conditions were terrible, as these were the first modern "concentration camps" (although without the gas chambers). Over 26,000 Boer women and children died. The Boers have never forgotten this. Over 6,000 Boer troops, out of a guerrilla force of 35,000, were also killed. The British lost 8,000 men out of an army of 290,000. The two Boer republics were incorporated into the British colonies of Cape and Natal, and the Union of South Africa was formed as a British dominion.

South African forces fought in World War I and South African dip-lomats participated in the Treaty of Versailles Peace Conference. As part of the spoils of war, the League of Nations gave South Africa an ad-ministrative mandate over the former German colony of Southwest Africa, today's Namibia.

Afrikaaner political strength began to grow in the late 1930s. They organized and took advantage of the colonial democratic political ma-chinery. The RSA sent troops to help Britain during World War II, most notably serving in North Africa against Rommel's Afrika Korps.

In 1948, capitalizing on white working-class fear of losing their jobs to cheaper black labor, the Afrikaaner National party took control of the dominion's parliament. The National party's apartheid policies were developed to ensure that all political and economic power (and choice jobs) remained securely in white hands. The Afrikaaners decided to dispense with dominion status and the republic was officially born in 1961.

Namibia

After World War II the UN assumed responsibility for all former League of Nations mandates. The league's mandate system was essentially a way of dispensing with territory that the "First World" nations found troublesome. From the point of view of the mandated it smacked of a new kind of colonialism.

Since World War II, UN policy has been to turn the mandates into self-governing countries. The UN officially terminated the RSA's mandate in 1966. The RSA said it was preparing Namibia for independence, but was really hoping to hang on to this thinly populated and resource rich area. In the 1960s Ovambo tribal dissidents decided the preparations had been taking too long. In 1966 the South West Africa Political Organization (SWAPO) began guerrilla (of over 90 percent Ovambo) raids into Namibia. In 1973 the UN recognized SWAPO as the "authentic" representative of Namibia.

With the MPLA-Cuban 1976 victory in Angola, SWAPO moved its operation base from Zambia to Angola. After the Portuguese withdrew from Angola, the guerrilla war for control of the former colony at first favored the pro-Western UNITA forces. Part of UNITA's success was due to support from South African logistics support. The South Africans wanted to ensure that a non-Communist regime came to power in Angola as well as one that would not give SWAPO a sanctuary. Until 1984 and the South African–Angolan disengagement agreement, South Africa continued to provide UNITA with arms and logistics support, and the SADF launched occasional raids on SWAPO base camps. South Africa maintained a small number of troops on the Angolan side of the Angola-Namibia border. By 1987 the Cubans and South Africans decided it would be mutually beneficial for the Cubans to go home and the South Africans to leave Namibia. Both sides thought they were getting the better of the deal, at least officially. Cubans serving in Angola were paid for by the Russians, who eventually decided that this was an expense they could no longer afford. This was particularly true in light of the failure, year after year, of the Angolan Army attacks into UNITA strongholds. While independence for Namibia leaves Angola with no South Africans on its border, nothing was said about continued assistance for UNITA by the United States and South Africa. The Communist government in Angola was not popular with most of the population, and UNITA showed no willingness to roll over and die.

Angola

After 1976 when the MPLA drove the UNITA into the bush, Angola was to be another "people's republic." But the UNITA not only managed to hang on (with South African and CIA support) but also did well against the MPLA and its Cuban allies. In the fall of 1990, despite signed agreements, the Angolan civil war still lurched forward. Because of its proximity to South Africa and the desperation of the tiny local Communist party, Russia and Cuba poured billions of dollars and thousands of troops into Angola to keep the rebels at bay. In many respects, the UNITA and FNLA rebels were not far politically from the Marxists in power—the major cause of the dispute was ethnicity. Three tribes make up 75 percent of the population, and the civil war is fought largely along these divisions. The rebels have since softened their stance on socialism, not wishing to bite the hand that arms them. The high level of civil disorder in the countryside, where most of the people live, has created the lowest life expectancy in Africa. Mutual exhaustion may bring peace.

Zimbabwe

The political situation with Zimbabwe (before 1980, a white minority ruled Rhodesia) remains hostile but pragmatic. Economics force the Zimbabwean government to deal with the RSA and to support a largely free-market economy despite continuing official support of state socialism. Botswana remains economically dependent on Pretoria.

Mozambique

Mozambique (a Portuguese colony until the 1970s) has been ruled since the Portuguese left by the FRELIMO—the Mozambican Liberation

Front. Nominally Marxist, the FRELIMO really controls little beyond the city of Maputo and other major towns. The FRELIMO initially allowed the ANC to operate out of Mozambique, but South African raids into Mozambique and diligent patrolling of the border areas made ANC guerrilla activity difficult to sustain, although nearly a hundred terrorist acts a year were recorded in South Africa during the 1980s. By the late 1980s, the South African–Mozambique border region was quiet.

All was not quiet, however, inside Mozambique. When Mozambique offered support for ANC guerrillas, South Africa responded by backing antigovernment groups in Mozambique. Unlike Angola, where the South African-backed UNITA guerrillas were well organized and had substantial local support, the RENAMO (Mozambique National Resistance) movement in Mozambique quickly degenerated into numerous uncoordinated bandit groups. This was partially because of the disastrous economic conditions brought on by the socialist government; Mozambique never had a strong economic base to begin with and a decade of socialism made things much worse. South Africa withdrew nearly all support for the RENAMO in the late 1980s. But by then the savage partisan warfare and banditry had acquired a life of its own. The RENAMO lacks a centralized leadership, and getting people to agree to stop the war is a haphazard affair and explains why negotiations over this conflict will drag on into the mid-1990s.

The "Homelands"

The RSA continues its policy of establishing "tribal homelands" in the least productive areas of the country. South African police units have forceably removed black villagers to these new "homelands." These "homelands" have a Russian *gulag*-like reputation. Black moderates as well as radicals refer to the "homelands" as concentration camps.

The Zimbabwe and Namibia situations have great import for the future of South Africa. In both nations there are (smaller) white minorities trying to coexist with poverty-stricken, less-educated, and culturally different black majorities. Zimbabwe did not collapse during the 1980s under black majority control. Many whites left, but those that stayed prospered. Namibian whites have been working to accommodate black majority rule since before independence, the South African government having made it known in advance that it was eventually going to withdraw. Had Namibia become another Zaire or Uganda, Namibian independence would have been more difficult to pull off and South African whites would be much less willing to share power.

LOCAL POLITICS

As befitting an African nation with dozens of ethnic groups, South African politics is quite complex. No simple Democrats and Republicans here.

Apartheid—Boer policy of enforced racial separation. Apartheid divides the population into whites, coloreds (which includes mixed black-white, at least where it still shows), Asians (Chinese and Indians, except Hong Kong Chinese and Japanese, who have enough money to become officially "white"), and blacks. Whites get all the advantages like wealth and democracy. Blacks get herded on to reservations, and their employment and life-style options are severely limited. The South African parliament is all white, although a nonwhite assembly exists largely for "advisory" functions. The judiciary has limited power to review parliamentary acts. Various "councils" for coloreds and blacks have been established to give the veneer of democracy to these groups. In the late 1980s, many Afrikaaner leaders saw that apartheid could not be sustained forever and began to dismantle it. The ANC (and even the Communist party) was legalized once more, and slow progress was made toward some kind of universal democracy.

National party—Afrikaaner party in power since World War II. Though it was the creator of the apartheid system, the National party has a growing number of moderates calling for change in the rigid apartheid system. The moderates are now a majority, although the party threatens to split in two with the diehard apartheid advocates going their own way.

Herstigte Nasionale party (Reconstituted National party)—Far right-wing splinter of the National party. It is religiously oriented, Calvinist, and a strong advocate of rigid apartheid. As the National party edges closer to complete democracy, this far-right party grows.

Conservative party of South Africa—Formed in 1982, another National party splinter group. It opposes all calls for power sharing.

New Republic party—Party that advocates a new federal republic with each racial group self-governing. It wants a multiracial central government with whites in control of principal positions. This has become a favored option of moderate National party members.

Progressive Federal party—Party that advocates a democratic federal system and elimination of apartheid. Many of its members are South African English. The non-Boer whites always were more disposed to complete democracy.

African National Congress (ANC)—Organization that has several wings. The most troublesome at the moment is the "Spear of the Nation," the military wing. This crowd is not eager to turn in their weapons. The ANC, a banned party for several decades, advocates a "nonracial socialist system" and democracy. It is the principal sponsor of anti-South African government guerrilla activity. Originally nonviolent, after years of frustration it came to advocate the violent overthrow of apartheid. The release of Nelson Mandela from prison in 1989 made the ANC a major, and growing, force in South African politics. Mandela's release and legalization of the ANC have put the "armed-struggle" wing on the defensive. The continuing effectiveness of South African police actions against ANC activists has also made a peaceful approach more appealing.

The Comrades—Youth group against apartheid. With so many unemployed adolescents and young men in the black urban areas, nature and politics took its usual course. These youths organized into gangs, the better to keep the revolution going. Many were kept under control by ANC leaders, but many more became a force unto themselves. Calling themselves the Comrades, they used vigilante-style justice to punish real or imagined transgressions against the movement (to bring democracy to South Africa or to at least get rid of apartheid). While the local police (largely black) and the SADF were equipped to deal with the Comrades, the local black population was not. Caught between the police and the Comrades, the black population is not getting a very good introduction to the future ANC government. Moreover, the Comrades are becoming more difficult to control. Boycotting school and becoming more unemployable, many Comrade groups are turning to crime against the very people they profess to liberate from government oppression.

South African police and intelligence agencies—Law-enforcement and intelligence-gathering organizations numbering 60,000 people (plus over 30,000 reserves) and another 10,000 paramilitary and police in the four black "homelands" (containing about 7 million people). Most of the police see to normal police functions, but several thousand are employed running an extensive informer and intelligence-gathering operation among the entire South African population. Much like Israel's MOSSAD (which has provided some assistance to the South African police), the police have been able to keep one step ahead of the opposition. For heavy-duty antiriot duty, the SADF is called in.

Pan-Africanist Congress (also Pan-Africanist Congress of Azania—PAC)—Banned splinter faction of the ANC. PAC advocates black-controlled government and is increasingly a refuge for disenchanted ANC members who don't agree with the ANC's conciliatory approach.

Indian National Conference of South Africa—Indian and colored-based political party. The party was banned but some members participated in the system through splinter groups, and now the entire party is out in the open again.

Black People's Convention—Advocates of black organization outside of the "white racist political regime." Strong among urban blacks. This group was part of the Black Consciousness Movement.

South African Black Alliance—Black and colored coalition advocating nonviolent change in system.

Colored Labor party—Asian and mixed-race party considered by the National party to be an opposition group.

Colored Federal party—Asian and mixed-race party that tends to be more progovernment.

"Tribal Homelands"—States behind which is the concept that if black tribes are recognized as being citizens of a nation other than South Africa, their disenfranchisement from South African politics is made legitimate.

Dutch Reformed Church—Religion in South Africa that is the cultural as well as religious heart of the Boers. Extreme Calvinism (a very narrow interpretation unfair to John Calvin) concerning predestination of "God's Elect" is used to justify apartheid.

South African Defense Force (SADF)—South Africa's Army, Navy, and Air Force. While led largely by whites, many of the troops are black. Most of the police, who are also heavily armed, are black, which is another curious aspect of South African society. Blacks cannot have the vote, but they are regularly armed and given military training. The fighting in Angola and in Namibia was done largely with black troops (who constituted up to a third of the soldiers). Putting so many blacks in combat units was a significant move toward ending apartheid, as military service is universally seen as a major impediment to denying blacks the vote and full equality in political affairs.

Nuclear weapons—Bearers of Armageddon. South Africa, many fear, may have nuclear weapons. If it does, what happens as the political situation frays and changes? This is an interesting question that is rarely raised during discussions of post-apartheid politics. This issue will become big and loud when the time comes to actually change the form of government in South Africa. Most likely, the nuclear weapons will be destroyed under international supervision. The other nuclear powers would not be keen to see a nation run by the ANC (which still preaches "revolutionary unity" with the likes of Libya) in possession of nuclear weapons.

Broederbond—"Secret" Afrikaaner society dedicated to Afrikaaner cultural and political control. It is probably a participant in the increasing number of terrorist actions against blacks.

DeBeers—Giant South African mining consortium that monopolizes, along with Russia, the world's diamond business. In 1990 it paid Russia a billion dollars just for marketing rights to a Russian diamond horde. The Russians needed the dollars, and only DeBeers could unload that many diamonds and pay up front in cash.

Congress of South African Trade Unions (COSATU)—Black organization that is, in many respects, more important than all the political organizations fighting apartheid. Labor, especially cheap black labor, enables South Africa to continue economic growth despite the ANC and foreign sanctions. Blacks are paid so little (on a par with most other Third World workers) because so many of them are chasing so few jobs. Half the population (and most of the blacks) are still living in the "homelands" (somewhat similar to Indian reservations in the United States). A job in the urban-cash economy is seen as far superior to subsistence farming, and despite strenuous government controls, young blacks continue coming into the cities looking for work. Overall unemployment is nearly 20 percent, mostly black. Black literacy is under 50 percent, but there are enough skilled and educated blacks to fill any jobs that become available. Where the COSATU becomes a potent force is in its implied threat to upset the social apple cart. White workers get paid on a Western scale, while most black workers get paid on a Third World scale (one fifth to one tenth as much as whites). The huge surplus of eager black workers makes it difficult to sustain labor unions, but the COSATU has done it, even if it represents less than 20 percent (under two million) of black workers and has had its major strikes broken. The COSATU faces a formidable task in the future. Only a portion of black workers will be able to get jobs in the cash economy, and the COSATU may find itself deciding who shall join the cash economy and who shall remain in Third World poverty. In performing this function, the COSATU will acquire considerable political power and find itself in the position of defending white-dominated industry. The only alternative is the destruction of South Africa's Western-style economy and the loss of the COSATU's reason for being. The COSATU may well self-destruct, as many of its key leaders are senior members of the South African Communist party (which has largely ignored the collapse of Communist parties elsewhere).

Rand Monetary Area/South African Customs Union—RSA-run economic group that includes Botswana, Swaziland, Lesotho, and Namibia. The rand is the basic currency in RSA.

South African Coal, Oil, and Gas Corporation (SASOL)—Company that has been instrumental in developing coal gasification and liquefication processes to produce oil from coal. The idea was to use the RSA's abundant coal reserves to overcome an international oil embargo instituted because of apartheid policies. SASOL plants have suffered several guerrilla attacks but continue to operate.

Steve Biko—Former head of the Black People's Convention, who died from injuries received while being held by the South African police. His name is still a rallying point, for Biko led anti-apartheid activists. Biko's original Black Consciousness Movement became the National Forum, which, in turn, spawned the Azanian People's Organization (AZAPO). This last outfit is leftist and dedicated to eliminating all white involvement in a future "Azania" (South African) government.

KwaZulu—Area where Pretoria attempted to create a Zulu "homeland" and the Zulus refused to accept it. The Zulus run the area as they see fit, and the white government goes along because of Zulu opposition to the ANC.

Mogopa—Village west of Johannesburg, from which black families were forceably removed to new "homelands" in 1984. Mogopa has been used as an international symbol of the resettlement policy.

Soweto—Black African suburb of Johannesburg, which has been the scene of several protests against apartheid and several brutal confrontations with RSA police. It holds nearly a million blacks, most of whom are there illegally.

Nelson Mandela—South African politician held in prison since the 1960s, then finally released in 1990, resuming his leading position in the ANC leadership. Now in his seventies, Mandela is still vigorous but not in control; a number of other ANC leaders, some still living in exile, predominate. Nevertheless, his release was initially a big boost to the ANC.

Inkatha—Zulu nationalist group led by Chief Mangosuthu Buthelezi, the hereditary leader of the Zulu nation. He has assumed a characteristically Zulu approach to the political situation. While the Zulus have had their battles with the Boers, they also feel a certain kinship with them. For example, when scholars looked into the genealogy of the Boers, it was discovered that many had blacks in their ancestry (between 30 and 40 percent). A common Boer response was, "Well, that's probably true, but it's *Zulu* blood." The Boers and the Zulus have both suffered oppression from the British. They both are feared by other blacks because of past conquests and because they tend to keep their combative traditions alive, much to the distress of other South African ethnic groups. Buthelezi, a university-trained leader with considerable speaking and administrative skills (and a substantial ego), regularly points out that the whites have the firepower and would not hesitate to use it against blacks (especially the Boers) if it came to a fight. Partially for this reason, the Zulus are readier to work with the whites for some kind of accommodation. This puts the Zulus at odds with the ANC and regularly produces thousands of dead and wounded when Zulu and ANC supporters clash in black-populated areas. Thus, the Zulus represent a more conservative black attitude to the ANC program for political reform. However, the ANC is becoming more conservative in its own outlook. But meanwhile the armed partisans from both sides continue to fight it out in the black areas. Buthelezi has his own agenda, and no one is sure if he's simply being a statesman or a proponent of past Zulu hegemony in South Africa. The ANC largely represents the Bantu peoples, who have been kicked around in the past by both Zulus and whites and feel that, this time, it's going to be different.

Desmond Tutu—Anglican bishop and South African moderate, who is a major figure in the national reconciliation effort between black tribes and Boers.

Namibia

Ovambo tribe—Largest tribe in Namibia with approximately 500,000 members (out of the Namibian population of 1.1 million). SWAPO is predominantly Ovambo, and domestic tranquility in Namibia depends largely on how effectively the Ovambo can use their majority. The Ovambos are also the largest tribal group in Angola, and so it goes.

South Africa and Its Neighbors

	Population (in millions)	Population (per sq. mile)	Percent Muslim Population	Percent of Arable Land	Per Capita GNP	Average Life Expectancy
So. Africa	39.0	83	1	10	2,400	63
Botswana	1.3	6	0	2	1,300	59
Namibia	1.4	5	0	1	1,100	59
Zimbabwe	10.3	68	0	7	540	61
Mozambique	14.4	29	10	4	100	47
Zambia	8.0	27	1	7	240	55
Angola	8.6	18	0	2	600	43
France*	56.0	252	2	34	14,000	75

*Included for comparison.

Note that South Africa, like the rest of Africa, has two economic classes—those that have and those that don't. There are jobs (in the Western sense) for only about half the labor force. This is three to four times the rate of the rest of Africa. The haves in South Africa tend to be white, or at least nonblack. Thus the per capita GNP for the non-middle-class South African blacks is about five hundred dollars. As low as this is, it's about five times what the black Africans outside of South Africa get in similar circumstances. Although many of the South African blacks in the rural areas live about as primitively as those in the rest of Africa, there is more access to jobs in the cash economy of the urban areas. The family customs of African blacks see to it that much of the cash earned finds it way back to kin in the bush.

Botswana and Namibia do well economically because they efficiently exploit valuable natural resources (particularly diamonds). However, 75–90 percent of the population is still engaged in subsistence agriculture, thus keeping most of the cash among a small part of the population.

POLITICAL TREND CHART

SOUTH AFRICA

A slight economic downturn but a big upturn in justice.

	1990 (Racist Autocracy*)	1996 (Representative Democracy†)
Government Effectiveness	4	3
Government Stability	2	5
Political Cohesion	2	4
Repression Level	6+	5
Economic Development	6	5+
Education Status	5	5

NOTE: 0 = minimum; 9 = maximum.
*With democratic trappings.
†With tribes as political parties.

REGIONAL POWERS AND POWER INTEREST INDICATOR CHART

WARS OF SOUTHERN AFRICA (SOUTH AFRICAN CIVIL WAR, ANGOLA, MOZAMBIQUE)

The Western powers have the greatest interest in stability and prosperity in South Africa, particularly since the Communist collapse of 1989.

	Economic Interests	Historical Interests	Political Interest	Military Interest	Force Generation Potential	Ability to Intervene Politically	Ability to Promote Economic Development
U.S.	7	4	6	3	6	5	6
So. Africa	9	9	9	9	8	3	5
UK	7	7	7	4	3	4	4
Cuba	2	4	7	5	5	3	0
"Arabs"	4	9	7	3	3	4	3
France	6	7	7	3	4	7	6
Russia	2	1	4	3	2	2	1
Portugal	4	7	4	1	1–	2	1

NOTE: 0 = minimum; 9 = maximum.

PARTICIPANT STRATEGIES AND GOALS

Boers—The Boers dominate South African politics, thus they *are* South Africa and call the shots in the government. As far as the radical Boers are concerned, the bloody British imperialists (who happen to be South African citizens just now) can split for England and stay there— after they've served in the SADF. But the Boers have no place to go, and South Africa is short of white soldiers. The RSA government can't keep calling up reservists up to twelve months a year without paying an economic price. Black troops in the SADF have proven themselves time and again to be superb soldiers, doing things like shooting Cubans in Angola and chasing down black guerrillas on the border. Many Boers, however, fear the demobilized black soldiers. Running a racist regime gets mighty tricky when the folks in charge discover how dependent they are on the oppressed. Many Boers have accepted the demise of apartheid, if only to avoid a race war led by black SADF combat veterans. Although Boers have traditionally left a lot of the commercial empire building to the English speakers, several generations of college-educated Boers have been in business and the professions long enough to realize that the old ways won't work in the late twentieth century. The only remaining problem is, which solution (there are several contending replacements for apartheid) will work best?

Radical Boers—This group prefers to fight to the bitter end. South Africa, according to the radicals, is under a "total onslaught." To defend against this assault requires a "total strategy"—military might, psychological intimidation, and political apartheid. The trekkers in the Transvaal didn't bend, and they didn't have decades of black misrule in other parts of Africa staring them in the face. The Radical Boers (for want of a better term) have a basically racist outlook mingled with some biblical quotes, a little old-time religion, a big dose of paranoia, and a firm belief that they can shoot their way out of the current spirit of change spreading ("like a cancer") throughout the Boer community. Many Boers will now accept change but want strong political guarantees of Boer existence and identity. Doubts that this moderation can be accomplished without the Boers' being "swamped in the black sea" allow Radical Boers to keep their militant wing operating. The Boers also want to maintain their economic gains in a continent swamped with poverty. That poses the same problem—if apartheid ends, black labor won't be as cheap. The Boer moderates are having more success pointing out that abler, and better-paid, black labor will bring more wealth to all. But the Radical Boers read the accounts of black slaughtering black over tribal, ethnic, or "racial" (light-skinned Tutsi versus dark-skinned Hutu) differences. Over a hundred years ago the triumphant Zulu army greeted the Boer trekkers with piles of non-Zulu skulls. Many Boers are too busy looking over their shoulders at skulls to face forward and deal with a new South Africa. This is one group that would use nuclear weapons if they could get their hands on them. The Radical Boers are already bombing and machine-gunning their opponents, making a peaceful resolution of South Africa's problems that much more difficult.

Black moderates—Several moderate groups look to the white English liberals, foreign governments, churches, and international human rights groups for support in forcing an end to the apartheid segregation. They demand democratic representation and an end to the "homelands" policies, and they are willing to guarantee Boer rights. Once again, the sticky point is how this can be accomplished, given the violence Boer radicals and black radicals are capable of wreaking on one another and on well-intentioned moderates.

Black radicals—South African blacks, and a few whites, think compromise with the Boers is impossible. They hold that violence and war are the only solution, with the Boer regime being destroyed, which after the leftist rhetoric is sifted out, means killing the Boers. The Communist bloc events of 1989, and elsewhere in Africa throughout the 1980s, have put the radicals' Marxist proposals into some disrepute.

ANC—With Nelson Mandela out of prison and the ANC a legal party once more, the ANC has a more difficult time of it. Running a revolution is one thing, running a government will be a much more daunting task. Many ANC leaders see their organization (and themselves) as the typical African "single party" to unite and run what would be the strongest black economic power in the world. Even Nigeria, with three times the population, does not have the economic muscle of South Africa. What the ANC has to come to grips with is a multiparty system, the only system that is likely to work in South Africa. The unreconstructed Communists, who form a large part of the ANC's inner circle, do not look favorably on power sharing of any kind.

Inkatha—Over 20 percent of South Africa's population is Zulu. Although many Zulus favor the ANC, many non-Zulu blacks lean toward Inkatha's less radical and more accommodating (to the whites and other groups) approach. Inkatha is trying to broaden its appeal in order to become a major force for moderates and conservatives of all ethnic persuasions. At the very least, Inkatha would resist the Bantu-led ANC grab for total power. It would be one of those sublime ironies to see the Zulus and Boers uniting to oppose a single-party Bantu (ANC) government.

Anti-apartheid religious and human rights groups—Washington's policy during the 1980s was called "constructive engagement"—creating a dialogue with the Boers, urging them to deal with black African moderates and to then open the democratic process to all South Africans, black and white. This was to be a change from confrontational policies. Critics said past policies of open condemnation and threats of economic sanction only increased the Boers' paranoia and inflexibility. Many Americans opposed this policy. Anti-apartheid activists maintain that the United States could drastically undermine South Africa's apartheid system by pressuring companies to "disinvest" and enforcing economic embargoes. Washington is firmly against apartheid, but the truth is that neither policy seems to have affected the Boers, who have stubbornly shown an ability to do without the West and have ignored moral suasion. Some countries (Israel and Taiwan) have been willing to sell weapons to the South Africans. Other countries (Saudi Arabia and Iraq) sold South Africa oil. South Africa continues to be a major trading nation, buying and selling vast quantities of goods on world markets. The U.S. policy has been a boon to the moderate groups in South Africa, who have gained more power and pushed through more reform. The withdrawal from Namibia and release of Nelson Mandela are but the two most obvious results of these policies. But the campaign against the South African government has not been without costs. The economic sanctions have slowed the South African economies' growth rate. Those most likely to lose their jobs, or not get one in the first place, are the chronically underemployed blacks. This side effect of economic sanctions has led to lethal disputes among South African blacks. These "side effects" of sanctions (if one can call tragedies side effects) are all too often ignored by religious and human rights sanctions advocates safely ensconced in the West.

United States—The United States is trying to act as a credible third party, but it is often portrayed as the "protector" of the South African racist regime. Perhaps, although that line often serves ends other than that of changing U.S. foreign policy. But the United States has also shown itself to be a reliable oil-trading partner with the Angolans, and the Luanda regime is discovering that people don't live on ideology alone. The U.S. strategy succeeds in moving both sides from temporary disengagements to a permanent cease-fire. The United States wanted the Cubans out and that was achieved. The United States also wanted to see a free and open election in Namibia, which meant a South African withdrawal. This tit-for-tat diplomacy is what the United States calls "linkage." All of this took time, money, and a lot of luck; but for once Washington wasn't just dreaming—U.S. diplomacy actually pulled it off. The next miracle will be a democratic South Africa. After the last act, the South Africa goals may be achievable.

Cuba—Angola had been one of the Cubans' steady duty spots since 1975. Fidel paid his dues to Moscow by providing a mercenary army for duty in the Third World. Put crudely, Cuba exchanged human cannon fodder for cheap oil. This way Cuba got directly involved in more armed conflicts than either superpower. As long as the Cold War lasted, it was a good game for El Jefe Maximo—the classic Latin tough guy, strutting his stuff on the world's stage. Shipping out the troops also helped Havana solve a chronic unemployment problem that could be hidden under the guise of "aiding worldwide socialist revolution." But Angola was, in some ways, a free ride for the East bloc. One source claims the Angolan MPLA government paid a hundred dollars a day for each Cuban mercenary. Most of this Angolan hard currency came from royalties on oil sold to the United States. Indirectly, U.S. consumers were paying for the Cubans. Fidel's pitching career may have been hampered by a lack of zip on his fastball, but when it came to making Washington look like a city of fools, for a long time Señor Castro proved to be a major league ace. Yet in southern Africa, Fidel did not win the ball game. Economic collapse in the East bloc, and political turmoil to match, have made the cost of propping up Cuba irksome. Castro's refusal to consider reform brought sharply worded articles in *Pravda* pointing out that if Fidel doesn't come to heel, he's going to have to live off sugarcane instead of Russian oil and wheat. The Cubans are rapidly pulling out of Angola, ending the economic and social benefits for Fidel. And the AIDS that many of these troops picked up in Angola went home with them.

POTENTIAL OUTCOMES

1. 45 percent chance through 1996: South Africa establishes a new government (that works) with all citizens obtaining the vote (in one form or another). It's wide open as to just what form this

would take. Some Boers push for ethnic areas for all groups, but this would not work completely—it never does. Even multiethnic democracies like Switzerland and Belgium end up with a lot of intermingling. Because the better-educated and wealthier whites tend to be where the jobs are, there would be a constant influx of blacks looking for work (and finding it). Many blacks push for "one person, one vote," allowing things to be sorted out after elections. What is needed is a form of government where consensus rules. The whites will continue to control the wealth for some time, and if they feel oppressed enough, they will leave and take most of the jobs their wealth and talents currently provide. This was the lesson learned, and acted upon, in Zimbabwe. The Zimbabwe example is everyone's foundation for the new South African constitution. Still, look for the political parties to retain tribal bases.

2. 35 percent chance through 1996: A new multiracial and multitribal South African government is established but doesn't work. Various factions (especially well-armed and organized Boer radicals) wage terror and guerrilla war against the new government. The tribally based political parties fail to reach democratic compromises. Street trouble continues but civil war does not erupt.

3. 20 percent chance through 1996: There is civil war in South Africa—the ANC, Inkatha, Boers, and other groups go at it with whatever weapons are available. If this occurs, there is a 75 percent chance of a division of South Africa into "tribal enclaves"—microstates organized by race and tribe. South Africa is functionally renamed "South Lebanon."

COST OF WAR

Based on GDP and a GDP/arms-expenditure analysis of a similar "out-of-the-way" nation (Australia), South Africa spends several billion dollars a year above its "normal" defense requirements in order to wage war with its neighbors and its own black inhabitants. Though the RSA thought the Angolan, Namibian, and Mozambican disengagements would allow it to reduce defense expenditures, the defense budget remained high. Including police and internal security budget items that are really paramilitary in nature, defense costs are over 10 percent of the GNP.

The economic cost to the entire South African economy is more difficult to measure, as the South African economy is based on cheap black labor. The human cost was several thousand lives a year when the fighting in Angola, Namibia, and Mozambique was all going strong. About 8,000 to 10,000 lives a year were lost due to combat, apartheid violence, or destruction of homes and food sources. This figure would include deaths in the tribal "homelands" that South Africa administers as well as SADF, Angolan, Cuban, SWAPO, ANC, and Mozambican combat deaths. Civilian deaths in Angola and Mozambique are not included in this estimated figure. How many people die due to UNITA–MPLA combat, or to starvation brought on by economic dislocation and destruction, by theft, by economic mismanagement due to ideological considerations wrought by adherence to Marxist theory, or by corruption is, at the present time, anybody's guess. The figure of over one million starvation- and drought-related deaths between 1981 and 1989 for the whole of southern Africa (including Zambia, as well as the RSA and the other states we've discussed) gives some idea of the potential magnitude of the civilian casualties that could be attributed to the warfare and political instability. Currently, the chief source of fatalities is among blacks fighting one another in the "homelands" (especially in Natal, Zululand) and in the urban black areas.

WHAT KIND OF WAR

The South African Defense Forces (SADF) is the most effective in Africa. Its peacetime strength is only 100,000 (with less than 10 percent black volunteers, although this is increasing).

Nearly all white males are conscripted for two years of service and a further twelve years in the Citizen Force. This last group is the real backbone of the SADF. Including the armed and trained Citizen Force, reserves and volunteer "commandos" give white South Africa nearly half a million troops (there are also over three million private firearms in the possession of the white population). These men are trained in the Boer tradition of aggressive, independent-minded bush warfare. It's no wonder that the ANC (or anyone else) has not been able to get a respectable guerrilla war going. With five thousand armored vehicles (mostly light, wheeled types) and over three hundred combat aircraft, the SADF can, and continually does, pounce on any incipient armed opposition. None of South Africa's neighbors has the means or desire to take on the SADF. The Cubans mixed it up with the SADF in Angola and came off second best (Fidel's press releases notwithstanding). What fighting does take place regularly is very low-intensity. The SADF keeps the lid on by making aggressive and constant patrolling a way of life. The Boer tradition of quick and violent retribution on the battlefield is well known among potential opponents to the apartheid government. Everyone lives in fear of the black population getting worked up and forgetting. The result would be a bloodbath no one wants.

THE TRIBES OF SOUTH AFRICA

Tribal population figures here are approximate and vary widely according to sources. Outsiders tend to play down the importance of tribalism in South Africa, as well as Africa in general, which is a grave error. Throughout the continent, one's tribe looms larger in an individual's life than does one's nationality. Only the 10 percent of the people at the top of the economic pyramid in African countries pay much attention to nationality. And even this educationally and economically advantaged minority keeps one foot firmly planted in tribalism.

Tribalism still plays a strong role in most other parts of the world, although it is often shrugged off as just another form of nationalism or, more accurately, ethnocentrism. But this is a false perception of the problem. Tribalism is grounded in common language and customs. In other words, it's what we would call ethnicity. Thus many Italians in America whose ancestors came from Sicily consider themselves more Sicilian in ancestry than Italian. The dialect spoken in Sicily is unique, as are many of the customs there. Irish Catholics coming to America from the Republic of Ireland set themselves apart from Irish Protestants from Ulster. And so it goes, even in the great melting pot of nationalities.

In South Africa, each ethnic group (tribe) is distinguished by a different language and customs. Among the blacks, some tribes even have different physiology and thus look quite different too. For this reason, the Boers set up a separate category for "coloreds," the descendants of marriages and liaisons between whites and blacks where it was still obvious that there was a black ancestor. By applying to the authorities, descendants who can now "pass" as white can have that valuable appellation stamped on their documents. Of course, the coloreds have long since picked up most of the white language (usually English) and customs.

The diverse ethnic groups of South Africa are what may well save it from a race war. Unlike most other African nations, there is no one tribe large enough to dominate the others by sheer weight of numbers. The Boers, of course, did it with superior technology. But increasingly, other ethnic groups in South Africa are gaining access to that technology. Indeed, one of the more progressive forces in the country are the corporations, who can never get enough skilled workers. Education and technical skills weaken the ethnic ties. The corporation replaces many of the security functions of ethnic groups. But for now South Africa has a plethora of ethnic groups.

Urban living has also created some twenty-eight million blacks who don't really belong to a tribe anymore but have simply become urban dwellers who consider themselves "South Africans."

Click-language Speakers

Click-language speakers are relatively primitive people who were the earliest to live in the South Africa area; they are included here for historical purposes.

Khoikhoi (more popularly known as Hottentots)—Some two hundred thousand lived in southern Africa as late as 1660. The tribe is now extinct and its descendants have merged into the colored South Africans. The Khoikhoi were the first migrants to South Africa, having been pushed south from the central African rain forest by iron-equipped Negro tribes migrating from Nigeria.

San (also called Bushmen)—No longer found in South Africa, thirty thousand live in the Kalahari in Namibia and Botswana. The San were the original South Africans, who just wandered into the area many thousands of years ago.

Bantu Speakers

Bantu speakers, one of the larger ethnic groups in Africa, are now fragmented into many groups with mutually incomprehensible languages and dialects.

Bantu speakers, Sotho group

North Sotho (also called Pedi)—Three million live in the RSA on reserves in eastern Transvaal.

South Sotho—Three million live in the RSA near Lesotho; another million live in Lesotho.

Tswana—Three million live in the RSA in western Transvaal, in eastern Cape Province, and near the Botswana border.

Bantu speakers, Nguni group

Xhosa—Nearly six million live in the RSA in Cape Province; others are nominal residents of the Transkei "homeland."

Zulu—Over seven million live in the RSA in Natal. The original Zulus were a Nguni clan.

Swazi—Nearly a million live in the RSA.

Ndebele—Several hundred thousand live in the RSA, mostly near the Zimbabwe border, and many have migrated to Zimbabwe.

Bantu speakers, Tsonga group

Tsonga—Over one million live in the RSA near its border with Mozambique.

Afrikaans Speakers

Boers—A white tribe of nearly four million in number, the Boers are a rather heterogeneous tribe of Dutch, French Huguenot, German, and (apartheid to the contrary) black African ancestry who adapted to the Dutch Boer life-style. They are more likely to live in the rural and interior areas than are the Anglos.

English Speakers

Indians and Asians—Over one million live primarily on the southeastern coast on either side of Durban.

Anglos—The majority of Anglos are South Africans of English descent, but there are immigrants from a number of other European countries. Approximately two million in number, they make up the majority (or large minority) in most cities and form a majority, with the "coloreds," in the western half of the country.

"Coloreds" (according to apartheid definition)—Nearly four million people of mixed (white, black, Indian, etc.) parentage, coloreds form most of the population of the western half of the country (where blacks are a minority). They could be called the "South Africans of the future" and are living proof that the races can get along on intimate terms.

Foreign Workers

Despite the abundance of unemployed South African blacks, some of the South African mining companies prefer to hire workers from adjacent nations. This is largely a matter of labor politics. The foreign workers are hired on short-term contracts and sent back across the border when the contract is up (or because of labor unrest). Most of these workers never go beyond the mining sites in the border regions. There are nearly a million workers in the mining industry, of which an increasing percentage are foreigners.

CHAPTER 10

ZAIRE AND CENTRAL AFRICA: THE HEART OF DARKNESS

INTRODUCTION

The center of Africa, largely occupied by Zaire, is truly the Heart of Darkness. Poor in agricultural resources and rich in typically abundant tropical diseases, the area can at best support large populations on a precarious and debilitated subsistence basis. The endemic diseases blind and cripple large numbers of the adult population and kill off many of the children and anyone lucky enough to make it past age fifty. Added to this arduous life-style is a persistent state, or threat, of war.

Zaire and its neighbors in central Africa each fight several wars. There are the internal ones, fought over which of the country's elites will be in power. Then there are the endemic tribal conflicts, often seen as the battles between the separate provinces that but for colonialism would be different tribal entities. Then there are the outside interests—like the Angolans who sponsor to some degree the Katangan reinvasions—and these battles become minor border wars. Sometimes this favor is reciprocated by Zaire, which until 1982 sponsored a revolt in Angola's Cabinda Province. Most nations have at least one ongoing border dispute with a neighbor because religious and ethnic animosities flare up continuously. Finally, there's the war with the International Monetary Fund (IMF), the world body that tries to cycle cash from the relatively wealthy to the definitely poverty-stricken. Zaire is losing this war in a big way, and dragging the banks of its "allies" to the brink.

Almost every nation in Central Africa suffers from similar problems, the only difference being in degree.

SOURCE OF CONFLICT

Zaire's problems are classic examples of a form of government endemic to Africa since the departure of the colonial governments in the 1960s. This uniquely African form of one-man rule resulted in a steady, severe decline in economic performance and an increase in violence. Economic growth has declined several percent a year through the 1980s and most Africans find themselves much worse off in 1990 than they were in 1980.

One of the primary causes of the prevalence of dictatorships was the colonial legacy. Borders were drawn in European parlors on the basis of who had explorers and troops where and/or who was currently in political hock to whom. Tribal areas, cultural development, language, etc. were given little consideration. The racist colonialists thought the natives were all "wogs" anyway, and besides, if things went bad, the empire's troops would bring order out of the chaos. But the colonial empires broke up, and the world wars accelerated the process. The Belgians tried to keep their Congo (Zaire) and succeeded for fifteen postwar years or so, but controlling tens of millions of people living in central Africa is a big task—central Africans have trouble doing it and they live there. Zaire has over two hundred different ethnic groups.

Here's the gist of the problem: When the colonial power leaves, there's inevitably a power vacuum, no matter how well prepared the country seems to be for independence. The colonial physicians, engineers, and other skilled personnel often leave with the colonial army, and if no locals have been trained to take their places (for example, 1960 Zaire—then the Belgian Congo—had three native MDs), economic and political disruption follow. The colonial powers made either weak attempts (Britain in Nigeria) or none at all (France and Belgium) to give their former colonies a sense of national identity or the technical means to run a country and an economy. This has been a cause of great suffering.

When there is no effort or desire on the part of the newly independent to reorganize the country into nations along tribal lines, the real bickering starts. It is exacerbated if single tribes are divided by national boundaries—like the Somalis, many of whom are located in Ethiopia.

Zaire, compared to other former middle African colonies, had a diversified economy when it achieved independence, but the seven years of warfare from decolonization in 1960 to 1967 stymied development. The invasion of Shaba in 1977 by the Angolan-backed Katangan gendarmes began another series of internal and external conflicts.

The precolonial form of government in Africa came in as many varieties as would be expected from an area with over a thousand distinct ethnic groups. But one common thread was a form of cooperative tribalism—Africans organized themselves for work and play. The tribes had chiefs, but these chiefs were selected by various forms of election. An old African saying sums it up best, "No people, no chief." In other words, a bad chief would find his people wandering off until there was no tribe to oppress. The African concept of nationhood was based on the allegiance of the people, not occupation of a lot of real estate. The Europeans brought into Africa their concept of territorial entities and control over large numbers of people. Colonial administrators tended to appoint chiefs and ignore pleas for removal of bad ones. Many of the postcolonial African nations became large fiefs for those in power. By controlling the bank accounts and the army, Africa was left with a perversion of its ancient tribal system.

After over two decades of watching Africans run their own affairs, and receiving more foreign aid per capita than any other region in the world, it became apparent that there were certain uniquely African elements at work. The most successful dictators were the ones who combined the technology of the West with the traditional tribal-control mechanisms of Africa. So the longest surviving African dictator, Joseph Mobutu, set up a communications and propaganda system, and spent much of his time visiting small villages throughout Zaire dressed as a traditional chief. These images were constantly in circulation throughout the nation. Mobutu's less successful peers in other African nations soon found themselves dead or in exile, as many of their own people began to grope, often with AK-47 in hand, for a better, or at least less painful, form of government.

Shaky government is not new to Africa. Before the European colonial administrations arrived, most of Africa was a patchwork of largely independent ethnic entities. The poor communications in most of Africa made nation (or, more often, empire) building a daunting task. Those empires that were occasionally built up rarely survived long. Long-term, stable national governments are a relatively recent development. Africa had not gotten that far by the 1800s, and Europe itself was pretty new to it at that point. Ethiopia and Liberia escaped the colonial experience and proved no different than their colonized brethren when the Europeans left. The basic fact was that most of Africa was not as well equipped to move into the industrial age as other areas were. There's no mystery about this. Lacking literacy, mechanization, strong agricultural resources, and ample natural transport routes, what happened in Africa is not surprising.

Easily overlooked by non-Africans is the "tribal" issue. There are over a thousand different ethnic groups in Africa, at least in terms of groups having a distinct language and customs. Many nations have over a hundred of these ethnic groups within their borders. No other region in the world has such a density of ethnic groups and this plethora of ethnic groups is a severe obstacle to nation building. Combined with Africa's other handicaps, the poor economic development and endemic conflict should not be surprising.

Zaire is little different from its neighbors in nearly all respects. A study of Zaire is a study of the bulk of sub-Saharan Africa.

WHO'S INVOLVED

Zaire—The central government of President Mobutu is located in Kinshasa. It is the personal fiefdom of Mr. Mobutu.

Zairian ethnic and religious groups—With over two hundred such groups spread among the population, these are not at all unified players in the political game; moreover, the existence of their immense divisions leaves Zaire open to constant internal disputes. The government's game is to play the groups off one another. Mobutu's policy of "national homogeneity" is a political masquerade.

Opposition parties—In the afterglow of falling dictatorships (particularly Communist ones), even Mobutu has had to pay some attention to local demands for a more pluralistic form of government. This could prove interesting, as nearly everyone in Zaire who is anyone (in terms of education and skills) is on Mobutu's payroll or, at the very least, on the list of people he has done favors for. Where the opposition parties will come from, who will lead them, and to what effect will be an interesting event.

Opposition groups—In a typical African situation, Zaire possesses over two hundred African ethnic groups, with the majority being Bantu.

The four largest tribes—the Mongo, Luba, Kongo (all Bantu), and Mang-betu-Azande (Hamitic)—make up nearly half the population. Mobutu has made strenuous efforts to prevent anyone from making these tribal group-ings into a power base. As half the population is Roman Catholic (another 20 percent is Protestant, plus 10 percent Kimbanguist, 10 percent Muslim, and the remainder traditional beliefs), control of the Catholic clergy has always been high on his list. The most worrisome source of opposition is from the urban population. Overall, about half the male (and a third of the female) population is literate. There is more literacy in the urban areas, which contain about a third of the population. Although 75 percent of the labor force is in agriculture, only 10 to 15 percent are wage earners. This includes most of the educated classes—the people with the means to get the urban population stirred up.

Katangan rebels—Remnants of the old Katangan gendarmerie, these are leftist elements from Angola who are still organized into a combat force and waiting in Angola. They have a really well-disciplined mer-cenary organization that could be a danger to Angola or anyone who harbors it. They constantly threaten to invade Shaba Province (as they did in 1977).

Wild Cards

Angola—Elements of the "old Marxist" MPLA have served as out-side sponsors of Katangan rebels.

France—Zaire is a member of the French "union" of former colonies, and as such, Mobutu (or his potential opposition) has some call on the use of French economic and diplomatic muscle, not to mention the ever-ready French 11th Airborne Division and Foreign Legion.

CIA—America's intelligence agency has several major operations in Zaire and cannot help getting mixed up in local affairs.

GEOGRAPHY

The Belgium Congo has been renamed Zaire, and the Congo River has been renamed the Zaire River (this should clear up any lingering discrepancies). However, Zaire remains the same equatorial land of 2.3 million square kilometers that it was when King Léopold II of Belgium was the sovereign.

Terrain varies from grasslands and savannas to mountains to tropical

rain forests. Basically it's a vast central basin which is a low-lying plateau, with mountains in the east. Approximately 80 percent of the country is forest and woodland. There is dense tropical rain forest in the central part of the country and the eastern highlands, with periodic droughts in the south. The climate is tropical: hot and humid along the Zaire River, cooler and drier in the southern highlands, and cooler and wetter in the eastern highlands.

The population is almost 36 million with 30 percent of it living in cities. Kinshasa has a population of over 4 million. Over half the people are Christian and the rest are members of tribal syncretic and animist sects.

Zaire borders Angola, Zambia, Tanzania, Burundi, Rwanda, Uganda,

Sudan, Central African Republic, and the Congo. It has large deposits of copper and cobalt as well as zinc, manganese, gold, and other minerals. The Shaba region, especially the mining area of Kolwezi, is particularly rich in mineral deposits. Shaba, formerly called Katanga, borders on Angola, Zambia, and Tanzania.

Some statisticians estimate that Zaire alone has 13 percent of the entire world's potential hydroelectric power. Its land and climate make it a potential African breadbasket, but so far agricultural development has not even kept pace with expanding domestic food needs.

HISTORY

Migrating Bantu tribes from Nigeria entered the Congo basin around A.D. 700, driving the more primitive Bushmen inhabitants south and east. In 1482 the Portuguese explorer Diogo Cam surveyed the Congo River's estuary, which was the heartland of the Bakongo kingdom. Because of the thick jungle and native tales of wild interior tribes, few Europeans attempted to penetrate beyond the coast. Besides, the Bakongos proved to be reasonable trading partners, supplying the Europeans with slaves and ivory. The hinterland remained relatively unexplored by Europeans until Henry Morton Stanley (of "Dr. Livingston I presume?" fame) passed through present-day Zaire in the 1870s. Belgium's King Léopold II, after hiring Stanley as an explorer and adviser, claimed the Congo area at the Berlin Conference of 1885.

The Congo was Belgium's most important colony, but the Belgians did little to improve native education or living standards. Their primary interest was in extracting Zaire's plentiful natural resources and shipping them to resource-poor Belgium. There were several native anticolonial movements, most of them religiously inspired, including Kimbanguism and the Kitawala sect.

French-African decolonization in the 1950s made Belgium's already shaky hold on Zaire completely untenable. Zaire (then still called the Congo) became independent on June 30, 1960. Patrice Lumumba became prime minister and Joseph Kasavubu president. Peace lasted less than a week: The Army mutinied, Belgian troops acted to protect colonials living in Zaire, and Katanga Province (now Shaba), under the leadership of Moise Tshombe, seceded from the new republic. UN peacekeeping forces showed up but Lumumba demanded they be placed under his direct control. The UN commander refused on the grounds that that was not part of his mandate. Lumumba then startled the world by requesting direct Russian aid.

This was too much. Exercising his powers as president, Kasavubu tried to fire Lumumba, but Lumumba refused to leave the government. He tried to remove Kasavubu. Col. Joseph Mobutu (the current president) led a military coup that toppled the unmanageable government. He threw out all East bloc diplomats and advisers, put Lumumba in prison, then returned Kasavubu to power. Meanwhile Lumumba died from mysterious causes; he was probably assassinated by his rivals. But Lumumba has his memorial—the KGB-run Patrice Lumumba University in Moscow for "students from the developing world."

In 1961 Zaire was in shambles. The reborn Kasavubu government faced a half dozen dissident groups, chief among them being a "pro-Lumumba people's government" in Kisangani, run by the ex-vice premier and Lumumba loyalist Antoine Gizenga; Moise Tshombe down in Katanga; and a Baluba-tribe separatist rebellion in Kasai, brought on by confusion, combat, negotiations, and UN troops. Gizenga and his followers returned to the government, but Katanga held out until 1963.

Katanga's reintegration and the UN withdrawal in 1964 didn't produce internal stability. A tribal rebellion erupted, directed by former Lumumba ally Pierre Mulele. Another revolt broke out in Kivu Province, led by another Lumumba faction. In July 1964 Tshombe was named head of the central government. He directed a counterattack on rebel strongholds and got strong support from Belgium.

In late 1965, further political infighting resulted in the fall of the Tshombe regime. Mobutu, now a lieutenant general, led another military coup and installed himself as president, a position he still holds as of early 1991. In July 1966 white mercenaries and Katangan rebels, many of them former members of the national army and police forces, launched another drive on the central government. Combat ensued and was renewed a year later. By late 1967 the insurgency had been defeated and the Katangans withdrew into Angola.

They returned in 1977 with a fast-paced invasion that overran Shaba Province. Mobutu asked for French and Belgian assistance. He was provided with a regiment of the Moroccan Army, which pushed back the rebels into Angola, where they fought a series of holding actions, avoiding pitched battles with the Moroccan forces. In May 1978 the rebels launched another offensive, this time directed at the mining town of Kolwezi. This was a most calculated invasion, one designed to strike at Zaire's economy. When the rebels took Kolwezi, they machine-gunned Belgian and French technical advisers and mining personnel as well as Zairian civilians. The rebels may have killed as many as two hundred foreigners and five thousand Zairians. France responded by sending the Foreign Legion. The legionnaires and the Zairian Army routed the rebels and drove them from Shaba. Belgium provided a paratroop battalion.

Since 1978 the Zairian government has been plagued with economic difficulties that have compounded some of the internal tribal contentions. The French used the situation as an opportunity to draw Zaire into the successful "union" it had established with its former colonies to the north since independence in 1960.

The overt war is in a quiet phase. Katangan rebel groups remain in their Angolan havens. Some bandit activity around Lake Tanganyika may be caused by former rebels on the lam. Muttering in the urban areas about the need for multiparty democracy and other heresies grow in response to the fall of dictatorships in Europe, Latin America, and Asia.

The more serious conflict is on the economic front. Accurate figures for Zaire's war with the IMF are hard to obtain, but sources cite an inflation rate of nearly 100 percent. International debt is over $7 billion. This figure compares to a 1987 GNP of slightly more than $5 billion. Zaire's economic situation is typical of sub-Saharan Africa (except South Africa). Consider the grim statistics for this region. While world economic activity increased several percent a year through the 1980s, sub-Saharan Africa's *fell* over 2 percent a year through the decade. Africa's share of world trade is now 1.5 percent, in 1960 it was 3 percent. Return on investment in the area is 3 percent versus 30 percent in 1960 and a current 22 percent in Asia. This is the major reason for the reluctance to invest in Africa. Not that a lot of money doesn't flow into the area. Despite the fact that Africa receives more aid per capita than any other region in the world, the region's external debt equals its GNP. It costs a lot more to do business in Africa (over 50 percent more than in Asia), and with many other underdeveloped nations clamoring for new investment, Africa comes up dead last in the investment potential department. Zaire is one of the worst examples of this syndrome.

Internal development is at a standstill despite President Mobutu's policy of "national homogenization," an alleged attempt to forge a national identity for Zaire. The actual policy is to spread around as many economic goodies as possible among the tribes while keeping the elites

in the federal district of Kinshasa supplied with new Mercedeses. This
works when copper prices are high; when they aren't, the country's
consensus begins to break down.

Mobutu does feel confident enough about the internal and external
situations that he has lent Chad and France 2,000 troops for duty in Chad.
But then he also owes France a thank-you for the Foreign Legion's
assistance in 1978. In Chad his troops are given an opportunity to train
and gain field experience. Perhaps Mobutu's strongest form of insurance
was to strike a deal with the American CIA to provide logistical bases
for U.S. support of Angolan rebels. These CIA bases are the largest U.S.
intelligence presence on the continent and form the source for many other
intelligence-gathering operations in surrounding states. As a result, the
CIA has a strong interest in keeping Mobutu in power. Mobutu further
cements his position by maintaining good relations with South Africa.
At the same time, he positions himself as a leader in the fight against
apartheid and the promoter of anti-Communist rebellions in Africa. The
events of 1989 in the Communist world have shown Mobutu's policies
to be wise (or just lucky). The many African nations that threw in with
the Russians are now out of luck (and foreign aid). Mobutu's gamble
with respect to maintaining good Western relations has paid off. All of
this external support may be needed if meaningful opposition develops
within Zaire.

LOCAL POLITICS

Zaire, nominally a federal republic, is a strongman-type dictatorship
backed by the Army and a consensus of tribal leaders.

Mobutu Sese Seko—Formerly Joseph Mobutu, now the president of
Zaire and referred to as the "Guide." Essentially a strongman dictator
backed by the Army, he still appears to be the only consensus leader.

Popular Movement of the Revolution (MPR)—Only legal political
party, a Mobutu front.

Katangan rebels—Remnants of the old Katangan gendarmerie, some
renegade Lumumba backers, leftist elements, now perhaps 2,000 strong.
They are essentially an exile army in Angola. Evidence shows that Cuban
and East bloc advisers have trained and rearmed the rebel units, but some
of these guys were first-class French- and British-trained mercs to begin
with.

The Bakongo—Largest ethnic group with 2.5 to 3 million members. A Bantu tribe, they are only 10 percent of the population, which illustrates the ethnic diversity of the country.

Baluba, Balunda, Mongos—Other major Zairian Bantu tribes.

Manbetu-Azande—Major Zairian Hamitic tribe.

Lingala—Zairian patois, the language used by the Zairian Army and the closest thing to a national Zairian language. Government "nationalization policies" encourage its use. Zaire may have as many as 650 local languages and dialects. The plethora of languages and ethnic groups makes it difficult for someone without an army, aircraft, and radio stations to oppose someone (Mobutu) who has.

Kimbanguism—Syncretic tribal religion with 3 to 4 million members, whose full name is "The Church of Christ on Earth by the Prophet Simon Kimbangu."

CIA—Intelligence presence whose logistical bases and large number of operatives, plus the implicit obligation of the U.S. government for this hospitality, make additional U.S. support in time of internal crises a major asset for Mobutu and his followers. At the very least, it gives Mobutu an assured exit from Zaire to a comfortable exile should things get too hot. Moreover, the United States is unlikely to support any legal action against Mobutu for any economic or other crimes committed while he was in charge. Mobutu knows too much about CIA operations.

POLITICAL TREND CHART

ZAIRE

A mess getting messier.

	1990	1996
		(Military Dictatorship)
Government Effectiveness	3	2
Government Stability	3	1
Political Cohesion	2	1
Repression Level	7	6
Economic Development	1−	1−
Education Status	1−	0+

NOTE: 0 = minimum; 9 = maximum.

REGIONAL POWERS AND POWER INTEREST INDICATOR CHART

ZAIRIAN CIVIL DISINTEGRATION

South Africa, for all its own problems, is the major foreign power in Zaire's future and the best hope of saving Zaire.

	Economic Interests	Historical Interests	Political Interest	Military Interest	Force Generation Potential	Ability to Intervene Politically	Ability to Promote Economic Development
U.S.	7	4	6	3	6	5	6
So. Africa	9	9	9	9	8	3	5
"Arabs"	4	9	7	3	3	4	3
France	6	7	7	3	7	7	6
Russia	2	1	4	3	2	2	1
Belgium	6	7	5	2	1	3	2
Nigeria	3	2	4	4	2	1	1

NOTE: 0 = minimum; 9 = maximum.

PARTICIPANT STRATEGIES AND GOALS

Zaire's central government—Mobutu continues to play the internal payoff game and hopes the IMF doesn't close the bank. Growing demands by the urban population for democracy loom as the largest problem, and the problem is made worse by increasing economic problems caused by declining prices for export goods and rampant corruption. Potential problems in Shaba Province shrink by comparison. But the government must ensure that Shaba is adequately defended in order to forestall another invasion—Shaba is economically vital to Zaire's existence and everyone knows it. While 75 percent of the population produces 30 percent of the GNP by scratching a living out of subsistence farming, the raw materials industries generate the majority of the GNP, using most of the remaining people. As for internal politics, the increasing use of the Lingala language and educational development programs are crucial to national survival, but these programs will take a long time and a lot of political stability to be successful.

Katangan rebels—This group is biding its time and waiting for another opportunity to return to Shaba. They have suffered from the waning fortunes of the Communist Angolan government. But if the CIA wanted to play rough with Mobutu, a deal could always be made with the remaining Katangan rebels.

France—France is increasingly keen on getting competent leadership in the French "Union" states. For over twenty years France has been tolerant of unsuccessful African attempts to reinvent some form of state socialism. France's economic and monetary ties to the French "Union" states are getting expensive, and patience is wearing thin. The French Foreign Legion and 11th Airborne Division may become a means of political reform in more nations.

United States—Once South Africa appears on its way to democracy, the focus will shift to the more depressing situations in the rest of Africa. The Heart of Darkness dictators have been getting away with murder (on a vast scale) and plunder (big-time) while the Western media spotlights South Africa's problems. Once South Africans get less attention, the United States will either feel compelled to twist some arms or, quite likely, continue to ignore the mess. The CIA may become the major cause of U.S. involvement here, as the U.S. military and intelligence agencies are looking for something to justify their large budgets now that the Cold War is over. "Saving Africa" has a nice ring to it, especially if you're a general or CIA honcho about to have your budget torn to ribbons.

Potential Outcomes

1. 60 percent chance through 1996: There is the same old suffering with increased agitation for more power sharing. Look for increasing corruption in an already corrupt kleptocracy.
2. 30 percent chance through 1996: Utter disintegration into separate nations and tribal areas may occur, with Katanga as a viable independent country. This goes to 60 percent if Mobutu dies.
3. 10 percent chance through 1996: A successful tribal federation system is established, which goes to 40 percent if Mobutu dies and is not succeeded by someone like him.

Cost of War

Since independence (1960 for most nations), the region has suffered over 1.6 million deaths directly attributable to warfare, rebellion, and other forms of civil strife—out of a population of some 150 million people. The collateral damage was more significant, as the fragile economies involved were further weakened, which is the primary cause of local life expectancy being five to six years lower than in India (a country with a lower per capita GNP, but also with a lower level of violence).

The most prominent of these conflicts were the Zaire civil wars (1960–65, 100,000–110,000 dead), the Angola rebellion against Portugal (1961–75, 120,000 dead), subsequent civil war (1975–present, 60,000 dead), Ugandan civil disorder (1966–present, 650,000 dead), the Burundi-Tutsi massacres of the Hutu (1972, 210,000 dead; 1988, 33,000 dead), and Sudan civil wars (1983–present, 500,000 dead).

What Kind of War

While there are over a thousand armored vehicles in the region, most of them are not maintained effectively, and even those that are running

Zaire and Its Neighbors

	Population (in millions)	Population (per sq. mile)	Percent Muslim Population	Percent of Arable Land	Per Capita GNP	Average Life Expectancy
Zaire	36.0	40	10	3	170	52
Congo	2.4	18	2	2	1,050	56
Central African Republic	3.0	13	15	3	410	47
Sudan	26.0	27	70	5	340	53
Uganda	18.0	198	16	25	210	50
Rwanda	7.6	752	9	29	340	51
Burundi	5.7	532	1	43	240	51
Tanzania	26.0	76	33	5	250	52
Zambia	8.0	27	1	7	240	55
Angola	8.6	18	0	2	600	43
France*	56.0	252	2	34	14,000	75

*Included for comparison.

well don't have many places to go. The Heart of Darkness is also the heart of the African rain forest. In addition to the jungles, there are numerous swamps (not all of which announce themselves to the unwary tank driver). The flat, dry areas are filled with rocky outcroppings and gullies. While there is some good tank terrain, there's nothing there for tanks to fight over. In other words, this is not the best terrain for mechanized warfare.

This is infantry country—geographically, psychologically, and culturally. The population is spread out in thousands of small settlements. The people (armed or not) respond well to a disciplined platoon of heavily armed infantry. All that's worth having is concentrated in a few urban areas or industrial sites and light-armored vehicles and infantry also work best in these areas. Countries in this region tend to keep their heavy vehicles in the built-up areas, where they can be used most effectively against unruly urban citizens and where they are most likely to avoid mechanical (or loyalty) breakdowns.

QUICK LOOK AT OTHER CENTRAL AND SUB-SAHARAN AFRICAN CONFLICTS

Congo—This was the part of "Greater Zaire" that got away (Belgium got the rest of the Congo River basin), the part that joined the French Union. Its official national title is The People's Republic of the Congo. The illusion of socialism is kept alive by large oil revenues, and by the majority of people (75 percent) tending their subsistence farms out in the bush in physical and political isolation from the urban and better-educated minority, who are living off foreign exchange. Weak oil prices and ill-conceived and -executed development projects have piled up the foreign debt and domestic discontent. While the Congo looks like a paradise compared to its neighbor Zaire, there is trouble brewing—for all the usual reasons.

Central African Republic (CAR)—The Central African Republic was, for a few years, the Central African Empire (run by Emperor Bokassa I). This short-lived imperium spent a great deal of one year's GNP on the coronation of the emperor, who was later run out of the country on charges of embezzlement, child abuse, and cannibalism. Well, some emperors are like that. Ask the Romans about Caligula. Now the present-day Central African Republic is not doing much better. It's about the size of Texas, and equally hot and flat. Three ethnic groups make up 75 percent of the small population. There is only 20 percent literacy, 30 percent unemployment, and a massive trade deficit and foreign debt. The form of government is one-party rule, and, like Zaire, it is part of the French Union. A sad case, not likely to get any happier.

Sudan—Sudan's travails are covered in the previous chapter. Some of the tribes in northern Zaire are related to those in southern Sudan.

Uganda—Although Uganda is blessed with rich, well-watered farmland, it suffered one of the great tragedies in Africa. It was cursed by a particularly evil postcolonial dictator: Idi Amin. This fellow belonged to one of the smaller Muslim tribes in the northern part of the country and had illusions of grandeur that proved fatal for over a million Ugandans. In 1978, by the time Amin was run out of the country (into comfortable exile in Saudi Arabia), the Ugandan economy was a shambles. For one thing, Amin had expelled the Indian minority, which, in a common African development, had run most of the retail and wholesale trade. The tribal civil war that erupted in the wake of Amin's departure still goes on. The country has become something of an African Lebanon, although not as well organized or thoroughly covered by the Western press. (Perhaps because none of the locals thought to seize Western hostages.)

Rwanda/Burundi—These two nations have much in common. Both lie in the fertile highlands surrounding Lake Victoria, and both are populated largely with Hutu people with a significant Tutsi minority. In the 1500s the Tutsi (or Watutsi) moved south from their original home in the Sahel. Lighter-skinned (an important point for the Tutsi) and a foot taller than the local Hutu, they did not take long to take over and install their own brand of apartheid. The area eventually evolved into two Tutsi-ruled empires, each roughly covering the territory of modern Burundi and Rwanda. In 1899 the Germans moved in and made both areas colonies. The British replaced the Germans in 1916 and passed the area over to the Belgians in the 1920s. It was assumed that when the areas became independent nations, the Hutu (over 80 percent of the population) would run the place. The more aggressive and warlike Tutsi had other ideas, and the Hutu knew it. In 1959 the Hutu of Rwanda rose up against the Tutsi (who held most of the positions of local power), slaughtered thousands of them, and then drove several hundred thousand into exile (mainly into Uganda). In 1990, several thousand of these exiles formed an army and attempted a comeback.

After 1959, the Tutsi in Burundi took the hint and were successful in repressing the Hutu rebellion that occurred in 1965. Being 14 percent of the Burundi population (contrasted with only 9 percent in Rwanda), the Tutsi were numerous enough, and savage enough, to hold on to their power. Periodic massacres of the Hutu have kept that majority people out of power. The Tutsi apartheid differs from the Boer (South African) version in several respects. First, the Tutsi don't bother with a lot of laws attempting to legitimize their power. They state it simply and unequivocally: Tutsi rule, Hutu obey. While the Tutsi generally keep to themselves, there is some intermarriage. Every area has some Tutsi settlements, and they often share the same villages with the Hutu. With over 90 percent of the population engaged in farming or herding (a Tutsi specialty), control is maintained by the Tutsi monopolizing the armed forces and police jobs, as well as most civil service positions. Tutsi apartheid also differs from the Boer version in that it delivers no economic benefits to the oppressed Hutu. Moreover, the Tutsi control system relies on outright slaughter, not the less lethal police and legal controls found in South Africa. The Tutsi do have one big advantage over the Boers: No one pays much attention to their version of apartheid. While a riot with a few dozen deaths in South Africa grabs world headlines, periodic slaughters of tens of thousands of Hutu merit only the briefest of mentions in the press. Some of the more progressive Tutsi leaders are attempting to reach an accommodation with the Hutu. But with all the bad feeling engendered by the regular massacres, it is unlikely that a peaceful solution will be achieved in this decade.

Tanzania—More typical of sub-Saharan Africa than Zaire, Tanzania is a one-party state run by the "Revolutionary party." The party, in this case, is superior in legal and de facto power to the government. Not that it matters much, as 90 percent of the population fights a losing battle trying to scrape a living out of an arid landscape. Twenty years of poorly implemented socialism caused the ruling party to loosen things up economically in 1986. This proved an immediate success, although the rate of improvement was so small that it will take a decade or more to make a significant difference. Over a hundred different ethnic groups live in the country, only 1 percent of which (being mainly Arab) is not black African. A third of the population are Muslim, mainly near the coast where Arabs have long traded. Another third are various Christian denominations and the remainder hold traditional (animist, etc.) beliefs. Literacy is high, at nearly 80 percent. This, coupled with the government's new economic policies and a growing demand for multiparty democracy, may offer the country a better outlook for the upcoming century.

Zambia—Zambia is another one-party "democracy" with a failing economy and over sixty different ethnic groups. The economy was expected to thrive through massive copper exports, but the price of copper fell through most of the 1980s and local mismanagement did the rest.

Liberia—In September 1990 the government of President Samuel K. Doe was toppled when he was assassinated by insurgent forces under the command of Prince Yealu Johnson. Rival rebel forces loyal to former Doe aide Charles Taylor were also besieging Monrovia, the capital. The Liberian civil war was chaotic and anarchic, with all sides being accused of atrocities against one another and civilians. Tribal tensions and historical hatreds powered a general dislike of President Doe's corrupt regime. Doe's regime clearly favored his Krahn tribe; both Johnson's and Taylor's rebel groups (at one time in an alliance, but were unable to agree who would be president) drew strength from the Gio and Mano tribes. The sixteen-member Economic Community of West African States (ECOWAS) sent forces; nations contributing troops included Nigeria, Ghana, Guinea, Gambia, and Sierra Leone. Complicating its own politics is, oddly enough, the Liberian heritage. The nation was founded by freed American slaves in 1847. The freed slaves, through the "True Whig" party, became the upper, ruling class in Liberia and thoroughly dominated the tribal Liberians until 1980 when Doe, then a master sergeant in the Army, overthrew the government of President William R. Tolbert, who was executed. In his own turn Doe was executed by rebels (after ritual torture documented on videotape) sometime in late 1990.

The trends in Liberia:

1. 40 percent chance through 1996: The post-Doe government turns into the same corrupt and tribally biased regime the old one was.

2. 40 percent chance through 1996: New civil war erupts. Tribal fighting spills into neighboring nations. The Taylor, Johnson, and remnant Doe regime supporters in the Army and in the People's Progressive party renew the political struggle. No line on who wins.

3. 15 percent chance through 1996: U.S. political pressure and economic aid help forge a fragile but functioning democracy.

4. 5 percent chance through 1996: Anarchy continues as the new government falls but has no replacement. Civil war becomes tribal battling. ECOWAS nations reoccupy Liberia for the long term.

QUICK LOOK AT TRIBALISM
AND COLONIALISM

Africa was not a blank slate when the Europeans began showing up four centuries ago. For nearly three thousand years there had been extensive intercourse (economically, culturally, and otherwise) between Arabs in North Africa and the Negro, Nilo-Saharan, and Cushite peoples in the Sahel and farther south. The Arabs were more technologically advanced, and this led to various forms of domination over the sub-Saharan peoples. For thousands of years the Arabs have been sending technology, trade goods, and armies south and bringing gold, slaves, and mercenaries back north with them. The black Africans were apt students, and because they always outnumbered the Arabs south of the Sahara, the empires and kingdoms that developed were often run by blacks who had adapted Arab technology and, later, religion (Islam). Out of this developed an antagonism between Arabs and blacks that persists to the present. It was this mélange of Arab and sub-Saharan cultures that greeted the Europeans when they first ventured into Africa. At first, the best the Europeans could do was establish trading posts down the west coast of Africa; the Arabs controlled the east coast and North Africa. It wasn't until the European nations conquered the Arab states in North Africa in the 1800s that large-scale colonization of Africa took place.

A century earlier, in the 1700s, the largest European commercial venture in Africa was transatlantic slave trade. The Arabs had been slaving in sub-Saharan Africa for over a thousand years, but because they largely used land routes, only a few thousand blacks were sent north in chains each year. The Western Hemisphere plantations (mostly in the Caribbean and Brazil), however, were able to take over a hundred thousand slaves a year. The Arab and black kingdoms on the west coast of Africa saw this as a great opportunity. While wars in this area were frequent, and slaves were usually taken (although some tribes, like the Ashanti, used some of their captives for human sacrifices), there had never before been a market like the one the Europeans created with their huge sailing ships full of trade goods to exchange for all the slaves the stronger kingdoms could capture. So for over a century the west coast of Africa was in turmoil as the strong tribes raided the weak ones for slaves. Many tribes fled the area for points south, causing ethnic rearrangements that persist to this day.

The Europeans suppressed the slave trade in the early 1800s, bringing on a period of prolonged economic depression to the area. This coincided with the European conquest of the Arab states in North Africa and the realization by the Europeans that the only continent left to conquer was Africa. Advances in medicine had now made Africa less lethal for Europeans, so the Europeans moved in full-time and in significant numbers. Before the better medical care of the 1800s, most Europeans would not survive more than a year among the ample tropical diseases of sub-Saharan Africa. After that, though, with a measure of medical protection, large numbers of Europeans ventured into the heart of Africa.

What they found was the most complex patchwork of tribes, kingdoms, and empires that has ever been known to exist on this planet. Over seven hundred separate languages are spoken in Africa, and over a thousand different ethnic groups exist. In all of Europe (at the time), there were fewer than a hundred ethnic groups, and most of these were concentrated in fewer than a dozen highly organized nation-states. As the British discovered in India, such a multiplicity of different (and often mutually hostile) ethnic groups makes it easier to divide and conquer. Superior weapons helped also. Skin color helped, as the Arabs were lighter-skinned, better-armed, and had put the fear of paleface warriors into the black Africans. To many black Africans, the Europeans were just another form of Arab. With few exceptions (the Ashantis and Zulus, for example), the black Africans were unable to put up much meaningful resistance to the European inroads, so the European invasion was much more rapid and thorough than the Arab one had been. In less than a century, all of Africa had been carved up by the various European colonizers.

Twentieth-century population growth combined with fifteenth-century tribal politics and a veneer of European technology and customs had a strange effect on Africa. Colonialism brought many things, such as education for a small number of the locals and some infrastructure. Medicines, disease control, and suppression of warfare enabled the population to grow rapidly. In general, similar progress was not made in agriculture or the economy. But the most lasting contribution was borders. African kingdoms had existed for thousands of years, but they had always been very temporary affairs. Poor communication in the continent is the main reason for the thousand or so ethnic groups, and the most an able conqueror could expect to do was hold a large area of antagonistic tribes by force of arms for a few decades (or for as long as a century, if there were a string of good leaders, which was quite rare). The tribes themselves were wont to move around when the action became too uncomfortable, so there was little consciousness of "this land is our land" and all that it entails. The European colonial administrators changed all that. They had surveyors, maps, intrepid explorers, engineers, steamboats, roads, and railroads. The Europeans drew borders on maps, and after the Europeans left, the one thing the Africans did not trifle with was those borders. Naturally, this left several dozen African nations to divide those thousand ethnic groups among themselves. This presents a daunting problem for the Africans. Worldwide, ethnic antagonisms are a major burden for nations that suffer them. Canada, most of Latin America, Russia, India, and Ireland are only some of the examples that pop up in the news frequently. Even the United States, a veritable melting pot compared to most other polyglot countries, is constantly struggling with ethnic disputes. Most African nations have barely begun dealing with the problem. Ironically, South Africa is much farther down the road of planned ethnic accommodation than most other African nations. But then South Africa has relatively fewer ethnic groups than most other African nations.

For African nations to move their populations out of medieval economic conditions, they will require technology. After trying, and failing, to adopt a Russian-type socialist economy during the last twenty-five years, Africa is now back to the Western model of economics. But this implies a well-educated population, free-market economies, efficient government, and a stable political atmosphere. Few of these conditions are present in most African nations. All they have as a result of the colonial experience is a small, educated elite and borders.

QUICK LOOK AT THE FRENCH "UNION"

Most of the nations on Africa's west coast, from Senegal to Zaire, are part of a loose economic, commercial, diplomatic, and military union with France. Until 1960 most of these nations were French colonies. Unlike Britain, France did not abandon all its many ties to its former colonies; in fact, the French were unique in their efforts to integrate the educated elites of these nations into French culture, politics, and commerce. In the 1950s, several of these French Africans even served in the French government (by virtue of the colonies electing representatives to the French national legislature). At least among these elites, there was a confidence resulting from French education and participation in French government that enabled them to eagerly enter into a mesh of treaties and agreements before and after the colonies became independent nations. In addition to some hundred thousand French citizens continuing to work in the former colonies (in government, military, and commercial sectors), these African nations link their currencies with the French franc and use the French central bank with their own. There is free trade between France and the former colonies as well as a web of commercial arrangements. Since 1960, French troops have intervened more than a dozen times to stymie local coups, rebellions, and, in Chad, foreign invasions. While only 10 to 20 percent of the people in these nations speak French to any degree, the top 5 percent of the population that makes up the national leadership are thoroughly Frenchified. In many cases there are third- and fourth-generation Africans who have grown up speaking French from an early age and obtaining the same education and indoctrination available to the middle and upper classes in France. Some nations that were reluctant to join this French ''union'' in 1960 later did so because of the obvious benefits.

The strong French ties with the former colonies have not solved most of the problems these nations, like most others in Africa, have been afflicted with. But there has been a greater degree of political and economic stability. Zaire came to the ''union'' only in the 1970s. This was because Zaire was a former Belgian colony, and, initially, France had its hands full with its own former colonies. Now other nations that were not originally French colonies are edging toward joining. These relationships with France are not panaceas, but they do provide these still-struggling nations with another resource to get them over the numerous problems they continue to encounter.

Zaire signed a Military Assistance Agreement with France in 1974 (as have fifteen other African nations). Six African nations have defense agreements with France (seen as insurance policies by the African heads of state). Mobutu might like such an agreement, but the French would like to see what develops after Mobutu dies or is otherwise removed from the scene.

QUICK LOOK AT GETTING BY IN CENTRAL AFRICA ON $200 A YEAR

One aspect of central Africa's situation requires a few additional comments. Note that many of these nations have extremely low per capita GNPs. Most of the people in the region have average individual cash incomes of $200–$300 a year. But dollar figures are misleading. Most of these people don't get anything near the average $200–$300 per person a year. The people in this region work as subsistence farmers, growing most of the food they require, or gathering fruits and other items in the bush. Many maintain herds of cattle. This is as it has been for thousands of years and several hundred million people in Africa get by in this fashion. They live in a tropical climate, so they do not require the additional housing and clothing needed in areas where a winter must be survived each year.

If these farmers had to buy food in the local markets (which exist for the minority that perform other tasks), it would cost several hundred dollars a year per person just for the food most produce themselves. Shelter is also created by the families out of local materials. Other items are obtained through barter. In practice, the subsistence farmer sees only $100 or so in cash each year for an entire family (averaging over six people). This cash is quickly spent on manufactured items that cannot be procured locally by family members. This includes clothing, farm tools, medicine, and such "luxury" items as portable radios and education fees for the children. A small percent of the population does have a substantial cash income, and some of these families live in the Western style with many of the essentials and luxuries Americans are familiar with.

Subsistence farming is, as the term implies, a precarious way to live. The average life span in this part of Africa is over twenty years less than in Europe and North America. But the conditions people live under are not poverty to many of those who have lived this way for thousands of years. Our life-style appears to these people to be quite unbelievable. But the Western way of life is a rare and rather recent development. Ecologically, the Western life-style may not be sustainable for most of the world's population. This is particularly true in Africa, which is relatively deficient in key resources (such as water and highly fertile land) and not overly endowed with many other items. Africa may have to seek another way, not because it wants to, but because it has to.

QUICK LOOK AT AIDS IN AFRICA

AIDS may or may not be of African origin. However, tropical areas are the source of more diseases than are temperate or arctic areas simply because it's easier for more life-forms to proliferate without the annual onset of freezing weather. For this reason, arctic people (Eskimos, etc.) often find the common cold lethal because the cold germ rarely survives in areas where winter is the longest season. Diseases similar to AIDS began showing up (to Western medical personnel) in the 1960s. That AIDS first spread widely in the West was largely due to a mobile, sexually active homosexual population. AIDS may have existed in parts of Africa for centuries, but was unable to spread because so many isolated populations had no way to pass it on. But things changed in Africa after World War II. Many roads, albeit primitive ones, were built and truck traffic became much more widespread and intense. Fewer Africans lived in total isolation. Globe-trotting Westerners, or equally mobile African elites, may have moved the disease from Africa into the West. Whatever the case, the wildfire spread of AIDS in Africa can be traced to sectors of the population that move around a lot (truck drivers and the small middle class).

Prostitution in Africa is widespread, and most of these women quickly become infected. Attitudes toward casual sex are different in Africa than in the West, and poor medical care and hygiene, plus certain sexual practices, make it easier for AIDS to spread via heterosexual contact. AIDS is spreading virtually unchecked in Africa, and until recently most

African governments had a policy of denying the existence of AIDS within their borders. Huge death rates in some regions have gotten the attention of the local governments, but there are few resources to deal with the disease or its spread.

In the 1990s, AIDS is expected to become a major killer on this continent long noted for its multitude of lethal and disabling diseases. Estimates of over 10 percent infection on the continent and eventual loss of an even higher portion of the population are not unreasonable. AIDS is a relatively silent killer, even though it kills a disproportionate number of relatively affluent people in their prime. Many rural areas are discovered to be heavily infected only after someone notices the empty villages and untilled fields.

Endemic warfare and economic collapse may get most of the attention in Africa, but it's quite likely that AIDS will have the biggest impact for this decade and on into the next century. Even if a cure is discovered soon, getting it to the widely dispersed population will not be easy. Some nations will suffer more than others. The nations covered in this chapter are the most affected. South Africa has taken measures to keep the disease out and to control it when it is found within its borders. But South Africa has more resources than does the rest of sub-Saharan Africa. For the Heart of Darkness, AIDS may be the ultimate burden.

PART FOUR

ASIA

The most populous and, not surprisingly, the most blood-soaked and fought-over region is Asia. Because Asia is relatively isolated from Europe and the Americas, the enormous conflicts that take place in Asia are relatively unknown to Westerners. But as technology, long-range missiles, and nuclear weapons reach Asian nations, events in these far-off lands can no longer be ignored.

CHAPTER 11

BURMA'S BITTER ROAD: THE SILENCED HELL OF MYANMAR

INTRODUCTION

The idea was horrifyingly simple: Burmese society, in order to realize socialist perfection, would internalize development. Burma would curl upon itself like a political lotus, a "Marxist-Buddha" rejecting the virus of bourgeois values, the disease of capitalism, the legacy of "Western imperialism"—and the grim reality of its own ethnically fractured and poverty-stricken hinterland. Burma went socialist and wrecked its economy. But for decades Burma—recast by Gen. Ne Win's brutal regime as "Myanmar" (Union of Myanma, a transliteration of the name in Burmese), a nomination intended to exorcise any lingering British imperial ghosts—has been less of an Asian Albania and more of an anguished battlefield—a hushed battlefield outside the focus of network video cameras and the concerns of the external world.

SOURCE OF CONFLICT

Burma is the perfect place for catchphrases describing a national state of self-inflicted economic destruction, political oppression, military corruption, social degradation, and ethnic partisanship. What was in the mid-1950s a rice-exporting nation and a comparatively literate society (an adult rate of 80 percent by some estimates) has become a net rice importer, a land of jailed intellectuals, and one of the world's more devastated economies.

The long-running military regime under the dictatorial control of Gen. Ne Win, a regime espousing a curious concoction of socialism and Buddhism, stifled private markets, shut down foreign trade, and produced the current appalling economic catastrophe. Ironically, the isolationist policies, intended to promote independent economic development and to reinforce political neutrality, made the country even more dependent on foreign aid. To this potent mix, add a host of failed promises to historically antagonistic indigenous ethnic groups, creeping environmental destruction in the jungle, a never-ending drug war for control of the opium trade, and the looming strategic interests of two nuclear-armed and mutually suspicious "super" regional powers, China and India. Myanmar is a series of small yet bitter wars that could explode into a battlefield in the Indo-China conflict once India secures its Pakistani flank—a future regional battleground in the multipolar, post–Cold War world.

WHO'S INVOLVED

Burma/Myanmar's armed struggles might be *very* loosely organized into five overlapping conflicts.

"The War for Democracy"

The war for democracy refers to the internal struggle fought in Rangoon, the central Burma "divisions," and the cities.

Ne Win regime(s)—These regimes have existed (and exist) under several guises: as the military, as the National Unity party, and as the State Law and Order Restoration Council (SLORC). They are always tied to the secret police. Ne Win's cadre of military officers is strong, entrenched, and wealthy, and it will continue to pose a severe threat to the emerging democratic movement whether or not the military is officially in power and long after Gen. Ne Win has gone. In the fall of 1990 Gen. Saw Maung was in nominal control.

National League for Democracy—This is a "spectrum" party of democratic dissidents that managed to win a solid majority of the seats in the open election held in May 1990. It is led by the dissident Gen. Ti

Oo and Daw Aung San Suu Kyi, the daughter of the Burmese revolutionary hero Au Maung.

Other democratic groups—There are several, including the All-Burma Students Democratic Front and the Democratic Alliance for Burma.

Burmese Communist party (BCP)—No longer a major player, this group still has some five thousand armed partisans. It might better be classified as a player in the drug wars, since until mid-1989 it controlled many Shan State poppy fields. Because many of its members are from minority groups, the BCP could also be described as a player in the ethnic wars. It is based in Shan State, and its original cadre was from Red Flag and White Flag Communist groups who fled to the hills in 1948. Its allies include the small Shan State Nationalities Liberation Organization and the Pa-O Liberation Army.

"The Opium War"

The opium war is nothing but more of the same old news. Opium trading has been a way of life in Burma's rural Golden Triangle region. Growing poppies is easy, moving the narcotic "base" is relatively simple, and the payoff is huge. The Golden Triangle region (see the map) is mountainous, jungle-covered, and isolated. There are strong political overtones, especially among the Shan peoples. The drug war has dragged on for more or less fifty years. (Before that it was something of a smugglers' war, opium being one of the more important items.) The forces involved include the BCP; the Chinese Nationalist (Kuomintang) forces who were operating in China's Yunan Province and could not escape to Taiwan; the Laotian Royalists who fled the Communist Pathet Lao takeover in Vientiane; some Pathet Lao forces; and of course a sprinkling of just plain mountain bandits. The total 1989 crop (based on U.S. figures) was over 2,000 metric tons of opium. The 1990 crop came in around 2,200 tons. That makes Burma the largest opium producer in the world. In February 1990 the DEA estimated that 80 percent of the heroin coming into New York City originated in the Golden Triangle region.

Burmese Army—The Army is sometimes chasing after the druggies, sometimes not, but is always in on the take.

Various "drug armies"—This is a weak description for failed guerrilla movements looking for cash, various ethnic forces operating a sideline business, a few big-time drug lords, and a host of bandits. These include:

Kuomintang (KMT) Opium Army (also Chinese Irregular Forces)—
This is now a rather ill-defined group broken into at least two major
"subarmies," the 3rd Chinese Irregular Forces and the 5th Chinese Irregular Forces. (The 5th has a sub-subgroup called the Yang hwe-kang
Group, named for its leader.) These troops are the descendants of remnants of various Yunan (Province) Nationalist Chinese forces and the
93rd Chinese Nationalist Army. After the Maoist victory in 1949, the
Nationalists fled China and entered Shan State and went into the opium
business. In 1953 and again in the early 1960s, several thousand were
evacuated to Taiwan; however, several thousand stayed. The dope business was lucrative. The KMT Opium Army suffered a major defeat in
1975 when the Burmese Army attacked its headquarters and disrupted its
drug operation. It may now be considered something of an "ethnopo-
litical" group which has up to 4,000 troops, and was at one time allied
with the Shan United Revolutionary Army (2,000 troops, not to be con-
fused with the SUA).

Shan United Army (SUA)—Operating under the guise of Shan nationalism, this is in fact a well-organized drug cartel. It claims to have
6,000 men under arms.

Laotian interests—Laos produced 300–400 tons of opium in 1990.

Thai Army—Like the Burmese Army, it sometimes chases druggies,
and is always in on the take. It launchs occasional forays into the Golden
Triangle, and in the mid–1980s it dealt the Shan United Army several
harsh blows. Thai Army officers are also deeply involved. In 1989 a U.S.
grand jury indicted Maj. Gen. Vech Pechborom on heroin-trafficking
charges. In 1990 Thailand produced 50 tons of opium, down from 150
tons in 1970.

U.S. Drug Enforcement Administration (DEA)—Ineffective as a
fighting force, the DEA is improving as an intelligence source. It does
get some cooperation from Thailand's Office of Narcotics Control Board.

"The Teak War"

This is the name applied to the battle over hardwood logging in Karen
State's jungles and forests (Thailand's hardwoods have been logged out).
The demand for hardwoods (largely from Japan) has produced a "smug-
gling" war with the Karen people caught in the middle. Thai and Burmese
Army interests don't care much about the jungle and "the ecology," and
there is a very real risk of irreversible damage to the forests. As of January

1990, Thai interests had over twenty logging concessions in Burma. Ne Win's government had allowed the concessions as a means of obtaining hard currency and as a way to get Thai cooperation against Karen rebels.

Karen peoples—An ethnic group in the Thai border area, the Karen have long been involved in the logging trade. They have been using the "British Burma Selection System" for logging—a system of staggered cutting that is intended to keep tree supplies up.

Burmese Army—They're after the cash and an increased Karen body count.

Corrupt Thai Army officers—Many are involved with the logging concessions in Burma.

"The Ethnic Conflicts"

These conflicts involve armed separatist movements, elements of Red and White Flag Communist forces. Over thirty identified armies were operating in Burma in 1988, with the total troop figures ranging from 35,000 to 55,000. (The lower figure seems more likely.)

Burmese Army—This is the central government's forces.

"People's militias"—Irregular local defense forces organized by the central government, these are intended to defend the towns and hamlets. They are allegedly allies of the central government, but their loyalties are highly questionable. One of the largest and best organized is the Shan State Volunteer Force (SSVF). The SSVF, which has 500 troops, was organized by the Burmese government in 1980 as an antiguerrilla militia.

Karen peoples—These people were pushed into the Thai border area east of Rangoon (Yangon). The primary active force is the Karen National Union, with 7,000 troops in the Karen National Liberation Army. Karen groups have been fighting the Burmese "governments" more or less continually since the turn of the century and the Karen rebellion may be the longest-running war ever in the world (the "Teak War" is part of this struggle). There are approximately 3.7 million Karens in Burma (if Kayah are included), with about 1 million in Karen State; many are Christians. The Burmese Army launched a major attack into Karen State in 1984, with several attacks also in 1987 and 1988. In 1989 the Burmese Army took Karen strongholds along the Moei River, allegedly with Thai Army support. In December 1989 and the spring of 1990, the Burmese Army took Karen and Mon positions at Thay Baw Bo and Three Pagodas Pass. Perhaps 40,000 Karen and another 10,000 Burmese dissidents (including many students who participated in the September 1988 riots) are living in refugee camps in Thailand. The Karens are particularly reviled by Ne Win, possibly because many Karens readily served in British colonial military and paramilitary forces (a common, and understandable, practice among minorities during colonial rule).

Kayah (also Kalenni or Red Karens)—The Kayahs generally get along with the central government but they support two small insurgent groups: the Kayah New Land Revolutionary Council and the Karenni People's Liberation Front. Both have token combat forces of less than 100 troops each.

Kachin—The Kachin Independence Army has 5,000–8,000 troops. There are 500,000 Kachin in Burma, mostly in Kachin State along the Chinese border. The largest military group is the Kachin Independence Organization (KIO) (6,000–8,000 troops), which was once an ally of the Burmese Communist party, but is primarily an ethnic-based defense force.

Mon—There are 500,000–600,000 Mon in Burma, and several small Mon resistance groups operate in both Karen and Mon states.

Chin—There are approximately 500,000 Chin in Burma. The small "Chin Group" operates in southern Chin State.

Wa—A key hill tribe on the opium trail near the Thai border, the Wa at times have been everyone's ally and everyone's enemy. There are about 500,000 in Burma, and three small combat groups have been identified: the Wa National Army (two factions) and the Ai Hsiao-shih group, each with 100 to 200 troops.

Shans—A large (4.2 million in Burma) and diverse ethnic group, Shans are found in several states and divisions. Originally the Shans in Shan State were granted the right (in 1947) to secede from the "Burma Union" after ten years of unity. Shan *sawbwas* ("chiefs") were stripped of power in 1959, sparking an uprising. The Shans once ruled the Burmese (see p. 402). There are several armed organizations, including the Shan State Army of 4,000 troops. Some Shans claim that "Siam" (as in Thailand, the Kingdom of Shan) is the same word as "Shan," making Thailand the greatest Shan state.

Arakans—There are 2.3 million Arakans living in Burma.

Other ethnic groups—The Lahus (Lahu State Army), the Pa-O (Pa-O National Organization), and the Paluang (Paluang State Liberation Army).

"Burmese Muslims"—Muslims, drawn from various ethnic groups, at one time may have been influenced by Pakistan. Many live in Rakhine Province (formerly Arakan State). Their numbers include some Bangladeshi refugees bounced between Burma and Bangladesh. The Rohingya Patriotic Front, led by Mohammad Jafar Habib, has been identified as a Muslim dissident group, though it may not be religiously oriented at all. The organization may be the same one as the Arakan Liberation party.

"Hindus"—Various "Indians" who have settled in Burma are distrusted by the Burmese, as Indians are considered by some Burmese to have been in league with the British.

"Chinese"—These are the ethnic Chinese in Burma, many of whom speak only local languages. One group is called "Kohang" Chinese.

Naga peoples—Once noted as headhunters, this small group lives along the upper reaches of the Chindwin River. The Nagas living in neighboring India are at odds with New Delhi over autonomy. Inside Burma, Naga separatists are semiactive, but in their cut-off territory, the Burmese government is only semipresent. There are fewer than 100,000 in Burma.

"The Sino-Indian Battleground"

Geography breeds the potential for bigger trouble between India and China. Britain and Japan fought over Burma as a land route from China to India and vice versa. It is an example of a potential regional battleground, already filled with internal troubles, anarchy, and a tribal/drug war in the hills. While a big battle is unlikely, the potential for political intrigue, sponsored terrorist activity, and destabilization is very high.

Wild Cards (in all five conflicts)

India—Big, nuclear, and on the border.

China—Bigger, nuclear, and on the border.

Japan—Burma could be a "foreign aid" success story for yen diplomacy, if the NLD assumes control, the ethnic wars die down, and China and India play along.

United States—With a navy and paratroopers, the world's superpower has it in for drug lords, sort of.

Wild Cards (Sino-Indian battleground)

Russia—The bear still has bombers and guns—for sale.

Vietnam—A potential Indian ally (anyone who makes trouble for China has a friend in Hanoi).

Pakistan—Anyone who makes trouble for India has a friend in Islamabad.

GEOGRAPHY

Burma covers 676,500 square kilometers, about the size of Texas. Administratively, Burma is carved into seven minority peoples' districts, called states, and seven "divisions" where ethnic Burmese dominate the population.

Elevations run from sea level (the Bay of Bengal and the Andaman Sea) to 5,900 meters in the edge of the Himalayas, as that roof of the

world dominates the northern tip of Kachin State. The central region is crossed by the Irrawaddy River, which passes the city of Mandalay (Mandalay Division) and comes to a delta in the lowlands south of the capital, Rangoon (now Yangon, in Rangoon Division). The major population centers lie along the Irrawaddy. Mountains cut the jungle of the Thai border (the Dawna Range in Karen State) and continue down into Mon State and Tenasserim Division along the Isthmus of Kra. Shan State is a trackless morass of hills and jungle that nestles among the trackless morass of hills and jungle that comprises northern Thailand, Laos, and China's Yunan Province. Chin State, which abuts Bangladesh and India, is also mountainous. Sagaing Division, which is bisected by the Tropic of Cancer, follows the Chindwin River valley and lies between India and Kachin.

The Irrawaddy plain and delta areas are fertile, making Burma an agriculturally productive land—at least potentially. Blessed with climactic conditions and soils ideal for rice production, Burma was once one of the world's leading rice exporters. During World War II, two of Japan's major goals in Burma, after cutting off the resupply route to China and gaining a jumping-off point for an attack on India, were to acquire Burmese "food basket" assets and petroleum.

The nation has a population of 38 to 42 million. Census data is highly unreliable (the last real census was conducted in 1931), but (for Asia) the region is relatively underpopulated. In the Burmese political divisions (particularly in Rangoon, Mandalay, and parts of Pegu), the people are highly literate and comparatively well educated. Burma, despite years of Ne Win, still has a potentially first-rate higher-education system. About 85 percent of the Burmese population is Buddhist. Many Karen as well as Chin and Kachin are Christian (converted by American missionaries). There are a number of Muslims living primarily along the Bangladeshi border.

The country possesses significant oil and gas deposits. While some of the old oil fields in Magwe Division are playing out, several areas may contain even more oil (including offshore along the Tenasserim Division). Oil production facilities, however, lack spare parts and equipment.

Burma is dotted with mineral deposits (tungsten), gems, and precious hardwoods (teak)—at least it has hardwoods until the Thai and Burmese armies' buzz saws cut their way through Karen lands and the Japanese lose their taste for fancy "natural wood" furniture. Kachin State has several jade mines, and ruby smuggling takes a backseat to drug smuggling, but it's there.

The trail from lovely poppies to deadly street heroin—the Opium Trail—begins in the Golden Triangle. Though for what it is and does the figurative "Opium Trail" is in superb condition, the same cannot be said for Burma's real roads. The Burmese road network and general transporation infrastructure are either in terrible shape or nonexistent. Shan State is particularly isolated—but then the Opium Trail *is* Shan State.

From a strategic perspective, Burma sits across the major India-China land route (hence the Burma Road of World War II fame). The northern Burmese country is tough, but a Chinese thrust from Yunan Province to the upper reaches of the Irrawaddy would bypass the even tougher Himalayas and make a strike at India's eastern districts at least plausible. New Delhi knows this—the Japanese played a similar game in World War II. Superpower tangling over the "strategic asset" of an Indian Ocean coastline and the potential for "dual use" air bases in the Kra Isthmus region (bases that could launch aircraft into either the South China Sea or the Indian Ocean) have diminished with the Soviet loss of the Cold War, but the geography is still there (for an India interested in extending military influence into the Gulf of Thailand?).

HISTORY

Burma has a long and complex history. Mongolian tribes (the Mons) and Tibeto-Chinese peoples (the Burmans) invaded in the latter half of the first millennium. The first strong "Burmese Buddhist" state was founded in A.D. 1044 (the Kingdom of Pagan and the Temple Builders Dynasty). Tartar and Chinese forces (at the initial direction of Kubla Khan) finally destroyed the state in 1287. After the collapse, several "princelet" kingdoms formed in Upper and Lower Burma, all under nominal Chinese suzerainty. The Shan Dominion (1287–1531) was one of the more powerful and the Shan recall with delight the time they ruled the Burmese.

Basically, Burma fell into two "spheres of influence," Upper and Lower Burma. In 1755 the Upper Burmese warlord Alaungpaya ("embryo Buddha") broke the Mon hold on Lower Burma, burned the city of Ava, and built a new capital called Yangon (or Rangoon, translated roughly as "the end of strife"). Strife, however, didn't end. From 1765 to 1769 the Chinese launched a series of invasions from Yunan, threatening the rebuilt city of Ava. The Chinese forces agreed to withdraw after climate and disease weakened their troops and the Burmese cut off their supplies. French prisoners, captured by the Burmese in a failed French colonial escapade, helped the Burmese man their artillery in several battles against the Chinese. Several thousand Chinese prisoners stayed in Burma and interestingly enough, many of them became royal gardeners.

In 1785 Alaungpaya's son, Bodawpaya, annexed the province of Arakan which gave Burma an Indian border. Burmese "expansionism" ran smack into the British version.

Enter the Lion

The British conquered Burma—sort of—in the nineteenth century. The British were in the area primarily to make money, not war. Meeting continual resistance in the jungles and hills, they fought three wars against the Burmese kingdom. The First Anglo-Burmese War (1824–26) ended with Arakan and Tenasserim being ceded to the British East India Company. The Second Anglo-Burmese War (1852–53) extended British control up the Irrawaddy to Pegu. And the Third Anglo-Burmese War (1885) ended with the complete annexation of Upper Burma. Burma became part of British India.

Burma was an uneasy conquest. Several open revolts occurred in the 1930s. Burmese petroleum workers launched a series of bitter and politically telling strikes in 1938.

World War II

The Japanese invasion in 1942 broke the British rule. The fact that the Japanese attack ushered in the demise of British control is fondly remembered in Burma, making Burma one of the few places in continental Asia where the Japanese aren't totally despised for their World War II depredations. The Japanese trained a group called "the Thirty Comrades" (also translated as "the Thirty Heroes"), a group of young military officers and political leaders, including U Aung San and Ne Win (the nom de guerre of Shu Maung). The Thirty Comrades, who organized Burmese forces to help fight the British and the Indians, would play a central role in twentieth-century Burmese history.

In late 1944 the Thirty Comrades switched sides. While the switch may appear opportune, the outcome of World War II, from the perspective of combat in the "CBI" (the China-Burma-India theater during 1944), was not regarded as a certain Western Allies' victory. The fact is, Japanese imperialism had proved to be more brutal and cruder than the British version. The aim of the Thirty Comrades, however, was to not have any outside control. Remember, though, that many of the Karens consider the Burmese to be "outsiders"—imperialists taking Karen land.

The Thirty Comrades' military and political organization convinced any would-be British colonialists that an attempted return to power would meet with a long and bitter war. U Aung San, at a meeting in Panglong, promised the Shan equality, autonomy, and the right to preserve their culture in the new Burmese nation if they would promise to give him political support against the British. This was promised to all of the ethnic minorities—only the Karen refused to take Aung San at his word.

As "a reward" to Burma for switching sides against the Japanese, the British agreed to Burmese independence. In 1947, however, before independence, U Aung San and a half dozen colleagues were assassinated by a political rival. Aung San's death was a major loss—he was the key hero of the independence movement and the founder of the Burmese Army. In January 1948 Burma became independent, with U Nu as prime minister and Ne Win in charge of the armed forces. Ne Win claimed that though Aung San was the first father of the Army, he was the second.

The new Burmese government moved to assert control over the hinterland. The Burmese Communist party began an insurgency. Ethnic strife began to simmer when promised autonomy failed to blossom.

The Burmese Way to Socialism

In the early 1950s, despite the low-grade insurgencies, a prosperous Burma was exporting large quantities of rice to a recuperating Japan. Burma also had a literacy rate of 80 percent (while what might be considered literate is arguable, it was inarguable that Burma had a leg up on Asian development).

In 1958 Ne Win took control in a "temporary" military government. This was replaced in 1960 by a government under U Nu. Then 1962 rolled around, and a dissatisfied Ne Win imprisoned U Nu, swept the democrats from power, and established a single-party state.

Ne Win's new ideology, the "Burmese Way to Socialism," was an amalgam of isolationism, Buddhism, and Marxism braced by a healthy dose of militarism, single-party control, and a tough secret police force. It was also a raging economic disaster: Trade and contact with the outside world were restricted and, in some cases, eliminated. The ethnic insurgencies picked up steam. The demand for drugs in the West put money into the various insurgencies and increased corruption in the Burmese Army.

In 1987, after a series of demonetizations by the Ne Win regime, the already weakened economy collapsed. The overall production of goods fell by a third. Even the production of beer, regarded as an essential good in Burma, dropped disastrously. The urban population then tried to get beer supplies by bartering with hill tribes who lugged Chinese brew over the border. Too, Burmese petroleum production dropped to 15,000 barrels a day—a minimum of 35,000 a day were needed to keep the country going.

In 1988 the country erupted. In March and April 1988, riots broke out and the Burmese Army shot several hundred demonstrators. In July 1988, in what was viewed as an attempt to placate the demonstrators while retaining dictatorial control, Gen. Ne Win resigned as chairman of the ruling Burmese socialist party and offered a referendum on a multiparty system. In August and September 1988, riots broke out again, and 3,000 people were killed. Ne Win brought civilian U Maung Maung in as president. During the September riots, student and protest leaders organized food delivery to protesters using a "block leader" structure—the beginning of an organized and resilient democratic political force. The students were assisted by many Buddhist monks and the regime perceived the overt Buddhist support as another major threat.

In January 1989, in anticipation of the promised multiparty balloting, 170 new political parties formed—50 of which backed the regime.

In March 1990, the Maung Maung regime attempted to destroy several areas known to support the NLD. In a move reminiscent of Khmer Rouge mass migrations, the government attempted to relocate urban neighborhoods into "new towns." Admittedly, one of the new towns, Shwe Pyitha, seemed to be intended for National Unity party supporters; it may have been intended as a gerrymander that would guarantee NUP representation. An estimated 250,000 people were forced out of Rangoon.

In May 1990 the National League for Democracy, with Daw Aung San Suu Kyi in the lead, swept nearly 70 percent of the seats in the legislature—ninety-three parties actually participated in the election. As of early 1991 the military government remained in control, and Daw

Aung San Suu Kyi remained in jail. And in early 1991 the military government ordered a new crackdown on dissidents.

Local Politics

National League for Democracy (NLD)—Party led by Gen. U Tin Oo and Daw Aung San Suu Kyi.

Daw Aung San Suu Kyi—Key civilian leader of the National League for Democracy and the daughter of Aung San (the Burmese independence leader assassinated in 1947). Raised in England and married to an Oxford professor of Tibetan studies, she returned to Burma in 1988 to care for her dying mother. Her emergence challenged Ne Win's "myth" of legitimacy. She has two political handicaps: She is a woman in a male-dominated culture and she has lived most of her life as an expatriate.

U Tin Oo—Opposition leader. Ne Win sacked him as defense minister in 1976 when Tin Oo failed to report a planned coup. He may have some backing in the military and among some Japanese officials.

National Democratic Front—Very loose organization of major ethnic armies. Its members include the Lahu State Army, Arakan Liberation party, Karenni National Progress party, Karen National Union (political arm of Karen National Liberation Army), Paluang State Liberation Organization, and Shan State Army.

State Law and Order Restoration Council (SLORC)—Organization led by Gen. Saw Maung, leader of military that overthrew the Socialist Program party in September 1988.

Burma Socialist Program party—Ne Win's party renamed the National Unity party (NUP) for the 1990 elections. Eighty-year-old Gen. Ne Win controls the party. Sein Lwin, another former general and aide to Ne Win, is also a major figure. In 1988, U Maung Maung became party chairman and president of Burma. A civilian, viewed by some Burmese as a moderate, he is thought to have little control over the party.

Burmese Army—Burma's regular army which has under 200,000 troops divided into nine regional commands and nine light infantry divisions, each with ten battalions. The forces are armed with light weapons; their heavy support is mortars and recoilless rifles. The Army possesses a few light antiaircraft artillery pieces and some artillery. Seven divisions are assigned to insurgent combat. The 11th and 22nd Infantry Divisions are the army's "security" divisions and the chief political units. The commander of the 22nd Light Infantry Division which was responsible for most of the 1988 massacre, was Col. Tin Hla, who is closely aligned with Gen. Khin Nyunt, another antidemocratic hard-liner. The 99th Infantry Division operates in Shan State, and its commanders tend to get very rich—if they look the other way when the opium caravans are moving. As of 1983, Burma Rifles, Kachin Rifles, Chin Rifles, Shan Rifles, and Kayah Rifles, all these battalions, despite their ethnic designations, were ethnically integrated in order to diminish the likelihood of ethnic mutinies.

Burmese Communist party of Burma (BCP)—Party that experienced a major mutiny in April 1989. The mutineers hit the party headquarters in Pangghsang (Shan State) and killed several members of the central organization. The Maoist leaders fled to China. The BCP has broken into several ethnic factions.

Insein jail—Notorious prison north of Rangoon.

Directorate of Defense Services Intelligence (DDSI)—Secret police force run by Ne Win.

Defense Services Academy—Officers' training school in Maymya and source of Ne Win old-boy network.

Burma Relief Foundation—Group that sends funds to help students hiding out along the Thai border.

"Tea money"—Bribery, the means of the government in Rangoon (equivalents: "*mordida*" in Mexico, "palm grease" in Texas, anything from a lobbyist in Washington).

U Aung Gyi—Opposition leader, a former brigadier general, who is regarded as a moderate. As a businessman, he has run several teahouses. He was briefly imprisoned by U Sein Lwin.

U Min Ko Naing—Student leader during the 1988 protests, an articulate and street-smart rabble-rouser.

Khun Sa—Leading local warlord up north involved in the drug trade, and the head of the Shan United Army.

Sangha—Buddhist monastic system (Buddhist monks are highly regarded in Burma).

U—Title for respected elders ("uncle"). Burma's U Thant was the UN secretary general.

Daw—"Royal" or "royalty"; as a term of address, it can indicate a person held in high esteem.

Maung—Title for a younger man (equivalent of "mister").

Kala—"Foreigner" (a pejorative for the British and Indians).

Political Trend Chart

Burma

The numbers are good only if a popular democracy succeeds in taking power.

	1990 (Military Authoritarian)	1996 (Representative Democracy)
Government Effectiveness	3	1
Government Stability	3	2
Political Cohesion	1	3
Repression Level	7	6
Economic Development	1	2+
Education Status*	4	5

NOTE: 0 = minimum; 9 = maximum.
*Urban population only.

Participant Strategies and Goals

Ne Win Burmese military—Their aim is to retain power, either through direct control or through police and corruption control.

Burmese democracy movements—These are trying to establish a representative democracy and revive the economy.

Drug warriors—Always after lucre, they continue to play the indigenous peoples off the central government and the Laotians off the Thais and the Burmese (etc.). They also continue to pay off the Thai and Burmese armies and supply the West with heroin.

Indigenous ethnic guerrilla groups—These want to wear down the central Burmese government until autonomy is granted.

DEA—The DEA continually pesters the Burmese and Thai governments to go after the big drug smugglers. The strategy, as in South America, is to attempt to dry up narcotics production sources.

India—The Indians are watching the Chinese through the Burmese lens, and helping the central government (whoever it may be) keep the Naga under control.

REGIONAL POWERS AND POWER INTEREST INDICATOR CHART

BURMA

Burma travels in India's orbit, although India tries to distance itself from the increasingly messy Burmese situation.

	Economic Interests	Historical Interests	Political Interest	Military Interest	Force Generation Potential	Ability to Intervene Politically	Ability to Promote Economic Development
China	2	5	6	6	8	8	1
India	4	7	8	7	7	9	2
Vietnam	0	1	4	2	1	1	0
U.S.	2	2	5*	4	4	4	4†
Japan	5	3	4	2	1	7	6‡
ASEAN	5	5	7	5	1	4	3

NOTE: 0 = minimum; 9 = maximum.

*U.S. political interest fluctuates with U.S. interest in the "drug war."

†U.S. development aid in 1987 was only $15 million.

‡Japanese 1986 economic aid was $245 million but plunged 1988 to around $30 million. It was a not-so-subtle attempt to urge Ne Win into political reform.

China—The Chinese are returning the favor to India.

Japan—The Japanese are encouraging the democratic movement so then they can offer aid once it is in power which could be a big success for yen diplomacy and improve Japan's international political standing. The Japanese aren't as soundly disliked in Burma as they are elsewhere in Asia; after all, Japan helped get rid of the British, and the Burmese remember.

POTENTIAL OUTCOMES

"The War for Democracy"

1. 55 percent chance through 1996: The New League for Democracy eventually assumes control of the government, but the control is weak, especially in the outlying areas. The division commanders in ethnic states essentially become local warlords (see p. 408—the government effectiveness rating is very weak).

2. 25 percent chance through 1996: Ne Win's clan retains power by hook, crook, and secret police. The NLD leaders are back in jail.

3. 10 percent chance through 1996: An intra-Burmese Army rebellion sparks long-term civil war. Ethnic states are effectively separate nations—Burma essentially splits into a Mandalay-centered state and a Rangoon-centered state. There may be possible intervention by United Nations forces or the Indian Army.

4. 5 percent chance through 1996: An authoritarian "people's government" emerges from the anti–Ne Win elements in the Army. Look for "friends" in Beijing.

5. 5 percent chance through 1996: The NLD democratic government stabilizes the country. Massive aid from Japan and local initiative turn the economy around. The military focuses on war in Shan State. (Essentially outcome 1, but the government's effectiveness is a "4" or better and stability is a "6." Political cohesiveness improves.)

"The Opium War"

1. 99 + percent chance through 1999: No sweat on this analysis: the same struggle with different players. The drug smugglers fight it out, retreat, or call on their erstwhile political allies.

2. <1 percent chance through 1999: The poppy fields are destroyed and the insatiable U.S. demand for hard drugs abates . . . Now, about that bridge to Brooklyn . . .

"The Teak War"

1. 55 percent chance through 1996: The military pressure on Karen loggers by the Burmese Army (with implicit Thai assistance) is successful. Enter the buzz saws. The hardwoods in Karen State are depleted and the land is ecologically damaged—but rich folks in Japan and the United States have fantastic dinner tables.

2. 20 percent chance through 1996: The international pressure exerted by the United States and Japan and Burma curbs logging. The Japanese act to diminish the market for hardwoods, and as a result, some forest is saved. The killing of Karens by the Burmese Army continues. (If this occurs, there's a 99 percent chance the Burmese government, of any stripe, will trade "ecological protection" for foreign aid.)

3. 10 percent chance through 1996: The New League for Democracy reins in the Burmese Army. The Burmese Army blunts Thai interests. The Karen war dies down, and some forest survives.

4. 10 percent chance through 1996: Civil war in the central Burmese political divisions takes the Burmese Army's mind off of logs and Karens. Forests are saved—for a while.

5. 5 percent chance through 1996: Karen insurgency drives the Burmese Army out of border areas.

Ethnic Insurgencies

Much depends on the kind of government in Rangoon. A democratic regime willing to grant various degrees of autonomy increases the chance of pacification of some groups. Other insurgents, particularly those in Shan State, would perceive the democrats as being far weaker.

Shan State

1. 95 percent chance through 1996: We have virtually no projection here, literally a picture of the present. Same chaos.
2. 5 percent chance through 1996: There is pacification of the ethnic forces *not* involved in the drug trade (by democratic government only).

Karen State

1. 80 percent chance through 1996: Same on-again, off-again struggle.
2. 10 percent chance through 1996: Karen State becomes an autonomous Burmese province (with local rule). There's a 40 percent chance if democratic forces rule in Rangoon.
3. 10 percent chance through 1996: Karen insurgents are militarily defeated; this requires implicit Thai aid to the Burmese Army.

Sino-Indian War with Burma as the Battleground

1. 10 percent chance through 1996: Not a big chance, but potentially a big problem for the Burmese.

COST OF WAR

The low-level insurrections and guerrilla warfare since the late 1940s have killed about a thousand people a year. Some years, like 1989–90, the killings have been higher, while for years at a time the body count has been quite low. The economy has collapsed during the 1980s to the point where deaths from want of food, medicine, and other necessities are causing the death rate to increase. These deaths are as real as those caused by combat. The economic disruption created by the insurrections and corruption also has a cost, amounting to several billion dollars a year and appreciably lowering the per capita income.

WHAT KIND OF WAR

This is classic "low-intensity warfare." No one, including the Burmese Army, can afford heavy or elaborate weapons. Most of the fighting is done in the bush   a war of patrol and ambush by small groups. The few attempts at elaborate operations with large units have generally been disasters. Not a lot of urban combat, yet.

CHAPTER 12

TROUBLE ON THE SUBCONTINENT: INDIA, PAKISTAN, AND SRI LANKA

INTRODUCTION

The ethnic wars in Sri Lanka (formerly Ceylon) have been a microcosm of several similar conflicts troubling neighboring India. To make matters even more dicey, the Indian subcontinent, with nuclear arms stashed in the saber-rattling states of India and Pakistan, is one of the more likely sites for the next use of nuclear weapons. India has had nuclear weapons since the 1970s, and if Pakistan doesn't have them as of late 1990, then trust that Islamabad is but a few short steps from assembling its own. A constant state of tension between these two regional powers, the atomic weapons, and the exacerbating ethnic turmoil make the area a potential post–Cold War, thermonuclear combat zone.

Sri Lanka was one of four nations created when Britain's Indian empire was granted independence in 1947. Burma too was one of the newly independent states (see chapter 11). Another was Muslim Pakistan, separated by Hindu India into East and West Pakistan. The 1971 Indo-Pakistani War broke the ungainly arrangement into the current states of Pakistan and Bangladesh.

India itself is less a nation and more a teeming continent of many different ethnic states that somehow find themselves united as the world's largest functioning, though creaky, democracy. All four parts of the former British Indian territories have continued to suffer discord because of their complex ethnic and religious makeups.

SOURCE OF CONFLICT

Sri Lanka has long been considered a paradise. The climate is mild and the land fruitful. The native Sinhalese people have been peaceful Buddhists for many centuries. When European ships sailed into the area four hundred years ago, it was not long before Sri Lanka fell under British control. Not satisfied with the casual work habits of the Sri Lankans, the British imported more eager workers from the nearby Indian province of Tamil Nadu, who were Hindus. There had always been a Tamil minority on the island, but this new policy made it larger. When Britain left in 1947, the Tamils were a substantial minority (over 10 percent). While the Sri Lankans owned most of the land and industry, the more ambitious Tamils had been trained by the British to assume civil service jobs; in turn, the Tamils sought higher education and professional training. This did not cause extraordinary anxiety among the Sinhalese, but eventually each group began to resent the other's advantages, and armed unrest followed.

While India is a relatively isolated subcontinent, shielded by oceans, mountains, and jungles on most of its periphery, there is one primary gateway for invaders. This open door is in the northwest, where Asiatic and Aryan tribes have been constantly riding in through the centuries. It's also been a two-way street, as most European languages can trace their roots back to "Indo-European"—a "theoretical language" constructed by philologists that suggests the common roots of most of the languages found in the vast area running from India to Iceland.

The subcontinent has had long periods of unity over the centuries, but only as long as the current emperor could hold the numerous ethnic groups together through a combination of military power and skillful diplomacy.

The simplest facts illustrate the polyglot culture: Contemporary India has sixteen major languages and hundreds of minor ones. The major language, Hindi, is spoken, or understood, by about half the population. English, a colonial "leftover" from the years of British domination, is spoken or at least partially understood by 15 to 25 percent of the population, particularly the commercial, administrative, and educated classes. English, to pun, serves India's interior commerce as a lingua franca.

This subcontinent English has now developed into a unique Indian dialect. Interestingly, English has become one of the elements that holds India together. There is an ethnic plus: As a language not native to India, its use does not displace one local language in favor of another. Yet English also carries a political downside: English is the language of the (sometimes) despised former rulers.

Many elements divide India's numerous peoples. Not only do the thirty-one states and territories possess different languages and customs, but many of their inhabitants practice different religions and prefer to wear distinctly different clothing that emphasizes their cultural heritages. Yes, in India, wearing turbans can cause trouble, because of what a turban can signify.

Unfortunately, religion is one of the most divisive elements in the region. Most people are Hindu, but the next largest group is Muslim. Islam came to India at sword point as several waves of Muslim invaders swept across the Indus River in the northwest. The last major incursion, by central Asian tribes under Babur in the sixteenth century, established the Mogul empire. Islam ruled across northern India.

Hinduism is a native Indian religion which developed over a thousand years before Christianity. Buddhism began 2,500 years ago as a "Protestant" form of Hinduism. These two religions still hold the devotion of over 80 percent of the people living in India. But 11 percent are Muslim, 3 percent Christian, and over 2 percent Sikh. In India, like in China, small percentages add up. That's why "over 2 percent" of 800 million people adds up to about 18 million Sikhs. That's three times the population of the nation of Austria.

Pakistan and Bangladesh are both over 90 percent Muslim, and Sri Lanka is 70 percent Buddhist.

As for political rules of thumb, on the subcontinent the Christians tend to keep their collective heads down, and the Buddhists generally practice pacifism, with a few noteworthy exceptions. Hindus, Muslims, and Sikhs, however, have had a long tradition of conflict. The violent interaction of these religions creates the sparks that set off bloody and sustained confrontations.

Despite the normal desire to get along and get on with their lives, there are several reasons why violence flares up between Muslims and Hindus. First, there are the obvious differences in religious practice. Hinduism is the ancient religion of India that worships an array of gods (or the different "forms of God"). Islam is a much more recent phenomenon (seventh century, A.D.), and as a Semitic monotheism, counts Jesus and Moses among its prophets (see chapter 3 for more on the subtleties of Islam).

Because the Muslims who entered India were conquerors (another lingering historical sore point), they took over many Hindu holy places and adapted them for their own use. The Hindus never forget this, and both sides are willing to fight to the death over disputed religious sites. And there is one other exacerbating trouble: Although Muslims within India are loyal citizens, India's chief rival in the area is Muslim Pakistan, and this creates yet another flash point between the two communities.

WHO'S INVOLVED

Sri Lanka: Hell in Paradise

Tamil Nadu (formerly Madras)—A large province in southeastern India, Tamil Nadu contains over fifty million Tamils, who are ethnically the same as the Tamils in Sri Lanka.

Sinhalese—The native people of Sri Lanka are Sinhalese. Not much different in appearance from the Tamils, they practice Buddhism rather than Hinduism and consider themselves the only true inhabitants of Sri Lanka.

Tamils—Through the twentieth century, the British colonial government recruited Tamil Nadu workers for their plantations on Sri Lanka (Ceylon). The Tamils maintained their ethnic identity, living apart from the native Sinhalese.

Tamil Tigers (also Liberation Tigers of Tamil Eelam)—This terrorist organization is dedicated to the creation of an independent Tamil state (Tamil Eelam) in Sri Lanka.

People's Liberation Front (JVP)—A Sinhalese Marxist revolutionary government, the JVP staged an unsuccessful rebellion against the Marxist (but not Marxist enough, or pro-Sinhalese enough) Sri Lankan government. The JVP, legalized in 1977 but outlawed again in 1983, is nearly as bloody-minded as the Tamil Tigers.

Sri Lankan Army—Sri Lanka never had much of a military tradition, so its postcolonial Army was not very effective. The Army tends to act in an undisciplined and heavy-handed way against the Tamils, provoking similar terror from the Tamil Tigers.

The Indian Internal Situation and the Indo-Pakistani Conflict

Hindus—This group constitutes over 80 percent of India's population, nearly a third of which speak Hindi or Urdu, the principal languages of

India. The Hindu religion is probably the strongest unifying force in the country. Ironically enough, religious intolerance among many Hindus is also what is pulling the nation apart.

Indo-Aryans—These are the northern Indians of light complexion. While race is not as important a matter as religion is in India, it still plays a role and the Indo-Aryans tend to keep their distance from the darker-skinned Dravidians.

Dravidians—These are the darker-skinned inhabitants of southern India. Descended from the original (thousands of years ago) inhabitants of India, they were gradually pushed south by the waves of lighter-skinned Aryan invaders coming across the Indus River.

Upper castes—The caste system, originally part of the Hindu religion, is technically outlawed, but in practice it still survives. The caste you were born into is usually the one you stay in. The upper three castes comprise about 150 million people (the lowest castes comprise about the same number—everyone else is in between). Not surprisingly, the vast majority of the wealthy and educated people belong to these three castes, whether or not they take advantage of the caste system. The high-caste people also tend to have lighter complexions, further stirring up social animosities.

Untouchables—Technically, this is one of the lowest (if not the lowest) castes, which comprises about 15 percent of the population. These are people who do the most unappealing work having to do with blood, dead bodies, and excrement, which is a religious thing having to do with "purity" (nearly every religion has some variation on this). It's still taken seriously, even by those who are not particularly religious. The lower-caste people are, literally, untouchable or worse by upper-caste people. For example, if the shadow of a lower-caste person falls on the food a higher-caste person is eating, that food becomes "unclean" and cannot be eaten. Many laws have been passed to liberate the lower castes (and the majority not belonging to the upper castes) from ancient bias and discrimination, but naturally these laws have not been nearly as effective as people hoped. The lower castes in general, and the Untouchables in particular, are a constant source of (quite justified) agitation for social justice. Just one more vexing problem for India's leaders to contend with.

Indian middle class—Taken as a whole, India has an enormous economy, and about 100 million people operate the bulk of it and reap most of its benefits. The middle class, a recent phenomenon, is one powerful group that has something of a national outlook and an already apparent impact on international trade. These people tend to be the English-speaking opinion leaders, who have a strong vested interest in the economic and political well-being of India.

Indian Army—India has long had a strong military tradition. Hindus have a caste for soldiers and the profession is seen as a respectable one. On top of this was laid the British military tradition, which stressed a high degree of professionalism and technical proficiency. The relatively low military spending per soldier, the warrior tradition of the Indians, and the professional attitudes taken over from the British have produced a rather efficient Army at relatively low cost. Another adopted British tradition is officer reluctance to get involved with politics. This has made the military a stabilizing force in the country without the threat of the generals taking over the government. The downside of this is that the military doesn't really feel comfortable (or capable) when called upon to deal with cases of civil unrest. The troops tend to be heavy-handed in such political situations, making matters worse rather than better. Also, the military is another of the national institutions that manages to blend the major ethnic groups in an effective and nonviolent fashion. The Indian Army fields several first-rate divisions that troop for troop are the equal of any other power around the globe.

Indian government bureaucracy—Originally modeled after the efficient British bureaucracy, the Indian version soon became immobilized by politics. Unlike the military, the civil service quickly became corrupted by political patronage and, to a lesser extent, graft. Part of this was due to a typical Third World condition: low civil service salaries. Worst of all, the bureaucracy became obstructionist and self-serving. Nationalist and socialist attitudes encouraged growth in the bureaucracy as a means of exerting better control over the economy which had the result of crippling the economy with reams of red tape. Even bureaucrats with good intentions were hobbled by the huge amounts of regulation and administration. In the 1980s, the harmful effects of this civil service finally were widely recognized. Efforts to reverse the ill effects of the bureaucracy have not been strikingly successful: Over ten million civil servants are a political, economic, and social force to be recognized.

Muslims—There are 300 million Muslims in this region. The largest number, some 110 million, are in Pakistan, with another 95 million in Bangladesh. Despite the millions of Muslims who fled from India to neighboring Islamic areas, 11 percent (90 million) of the population of India is still Muslim. This will add up to nearly 100 million Muslims by the end of the century. Already, India is one of the largest Muslim nations in the world. But the Indian Muslims exist in "a sea of Hindus" (their words). Although most of the Muslims are in northern India, a large number of Muslims are still found dispersed throughout the nation, with the largest clumps normally being all-Muslim villages near cities or all-Muslim ghettolike neighborhoods in urban areas.

Sikhs—Sikhism is a religion founded in the 1400s as something of a cross between Islam and Hinduism. It eliminates the caste system and promotes individual effort and fierce defense of the religion. Every Sikh is considered a warrior, and the common name each male assumes ("*singh*") means "lion." Thus you have a very macho and unified group—and you know what that usually means. As a consequence, the Sikhs eventually (in the early 1800s) controlled the northwestern Indian province of Punjab, where Sikhism first developed. Their discipline and military prowess made them popular with British administrators and generals. There are only about 18 million Sikhs, most of whom are in Punjab (where they are a majority). They have been successful in commerce (another form of warfare to many Sikhs) and the professions and are found throughout India.

Kashmir and Kashmiris—India's two thirds of the old state is called the "State of Jammu and Kashmir." Pakistan refers to its portion of Kashmir as "Azad Kashmir," or "Independent (or Free) Kashmir." Indians call the Pakistani third "Pak-Occupied Kashmir." The State of Jammu and Kashmir is an Indian province on the Pakistani border, with the state capital in Srinagar. It is the only state in India with a Muslim majority (65 percent), most of whom live in the Kashmir valley. Many Buddhists live in the Ladakh region (the northeastern quarter). In 1947 Jammu and Kashmir became part of India, rather than of Pakistan, because of larger political considerations, not due to the desires of the population. The political consideration? Pakistan's abortive invasion in 1948, launched after Indian troops moved into Kashmir to suppress a Muslim-led revolt against the local (Hindu) maharaja. When India gained its independence in 1947, those provinces ruled by Indian nobles (and controlled by the British) had the option to remain independent or, if they were in an area between Hindu and Muslim regions, to go with one nation or the other. Once the Indians were in control, they did not allow any of the nobles to stay in power. Most of the aristocrats complied when they got the word, but a few required the threat or use of military force. One special case was Kashmir, a wealthy province between Pakistan and India, whose population was (and still is) mostly Muslim, with a sizable

Hindu minority in the eastern Jammu region. The maharaja was Hindu, and he thought he could get away with the independence option. It didn't work. Islamic irregular troops started moving in from Pakistan, Indian troops entered next, then regular Pakistani troops followed. The war was brief, and most of Kashmir became Indian, complete with its Muslim majority. Pakistan has been attempting to rectify the situation ever since. The fight left a jagged cease-fire line cutting the province, and has sparked two more wars. Interestingly, the leader of the 1940s Muslim guerrilla force was Muhammad Abdul Qayyum Khan, who in 1990 was the president of Pakistani Kashmir. The Jammu and Kashmir Liberation Front is the largely Muslim organization that creates most of the local mayhem. The Indian National Conference party, which is an arm of the Congress party, has many Muslims in its hierarchy.

Border tribes and border states—India is a triangle with two sides bordering on ocean. But the third side is covered with a jumble of ethnic groups that are antagonistic with India for one reason or another. Starting in the west there is Pakistan, which is fully covered elsewhere in this chapter. Next there are the Chinese forces in Chinese-occupied Tibet, where there is an ongoing border dispute. Next there is Nepal, over whom India exercises considerable influence and with whom India has always had uncomfortable relations. To the east of Bangladesh lies a large territory (connected to India by only a thin strip of territory north of Bangladesh) populated by a mélange of tribes, and boasting India's only domestic source of oil. For years these tribes lived in relative isolation from one another and from the teeming Indian populations to the west. But since World War II, population pressures in India have sent millions of Indians (23 million now) into these sparsely populated territories in search of living space. The tribes were not happy with this, and the warfare resulting, while low-level, has been persistent and intractable. Some of the rebellions were settled (or at least died down) in the late 1980s. But the largest movements, in Assam and Nagaland, grow larger. These groups use bases in Burma and Bangladesh.

Pakistan—Although poverty-stricken and rent with ethnic strife, Pakistan is one of the largest, and possibly the strongest, Muslim nations in the world. It is the one Muslim nation closest to having nuclear weapons; in fact, it may already have them. The peoples occupying Pakistan have, over the ages, periodically invaded—and often conquered—India. There are several current border disputes and no love lost between the two nations.

Pakistani tribes—Pakistan is largely populated by Punjabis. But these make up only two thirds of the population. Other major groups are Sinds (13 percent, related to Punjabis), Pathans (9 percent, the major group in Afghanistan and related to the Iranians), Urdu speakers (8 percent, speaking a Hindi dialect), Baluchis (3 percent), and a few others. The Baluchis are the biggest problem, as these people, scattered across three nations (including Iran and Afghanistan), do not have their own country and would like one. The other groups are less of a problem as they have some place to go to.

Other Players in the Region

Russia—After the Indian border war with China in the 1960s, India became quite cozy with Russia. All this can be considered just good power politics. Russia and China had nuclear weapons in the 1960s, India did not. Russia's relations with China were strained, and Russia was willing to sell inexpensive, but fairly modern weapons to India. Getting close to Russia increased India's stature among Third World nations (at least until Afghanistan). And so on. As a consequence, China is the friend of Pakistan (which has a rather cool relationship with Russia). Russia's invasion of Afghanistan further alienated the Pakistanis, as Islamabad saw the potential of an "Indo-Soviet Pincer" attacking Pakistan. Russia's defeat in and current retreat from Afghanistan have somewhat mitigated that strategic threat. Still, Russia did seize and officially incorporate the Wakhann Corridor (the strip linking Afghanistan to China) into the Soviet Union. Unless the Russians officially withdraw, that means Russia now abuts the subcontinent's nest of troubles.

China—In the 1950s China occupied Tibet (as it had done so many times in the past centuries). A vaguely drawn border in the mountain wilderness separating China and India became the subject of a dispute which escalated to combat. The Indians lost and became quite upset about this. Since the 1960s, diplomatic relations between the two countries have been relatively frosty, with Pakistan, in turn, having become an ally of China, who through the 1970s was Pakistan's major arms supplier. China's official line is that Kashmir is "a bilateral" Indian and Pakistani problem (although China also occupies a portion of "Greater Kashmir"). China, however, still continues to supply Pakistan with political support and considerable cheap but reliable arms, and is always "a threat to move" on India.

United States—Despite the area's need for economic aid from the United States, a number of local conditions have caused Washington to maintain a low profile in the region since World War II. India's alignment with Russia in the 1960s, and India's desire to be regarded as the leader of the Third World nations, created an antagonistic attitude toward the United States. Until the Russian invasion of Afghanistan in 1979, Pakistan had been generally lukewarm toward the United States because of America's support for Israel. As a major Muslim nation, Pakistan could not be seen as too close to Israel's biggest ally. Yet in the 1971 Indo-Pakistani War the United States tilted toward Pakistan and sent a carrier-led task force into the area.

Afghanistan—Although not technically a part of the region, the Russian invasion of Afghanistan put India in an embarrassing position and enabled Pakistan to assume a closer relationship with the United States. Most U.S. aid for the Afghan resistance was funneled through Pakistan, where the Pakistanis took a large cut off the top. In addition, Pakistan received substantial military and economic aid for itself. Most aid for the millions of Afghan refugees who fled to Pakistan came from the United States. With Russia now out of Afghanistan, Pakistan continues to maintain good relations with the United States. This is not unwelcome to Pakistan, as it always looked to the United States for support against India. The United States is usually reluctant to give support but, under the current circumstances, may have a hard time avoiding involvement.

Britain—Britain continues to maintain good diplomatic and commercial ties with its former colonies in the region. The former colonies tend to regard Britain's several centuries of occupation more favorably than most of its other former colonies do. The colonial period was one of relative peace and prosperity and also laid the foundations for current national institutions. Before Britain arrived, the political situation had been much more unsettled and violent.

Burma—Long a sleepy little area, with several organized states on the coast and many intractable tribes inland, Burma was taken over by the British in the 1800s and given its current borders and ethnic makeup. As arguably the world's largest producer and exporter of opium and other drugs, Burma has done more damage to the United States than any other nation in the region. After independence in 1948, Burma chose socialism, which ruined an already weak economy. The drug lords in the mountains thus became the largest economic force in the nation and an invulnerable political one as well. The situation within Burma continues to fester and become more unstable. The Naga tribe's long-running rebellion in India has a sideshow in Burma (see chapter 11).

Geography

Given all India's other complexities, its geography is relatively simple. Most of India is a 2,000- to 3,000-foot plateau, with lower coastal areas, plus the large river valleys of the Indus (in Pakistan) and Ganges rivers (on the east coast). In the north the landscape rapidly goes uphill into the Himalayan Mountains. Most of the continent is well-watered, particularly in the west and in a narrow band along the east coast. The northwest is the driest area.

The climate, except in the far north and in the Himalayas, is generally warm year round. Most Indians have never seen, or rarely see, snow and

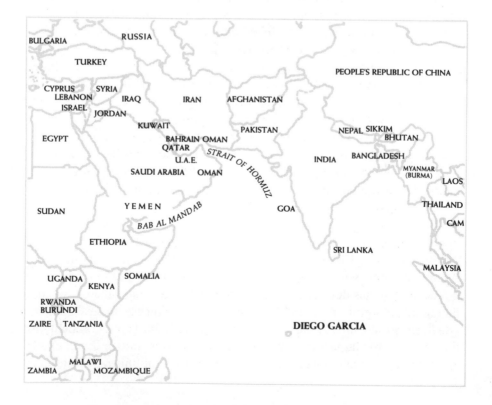

ice. The northwest, for several hundred miles east and south of New Delhi, is hot and dry, an extension of the hot, dry region that causes the Saharan, Saudi Arabian, Iranian, and Pakistani desert areas. To the south and west, the climate actually improves in many respects.

Most of the land is suitable for farming, with intensive rice farming predominant along the coasts (and into the upland plateau). Wheat and similar crops are grown in the north. In the northwest, particularly along the Pakistan border, the land is drier and more primitive agriculture and grazing are predominant. In the far south, and in much of Sri Lanka, large-scale plantation farming is common.

The population is dense everywhere, but particularly in the rice-farming and river valley areas. This is because India is the southernmost recipient of the huge quantities of moisture that blow in off the Pacific on to the east coast of Asia (from Korea southwest to Sri Lanka). As a consequence, the huge eastern coast of Asia is better supplied with water than the eastern part of the United States. This enables intensive agriculture to flourish in this largely tropical and semitropical area. The result has been a degree of intensive (although relatively unmechanized) farming that supports over half the world's population, including India.

Language is also an important aspect of the geography. There are three major language groups in the area: Indic (Indo-European), Dravidian, and Asiatic (Oriental). The Indic group is the source of most European languages. The principal one in India is Hindi (and a closely related dialect, Urdu), which is spoken across northern India, east of the Indus River valley. A quarter of India's population speaks Hindi, and the majority at least understands it now due to the showing of Hindu-language movies on TV throughout the nation. Those in the Indus River valley, and much of Pakistan, speak other Indic languages, such as Punjabi and several other related tongues. Due south of Pakistan, Rajasthani is widely spoken. In the east, Bengali, a close relative of Hindi, is spoken (largely in Bangladesh). Another similar tongue, Marathi, is spoken across much of central India. Nepali is spoken in Nepal, and a half dozen other related languages are spoken across northern India. Sinhalese (an Indic language) is spoken only in Sri Lanka.

People in the western portions of Pakistan speak a number of Indo-European languages related to Farsi (or Persian, the language of Iran), chief among which are Pashto (the language of the Pathans of Afghanistan) and Baluchi.

Southern India speaks a non–Indo-European language: Dravidian (the original language of India before the Indo-Europeans arrived). This is actually a number of separate languages, the principal ones being Telugu (in central India along the east coast), Tamil (in the far south and Sri Lanka), Kanarese (in south central India), Malayalam (on the southwest coast), and several other variants.

Various Asian languages are spoken along the northern border and in scattered interior areas (invaders and colonists who retained their language and customs). The principal one is Sino-Tibetan, the language of Tibet that is similar to Chinese (see chapter 11).

HISTORY

The Indian subcontinent is one of the world's original cradles of civilization, along with China, Egypt, and the Tigris-Euphrates rivers area. Highly organized communities developed there over five thousand years ago, most notably in the Indus River valley region.

For centuries, invaders from the Asian plains rode across the Indus River into northern India. The first of these were Aryan (Caucasian) nomads, who came across the Indus River 3,500 years ago. These Sanskrit-speaking peoples pushed the original inhabitants of India (the Dravidians) south, except for Sri Lanka, where northern Indians settled and excluded Dravidians. The Sanskrit-speaking Aryans merged with Dravidians in the north to form the classic Indian civilization. Until the last century or so, there were few Indians east of modern Bangladesh. Burma long served as the border between Indo-European and Oriental peoples, with a small number of tribal peoples and the Arakan mountains as buffers.

The first major Islamic invasion occurred in the 1200s. Modern Indian history begins with the arrival of the central Asian (and Muslim) Moguls in the sixteenth century and the first seaborne European traders a century later. Eventually, the British supplanted the Portuguese and French in the eighteenth century and gradually brought the entire subcontinent under a single colonial control in the early nineteenth century.

The Mogul Empire controlled India by the simple expedient of seizing and garrisoning the major population centers. Most of the population lived, then as now, in the countryside and were often ignorant of any new conqueror. The Moguls collected taxes, built monuments to themselves, and generally lived it up. They wore themselves out trying to extend their conquests to the south of India (ruled by another set of Muslim overlords). By the eighteenth century, the Muslim ruling class was suitably weakened, which made European inroads that much easier. The Moguls' lasting contribution to the future was to leave millions of Muslims scattered across northern, and predominantly Hindu, India.

The British conquest of India was not a strictly military venture; in fact, the British influence was largely economic and diplomatic, with Her Majesty's soldiers being something of a fragile extrapolitical "spine." From the earliest European encounters with India, the overriding motive was profit, not plunder or empire. Indeed, until the mid-nineteenth century, most of British-controlled India was run by commercial enterprises. Accountants had more say than soldiers, as British diplomacy almost invariably had an immediate economic underpinning. As a result of this approach, there was comparatively little violence in Britain's "conquest" of India. (It was more a leveraged buyout than a hostile takeover.)

The British also knew how to play one rival Indian ethno-religious group or "ministate" off against another. Britain's gradual conquest of India was greatly facilitated by the extensive fragmentation of the area into scores of political entities. Britain's initial involvement was often to assist one faction against another. Local customs and sensibilities were generally respected when the British administration took over, and in half the country areas, local nobles were left in control. All Britain wanted was "to keep the peace" (which meant a stable status quo) and facilitate commerce. Most Indians were quite content with this and many served in the British civil service and Army. The majority of the Indian population had little exposure to the British, except to enjoy the lack of invading armies or the local feuds between nobles.

The British also built up a commercial and transportation infrastructure (roads and railroads) that still benefits modern India. Yet the British were almost invariably overbearing, wrongheaded, and outright racist in their colonial administration of India. Many Indians feel the British needlessly involved the Indian Army in the United Kingdom's European conflicts (i.e., World War I and World War II). Memories and contentions such as these have produced a case of lingering friction between India and Great Britain. After all, the British were just another foreign conqueror, although they had the good grace to depart when the imperial era was over and, unlike the Muslim invaders, did not leave a large minority behind.

By the twentieth century, educated Indians began to agitate for independence. The original British conquest of the country was a haphazard affair and increasingly a relic of a past age. Eventually, the British saw the handwriting on the wall and, in the face of a well-organized and supposedly nonviolent revolution, turned control of India over to the Indians in 1947. Lord Louis Mountbatten orchestrated a British withdrawal. There would be two Indian nation-states, one primarily Muslim and the larger Hindu.

That's when the wars began once more.

Warfare has been a constant presence in the region since World War II, but deaths have been relatively low. On a per capita basis, there have been fewer war-related deaths in the Indian region since World War II than in any other region.

India and Pakistan have fought three wars to date, minor ones in 1948 and 1965, and a major one in 1971 which resulted in the loss of Pakistan's eastern portion which became the nation of Bangladesh. Serious disagreements remain between Pakistan and India over who will control the Indian state of Kashmir (which is largely Muslim).

In 1974, India exploded a nuclear weapon. India's nuclear arsenal has probably grown since then even though no further nuclear explosions have been detected. Pakistan has redoubled its own efforts to manufacture nuclear weapons and will probably have several by the early part of the 1990s.

Normally, a war between India and Pakistan is a pretty uneven contest, with India the likely winner. Pakistan's first-line forces, however, are excellent, and a short, minor war is a more even affair. India's huge arms buildup in the late 1980s may have shifted the power balance so strongly in India's favor that New Delhi would most certainly prevail in a long, major conventional war. When both sides have nuclear weapons and become locked into a desperate border battle, however, nuclear warfare looms likely—especially if one side (Pakistan?) begins to feel hard-pressed. It looks as if even more bitter, brutal, and destructive Indo-Pakistani wars are in the offing, with Jammu and Kashmir as the most likely trigger point.

India also has a long-running conflict with another regional power, and one that is definitely nuclear: China. In 1962, a dispute over a Chinese-built road running through a slice of territory claimed by India set off a series of border clashes between the Chinese and Indian armies. China attacked Indian positions in Arunachal Pradesh (northeastern India, near the Burmese border) and also seized some territory in the Ladakh region of Kashmir near the Kongka Pass. After a month of combat, China won its objectives and declared a unilateral cease-fire.

In 1967, the Sino-Indian conflict erupted once again, this time in the Nathu La Pass on the Sikkim-Tibetan border. In 1986, India accused China of sending troops into Indian valleys in Arunachal Pradesh.

LOCAL POLITICS

India

Ethnicity pervades Indian politics, further complicated by the Hindu religious caste and social classes. With the ethnic mix in India, that makes for an extremely complex series of internal political arrangements. While there are pressing economic and social welfare issues, these all take second place to the increasingly violent ethnic troubles. Going into infinite detail over the various ethnic political parties (and the subgroups of the Congress party) would miss the grand scope, so this section will address India's local politics in a more general manner.

Congress party (also Congress "I" party—the "I" standing for Indira, as in Indira Gandhi)—Politically, the party dominating India's democracy since independence. This is the party that grew out of the nonviolent independence activities of Mahatma Gandhi, the spiritual father of modern India and a heroic individual by any standard. Acutely aware of India's volatile ethnic mix, Gandhi strove to persuade people to overcome it. But his efforts failed, as nearly a million Muslims and Hindus died in an orgy of ethnic violence. Twelve million people fled their homes to reach sanctuary in areas occupied by a majority of their kinsmen.

The Congress party grew fat, lazy, and corrupt as dominant parties tend to do. First Jawaharlal Nehru, then his daughter, Indira Gandhi, in 1966, and finally his grandson, Rajiv Gandhi, in 1984, were elected to head the government and the Congress party. This forty-year dynasty kept the nation together and put out a lot of domestic and diplomatic fires. But the Nehru dynasty also created a lot of political baggage that India now has to drag behind it. For one thing, the monolithic rule of the Congress party created a lot of corruption and inertia in the government. Even though Rajiv was voted out of office in 1989, it was by what is essentially another branch of the Congress party.

Despite V. P. (Viswanath Pratrap) Singh's victory over Rajiv Gandhi, there is still no comparative national opposition power of any note. In 1969 the Congress party split into New Congress and Old Congress parties. Indira Gandhi led the New Congress party to victory. Subsequent moves to maintain her new position led to decisions that stirred up too many voters and got Indira voted out of office in 1977. Her opponents were even less able to consolidate their power and Indira was voted back into office in 1980. She was assassinated by Sikh extremists in 1984 and succeeded by her son, Rajiv. Many Indians expected Rajiv, a member of the post–World War II generation, to shake free of the old ward-heeling politics of the past. He tried, but had little success. V. P. Singh, who defeated him in the 1989 election, essentially forged a coalition (the National Front) whose sole source of unity was to defeat Rajiv Gandhi. Many members of the National Front are closely associated with the Congress party, including Singh, who was Gandhi's finance minister until resigning in 1987. Singh played a dangerous game when he stirred up expectations among various ethnic and caste groups in order to get their support, and the subsequent riots over ethnic and caste policies were a direct result of Singh's political maneuvering to get Rajiv Gandhi out of office. It cost him. Singh fell and subsequent coalitions are shaky.

In India, most of the significant opposition to the central government comes from the different states (which are generally dominated by one ethnic group or another). In other words, it's individual ethnic groups against the national government—not a very healthy situation for a nation made up of so many distinct ethnic groups occupying their own separate states. The Congress party has maintained its hold on power and national unity by using its vast patronage power to dole out jobs and favors to key people in the thirty-one states and territories. Jobs are given out to maximize their political effect, not to obtain the greatest efficiency. Rajiv quickly learned what his mother and grandfather knew well: You cannot afford to upset the balance of power in too many of the states and territories. While ethnic and religious riots might make the headlines, loss of support among local politicians can get you voted out of office. The Dravida Munnetra Kazgham (DMK) party in the southern state of Tamil Nadu (near Sri Lanka) is an example of an ethnic, state-based party. The DMK has participated in the National Front coalition. The Akali Dal (also the United Akali Dal) is a Sikh party confined to Punjab. V. P. Singh's Janata Dal operates in several states, but is a ragtag collection of local parties.

Ethnic groups, caste, and the "language factor"—Significant elements of ethnicity looming large in Indian politics. People will eventually vote for and against economic measures, but they can be quickly stirred up by religious and ethnic issues raised by local opportunists. A case in point is the status of religious sites that originally were Hindu but were later usurped by Muslim invaders. It doesn't take much for a local Hindu politician to make an issue of one of these holy places and the national government expects the local politicians to take the heat. If the local Congress party leaders can't, or won't, handle the issue, the voters will momentarily be lost to the Congress party. A guerrilla group based in central and southern India, the People's War Group, claims to wage war for the lower castes. This group has attacked trains and local officials.

While raising religious issues is most popular in the north, where most of the Muslims are, throughout most of non-Hindi India the topic of Hindi cultural domination is a surefire way of turning a crowd into a raging mob (or at least changing their votes). North central India is the heart of the nation, where much of the population resides, and is largely a Hindi-speaking area.

Language is another explosive issue. In 1947, it was thought that English would be an ideal national language for government and commercial affairs. Most senior officials already spoke English, which was a popular second language among many educated people (who made up no more than 10 to 20 percent of the population, depending on how you define education). Most Indians spoke only one language and lived their entire lives within the confines of the village they were born in. But many Indians, particularly those working in retail trade, and especially those in areas where more than one language group lived, spoke more than one language.

The Hindi speakers soon began to push the use of Hindi as the national language, arguing that it was an Indian language, related to the various languages spoken by 70 percent of the population (most of the remainder spoke Dravidic languages). The Hindi speakers were able to have Hindi made the "official" language with English the "associate official" language. But this was a costly victory. Emotions were stirred up on the "Hindi Domination" issue and the Congress party suffered a lot of damage for this one. In 1990, Hindi speakers launched yet another drive to make Hindi the national language.

Communist and socialist parties—Other less influential parties in India. India was not immune to the spread of Communist and socialist ideas in the post–World War II era. Although the Indian democracy was set up on the much-admired British model, Britain was also practicing a great deal of socialism after World War II and India picked up on this. Although the Indian Communist party never attracted a large following, there was a desire to "build India" without coming under the economic control of large foreign corporations. What resulted was not so much socialism (as there wasn't a great deal of surplus wealth to "socialize") as strong government guidance of commercial development. In many ways, this worked. Agriculture was supported, which was a significant departure from the practices of other Third World nations. India had a plentiful supply of local entrepreneurs, and the Western-style university system the British had left behind turned out a torrent of well-educated Indians. The Communist party of India (CPI) remains active and is pro-Moscow, whatever that may mean in the 1990s. The Communist party —Marxist (CPM), however, is powerful in the states of West Bengal and Kerala and behaves more like a "state" party. Several small leftist groups and splinter parties advocate the violent overthrow of the New Delhi government.

India as a "Third World common market"—An interesting way to look at India's internal organization (or disorganization, as the case may be) which considers "the Republic of India" as a sort of Third World common market comprising all the parts of India. Hundreds of millions of people operate in one vast economy under more or less one overall "economic government" that sets the pace for thirty-one "local nations." In some ways, if compared to the situation inside India in 1947, the "results" produced by this arrangement look encouraging. Despite a meager 36 percent literacy rate and a steadily growing population, India's economy grew stronger and India began to feed itself. Both of these accomplishments are rare in Third World countries. Note, however, that 64 percent of the population remaining illiterate forms a large pool of people who rely solely on radio and TV (or other forms of mass rumor and hearsay) for their political information and thus may be swayed by whoever controls the radio and TV media. This is especially true with radio, which is accessible to nearly everyone in India; but even television is found in remote areas, and large numbers of people will see important events on those isolated receivers.

By other comparative slide rules, however, the Indian common market has done poorly. In 1950 India accounted for 2 percent of total world exports and 6 percent of exports generated by Third World countries. In 1980 India's share in each category had shrunk to 0.4 percent and 1.4 percent. In 1955 India was the world's tenth-ranked industrial power; in 1975 it ranked twentieth. China, even hobbled by Maoism, produced a 5.2 percent growth in real GNP per person between 1965 and 1987.

India's real per capita GNP growth during the same time frame was 1.8 percent. Why? Because of the New Delhi-led bureaucracy that runs the whole show. Inefficiency percolates through the system. India is an economic "success" partially because it has avoided doing as badly as many experts expected.

Pakistan

Pakistan has serious problems with internal stability. While 60 percent of the population is Sindi (an Indic group speaking a language similar to Hindi), the rest are diverse groups and not happy with Sindi domination. Should the Punjabi, Pathan, Baluchi, and Dravidian minorities get out of hand, the Sindis would end up with only their densely populated home regions along the lower Indus River valley and the Karachi and Islamabad urban areas. To further complicate matters, over 15 percent of the population is Shiite Muslim (the others are main-line Sunni Muslims). The Shiites are the majority in neighboring Iran, which would also not ignore an opportunity to participate in a partitioning of Pakistan. Neighboring Afghanistan, still working out the aftereffects of the Russian invasion of the 1980s, also has claims to that large part of Pakistan occupied by Pathan people. Pakistan is, if anything, inherently more unstable than India, with the same multiplicity of different ethnic groups. Even Indian Muslims who migrated to Pakistan in 1947 have their own small party, the Mohajir Qami Movement, which has a militant wing.

Political party activity was banned during martial law, which was in effect from 1977 to 1985.

Pakistan People's party (PPP)—Party led by President Benazir Bhutto until she was deposed in August 1990. Her father, Zulfiqar Ali Bhutto, was PPP head and elected president in 1971. Then he was deposed by the Army, under Gen. Muhammad Zia-ul-Haq, in 1977 and later hanged. Zia died in 1988 when a plane he was flying in mysteriously crashed and blew apart.

Other parties—National Democratic party (which draws support in North-West Frontier and Baluchistan), Jamaat-i-Islami (conservative religious party), and fifteen other parties active in 1990.

Pakistan Army—The world's seventh largest armed force with its 430,000 ready troops plus reserves.

ISI—Pakistani military intelligence service.

A Quick but Nutritious Subcontinent Political Smorgasbord

The "Agni" ("Fire")—Indian-developed intermediate-range ballistic missile (IRBM) which is nuclear-capable. Weight: 14 tons. Length: 19 meters. Range: in excess of 1,000 kilometers. It consists of SLV-3 solid-fuel booster and, as a second stage, the "Prithvi" battlefield support missile. India may be experimenting with a fuel-air-explosive (FAE) conventional warhead.

"Angrezi hatao!" ("English out!")—Cry of Hindi radicals. Hindi, a Sanskrit-based language, is spoken by 300 million people, but is common only in the northern central states of India.

Azad Kashmir—Pakistan's name for its third of Kashmir.

Jammu and Kashmir Liberation Front (JKLF)—Largest of over twenty-five dissident groups active in Indian Kashmir.

Maulvi Muhammad Farooq—"The Mirwaiz of Kashmir," the hereditary Islamic leader in Kashmir, who was assassinated in May 1990. He had been a force behind Kashmiri separatism since 1964 when he founded the pro-Pakistan Awami Action Committee.

Siachen Glacier—World's highest battlefield, located in Pakistan's Baltistan area only forty kilometers from K-2, the second highest peak in the world. India and Pakistan have been shooting at each other for years in this mountainous area, where walking—much less combat—is difficult. The air is so thin that many troops pass out from lack of oxygen. India occupies the glacier (4,000–5,500 meters in altitude) with one reinforced battalion drawn from its 3rd Mountain Infantry Division (which is equipped with Indian-made snowmobiles). Pakistan has nearly two brigades of infantry, at the more habitable altitudes of 4,000–4,400 meters. Most of the fighting is confined to sporadic artillery duels and some sniping. Although the area has no strategic value, Pakistan's former president Zia-ul-Haq, once said of the Siachen Glacier, "It is of no great value for us but we have to fight for it." Frankly, India may be the aggressor in this area, having apparently violated a boundary agreement that put the cease-fire line at a point drawn from a cairn in the Karakoram Pass east of the glacier—but the boundary seems fuzzy (definitely icy) to begin with. Still, Siachen illustrates some of the "glacial" intractability of the Indo-Pakistani confrontation.

MacMahon Line—Line separating Indian and Chinese forces in the Tibetan border region.

Janata ("people's")—Widely used term in Indian politics.

Bharatiya Janata party—Hindu-based party that has been a coalition member with the Janata Dal.

Committee for Resisting Birth Control—Muslim fundamentalist group active in Bangladesh.

Tamil National Army—Artificially created Tamil Army, organized by departing Indian peacekeeping force in late 1989.

People's Liberation Organization of Tamil Eelam—Political group once associated with the Liberation Tigers of Tamil Eelam. It was one of the first ethnic Tamil armies in Sri Lanka to agree to negotiations in 1987. Some of its former fighters became involved in the aborted Maldives coup of 1988.

Maldive Islands—Island chain in the Indian Ocean south-southwest of India, with a population of around 200,000. This was the scene of an attempted coup in December 1988. Local Maldivians (who may be involved in a drug-smuggling cartel) hired Tamil mercenaries to overthrow President Maumoon Gayoom's government. India intervened with troops and ships and put the coup attempt down within a day.

PARTICIPANT STRATEGIES AND GOALS

India (The Indian Government in New Delhi)

The overriding goal of the Indian government is to maintain itself as the central government of India and the decisive power in the region. Not an easy task. Its strategy to date has been to deal with each local disturbance as it comes along. Internally, most Indians accept the fact that the nation is multilingual, multicultural, and possessed of several different religions. The most dangerous situations have developed, not unnaturally, in border areas.

India has decided to try and become the region's "policeman." Between 1985 and 1989 India bought nearly $18 billion worth of weapons, making it one of the world's leaders, especially in spending on conventional arms. Tanks, artillery, jet aircraft, aircraft carriers, and nuclear subs "leased" (although recently returned) from Russia are included in its weapons mix. Call it Indian gunboat diplomacy. The spending on the Indian Navy gives India the ability to intervene anywhere in the Indian Ocean from Singapore to Madagascar. The December 1988 action in the Maldives demonstrates this policy.

Last, if Russia continues to concentrate on its internal troubles, India may well increase its contacts with Vietnam, as a hedge against China.

POLITICAL TREND CHARTS

INDIA

Actually, India's economy could just as easily drop to a 3 − as it could go up to a 5 −. The key? War with Pakistan.

	1990	1996
		(Authoritarian Democracy)
Government Effectiveness	6	6
Government Stability	6	5
Political Cohesion	5	4
Repression Level	5	6
Economic Development	4	5 −
Education Status*	4	5

NOTE: 0 = minimum; 9 = maximum.
*Urban population only.

PAKISTAN

See the comments on the chart for India.

	1990 (Authoritarian Democracy)	1996 (Military Authoritarian)
Government Effectiveness	5	4
Government Stability	4	3
Political Cohesion	4	4
Repression Level	6	7
Economic Development	3	4 −
Education Status	4	4

NOTE: 0 = minimum; 9 = maximum.

SRI LANKA

Could become another Lebanon if the Tamils are not crushed and foreign support is kept out.

	1990 (Authoritarian Democracy*)	1996 (Military Authoritarian)
Government Effectiveness	3	4
Government Stability	3	5
Political Cohesion	3	5
Repression Level	5	7
Economic Development†	2+	3
Education Status	3	6

NOTE: 0 = minimum; 9 = maximum.
*Sri Lanka has a history of functional representative democracy.
†The economy is already in relative shambles.

For theoretical purposes, since it is unlikely that these states will exist:

"FREE STATE OF PUNJAB"

A viable nation, as are many other Indian regions.

	1996 (Religious Authoritarian*)
Government Effectiveness	4
Government Stability	3
Political Cohesion	6
Repression Level	6
Economic Development	2
Education Status	3

NOTE: 0 = minimum; 9 = maximum.
*What does this mean? There will be elections but this will be a Sikh state where theological considerations call the ultimate shots. The Sikhs, however, are reasonably tolerant of other religions. There may, however, be a great deal of resentment left for the Hindus.

"GREATER KASHMIR"
Another part of India that could exist as a separate nation.

	1996 (Democratic Authoritarian*)
Government Effectiveness	6
Government Stability	6
Political Cohesion	6
Repression Level	7†
Economic Development	4
Education Status	3

NOTE: 0 = minimum; 9 = maximum.
*But with a strong Islamic religious bent.
†Against the remaining Hindus; 3 for everyone else, including Buddhists.

Sri Lanka

Sinhalese government—One doubts that the Sinhalese would have ever started their campaign against the Tamils if they knew they would have gotten out of it as vicious a group of terrorists as the Tamil Tigers. At this point, the Sinhalese have several options:

1. Kill all the Tamils. Unlikely, as they haven't got the means or the stomach for it, nor would world public opinion let them off easily. Besides, the Sinhalese are Buddhists, with an ancient tradition for pacifism.

2. Expel all the Tamils. But no one will have them—even India is in no position to accept 3 million refugees. And while their kinsmen in Tamil Nadu support the Tamils, this support does not extend toward taking all of them back to their ancestral homeland.

3. Partition the country. This is what is happening already, even though radical Sinhalese are inclined to resist this one to the death, Buddhist pacifism notwithstanding.

4. Return to the previolence situation, the "tropical paradise." But hell has been let loose and too many people are now out for revenge or to attain radical solutions to the situation for this option to be likely.

REGIONAL POWERS AND POWER INTEREST INDICATOR CHARTS

INDO-PAKISTANI WAR (AND KASHMIR)

As the Kashmir problem heats up, it is well that the Cold War has subsided, as this is one issue that all the superpowers are connected to.

	Economic Interests	Historical Interests	Political Interest	Military Interest	Force Generation Potential	Ability to Intervene Politically
Pakistan	9	9	9	9	7	0
India	8	9	9	9	8	9
U.S.	4	6	6	6	2	4
China	6	7	8	8	5	4
Russia	1	3	4	3	2	2
Britain	5	7	6	2	1–	3
Japan	5	3	6	1	0	3

NOTE: 0 = minimum; 9 = maximum.

SRI LANKA

Seen primarily as India's problem (as the local superpower). Unless the Tamils start global terrorism (always a possibility), the rest of the world will largely ignore the situation.

	Economic Interests	Historical Interests	Political Interest	Military Interest	Force Generation Potential	Ability to Intervene Politically	Ability to Promote Economic Development
India	7	7	8	7	8	8	8
U.S.	5	4	3	4	5	4	5
Sri Lanka	9	9	9	9	6	8	6
Tamil	9	9	9	9	5	8	5
Pakistan	1	2	7	3	1	3	0

NOTE: 0 = minimum; 9 = maximum.

TIBET AND INDIA-CHINA BORDER

Important to India, China, Pakistan, and, of course, the Tibetans. No one else really sees any significant reason to get involved.

	Economic Interests	Historical Interests	Political Interest	Military Interest	Force Generation Potential	Ability to Intervene Politically	Ability to Promote Economic Development
China	3	5	6	7	7	8	2
India	4	6	7	7	5	5	3
Pakistan	1	5	7	6	2	2	1
U.S.	0	3	4	2	0+	1	2
Russia	1	2	4	4	1	1	0
Taiwan*	0	4	5	1	0	1	1

NOTES: 0 = minimum; 9 = maximum.

Also see chapter 11.

*"The Republic of China" supports Beijing's territorial claims.

5. At least, as a fall-back position, lower the level of violence and achieve a semblance of normalcy. This is most likely, especially if India does not allow support from its Tamil Nadu Province and its 56 million Tamils.

Some form of accommodation may still be possible. In 1988 an executive order by President J. R. Jayawardene merged Sri Lanka's northern and eastern provinces—a key Tamil demand.

Tamil Tigers—Shoot to kill, and hide when the Indians show up.

Kashmir

Kashmiri separatists—Separatist Muslims have begun to take matters into their own hands. Their "struggle" is three-pronged: political, diplomatic, and armed. Members of the Jammu and Kashmir Liberation Front (JKLF) cooperate with Kashmiri activists in Pakistan and camps have been set up to take in refugees from across the border. The Kashmiri rebels claim they receive no military aid from Pakistan, but there is good reason to believe the camps provide the refugees with arms as well as food and shelter. Some Kashmiris concede that current members of the JKLF received military training in Afghanistan in the early 1980s—training presumably arranged by the Pakistani intelligence services. Members of the front are trying to use the "international climate of devolution" (i.e., the troubles in the devolving Soviet Union and the changes in Eastern Europe) to aid the Kashmiri separatist cause. Assassination, terrorism, and ambushes against Indian troops keep the pot boiling. The aim is to convince New Delhi that neither a war with Pakistan nor a guerrilla war in Kashmir is worth the effort. One of their diplomatic and political arguments is that the trouble in Kashmir isn't strictly religious. Kashmir suffers from a low level of industrial investment, poor communications, and poor transportation services. Even the Buddhists in the Ladakh region of Kashmir agree with this and they blame New Delhi. Final goal: A Great Kashmir (?) that is semiautonomous from both Pakistan and India?

Pakistan

The major fear of Pakistan is that India will take advantage of increased instability within Pakistan to absorb the nation within India. Since

1948 India has claimed 32,000 square miles of Pakistani territory. While this would double the number of Muslims in India, the Hindus would still constitute two thirds of the total population.

Pakistan also fears that India's new naval muscle may be put to use blockading Pakistani ports. As well it feels that its province of Sind is the likely target of an Indian armored thrust if a new war breaks out.

The Pakistan strategy vis-à-vis Kashmir is to press for a "local plebiscite" in Kashmir (as called for by the United Nation in 1949). Islamabad believes the Muslim majority would vote either for a separate Kashmiri nation or (more likely) for union with Pakistan. Resentment over Indian support for Bengali Muslim separatists in 1971 (and the Indian invasion of east Pakistan) fuels Pakistan's brinkmanship.

Pakistan is increasing its arms expenditures. Over 50 percent of its yearly budget ($7 billion) is allocated for defense. (Pakistan had a 1989 GNP of around $39 billion. Over 9 percent of a Third World economy's GNP goes for defense.)

Pakistan has another card to play on the "other front": India can never forget that China is Pakistan's ally, and that Chinese divisions still occupy Himalayan territory (or so India claims).

Pakistan can rely on a highly trained and highly motivated regular army—its hole card in a short conflict. Pakistan, in fact, has provided forces to a number of regimes throughout the world. Up until late 1988, Pakistan had nearly 10,000 men (an armored brigade plus) serving in Saudi Arabia. This earned Pakistan hard currency as well as trained their troops. Allegedly, the Pakistanis decided to withdraw their troops from Saudi Arabia when the Saudis asked Pakistan to provide an "all-Sunni Muslim" force. Pakistan refused since it relies on its Shiite minority. (To do otherwise would have caused political problems in Pakistan.)

Punjab

The Sikh majority in Punjab is neither fish nor fowl, or, rather, neither Hindu nor Muslim. The Sikh religion developed during the 1400s, and except for a short period in the 1800s, the Sikhs were never able to make an independent Sikh state out of their home province of Punjab. During the 1947 partition, over a third of the Sikhs found themselves in Pakistani territory and many of them were killed before they could get into the Indian portion of Punjab (where the Sikhs were likewise killing many Muslims). For several decades, this mutual massacre precluded any cooperation between independence-minded Sikhs and potential Pakistani support. But this animosity faded after several decades of prosperity and Indian-Pakistani hostility.

By 1981, the idea of the independent Sikh state of Khalistan ("Land of the Pure") in the Punjab became popular once more. Led by the principal Sikh holy man, the Sikhs asked the Indian government to grant Punjab autonomy just short of complete independence. The government rejected this and Sikh terrorists then began to kill Hindus in the Punjab. In 1982, a group of Sikhs declared holy war against India and the killing intensified, now including Sikh government officials in Punjab. Prime Minister Indira Gandhi refused to crack down, feeling that this would inflame a larger portion of the Sikh population (many of whom lived outside of Punjab). She was correct in feeling that the majority of the Sikh population was against the terrorism and not terribly keen on independence. Strong antiterrorism measures by the Indian police and Army could get out of hand and launch much of the population into rebellion. One side effect of this policy was to allow a group of Sikh holy men and terrorists to turn the Sikh Golden Temple (the principal holy place of the Sikh religion) in the city of Amristar into a heavily armed fortress. From this redoubt, many of the terrorists operated.

In 1983 the terrorism intensified. Bus and trainloads of Hindus passing through Punjab were massacred by terrorists, and Hindus in neighboring states began to riot against local Punjab minorities. Finally, in June 1984, Gandhi ordered the Army to storm the Golden Temple, root out the terrorists, and disarm the place. This was done at great cost in life to the largely Hindu soldiers and the Sikh defenders. The expected repercussions were not as bad as expected—some Sikh troops mutinied, but the vast majority remained loyal. There was more fear of large-scale insurrection among the Punjab Sikhs than actually occurred. Nonetheless, the state of Punjab was put under what amounted to martial law. Stymied in their attempt to create a regular military force, the Sikh rebels resorted to wide-scale terror and assassination. One of the principal victims was Indira Gandhi herself, and she was killed in October 1984. Over three thousand people were killed in the Punjab and neighboring areas in 1984. But the Army and police actions did cause a momentary pause in the killing.

From 1985 to 1990, the killings escalated. In 1985, only 6 or 7 people a month were killed. This went up tenfold in 1986 and then more than doubled again in 1987. By 1988, over 150 people a month were being killed in the Punjab by terrorist action (although over a third were terrorists themselves). The killing continues.

The Indian government has accused Pakistan (and the CIA) of supporting the Sikh rebels, and there may indeed be some Pakistani support. But the primary cause is a fanatical core of Sikhs who want independence and revenge (in no particular order at this point).

The state of Punjab is not turning into another Lebanon, as there is no multiplicity of militias. Most of the Sikhs and nearly all of the local Hindus want no part of the violence. The majority of Sikhs have yet to reach the point where they will go to war with the terrorists (still led by a number of Sikh holy men). The local Hindus are moving out of the Punjab in larger numbers, and the Indian Army and Punjabi police simply intensify their antiterrorism efforts. Hindu resentment of terrorists' killing Hindus has caused anti-Sikh riots in other parts of India, causing some Sikhs to move back to the Punjab. All of this plays into the terrorists' hands, but probably not sufficiently enough to create an independent Sikh state. Punjab could become a pawn in some future India-Pakistan war, as the Pakistanis have already made noises about their willingness to recognize an independent Sikh state. This is somewhat farfetched, as Punjab is well integrated into the Indian economy and has substantial non-Sikh minorities (mainly Hindus). Until the current generation of rebels gets older, expect this situation to continue as a festering sore for India.

Northeastern Border Tribes

These tribal wars are messy affairs, but unlikely to generate international—or national—complications. There are too many different tribes fighting with too few resources in too disorganized a manner to have any real effect. The Indians use a combination of carrot (aid, concessions) and stick (increased police, Army activity) to manage these uprisings. The tribes are outnumbered and increasingly hemmed in by the much more numerous Indians. This is the chief grievance of the tribes —the encroachment of the Indians and their modernity—and the primary reason why the tribes are unlikely to succeed in their secessionist endeavors. Demographics will out. One of the longest-lived of these secessionist revolts is in Nagaland, in the Assam region near Burma. The British fought and conquered the Naga during the nineteenth century. The tribe had a great deal of local control in its mountain area. When India became independent, the Naga asked for a separate independent state. New Delhi said no. An insurgency began that ran on and off until 1963; at one time India had several divisions deployed in Nagaland. Then

NATIONS OF THE INDIAN REGION

	Population (in millions)	Population (per sq. mile)	Percent Muslim Population	Percent of Arable Land	Per Capita GNP	Average Life Expectancy
Pakistan	111	336	97	26	360	52
India	850	670	11	57	330	57
Bangladesh	115	2,050	83	80	115	50
Burma	40	154	0	15	210	54
Sri Lanka	18	710	7	33	340	69
Nepal	19	336	0	17	160	52
France*	56	252	2	34	14,000	75

*Included for comparison.

India made Nagaland a separate state inside the Indian republic in 1963. In the mid-1960s, a Naga faction demanding full sovereignty went back to the bush, where they still operate along the Burmese border. Other northeastern "tribal" groups who have fought with the Indian government include the Mizos and the Tripurans. Their hope? Hold out long enough that if civil war comes to India or the Indians and Pakistanis nuke each other, they will be able to form a tribal state out of the chaos.

China

Kashmir borders China, as does an adjacent portion of Pakistan. The remainder of the border between India and China is actually between India and Tibet. In general, China tries to act as if it really has no quarrel with India. However, India insists that some mountain wilderness in Kashmir, occupied by the Chinese because it contains one of the few roads from China to Tibet, belongs to India. India claims 15,000 square miles occupied by China, and another 1,100 square miles ceded by Pakistan to China. The Indians also support an independent Tibet, while the Chinese support (and enforce) a Tibet as a part of China. India is unwilling to take on China in a war, even though China would have to supply its forces over hundreds of miles of difficult and inhospitable Tibetan mountains or deserts. The war would have to be fought in the world's highest mountains and there's really not enough to be gained from such a war to make it worthwhile. The antagonism between Russia and China makes it easy for India to cozy up to Russia and for Pakistan to become friendly with China. Everything cancels everything else out, until someone drops a match—or a nuke.

POTENTIAL OUTCOMES

Pakistan-India

1. 33 percent chance before 1996: A short, minor war occurs, a clash of two divisions or less per side on the primary front, with gains or losses of territory measured in a couple of dozen kilometers or less. The time of actual fighting is a week or less, with limited air strikes on military targets near cities, and lots of

shooting in the mountains, but the fighting sputters out as the United Nation brokers negotiations. In this scenario, there is a 50 percent chance that Pakistan slightly improves its political and military situation in Kashmir, a 40 percent chance India does, and a 10 percent chance of "who knows." (There may be several of these clashes.)

2. 25 percent chance through 1996: There is "hesitant peace," continuing ethnic troubles in Kashmir, and saber rattling by New Delhi and Islamabad. Shooting may occur on the Siachen Glacier. (This increases to a 40 percent chance if the Indian Army suppresses Punjab or if New Delhi annexes Sri Lanka.)

3. 20 percent chance through 1996: Major war, an all-out conventional slugfest occurs, stopped only by the explicit threat of one side (probably Pakistan) to use nuclear weapons or by one side suing for peace. This could last from days to months with a 70 percent chance of a relative Indian victory (India makes significant geographic gains in Kashmir area).

4. 20 percent chance through 1996: There is nuclear war, a "supermajor" war in which both sides use nukes and both sides experience heavy civilian casualties. (Both sides move their economic development back thirty years.) No real winner, but if the nuclear war does occur, there's a 75 percent chance Indian forces will occupy a significant part of radioactive Pakistani Kashmir if India is the first to use nuclear weapons (so the Indians claim a "glowing" victory—of a most cruel and terrible sort).

5. 2 percent or less chance through 1996: A "negotiated solution" to the Kashmir problem is reached. Kashmir is either made "autonomous" along the lines of Punjab autonomy or joins Pakistan. A protectable outcome—but don't even bet the ant farm on it.

Sri Lanka

1. 50 percent chance through 1996: The civil strife of the 1980s continues. The Tigers rise and fall. There is no resolution, no new accommodations.

2. 20 percent chance through 1996: The military suppresses the Tamil separatists. The Sinhalese have the numbers, the growing

hatred of the terrorists, and, increasingly, the military capability. The 1987 Indian intervention was caused largely by Sinhalese ruthlessness, and success, at cornering large numbers of rebels. The Tamils of India were outraged and put pressure on the government to allow aid to get through the Sri Lankan blockade. Now the Sinhalese are even bitterer, and with greater numbers and resolve they could put down the Tamil rebellion. The cost, however, would be great and the aftermath would likely lay the groundwork for yet another rebellion in the future. Outcomes 1 and 2 reflect the likelihood of some type of military-authoritarian government taking power in Sri Lanka (see p. 437). This goes up to a 30 percent chance if there is a major Indo-Pakistani war. Indian military attention would then be almost completely drawn to Pakistan. If India "won," significant Indian forces would be engaged in occupying territory taken from Pakistan.

3. 20 percent chance through 1996: Sri Lanka is politically partitioned which would involve setting up part of the country for the exclusive use of the Tamils. It would be similar to the partition that took place between India and Pakistan in 1947 and involve a great deal of intense and immediate violence.

4. 5 percent chance before 1996: India annexes Sri Lanka. Actually, India does not want to try this for several reasons. For one thing, it discovered how difficult it was to deal with this sort of conflict when it sent troops into Sri Lanka in 1987, and withdrew them two years later without having achieved much success. There is also the world opinion of India as a peaceful state in a warlike world. India cherishes this image, which is increasingly tarnished by Indian military operations. Annexation, however, is always a possibility and a difficult one to estimate.

5. 5 percent chance before 1996: Sri Lanka expels the Tamils, which an increasing number of Sinhalese see as a viable option. It really isn't, for the simple fact that there is no nation out there willing to take in three million Tamils. The Tamils of Tamil Nadu have grown impatient with the war their kin are waging in Sri Lanka. Support in Tamil Nadu is gradually evaporating, and even the thousands of Sri Lankan Tamils who have fled to India are being made to feel uncomfortable. Tamil Nadu is no longer willing to provide training bases and supplies for the Tamil rebels of Sri Lanka. However, if the level of violence was high enough, and

the Indian government maintains its reluctance to get involved once more, a major evacuation of Tamils from Sri Lanka remains a distant possibility.

Punjab

1. 35 percent chance before 1996: Military suppression of the Punjab separatists by the Indian government occurs. Essentially, this entails an Indian Army invasion of Punjab and a brutal anti-insurgent war that in six months eliminates most of the resistance. Civil strife, however, continues for decades.

2. 35 percent chance before 1996: There is a continued cycle of the late 1980s' unrest and violence, with bombs and terrorism and military reprisal.

3. 25 percent chance before 1996: New Delhi grants autonomy for Punjab, wherein the state operates as its own nation with India responsible for defense and foreign affairs.

4. 5 percent chance or less through 1996: Outright national independence is given to Punjab.

Pakistan: Internal Situation

1. 66 percent chance through 1996: No significant change occurs from the rickety status quo, despite war with India

2. 15 percent chance through 1996: Civil war is sparked by war with India or rebellions on Afghan border. Islamabad eventually gets control, and minor border adjustments result. Pakistan is greatly weakened vis-à-vis India. This jumps to a 40 percent chance if Indo-Pakistani war goes nuclear.

3. 10 percent chance through 1996: There is partition, brought about by war with India, civil war, or (less likely) by a vote in Kashmir which produces an autonomous Kashmir.

4. 3 percent chance through 1996: The whole of Pakistan is annexed by India, as a result of Indo-Pakistani war.

5. 1 percent chance through 1996: The Indian state of Kashmir and Jammu becomes part of Pakistan either through war or plebiscite.

India: Internal Situation

There is a fair chance of a civil war breaking out in India through the end of the decade, sparked either by a war with Pakistan or one of the inevitable local squabbles. The language issue could set it off if Hindi radicals try to get rid of English. Yet the Congress party is resourceful and resilient—and adept at diffusing these issues. Still, for argument's sake, let's say there is a 10 percent chance of an extensive, armed civil conflict erupting inside India (excluding Punjab and Kashmir and the ongoing troubles with the Naga). This is, admittedly, a rather high figure, but India has a lot of factions that could radicalize on the drop of a rupee. For further argument, the possibility of civil war rises to 30 percent if a nuclear war erupts and extremist factions see the resulting chaos and fear as their best opportunity . . .

India and China

There exists a slight chance that India and China will come to blows through 1996. China certainly might shake the arrows if Pakistan and India got into a major war that lasted over a couple of weeks.

COST OF WAR

The massacres began with the million killed during the partition that accompanied India's and Pakistan's independence in 1947. The ensuing wars between Pakistan and India were relatively bloodless as major wars go: The 1965 war killed about 20,000 people, and the 1971 war another 12,000. The 1962 war between China and India resulted in 5,000 deaths. The formal wars have not been the chief cause of death by violence, but the civil unrest that sometimes leads to war. The 1971 Pakistani civil war killed over 300,000. Left-wing rebellions in Sri Lanka during the 1970s killed as many as 3,000. The Tamil separatist activity during the 1980s has killed nearly 20,000 to date. Another 20,000 have died in the Punjab to date. Several thousand have died in Burma since unrest began in the late 1980s. The fighting in the tribal areas has caused over a thousand deaths since the 1970s. Over a thousand have died in Kashmir since 1989.

But the biggest death toll could occur during a future war between

India and Pakistan if either nation used its nuclear weapons. While the Pakistanis may not have operational nuclear weapons yet, they could get their hands on chemical weapons and these could be just as deadly. The casualty toll in a nuclear or chemical war would easily be in the hundreds of thousands and could go into the millions if things got out of hand.

WHAT KIND OF WAR

India has fought several large wars in the classical style, with masses of tanks and aircraft slugging it out amid large quantities of infantry. These battles are usually fought in the open plains of northern India, which favor mechanized operations. But this is the exception. The more common form of armed violence is somewhat unique to this part of the world. Again and again, small bands of rebels walk into a village, or stop a bus, and slaughter as many unarmed civilians as they can. The rebels then depart, either to camps deep in the forest, or to their own civilian identities. The security forces often reply by doing a little slaughtering of their own. Sometimes, the security forces and rebels actually fight it out, but this is less common than the killing of civilians.

QUICK LOOK AT NEPAL

In late 1989 and 1990 Nepal went through a series of sudden changes—changes that began to bring the mountainous Shangri-la into the twentieth century. In April 1990 King Birendra, the heir of the Shaha dynasty, invited a loosely formed but vocal national opposition to form the nation's first multiparty government in twenty-nine years. Nearly three hundred people were killed in riots and shootings leading up to the king's decision to share power.

For generations Nepal had an absolute monarchy, though often real control was in the hands of courtiers. The kingdom's only experience with democracy lasted less than two years and was halted in 1961 when King Mahendra, King Birendra's father, dismissed the Nepali Congress-led government due to "corruption and inefficiency." The *panchayat* ("council") system was formed, which was a pyramid of council groups that ran from villager to king. If it sounds feudalistic, well, it was business as usual.

The Nepali Congress party, although banned, maintained close ties with the Indian Congress party. In 1989 India imposed an economic blockade on Nepal, which sent prices skyrocketing. This added fuel to the already disenchanted Nepalese living in the urban capital of Katmandu.

Nepal is a country of 17 million people, 93 percent of them engaged in agriculture even though only 14 percent of the land is arable. Their per capita income is $170. Not all of the people are antimonarchist. Nepal's famous Gurkas (who have served as mercenaries in the British and Indian armies) tend to be proroyalist. In some mountain villages the king is treated as a deity. However, Nepal's biggest industry has become tourism, and tourism has opened up the country both politically and socially.

In the last decade, deforestation has become a severe problem. The poor Nepalese rely on the wood for fuel. The Nepalese are hoping to

open up potential oil and gas reserves along their valley border with India.
This may mitigate the deforestation problem.

LOCAL POLITICS

Nepali Congress party.
United Left Front—Seven-party, left-leaning coalition group.
Pashupati Temple—One of Hinduism's holiest shrines. Located in
Nepal.

POLITICAL TREND CHART

NEPAL

The economy could improve if hydroelectric comes on line and environmental degradation is halted.

	1990 (Authoritarian Monarchy*)	1996 (Authoritarian Democracy)
Government Effectiveness	7	7
Government Stability	5	6
Political Cohesion	7	7
Repression Level	6	4
Economic Development	2 +	4 −
Education Status	2	2

NOTE: 0 = minimum; 9 = maximum.
*Authoritarian monarchy changing to an authoritarian democracy based on limited representative government and constitutional curtailment of the king's powers.

REGIONAL POWERS AND POWER INTEREST INDICATOR CHART

NEPAL

Another sideshow (literally) up in the mountains. Most people have no idea where Nepal is, or why.

	Economic Interests	Historical Interests	Political Interest	Military Interest	Force Generation Potential	Ability to Intervene Politically	Ability to Promote Economic Development
China	1	3	5	7	5	4	1
India	5	5	7	8	8	8	7
Pakistan	1	2	5	2	1–	2	0
U.S.	2	2	3	1	1	3	4
Russia	0	1	1	1	1–	1	0
Gurkas*	8	9	8	6	6	5	—

NOTE: 0 = minimum; 9 = maximum.
*Potential rebel force, probably promonarchist.

QUICK LOOK AT INDONESIA: STRAITS JACKET

EAST TIMOR, THE MOLUCCANS, IRIAN BARAT

The Indonesian central government in Jakarta has been waging a quiet but ugly war on the island of East Timor. East Timor, formerly a Portuguese colony, went through several upheavals—including a short-lived, left-leaning rebel front—and then the Indonesians invaded in 1975, claiming that **(1)** East Timor was Indonesian all along, and **(2)** a pro-Communist government in East Timor would not be tolerated. A new East Timorese liberation front named Fretilin was created, but it has not had much success. The East Timorese have no allies, little opportunity to acquire weapons, and no public relations firm trying to interest the Western press in their cause. The best estimates suggest that anywhere from 90,000 to 200,000 people have been killed in East Timor since the Indonesians invaded. It has been a silent massacre, killing a higher proportion of the population than during the Khmer Rouge terror in Cambodia during the 1970s.

The South Moluccans, at least those exiled in the Netherlands, understand media attention. Hijacking Dutch trains, blowing up Dutch school buildings, threatening the assassination of Indonesian ambassadors—the South Moluccans know how to grab headlines in the West. But they have not been successful at creating an active guerrilla movement in the islands to challenge the Indonesians. Press reports in 1984 had the Moluccans looking to the East bloc for support. That support never developed, and now the East bloc has dissipated.

The Moluccans believe they were promised an independent Moluccan state when the Dutch turned the Dutch East Indies loose. Decolonization of the Indies, however, was not a planned or calculated Dutch policy. It was brought about by a Japanese invasion at a time when post–World War II Holland, with its own home country shattered by the Germans, was in no mood to properly oversee the division of its old Far Eastern island empire. Javanese and Sumatran imperialists (the Moluccan names for the Indonesian government) took advantage of a power vacuum and assumed control. Forty-five years later the Moluccans remain angry.

The Indonesian government also has a low-level war going on in Irian Barat, the former colony of Dutch New Guinea, which Jakarta formally annexed in 1963. There was little consultation with the inhabitants, a collection of near Stone Age tribes and a few fishing villages. Some of the tribes in the mountain jungles, according to missionary sources, still occasionally practice ritual cannibalism, and now and then—as the stories go—a little head-hunting also still occurs. But bows and arrows and spears and a few submachine guns are no match for Indonesian troops armed with automatic rifles and helicopters. The Free Papua Movement has failed. Support from Papua New Guinea, the other half of the island of New Guinea, is now virtually nonexistent.

Indonesia has over 170 million people. The cultural and economic spectrum of the nation runs from the ultra high tech of the Indonesian petroleum industry to the stone-ax technology (circa 25000 B.C.) of mountain tribes on Irian Barat.

The political spine of Indonesia, however, runs through the islands of Java and Sumatra. The island of Java has over 100 million inhabitants. Jakarta, the capital, is one of the world's most densely populated cities. Over 300 ethnic groups populate an island chain of 2 million square kilometers and 13,000-plus islands, which run from the Straits of Malacca and Malaya nearly to Australia, a distance of over 5,500 kilometers. Almost 90 percent of the Indonesians are Sunni Muslim. The island of Bali is Hindu, a holdover from the days when the whole of Indonesia was either Hindu or Buddhist. The South Moluccans (the island of Ambon) are primarily Dutch Calvinist. Religious differences exacerbate the problems between the South Moluccans and the rest of Indonesia.

Indonesia may itself be ripe for a wave of Islamic fundamentalism. The military-sponsored regime tends to be Western oriented and is open to fundamentalist charges of "co-option" by Western influences. There are also tensions between the Javanese and the ethnic Chinese who make up a large portion of the merchant class and run many banking institutions.

POLITICAL TREND CHART

INDONESIA

Internal trouble could produce the economic slide.

	1990	1996
		(Military Totalitarian)
Government Effectiveness	7	6
Government Stability	5	3
Political Cohesion	5	4
Repression Level	7	7
Economic Development	4 −	3 +
Education Status	3	3

NOTE: 0 = minimum; 9 = maximum.

At the same time Indonesia is experiencing a democratic awakening. As aging President Suharto nears the end of his fifth term (1992), this awakening affects the military and its "New Order" control over the country. The Indonesian military claims to serve two functions: to defend against external and internal threats and to take a leading role in promoting internal political life and development. Through a system of "Korems and Korams" (essentially military districts), the Indonesian military elites often do more than merely encourage development projects and economic activity—they direct them as well. Charges of corruption are rife but the proof hazy. Still, even the Army has complained that President Suharto's immediate family has benefited from influence peddling, and this has led to friction in the military. The years 1992 and 1993 may be difficult ones in Jakarta as the military seeks to navigate a time of transition to new— and possibly "more civilian"—leadership.

REGIONAL POWERS AND POWER INTEREST INDICATOR CHARTS

THE WAR IN IRIAN BARAT

Why is this conflict ignored? Take a gander and make a guess.

	Economic Interests	Historical Interests	Political Interest	Military Interest	Force Generation Potential	Ability to Intervene Politically	Ability to Promote Economic Development
Indonesia	2	4	4	3	4	9	2
Japan	1	1	1	0	1	7	8
Australia	2	3	4	4	5	4	3
China	0	0	1	0	0	1	0
Malaysia	1	1	2	1	0	2	0
U.S.	0	0	1	0	8+	8	7

NOTE: 0 = minimum; 9 = maximum.

INDONESIAN CIVIL WAR/CONFLICT THAT LEADS TO A CLOSING OF THE STRAIT OF MALACCA

On the other hand, this would make instantaneous headlines.

	Economic Interests	Historical Interests	Political Interest	Military Interest	Force Generation Potential	Ability to Intervene Politically
Indonesia	9	9	9	9	7	9
Singapore	9	9	9	9	4+	7
Japan	8+	8	9	8	3	6
Australia	7	7	8	8+	3	6
India	3	5	6	6	3	4
China	5	4	6	7	2	4+
Malaysia	8	9	9	9	4	7
So. Korea	6	3	6	4	1−	2
U.S.	8	7	8	8+	6+	8
Philippines	7	7	9	8+	2	5
Vietnam	2	3	5	3	1	1

NOTE: 0 = minimum; 9 = maximum.

QUICK LOOK AT THE PHILIPPINES: THE SICK MAN OF ASEAN

The Philippines were the first Asian nation to be deeply influenced by Western culture and economics. A Spanish colony taken by the United States in the Spanish-American War, the country was once one of Asia's most progressive and educated societies, possessing a strong foundation for the expansion of democratic institutions.

In February 1986, those democratic roots and aspirations were powerful enough to topple dictator Ferdinand Marcos. Marcos attempted to deny Corazón Aquino, the widow of the slain opposition leader Benigno Aquino, a victory at the ballot box. With aid from the United States and world opinion, Mrs. Aquino essentially toppled Marcos in a democratic coup reinforced by armies of voters.

Still, the basic political and economic afflictions that the Marcos regime exacerbated remain. Democracy is fragile, and poverty and corruption are persistent. Since coming to power, Mrs. Aquino has faced over a dozen military coup attempts. The script goes something like this: A renegade officer will collect a battalion or two of mutineers and seize one or two Army bases, the objective being to provoke other disgruntled military units and create a wave of mutinies. The chaos will force the government to fall. The Reform the Armed Forces Movement, a right-wing underground group of current and retired military officers, has been implicated in a number of coup attempts.

The Philippines are still involved in the low-budget but high-risk military and political controversy over the Spratley Islands. Potential oil deposits, political one-upmanship, and old suspicions drive this dispute over a scattered South China Sea archipelago. The Spratleys are just one of two island chains in the region in dispute, by Malaysia, Taiwan, China, Vietnam, and the Philippines. Vietnam and China have fought small naval battles as well over the Paracel Islands off the Vietnam coast. Some islets occupied by the Filipinos are almost inundated at high tide.

The Communist New People's Army's insurgency still lingers. Despite the acceptance of amnesty by many Communist leaders and deep internal struggles in the Communist movement, as of late 1990 the Communists still claimed to have 10,000 guerrilla troops. Communist remnants often unite with anti-U.S. radicals in protests, violence, and terror directed at the U.S. military bases at Subic Bay and Clark Field. The United States, by 1996, may well close one of these facilities (or both) and move operations to Guam, Tinian, or Japan.

Several ethnic groups, most notably the Muslim Moros, fight a guerrilla war in the bush. The Philippine "Moro" (Muslim) insurgency is centered in western Mindanao. (Mindanao and Sulu are essentially occupied by the Philippine Army, which gives the Moro militants lots of targets.) Attacking the Army, however, makes Moro villages and barrios vulnerable to reprisal. Muslim Indonesia has not been very helpful to the Moros, fearing Philippine "stimulation" of Indonesia's many ethnic antagonisms.

The Moro National Liberation Front (MNLF) is the key resistance group. But Moro activists must fight more than the Manila government. The "Datu" system—the old Moro "headman" system, originally a flexible means of allowing a man with natural leadership abilities to become a tribal leader—has evolved into a rigid hereditary system over the years. The Moro "tribal" organization has been helpful in keeping the insurgency going but has been a dismal failure in establishing a political framework that can challenge Manila.

Despite the rise of democracy, there has as yet been no broad-based power sharing among the Philippines' many ethnic and economic groups. A small number of wealthy families still controls the destiny of the nation and is reluctant to share power. During the 1990s, look for the Philippines' basic problems of political instability, ethnic conflict, and economic dislocation to continue.

POLITICAL TREND CHART

PHILIPPINES

The Philippines should shake off some of the legacy of the Marcos corruption in the 1990s.

	1990	1996
	(Authoritarian Democracy)	
Government Effectiveness	6	6
Government Stability	3	3
Political Cohesion	4	4
Repression Level	4	5
Economic Development	3	4
Education Status	3+	3+

NOTE: 0 = minimum; 9 = maximum.

REGIONAL POWERS AND POWER INTEREST INDICATOR CHARTS

WAR OF THE SPRATLEYS

The antagonists might get really violent if significant amounts of oil are actually found in and around these rocks in the ocean.

	Economic Interests	Historical Interests	Political Interest	Military Interest	Force Generation Potential	Ability to Intervene Politically
Philippines	7	7	8	8+	6	6
Vietnam	7	7	8	7	7	5
China	7	6	7	8	7+	7
Malaysia	5	7	7	7	1	3
Taiwan	2	3	5	2	0+	1

NOTE: 0 = minimum; 9 = maximum.

In addition, there are the "interested parties" concerning the Spratleys issue.

INTERESTED PARTIES

	Economic Interests	Historical Interests	Political Interest	Military Interest	Force Generation Potential	Ability to Intervene Politically
Indonesia	3	5	7	5	2	4
Singapore	5	6	8	4	0	3
Japan	7	7	8	7	3	8
Australia	2	6	8	7	3	5
India	1	2	6	3	1–	2
So. Korea	2	3	7	5	1	2
U.S.	6	7	8	7+	8+	8

NOTE: 0 = minimum; 9 = maximum.

QUICK LOOK AT CAMBODIA
AND THE GREAT INDOCHINA WAR

The twentieth century's "Great Indochina War" continues to sputter on—with tragic consequences—in the sad confines of Cambodia. As of fall 1990, the pro-Western forces loyal to Cambodian Prince Norodom Sihanouk, a Marxist puppet government loyal to Vietnam, and the still-strong Khmer Rouge tangle with each other over the corpse of a country.

The Khmer Rouge, orchestrators of one of this century's most grievous genocides (20 percent of Cambodia's population was killed in the late 1970s), refuses to fade away. It is still propped up, at least with arms and ammunition, by China. China, at odds with Vietnam, finds it "useful" to keep Hanoi bogged down in Cambodia. The government in Beijing doesn't seem to mind an association with mass murderers.

The Western powers have flip-flopped through a series of promises to back then not to back the "Sihanoukists." A potential rapprochement with Vietnam could be in the works (1991 or 1992), which explains some of the diplomatic hedging. Another reason is that the Sihanouk faction is weak "in the field"—its combat forces are largely ineffectual. Even massive Western support might accomplish little.

The third party to the conflict, the Vietnamese-backed Cambodian government, has few international supporters and what has been described as "fragile" local support. Some suspect local (Cambodian) support for the regime stops outside of Phnom Penh. Though Vietnam has withdrawn most of its occupying forces, a number of sources suggest that some Vietnamese "volunteer labor groups" along the Cambodian-Vietnamese border areas are actually infantry battalions. Whether factual or not, the Cambodian regime relies heavily on Vietnam.

The Great Indochina War, which began as resistance against the French colonial masters in the 1930s, has been a hell for all participants. What the United States thinks of as the Vietnam War was only one particularly awful twelve-year slice of what has now been six decades of combat. An agreement to end the struggle in Cambodia will be a step toward more peace and less war, but few believe the members of the "psychotic wing" of the Khmer Rouge will ever put their arms down.

QUICK LOOK AT CHINA:
UNDER THE VOLCANO

WAITING FOR CHANGE, WAITING FOR THE NEXT EXPLOSION

Mao tried to create a policy of permanent Chinese socialist revolution. While in power, Mao made dozens of attempts to "institutionalize" his version of change from the late 1950s to the early 1970s. All of them failed, the Red Guards Cultural Revolution being the old man's last gasp. Now, after a decade and a half of economic experimentation—and recovery from the Cultural Revolution—the un-Confucian but very Chinese political cycle of harsh central control replaced by harsh paroxysm is set once again. China has once again moved from a sleeping (this time Communist) giant, to an Asian political and economic volcano set to erupt.

In the mid-1980s, the government relaxed the central planning and control of the economy—the typical prescription of Communist nations. This brought forth annual double-digit growth in the economy. It also brought forth calls for democracy. The Communist party resisted demands that it share power. China is on the verge of another armed civil revolution, its third of this century (not counting the minor revolutions, civil wars, invasions, and sundry purges). The June 1989 Tiananmen Square incident was just a foretaste.

In China, the twentieth century has been a busy one: In 1900 China was ruled by a feudal nobility; a "republican" (Kuomintang, etc.) dictatorship had nominal rule through World War II and the 1940s; and a Communist dictatorship, with varying degrees of Marxist orthodoxy but an invariant reliance on military control, has ruled since, taking control of the mainland in 1949.

The current situation in China is an ancient one, with a few novel twentieth-century twists. China has maintained its national identity for thousands of years because it was always able to overcome periods of disorder and reestablish a central government. In fact, the Communists did just that in the late 1940s, thus ending fifty years of internal disorder. But another pattern in Chinese history is a central government that grows corrupt and inefficient, which is what the Communists have managed to do in the relatively short span of forty years. As in centuries past, the educated classes, the merchants, the military, and the provincial constituencies all agitate for their own version of a better central government. More than in the past, China is less isolated from events in the rest of the world (the collapse of communism in Europe, etc.) and possesses much more efficient internal communications (radio, TV, fax, etc.). As in the past, the farmers, who form a majority (80 percent) of the population, sit on the sidelines, waiting to see who will most likely prevail.

The current revolutionary climate is centered in the urban areas, as usual. This time the struggle, both politically and militarily, will be decided in the cities, and it may well be bloody. Most of the conscript soldiers of the People's Liberation Army (PLA) are farmers' sons and not all that reluctant to gun down unruly urban folk.

The situation in China is complicated by the existence of Taiwan (the Republic of China), the looming move of Hong Kong from British to Beijing rule, the still-uneasy relationship with Russia, and a growing uneasiness with that post–Cold War industrial superpower, Japan.

Yet this lurking Chinese civil war is very much a war of economic performance and public opinion. And it's not so much a matter of the rebels winning as it is the government losing. In many respects, the pattern of the Communist governmental and economic muddle in China mirrors that of Russia—the mess is very difficult to get out of. If the civil war moves to shooting, it could become a civil conflict with nuclear weapons. In the past, Chinese warlords have shown few scruples. Bitter tea, indeed.

POLITICAL TREND CHARTS

"MAINLAND" CHINA
More democracy, but less order and regimentation.

	1990 (Socialist Totalitarian)	1996 (Authoritarian Democracy)
Government Effectiveness	7	4
Government Stability	7	4
Political Cohesion	6	4
Repression Level	7+	6
Economic Development	4	4+
Education Status	4	4+

NOTE: 0 = minimum; 9 = maximum.

TAIWAN ("REPUBLIC OF CHINA")
Not much chance but economic progress continues.

	1990	1996
	(Authoritarian Democracy)	
Government Effectiveness	8	7
Government Stability	7	7
Political Cohesion	7	7
Repression Level	5	5
Economic Development	7+	7
Education Status	5	5

NOTE: 0 = minimum; 9 = maximum.

REGIONAL POWERS AND POWER INTEREST INDICATOR CHARTS

CHINESE INTERNAL STRUGGLE

	Economic Interests	Historical Interests	Political Interest	Military Interest	Force Generation Potential	Ability to Intervene Politically	Ability to Promote Economic Development
Russia	3	4	7	7	6+	2	1–
Japan	7	7	8	8	1	4	7
Vietnam	2	7	7	8	3+	1	0
U.S.	4	4	6	4	3	5	3
India	1	2	4	3	2+	1	0
Taiwan	9	9	9	9	3	3	7

NOTE: 0 = minimum; 9 = maximum.

Russo-Chinese Border War

	Economic Interests	Historical Interests	Political Interest	Military Interest	Force Generation Potential	Ability to Intervene Politically
China	6	8	9	9	8	6
Russia	7	8	9	9	9	7
Japan	7	7	6	6	1 –	7
Vietnam	1	3	7	8	3	2
U.S.	4	2	7	7	2 +	8

NOTE: 0 = minimum; 9 = maximum.

ON THE SOUTHERN FRONT

	Economic Interests	Historical Interests	Political Interest	Military Interest	Force Generation Potential	Ability to Intervene Politically	Ability to Promote Economic Development
China	3	6	7	8	9	8	4
Russia	0	2	3	2	3	3	0
India	3	7	8	8	7	8	1
Pakistan	3	6	7	7	2	4	0
U.S.	1	2	5	2	1	5	3

NOTE: 0 = minimum; 9 = maximum.

Potential Outcomes

China's politics move slowly, but when its politics pick up, the world soon knows about it. In 1990, an aging Communist leadership was attempting to hold on to power, keep the economy moving, and stamp out a rising clamor for democracy and political reform. There are several ways the situation can go.

1. 50 percent chance through 1996, 70 percent chance after that: China goes democratic. While there are still Communists willing to carry on, and most of the population doesn't really care who's in charge, the key people in the modern sectors of the economy—plus most of the urban population—do want more shared power. History is on their side, as the growth of democracy in Europe (and India) was a result of a larger number of educated people getting involved in an increasingly complex decision-making process. The odds, and history, favor the democrats.

2. 30 percent chance through 1996, 10 percent chance after that: China remains a socialist dictatorship. The party is not without its adherents, and there *is* a younger generation of party functionaries eager to continue Communist party rule into the next century. Moreover, the bulk of the population couldn't care less who runs the country as long as there is peace and prosperity. Remember, democracy is an alien concept to the Chinese. They are a conservative people, not given to risking what little they have for the cause of an alien and unfamiliar concept (but then, they *did* adopt communism . . .).

3. 15 percent chance through 1996: There is a Chinese nonnuclear civil war. The Communists have already demonstrated that they are not willing to go without a fight. Civil war tore the country apart earlier in this century and could do so again.

4. 5 percent chance through 1996: There is a Chinese nuclear civil war. While a civil war is possible, nuclear civil war is less likely. Though particularly rabid individuals might want to resort to nuclear weapons, it's unlikely that any organized group would. After all, who wants to run a China replete with radioactive wreckage and hundreds of millions of corpses. But the nuclear weapons do exist, and someone could use them.

QUICK LOOK AT KOREA:
THE STRANGE KINGDOM

Korea is an ancient nation. The division of Korea is something of a historical aberration—the nation was unified for most of the last thousand years, though the majority of that time it was a vassal state of China or Japan. After its split by Russia in the aftermath of World War II into the Communist totalitarian North and the sometimes democratic but increasingly economically successful South, the problems associated with reuniting the country have complicated East Asian diplomacy since the 1950s. There is no doubt: Both Koreas want reunification. The radically different political systems put in place by superpower patrons, however, make this very difficult, even in the post–Cold War environment.

Sixty-eight million Koreans are separated by an armistice line and historical superpower interests. A World War II political decision divided the country into Communist and non-Communist halves. An unsuccessful Communist military invasion in 1950 produced the current stalemate. North Korea's military strongman, Kim Il Sung, has dynastic ambitions—he plans to have his son succeed him as dictator.

While there is a superficial resemblance to the former division of East and West Germany, the two Koreas are much more firmly divided. The physical divider is a case in point. Unlike a Berlin Wall with its attendant East German border barriers, the Korean demilitarized zone (DMZ) is a massive structure.

The DMZ marks the frontline positions of UN and Chinese troops when the cease-fire went into effect in 1953. Each side withdrew 2 kilometers, leaving a 4-kilometer-wide neutral zone which stretches some 240 kilometers from one side of the peninsula to the other. Within the DMZ, nothing but the wreckage of war (as of 1953) and wildlife remain. The DMZ contains many old mine fields, human skeletons, and other military debris. The wildlife in the DMZ flourishes, including many of the few remaining specimens of the Korean tiger. The grass grows wild, being over two feet high, along with sundry brush and some trees. Both sides occasionally burn off the brush to make it more difficult for infiltrators to get through.

Some 500–1,000 meters from the north and south edge of the DMZ is a barbed wire fence (electrified in many places) with a 10-meter clearance area on either side of it. Some sectors of the fence have other sensors nearby, and the entire fence is covered by a series of small bunkers (for two to three men) which are usually occupied only at night or when the political situation heats up. Sometimes these bunkers are connected to each other by a trench, but they are there mainly for observation purposes. Nothing larger than a machine gun is used in them. About 300 meters behind the fencelike bunkers is a double barbed wire fence, another cleared zone, and platoon-size bunker systems (each concrete bunker can hold four to six men) connected along the length of the DMZ by trenches and tunnels. Where appropriate, there are also antitank obstacles in the form of thick concrete pillars or 10- to 30-foot earth and stone walls. Also found in this area are concrete artillery positions, underground ammo dumps, command centers, and so on. In effect, there's a fortified line stretching across the peninsula. Each kilometer of DMZ frontage is held by 100–200 troops in peacetime, with several hundred more behind the lines and over a thousand men per kilometer for wartime deployment.

Nearly a million acres of Korean real estate (almost 1 percent of both countries) is taken up by the DMZ and adjacent military areas. Unlike the old Berlin Wall (and the border between East and West Germany), the DMZ is heavily fortified and manned on both sides. Moreover, the North Koreans have been digging tunnels under the DMZ for over twenty years and regularly send infiltrators across. The DMZ is an active zone of military operations, just waiting for a spark to set it off. The DMZ is the Eastern European iron curtain writ very large.

Kim Il Sung is still obsessed with reunification on his terms, through military force and subversion. Economic prosperity in the more populous South makes subversion difficult and another invasion a precarious undertaking.

Still, most Koreans desire reunification. To this end there have been on-again, off-again talks between the two Koreas, and North Korea has eased up on its terrorist war against South Korea.

The United States stands staunchly behind South Korea, while Russia continues to support its neighbor, North Korea. Yet the Kremlin now advises North Korea to "reform" economically and politically. And the Kremlin has already begun to develop closer relations with South Korea. China waits and watches. And while Russia makes diplomatic and economic moves toward South Korea, Japan worries.

As this is written in early 1991, the North and South continue to make further preliminary moves toward reunification. But this cannot take place until the Communist government in the North undergoes some substantial changes. Along with Cuba, North Korea is the last of the old-line dictatorships that survived the upheavals in the Communist world during 1989. While there are many special interest groups in the North that would lose much through reunification, nearly all Koreans would be swept along if serious reunification efforts begin.

Still, given the two generations of hate and the large armies in place, the situation could turn ugly. North Korea has been one of the most (if not the most) isolated of the Communist dictatorships. Heavily militarized and closely supervised, the population and its controllers might react in unpleasant ways to a change in government.

The current situation developed from the very bloody Korean War which left in its wake two heavily armed and extremely determined adversaries (the North and the South) locked in a bitter stalemate. The huge disparity in living standards (and political freedom) between North and South Korea increases potential instability in the North. The North's economy, along with other Communist economies, has declined over the years. It has now reached a point where the shortages are rampant.

Militarily, an armed struggle between the two Koreas would be similar to World War I. Both sides still adhere to a doctrine of frontal assault until the objective is taken or the attacker is demolished. Since the DMZ is 240 kilometers of mostly mountainous terrain, and the largest open area is the 100-kilometer front only 24 kilometers north of the South Korean capital of Seoul, both sides concentrate their best forces on this front.

The political situation in the two Koreas is, on the surface, quite different. But looking closer reveals interesting similarities. In the North exists a classic example (perhaps the "best" one) of Communist military dictatorship. Up to a third of the GNP goes to the military and secret police. The Army, secret police, and Communist party keep a wary eye on one another, creating a balance of terror that makes reform difficult. Added to this standard Communist setup is Kim Il Sung's attempt to pass power on to his son. This is unlikely to work, but it adds an interesting bit of political color to an otherwise drab situation.

In the South there was a military dictatorship for years, but always with the security organizations (the Korean Central Intelligence Agency [KCIA] and the military security agencies) keeping an eye on the military and the population. The more dynamic portions of the economy are concentrated in huge, government-supported and (to a lesser extent) -directed corporations called *chaebol*. While there was more individual and economic freedom in the South, it was still a police state. Then came the democratic revolution of the late 1980s which resulted in free elections and a more democratic government. But otherwise, things remained as they were. That is, the South was still largely an authoritarian society with a highly concentrated economy.

Both the North and South do have one other thing in common: a particularly strong feeling of national identity. This is well exemplified by the "Juche" philosophy in the North. Modern dictatorships usually come with some kind of new political philosophy to explain and justify their tyranny. Kim Il Sung's particular secular religion is uniquely Korean and is called Juche. What makes it so "Korean" is its emphasis on the uniqueness of the Korean character and a particular emphasis on the need to unite Korea under the Juche banner. Combining nationalism, collectivism, and shards of several Oriental and Western philosophies, Kim has made Juche the state religion, or philosophy anyway. Some believe it, but hardly anyone dares criticize it in the North. In the South, the basic elements of Juche are accepted and fuel a broadly accepted desire for unity.

The problem with Korean reunification is that it could degenerate into a large-scale Lebanon (possibly nuclear). On the other hand, a peaceful change somewhat resembling the recent German reunification is not inconceivable—just unlikely. Yet the Northerners have fewer options than the East Germans did. There is no wide access to the South Korean media, nor are there neighboring nations that dissatisfied Northerners can escape to. North Korea is very much a prison, and an inmate rebellion would be a very risky and bloody exercise.

Koreans demonstrated that they were quite capable of killing one another in 1950–53, and both populations have been exhorted, for over three decades, to do it again. The well-entrenched, and increasingly inept, bureaucracy of the North has everything to lose with reunification. The South would gain a bankrupt and economically alien North. The prospects for peaceful, or even uneventful, reunification are not bright.

A united Korea would be the third strongest (economically and militarily) nation in the region (after China and Japan). Note that a united Korea has about the same population as Vietnam, but ten times the economic power.

POTENTIAL OUTCOMES

Continuation of the current stalemate. The cost of trying to change things is too high.

1. 40 percent chance through 1996: There is a peaceful reunification of Korea.

2. 36 percent chance through 1996: The status quo continues.

3. 15 percent chance before 1992: North Korea has a political breakdown, civil war, and reunification with wealthy South Korea.

4. 5 percent chance before 1992: North Korea has a political breakdown, civil war, and reestablishment of a Communist government.

5. 2 percent chance before 1992: There is an unsuccessful North Korean invasion and subsequent reunification by South Korea (not as long as the superpowers don't approve, but . . .).

6. 1 percent chance before 1996: There is an unsuccessful North Korean invasion and return to the status quo—as long as Kim Il Sung has the means, this is a possibility.

7. 1 percent chance before 1996: North Korea makes a successful conquest of South Korea—unless South Korea weakens considerably in military strength (through internal disorder), which is highly unlikely.

Korea and Its Neighbors

	Population (in millions)	Population (per sq. mile)	Percent Muslim Population	Percent of Arable Land	Per Capita GNP	Average Life Expectancy
Korea (whole)	68	820	0	21	2,000	69
No. Korea	22	472	0	19	500	68
So. Korea	46	1,195	0	22	2,600	69
Japan	124	845	0	13	15,000	78
China	1,100	297	1	11	300	69
Mongolia	2	3	0	1	400	63
Vietnam	67	520	0	24	200	60
Russia	290	34	11	11	1,400	68
France*	56	252	2	34	14,000	75

*Included for comparison.

POLITICAL TREND CHARTS

SOUTH KOREA
Stronger democracy, stable economy, steady prospects.

	1990 (Authoritarian Democracy)	1996 (Representative Democracy)
Government Effectiveness	7	7
Government Stability	6	7
Political Cohesion	7	8
Repression Level	5	3
Economic Development	7+	7
Education Status	5+	6

NOTE: 0 = minimum; 9 = maximum.

NORTH KOREA

	1990	1996
	(Socialist Totalitarian)	
Government Effectiveness	8	5
Government Stability	7	4
Political Cohesion	8	3
Repression Level	9	9
Economic Development	3	2
Education Status	2	2

NOTE: 0 = minimum; 9 = maximum.

"UNITED KOREA"

	1996 (Representative Democracy)
Government Effectiveness	5
Government Stability	4
Political Cohesion	4
Repression Level	5
Economic Development	6
Education Status	6

NOTE: 0 = minimum; 9 = maximum.

REGIONAL POWERS AND POWER INTEREST INDICATOR CHART

SECOND KOREAN WAR

	Economic Interests	Historical Interests	Political Interest	Military Interest	Force Generation Potential	Ability to Intervene Politically
No. Korea	9	9	9	9	8+	7
So. Korea	9	9	9	9	8	8
U.S.	5	8	8	8	7	7
Russia	3	7	6	8	5	6
China	6	8	9	8+	7	7
Japan	7	8	9	9	3	5

NOTE: 0 = minimum; 9 = maximum.

QUICK LOOK AT JAPAN:
THE RED SUN ALSO RISES, AGAIN

Since World War II, no one (except Japan's neighbors) has thought of Japan as a real or potential military threat. Japan was thoroughly defeated and devastated by the United States during World War II. This was the first time Japan had ever lost a war or been occupied by a foreign army, and it had a traumatic effect on the nation and caused some profound changes. One significant change was the introduction of functioning (by Japanese standards) participatory democracy. Another was the adoption of a constitution (at the point of American bayonets) that forbade Japan the right to possess offensive military capability and to use what armed forces it might possess beyond its own territory.

Both the new democracy and the prohibition of armed "adventures" worked, sort of. Japan's democracy is still uniquely Japanese and many of the same groups (merchants, aristocrats, etc.) that dominated past governments now dominate the post–World War II ones. Thus for the past forty-plus years, a Japanese Self-Defense Force (JSDF) has grown into the most capable, and arguably the most powerful, armed force in the region. Although the JSDF has only 250,000 troops (all volunteers), they are eager, well-trained, and well-equipped. They have also not lost the traditional Japanese "code of the warrior." Man for man, these troops are more effective than any other in the region (most other Asian armies are largely sullen conscripts).

In a national emergency, the armed forces can be brought up to 300,000 combat troops, made more effective by the extensive use of civilians for support jobs. Japan possesses the strongest navy in the region, with fifteen subs and over fifty destroyers and frigates. The Air Force has four hundred modern combat aircraft, and the ground forces comprise fourteen divisions (with over a thousand tanks). Most important, this force is backed by the strongest industrial economy in the region.

What Japan does not have, and is not likely to have any time soon, is nuclear weapons. This eliminates any Japanese threat to nuclear-armed China. Korea, even after a reunification and demobilization, would have larger ground forces and nearly equal air forces. To the south it's a different story. Southeast Asia has much to fear from economic, and perhaps even military, domination by Japan. With a growing number of economic interests to protect in a region long beset by internal and international conflicts, Japan will be under increasing economic, and domestic political, pressure to maintain its supply of raw materials and its access to markets. A new generation of Japanese is coming of age who never witnessed the sky growing black with masses of American bombers or experienced the rain of bombs that fell on Japan for over a year during World War II.

Already, many Japanese are urging a change in Japan's constitution in order to allow Japan a greater military role in world affairs. Ten years ago such a change would have been unthinkable. But the votes to stop such a move are dying off with the World War II generation. Japanese military and political ineffectuality in the face of the Iraqi attack on Kuwait embarrassed many. The memories of Japan's first lost war are fading while the visions of an ever-stronger Japan conjure up in many Japanese the image of military and economic power. The return of the "Northern Territories" (Kuril Islands) to Japan by Russia will further pale those World War II memories—as well as resolve a sticking point in Russo-Japanese relations.

PART FIVE
THE AMERICAS

Geographically and culturally isolated from the rest of the world, the Americas are populated as well by refugees from the rest of the world's trouble spots. As a result, the wars in the Americas tend to be relatively low-key and largely internal. Revolution and internal disorder are the norm. Yet there is a lot of that, particularly in Latin America, where the transition from eighteenth-century colonial rule to twentieth-century participatory democracy has not been completed.

CHAPTER 13

CENTRAL AMERICA

INTRODUCTION

Revolutionaries battle other revolutionaries, and both fight the old *patrones* ("landowners") in Latin American nations who never made "democratic capitalism" work for anyone but a small, wealthy minority—that isn't democracy, that's oligarchy; and it hasn't been capitalism either, but a curious form of national mercantilism and a large dose of common corruption. For these reasons, and a host of other ethnic, cultural, economic, and geographical factors, violent administration of and quick changes in local government have been the centuries-long norm in Central and South America.

The (U.S.) Monroe Doctrine of 1823 supposedly put such mayhem off limits to nations outside the Americas, but it didn't prohibit the United States from intervening economically and militarily. If the local tough guys got out of line, here came the U.S. Marines and many of the nations affected by this yanqui intervention saw little difference between American and European interference. Central America has long suffered from the "Pistolero Effect" in which oligarchs or bandits in the guise of revolutionaries (or not in the guise, as the case might be) toss out the reigning fascists and bring in their own clique. But these revolutions bring about few changes.

During the Cold War period, the Monroe Doctrine became hard to enforce. The CIA held the line in miserable Guatemala (1954), shutting

down the leftist-yet-elected Arbenz government and leaving the land in the control of a feudal (but anti-Communist) military. Fidel Castro then tossed out the corrupt Batista regime and turned Cuba red. Russian guns and Cuban advisers started mixing with local troubles, and political and social problems that were once ignored became international concerns.

With the collapse of Eastern European communism, and the dismal (and now very corrupt) failure of Castro's revolution, the danger is that Central America's troubles will once more disappear in the backwater eddies of international politics. The trouble is, all the old social and economic inequities still exist, the fratricidal hatreds are still present, and all the guns are still around.

SOURCE OF CONFLICT

Central America, Spain's colonial backwater, long avoided the twentieth century's tides of social, economic, and political change. Dualistic market (markets seriously restricted by political access) and barter economies, the *patrón* system of landownership (vesting all authority, to include life and death legalities, in the large estate landowner), submission to outside economic interests (such as U.S. fruit companies), and governmental failure to integrate the hinterlands into the national economic and political fabric, all combined to produce countries needing not one but several revolutions. Yet revolutionary slogans and firepower cannot solve problems created by 450 years of neglect. Solutions require education, capital, and stability. All of these take peace and time. In Central America, peace has been in short supply.

Despite the relative subsidence of the East-West bloc confrontation, the basic political situation in the Central American countries remains unchanged. With the exception of Belize and Costa Rica, the short story of Central America has been the sad fact that the genuine social revolutions have been co-opted by outside interests who have little real commitment to the betterment of the people. These revolutions were long overdue. Inequitable distribution of wealth, lack of social and economic opportunity for all but the elite, and inhumane military regimes created a social and political climate where rapid, revolutionary action was inevitable. Cuba's armed revolution, under the overt name of "new socialism" (and covert Kremlin expansionism), produced a new form of mass, endemic poverty. The Sandinista revolt produced a new class of privileged—the Sandinist bureaucratic functionaries, the Sandinist Army, and various "philosophical friends." Central America's unanswered question remains: What kind of revolution could make change stick? After the revolutionaries toss out the government they are the government. Now the real problems begin.

Old political debts are one of the new government's biggest problems.

Revolutionaries turn to outside sources for arms, and getting arms is sort of like getting a loan from the Mafia—when you owe, you really owe. Though the revolution arises for indigenous reasons, the outside source exerts a strong influence upon the revolutionaries. The revolutionaries must then resist their own allies who are agents of the outside supporter. The outside supporter then demands its payoff. It's an old tactic; for example, the United States organized and funded Panamanian revolutionaries and then extracted the Canal Zone as its payment. Seeing the same old imperialism, supporters of the revolution began to fall away, charging their former cohorts with "selling out the revolution." The remaining revolutionaries must face the new reality of running the country. They are forced to make unpopular decisions—they may choose to pay their political debts at the expense of a frustrated populace. These revolutionaries, now called the government, become increasingly isolated. The old revolutionary vanguard becomes the new elite. Commissars become *patrones*.

The Sandinista regime in Nicaragua, curtailed though not toppled by Mrs. Violeta Chamorro's democratic electoral victory in February 1990, was in deep political hock to Havana and Moscow. In the politics of payoff, that meant the Sandinistas promoted policies of virulent anti-Americanism and military support for Marxist guerrillas in El Salvador and elsewhere. In the context of the Cold War, the idea was to "keep the Third World stewing" and portray the West, the United States in particular, as the enemy of the developing world. While this was good policy from the perspective of an imperial Kremlin, it was bad policy for a government in Nicaragua—at least if that government were genuinely interested in nation building. The U.S. government disliked the Sandinista rhetoric and perceived the Sandinista arms buildup on the Central American isthmus as a strategic threat. What had been a popular anti-Somoza revolution, led by the Sandinistas then co-opted by their more "Bolshevik" element, became a superpower game. This was sad and wasteful—the last thing the Nicaraguans needed was more conflict. Public weariness of war did the Sandinistas in as much as their aggressive bureaucracy (the new *patrones*) and economic failure.

Sandinistas wanted to build an army of 600,000 troops. Just before the election the regular Army consisted of 97,000 soldiers backed by 250,000 "militia" troops—Sandinista labor groups, government workers, and other paid-off factions. As late as December 1989, as many as five hundred Cuban military advisers were still in the country but there was no evidence that Cubans had flown any combat helicopter missions. Nicaragua received aid from several nonbloc sources, including 5,000 G-3 automatic rifles shipped by Papandreou's Greek government.

The Russians weren't the only power pulling guerrilla strings. When the Sandinistas talk about the CIA controlling the contras they aren't far off the mark, but the revolutionary who refuses superpower beneficence has the proverbial tough row to hoe. Edén Pastora, the former Sandinista and five-star revolutionary hero, defected from the Sandinista junta because of the overwhelming East bloc influence. But he didn't want to make the mistake of getting into the same situation with Uncle Sam so he refused to deal with elements he (still) considers to be controlled by Washington.

The isthmus between the North and South American continents really is the strategic neck of the Western Hemisphere. That's the geographic fact that drove the superpowers' game. As that game subsides, the old troubles return, but the United States remains particularly sensitive to the Panama Canal's still useful sea link. The U.S. invasion of Panama in December 1989 attests to that fact.

Where are those who would deal with the fundamental human problems that fed the covert war between the superpowers and continue to provide the background for future armed disputes? Moderates—and there are many who want change without bloodshed—get shot by right-wing death squads or get assassinated by left-wing terrorists, and the old oligarch elites run to Miami. The revolution turns sour and the revolutionaries start tooling around Managua in Mercedeses. The face of power is changed in a monitored election but the old resentments of the heart don't change.

The peasant who spilled his blood for the revolution sees his new farm taken over by the "State." Back in the woods, the Indians continue to starve. In fact, in Guatemala the government continues to fight an Indian war. In future wars between the elites the Indians will continue to suffer.

The change will succeed only if there is peace. But with the automatic rifles and grenade launchers still near at hand, the uneasy *pistoleros* ("gunmen") in from the hills, the Red fascists with "their people" still in the Army and the police, the right-wing militarists with death squads in the back room, and tattered economies controlled by a wealthy elite and a corrupt bureaucracy, peace in the Central American backwater remains a ragged, distant prospect.

WHO'S INVOLVED

United States—The Colossus of the North, Washington has tended to support whoever claimed to be anti-Communist and provided local stability. Now it tries to promote "democratic change"—in the interest of local stability—and a drug-free body politic. Its promotion efforts can include military invasion—witness Panama, December 1989.

Cuba—Fidel is old, but the last true Communist may want to go down in "glory"—whatever kind of bloody hell that is. Allegedly, Castro has five million automatic weapons stashed on his island. Cuba has trained revolutionary cadres throughout Latin America.

Nicaragua

The "new democratic" Nicaraguan regime—This fractured collection of moderate democrats, socialists, and anti-Sandinista leftists and revolutionaries united against increasing Communist subversion and domination of the Nicaraguan revolution, then won an open election (see p. 192).

Nicaraguan Sandinistas—These are the remaining "revolutionary vanguard" and militarized political elites of the anti-Somoza revolution.

United States-backed anti-Sandinista groups—Remnants of the overt "covert army" backed by the CIA and based in Honduras, they are now inside Nicaragua and allegedly disarmed.

"Miskito" Indians—These Creole and native American peoples live in eastern Nicaragua.

El Salvador

El Salvador government—The divisions and tensions between moderates and the right wing are deep.

Left-wing El Salvadoran guerrillas and terrorists—Many of these were trained by Havana.

Right-wing El Salvadoran groups and "death squads"—These are the guerrillas and terrorists with money and governmental protection.

The people of El Salvador—They are trapped in the cross fire between murderous old oligarchs and murderous ideologues.

Guatemala

Guatemalan government—It's always armed, at times it's even civilian.

Guatemalan military—This presence is a power unto itself.

Left-wing Guatemalan revolutionaries—What's left of them.

"Guatemalan" (Mayan) Indians—Still the resentful underclass.

Panama

United States—As creator of the canal, and the nation of Panama, it still feels responsible for both.

Other major players—"Elected" Panamanian government, underground elements of "old" (Torrijos/Noriega) Panamanian National Guard tied to drug running, Castro, and (yes) former CIA operations.

Wild Cards

Honduras—This seems to be a regional "moderate democracy," but only in comparison to El Salvador and the deposed Sandinista dictatorship.

Costa Rica—In the area, Costa Rica is comparatively rich and comparatively defenseless.

Contadora Group—Mexico, Venezuela, Colombia, and Panama are nations seeking negotiated solutions to Central American conflicts.

Colombian, Central American, and U.S. drug cartels—These are the bad guys with money, guns, and lawyers.

Catholic Church—It is split between an old-guard wing and a Marxist-influenced, social-activist "liberation theology" wing.

"Insurgent" Protestant evangelical organizations—Especially active in Guatemala, these groups represent a challenge to several traditional Latin American means of social control (i.e., the Catholic Church, militarism, and, for that matter, Marxism). The message is self-help, but they also go in for ecstatic preaching, personal testimonials, and plate passing. (American cable TV preachers become authority figures . . . they may make many wistful for the bad old days of Jesuits and Castro.)

Belize—Guatemala has moved toward renouncing its long-term claim to Belize, but a Guatemalan military dictatorship, suddenly in need of a "foreign enemy" that could deflect domestic discontent, might find the claim to Belize worth resurrecting. (Like the Argentine junta of 1982, this dictatorship would make a Falklands mistake and involve a Super Wild Card—Great Britain.)

Super Wild Cards

Russia—Old habits die hard. Despite Russia's and the "Soviet Union" 's massive internal troubles, an overt threat by the United States toward Cuba could lead to at least the threat of renewed Kremlin troublemaking or support—a Russian infantry brigade is still based in Cuba. The Russians may play an important political role, however, in the politics of constructing a post-Castro Cuban government, especially if the change is evolutionary rather than revolutionary.

Great Britain—With troops in Belize, the Lion is there.

GEOGRAPHY

Central America may be seen as a mountain range dividing two coastal plains, with the Caribbean coastal lowlands forming the eastern margin. They're flat, swampy, and largely covered by tropical forest, and the region's hurricanes, poor soils, and insects discourage settlement. The coastal lowlands tend to get left to the Indians and the poor.

The Pacific coastal plain is narrower than its Caribbean cousin. Weather patterns give it a tropical wet-dry climate. There are more deciduous forests there than on the other coast and some open grasslands. The western plain is widest around the Gulf of Fonseca between El Salvador, Nicaragua, and Honduras.

The mountains sweep down the isthmus in a long arc of parallel ridges. The western range is volcanically active, the eastern range, especially in Honduras and Guatemala, is very rugged. The backcountry tends to remain culturally and economically isolated: Mayan Indians in the Guatemalan highlands remained relatively untouched by the dominant Spanish society well into the twentieth century. The isolated mountain regions and the relatively empty wetlands provide excellent rebel staging areas.

The people of El Salvador and Honduras tend to cluster in the *tierra templada*, a temperate and less disease-ridden zone that runs from roughly 800 to 1,800 meters above sea level. This also holds true in Guatemala and Costa Rica.

Nicaragua is the largest Central American country, with 148,000 square kilometers. Honduras has an area of 109,500 square kilometers and Guatemala 109,000. Next comes Panama with 77,300 and Costa Rica with 51,000. Belize covers 23,000 square kilometers and tiny El Salvador nearly 21,500.

Coffee is the region's primary export crop. Bananas and other agricultural products follow in importance. Dependence on these crops makes national economies highly vulnerable to price fluctuations: Even a shift of fifteen to twenty-five cents in export coffee prices can have a major effect. Only in Costa Rica is industrial activity a larger portion of the GDP than agriculture.

Some 26 million people live in Central America. Guatemala has a population of 8.4 million, with 55 percent Ladinos and Mestizos, 36 percent Mayan Indians (many of whom in the mountains do not understand Spanish). Over 90 percent of Honduras' 4.5 million people are Mestizos.

El Salvador has around 5.2 million people, with Mestizos making up 89 percent of its population, Indians 10 percent, and white Europeans 1 percent (1.5 million people live in the capital, San Salvador). Nicaragua has almost 3 million people, 69 percent Mestizos, 17 percent white Europeans, 9 percent Caribbean blacks, and 5 percent Indians. The mountains break around Nicaragua's lake district and Nicaragua's largest population centers lie along the shores of Lake Managua and Lake Nicaragua.

Costa Rica has a population of 2.7 million, 97 percent of European origin, the majority of whom trace their ancestry to Spain. The relative homogeneity of Costa Rica's population (combined with a higher level of education and health) is a major factor in Costa Rica's comparative stability. Cynics say Costa Rica is stable because most of the Indians have been killed off. This overstates the case, but not by much. There are 20,000 Indians in Costa Rica, roughly the same number that inhabited Costa Rica in 1525. Belize, on the other hand, is highly heterogeneous, though the population is small. In a population of only 170,000, 50 percent are Creole blacks of Caribbean origin (most in Belize City and its coastal area), 20 percent are Mayan Indians, and 20 percent are Mestizos. The British infantry battalion stationed at the airport in Ladyville and at Hold Fast Camp gives Belize a lot of local stability and political confidence. The key political question fought between Belize's political parties is which one of them can best assure that the British will stay. English is the official language of Belize, though Spanish is widely spoken, especially along the Mexican and Guatemalan borders.

Panama has a population of 2.3 million, 70 percent Mestizos, 14 percent Caribbean/West Indians, 10 percent white Europeans, and 6 percent Indians. Spanish is the official language, but 15 percent of the population speak English as their native language.

In all of these countries, with Belize as something of an exception, the ''Europeans'' tend to control the political processes and the economy, which seemed to be the case even in Sandinista Nicaragua.

Rapid population growth gives another dimension to the region's problems. The regional rate of increase is over 3.2 percent per year. Honduras sports a whopping 3.6-plus percent growth rate. That gives already struggling Honduras another 125,000 or so mouths to feed annually. Decline in infant mortality rates, due to improved nutrition and health for children, has helped produce these high growth rates. The powerful Catholic Church opposes birth control programs.

Population growth is also a problem for land reformers. More and more peasants must be settled on smaller and smaller farms. This problem is already apparent in El Salvador, which has the highest population density in all of Latin America. If the birthrate isn't controlled, revolutions of any stripe simply won't make any difference in terms of solving the problem of poverty. Another ten years at the present birthrate will render any productivity increases or revolutionary redistribution of wealth meaningless.

HISTORY

Regional Overview

Spain conquered Central America between 1502 and 1540. The conquistadors didn't find much gold in Nicaragua, El Salvador, and Honduras, but they did take the best agricultural lands and established large private land holdings for the Spanish overseers. In Panama (for years a province of Colombia), at the isthmus, they found a route that opened up the west coast of South America. The Indians either retreated into the hills or became slaves.

Guatemala, Nicaragua, Costa Rica, El Salvador, and Honduras were provinces under the captaincy general of Guatemala. In 1821 they broke with Spain during the Latin American revolt.

At first Mexico tried to keep all of the Central American provinces in one large union, but El Salvador insisted on Central American autonomy. Mexican forces invaded El Salvador in 1823 (Mexican imperialism is not a foreign notion in Central America). El Salvador, looking for an ally, asked the U.S. government to make it a state. The United States was cool to the idea, but a revolution in Mexico led to a Mexican withdrawal. Later that year the five Central American provinces of El Salvador, Nicaragua, Honduras, Costa Rica, and Guatemala formed the Federal Republic of Central America. The union dissolved in 1838, with much mutual bickering and recrimination, and Honduras seemed to be the only nation interested in continuing the arrangement. (In fact, until 1922, the reestablishment of the Central American federation was a major feature of Honduran policy.) There have been several union proposals made since the breakup, but they have failed to arouse much enthusiasm.

British and German investments in the 1850s, primarily in coffee plantations, did return some capital to the region, but they also tied the local economies to one or two crops. In the twentieth century, large U.S. firms began to acquire banana and coffee plantations in the area. Native businessmen and politicians tended to become the local representatives of foreign investment interests.

One of the major historical factors, U.S. Central American policy, could be summed up as unqualified support for any pro-U.S. regime. As long as foreign powers stayed away, as long as U.S. citizens weren't threatened, as long as American business interests weren't complaining, and as long as national borders weren't violated, Washington couldn't have cared less.

El Salvador

El Salvador's history is one of frequent revolutions. Since the 1930s all but two governments have been led by the military. In 1979 a civilian-military group overthrew President Carlos Humberto Romero. Young officers and Christian Democrat allies formed a new junta in early 1980 and began a series of economic reforms which included the expropriation of all estates larger than 1,250 acres, nationalization of export marketing, and nationalization of the banks. The right-wing objected and many wealthy landowners left the country, and the left-wing opposition, centered on the Democratic Revolutionary Front (FDR), refused to join the government. Members of the radical Popular Liberation Forces (PLF), already waging a low-level war in the countryside, saw the splintering of its center and right opposition as an opportunity. The civil war was on.

Centrist socialist José Napoleón Duarte tried to forge a moderate political center in the midst of the turmoil, but he was foiled by radicals of the left and right and by his own failing health. In 1989, Alfredo Cristiani of the right-wing Arena party was elected president. The leftist FMLN guerrillas launched a "final" offensive on November 11, 1989, which marked a new phase in the war: For the first time in the conflict, the left-wing guerrillas tried to seize and hold territory. Focusing on the big prize—San Salvador—packets of guerrilla forces infiltrated through the eastern and northern working-class neighborhoods (Soyapango, Zacamil, Ciudad Delgado, Mejicanos). From there they launched attacks into the upscale suburbs (Escalon) in an attempt to "take the war to the wealthy." The strategy was to tie down Army units with attacks on headquarters and economic sites, then hit political targets. After eleven days the offensive sputtered: The guerrillas withdrew, leaving some 460 dead (5 percent of their total strength). While the assault was, from a military perspective, a defeat for the guerrillas, the FMLN did score on the political front. It shredded the El Salvadoran government's claims that the rebels could no longer mass forces. The rebels won a political victory, of sorts, when right-wing death squads murdered six Jesuit priests and provoked international outrage.

El Salvador continues to suffer from the disruption and violence of its two separate but related wars. The political right and political center fight an overt main-force guerrilla war against the rebel left. Then there is the terror war. The far right wages a "death-squad" war against the center and left-wing elements that have not gone underground. The far left murders its centrist and right-wing opponents. Moderates die in between, along with peasants, students, American nuns, and journalists. The political compass points in several directions at once: army coup d'état, open elections, more civil war, internal collapse. In July 1990 the El Salvadoran government had 57,000 troops under arms. Estimates of hard-core guerrilla strength ran from 7,000 to 10,000. The government had promised to cut the Army to 18,000 troops once a peace treaty was signed, but after some 70,000 deaths and $4.5 billion in U.S. aid, the war sputters on. As the left and right negotiate, the economy declines.

Nicaragua

In the seventeenth, eighteenth, and nineteenth centuries, Spaniards in Nicaragua fought a number of battles with the Miskito Indians of the Caribbean coast. Great Britain supported the Miskitos and even controlled a small strip of the eastern coast until the late 1800s.

After the breakup of the Central American federation, Nicaragua experienced nearly a hundred years of instability. American adventurers, the notorious William Walker being the most prominent, fueled the ongoing disputes between polarized liberal democrats and supporters of the old patriarchal elite.

The United States intervened on a number of occasions. U.S. Marines were in and out of Nicaragua between 1912 and 1933, when Roosevelt finally withdrew them as part of his Good Neighbor Policy—the United States was also involved in the Great Depression.

Before the Marines left, they placed Anastasio Somoza García into power. The Somozas controlled the country until 1979, when Anastasio

Somoza Debayle was overthrown by the Sandinistas. The 1979 revolution was popular—businessmen, church groups, peasants, the middle class, and ideological opponents banded together to topple the Somoza regime.

The Sandinista junta became increasingly militant and anti-United States. East bloc military advisers entered the country, along with a flood of small arms and antiquated tanks and helicopters. The Sandinistas doubled, then tripled the size of their armed forces; the reason given was to thwart a U.S. invasion. The Sandinistas frightened Honduras and shook Costa Rica's complacent worldview. CIA-sponsored contras (anti-Sandinista forces) operated against the Sandinistas from bases in Honduras and from camps inside Nicaragua.

In the mid-1980s, several Sandinista revolutionaries broke with the regime and had their own guerrilla groups operating from inside Nicaragua and from Costa Rica. Ham-handed and ideological Sandinista attempts to control the Miskito Indians of the Caribbean coast backfired and produced an Indian revolt. The Sandinista junta beefed up the secret police, imposed press censorship, and shut down the offices of human rights groups who objected to Sandinista junta policies. That led to further defections from the anti-Somoza ranks.

The Sandinistas, however, knew how to take care of their own. They expanded the governmental bureaucracy and stuffed it with Sandinista supporters. They confiscated opposition goods and real estate, and redistributed them to their guys and gals. The Sandinistas could also rely on old-fashioned anti-yanqui emotion: The junta blamed the abysmal Nicaraguan economy on the U.S.-imposed embargo and "contra terrorism."

In late 1989, outside pressure and economic decline forced the Sandinista junta to agree to open, internationally monitored elections. The Sandinistas believed, with good reason, that they could win an open election by playing on anti-yanqui sentiment, portraying themselves as the saviors of Nicaragua from the Somoza scourge, and by—when appropriate—sabotaging the opposition.

In one of the more surprising electoral results to ever come out of Central America, Mrs. Violeta Chamorro and her UNO party defeated the Sandinistas in February 1990. The election was witnessed by two thousand foreign observers. The war weariness of the populace (30,000 Nicaraguans killed) was a major factor in her election, as well as popular disenchantment with the Sandinistas which ran deep. Even Masaya, the first town of any size to rise against Somoza and long considered hardcore Sandinista territory, spurned the FSLN in favor of the National Opposition Union (UNO).

Mrs. Chamorro was inaugurated in April 1990—after the Sandinistas had rammed through legislation exempting them from prosecution for theft and other crimes. In what was viewed as a troubling compromise on Chamorro's part, Sandinista Humberto Ortega remained in charge of the Sandinista People's Army (Ejército Popular Sandinista—EPS). Contra forces returned to Nicaragua and began a slow (and begrudging) process of disarmament.

The rebels' demobilization gave Mrs. Chamorro the political opportunity to slice up the EPS. The Chamorro government planned to first shrink the Army to less than 40,000 troops and end the bitterly divisive Sandinista military draft, then turn the force into an even smaller and professional border guard.

This struck at the heart of Sandinista power. The question in Nicaragua remains who in the military is loyal to what and to whom. Old Sandinista military officials still remained in control as of early 1991.

Honduras

Given the region's reputation, during the last quarter of the twentieth century, Honduras has been an island of comparative tranquility. Maybe it's despair at the endemic poverty. Maybe it's the fact that in the first sixty-odd years of this century Honduras experienced over a hundred internal revolts and government changes—turmoil even more marked by the fact that the Andino administration ruled from 1932 to 1948 and provided a relative source of calm and stability. Honduras did receive a visit from the U.S. Marines in 1912, and the partisan left-right political clashes typical of the region do occur. In Honduras, though, oddly enough these clashes have never produced the polarization found in Guatemala, El Salvador, and Nicaragua. Though plagued by military coups, Honduras has enjoyed periods of national cooperation. Ever since their highly successful national strike in 1954, Honduran labor unions have held a great deal of political power.

Guerrilla activity in Honduras has been minimal, though spillover fighting along guerrilla infiltration routes around the Gulf of Fonseca (between El Salvador and Nicaragua) has concerned the present government. The removal of contra forces from Honduras has been a major relief to the entire nation.

The 1969 Soccer War between El Salvador and Honduras didn't officially end until 1980, when the two countries finally agreed to settle lingering border differences. Rivalry over a series of soccer matches sparked the brief five-day fight. The real issue was, from the Salvadoran perspective, Honduran so-called mistreatment of Salvadoran migrants. From the Honduran perspective it was illegal Salvadoran immigration. Given El Salvador's current internal disruption and the mutual threat presented by instability in Nicaragua, a Soccer War rematch is highly unlikely. The war, however, was indicative of several things. In main-force, conventional combat, the Salvadoran Army can be an effective offensive force. The Honduran Air Force performed well, and in 1990 the Honduran Air Force is even better. Though effectively limited to one squadron of high-performance fighter-bombers and outnumbered by what was, until February 1990, a rapidly growing Nicaraguan Air Force, the Honduran Air Force has a corps of superb pilots. The Hondurans believe this compensates for their weak ground forces (in 1990 a strength of some 23,000 poorly equipped troops). The Honduran pilots believe they are more than a match for any potential opponents, be the opposition Guatemalan, Salvadoran, Nicaraguan, Cuban, or mercenary.

Belize

Belize is increasingly recognized as a major zone of early Mayan Indian development. With sites excavated at Altun Ha, Xunantunich ("Maid of the Rock," near the Guatemalan border), and El Pilar, archaeologists have begun to focus on the area's importance as a pre-Columbian center of Mayan civilization. Columbus passed the Belizean coastline on his fourth voyage in 1502, but the first European settlements were begun in 1638 by shipwrecked Englishmen.

The area around Belize City was a perfect haven for pirates—shallow-water approaches discouraged deep-draft men-of-war from chasing the swift pirate craft, and if the soldiers did land there was lots of jungle in which to slink. Over the next 150 years the area attracted runaway slaves, adventurers, thieves, and loggers. Mahogany paid for a trek into the hinterland.

Foreign powers exerted little control over the area. Britain "officially" recognized Spanish dominion during the 1700s, then with the collapse of Spain's continental empire, the area was up for grabs. Still, Britain didn't formally establish British Honduras as a colony until 1840. Guatemala's on-again, off-again claim to Belize is based on eighteenth-century treaties between Spain and Britain.

In June 1973 the colony changed its name to Belize. It became independent in September 1981. Belize has one of the finest barrier reefs in the world which the government hopes to use as a means of attracting more tourists. There may also be significant oil fields in the area, on the trend running from Mexico's Yucatán fields.

Guatemala

With the great city of Tikal as an archaeological testament, Guatemala was the center of Mayan civilization. Parts of Guatemala came under Spanish control in 1524 after the defeat of the Mayas by the conquistador Pedro de Alvarado. Guatemala seceded from Spain in 1821, at first as part of Mexico, then as a chief architect (in an attempt to maintain the captaincy general of Guatemala) of the ill-fated Central American federation. After the federation collapsed, the cycle of Guatemalan internal politics was bitterly established: long periods of military dictatorship infrequently interrupted by brief, unstable democratic governments.

In 1944 "the October revolutionaries" overthrew Gen. Jorge Ubico's dictatorship, then a period of attempts at social change was begun by President Juan José Arévalo in 1945–50.

In 1952, Colonel Jacobo Arbenz Guzman, Arévalo's successor as president, gave the underground, Communist-run Guatemalan Labor party (PGT) legal status and by 1954 it controlled several labor organizations and key posts in the government. The "red flag" went up in Washington and the Guzman government was toppled by a CIA-aided Army coup.

Guatemala was governed by a series of military juntas or military-"sponsored" civilian governments until 1985, when a civilian president, Vinicio Cerezo Arévalo, was elected. One of the more interesting military governments was headed by Gen. Efrain Rios Montt, who took power in March 1982 and ruled for sixteen months. He denounced death-squad activity and set in place a number of "populist" programs, the majority of which, however, were designed to gain Indian help in fighting leftist guerrillas. Rios Montt belonged to a fundamentalist Protestant Church sect and was viewed with suspicion by the influential hierarchy of the Catholic Church. His regime was characterized by bitter anti-Communist repression. Rios Montt was toppled in October 1983 but retains a significant following in Guatemala. Guatemala went through a difficult election in 1990. Shaky civilian rule continued. The Army watches.

Costa Rica

Columbus landed in the Costa Rican region in 1502. The Spaniards began to settle the area in 1522. Despite its name ("Rich Coast"), Costa Rica wasn't a land of mineral wealth—no gold, no gems—and had an Indian population adept at escaping Spanish slavers. The land wasn't particularly productive agriculturally, either, so Costa Rica developed as a backwater's backwater—a land of small, often-struggling farmers and landowners. Costa Ricans often think this experience helped lay the foundations for some of their egalitarian traditions.

Costa Rica seceded from Spain in 1821. In the midst of the turmoil associated with the Central American federation, Costa Rica took its Guanacaste Province from neighboring Nicaragua. This is still remembered—by the Nicaraguans. When the Sandinistas made noises about chasing Edén Pastora's ARDE guerrilla group into its Costa Rican sanctuaries, the fact that Guanacaste had been Nicaraguan territory was an unspoken irritant.

Costa Rica held its first free election in 1889. Since that time Costa Rican democracy has proved quite resilient. Only two events mar the record: the short-lived dictatorship of Federico Tinoco (1917–18) and the disputed 1948 presidential election. Two thousand people died that year when the Army, allied with a Communist-led guerrilla force, attempted a coup. José Figueres Ferrer (known affectionately as Don Pepe), the leader of the revolt against the coup, established an interim regime which wrote a new constitution that guaranteed universal suffrage and abolished the Army. He served three nonconsecutive terms as president.

Costa Rica's Civil Guard is essentially a police force trained for border surveillance and patrol in the urban areas. The Rural Guard polices the backcountry. The total force is around 4,000 men. During the height of the Sandinista tensions, the Civil Guard clashed with Nicaraguan forces along the border, but Costa Rica relies on the Organization of American States to defend its borders. This means Costa Rica's borders are guaranteed by the armed forces of the United States, but because of the so-called sensitivities of small nation politics, no one is supposed to say that out loud.

Panama

The first European explorers reached Panama in 1501, then in 1513 Vasco Nuñez de Balboa crossed the isthmus and encountered the "Southern Sea'' (Pacific Ocean). From that point on, geography made Panama a strategic asset for any power wishing to operate in both the Pacific and Atlantic oceans.

The Spaniards transshipped Incan gold and silver from the Pacific, across Panama, to their Iberia-bound treasure galleons, dreaming of a canal across the isthmus—gold-humping mule trains and Indian slaves were slow and a pain to maintain.

Panama seceded from Spain in 1821 and joined the new Republic of Greater Colombia. Three times during the nineteenth century, Panamanians attempted to secede from Colombia. In 1903, after Colombia refused a U.S. bid to build a canal across the isthmus, the United States bankrolled and protected a Panamanian secessionist movement. The Panamanians declared independence and Colombia decided it didn't want to fight the U.S. Navy.

In 1914 the United States completed the eighty-three-kilometer-long canal in its sixteen-kilometer-wide Canal Zone. The Canal Zone was Panamanian territory but was completely administered by Washington.

From 1903 to 1968, an often-less-than-democratic government ruled in Panama, with local trading and business families actually controlling most of the politics. Still, the Panamanians resented U.S. control of the canal and the Canal Zone and demonstrations against U.S. control became more frequent and more heated.

In 1968, Brig. Gen. Omar Torrijos Herrera overthrew the newly elected president. From that time on, until the U.S. invasion in December 1989, the Panamanian National Guard, later renamed the Panamanian Defense Forces (PDF), was the arbiter of power, even under the guise of civilian rule. Constitutional democracy was supposedly restored in 1984, but in Panama, 1984 really was 1984—the military dictatorship was increasingly entrenched.

In February 1988, the head of the PDF, Gen. Manuel Antonio Noriega, was indicted by a U.S. grand jury on drug-smuggling charges. The civilian president of Panama, Eric Arturo Delvalle, attempted to remove Noriega from command. Noriega took over the government and conducted a bizarre anti–United States campaign that included hobnobbing with the Sandinistas and Cuba's Fidel Castro. He stifled the May 1989 elections. Then there was the poignant, and widely published, photo of bleeding vice presidential candidate Guillermo ''Billy'' Ford being whipped by a member of Noriega's paramilitary ''Dignity Battalions''—a streetwise force of brutal thugs paid off by Noriega and the PDF (and suggested by

Castro). In the fall of 1989 Noriega foiled an attempted coup by lower-ranking PDF officers.

If anything, Noriega began to swagger; he seemed to think himself invincible. In early December, harassment of U.S. personnel in Panama increased and after a U.S. Marine lieutenant was murdered, the United States struck.

In an operation code-named "Just Cause," U.S. airborne rangers hit the Panamanian control points and airfields as mechanized infantry and attack helicopters assaulted PDF headquarters. Marine units in light assault vehicles (LAVs) screened escape routes. U.S. special operations forces hit houses where intelligence sources suspected Noriega had been hiding and AC-130 "Spectre" gunships pinned down PDF forces. A total of 24,000 U.S. troops took part, destroying the PDF in less than eight hours. As a sidelight, two U.S. Air Force F-117A Stealth fighter-bombers participated in the action. One aircraft dropped a two-thousand-pound bomb near a barracks, stunning the PDF troops inside the building. The other F-117A completely missed its target. Initially the U.S. Air Force touted the strike as an example of successful use of high-tech weapons but was forced to retract its original claims.

(Several sources reported that Cuban Mig-21s shadowed U.S. C-141 jet transports ferrying paratroopers from North Carolina to Panama.)

Noriega eluded capture for several days. He eventually sought asylum in the Vatican embassy and a car was sent by the papal nuncio to pick Noriega up outside of a Dairy Queen ice-cream shop. U.S. troops bombarded the embassy compound with highly amplified heavy metal rock and roll, which the young soldiers and local Panamanian kids loved. The Vatican protested to Washington, and after considerable wrangling, the Vatican "urged" Noriega to turn himself over to the United States for trial as a drug smuggler. Yet more than a year after Noriega's fall the Panamanian economy still lay in shambles, the new police forces were unreliable, and the government remained ineffective. All the old troubles.

Local Politics

Belize

Belizean political parties—People's United party (PUP) and United Democratic party (UDP), the main parties in Belize. There are three smaller parties: Toledo Progressive party, Belize Popular party, and Christian Democratic party.

British Forces, Belize—One infantry battalion with an artillery battery (105-mm guns) and supported by a flight of Harrier jump jets.

Belmopan—Newly built "national capital." With the exception of the bureaucrats, few people want to live there since all the action (what there is of it) is either in Belize City or in the resort area of Ambergris Cay.

The Lions Club—In Belize City a particularly active and potentially politically influential business organization.

Guatemalan and Salvadoran refugees—A touchy subject. The influx of refugees from war-torn nations may have long-term demographic consequences for Belize.

Costa Rica

Costa Rican political parties—National Liberation party (PLN) and Social Christian Unity party (PUSC), the major parties. The PLN is a member of the Socialist International. Other parties include Costa Rican Socialist party, Costa Rican People's party, and Popular Vanguard party.

Servicio de Parques Nacionales de Costa Rica (Costa Rican National Parks Service)—"Good-guy" government agency. Costa Rica has made a valiant attempt to preserve its natural habitats. It also has an eye on increasing tourism.

El Salvador

Democratic Revolutionary Front (FDR)—Salvadoran leftists. Guillermo Ungo heads a small opposition socialist democratic party, and Rubén Zamora is a former Christian Democrat. The FDR is aligned with the FMLN as the FMLN–FDR, forming part of the Unified Revolutionary Directorate (DRU).

Farabundo Martí Revolutionary Front for National Liberation (FMLN)—Guerrilla alliance whose chief group is the Salvadoran Communist party. There are three other members: the Popular Liberation Forces (PLF, a group with a Maoist orientation), the People's Revolutionary Army, and the Armed Forces of National Resistance, which are both splinter groups of the Communist party. The fifth guerrilla group is the Central American Revolutionary Workers party. In mid-1983 an even more radical group, the Clara Elizabeth Ramírez Front (CERF), split from the PLF. The PLF may have fractured more in the aftermath of the November 1989 FMLN offensive and the Sandinistas' defeat in the February 1990 Nicaraguan elections. FMLN's chief combat leaders are Joaquin Villalobos and Gustavo Anaya. Head of "General Command" negotiating team is Shafik Handal. Villalobos now talks of negotiations.

Arena party—Right-wing nationalist Republican alliance headed by President Alfredo Crisitani. The real power may be Maj. Roberto d'Aubuisson, suspected death-squad organizer. The Salvadoran Authentic Institutional party is another right-wing group.

Christian Democratic party—Party of nominal moderates.

Salvadoran Army (Fuerza Armada)—Main source of political power in the country. The Air Force is armed with U.S.-supplied A-37 Dragonfly light attack jets. U.S. advisers have improved El Salvador's weapons' reliability and organization. The most successful counterguerrilla units of PRALs (long-range recon patrols) are units of three to twelve men who operate in guerrilla country.

"Death squads"—Name usually applied to right-wing terror groups who seek to enforce their aims by "making examples" of those who oppose them. Estimates vary, but death squads may have murdered as many as five thousand people since 1980.

The Six Jesuits—Jesuit priests and scholars murdered by death squads during guerrilla offensive in November 1989.

Salvadoran Institute for Agrarian Transformation (ISTA)—Government bureau with the task of administering land reform.

Guatemala

Christian Democratic party (DCG)—As of 1990, the largest and most powerful party, though ultimate control lies with the Army.

Union of the National Center (also National Centrist Union) (UCN) —Led by Jorge Carpio Nicolle, a party capable of challenging Christian Democrats.

Other parties—National Liberation Movement, Nationalist Authentic Center (Authentic Nationalist party), Democratic Institutional party, Democratic Party of National Cooperation, National Renewal party, and Social Democratic party. The Revolutionary party (PR) is actually a moderate party.

Army of Guatemala—Main source of power in the nation, with 35,000 total troops. When the U.S. military arms embargo started to bite into the Army's capabilities, its senior officers turned to the international arms market for spares and simultaneously began to develop indigenous light-weapons-repair capabilities. As many of the rebels were now better armed, the Army sought to capture weapons from them. Its elite forces have allegedly been trained by the Israelis. In 1988 the Army also took command of the Treasury Police and National Police.

Guatemalan Labor party (PGT)—Communist party of Guatemala which has been outlawed.

Guatemalan National Revolutionary party (URNG)—"Unified" organization of three former left-wing guerrilla groups: the Guerrilla Army of the Poor (EGP), the Revolutionary Organization of the Armed People (ORPA), and the Rebel Armed Forces (FAR). Now the URNG also includes the Guatemalan Labor party and its small armed contingents.

Secret Anti-Communist Army (ESA)—Guatemalan death-squad organization allegedly run by high-ranking regular Army officers.

The White Hand—Right-wing terrorist force.

National Inter-Agency Coordinating Office (Coordinadora Inter-Institucional Nacional)—Advisory bodies set up in each Guatemalan province. The officers and advisers on the boards, who report directly to the regional military commander, have the task of coordinating all civilian agencies operating in the province. These boards are how the military keeps its thumb on all aspects of the government.

Panzos—Site of 1978 Army massacre of Indian population.

Drug producers—In 1989 world's sixth-largest producer of opium poppies.

"Bullets and beans" ("*fusiles y frijoles*," literally, "guns and beans")—Gen. Efrain Rios Montt's strategy of providing food, shelter, and protection for villages that would turn against leftist guerrillas. Montt, a Protestant evangelical, ran the military dictatorship in the early 1980s.

Honduras

Army of Honduras—The strongest power group in the country, with 23,000 troops. At present, though, Honduras is nominally a liberal democracy.

Honduran political parties—National party (PNH) and Liberal party (PLH), the largest and strongest parties. Both are centrist. The Liberal party exists in three main factions: Rodista, FUL, and ALIPO. Two other parties both attract approximately 5 percent of the electorate: National Innovation and Unity party (PINU) and Honduran Christian Democratic party (PDCH). "Unregistered" parties include: Communist party of Honduras (PCH) and Socialist party of Honduras (PASO).

Other political groups—Association of Honduran Campesinos (ANACH), Honduran Council of Private Enterprise (COHEP), Confederation of Honduran Workers (CTH), United Federation of Honduran Workers (FUTH).

Gen. Francisco Morazán—National hero of Honduras, who tried to keep the Central American federation together as a potential guerrilla force. His organization, the Morazán Liberation Front (considered at one time to be a Sandinista puppet, may actually be a Marxist splinter group controlled by no one), killed two U.S. soldiers in an attack in April 1990.

U.S. armed forces in Honduras—U.S. military presence there which includes the National Guard and Reserve forces. Many of these units were engineer formations engaged in building roads and airfields that were intended to support a U.S. attack on Sandinista Nicaragua. The Hondurans didn't want the war, but if the yanquis leave, the roads and airfields stay behind . . .

Nicaragua

Former Sandinista junta—Headed by former president Daniel Ortega Saavedra, includes his brother, Humberto Ortega, and head of the secret police, Tomas Borges. They are the "Castroite wing" of the revolution against Somoza.

Sandinista Front for National Liberation (FSLN)—Original umbrella group for opposition to Somoza. As the moderates left in disgust or fright, the FSLN became increasingly Marxist and anti-U.S.

National Employees Union—Sandinista-controlled union of government civil service workers.

Turbas—Pro-Sandinista street mobs used to terrorize opponents.

National Opposition Union (UNO)—"Fourteen-party bloc" umbrella organization of opposition to the Sandinista junta. Covering the spectrum of politics from right to left, it includes: National Conservative party, Conservative Popular Alliance, Conservative National Action party (a splinter group of the Conservative Democratic Movement), Democratic party of National Confidence, Independent Liberal party, Liberal party, Liberal Constitutionalist party, National Action party, Nicaraguan Democratic Movement (MDN) (headed by Alfonso Robelo), Nicaraguan Socialist party (formally a pro-Moscow Communist party, now social democratic), Communist party of Nicaragua (splinter group of Nicaraguan

Socialist party), Popular Social Christian party, Central American Integrationist party, and Social Democratic party (which includes key Chamorro advisers, Alfredo César and Pedro Joaquin Chamorro, her son).

Other Nicaraguan political parties—Democratic Conservative Movement (PCD) and Central American Unionist party.

Contras—Anti-Sandinista guerrillas whose main group was the Nicaraguan Democratic Force which fielded over 8,000 troops. The total force in the field at the time of the February 1990 election was 16,000. Col. Enrique Bermúdez, a former Somoza officer, was deposed as their leader. He was murdered in 1991, allegedly by Sandinistas. Re-contras have returned to the hills. Commander Rueben and Commander Franklin (noms de guerre) replaced Bermúdez.

Misurasata—Miskito, Sumo, and Rama Indian organization whose leader is Stedman Fagoth Muller. The Miskitos fielded 3,000 guerrillas. Misurasata is an important force for Indian rights and autonomy and is associated with Yatama, another Miskito organization.

La Prensa—Nicaraguan opposition newspaper owned by the Chamorro family. It was frequently shut down by Somoza and the Sandinista junta.

Chamorro clan—Political publishing family. Violeta Barrios de Chamorro (Dona Violeta) is the widow of Pedro Joaquin Chamorro Cardenal, the former publisher of *La Prensa*, who was murdered by order of Somoza in 1978. Two of her four children, Pedro Joaquin Chamorro and Cristiana Chamorro, joined her in the UNO. Her other two, Carlos Fernando Chamorro and Claudia Chamorro, were militant, high-ranking Sandinistas. Carlos edited the Sandinista newspaper, *Barricada*.

Edén Pastora—With a nom de guerre of Commander Zero, the Che Guevara of the anti-Somoza revolution who led the assault on Somoza's private bunker and revolted against the Sandinistas (see ARDE). Though personally popular, he is regarded by the left, right, and center as an unpredictable (and therefore dangerous) romantic.

Democratic Revolutionary Alliance (ARDE)—Anti-Sandinista guerrilla group once led by revolutionary socialist Edén Pastora. It was based in Costa Rica but faded from the scene after 1987.

Gen. Augusto Caesar Sandino—Nicaraguan national hero who fought the U.S. Marines to a stalemate in the 1920s and 1930s. When the Marines left in 1933, he left the backcountry and made peace with the new government. He was murdered during dinner with President Bautista by the National Guardsmen under the command of Anastasio Somoza. The Sandinistas take their name from Sandino.

Sandinistas' foreign supporters—Often nicknamed "Sandalistas," a legion of "leftish" groups and small political organizations in the United States and Western Europe who are attracted by the Sandinistas' revolutionary aura and romantic rhetoric. They enjoy protesting in front of the American embassy and speak of being in "internationalist solidarity" with the Sandinistas. The groups include: Veterans for Peace, Bikes Not Bombs, Nicaragua Network, Witness for Peace, and dozens more. Many Sandalistas expressed "utter shock" and "disorientation" at the results of the February 1990 Nicaraguan election.

Panama

Panamanian political parties—Authentic Panamenista party (PPA), Christian Democratic party (PDC), Labor party (PALA), Republican party (PR), Nationalist Republican Liberal party (MOLIRENA).

Remnant pro-Noriega party—Democratic Revolutionary party (PRD).

Panamanian Defense Forces (PDF)—New name of the Noriega-led National Guard. Its organization was destroyed by U.S. forces in the December 1989 invasion.

Panama Canal Treaties—Treaties signed on September 7, 1977, by U.S. president Jimmy Carter and Panamanian dictator Gen. Omar Torrijos, and that went into effect in October 1979. The treaties govern the operation and defense of the canal and guarantee the canal's neutrality. Panama will take over full operation of the canal in December 1999.

Panama Canal Commission—U.S. government agency with the task of running the Panama Canal and training Panamanians to take over the canal operations in 1999.

Canal Alternative Study Commission—Established by the United States, Japan, and Panama, a commission studying the feasibility of a new sea-level canal through the Panamanian isthmus.

Answer to the Canal Trivia Question: The Pacific (Balboa) end of the canal is actually east of the Atlantic (Colon) end. (The canal is cut northwest to southeast, from Atlantic to Pacific.)

Extended Local Politics

Central American Common Market (CACM) (MERCOMUN)—Established in 1960 by Guatemala, Honduras, El Salvador, Nicaragua, and

Costa Rica (though Costa Rica didn't formally join until 1963), a venture designed to promote Central American trade and develop local industries. However, industry ended up being concentrated in the countries with lowest wage rates. Honduras withdrew in 1971. It is now nonoperative —a good idea but failed venture.

U.S. Congress, U.S. public opinion, U.S. newspapers and TV networks—Considered by many Latin Americans to be the most important political battleground in Central America.

POLITICAL TREND CHARTS

BELIZE

Light industry and tourism fuel the economic uptrend.

	1990	1996 (Representative Democracy)
Government Effectiveness	5	5
Government Stability	5	6
Political Cohesion	5	5
Repression Level	3	2
Economic Development	3	4
Education Status	4	4 –

NOTE: 0 = minimum; 9 = maximum.

COSTA RICA

Stability continues. Getting rid of one's armed forces has at least one shining example of success.

| | 1990 | 1996 |
		(Representative Democracy)
Government Effectiveness	7	8
Government Stability	7	8
Political Cohesion	8	8
Repression Level	1	1
Economic Development	6 –	7 –
Education Status	6	6

NOTE: 0 = minimum; 9 = maximum.

EL SALVADOR

The reason the 1990 economic development is a "3" is because of all the money the United States has pumped into the country. Still, a 1996 "4 –" is possible if there is an end to the civil war and coffee prices are stable.

| | 1990 | 1996 |
		(Democratic Authoritarian)
Government Effectiveness	4	4
Government Stability	3	4
Political Cohesion	3	4
Repression Level	8	6
Economic Development	3	4 –
Education Status	3	4

NOTE: 0 = minimum; 9 = maximum.

GUATEMALA

The chart suggests that the military will dispense with the civilian cover story.

	1990 (Democratic Authoritarian)	1996 (Military Authoritarian)
Government Effectiveness	3	4
Government Stability	3	3
Political Cohesion	4	4
Repression Level	8	7
Economic Development	3 −	3
Education Status	2	3

NOTE: 0 = minimum; 9 = maximum.

HONDURAS

Next to no progress.

	1990	1996
	(Democratic Authoritarian)	
Government Effectiveness	4	4
Government Stability	5	6
Political Cohesion	5	6
Repression Level	5	5
Economic Development	2	3 −
Education Status	2	2

NOTE: 0 = minimum; 9 = maximum.

NICARAGUA

First Somoza robbed the country. Then the Sandinistas stole the revolution. Then the Sandinistas robbed the country. But Nicaragua has too much economic potential to remain the mess it was in early 1990.

	1990 (Representative Democracy)	1996 (Democratic Authoritarian)
Government Effectiveness	2	4
Government Stability	2	3
Political Cohesion	2	4
Repression Level	6*	4
Economic Development	2	4 –
Education Status	3	3

NOTE: 0 = minimum; 9 = maximum.
*Sandinista = 6; UNO = 4.

PANAMA

If global economic activity is vibrant, Panama could do well.

	1990 (Representative Democracy)	1996
Government Effectiveness	1*	4
Government Stability	2	5
Political Cohesion	3	4
Repression Level	5	3
Economic Development	3	5
Education Status	4	5

NOTE: 0 = minimum; 9 = maximum.
*Representative democracy enforced by foreign troops.

REGIONAL POWERS AND POWER INTEREST INDICATOR CHART

PANAMA

The drug cartels are still a major player, Cuba still has its hand in, and Mexico is eager to have less unrest on its southern border.

	Economic Interests	Historical Interests	Political Interest	Military Interest	Force Generation Potential	Ability to Intervene Politically	Ability to Promote Economic Development
U.S.	7	7	8	8	9	8	6
Drug Cartels	9	1	3	1	2	4	1
Cuba	2	6	5	2	3	2	0
Mexico	3	5	6	3	3	4	1

NOTE: 0 = minimum; 9 = maximum.

PARTICIPANT STRATEGIES AND GOALS

The United States wants to **(1)** defend the Panama Canal, **(2)** defend Mexico and the southern U.S. border, and **(3)** bring moderate, popular, and pro-U.S. governments into being.

U.S. neglect of Central America is dramatically balanced by a record of sudden frenzied concern, which ends when American isolationism reasserts itself, or when the region "stabilizes" either through democracy (Costa Rica) or strongman government (everybody else), or when a depression causes the United States to focus on itself (FDR and the Good Neighbor Policy in 1933).

U.S. economic interests in the region are only outclassed by Western Europe, Canada, Japan, and Persian Gulf oil.

Washington is trying to use economic and military aid to bring about social and political reforms in Central America. Negotiations by opposing factions, free elections, and land reallocation are part of the policy. This affects the use of American combat forces as well as the aid packages. A Cuban-style dictatorship merely substitutes one ruling oligarchy for another. Another side counters with the analysis that Central American revolutions are inevitable and anger at U.S. support for the old oligarchs is understandable. If the United States would stop supplying arms to the regimes in power, and then opened negotiations with the rebels, U.S. policy aims would be far better served. The first side then responds that "the Bolsheviks would subvert the Mensheviks," i.e., moderate democratic rebels who would opt for genuine coexistence and reform would be toppled by pro-Moscow extremists. So the arguments go.

The bipartisan Central American Policy Commission, chaired by Henry Kissinger, represented an attempt to overcome this policy hiatus. The commission's report reveals an understanding of the economic and social origins of Central America's problems, which are often glossed over by those who see the world as a struggle between the superpowers. The committee's recommendations stressed educational reform and highlighted the need for extensive development of basic transportation services and agricultural revitalization. Translated, this means teaching kids, building roads, and growing plants. All of these take time. War kills teachers and kids, destroys roads, and burns cornfields.

So what do you do in the short run, while people wage war against one another? The basic U.S. policy dilemma remains. Peace is essential to solving these human problems.

Essentially, Nicaragua, El Salvador, and Honduras represent three different U.S. strategies. In Nicaragua the United States withdrew its support from Somoza and encouraged the Sandinista revolution. An anti-American "socialist" clique threw out the moderates and ten harsh and bitter years of war resulted. The democrats' hold on power in Nicaragua remains tentative.

In El Salvador the United States has practiced a policy of providing "just enough" military and economic aid to sustain the government. In Honduras the United States has built military support and training facilities and essentially established a policy of bilateral defense, which promises the use of U.S. troops to defend Honduras. With the collapse of the Sandinista regime (whether temporary or not) the immediate importance of Honduras fades, though the commitments remain. The Honduran policy may work as a crude model for economic development programs, as long as Honduras maintains a liberal democratic government. Should a dictatorship return to power, the United States is back in the bind of supporting what could become an unpopular and oppressive regime.

Panama represents a fourth U.S. strategy: When everything goes wrong, invade. This strategy is often called "The (Teddy) Roosevelt Corollary to the Monroe Doctrine." Here's the gist of that: Whenever a government becomes "incapable of behaving properly," the United States, in support of its "civilizing mission" associated with the Monroe Doctrine, can act as the hemispheric police force. That strategy, of course, leads to other troubles.

Nicaragua

UNO—The UNO's aim is to reconstruct the economy, attract U.S. and foreign aid and investment, disarm the contras, and cut the Sandinista-leaning Nicaraguan Army back to a token border guard force, and to maintain the fractious UNO as a coherent political force. The government must weed out Sandinista sympathizers in the governmental bureaucracy. If the Sandinistas attempt an armed coup, the UNO can appeal to (1) Nicaraguan nationalism to stop it, (2) international opinion to stop it, or (3) in extremis, the United States for military assistance (Roosevelt Corollary time).

Sandinistas—The idea is to regain power by using strength in civil service unions, the Army, and old secret police networks. They need to stymie the UNO government's attempts to rein in inflation and privatize businesses with strikes and demonstrations; to create chaos, then either win an election or seize power through an armed coup. The Sandinistas speak of this strategy as "rule from below." The UNO and Mrs. Chamorro will have nominal control, but they will control the guns and the paper pushers. The Sandinistas remain a potent and well-organized opposition. They are counting on UNO fracturing into a dozen squabbling factions.

El Salvador

Government—What is the government? That's the first question. Is it the Army, as some maintain, or a hazy coalition of moderates and conservatives who are caught in a cross fire between the extreme right-wing and the left-wing guerrillas? Land reform has been a central issue. The government developed a strong land-reform policy but its implementation has been sporadic, and right-wing critics have tried to stop the program. In fact, President Cristiani's government has blocked implementations of part of the program. Moderates in El Salvador, those that have not fled or been slain, press for a centrist "government of national reconciliation" that seeks to bring in all but the most extreme political elements. This is almost as impossible as trying to stop right-wing death squads and left-wing guerrilla raids and terror bombings. The government is trying to **(1)** convince the peasants that reform is progressing, **(2)** stop left- and right-wing violence, and **(3)** ensure continued U.S. support. The government also claims that stopping outside support for left- and right-wing violence is beyond its means. Right-wing death squads are paid for by wealthy exiles living in Miami and elsewhere.

Several analysts in the United States have concluded that the government cannot "win" the war outright.

Right-wing groups—This clan has become a different kind of rebel, but nevertheless a rebel. They want to maintain the old economic system at all costs, which means stopping and then rolling back land reform. Assassination and terror are their tactical means. They don't want labor organizers or "meddling" clergy who talk about the health needs of peasants—those folks are just engaged in "stirring up trouble." They argue that the old patriarchal system provided a "kind of stability."

Left-wing rebels—The rebels aim to "stay in the field." They will keep up the tactics of hitting isolated Army posts, seizing and holding villages until the Army responds, and tackling government main-force units when such units are vulnerable. The guerrillas are very successful at operating out of their sanctuaries. Urban hit-and-run raids and "economic disruption" also play a part. The rebels dynamite electric generators, bridges, and railroads. This damages the economy. Shooting up buses and trucks further weakens the transportation and distribution networks. And the right wing rebels have no monopoly on terror. Assassination of key opponents remains a classic revolutionary tool—the trick is to shift the blame to someone else. Analysts are split as to the left-wing rebels' genuine willingness to negotiate. The end of Nicaraguan Sandinista direct supply of guerrilla operations, however, puts a logistical tether on the ambitions of the hard core.

The Other Players

Honduras—Honduras doesn't want to be left out of the aid windfall: The Hondurans argue that when the United States needed a place to put the contras, they provided one. Honduran democrats have tried to make a deal with the military and with right-wing elements for the maintenance of free elections. They argue that it is easier to get military and economic support from Washington if Honduras remains a democracy. This means new weapons and supplies for the Army, funds for capital investment, and a significant kick to the weak Honduran economy.

Guatemala—The Indian wars continue. Poverty continues. Corruption pervades. The Guatemalan Army's strategy is simple: When the situation gets too chaotic, step in and seize power. Whoever rules Guatemala, however, must address the entire spectrum of troubles. Per capita productivity declined by over 15 percent between 1980 and 1985. This is a nation in malaise.

Belize—The best idea is to keep the British in Belize, and to try to sell the country as an English-speaking destination for tourists and a site for light industrial development.

Costa Rica—Costa Rica needs to support the democratic government in Nicaragua (that keeps troubles away from the borders) and pay off its own mounting debts.

POTENTIAL OUTCOMES

Nicaragua

1. 35 percent chance through 1996: Severe instability wracks the democratically elected Chamorro regime; the UNO fragments;

and an ''authoritarian democratic'' but non-Sandinista (so as not to antagonize Washington) regime comes to power. (Contingent factor is foreign economic aid. See outcome 3.)

2. 25 percent chance: Sandinistas regain power through elections and/or ''military leverage'' (i.e., threats and intimidation). If this happens, there is a 70 percent chance of a new Indian and contra insurgency.

3. 25 percent chance: The UNO coalition stabilizes; the Sandinista Army is demobilized and a new army is formed as a ''border guard''; and a new Nicaraguan constitution is instituted using Costa Rica as a model. Note: This increases to an overall 75 percent chance if massive economic aid arrives in the 1991–94 time frame. (Massive is defined as $400 million or more. It would be unfair to assume that the United States should foot the bill, given the aid promised to the Sandinistas by Western European governments.)

4. 15 percent chance: A U.S. invasion of Nicaragua is provoked by a Sandinista power grab. This goes to a 90 percent chance if Cuban units are discovered aiding the Sandinistas in Nicaragua —a ''Panama situation'' will result and a Sandinista-inspired insurgency will begin in the hinterland.

El Salvador

1. 40 percent chance through 1996: Same old story—bloodshed, poverty, guerrilla war, coup d'état. The United States continues its program of giving just enough military and economic aid to sustain pro-U.S. forces and to enrich crooked right-wing generals. This drops to a 20 percent chance if rebel supply sources in Nicaragua dry up.

2. 40 percent chance: The moderate liberal democrats succeed in controlling the right-wing elements; the non-Communist left enters the political process, and reconstruction begins. This increases to a 60 percent chance if effective U.S. economic aid materializes ($200 million in direct economic assistance). In order to be effective, the aid must be coupled with controls limiting effects of local corruption. Note: A major political indicator for this outcome: successful prosecution of death-squad members for murder and terror activities.

3. 15 percent chance: There is a right-wing military victory. This goes up to a 35 percent chance if the Sandinista regime regains power in Nicaragua. (Extremists benefit by Sandinistas' holding power in Managua.)

4. 5 percent chance: There is an outright leftist rebel military victory. This goes up to a 40 percent chance if the Sandinista regime regains power in Nicaragua and to a 50 percent chance if the U.S. Congress cuts off military and economic aid to the El Salvadoran government.

Guatemala

1. 85 percent chance through 1996: Want a safe projection anyone can make? There is the recurrent cycle of bloodshed, poverty, low-grade guerrilla war, Army coup d'état, and the taking of Indian lands in the mountains.

2. 14 percent chance: Incremental progress is made on integrating the Indians into the nation and addressing the chronic problems of poverty and illness. This increases minimally if the Chamorro regime stays in power through 1992 and shows the region that civilian governments can accomplish many things the military cannot.

3. Small chance: The Guatemalan Army is abolished.

4. Less than a small chance: The Guatemalans attack Belize. After the resulting Belizean-British victory, it could lead to the abolition of the Guatemalan Army.

Honduras

15 percent chance of an Army coup d'état by 1996; an 85 percent chance of stability of the present regime.

Panama

15 percent chance through 1996: There is a reemergence of a military-backed strongman. If this happens, there is a 95 percent chance of another U.S. invasion.

Side bet: Pressure in the United States increases for the renegotiation of defense aspects of the Panama Canal Treaty, which might entail a "new" U.S.-Panamanian regional defense treaty. And permanent U.S. troops.

Cost of War

Central America is a poor region to begin with; the accountants won't come up with large numbers from the war damages. The human cost is higher, as most of the wars have degenerated into endemic banditry and lawlessness. The rule of law is supplanted by the law of the pistol (or AK-47). The loss of 10 to 50 percent or more of the local GNP during each year of these conflicts, plus thousands of fighters and civilians, has done little to improve the standard of living in the region.

What Kind of War

Central American wars have followed a familiar pattern: Small groups of infantry chasing each other through the bush. Military assistance from superpowers (usually the United States, sometimes Russia) has provided some major-league gear, but the addition of tanks, heavy artillery, and jets is usually overdoing it. Central America is light-infantry country, particularly when the locals are fighting one another. It almost always *is* locals versus locals, so warfare remains a relatively low-key, but still quite bloody process.

QUICK LOOK AT CUBA—VIVA FIDEL!: THE LAST DAYS OF THE CASTRO REGIME

For years Fidel Castro reveled in his role as a thorn in the side of U.S. policy. Castro provided Cuban troops to "Third World struggles for liberation," touting the Soviet Union as "the natural ally" of the Third World. He supported Marxist insurgencies throughout the hemisphere— from Bolivia and Brazil to Nicaragua and El Salvador. He gloated on the toasts of the American left.

But the end of the Cold War has left El Jefe Maximo ("the supreme leader") rotting on the dictatorial vine. Even his old left-wing buddies are shunning his repressive and poverty-stricken junta.

This trouble has been brewing for a long while. The economic devastation in Cuba can no longer be hidden by boasts about "free medical care." Cuba has been notoriously cruel to its AIDS victims, even to Cuban soldiers who picked up the disease while in Angola. The looming (and actual) loss of Russian aid makes life in Red Cuba even harder. Castro had been reselling discounted Russian oil elsewhere on the world market, earning hard currency. The Russian oil spigot is closing: In late 1990 the Castro regime began cutting back on railroad operations and was shopping for a million bicycles. Bikes don't need gasoline, just legs fueled by carbohydrates. Loss of Russian economic aid portends loss of Russian military backing. The Castro regime then becomes even more open to Washington saber rattling.

Other external pressures are also increasing: Cuba's international debt is one problem, and accusations of human rights abuses, a sensitive issue with Fidel, won't go away. Castro, who at one time could finesse the human rights investigators by mumbling ''progressive'' mumbo jumbo and pointing to the onerous Somoza junta in Nicaragua and Guatemala's murderous military regimes, seems to have lost that touch. His own regime is one of the worst human rights violators in the hemisphere, and the world knows it. Cuba has also been involved in the drug trade—at the very least allowing drug-running aircraft and ships protection in Cuban airspace and waters.

In 1988 and 1989, Castro put to death several senior Army officers, including the Angolan war hero Gen. Oscar Ochoa, claiming they were guilty of drug running. Perhaps—but in that case Fidel should have shot his entire intelligence staff. Many opponents of the Castro regime think it more likely that Castro shot Ochoa because he was a potential political threat to him—Ochoa was regarded as a hero by his troops. Many former Cuban soldiers who served in Angola, South Yemen, and Ethiopia are openly disgruntled with the increasingly harsh conditions inside Cuba. With a leader like Ochoa, they could represent a threat.

Finally, Fidel himself is getting old. Combat fatigues don't hide the paunch; his face sags; and he doesn't look like the future, even in Berkeley, California. Still, Castro styles himself as the true believer in communism. More likely, he is the ''Last Romantic''—the romantic Communist revolutionary, faithful until the last, despite the ugly reality of national poverty and fascist repression, his own handiwork.

POTENTIAL OUTCOMES

1. 40 percent chance through 1996: The Castro regime is replaced by more ''peaceful means'' and representative democracy nurtured by Cuban exiles returning from the United States is established. The chance goes to 90 percent if Fidel dies a ''natural death'' before 1994. So, how might this occur? The obvious scenario (in Fidel's case) includes lung cancer and a Nelson Rockefeller demise. There are several other interesting ways. One is the Alzheimer's scenario: Fidel gets old fast. He is replaced in a ''bloodless'' Cuban Army coup, and progressives in the Army liberalize the system. The doddering Castro is put out to a well-foddered (and well-policed) pasture. Another scenario: Fidel risks a ''Nicaraguan election'' (or a democratic referendum like the one that got Chile's General Pinochet) which is internationally monitored and allows all Cubans to vote freely. Then Castro gets surprised just like the Sandinistas. (Not too likely an

outcome, but possible. What might bring an open election about is that there's a decent chance that Fidel would win the presidency, making for an interesting clash of values with a democratic legislature.)

2. 30 percent chance through 1996: Vive Fidel! El Jefe lives. Fidel stuffs all coup attempts and continues to strut his anti-yanqui line, though the Third World is now more interested in yen and Eurodollars. The Cuban Communist regime continues to ossify (under this scenario, repression level in 1996 is an 8+).

3. 15 percent chance through 1996: Castro is assassinated or replaced by members of the secret police or disgruntled Army troops in a coup. A "Menshevik" military dictatorship comes to power, possibly with strong drug cartel ties. (The repression level is 6.)

4. 15 percent chance through 1996: A coup attempt against Castro fails, but Castro cannot suppress the rebels. Civil war breaks out on the island. If this occurs, there is a 60 percent chance of U.S. military intervention on the anti-Castro side, especially in the Guantánamo Bay area.

POLITICAL TREND CHART

CUBA

Getting rid of Castro will lead to a Cuban renaissance. But if Fidel stays in power, toss out the economic recovery.

	1990 (Totalitarian Socialist*)	1996 (Representative Democracy)
Government Effectiveness	8	6
Government Stability	7	8
Political Cohesion	7	8
Repression Level	8 −	2
Economic Development	2	6
Education Status†	4	6

NOTE: 0 = minimum; 9 = maximum.
*Red fascist.
†Urban population only.

REGIONAL POWERS AND POWER INTEREST INDICATOR CHARTS

CUBA

Russia's leaving the stage has made a significant difference, although Cuba was heading for trouble anyway. Keep an eye on the Cuban exile community.

	Economic Interests	Historical Interests	Political Interest	Military Interest	Force Generation Potential	Ability to Intervene Politically	Ability to Promote Economic Development
U.S.	5	8	8	9	9	6	8
Post–Cold War Russia	1	7	6 –	4	1 –	3	0
Cold War Russia	5	7	9	8	2	8	3
Cuban Exiles	8	9	9	9	1 –	4	9

NOTE: 0 = minimum; 9 = maximum.

THE CARIBBEAN

Although technically it's the United States' backyard, other powers have been allowed to do their thing as long as they didn't leave a mess.

	Economic Interests	Historical Interests	Political Interest	Military Interest	Force Generation Potential	Ability to Intervene Politically	Ability to Promote Economic Development
U.S.	6	8	8	9	9	8	9
Castro Cuba	4	9	9	7	2+	5	0
Venezuela	5	6	7	4	1	4	2
Netherlands	6	7	6	4	1	4	5
U.K.	2	7	4	2	1+	3	4
Brazil	2	2	4	3	1	2	2
Colombia	4	6	7	5	1	3	2

NOTE: 0 = minimum; 9 = maximum.

And, for the sake of argument:

THE CARIBBEAN

The drug trade has brought two new players into the action. This, however, is remarkably similar to the rampant smuggling and piracy that were suppressed only a century ago.

	Economic Interests	Historical Interests	Political Interest	Military Interest	Force Generation Potential	Ability to Intervene Politically	Ability to Promote Economic Development
Colombian Drug Cartels	8*	0	8	9†	1−(‡)	5+	1
U.S. Coast Guard	1	7	8	8	2−	3	0

NOTE: 0 = minimum; 9 = maximum.

*Economic interest in New York, Los Angeles, Miami, Houston, Chicago, Detroit, and Washington, D.C. is a 9+.

†Military, in this case, is broadly defined.

‡The power of cartels is money and terror, hence 5+ for political intervention capability.

QUICK LOOK: MEANWHILE, ELSEWHERE IN THE CARIBBEAN

The countries of the eastern Caribbean have several common characteristics that make them prone to political instability, violence, and war.

SMALL IS NOT BETTER

Many of these nations are small in size and population, as shown by the table on p. 534, which also shows the annual per capita income. In comparison, the United States has a population of 67 per square kilometer, and a per capita income of nearly $15,000 (Russia $1,600, Japan $16,600, other industrialized nations $5,000–$14,000).

Size tends to create more stability than wealth does. It's a matter of arithmetic: It takes more troops to terrorize two million people than to terrorized two thousand. Thus the Caribbean's micronations are prone to the adventures of the powerful—the United States, Britain, France, and wealthy drug lords. During the height of the Cold War the Cuban Communist regime was quite adventurous, but smart enough to avoid being foolhardy. When it has been foolhardy, its more powerful neighbor, the United States, has intervened (the Dominican Republic and Grenada, and Nicaragua to some extent). As the Cold War fades, Cuba's taste for leftist revolutionary adventure, outside of the occasional burst of nostalgic anti-American rhetoric, appears to wane.

ISLAND NATIONS OF THE CARIBBEAN

Nation	Population	Per Square Kilometer	Per Capita Income
Antigua (Br.)*	86,000	503.0	$2,200
Barbados (Br.)	256,000	583.0	3,100
Dominica (Br.)	85,000	195.0	1,200
Grenada (Br.)	110,000	148.0	690
Guadeloupe (Fr.)	330,000	187.0	3,870
Martinique (Fr.)	325,000	296.0	4,640
St. Lucia (Br.)	130,000	208.0	850
St. Vincent (Br.)	110,000	325.0	520
Trinidad/Tobago (Br.)	1,200,000	235.0	3,710
Guyana (Br.)	820,000	4.0	488
French Guiana (Fr.)	63,000	0.7	2,880
Suriname (Dutch)	400,000	2.2	2,800
Bahamas (Br.)	250,000	18.0	3,300
Cuba	10,500,000	90.0	1,500
Dominican Republic	7,300,000	388.0	1,200
Haiti	6,200,000	579.0	290
Jamaica (Br.)	2,300,000	203.0	1,100
Puerto Rico (U.S.)†	3,300,000	961.0	5,100

*In parentheses are the recent colonial associations (Br. = British, Fr. = French).
†Puerto Rico, given the large number of inhabitants who agitate to become the fifty-first state, really isn't a colony in the same sense as the Bahamas or Suriname were. Just what Puerto Rico is remains a classic question—for the United States, the UN, and Puerto Rico.

DIFFERENT KINDS OF INDEPENDENCE

The independence of these nations varies. The British, Dutch, and French controlled the area before the wave of decolonialization after World War II. The French states (Guadeloupe, Martinique, and French Guiana) are considered to be overseas departments of metropolitan (mainland) France. Like French citizens, the islanders may move freely to France and are eligible for relatively generous social welfare benefits. Anyone who gets out of line will either be arrested by the local gendarmes or face the tender mercies of the Foreign Legion. The Dutch treated Suriname in a like fashion as far as emigration and financial assistance were concerned. Suriname, however, is now an independent state, with the Dutch playing the role of a rich and, so far, indulgent uncle. The treacherous regime of Dési Bouterse sorely tested Dutch sympathies. His secret police force, which had close ties to Cuba, murdered a number of democratic advocates. His regime was far more gangland than ideological, however. The British were not as generous as the French and Dutch. Immigration was eventually restricted, and generous social benefits were not forthcoming. Interestingly, the former British colonies have been the most prone to disorder.

OUR GANG

The small size of these islands enables small, organized groups, like the Army or police or private armies backed by drug lords, to take over or establish de facto control. When there is no external authority to which the population can appeal, these takeovers can be long-lasting. Until the Russians entered the picture in the 1950s, these takeovers had generally been right-wing (conservative) or apolitical. The ruler operated on behalf of the wealthier families and generally avoided messy external political involvements. The emergence of a powerful, violent, and reasonably well-financed left led to the establishment of left-wing regimes, which in turn got involved, at least rhetorically, in external politics. These governments tended to operate on behalf of governmental bureaucrats and their police forces (the new wealthy). The 1989 collapse of communism in Eastern Europe actually changes little except the rhetoric. The truly nasty turn has been the extensive reemergence of drug and crime syndicates as major players in local governments. In certain areas Communists were much more reasonable than the Mob. With police officials on Caribbean islands averaging between $5,500 and $6,000 in annual income, there's a lot of room for bribery. The July 1990 "microrevolution" in Trinidad, which featured a fringe Islamic sect (Jamaat Muslimeen) with a demanding leader, is an example of how few people it really takes to shake up a Caribbean nation. Approximately 110 members (the equivalent of a weak infantry company) of the Muslimeen participated in the shoot-out and hostage taking, which nearly toppled one of the Caribbean's most populous and comparatively wealthy nations. Most of the rebels' weapons were bought on the open market through gun shops in south Florida.

DELICATE FINANCES

The economies are very fragile, usually dependent on tourism, raw materials, and cash subsidies from foreign nations (often the former colonial power). The tourism income varies with the state of the North American economy and the perceived friendliness and safety of the tourist areas. Cuba in particular has tried to establish a new tourist industry based on Canadian and European tourists rather than on those from the United States. Raw materials income depends on the state of the world economy and competition from other producers. Cash subsidies vary with the providing nation's political and economic climates.

REVOLUTION AS A CAREER

High unemployment provides a pool of capable and willing followers for an armed leader who preaches change, especially in situations where only change will improve a stagnant economy and prospects for the young and ambitious. Revolution becomes a job. The Muslimeen revolt in Trinidad was fueled by both poor economic circumstances and religious antagonism. The fact that the "Meen revolt" produced a negotiated settlement kept down the bloodshed but did little to solve the underlying economic troubles.

SELLING FRIENDSHIP AND POSITION

The Caribbean nations have little to offer their wealthier and more powerful neighbors other than friendship (they respect foreign citizens' economic and social indiscretions) and position (they cooperate militarily with their stronger neighbors). For many years Americans and Europeans had the islands to themselves, as there was no competition for friendship and position. When Russia entered the act, there was a political tug-of-war, as well as several shooting wars. With Russia departing, a poverty-stricken Cuba and swaggering drug barons are the Americans' and Europeans' competition.

SCOUNDRELS IN POWER

Small size, particularly when coupled with high unemployment, high education levels, national independence, and armed forces, produces a political climate ripe for tragicomic situations. The most apt comparison is to the frequent municipal-political scandals in the United States in which a group of scoundrels gets elected by making the most outlandish promises, then does as it wishes with the municipal finances and civil rights. The day of reckoning on the undeliverable promises is delayed by paying off potential troublemakers. The worst abuses are often in the smaller cities: Without the restraint, and threat of intervention by state and federal governments, small municipalities can get out of hand. Haiti, with its trail of right-wing dictatorships in league with a corrupt oligarchy, is a prime example of how bad things can get.

THE ARMY TO THE RESCUE

Think of what would happen if the corrupt city governments of the United States had ruled independent islands and kept small armies. In such isolation very little restrains local bully boys. The elected scoundrels cater to their favorite faction. Driven by jealousy or indignation, the Army often deposes the civilian government in order to "straighten things out." The only solution is for the bully boys to control the armed forces closely. Such is the case in Haiti.

THE FAILED PROMISE OF SOCIALISM

The socialist dictators have introduced two new versions of a couple of old ideas. First, there is to be no independent wealth. The state—that is, the leader and his gang—owns and controls everything. Second, this nifty new wrinkle is treated like a religion. Missionary activity is supported to convert the heathens (nonsocialist nations, especially those who economically oppress their citizens). Socialist dictatorships become fascist dictatorships with a propaganda shield, and the democratic socialist revolutionaries end up either dead or in exile. With the end of the Cold War and the collapse of most of Eastern Europe's totalitarian socialist regimes, the propaganda shield covering socialist dictatorships has slipped and in some cases fallen.

The Perils of Foreign Policy

Foreign affairs is a dangerous area for all nations, particularly small ones. The best approach appears to be, "Keep your head down and your mouth shut." For years, the Duvalier dictatorship in Haiti managed to stay in power by doing the right thing by its more powerful neighbors (the United States and Cuba)—Haiti stayed out of the U.S. and Cuban controversy. As for the flip side: When Grenada decided to go "pro-Cuban" and Grenada's Stalinist faction assassinated the more or less social-democratic front man, Maurice Bishop (head of the New Jewel Movement), the United States invaded in October 1983.

QUICK LOOK AT ECUADOR AND PERU: BORDER WAR, INDIAN WAR, AND THE SHINING PATH

Peru and Ecuador share a long, mountainous, and ill-defined border. The population of the region—where there is any—consists of Indians living in small, isolated villages.

The simmering border conflict between Ecuador and Peru, which so far has featured only minor infantry skirmishes and strikes by armed helicopters, isn't driven by national pride: There are strong indications that the border area sits on a significant pool of oil. The new Inca gold is Texas tea.

The Indians don't particularly care for the Mestizos (people of mixed blood) and white soldiers of either side. Ecuador and Peru have both followed a policy of neglect that cannot be characterized as benign. The Indians lack basic medical care, and their agricultural methods remain primitive. But the Indian peasants also want to be left alone. They are classic mountaineers.

The Indians confront Marxist ideologues with a quandary. According to Marxist-Leninist theory, the Indians should be rebelling. Enter Sendero Luminoso, the "Shining Path." Founded by extreme leftist intellectuals in Lima, and with a slight bow to Mao and Trotsky, in the early 1980s the Sendero Luminoso began a brutal series of terror attacks against the Peruvian government. The intent was to foment an Indian revolt. The intellectuals even called on the power of old Inca legends that say "sleeping" Inca kings would rise out of the Andes to kill the Spanish invaders. Naturally, the Leninists want the Indians to conclude that the Shining Path is that Incan resurrection.

To the Indians, leftist intellectuals from Lima are just central government Spaniards spouting a different verse of the old saw "you be like us, or else." The Sendero Luminoso hasn't been very successful at organizing the Indians. And the Indians have killed a number of the would-be guerrillas and, in one instance, massacred a group of journalists mistaken for the left-wing outsiders.

The Shining Path's founder is Abimael Guzman, who calls himself the "Fourth Sword of Marxism," an apocalyptic compliment to Marx, Lenin, and Mao. Unlike other South American guerrilla groups, however, the Shining Path doesn't seem to rely on outside advisers or arms shipments. Even before the collapse of Eastern European communism, "Senderistas" hated Moscow as intensely as they hate Washington. The Communist collapse has little ideological effect on the Shining Path's central clique: They are the only ones who really know how to make Marxism work. The Russians' failure is a subject of scorn.

Fall 1990 estimates on the Shining Path's strength ran from 25,000 to 35,000 guerrillas; in the summer of 1984, estimates were from 2,000 to 7,000 guerrillas. Recruitment and economic failure (highlight the latter) have increased Senderista appeal.

The Shining Path has exhibited a genuine nihilistic taste for general terror, and while a murderous problem for the Indians, it is also a threat to Peru's central government. Recent reports also mention Shining Path activity in Colombia, but that's already the stomping ground of the guerrilla organization M-19, which started as an urban-proletariat-oriented revolutionary group. M-19, however, has gone legit. They sponsor political candidates. They may also be in the cocaine business, depending upon whom you believe.

QUICK LOOK AT BOLIVIA, CHILE, AND PERU: THE LINGERING WAR OF THE PACIFIC

During the War of the Pacific (1878–84), Bolivia lost to Chile the port of Arica, its outlet to the sea. Over one hundred years later, Bolivia and Chile still have not resolved this loss and it remains a potentially explosive issue for the 1990s. The economic performance of all of these countries can either resolve or exacerbate the situation. The lack of a seaport provides Bolivia, or at least Bolivian military regimes, with a "legitimate" external excuse for poor economic performance—"it's not our fault." Bolivian calls for negotiations have been, for the most part, ignored and certainly rebuffed. Even Chile's new democratic government prefers to ignore this issue. But the argument over access to the sea through a national port isn't simply an issue of hurt national pride, and it isn't about an insignificant area (like Chile and Argentina's old dispute over islands in the Beagle Channel). When it comes to trade and tariffs, Chile and neighboring Peru have a geostrategic choke hold on Bolivia. The result: a brew for renewed conflict in a poor and suffering corner of the world.

QUICK LOOK AT THE COCAINE WARS: DRUG LORDS AND A NEW/OLD CONFLICT

Most wars are either revolutions or squabbles over territory. Very few are both, and a war going on now in South America, financed by the U.S. people (not the government), is spilling over into the streets of America. This is the Cocaine War.

The war starts in the foothills of the Andes Mountains in the backcountry of Colombia, Bolivia, and Peru. The soldiers are Israeli-trained gunmen and leftist guerrillas working together. The fighting continues down to the urban areas of Colombia, up through Central America and the Caribbean, and on into the United States. The war is over the control of the cocaine trade—the thousands of square miles of hill country where the coca leaf is grown, to the streets of urban America where most of the drug is sold. Nearly a million South American farmers, technicians, gunmen, pilots, sailors, soldiers, policemen, and accountants make up the drug producers forces. In North America, over ten million cocaine users pay out over $50 billion a year for the drug.

Until the late 1970s, the traffic in cocaine from South America to North America was relatively small and divided among dozens of small operators. But then one drug producer, then another, got organized and began moving larger quantities into an apparently insatiable market. In the early 1980s, an attempt by leftist guerrillas to cash in on the trade by kidnapping members of the drug rings backfired. The drug producers in Colombia united to fight the guerrillas, and succeeded. They decided to stay together, stamp out most of their competition, and grow even larger as a cartel. Thus was born the Colombian Cocaine Cartel. By the late 1980s, this cartel had increased cocaine production and distribution ten times more than its 1970s volume. It did this in one of the most consistently violent nations in the world—Colombia.

Colombia has suffered endemic violence, largely political, since the late 1940s. Over 300,000 people have died, and the annual death rate from violence is over five times that of the United States' (a fairly violent place to begin with). In the late 1980s, the annual deaths from shootouts, assassinations, banditry, and the like reached over 20,000. (An equivalent number of deaths in the United States would be 150,000, which is more deaths than the United States suffered in any single year of World War II.) There's a war going on down there in Colombia, and it's because of cocaine bought and consumed largely by Americans.

The Cocaine Wars are all about money and control of the coca-growing lands, with a few politics thrown in. In Colombia, where the per capita GNP is about $1,200 and the farming family in the bush makes less than $1,000 a year, cocaine can be the road to riches. Each acre of coca plants can produce 800–900 pounds of leaves a year. These the farmer sells to one of the cocaine cartels for anywhere from fifteen cents to several dollars a pound (depending on market conditions). The price is now on the low side because so many farmers are cultivating coca leaves. But the farmers are still able to get up to $200 an acre from a plant that requires relatively little effort to grow and harvest. And the farmers don't have to worry about lack of transportation to get their crops out. The drug lords take care of everything, and they pay cash. With 300–400 tons of cocaine coming into the United States each year, that means the farmers in the backcountry of Colombia, Bolivia, and Peru are producing up to 200,000 tons of coca leaves. That's over six hundred square miles of coca plants and over $80 million flowing into the farmers' pockets. Each 500 pounds of coca leaves ends up as 1 pound of cocaine, which can sell for over $10,000 in the United States. There's lots of profit to be made between buying a hundred dollars' worth of coca leaves in the bush, performing a few chemical operations on them, and getting the resulting pound of cocaine into the United States and the cash out. The Colombian cartels that control most of the business can thus garner over $10 billion a year from the cocaine trade. This is about a third of the total GNP of Colombia, and a 1984 cartel offer to pay off Colombia's $9 billion national debt in return for amnesty, while possibly not serious, was certainly within the cartel's means.

With such large sums of cash at stake, the cartel spares no expense in offering "gold or lead" to all who oppose it. If opponents can't be bought off, they are killed off. Thousands of Colombian police and soldiers have died, as well as dozens of judges and prosecutors. No one is safe, not even senior members of the government.

This type of conflict is nothing new; it has been going on in the Golden Triangle of Thailand and Burma since the late 1940s, where it is tolerated. Officials who are bought, stay bought. In America's backyard, there is less tolerance. In Colombia there is even less tolerance, and the nation is at war with the cartel and the cartel's billions.

Since 1988, Colombia has been, literally, at war with the cartel, and it hasn't been an easy battle. Casualties have been heavy on both sides. The Colombian cartel, unlike its counterparts in the Golden Triangle, has not managed to take over its own chunk of backcountry territory and keep it free of government troops. Moreover, the cartel is no longer a monolith but several major factions that still snipe at one another as they all struggle against the governments in the region. While the United States wants the government forces to prevail, the Latin American nations are wary of accepting direct military intervention from up north.

It's still up in the air whether this war can be won and, if so, how to do it. The drug demand in Yankee land remains.

QUICK LOOK AT BRAZIL

THE BRAZILIAN MILITARY

While Brazil's Army, in the main, consists of politicized generals and units chiefly designed for policing Brazil, it is capable of waging an offensive war beyond its borders. The Army has 197,000 troops (143,000 conscripts) but is being expanded to 290,000. These troops man eight infantry divisions and approximately twenty-five "brigade groups" which include armor, jungle infantry, and mountain warfare units. The Brazilian airborne brigade, which includes a special forces battalion, is highly trained. Brazil equips its light-armored formations with the "homemade" Urutu and Cascavel armored personnel carriers and recon vehicles—vehicles ideally suited for combat in South America.

The Brazilian Navy has nearly 50,000 sailors and marines. The Navy isn't strictly a coastal force. It deploys a small antisubmarine aircraft carrier, seven submarines, ten destroyers, and fifteen frigates and corvettes. Several of the ships are armed with modern ship-to-ship missiles. Brazil also maintains a large river (Amazon) warfare force. The Navy has flirted with the idea of buying or producing a nuclear submarine.

The Brazilian Air Force has over 50,000 personnel manning nearly 200 combat aircraft, and it is continuing to grow—in 1988 some 150 aircraft of all types were on order. The Air Force's technical capabilities are good—Brazilians know how to service their aircraft. Frontline fighters are aging French Mirage IIIs and U.S. F-5s. Their counterinsurgency squadrons operate the locally produced (by Embraer) Xavante aircraft. The Air Force wants to acquire long-range tanker and transport aircraft, as an increase in range means an increase in the strategic reach of Brazil's air power.

BRAZILIAN STRATEGIC SITUATION: SOURCES OF CONFLICT

Regional Sources

Suriname—Brazil is deeply involved in keeping a lid on the simmering crisis created by Suriname's dictator, Dési Bouterse. In 1980 Bouterse seized power in the former Dutch colony and in 1982 he conducted a bloody purge of his opposition. He has been, allegedly, backed by the Cubans. Brazil doesn't want a Marxist-influenced state on its northern border, so it has been training Surinamese officers and seeking to expand its influence in Paramaribo by offering a military assistance plan.

Land and border claims—(1) Brazil and hapless (hopelessly oppressed) Paraguay have a lingering boundary dispute in the Rio Parana area; (2) Brazil and Uruguay have several small border disputes; (3) Brazil claims a "zone of interest" in Antarctica. This claim also has a regional feature: It is a counterbalance to Chilean and Argentine claims on the Antarctic continent; and (4) Brazil has a lingering border dispute with Venezuela over the Parima Mountain range. This dispute traces back to Portuguese and Spanish colonial days but is now more relevant since Brazil's Roraima Province (which abuts the mountains) is proving to be "mineral rich." Much of the disputed area is inhabited by the Yanoamamo tribe. The border zone may hold gold, diamonds, and uranium.

International Sources

Economic—The overall Brazilian foreign debt in late 1988 was over $190 billion. The debt service was estimated at close to $20 billion a year. International Monetary Fund (IMF) belt tightening does not, and will not, sell in party-mad Brazil. In fact, the Brazilians aren't too worried about the debt—they view it as being unpayable. When asked about their foreign debt, Brazilians point a finger at the massive U.S. debt and shrug. Besides, since a Brazilian default could initiate a worldwide economic collapse, the Brazilians feel certain that the United States and its other Western lenders won't let that happen. Nevertheless the potential remains. Brazil's first priority goal is debt restructuring and repayment. All its developmental projects hinge on successfully resolving the foreign debt load.

Increasing Brazilian military and economic power—Regional competition and jealousy, in particular from Argentina, could produce severe international strains. Brazil's expanding power has created a great deal of apprehension. Venezuela and Argentina oppose Brazil's attempt to assume the mantle of Latin American leader (see goal 2). Brazil has maintained a long and strong influence within the Chilean and Bolivian military, which is another cause for Argentine fretting. While Brazil and Argentina have exchanged inspection groups who will monitor each other's highly sensitive nuclear programs, that "quiet" race, if it leads to bombs, could have a devastating result. In the fall of 1990, Brazil's civilian government confirmed that past military governments had begun a program intended to build a nuclear weapon. The civilian government says it has killed the program.

Arms industry fiascoes—Supplying Libya, Iraq, Iran, and a host of other volatile nations (perhaps South Africa) with weapons and munitions may make money, but it also invites a whole host of risks, including terrorist retribution and economic sanctions.

Brazil has one of the largest arms industries in the developing world. Its light-armored vehicles, attack aircraft, trucks, munitions, and—now —missiles provide jobs and foreign exchange. Brazil has astutely specialized in producing what it calls "sellable vanilla": tough, relatively unsophisticated but functional weapons that don't require a lot of detailed maintenance or a highly educated crew. In competing with inexpensive Russian equipment, Brazilian arms salesmen can point out that their stuff is "Western" and not that shabby stuff the Russians peddle. But basically the Brazilians sell on the basis of price and availability. Brazil has few (if any) qualms about selling weapons to any nation—in fact, Brazil supplied both sides in the Iran-Iraq War. Iraq made use of Brazilian equipment and ammunition in its invasion of Kuwait.

Brazilian Geostrategic Goals

Goal 1:   Resolving economic problems—The debt issue won't go away.

Goal 2:   Becoming the leader of Latin America—The Brazilians have one of the best-trained and most sophisticated diplomatic corps in Latin America. Given their nation's size, power, and savoir faire, they believe they are the natural regional coordinators of policy.

Goal 3:   Forging the "Industrialized Third World Co-Prosperity Sphere"—This might be a more subtle title for the last, long-range goal. As the Brazilians see it, with their nascent space program, strong arms industry, multiracial democracy (although there are plenty of racial tensions), and burgeoning population, their nation is a natural leader in a tier of nations including South Korea, Taiwan, South Africa, and perhaps Egypt. This loose collection conveniently ignores India. Supporting this upper tier would be another group of Third World nations who would be "happier" trading their resources for goods produced by other Third World nations, rather than goods produced by the "old" imperialists (Japan, Britain, France, etc.).

Goal 4:   Suppressing insurgent movements in the Western Hemisphere—This used to mean controlling Castro, but the economic failure of Cuba and the 1989 Communist collapse in Eastern Europe have lessened Fidel's appeal. Still, Brazil's military remembers the situation in 1964 and they put a great deal of the blame on "Castroites." The Sendero Luminoso ("Shining Path") Maoist guerrilla movement in Peru (and perhaps Ecuador as well) is being viewed with increasing alarm.

Long-Range Goal: Being the Brazilian route to world power—Call this reestablishing the "axis of Portuguese influence'' around the globe, this time under the direction of Brazil. Brazil would dearly love to have a direct (and directing) relationship with Angola and Mozambique, reestablishing to a degree the ''band of the Portuguese'' that once stretched from Guinea-Bissau to Formosa.

This new ''band'' through Africa is a geostrategic means of becoming a world power, similar to the French strategy of ''overseas departments,'' and might be accurately described as an economic-based form of neo-colonialism. (But please don't use that word in front of the Angolans.)

Brazilians assert that the cultural and linguistic frameworks are already in place. ''We all came from Portugal,'' the Brazilians say. Perhaps the United Kingdom's ''Commonwealth'' approach best describes this Brazilian aspiration: a loose confederation of former Portuguese colonies with the leadership supplied by Brazil. Even Portugal could join, as long as it was clearly third or fourth fiddle.

In the meantime, Brazil must contend with an economy that still has a lot of problems, a divisive ethnic mix, hidden agendas by various groups (the military was discovered, in 1990, to be secretly developing nuclear weapons and not telling the government about it), and several other problems that might just make Brazil one of those perpetual ''future supcrpowers.''

QUICK LOOK AT THE UNITED STATES AND CANADA: CONTROLLED ANARCHY ON THE ISLAND OF STABILITY

In parts of southern Missouri, Jesse James is still regarded as a hero— The United States has always been a relatively easy place to stage a riot or rob the stage. But the U.S. government is difficult to topple because democracy provides a way to at least give the appearance of overthrowing the ruling cliques every few years. Being rich also helps. So the United States and Canada remain stable.

One of the biggest reasons for democratic success in the United States and Canada is that they sit on a big island. The Mexicans to the south aren't the Germans; there aren't any Hapsburg empresses building armies next door in Greenland; and no Emirs live across the river. No one has ever heard of Attila the Eskimo (or, to be ethnically specific, Attila the Inuit). All of the local barbarians (i.e., the Native Americans) were massacred or destroyed by Eurasian diseases or, after being starved, placed in large desert relocation camps, euphemistically called reservations. The fact is, even the toughest of the North American tribes, the Comanches, just could never get an all-out invasion together like the Goths could. Comanche warriors were the world's greatest light cavalry, and the best they could manage was an extended cavalry raid, with a little looting, burning, and scalping. Yet even in the latter days of the twentieth century "Indian troubles" continue. Many Native American organizations have strong claims to land now owned by others. These claims involve billions of dollars and many are in litigation. Other Indian groups in the United States are pressing environmental degradation lawsuits against opponents.

Very low-grade "Indian war" occasionally breaks out in the United States and Canada. Shooting incidents involving Mohawks (some with obviously legitimate claims against the governments, others a criminal element engaged in drug-running operations) have erupted in both upstate New York and Quebec.

But in point of fact these fights are far less violent than the many civil rights riots that erupted in the United States in the 1960s and 1970s. The North American system is designed to let the steam out of polarized positions by allowing for loud political debate and occasional riots. This is then followed by a period of muddling compromise. Historically, the United States and Canada have had time to muddle through because there isn't a Hun at the doorstep. One can see the geographic analogy—the Atlantic and Pacific oceans serve as rather large English Channels.

Even the portending breakup of Canada has all of the features of muddling compromise. Initially, Quebec's separatist Parti Quebecois began to falter as soon as the French Canadians saw that all the English (and American) companies leaving Montreal for Toronto and Burlington meant a "Free Quebec" could get a nasty case of Third World poverty. This appears to have changed, as well as western Canada's attitudes about begrudging the Quebecers their language and Ontario its dominance.

Some governmental theoreticians argue that the Canadian parliamentary system is too weak for continental rule. Other observers argue that the impending U.S.-Canada Free Trade Pact will effectively counter political fracturing of Canada. Even if new political arrangements are reached, the pressing reality of economic cooperation will ultimately force separatists to cooperate with their former countrymen (or so the argument goes). If disunion comes about, it will scarcely matter since none of the new "nations" or political entities will present a military threat to one another.

What might an "altered" Canada look like? Quebec is in many aspects a genuine European nation-state—a "people" with cultural, linguistic, religious, and historical identity. The irony haunting the French Quebecois' claims is that their Mohawk minority is as equally unique in contrast to French culture as Quebecois claim to be in contrast to the rest of English Canada. The Quebecers show no signs of wanting to grant the Mohawks the same recognition they demand. (Ironique?)

British Columbia, interestingly, has most of the assets required to make it as a separate nation: access to the sea, strong industrial and educational bases, raw materials, and a well-educated populace with linguistic integration.

Oil-producing Alberta might be interested in joining the United States and would immediately find common ground with Alaska, Louisiana, Texas, Oklahoma, and California. The impoverished Canadian Atlantic provinces would be the best bets for joining the United States and extending the New England coastline. The remains of Canada might stick together, with Manitoba and Saskatchewan wary of being adjuncts to a "Greater Ontario." Ontario is still the home of the Royal American Regiment. Tories fleeing the American Revolution (and choosing to remain loyal to King George) put a mild but still present anti-U.S. disposition on Ontarian politics.

The wild card? If Canada breaks up, watch for Newfoundland to petition the United Kingdom to be taken over as a colony.

CHAPTER 14

THE UNITED STATES AND THE NEW AGE OF LITTLE WARS

INTRODUCTION

With the end of the Cold War, the chance of superpower confrontation escalating into World War III has diminished. Yet the opportunity for "little wars" and terrible regional conflicts (such as Iraq's invasion of Kuwait) may have increased. In truth, there are always dozens of brushfire conflicts occurring (as this book amply illustrates), but the paradox of the Cold War was that these conflicts were held in check by the superpowers as much as they were used by the superpowers.

The question now is how well can the United States (and other major military powers) deal with these new brushfire wars?

SOURCE OF CONFLICT

In the last two centuries there have been over four hundred wars, along with several conflicts that, while violent, did not quite qualify. (You have to draw the line somewhere.) Most of these wars were either territorial disputes or revolutions. There have been four mega-wars in this period (the Napoleonic Wars, the Taiping Rebellion, World War I, and World War II) which accounted for half the 150 million war victims during the period. The remaining wars were, to varying degrees, "little wars." With the introduction of nuclear weapons after 1945, and with most major powers obtaining these weapons of mass destruction, the major powers have—for the first time in history—been extremely reluctant to engage one another in war. While there were periods in the past where the major powers refrained from conflict with one another for a few decades, the period of major-power peace since World War II has been a record.

Rather than fight one another, and risk a nuclear holocaust, the superpowers have encouraged smaller nations with grievances to fight as proxies. Most of the wars fought since 1945 have had at least a bit of superpower conflict, and support, in them.

But now the Cold War is over and Russia is unwilling, and increasingly unable, to get involved in distant little wars. Domestic problems, and a large degree of self-sufficiency, make it easy for Russia to avoid any international police work. America's situation is quite the opposite. The United States is a maritime and trading nation. American firms do business all over the world, as do America's major allies. What goes wrong in numerous obscure parts of the globe has a significant impact on these trading nations. While the United States is the strongest militarily, many other trading nations have the capability to get involved in little wars.

WHO'S INVOLVED

United States Groups

The United States State Department—It's not that the State Department diplomats are warmongers, but they are charged with dealing in foreign affairs on a day-to-day basis and are, thus, often the first to run up against little wars when they break out. The CIA works closely with the State Department people (and the president) in dealing with real or potential little wars. But it is the State Department that is—in theory, and in practice—the most knowledgeable U.S. agency when it comes to little wars. Of course, the State Department works for the president, and if the president says keep a lid on things, or stir things up, that's what the diplomats and CIA operatives try to do. Note also that the vast majority of the CIA employees are gathering and collecting information. The State Department has far more people in contact with foreigners (although some of these diplomats are actually CIA employees). Put simply, the State

Department and CIA keep an eye on things and report back to the president, who then makes decisions which the State Department tries to carry out. If diplomatic means fail, the military comes in.

The United States Navy and Marine Corps—Of all the U.S. armed forces, the Navy has traditionally maintained the most contacts with foreigners. From its inception, the U.S. Navy has ranged far beyond American coastal waters. The United States has always depended on foreign trade, and the Navy was always out there to protect it from pirates and unfriendly foreigners in general. Over the years, the Navy's Marine Corps steadily grew with the increasing need for troops to be landed quickly on foreign shores. Before World War II, the U.S. Marines were often referred to as "State Department troops" because the Marines were the most readily available force when U.S. military action was needed. The ending of the Cold War brings with it a reduction of U.S. overseas bases. While the Navy will lose some facilities, it can still maintain substantial combat power off a foreign shore where the Army and Air Force cannot.

The United States Army—Until World War II, the Army had few overseas responsibilities. At the outbreak of World War II, the largest Army presence overseas was in the Philippines, and this was scheduled to end before the end of the 1940s. Since 1945, the largest overseas Army commitment has been Europe (the Seventh Army, with 250,000 troops) and South Korea (the Eighth Army, with 25,000 troops). The end of the Cold War makes both of these situations increasingly untenable. Having had a taste of foreign adventure, the Army is reluctant to give it up. Basically, the Army has been encroaching on the Marines' traditional turf, and a major interservice brawl is shaping up as the Army attempts to carve out a permanent piece of the "foreign intervention" market.

The United States Air Force—The Air Force did not exist as a separate service until shortly after World War II. Since then, the Air Force has followed the Army to the same foreign stations. Like the Army, the Air Force is in danger of losing its overseas bases. Unlike the Army, though, the Air Force has a better chance of keeping a piece of the foreign intervention business. Unlike the Army, too, with all its heavy equipment, the Air Force can rapidly fly hundreds of combat aircraft and their support units to most distant trouble spots. Although the Navy has its own large air force, most of the naval aviation flies from aircraft carriers. The Air Force can, in many instances, get its aircraft to a distant location faster than the Navy can.

Other Players

Great Britain—Long the ruler of a worldwide empire, Great Britain has seen its empire dissipate over the past fifty years, although not all the military responsibilities associated with that. Small British garrisons still dot the globe in out-of-the-way places like South America and Asia. Britain, like the United States, is a trading nation and still remembers how to solve particularly nasty commercial problems with armed force.

France—While never possessed of as large a worldwide empire as the British, the French were even keener on maintaining a well-rounded approach to diplomacy. In other words, the French maintain, and use, several regiments of light infantry for intervention in distant places. This is particularly true in Africa, where France has maintained closer ties with its former colonies than has any other colonial power.

Other European Economic Community (EEC) countries—Several other European nations also maintain "intervention forces" for either diplomatic (foreign trade) or nostalgic (former colonies) reasons. Belgium and Holland are two examples.

Russia—The 1960s and 1970s were something of a golden age for Russian diplomacy. As the leader of the "World Communist Revolution," Russia had diplomats, military advisers, and arms salesmen everywhere. But the Russians were never cut out for this sort of thing, and going into the 1980s it all began to fall apart. Communism and its economic system turned out to be more a liability than an asset, as dealing with revolution-minded foreigners was clearly something Russian (or any other) diplomats were never going to become particularly good at. Russia is still stuck with a lot of these diplomatic remnants (as in Cuba), and there is always national pride to consider. Failure can always be fogged over with an unwillingness to completely abandon poor diplomatic efforts. But Russia can no longer afford to play the game big time. Diplomacy is expensive and Russia needs the money for more important matters at home. Yet Russia is still a large and powerful nation which has many long and substantial diplomatic ties with its numerous neighbors, and with these, at least, Russia is still a potent diplomatic force.

China—Traditionally even more insular than Russia, China has historically felt that if foreigners wanted to deal with it, they could come there and present themselves. Attempts at diplomacy on foreign lands were not successful, and for much the same reasons as Russia has, China has withdrawn into itself once more. Too, as with Russia, China will continue to maintain a keen interest in relations with its many neighbors.

Third World "Little Warriors"—Like Russia and China, many a large Third World nation must maintain complex relations with its neighbors. Examples are India, Indonesia, Brazil, and so on.

The Outcasts—Several nations have become diplomatic outcasts in the past forty years and they maintain a very active diplomacy in order to better survive this pariah status. Chief examples are South Africa, Israel, Taiwan, North Korea, and a few others. These nations tend to sell anything to anyone for both the diplomatic and commercial access this provides.

GEOGRAPHY

The three most crucial geographical factors of the little war regions are ports, air bases (and commercial airports), and money. Put another way, the so-called geography of little wars consists of time and money. Little wars tend to occur in the most out-of-the-way places and the quickest way in is usually a local airport. The commercial air bases are often preferable to military ones as the commercial airport is often better equipped to handle heavy freighter aircraft. A port, preferably with its docking facilities intact, is another requirement if the little war is going to require more than paratroopers and light infantry. While Marines are theoretically capable of moving in quickly and efficiently without ports, there are few Marine forces that can do this and only one, the U.S. Marine Corps, that can do it on a large scale (a division or more of troops). Moreover, even the U.S. Marines have as their first objective the capture of a port so that they can better supply themselves. Moving goods by sea is a lot cheaper than by air, and in warfare, money is often a crucial factor.

There are nearly a hundred nations that are likely to involve little wars. For most of these nations, the wars loom large, locally, and at a greater cost than they can afford. These are usually conflicts with neighbors, like Iraq's invasion of Kuwait in 1990 (which was mainly about money). Others are forces moving a few hundred miles to join in a regional conflict, as happened in Saudi Arabia and Liberia in 1990. In most cases these little wars are small because it's so expensive to send armed forces any distance. It's more expensive still to actually use them at that distance and keep them supplied. Even light-infantry forces are expensive to move as the cost is ultimately more than just a round trip by aircraft. "Light troops" have a certain amount of heavy equipment (light vehicles and heavy weapons), and all this stuff is generally moved by air freight, an expensive proposition when large air freight planes cost $30,000–$50,000 a day to operate and can be used ten to twelve hours a day (which comes to about twenty-five cents per mile each ton is carried). Since each soldier in a little war requires at least a hundred pounds of supplies a day, the costs mount up rather quickly. Even a "light infantry"-type troop will require up to a ton of air freight capacity to get a soldier and his equipment and supplies to the battlefield. If the combat area is 10,000 miles away, it's going to cost $2,500 just to get him there. Each day the soldier is there will cost another $25 just for air freight. If the soldier gets killed, it will cost about $50 to ship the body back. If the soldier is wounded and has to be evacuated out of the area, the air freight bill goes to several hundred dollars. Thus air-freighting five thousand troops to a distant (10,000 miles away) hot spot will cost over $12 million and another $125,000 per day (nearly $4 million a month) just to fly the supplies in. After about a month, you can establish supply lines by sea, which costs only a small percentage of what air freight costs. But it can take twenty to forty-five days to travel 10,000 miles by sea, depending on what type of ship you use (fast ones cost more to operate) and which continents you have to sail around. But by the time seaborne supply has been established, the little war has been around for a while and is on its way to becoming a not-so-little war.

Aside from the cost of shipping the troops somewhere far away, there is the fact that not all the soldiers sent will actually be fighting. Even with our hypothetical force of five thousand light infantry, no more than half of them will actually be out there with weapons ready. The remainder (and they are usually the majority) are there for the ever-increasing number of support jobs (including taking care of all the supplies coming in by air and sea).

In terms of more traditional geography, little wars tend to be fought in places where the geographical conditions are, well, difficult. Little wars are often found in less-developed nations where nature has not yet been tamed. There are relatively fewer roads, more disease, bad water, and conditions that require more medical personnel and other support troops (engineers in particular).

HISTORY

The last major period of little wars was between the U.S. Civil War (1865) and World War I (1914). However, since World War II (1945), in the absence of any major-power war, there has already been a string of little wars which has gone largely unnoticed while the heavily armed superpowers glared at each other across the Iron Curtain in Europe. The concept of "little wars" is a matter of perception, and perceptions are changing as we move several generations away from the bloodbaths of World War I and World War II. To put things in perspective, from 1900 to 1945 an average of nearly two million people died annually in wars. From 1945 to 1990 the average annual deaths have been half that (a million a year). When adjusted for the enormous population growth since World War II, the annual death rate from wars, we find, was three times higher in the first half of the century than it was in the second half. Yet, the past four decades have been full of little wars—the superpowers just didn't concentrate on them. Instead they put most of their effort into the World War III that never came off and is now acknowledged to be a dead issue.

With a major war less likely, the military is now keen to pay close attention to the kinds of wars they usually fight. These are the dirty little wars that often lack support back home and frequently have ambiguous endings. America has had more of these than it likes to remember. Before Vietnam there was the Philippine insurrection and several major operations in Latin America. But now these wars are the only wars the military has, and without war, or the prospect of war, the public will perceive less need for armed forces. So, in a combination of common sense and institutional self-preservation, the military has gone back to the little wars.

LOCAL POLITICS

There are three areas where little wars are most likely to occur (and have done so over the centuries): Africa, the Middle East, and East Asia.

The most war-torn area is Africa; there the wars are not only little but also inconsequential as far as the more heavily armed industrialized nations are concerned. Over the past two centuries, although 22 percent of the wars have been in Africa, only 2 percent of the deaths have occurred there. Since World War II, the loss rate has gone up, but these wars are still generally ignored.

The Middle East has been the second most violent area over the past two centuries, with 20 percent of the wars and only 2 percent of the deaths. Again, the death rate has gone up since World War II, but not as much as in Africa since civilians are less likely to be victims of large-scale massacre in Middle Eastern conflicts. The industrialized powers do take an interest in these little wars, mainly because of the oil in the region, the Suez Canal, and, until recently, the area's proximity to Russia.

East Asia has had 16 percent of the wars in the last two centuries, and 44 percent of the war deaths. This is a densely populated area and includes China, Japan, and Vietnam—three nations long noted for their warlike proclivities.

Each of these three areas is of interest to the industrialized nations.

The Middle East, especially the Persian Gulf, contains most of the exportable oil in the world. The industrialized nations need this oil and will fight to retain access to it at an affordable price. The oil money that has poured into the region has bought huge amounts of arms and inspired even more ambitious plans for national conquest among the normally factious groups occupying the region. The region now attracts attention from the industrialized nations because several local despots are well on their way toward adding chemical weapons, atom bombs, and long-range missiles to their arsenals. Iraq's fate will not greatly discourage others in the region from being ambitious.

East Asian nations are important to the maintenance of a stable world economy. America has treaty obligations with Japan, South Korea, and several other nations in the region. East Asia also contains several unstable nations, China being the most worrisome. Civil war in China would likely be a number of little wars rather than one large conflict between two clearly defined groups. North Korea is another unstable country that could slip into civil war, or simply civil disorder.

When it comes to little wars, Africa is indeed the sad continent. There is an overabundance of little wars going on, but no particularly pressing interest on the part of the industrialized nations to get involved. The world's major military powers would like to see things calm down, if only to reduce the waste of economic aid. Currently this aid is either blown away on a hundred battlefields or stolen and deposited in hundreds of foreign bank accounts. As long as conditions are chaotic, and nonvital to outside interests, the African little wars will be of interest largely to those few journalists who happen to pass through.

REGIONAL POWERS AND POWER INTEREST INDICATOR CHARTS

UNITED STATES

America's interests, at all levels, span the globe.

	Economic Interests	Historical Interests	Political Interest	Military Interest	Force Generation Potential*	Ability to Intervene Politically	Ability to Promote Economic Development
Americas	8	8	9	9	9	7	8
Europe	8	8	9	9	7	6	6
Middle East	8	5	8	8	6	4	2
Africa	2	2	4	2	5	4	5
So. Asia	3	4	5	4	5	3	4
E. Asia	7+	7	8+	8	7	6	5

NOTE: 0 = minimum; 9 = maximum.
*Number (1–9).

A slight twist: Here we look at the various "expeditionary powers'" areas of interest.

FRANCE

France, despite the expense, continues to work at being a global player.

	Economic Interests	Historical Interests	Political Interest	Military Interest	Force Generation Potential*	Ability to Intervene Politically	Ability to Promote Economic Development
Americas	2	3	5	2	2	3	2
Europe	9	9	9	9	6	7	7
Middle East	7	8	8	7	3	5	4
Africa	8	8	7	7	5	7	8
So. Asia	3	5	7	2	1	4	1
E. Asia	6	3	6	2	1–	2	1

NOTE: 0 = minimum; 9 = maximum.
*Number (1–9).

United Kingdom

Britain knows its empire is gone, but old habits, and obligations, die hard.

	Economic Interests	Historical Interests	Political Interest	Military Interest	Force Generation Potential*	Ability to Intervene Politically	Ability to Promote Economic Development
Americas	4	8	7	2	2	4	2
Europe	8	8	9	9	4+	6	6
Middle East	8	8	8	8	3	6	3
Africa	7	7	6	6	3	7	4
So. Asia	3	4	6	2	2	5	1
E. Asia	5	3	6	2	1	3	1

NOTE: 0 = minimum; 9 = maximum.

*Number (1–9).

RUSSIA

The post–Cold War world has Russia returning to its traditional task: preventing Russia from falling apart.

	Economic Interests	Historical Interests	Political Interest	Military Interest	Force Generation Potential*	Ability to Intervene Politically	Ability to Promote Economic Development
Americas	1 –	2	4	4	2+	2	0
Europe	9	7	9	9	8+	7	2
Middle East	3	2	5	6	7	6	1
Africa	0	2	3	1	2	4	0
So. Asia	2	2	5	2	3	4	1
E. Asia	5	6	8	8	7+	4	3

NOTE: 0 = minimum; 9 = maximum.
*Number (1–9).

PARTICIPANT STRATEGIES AND GOALS

United States Groups

The United States State Department—The United States has traditionally been isolationist. This came about partially because the United States is geographically isolated from the rest of the world and partially because many U.S. residents have an immigrant attitude of wanting to leave the "old country's" strife and mayhem behind them. But the United States is part of a world economy, and as the Persian Gulf crises of 1990 demonstrated, it simply cannot ignore all of the little wars overseas. The State Department itself would prefer to settle all foreign disputes with diplomacy, which makes sense coming from diplomats. Besides, once the military gets called in, the State Department takes a very distant second place in the chain of command: Military solutions find more support among members of any U.S. president's staff, and after all, the State Department works for the president, not the other way around.

The United States Navy and Marine Corps—The Navy is a large organization that, like any large organization, will not go cheerfully (or willingly) through a downsizing. The Navy's position is that with at least a dozen carrier task forces (down from the current fourteen to fifteen) and three Marine divisions (a level mandated by law) the State Department troops would be numerous enough to take care of any conceivable little war. Perhaps it might need a little backup from the Army and Air Force, but those two services are there, preferably in skeletal form, to mobilize for the rare occasion when a little war grows into a big one.

The United States Army—As recently as 1940, the U.S. Army had only 150,000 troops (smaller than the post–World War II Marine Corps). The Cold War changed all that, but now that it's over, the Army faces a lot of pressure to shrink back to its 1940 size, or something close to it. With the Navy reasserting its traditional monopoly on little wars, the Army is in big trouble. Since World War II, the Army has built up substantial "little war" forces which include one parachute division, one air assault division, four light-infantry divisions, and a division of ranger and Special Forces (commando) troops. These forces exceed the strength of the Marine Corps, but as events in the Persian Gulf demonstrated, there are situations where little war forces are not enough. In the Persian Gulf a tank-heavy mechanized army was needed, which pleased the Army no end and put the Marines on the defensive.

The United States Air Force—The "blue suit" crowd is pushing its ability to rapidly deploy substantial firepower on short notice. This concept is also being used to support the long-range B-2 bomber and new transport aircraft (ostensibly to move Army units, but also capable of moving support units for Air Force combat aircraft). As a prime exponent of high-tech warfare, the Air Force is also promoting more (and quite expensive) research on new sensors (the better to spot war adversaries hiding in the bush or whatever). It's not as well positioned as the Navy, but better off than the Army. At least the Air Force can offer more tank-killing capability faster for the Marines.

Other Players

Great Britain—With acceptance of the decline of its empire and increasing budget problems at home, Great Britain does not want to increase its involvement in little wars. If it can get away with it, Great Britain will allow the United States to take the lead and send token contingents when asked.

France—More for glory than real national interest, France continues to maintain and use intervention forces, which are largely light infantry backed up by air power.

Other European Economic Community (EEC) countries—These nations will follow the lead of whoever jumps in first, as long as there is enough public support for another foreign adventure.

Russia—With an abundance of domestic problems, the Russians have neither the desire nor the resources to engage in military operations far from their borders. Although the Russians still maintain a large array of armed forces, they are having severe personnel problems. In addition, the Conventional Forces Europe (CFE) arms-reduction talks in Vienna are cutting Russian forces down further. Financial problems at home make overseas adventures prohibitively expensive, and there are increasing problems just maintaining all the equipment still in the inventory.

China—Like Russia, China has a multitude of internal problems and a traditional dislike of foreign adventures. Since the 1950s, China's foreign military involvements have been restricted to aid and advisers, and its economic and political problems are limiting even these operations. However, operations against bumptious neighbors are still a possibility.

Third World "Little Warriors"—The passing of the Cold War also eliminated the ability of major Third World nations to play one super-power off another and exact tribute from both. Without this aid, foreign military adventures become prohibitively expensive. Well, not always, but impoverished Third World military adventurers will have to check with their ministries of finance more so than in the past.

The Outcasts—With so many nations now cut off from access to free weapons or easy credit, the outcasts have more markets open to them. The outcasts tend to provide "technical advisers" with their weapons. While this does not mean you will encounter Israeli or South African troops in some little war, you are likely to find troops trained (and often well trained) by outcast advisers. This growing problem is producing some strange diplomatic side effects.

POTENTIAL OUTCOMES

1. 50 percent chance through 1996: The United States builds up a large intervention force and engages in only one or two expeditionary missions in the 1991–96 time frame.

2. 25 percent chance through 1996: The United States builds up a large intervention force and engages in three or more expeditionary missions in the 1991–96 time frame.

3. 15 percent chance through 1996: The United States maintains a large intervention force and does not use it in the 1991–96 time frame.

4. 10 percent chance through 1996: The United States cuts back its forces and does not engage in a major expeditionary campaign in the 1991–96 time frame.

COST OF WAR

Potentially, several hundred thousand people could be killed each year in the sundry little wars being fought around the world. Over a million are wounded or injured, and several times that number have their lives disrupted or even become refugees.

WHAT KIND OF WAR

The conventional wisdom is that most little wars will be infantry affairs. In many cases that is true, but as the Persian Gulf crises of 1990 and 1991 demonstrated, there are still times when a lot of tanks show up.

The current size of the U.S. tank force was determined by the need to possibly face Russia and the Warsaw Pact in a post–World War II standoff between the Communist and Western democratic nations. But the Warsaw Pact has disappeared in the last year, with East Germany and its three thousand tanks disappearing altogether. Intense negotiations are going on in Vienna to further reduce tank holdings in Europe and North America; thus it is immediately apparent that fewer U.S. tanks will be needed. The question is, how many will be needed in the 1990s.

That depends on how many other tank battalions you might have to fight. There are about 160,000 tanks in the world (as of early 1990). Three powers own half of them. Of the twenty-five nations with 1,000 or more tanks, five (marked with asterisks on the list) could be considered potential battlefield opponents. However, most of these potential foes are countered by nearby U.S. allies who have large tank parks of their own. Thus Syria would have to deal with Israel, Libya faces Egypt, North Korea must contend with South Korea, and Iran barely makes the cut. Iraq, then, was the worst case. To face this threat, the United States has fourteen tank-heavy divisions (six armored, eight mechanized) containing about 5,000 tanks. Another 10,000 tanks are used in tank-light divisions (including the three Marine divisions), held as replacements, or used to form new tank units.

NATIONAL TANK HOLDINGS
(EARLY 1990; SINCE THEN IRAQI AND EAST GERMAN TANK FORCES HAVE DISAPPEARED)

Russia	54,000
U.S.	16,000
China	11,000
W. Germany	4,950
Iraq*	4,500
Syria*	4,000
Poland	3,950
Israel	3,850
India	3,700
Turkey	3,600
Czechoslovakia	3,400
E. Germany	3,000
Libya*	3,000

No. Korea*	3,000
Bulgaria	2,550
Egypt	2,400
Romania	1,900
Vietnam	1,700
So. Korea	1,700
Greece	1,360
France	1,340
Hungary	1,300
Britain	1,200
Japan	1,200
Iran*	1,000
Jordan	975
Spain	840

NOTE: Iraq now (early 1991) holds around 800 tanks.
*Could be considered potential battlefield opponents.

The key question is, how much is enough? For one thing, it is increasingly difficult to get defense budgets through Congress. Assuming the Russian threat is gone, at least for the moment, there is the problem of all those other nations possessing tanks. How to deal with them? History, and any tank commander, will claim that the best antitank weapon is another tank, even though tanks are not usually responsible for most other tank losses. The tank was not invented to fight other tanks, but to spearhead the ground forces in the face of the strongest opposition. Sometimes that means other tanks, sometimes not. Whatever the case, the tank can move a lot of firepower around quickly and take care of itself in the bargain.

But tanks are heavy beasts and difficult to move anywhere in a hurry. Moreover, there is an abundance of other weapons that can destroy (or at least immobilize) a tank. Aircraft carry a wide array of weapons, including several types of mines. Mines are a favorite and cheap antitank weapon. The most numerous is the small (two to five pound) "track-buster" mine which immobilizes a tank by damaging (but not destroying) the track-laying mechanism. It can take several hours to a day or more to get a "track-busted" tank moving again. Missiles are also a favorite weapon, and most nations have more antitank missiles than they have tanks.

Thus the United States is faced with two primary questions. First, what is the most effective and economical way to neutralize enemy tanks, and second, how many tanks does the United States need for wars in the 1990s?

As events in the Persian Gulf demonstrated, the first U.S. antitank weapons to arrive on the scene were carried by U.S. ground-attack aircraft. Next came the antitank missiles (with trucks and helicopters to carry them) of the light infantry and Marines. Last came (by ship) the tanks. Without a month's warning, there is no practical way to get enough tanks to any faraway battlefield. It is possible, however, to get aircraft and light infantry there within a few days.

But, if a nation eventually plans to go on the offensive, it will need a sufficiently large tank force. Tanks are still key to speed and power in the offensive, though they are only part of the offensive equation.

Given the lineup of potential opponents, the United States needs fewer than half the tanks it now has, although it could use more antitank missiles and mines. (There are currently more effective mines in the works.) A true "light tank" would also come in handy to speed up offensive operations without waiting for the heavy tanks to be shipped in.

Light-Infantry Forces

Real light infantry is anything but a featherweight combat force, at least in terms of effectiveness. As has been demonstrated on many Third World battlefields, under the right leadership, well-trained and well-equipped light infantry can handle just about anything it encounters. Light infantry equipped with modern antitank missiles and supported by air power can even stop a mechanized force. However, there are many limitations when throwing light infantry against a mechanized foe. It can be done, but at great cost to your light troops.

Most Likely Little Wars

The places in the world where little wars are most likely to happen are the Balkans, Lebanon, South Africa, the Persian Gulf, and Pakistan (see the chapters on these).

PART SIX

A DATA BANK ON WARS PRESENT AND POTENTIAL

This section contains a statistical survey of currently active and most potential wars (even we thought Iraq going after Kuwait was a long shot, although Iraq had moved in that direction twice before in 1961 and 1973). There are two charts. One shows the conflicts themselves ("The World in Conflict") and the other, the basic economic and military information for all countries in the mid-1990s ("The Nations of the World").

CHAPTER 15

THE WORLD IN CONFLICT

This chapter presents a brief introduction to current international and internal wars which uses a standardized format and is supplemented by some explanatory notes. The next time you hear about some obscure conflict, a quick check in this chapter will bring you up to date on the background of the situation.

TERMS

Averages & Totals—Average and/or total for each column as appropriate will give a sense of proportion for each value for each nation.

Conflict—Common name for an active war. Potential wars have been designated by a descriptive name and the year of the start of the dispute that may yet lead to armed conflict.

Side—Name of a participant in the conflict. A country's name is given if a side is the government of the country. The term ''Insurgents'' is used for antigovernment forces from the same country. Note that often there are more than two sides in a war and that full information is supplied for every side in a conflict.

Year Began—Year that the (modern) version of the conflict began. Many wars are disputes that go back in one form or another for thousands of years. In the Middle East, for example, you have conflicts that have been raging for thousands of years. These disputes flare up every few

African Nations
 1 Liberia
 2 South Africa
 3 Gabon
 4 Guinea-Bissau
 5 Madagascar
 6 Ivory Coast
 7 Central African Republic
 8 Mauretania
 9 Botswana
10 Cameroon
11 Djibouti
12 Congo
13 Rwanda
14 Niger
15 Senegambia
16 Burkina Faso
17 Ghana
18 Somalia
19 Mali
20 Benin
21 Sierra Leone
22 Tanzania
23 Comoro Islands
24 Zambia
25 São Tomé & Príncipe
26 Chad
27 Swaziland
28 Nigeria
29 Lesotho
30 Cape Verde Islands
31 Malawi
32 Seychelles
33 Togo
34 Burundi
35 Zaire
36 Kenya
37 Uganda
38 Zimbabwe
39 Angola
40 Equatorial Guinea
41 Guinea
42 Ethiopia
43 Mozambique

American Nations
44 United States
45 Canada
46 Panama
47 El Salvador
48 Jamaica
49 Colombia
50 Brazil
51 Bolivia
52 Uruguay
53 Guyana
54 Paraguay
55 Peru
56 Mexico

57 Venezuela
58 Argentina
59 Chile
60 Ecuador
61 Trinidad
62 Guatemala
63 Haiti
64 Costa Rica
65 Honduras
66 Dominican Republic
67 Belize
68 Suriname
69 Nicaragua
70 Cuba

European Nations
71 Italy
72 Belgium
73 Norway
74 Germany

75 Britain
76 Luxembourg
77 Spain
78 France
79 Iceland
80 Denmark
81 Netherlands
82 Portugal
83 Greece
84 Turkey
85 Malta
86 Cyprus (Greek)
87 Switzerland
88 Sweden
89 Ireland
90 Finland
91 Austria
92 Yugoslavia
93 Cyprus (Turkish)
94 Albania

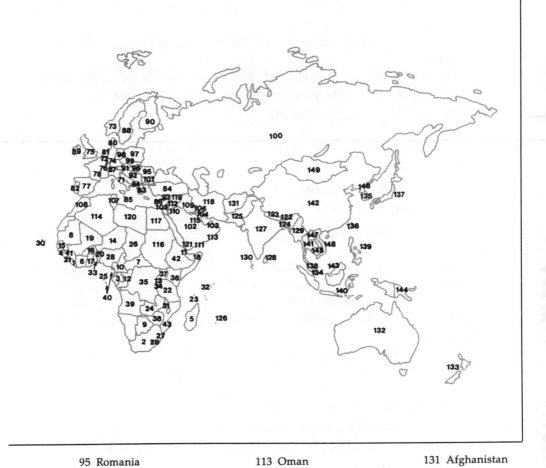

decades (or centuries) and are called "wars" but are basically the same dispute.

Type of Conflict—Indication of the nature of the conflict, using letter codes that are presented in order of increasing importance. (They are described here in no particular order.)

I: Ideological, including religious, conflict

R: Political/social revolution

S: Separatist movement

T: Territorial dispute

H: Historical antagonism

Danger Level—Relative danger to world peace represented by a participant in a conflict. The higher this value, the more likely the participant's warlike activities could trigger more widespread death and destruction. The key components of the danger level are the next three indexes.

Severity Intensity Index—Measure of the level of severity of the conflict (as of early 1991):

0:   Very-low-intensity terrorist activity

1:   Serious predisposition to armed conflict

2:   Sustained terrorist activity or regular forces on the scene

3:   Guerrilla activity or regular forces active

4:   Sustained guerrilla activity or regular forces very active

5:   State of war, continuous operations

6:   Lower-scale conventional operations such as in the Falklands or Lebanese wars

7:   Medium-scale conventional war, such as the Iran-Iraq conflict

8:   Full-scale conventional warfare, such as a nonnuclear superpower clash

9:   Nuclear exchange

Each side in a conflict will often have a different intensity level. This reflects different goals and means. A strong government when faced with opposition will bear down on it more severely than an emerging opposition group.

Probability Index—Percentage probability that the side will be engaged in active combat in the conflict at any given time in the next few years. Each side will often have a different probability index, reflecting differing predispositions to settling conflicts with violence.

Escalation Index—Possibility of the conflict spreading either vertically (intensifying) or horizontally (coming to involve more areas or countries):

1: No international impact beyond the nation(s) involved

2: Potential threat to neighboring states

3: Significant threat to neighboring states

4: No international impact beyond the nation(s) involved, with some chance of superpower involvement

5: Potential threat to neighboring states, with more superpower involvement

6: Significant threat to neighboring states, with significant superpower threat

7: Multiregional threat with superpower interest

8: As number 7 above but more so

9: Overwhelming international importance

Form of Government—Indication of the type of government of the side (combinations of types are shown as such):

Mon: Functioning monarchy

Dem: Functioning democracy

Dic: Dictatorship

M: Military government

OP: One-party rule

Soc: Soviet-style socialist regime

Jun: Junta (military leadership, applied to insurgent groups when no better information is available on the most likely type of leadership contained)

Government's Stability—Stability rating of the government on a scale of 1-highly unstable to 5-highly stable. This reflects the quality of the national leadership and whatever national governing organizations exist. A more stable national leadership usually means more predictable performance by that nation in pursuing or stopping its conflicts.

Forces—Approximate number in thousands of troops directly committed to the conflict. This number is often debatable, as the deployment of forces is usually flexible in "peacetime" wars. Other priorities like keeping your civilians in line and facing down other aggressors keep the order of battle (mix of units) in the immediate combat area quite flexible. The total forces involved in all conflicts can often exceed the number of troops available for each nation because a nation can have more potential conflicts on its hands than its available forces can handle. This is a particular fear of the Russians, surrounded as they are by numerous hostile nations.

Quality of Forces—Quality of the forces involved in the conflict. A nation often has available troops of vastly differing quality. The best troops are usually sent against the most dangerous enemy. Less qualified (but often more loyal) troops are used against restive civilians. Rated on a scale of 1-extremely poor to 5-excellent.

Endurance—Ability of each side to sustain the conflict at the current level of intensity, assuming the current political conditions continue. A single nation involved in multiple conflicts usually shows different endurance levels for each conflict. Rated on a scale of 1-poor to 5-excellent.

Losses—Number of casualties incurred in thousands. This includes killed, wounded, and missing, but not prisoners (assuming they survive). It covers the period from the beginning of the conflict (1945 for those wars that predate that year). Conflicts with fewer than 1,000 casualties are assigned the number 1,000 (shown as 1 on the chart). This is based on the reasonable assumption that it won't be long before this nominal number of casualties will be exceeded.

Refugees—Number of people in thousands displaced by the conflict, internally and internationally. These are people who were forced out of their homes either by the fighting or the threat of it. It does not include the much larger number of people who remained in their home areas as the fighting overcame them.

THE WORLD IN CONFLICT

Conflict	Side	Year Began	Type of Conflict	Danger Level	Severity Intensity Index	Probability Index (in %)	Escalation Index	Form of Government	Government's Stability	Forces (in thousands of troops)	Quality of Forces	Endurance	Losses (in thousands)	Refugees (in thousands)
Averages & Totals				14	4	62	4		4	31,512	3	4	54,371	60,632
Aegean	Greece	1945	TH	3	1	50	5	Dem	3	250	4	3	0	0
Aegean	Turkey	1945	TH	2	1	40	5	Dem	4	500	4	3	0	0
Afghanistan	Afghanistan	1978	IH	20	5	80	4	OP	2	150	1	5	100	6,000
Afghanistan	Insurgents	1978	IH	28	5	90	5	Jun	3	100	4	5	1,000	0
Angola	Angola	1975	I	22	5	70	5	OP	3	80	2	5	50	400
Angola	Cuba	1975	I	7	2	60	5	Dic	4	25	3	5	2	0
Angola	So. Africa	1975	I	3	1	50	5	DemDic	4	2	5	4	1	0
Angola	Insurgents	1975	I	9	3	60	4	Jun	4	40	2	5	10	0
Belize	Britain	1945	T	4	6	50	1	Dem	5	20	5	5	0	0
Belize	Guatemala	1945	T	3	5	50	1	MJun	3	25	3	3	0	0
Burma	Burma	1948	SIH	3	4	70	1	OP	4	160	3	5	10	100
Burma	Insurgents	1948	SIH	8	3	57	4	Jun	4	20	3	5	30	0
Burundi	Tutsis	1988	HR	3	3	90	1	Jun	5	7	4	2	3	0
Burundi	Hutus	1988	HR	0	1	20	1	OP	4	1	2	5	40	40
Cabinda	Angola	1975	SI	15	5	60	4	OP	3	8	2	5	1	50
Cabinda	Insurgents	1975	SI	8	3	55	4	Jun	4	4	2	5	1	0
Cambodia	Vietnam	1978	HI	35	7	80	5	Soc	4	160	4	3	100	0
Cambodia	Cambodia	1978	HI	15	5	60	4	Dic	2	20	2	3	120	400
Cambodia	Insurgents	1978	HI	12	4	60	4	Jun	3	40	3	5	2,200	2,000
Caucasus	Armenians	1988	TH	20	3	90	6	Jun	5	25	3	6	2	200
Caucasus	Georgians	1988	TH	6	2	50	5	Jun	4	20	3	6	1	0
Caucasus	Azeris	1988	TH	18	3	80	6	Jun	4	20	3	6	1	2
Caucasus	Russia	1988	TH	16	3	60	7	SocDem	3	200	4	5	2	0
Cent. America	Honduras	1945	TI	28	5	90	5	Dem	2	15	2	2	0	0
Cent. America	Nicaragua	1945	TI	20	4	80	5	Dem	3	50	2	3	0	0
Cent. Asia	Russia	1988	TH	16	3	60	7	SocDem	3	200	4	5	1	0
Cent. Asia	Insurgents	1988	TH	7	3	40	5	Jun	3	20	2	6	3	100

Conflict	Side	Year Began	Type of Conflict	Danger Level	Severity Intensity Index	Probability Index (in %)	Escalation Index	Form of Government	Government's Stability	Forces (in thousands of troops)	Quality of Forces	Endurance	Losses (in thousands)	Refugees (in thousands)
Averages & Totals				14	4	62	4		4	31,512	3	4	54,371	60,632
Chad	Chad	1965	IT	23	5	75	5	OP	2	6	2	5	30	200
Chad	Zaire	1965	IT	22	5	70	5	Dic	3	3	2	3	0	0
Chad	Nigeria	1965	TSI	19	6	50	5	Jun	3	150	2	3	0	0
Chad	France	1965	IT	31	6	85	5	Dem	5	3	5	5	1	0
Chad	Libya	1965	TSI	30	6	80	5	Dic	5	60	2	3	10	0
Chad	Insurgents	1965	IT	26	6	70	5	Dic	3	5	2	5	30	0
China 1945	Taiwan	1945	I	3	8	5	6	OP	4	500	4	3	10,000	0
China 1945	China	1945	I	3	8	5	6	Soc	4	1,500	3	5	20,000	5,000
China 1989	China	1989	R	17	7	40	5	Soc	4	1,500	3	5	10	20
China 1989	Insurgents	1989	R	7	3	40	5	Jun	3	1,500	4	5	10	20
Colombia	Colombia	1948	RSI	21	5	85	4	OP	4	60	3	5	250	500
Colombia	Insurgents	1948	RSI	6	2	65	4	Jun	3	4	4	5	25	0
Cyprus	Turkey	1945	TH	15	6	50	1	Dem	4	25	4	4	0	30
Cyprus	Turks	1945	TH	1	2	40	1	Jun	3	20	3	4	2	45
Cyprus	Greeks	1945	TH	1	2	60	1	Jun	3	40	3	3	1	0
Dhofar	Oman	1963	TSI	10	2	80	5	Mon	4	20	3	5	2	0
Dhofar	Yemen	1963	TSI	5	1	80	5	OP	4	25	3	5	4	0
Dhofar	Insurgents	1963	TSI	5	1	76	5	Jun	2	1	4	5	3	0
El Salvador	El Salvador	1979	IR	30	6	80	5	Dem	2	50	3	5	30	200
El Salvador	U.S.	1979	IT	10	9	10	9	Dem	5	5	5	5	0	0
El Salvador	Insurgents	1979	IR	33	6	90	5	Jun	4	7	2	5	30	0
Eritrea	Ethiopia	1961	SHI	33	6	90	5	MDic	3	250	2	4	500	300
Eritrea	Insurgents	1961	SHI	22	4	90	5	Jun	4	25	4	5	100	1,000
Ethiopia	Ethiopia	1974	ISH	33	6	90	5	MDic	3	100	2	6	1,600	1,200
Ethiopia	Insurgents	1974	ISH	17	4	67	5	Jun	2	60	3	5	20	0
Falklands	Britain	1982	T	12	6	40	4	Dem	5	20	5	5	1	0
Falklands	Argentina	1982	T	6	6	20	4	Dem	4	20	2	3	2	0
Guatemala	Guatemala	1960	R	21	5	86	4	MJun	3	17	3	3	5	50
Guatemala	Insurgents	1960	R	6	2	60	4	Jun	3	3	3	5	5	0
Guyana	Venezuela	1945	T	3	6	40	1	Dem	4	60	3	5	0	0
Guyana	Guyana	1945	T	15	6	50	4	Dem	2	3	3	2	0	0
Haiti	Haiti	1945	R	16	4	80	4	OP	3	20	1	5	1	0
Haiti	Insurgents	1945	R	4	1	80	4	Jun	2	1	1	5	20	0
Honduras	Honduras	1980	R	17	4	70	5	Dem	2	15	2	2	1	150

Conflict	Side	Year Began	Type of Conflict	Danger Level	Severity Intensity Index	Probability Index (in %)	Escalation Index	Form of Government	Government's Stability	Forces (in thousands of troops)	Quality of Forces	Endurance	Losses (in thousands)	Refugees (in thousands)
Averages & Totals				14	4	62	4		4	31,512	3	4	54,371	60,632
Honduras	Insurgents	1980	R	4	1	60	5	Jun	3	3	3	5	2	0
India	Insurgents	1990	I	4	4	90	1	Jun	3	400	1	5	5	0
India	India	1990	I	2	3	60	1	Dem	4	300	4	4	1	0
Indo-Pakistan	India	1947	HT	4	7	15	3	Dem	4	1,000	5	5	2,500	12,000
Indo-Pakistan	Pakistan	1947	HT	4	7	15	3	Dem	3	900	4	4	2,000	3,000
Iran	Iran	1979	ISH	22	5	90	4	OP	5	80	3	5	5	0
Iran	Insurgents	1979	ISH	6	2	65	4	Jun	4	20	3	5	25	0
Iran-Iraq	Iraq	1980	TH	8	1	90	7	OPDic	4	700	3	5	500	400
Iran-Iraq	Iran	1980	TH	9	1	90	8	OP	5	900	3	5	700	500
Irian Barat	Indonesia	1969	S	5	5	85	1	Dic	4	200	2	5	1	0
Irian Barat	Insurgents	1969	S	2	2	90	1	Jun	2	50	4	5	12	0
Israel-PLO	PLO	1948	T	12	2	80	6	Jun	3	16	3	5	12	2,300
Israel-PLO	Israel	1948	T	33	5	90	6	Dem	5	300	5	5	2	0
Kashmir	India	1988	RSI	28	5	90	5	Jun	4	600	4	4	1	5
Kashmir	Kashmir	1988	RSI	28	5	90	5	Jun	4	10	2	5	10	20
Kashmir	Pakistan	1988	RSI	2	1	30	5	Dem	3	500	4	5	0	0
Korea	So. Korea	1950	I	21	7	40	6	Dem	3	1,100	5	5	1,000	5,000
Korea	U.S.	1950	I	27	9	30	8	Dem	5	50	5	4	100	0
Korea	No. Korea	1950	I	31	7	60	6	MDic	4	900	4	5	2,000	3,000
Kosovo	Albania	1945	TH	10	3	55	5	OPDic	3	150	2	2	1	0
Kosovo	Yugoslavia	1945	TH	5	1	80	5	Soc	3	300	4	4	1	0
Kurdistan	Kurds	1961	SH	6	2	65	4	Jun	4	5	4	5	230	600
Kurdistan	Iraq	1961	SH	17	5	70	4	OPDic	4	12	3	5	40	0
Kurdistan	Iran	1961	SH	35	5	80	7	OP	5	50	3	5	5	0
Kurdistan	Turkey	1961	SH	12	3	80	4	Dem	4	2	4	5	2	0
Kuwait	Iraq	1990	TH	31	7	40	9	OPDic	4	1,100	3	2	150	2,000
Kuwait	UN	1990	TH	70	7	90	9	Dem	4	900	6	4	3	1,500
Laos	Laos	1975	IS	17	4	85	4	Dic	2	46	1	3	24	500
Laos	Vietnam	1975	IS	28	5	90	5	Soc	4	60	4	4	12	0
Laos	Insurgents	1975	IS	6	2	65	4	Jun	4	20	3	5	50	0
Lebanon	Lebanon	1975	HIS	28	5	90	5	Jun	2	15	2	3	12	500
Lebanon	U.S.	1975	HIS	24	7	40	7	Dem	5	35	5	3	1	0

Conflict	Side	Year Began	Type of Conflict	Danger Level	Severity Intensity Index	Probability Index (in %)	Escalation Index	Form of Government	Government's Stability	Forces (in thousands of troops)	Quality of Forces	Endurance	Losses (in thousands)	Refugees (in thousands)
Averages & Totals				14	4	62	4		4	31,512	3	4	54,371	60,632
Lebanon	Israel	1975	HIS	41	7	80	6	Dem	5	30	5	5	4	0
Lebanon	Syria	1975	HIS	41	7	80	6	OPDic	3	40	3	3	20	0
Lebanon	UN	1975	HIS	5	1	85	5	Dem	3	6	4	3	1	0
Lebanon	NATO	1975	HIS	27	6	60	6	Dem	3	2	5	5	1	0
Lebanon	Shiites	1975	HIS	28	5	90	5	Jun	4	18	2	5	5	0
Lebanon	Iran	1975	HIS	21	6	40	7	OP	5	1	3	5	1	0
Lebanon	PLO	1975	HIS	19	5	60	5	Jun	3	5	3	4	15	0
Lebanon	Sunnites	1975	HIS	33	6	90	5	Jun	4	5	2	5	50	0
Lebanon	Phalange	1975	HIS	30	6	80	5	Jun	4	15	2	5	40	0
Lebanon	Russia	1975	HIS	16	6	30	7	SocDem	3	2	4	3	1	0
Lebanon	Armenians	1975	HIS	7	6	20	5	Jun	3	25	4	3	1	5
Lebanon	Druze	1975	HIS	33	6	90	5	Jun	5	18	4	5	60	0
Libya	Egypt	1945	TI	17	7	40	5	OP	3	400	3	3	1	0
Libya	Libya	1945	TI	26	7	60	5	Dic	5	60	2	2	2	0
Libya	Sudan	1945	TI	12	5	50	4	OP	3	58	3	2	5	0
Malaysia	Malaysia	1968	I	11	3	75	4	Dem	4	80	3	5	3	0
Malaysia	Insurgents	1968	I	3	1	55	5	Dic	4	5	3	5	8	0
Malta	Malta	1980	TH	3	5	10	5	Dem	4	3	3	5	0	0
Malta	Libya	1980	TH	16	7	30	6	Dic	5	60	2	5	0	0
Maranon	Ecuador	1945	TH	4	6	50	1	Dem	3	45	2	3	0	0
Maranon	Peru	1945	TH	3	6	40	1	Dem	3	100	3	3	0	0
Middle East	U.S.	1948	TI	16	8	20	8	Dem	5	110	5	4	1	0
Middle East	Israel	1948	TI	48	8	70	7	Dem	5	400	5	3	1	0
Middle East	Jordan	1948	TI	24	7	40	7	Mon	4	80	4	1	1	0
Middle East	Syria	1948	TI	48	8	70	7	OPDic	3	200	3	2	4	0
Middle East	Lebanon	1948	TI	9	5	30	5	Jun	2	35	2	1	1	0
Middle East	Egypt	1948	TI	21	8	30	7	OP	3	400	3	2	1	0
Middle East	Iraq	1948	TI	36	7	60	7	OPDic	4	25	3	3	1	0
Moldavia	Russia	1990	TH	6	3	50	3	SocDem	3	200	4	2	1	5
Moldavia	Moldavia	1990	TH	3	2	40	3	Jun	3	10	1	5	2	2
Moldavia	Romania	1990	TH	1	1	20	3	Dem	4	150	2	4	0	0
Mozambique	Mozambique	1975	SI	17	5	70	4	OP	3	28	2	3	5	0

Conflict	Side	Year Began	Type of Conflict	Danger Level	Severity Intensity Index	Probability Index (in %)	Escalation Index	Form of Government	Government's Stability	Forces (in thousands of troops)	Quality of Forces	Endurance	Losses (in thousands)	Refugees (in thousands)
Averages & Totals				14	4	62	4		4	31,512	3	4	54,371	60,632
Mozambique	Insurgents	1975	SI	6	2	60	4	Jun	3	10	2	5	12	0
Nagaland	India	1956	SI	3	3	85	1	Dem	4	30	5	5	4	0
Nagaland	Insurgents	1956	SI	4	1	77	4	Jun	3	8	5	5	12	100
Nicaragua	Insurgents	1981	I	33	5	90	6	Dem	3	50	2	5	5	150
Nicaragua	Nicaragua	1981	I	21	4	70	6	Jun	2	10	3	5	5	0
Ogaden	Ethiopia	1964	TH	39	6	87	6	MDic	3	80	2	4	100	50
Ogaden	Insurgents	1964	TH	17	4	70	5	Jun	4	10	3	5	16	2,000
Ogaden	Somalia	1964	TH	27	4	90	6	OPDic	3	100	2	2	25	0
Oman-UAE	UAE	1945	T	12	5	40	5	Mon	3	25	2	4	1	0
Oman-UAE	Oman	1945	T	9	5	30	5	Mon	4	20	3	3	6	0
Pakistan	Pakistan	1972	SI	6	5	90	1	Dem	3	500	3	5	3	0
Pakistan	Insurgents	1972	SI	13	3	70	5	Jun	4	12	4	5	1	0
Persian Gulf	Bahrain	1945	TI	12	5	50	4	Mon	3	3	2	1	1	0
Persian Gulf	Qatar	1945	TI	12	5	50	4	Mon	3	20	2	1	1	0
Persian Gulf	U.S.	1945	TI	24	8	30	8	Dem	5	45	5	4	1	0
Persian Gulf	Saudi Arabia	1945	TI	41	7	60	8	Mon	4	50	3	4	1	0
Persian Gulf	UAE	1945	TI	12	5	50	4	Mon	3	25	2	3	1	0
Persian Gulf	Iran	1945	TI	47	8	60	8	OP	5	200	3	4	1	0
Peru	Peru	1980	R	4	4	90	1	Dem	3	40	3	5	2	0
Peru	Insurgents	1980	R	11	3	75	4	Dic	4	3	3	5	1	0
Philippines	Philippines	1972	SIR	6	5	90	1	Dem	3	60	4	5	50	0
Philippines	Marxists	1972	SIR	3	1	70	4	Jun	4	5	5	5	5	0
Philippines	Moros	1972	SIR	3	3	80	1	Jun	5	12	5	5	150	0
PLO	Arafat	1983	I	12	2	70	7	Jun	2	8	2	5	3	4
PLO	Insurgents	1983	I	10	2	60	7	Jun	2	10	2	3	5	0
Punjab	India	1984	RSI	17	5	90	3	Dem	4	100	4	4	4	150
Punjab	Sikhs	1984	RSI	17	5	90	3	Jun	4	35	3	5	15	70
Punjab	Pakistan	1984	RSI	0	1	10	3	Dem	3	500	4	2	0	0
Rwanda	Tutsis	1990	HR	4	4	90	1	Jun	5	1	3	3	1	4
Rwanda	Hutus	1990	HR	6	5	90	1	OP	4	6	3	4	2	0
Saudi Arabia	Saudi Arabia	1945	IS	21	4	85	5	Mon	4	50	3	5	1	0
Saudi Arabia	Insurgents	1945	IS	4	1	65	5	Jun	4	1	2	5	2	0

Conflict	Side	Year Began	Type of Conflict	Danger Level	Severity Intensity Index	Probability Index (in %)	Escalation Index	Form of Government	Government's Stability	Forces (in thousands of troops)	Quality of Forces	Endurance	Losses (in thousands)	Refugees (in thousands)
Averages & Totals				14	4	62	4		4	31,512	3	4	54,371	60,632
Senegal	Mauritania	1989	TH	6	2	50	5	Dic	3	12	4	6	2	0
Senegal	Senegal	1989	TH	6	2	60	4	DemDic	4	10	4	6	1	0
Sino-India	India	1962	SI	3	3	85	1	Dem	4	30	5	5	4	0
Sino-India	China	1962	T	2	7	20	1	Soc	4	250	3	4	2	0
Sino-Russia	China	1945	IT	4	3	15	8	Soc	4	3,000	3	4	2	0
Sino-Russia	Russia	1945	IT	30	9	30	9	SocDem	3	500	4	5	2	0
Sino-Vietnam	China	1979	TI	24	7	40	7	Soc	4	700	3	4	60	0
Sino-Vietnam	Vietnam	1979	TI	4	2	30	5	Soc	4	400	4	4	40	0
Somalia	Somalia	1988	TH	9	3	80	3	OPDic	3	60	2	4	60	0
Somalia	Insurgents	1988	TH	15	3	80	5	Jun	3	15	4	6	10	0
So. Africa	So. Africa	1975	R	17	3	90	5	DemDic	5	66	5	5	5	0
So. Africa	UDF	1975	R	7	2	70	4	Jun	4	25	3	5	1	50
So. Africa	Inkathas	1975	R	7	2	70	4	Jun	5	15	3	5	3	50
So. Africa	Radical Boers	1975	R	7	2	70	4	Jun	5	10	4	6	0	0
So. Africa	ANC	1975	R	7	2	70	4	Jun	4	20	3	5	3	50
So. China Sea	Vietnam	1945	TH	9	5	30	5	Soc	4	10	4	2	1	0
So. China Sea	Taiwan	1945	TH	5	8	10	5	OP	4	10	4	3	0	0
So. China Sea	Philippines	1945	TH	5	5	20	4	Dem	3	60	4	5	0	0
So. China Sea	China	1945	TH	19	6	50	5	Soc	4	20	3	4	1	0
Sri Lanka	Sri Lanka	1983	TS	17	5	90	3	Dem	4	90	3	5	15	200
Sri Lanka	India	1983	TS	1	1	20	3	Dem	4	300	4	3	4	0
Sri Lanka	Tamil	1983	TS	17	5	90	3	Jun	4	25	3	5	20	100
Sudan	Insurgents	1983	SH	17	5	90	3	Jun	4	30	2	5	500	600
Sudan	Sudan	1983	SH	17	5	90	3	OP	3	70	2	4	50	50
Sudan	Libya	1983	SH	1	1	20	3	Dic	5	50	2	2	1	0
Sudan	Sudan	1983	ISH	16	3	70	6	OP	3	58	2	5	50	0
Sudan	Insurgents	1983	ISH	9	2	60	6	Jun	2	3	3	5	250	100
Suriname	Suriname	1980	R	8	2	85	4	Dic	3	8	2	3	0	0
Suriname	Insurgents	1980	R	3	1	70	4	Jun	3	1	3	3	1	0
Syria	Syria	1975	SI	28	5	90	5	OPDic	3	235	3	5	5	0
Syria	Russia	1975	SI	11	6	30	5	SocDem	3	6	4	4	0	0
Syria	Insurgents	1975	SI	7	2	60	5	Jun	4	5	4	5	20	0

Conflict	Side	Year Began	Type of Conflict	Danger Level	Severity Intensity Index	Probability Index (in %)	Escalation Index	Form of Government	Government's Stability	Forces (in thousands of troops)	Quality of Forces	Endurance	Losses (in thousands)	Refugees (in thousands)
Averages & Totals				14	4	62	4		4	31,512	3	4	54,371	60,632
Tacna-Arica	Chile	1945	TH	2	6	30	1	Dem	4	100	3	3	0	0
Tacna-Arica	Peru	1945	TH	2	6	30	1	Dem	3	3	3	3	0	0
Tacna-Arica	Bolivia	1945	TH	3	6	40	1	Dem	2	2	2	3	0	0
Thailand	Thailand	1965	RS	17	4	85	4	MJun	4	200	4	5	2	0
Thailand	Insurgents	1965	RS	10	2	80	5	Jun	4	9	4	3	5	0
Tibet	China	1988	SH	9	4	90	2	Soc	4	200	3	4	5	0
Tibet	Tibet	1988	SH	1	2	30	2	Jun	4	15	1	4	20	10
Timor	Indonesia	1975	SI	6	5	90	1	Dic	4	250	2	5	400	200
Timor	Insurgents	1975	SI	2	2	75	1	Jun	3	50	3	3	50	0
Transylvania	Hungary	1989	TH	1	1	30	3	Dem	4	100	3	4	0	0
Transylvania	Romania	1989	TH	3	2	40	3	Dem	4	150	2	4	2	10
Uganda	Uganda	1979	SHI	4	4	90	1	Jun	2	10	1	3	12	200
Uganda	Insurgents	1979	SHI	1	1	80	1	Jun	1	6	1	3	60	0
Ulster	Britain	1969	HS	6	5	90	1	Dem	5	14	5	5	2	0
Ulster	Insurgents	1969	HS	8	2	85	4	Jun	3	1	5	5	2	0
Vietnam	Vietnam	1945	I	28	5	90	5	Soc	4	400	4	5	4,000	5,000
Vietnam	Insurgents	1945	I	2	2	85	1	Jun	3	12	4	5	2,000	5,000
W. Sahara	Morocco	1975	SI	20	5	80	4	Mon	4	75	4	5	100	0
W. Sahara	Insurgents	1975	SI	13	3	90	4	Jun	4	10	4	5	150	80
Yemen	Yemen	1972	TI	4	5	10	6	OP	3	50	3	4	3	0
Yemen	Yemen	1972	TI	4	5	10	6	OPDic	4	75	3	4	3	0
Yugoslavia	Yugoslavia	1945	SH	15	5	50	5	Soc	3	4	4	5	1	0
Yugoslavia	Croats	1945	SH	1	1	30	4	Jun	3	2	2	2	1	0
Yugoslavia	Albanians	1945	SH	10	2	80	5	Jun	4	2	2	2	1	0
Yugoslavia	Muslims	1945	SH	4	1	60	5	Jun	4	2	2	2	1	0
Yugoslavia	Macedonians	1945	SH	2	1	40	5	Jun	3	2	2	2	1	0
Yugoslavia	Serbs	1945	SH	1	1	20	4	Jun	3	2	2	5	1	0
Zaire	Zaire	1978	RSI	22	4	90	5	Dic	3	2	3	5	3	60
Zaire	Insurgents	1978	RSI	12	5	40	5	Jun	3	3	3	5	8	0
Zimbabwe	Zimbabwe	1981	I	28	5	90	5	OP	3	60	4	4	2	0
Zimbabwe	Insurgents	1981	I	9	2	70	5	Jun	3	1	3	5	3	0

NOTES ON THE CONFLICTS

Aegean—The dispute between Greece and Turkey over potential off-shore-oil deposits is exacerbated by long historic antagonisms and the declaration of independence by the Turkish-Cypriot community. It also spills over into other Greek-Turk border disputes.

Afghanistan—The Soviet Union withdrawal left a well-armed and desperate Communist government to fight a now splintered resistance movement. The rebels appear to have made little progress on the establishment of a unified front. Given the fundamental character of both sides, the war is likely to continue for some time. This has been the custom in the area for several thousand years.

Angola—Negotiations between South Africa and Angola settled matters in Namibia but not yet (as of 1991) in Angola itself. The antigovernment UNITA movement appears to be well entrenched in a classic Maoist "liberated zone," with the country virtually partitioned. It is possible that only the presence of Cuban troops maintains the allegedly Marxist regime in power—and now, the Cubans are leaving.

Belize—Argentina's defeat in the Falklands in 1982 appears to have cooled Guatemalan irredentist ardor, but the matter is of long standing. Britain made emergency reinforcements to its 1,500-man garrison in 1972, 1975, and 1977 in the face of saber rattling from Guatemala. Nevertheless, recent developments in negotiations may lead to a peaceful resolution. Meanwhile Britain is building up the new Belize armed forces and the country has received promises of aid in the event of invasion from either the United States *or* Cuba!

Burma—See chapter 11.

Burundi—An ancient animosity exists between the majority Hutu people and the minority (but in power) Tutsi. Sporadic massacres occur.

Cabinda—The externally supported insurrection against the Angolan regime appears to be quite durable, if low-level, and seems likely to continue for some time. Oddly, this struggle finds U.S. economic interests being protected by Cuban troops from a threat posed by an American friend, Zaire.

Cambodia—See chapter 12.

Caucasus—The Azeris and Armenians, possibly the Georgians, have a rather nasty and growing conflict with armed militias (obtaining weapons from plundered Russian armories) numbering in the tens of thousands.

Central America—See chapter 13.

Chad—The seesaw conflict in Chad will likely continue unabated, with the French-supported Habre government holding its own through most of the country while Libya maintains over 10,000 men in northern areas. No solution appears in sight and escalation is increasingly probable.

China 1945—The fifty-five-year-old Chinese civil war between the republicans (Taiwan) and the Communists continues while another struggle on the mainland is under way.

China 1989—This new struggle involves a new generation of Chinese to whom Taiwan is a foreign country and who have also laid claim to power. The Communist Old Guard must now struggle with their future (the rebellious students) as well as their past (Taiwan).

Colombia—See chapter 13.

Cyprus—Historic ethnic antagonisms on Cyprus have recently been exacerbated by the unilateral Turkish-Cypriot declaration of a federal state. Renewed armed conflict is barely restrained by the presence of some 24,000 Turkish, 4,000 British, and 3,000 UN troops.

Dhofar—Though the Dhofari insurgents suffered a severe defeat in 1975 by Omani, British, and Iranian forces while South Yemeni attentions were focused on Ethiopia, they remain in the field, albeit in greatly reduced numbers, and there is a serious possibility of a revival of the once broadly based insurrection.

El Salvador—See chapter 13.

Eritrea—See chapter 8.

Ethiopia—See chapter 8.

Falklands—Resumption of war is highly unlikely, and there is considerable movement toward normalization of relations with Britain, although new Argentine governments may occasionally engage in diplomatic threats for internal political purposes.

Guatemala—The insurgency lost considerable ground in the late 1970s but has begun to revive, due partially to a rising level of unrest in Central America as a whole, but primarily to unresolved domestic economic and social problems.

Guyana—Venezuela's claim to about 65 percent of Guyana surfaced in the early stages of the Falklands War. Although little has been heard of this since Argentina's humiliating defeat, Venezuela could revive it at any time for domestic political reasons. Should Venezuela choose to press its demands, Suriname, which has a similar claim on portions of eastern Guyana, would most likely be heard from as well.

Haiti—Enormous problems plague the most poverty-stricken and, despite the fall of the Duvalier regime, repressed state in the Americas.

The recent free election in the country suggests an increasing sense of hope, as does the recent need of the Dominican Republic to improve the security of its borders. Here is a nation so poor that, so far, it has not been able to support a guerrilla war.

Honduras—Honduras has a new and shaky democratic government, and great economic and social problems.

India—See chapter 12.

Indio-Pakistan—See chapter 12.

Iran—The fundamentalist Muslim government of Iran is confronted by resistance from a broad range of groups, including Kurds, rightists, monarchists, and leftists, some of whom are receiving aid from Iran's external enemy, Iraq. However, without unity among the insurgents it is doubtful that they can seriously threaten the regime.

Iran-Iraq—See chapter 3.

Irian Barat—The persistent tribal resistance to Indonesian control is likely to go on for some time with neither side gaining any significant advantage. Although the war complicates Indonesian relations with Papua–New Guinea, there is little possibility of conflict between the two despite occasional border violations.

Israel-PLO—See chapter 2.

Kashmir—See chapter 12.

Korea—See chapter 12.

Kosovo—See chapter 6.

Kurdistan—Long-standing Kurdish grievances sustain an armed insurgency in Iraq, Iran, and Turkey.

Kuwait—See chapter 3.

Laos—Limited royalist and tribal resistance to a Vietnamese-imposed Communist regime appears to continue, with neither side likely to secure victory in the near future. Vietnam's situation is complicated by a major guerrilla war in Cambodia, a small one back home in Vietnam, the necessity of retaining 300,000 men on alert on the Chinese frontier, and internal economic chaos.

Lebanon—See chapter 1.

Libya—Libyan adventurism and efforts to displace Egypt as the leader of the Arab and Muslim world led to one border war in 1977, plus assorted clashes with Sudan. Now allied with Sudan, and somewhat humbled by U.S. air raids and defeats in Chad, Libya is not as adventurous as in the past.

Malaysia—Although no longer representing a major threat to Malaysian stability that it did in 1948–60, the revived Communist insurgency is being viewed with great seriousness by the Federation of Malaysia, which has cooperated with Thailand to coordinate operations against the rebels across their mutual frontier.

Malta—Libyan pipe dreams could cause Qaddafi to make a try for Malta, which would cause Italy, and probably Algeria and Egypt, to intervene. Many thought Libya would not go into Chad—anything is possible, even likely, while Qaddafi is in power.

Maranon—A historic territorial dispute is kept alive in Ecuador for domestic political consumption and reasons of national pride. It is further complicated by occasional border clashes, with dangerous potential for adventurism.

Middle East—See chapter 2.

Moldavia—See chapter 7.

Mozambique—The South African-supported resistance movement, RENAMO, is anarchic. The inept socialist FRELIMO government is hard-pressed.

Nagaland—India continues to be unable to stamp out a tribal separatist movement that has peculiar links to the Western world through various evangelical Christian groups and that also occasionally finds support among other minority groups in northeastern India.

Nicaragua—In the long run, the situation here remains explosive.

Ogaden—Despite defeat in open war in 1977–78, the Somali insurgency in the Ogaden persists. This has created an enormous refugee problem for neighboring Somalia, which may be at the root of recent Somali efforts to seek a negotiated settlement with Ethiopia, itself experiencing pressing problems internally and in Eritrea. Nevertheless, tensions remain high and could spark a renewal of open warfare between the two states to reaffirm or to reverse Somalia's defeat in the field in 1979.

Oman-UAE—This is an old territorial dispute exacerbated by the efforts of the Sheik of Ras al-Khaimah, one of the emirs of the United Arab Emirates, to expand his territorial base, complicated by Iranian interests in Oman and the Persian Gulf.

Pakistan—The Pakistani government has been increasingly troubled by various tribal and political insurgencies. Baluchistan is a particular focus of unrest. Although at present the government seems capable of coping with the situation, the potential for a more serious problem remains high. All other political turmoil in the country pales before the ethnic problems.

Persian Gulf—The Iraqi invasion of Kuwait tilted the entire region.

The presence of significant Iranian ethnic and religious minorities on the Arab side of the Gulf and the existence of long-standing territorial claims will eventually cause confrontations. Iraq's actions merely delay it.

Peru—See chapter 13.

Philippines—The slow winding down of the persistent insurrection among the Muslim Moro tribes of the south may be complicated by the reemergence of the serious threat of military coup and rupture of the national Army. Also, the Communists have not fallen asleep.

PLO—The internal split in the PLO has resulted in open warfare between pro- and anti-Arafat supporters. The Iraqi invasion of Kuwait exacerbated the divisions.

Punjab—See chapter 12.

Rwanda—Here is a conflict similar to Burundi, except that the Hutus are in charge. Tutsi exiles invaded from Uganda in 1990.

Saudi Arabia—Strong religious and ethnic tensions mar the façade of stability and unity maintained by the Saudi regime. Iraq, Iran, and Yemen constantly threaten.

Senegal—Long-standing grievances between the largely black population of Senegal and its largely Arab neighbor Mauritania increasingly lead to threat of, or actual, warfare.

Sino-India—This is not likely to ever be a major conflict, primarily because troops have to get across the world's largest mountain range to get at each other. However, China backs India's archenemy, Pakistan, and Chinese nuclear missiles could conceivably be used if India nukes Pakistan.

Sino-Russia—Long-standing territorial and ideological disputes have been cooling recently, but a serious potential for war exists, particularly in the event of large-scale unrest in either nation.

Sino-Vietnam—Repetitions of the brief week's fighting in the spring of 1983 are likely, though a full-scale war is improbable but not impossible.

Somalia—The war with Ethiopia is accompanied by a brutal dictatorship that is having a hard time staying in power.

South Africa—Radical Boers are threatening their own terror campaign. See chapter 9.

South China Sea—The scent of oil in the Paracels and other islands has China, Vietnam, and maybe the Philippines squaring off for a possible violent resolution of their differences.

Sri Lanka—See chapter 12.

Sudan—See chapter 8.

Suriname—A military dictatorship in Suriname is at odds with most of its resident and expatriate population. The situation is compounded by differences between minority groups—none has a majority.

Syria—Internal resistance to the Assad Alawite regime has been relatively low since 10,000 actual and suspected rebels were killed in Hama in 1982, but the revival of more serious resistance is highly possible in a country ruled by a minority making up about 15 percent of the population. The trouble with Iraq is a threat.

Tacna-Arica—A territorial dispute going back to Chile's victory in 1879–84 is dusted off regularly for domestic political consumption and occasionally aired internationally by Peru and Bolivia.

Thailand—The government appears to have turned the corner in its efforts to suppress a persistent Communist insurgency. This is because of success in the field and in meeting the social and political needs of its people, friendlier links with China, and paradoxically, the Communist takeover of Cambodia, which presented a particularly unpleasant example of a ''worker's paradise'' in action. Cooperation with Malaysia in conducting antiguerrilla operations along their mutual frontier has been of critical importance as well. Efforts against the private armies of various drug lords remain frustratingly inconclusive, however, and there also appears to be Libyan-sponsored unrest among the country's tiny Muslim minority.

Tibet—Resistance to Chinese rule has been going on for centuries in Tibet. This threatens to turn into a full-scale guerrilla war, particularly if the Indians decide to support such an insurgency. Could be dicey, as both China and India have nukes.

Timor—Although perhaps the most poorly reported insurgency in the world, the anti-Indonesian movement on Timor seems to be surviving in the face of genocidal countermeasures, though it is not likely to achieve significant success either militarily or politically.

Transylvania—A centuries-old dispute exists over who should rule a province occupied by both Romanians and Hungarians.

Uganda—The government has had some success in resolving the anarchy existing since the overthrow of Idi Amin, but many revolutionary, local, and tribal armies control important areas, and like the regular Army itself, they are virtually indistinguishable from the numerous bandit gangs that also infest the bush.

Ulster—There does not appear to be any solution here in sight, since neither side is willing to undertake serious negotiations and neither is capable of securing victory.

Vietnam—A small-scale but persistent insurgency by remnants of the ARVN complicates Vietnam's internal situation, already suffering from economic disaster, the necessity of maintaining armies in Cambodia and Laos, and the threat of renewed war with China, all thereby contributing to the overall difficulty of solving any one of the problems.

Western Sahara—See chapter 8.

Yemen—Reunified Yemen could once more split into South and North and the bullets would fly.

Yugoslavia—See chapter 6.

Zaire—See chapter 10.

Zimbabwe—The political situation has settled down, while the economy has yet to achieve substantial growth. The strongest economy outside of South Africa, it is still crippled by socialist slogans.

LOW-LEVEL WARS

A number of movements that have resorted to violence in the form of terrorism do not meet our established criteria for qualification as a "war," since they are being dealt with largely by domestic police forces. In the list of these "wars" the "target" country is the primary entry. It should be noted that some of the groups are not active in the target country, but operate against its officials and diplomats, and even third parties, in other countries. Several of these groups are also involved with more serious combat in the disputed region causing the trouble in the first place. Some of these movements are "fronts" for groups wishing to embarrass particular nations, rather than genuine organic movements (at least one is based on a nonexistent ethnic minority).

Argentina: Leftist and rightist insurgents

Costa Rica: Leftist insurgents

France: Basque separatists, Bretons, Corsicans, Spanish anti-Basque activists, West Indian separatists

India: Mezo

Indonesia: Holy War commandos, South Moluccans

Italy: Red Brigades

Lesotho: Lesotho Liberation Army

Malaysia: Pirates along the coast

Netherlands: South Moluccans

Portugal: Ultra-leftist insurgents

Spain: Basques, "Canary Islands Liberation Front," Maoists

Turkey: Armenians, rightists, leftists, Kurds

United States: Puerto Rican nationalists, rightists, leftists

Venezuela: Leftists

Arguably, we could add countries that are involved in "assassination-level" wars.

Iran: Against exiled dissidents

Iraq: Against exiled dissidents

Libya: Against exiled dissidents

Nicaragua, Guatemala, and Canada's "Indian Wars"

North Korea: Against South Korean governmental officials and businessmen

United States (and other nations): Against drug producers and dealers

The "politically correct" in U.S. academia: Against free thought and creativity

OFF THE CRITICAL LIST

Beagle Channel—The advent of a democratic regime in Argentina, coupled with Chilean willingness to resolve the long-standing issue, and deft papal mediation, appears to have ended the danger of Argentine adventurism over these insignificant islands with possible offshore-oil deposits, a significant step from the situation that saw war virtually imminent in the late 1970s. This is an age-old sore point and can be expected to resurface.

CHAPTER 16

THE ABILITY OF THE WORLD'S NATIONS TO WAGE WAR

INTRODUCTION

Wars, or threats of wars, crop up in the most unlikely places at the most unlikely times. This chapter enables you to quickly become familiar with what's at stake and what's a plausible outcome. For example, one nation will be able to attack another with only its attack power and then only a fraction of that (rarely more than 80 percent of it). For a quick victory, the invader needs at least twice as much attack power as the defender has combat power. Anything less will usually result in a stalemate, with the attacker eventually losing. If one nation has to travel a long distance to confront another power, it needs control of the seas and a strong navy to ensure that. With the first edition of this book, one could have worked out the 1990 Iraqi invasion of Kuwait and the U.S. response. If the Iraqis had read this book, they might have thought twice about starting the Kuwait War. But then, the Iraqis thought the United States would not respond, just as the Argentines thought the British would not respond to their 1982 invasion of the Falklands. Political gambles usually overrule military prudence.

The data is taken from a number of sources, not all of which agree with one another. The data presented here is our estimate of what each nation will possess in the early and mid-1990s.

There have been several changes since the 1985 edition. The data base contains approximately the same number of nations (minus those lost through mergers, as in Germany and Yemen), yet there is less information for each nation. A survey of readers of the first edition found that, while most liked the data tables and many found them the strongest part of the book, all felt that not as much data was needed. So we reduced the number of items. Some of the now-absent information is still there in our computer data base, because it is needed to calculate items that are shown in the book. Sorry to disappoint the data buffs, but this edition was already much larger than the earlier one and we were faced with a shortage of space and a limited appetite for numbers among most of the book's readers.

One of the deleted columns from the previous edition's chart deserves special mention. This was the column where we listed the allies of each nation. These allies were the countries likely to provide military or political support in the event of war. In the 1985 edition, most of the world's nations leaned toward either Russia (a decreasing likelihood today) or the Western nations. Some attempted to be neutral, or received diplomatic and material aid pretty evenly from both directions. Many nations still receive arms from Russia, because Russia needs the money. Russia's economic and political problems have caused a sharp decline in nations receiving any other kind of support.

How to Read the Chart

Averages & Totals—Shows worldwide totals and averages (where appropriate) for all data on the individual nations. This is useful for putting each nation's numbers into some kind of context.

Summary Data

This chart summarizes and analyzes country data on the basis of geography (continent) and economy (degree of industrialization and, to a certain extent, politics) as represented by various "blocs" which are defined as:

Western Bloc—The EEC, United States, Israel, and Japan. Actually, there are a lot of other nations that are "associate members" of this bloc, such as Australia, New Zealand, and the European neutrals. But in our sense, we define the Western bloc as that group that tends to act in concert in most political matters and has the most political, economic, and military clout.

NDC—New developing countries with a per capita GDP of over $1,000 a year. Technically, these are nations that are on their way to industrialization; but by using the crude GDP yardstick, there are many nations that make it into this category not making a lot of progress in economic development. The best examples are the many nations with oil wealth that are spending more of it than they are investing. However, at least these states have the potential for economic development, and as such, tend to cooperate on what they perceive as common interests.

Third World—Poor nations of the world, those with a per capita income of less than $1,000 a year. Note that China and India comprise a disproportionate amount of certain items. Out of the Third World totals, these two large (and poor) nations hold about half the combat power; about a fifth of the land area; over half the population; a fifth of the GDP; a third of the military manpower; a fifth of the military spending, combat divisions, and AFV; and about a third of the combat aircraft and warship tonnage. Thus India and China are low-budget superpowers, if only because they both have large conventional armed forces and nuclear weapons.

EEC & U.S.—Formerly referred to as the NATO alliance, now it's just the EEC and the United States. This is still a formidable political/military/economic coalition, but without a unifying opponent like the Warsaw Pact (which has been disbanded).

EEC—The European Economic Community (the "Common Market"), containing most of the major European powers (Britain, Germany, France, Italy, Spain, etc.). Through the 1990s, the EEC is due to become even more united, and powerful.

Eastern Europe—Former Eastern European satellite states of Russia. As these nations become more Westernized in their economic strength, they will add to the power of Europe. Several of these nations will likely join the EEC in the 1990s, making the EEC even more imposing.

Russia—Still a superpower, but now in the shadow of the more powerful EEC to the West.

United States—Currently the most powerful nation economically and militarily. It will probably lose ground economically to the EEC in the 1990s and scale back its military strength accordingly.

Japan—A powerful nation, but lacking the population and resources to become anything as formidable as the EEC or the United States. At least not in the 1990s.

COUNTRY PROFILE

Country—Nation or bloc for which the information is provided.

Rank—Country's rank within each region by its war-making power.

War State—Degree of country's involvement in war: 1 = nothing much going on at all; 5 = pretty serious insurgency or disorder or armed tensions with neighbor but not out of control; 9 = major war.

Government's Stability—Indication of the ability of the government to act without fear of overthrow or disintegration on a scale of 1 = chaos (as in Lebanon), to 9 = rock-solid (as any government can get). Less stable governments often lead to war, either as attacker or victim.

War Power—Relative ability of the nation to engage in warfare—a combination of qualitative factors and the number of troops under arms. This is largely the nation's ability to defend itself. For a large nation like Russia and China, this combat capability is spread out along the nation's vast borders and, in effect, consists of up to half a dozen separate entities. This must be taken into account when considering the war-making power of a large country with long borders and many enemies. Even a country as relatively small as Iraq must disperse its forces over a wide area to counter a host of potential enemies. Once in the battle area, this value can change considerably depending on how the forces are deployed and used. If one side lacks sufficient supplies of food, fuel, and ammunition in the combat area, its war-making power degrades accordingly. Things are rarely equal on the battlefield.

Attack Power—Relative ability to make war beyond one's borders. This covers the resources needed to move combat forces long distances and keep them supplied. Nations with large fleets and air forces can do this. The superpowers, especially the United States, are unique in that they can move enormous amounts of combat power to any part of the globe—a capability none of the other nations possesses.

Total Quality—Overall qualitative value of the nation's military forces. This consists of the following items that were rated (but not shown on the chart): *Leaders*—officer quality and training. *Equipment*—quality and quantity of equipment available. *Experience*—quality of recent military experience, with an average rating indicating sound, but lengthy peacetime operations only. A politically active military would tend to be rated lower here. An armed force with recent combat experience would be rated higher. *Support*—quality of logistical apparatus, maintenance capacity, and general ability to sustain combat operations. *Mobilization index*—ability to rapidly expand forces beyond net mobilized manpower. This rating depends upon the unused portion of the country's ultimate manpower, the availability of equipment, and the availability of technical and managerial skills in the population pool. Thus a high industrialization index would tend to yield a higher mobilization index, as would a large population (even if it can only be armed as guerrillas). *Tradition*—quality of psychological factors such as culture, military history, and tradition.

Nukes—Degree of possession (or imminent possession) of nuclear weapons: 9 = having a lot of them; 7 = having a few; 4–6 = capability of building them and actually trying to do so; 1–3 = various degrees of not having them and having no intention to. Nations with nuclear weapons become a special kind of military power, one that another nation cannot force to the wall without risking unleashing a nuclear holocaust.

Geographic Profile

Area of Sq. Kilometers—Surface area of the nation in thousands of square kilometers. Larger nations require larger forces to cover all that territory. But the larger spaces also make it easier to defend, as the invader has to occupy more ground and travel longer distances in hostile territory in order to succeed.

Percent of Arable Land—Ultimately, a nation's power is based on its ability to feed itself. Nations that lack sufficient farmland to feed their population must either make money to buy food or beg for foreign aid.

Transportation Net—Efficiency of internal transportation system on a scale of 0 = none, to 9 = highly developed rail, highway, and riverine systems. A more efficient transportation system is a prerequisite for a strong economy and also aids in defending the nation. Note, however, that a poor net also inhibits an invader.

Military Environment Index—Suitability of the country for military operations on a scale of 0 = highly unfavorable conditions, to 9 = highly favorable. This is a combination of country size, terrain, climate patterns, border length, and location, plus the accessibility of vital civil, economic, and military resources to conventional external attack.

Population Profile

Population—Population density per square kilometer—a good indicator of how much civilians can be expected to suffer. The denser the population, the more likely civilians will be caught in the cross fire.

Population Total—Total resident population in millions, rounded and projected to 1991. Note that many (if not most) nations do not run a regular census and have only a rough idea of their populations. These are the best estimates based on several sources.

Percent of Literacy—Percent of the population technically able to read and write (often merely an indication of the ability to sign one's name). If a nation is not yet industrialized, this is a good indication of its potential to industrialize.

Percent of Urban Dwellers—Percent of the population living in cities and towns. Urban dwellers are usually better educated, although in nations with a low per capita GNP, urban dwellers are often unemployed, poor, and bloody-minded.

Average Life Expectancy—Given in years, a prime indicator of what the real quality of life in a nation is. It is more accurate than the GDP. The expectancy for females is usually 10 to 15 percent longer than for males, except in the poorest countries, where it is about equal.

ECONOMIC PROFILE

Industrialization Index—Indication of the degree of mechanization and flexibility in the country's production of goods and services on a scale of 0 = no industrial capability, to 9 = has highly developed and flexible industrial plants. This is one of the most telling indicators of a nation's potential war-making power, along with its GDP and population.

GDP—Gross domestic product in billions of dollars for the most recent year available, the total value of goods and services produced for internal consumption. A country's GNP (which is often used interchangeably) is a similar number, but it includes overseas activities. As with population data, the GDP is often difficult to calculate. International trade is easily tracked and valued, but most nations generate the bulk of their wealth internally and many nations have only crude internal accounting capabilities. As a consequence, GDP data is often an estimate. We have collected such data from several sources (the UN, banks, the government, etc.) and have come up with a reasonable composite.

Per Capita GDP—Value of the GDP in thousands of dollars. Note that nations with per capita GDP of only a few hundred dollars a year understate the actual income of the people. In these very poor nations much of the population is surviving through a noncash economy which usually involves subsistence farming (growing enough for themselves) as well as "underground economy" activity that often doesn't make it to the official GDP figures.

Living Standard Index—Indication of relative standard of living as expressed on a scale of 1 = virtual subsistence level, to 9 = that of the United States or better.

MILITARY CAPABILITY

Active Manpower—Number of men and women in active service in the armed forces, expressed in thousands.

Military Budget—Annual expenditures on defense in millions of dollars. Even more so than the GDP, this is another slippery figure. There is no standard way of accounting for military expenditures (although the more industrialized nations have reached some consensus in this area). We make our usual estimates based on all the (often conflicting) information available to us.

Percent of GDP—Defense expenditures as a percent of the GDP. This shows the emphasis the nation places on its military power.

Budget per Man—Thousands of dollars per soldier on active duty spent each year.

Reserve Forces—Reserve forces available in thousands. This is an indicator of the nation's preparedness for extended war. Reserves take time and money to prepare and maintain.

Paramilitary Forces—Paramilitary forces available in thousands. These include barracks police, part-time militia, coast guards, and volunteer defense workers. Nations that exercise more control over their population have relatively larger paramilitary forces. Often, especially in smaller nations, the regular forces spend most of their time performing traditionally paramilitary tasks such as keeping the population in check.

ARMY PROFILE

Mobilized Forces—Total ground combat force personnel upon mobilization, including ground combat elements of air and naval forces, marines, and air defense. This is generally what the nation will have to go to war with if it has some warning and at least a few weeks to get ready.

Available Divisions—Number of divisions available, assuming organized forces are grouped according to standard Tables of Organization.

These are basically the number of major combat units a nation can fight a war with.

Armored Fighting Vehicles—Total number of tanks, infantry combat vehicles, scout cars, armored assault guns, and amphibious assault vehicles. This is a good indicator of how mechanized and mobile a nation's ground forces are.

Combat-Capable Aircraft—Total number of combat-capable airplanes and helicopters. Once the war starts and one side gains control of the air, and keeps it, the other side is at a grave disadvantage.

Tonnage of Ships—Total tonnage of combatant and other ships in thousands of standard displacement tons. Tonnage is more important than the number of ships. A large number of smaller (and lighter) ships is a defensive measure that sacrifices offensive power and ability to send naval forces far afield.

THE GREAT DISARMAMENT OF THE 1990S

A note on the end of the Cold War. With the collapse of Eastern European communism, the virtual disappearance of the Warsaw Pact, and a major European arms reduction treaty, nearly all European nations are experiencing major declines in defense spending and force levels. This will continue through the mid-1990s, except for those few nations that have already developed serious disputes with their neighbors (Romania, Hungary, Bulgaria, and Turkey, for example). The long-festering economic problems of Russia and Eastern Europe must now be attended to, and this will put military affairs into the background for a decade or so.

LITTLE WARS AND TINY CONFLICTS

As the charts demonstrate, some nations have small armed forces and even smaller combat power. Thus a civil war in many African nations amounts to little more than a few thousand lightly armed troops firing a few shots and one faction deciding to flee across the border or into the bush. The winners move into the capital and take over. In many nations, be they in Africa or elsewhere, an ongoing rebellion would, in the days before CNN and satellite news, be considered little more than "a bandit problem." Put an eloquent bandit in front of a camera and you have a

NATIONS OF THE WORLD: REGIONAL AND BLOC SUMMARY

	Country Profile							Geographic Profile					Population Profile			
Country	Rank	War State	Government's Stability	War Power	Attack Power	Total Quality	Nukes	Area of Sq. Kilometers (in thousands)	Percent of Arable Land	Transportation Net	Military Environment Index	Population (per sq. kilometer)	Population Total (in millions)	Percent of Literacy	Percent of Urban Dwellers	Average Life Expectancy
Averages & Totals		2	6	11,771	5,363	6	2	261,359	15	4	5	48	12,637	63	41	63
Western Bloc		2	9	2,885	1,936	37	6	13,076	19	8	6	60	785	94	76	77
NDC		2	6	1,239	534	9	2	27,943	9	4	6	42	670	71	55	65
Third World		2	5	2,033	679	6	2	65,288	16	3	5	55	3,623	60	36	62
EEC & U.S.		2	8	2,268	1,545	31	6	12,677	24	8	4	52	655	97	72	76
EEC		1	8	1,268	745	19	4	3,511	27	7	6	115	405	95	69	75
Eastern Europe		1	6	252	83	12	3	1,145	38	6	6	110	126	93	51	71
Russia		4	6	800	640	16	9	22,141	10	4	4	13	292	95	62	69
United States		2	9	1,000	800	43	9	9,166	20	9	3	27	250	99	74	76
Japan		1	9	138	55	37	6	378	13	9	5	331	125	99	76	79
Africa		2	5	139	50	3	1	21,263	10	2	5	24	515	37	19	52
Americas		2	6	1,195	857	7	2	39,093	11	4	5	19	725	81	54	68
Europe		1	7	2,792	1,562	17	4	27,647	27	6	6	31	853	94	62	74

Middle East	2	6	1,295	668	12	2	11,755	8	4	7	23	272	51	53	65
South Asia	2	6	620	182	8	2	5,443	27	3	5	214	1,166	36	26	54
Southeast Asia	2	7	1,659	684	14	3	23,821	12	4	5	78	1,854	78	42	67

Percentage Analysis

Western Bloc	19%	52%	25%	36%	475%	164%	5%	30%	114%	8%	24%	6%	48%	84%	22%
NDC	3	11	11	10	39	-1	11	-38	6	14	-14	5	13	33	3
Third World	9	-15	17	13	-5	-3	25	5	-9	-2	15	29	-6	-13	-1
EEC & U.S.	-4	47	19	29	387	163	5	59	115	-16	7	5	53	73	20
EEC	-22	38	11	14	202	60	1	83	91	10	139	3	50	67	19
Eastern Europe	-27	9	2	2	88	28	0	159	48	22	128	1	48	23	13
Russia	127	4	7	12	152	266	8	-32	6	-24	-73	2	50	50	10
United States	13	57	8	15	571	266	4	35	139	-43	-44	2	57	79	21
Japan	-43	57	1	1	478	144	0	-12	139	-5	584	1	57	83	26
Africa	-10	-21	1	1	-56	-50	8	-33	-43	-5	-50	4	-41	-55	-17
Americas	7	10	10	16	2	-10	15	-29	-3	-2	-62	6	28	31	8
Europe	-23	29	24	29	162	53	11	80	71	9	-36	7	49	50	18
Middle East	35	-0	11	12	84	-3	4	-44	0	37	-52	2	-20	27	4
South Asia	13	-2	5	3	17	-11	2	82	-34	-11	343	9	-43	-37	-15
Southeast Asia	13	17	14	13	124	29	9	-20	18	-15	61	15	23	2	6

Nations of the World: Regional and Bloc Summary

Country	Economic Profile				Military Capability							Army Profile			
	Industrialization Index	GDP (in billions)	Per Capita GDP (in billions)	Living Standard Index	Active Manpower (in thousands)	Military Budget (in millions)	Percent of GDP	Budget per Man (in thousands)	Reserve Forces (in thousands)	Paramilitary Forces (in thousands)	Mobilized Forces (in thousands)	Available Divisions	Armored Fighting Vehicles	Combat-Capable Aircraft	Tonnage of Ships (in thousands)
Averages & Totals	3	$23,658	$1.9	4	53,807	$837,247	3.5%	$16	45,805	49,465	69,709	2,589	476,976	69,319	23,179
Western Bloc	8	$12,143	$15.5	8	5,194	$333,310	2.7	$64	6,587	818	5,535	220	93,935	14,170	12,505
NDC	4	1,653	2.5	4	4,847	78,086	4.7	16	7,028	10,154	8,764	314	48,491	5,479	1,464
Third World	3	2,747	0.8	3	13,629	97,193	3.5	7	9,861	11,514	16,633	622	92,786	13,693	2,910
EEC & U.S.	8	9,906	15.1	8	4,309	292,310	3.0	68	5,755	778	4,610	188	81,135	13,000	12,042
EEC	7	4,906	12.1	8	2,809	112,310	2.3	40	4,555	668	3,710	150	50,135	5,000	2,842
Eastern Europe	6	900	7.1	5	1,125	14,850	1.7	13	2,030	196	1,430	68	20,620	2,230	199
Russia	7	1,200	4.1	4	3,200	150,000	12.5	47	3,000	600	4,400	160	65,000	8,500	790
United States	9	5,000	20.0	9	1,500	180,000	3.6	120	1,200	110	900	38	31,000	8,000	9,200
Japan	9	2,200	17.6	8	240	35,000	1.6	146	132	20	280	14	1,800	420	440
Africa	1	$267	$0.5	1	1,072	$7,526	2.8%	$7	699	781	1,314	90	12,032	1,206	124
Americas	4	6,216	8.6	4	2,936	195,890	3.2	67	3,030	780	2,614	145	40,104	10,715	10,381
Europe	6	7,518	8.8	7	9,230	286,566	3.8	31	10,456	1,991	11,581	457	141,117	16,530	3,936

Middle East	3	457	1.7	4	3,834	62,890	13.8	16	3,102	709	4,346	174	47,200	3,711	262
South Asia	2	316	0.3	1	2,323	18,253	5.8	8	823	845	2,750	94	9,450	1,527	335
Southeast Asia	4	3,370	1.8	4	7,084	70,735	2.1	10	7,932	21,310	13,746	378	37,700	7,743	2,275

Western Bloc	138%	51%	726%	124	10%	40%	-22%	312%	14%	2%	8%	9%	20%	20%	54%
NDC	10	7	32	24	9	9	34	4	15	21	13	12	10	8	6
Third World	-12	12	-60	-6	25	12	-0	-54	22	23	24	24	19	20	13
EEC & U.S.	136	42	708	135	8	35	-17	336	13	2	7	7	11	19	52
EEC	101	21	547	114	5	13	-35	157	10	1	5	6	11	7	12
Eastern Europe	76	4	282	42	2	2	-53	-15	4	0	2	3	4	3	1
Russia	110	5	120	13	6	18	253	201	7	1	6	6	14	12	3
United States	170	21	968	155	3	21	2	671	3	0	1	1	6	12	40
Japan	170	9	840	127	0	4	-55	837	0	0	0	1	0	1	2

Africa	-65	1	-72	-62	2	1	-20	-55	2	2	2	3	3	2	0.5
Americas	19	26	358	4	5	23	-11	329	7	2	4	6	8	15	44.8
Europe	90	32	371	92	17	34	8	100	23	4	17	18	30	24	17.0
Middle East	-23	2	-10	12	7	8	289	5	7	1	6	7	10	5	1.1
South Asia	-40	1	-86	-60	4	2	63	-50	2	2	4	4	2	2	1.4
Southeast Asia	25	14	-3	23	13	8	-41	-36	17	43	20	15	8	11	9.8

NATIONS OF THE WORLD: EAST ASIAN NATIONS

Country	Rank	War State	Government's Stability	War Power	Attack Power	Total Quality	Nukes	Area of Sq. Kilometers (in thousands)	Percent of Arable Land	Transportation Net	Military Environment Index	Population (per sq. kilometer)	Population Total (in millions)	Percent of Literacy	Percent of Urban Dwellers	Average Life Expectancy
Averages & Totals		2	6	14,916	7,371	6	2	289,581	14	4	5	42	12,264	63	41	63
China	1	3	8	528	158	11	9	9,596	10	5	5	125	1,200	75	20	69
Vietnam	2	4	6	288	144	21	3	330	22	5	4	206	68	78	19	64
So. Korea	3	2	7	211	127	22	5	98	21	6	3	459	45	93	60	69
No. Korea	4	2	5	190	85	15	3	121	18	5	3	190	23	93	38	69
Japan	5	1	9	138	55	37	6	378	13	9	5	331	125	99	76	79
Taiwan	6	3	8	136	54	22	6	14	24	5	6	1,500	21	95	77	73
Indonesia	7	3	7	44	7	10	3	1,827	8	3	4	104	190	52	19	59
Australia	8	1	9	34	24	31	4	7,618	6	5	4	2	17	98	86	77
Malaysia	9	2	7	18	7	11	3	329	3	4	4	52	17	65	29	67
Philippines	10	3	4	18	2	8	3	298	26	4	3	221	66	87	32	66
Thailand	11	2	8	17	9	4	2	512	33	3	5	111	57	82	25	65
Singapore	12	1	7	16	5	19	2	1	4	9	8	3,000	3	87	100	74
Cambodia	13	4	2	11	2	10	1	177	16	2	4	40	7	48	25	48
New Zealand	14	1	9	5	3	24	3	269	2	8	5	15	4	99	77	76
Laos	15	3	4	3	1	4	1	231	4	2	5	17	4	85	15	49
Mongolia	16	1	7	2	1	7	1	1,565	1	2	7	2	3	80	50	65
Brunei	17	1	7	0	0	2	1	5	1	2	4	80	0	45	?	75
Papua–New Guinea	18	1	7	0	0	2	1	452	0	1	2	9	4	33	13	54

NATIONS OF THE WORLD: EAST ASIAN NATIONS

Country	Economic Profile				Military Capability						Army Profile				
	Industrialization Index	GDP (in billions)	Per Capita GDP (in billions)	Living Standard Index	Active Manpower (in thousands)	Military Budget (in millions)	Percent of GDP	Budget per Man (in thousands)	Reserve Forces (in thousands)	Paramilitary Forces (in thousands)	Mobilized Forces (in thousands)	Available Divisions	Armored Fighting Vehicles	Combat-Capable Aircraft	Tonnage of Ships (in thousands)
Averages & Totals	3	$40,613	$3.3	4	66,079	$1,501,009	3.7%	$23	64,559	59,035	89,567	3,363	742,878	96,049	30,747
China	4	$380.0	$0.3	3	3,000	$6,100	1.6	$2	1,200	8,000	4,000	95	13,000	4,500	700
Vietnam	3	14.0	0.2	2	900	800	5.7	1	2,000	1,500	2,600	68	4,000	240	45
So. Korea	7	190.0	4.2	5	620	6,000	3.2	10	1,500	9,000	2,000	46	2,200	470	140
No. Korea	6	21.0	0.9	3	840	4,000	19.0	5	400	1,800	1,200	46	7,200	800	55
Japan	9	2,200.0	17.6	8	240	35,000	1.6	146	132	20	280	14	1,800	420	440
Taiwan	7	95.0	4.5	6	400	7,000	7.4	18	1,600	30	1,800	30	2,000	500	290
Indonesia	2	70.0	0.4	2	280	1,400	2.0	5	100	500	330	14	500	90	160
Australia	9	210.0	12.4	9	70	4,500	2.1	64	30	5	60	4	900	90	140
Malaysia	2	38.0	2.2	4	110	800	2.1	7	45	190	120	7	1,020	55	44
Philippines	2	35.0	0.5	3	150	550	1.6	4	83	44	170	9	330	110	155
Thailand	2	54.0	0.9	3	255	1,800	3.3	7	510	105	700	16	1,300	145	52
Singapore	8	26.0	8.7	7	55	1,300	5.0	24	210	44	215	6	1,300	180	28
Cambodia	2	1.0	0.1	1	70	100	16.7	1	0	30	70	7	300	20	8
New Zealand	7	28.0	7.0	9	13	800	2.9	62	11	0	14	1	100	50	15
Laos	0	1.0	0.2	1	52	40	6.7	1	10	20	60	7	110	30	0
Mongolia	3	1.8	0.6	3	22	210	11.7	10	100	14	120	8	1,600	31	0
Brunei	2	3.2	8.0	6	4	300	9.4	75	0	3	4	0	0	12	1
Papua–New Guinea	0	3.0	0.8	3	3	35	1.2	12	1	5	3	0	0	0	2

NATIONS OF THE WORLD: SOUTH ASIAN NATIONS

Country	Rank	Country Profile							Geographic Profile				Population Profile				
		War State	Government's Stability	War Power	Attack Power	Total Quality	Nukes	Area of Sq. Kilometers (in thousands)	Percent of Arable Land	Transportation Net	Military Environment Index	Population (per sq. kilometer)	Population Total (in millions)	Percent of Literacy	Percent of Urban Dwellers	Average Life Expectancy
Averages & Totals		2	6	14,916	7,371	6	2	289,581	14	4	5	42	12,264	63	41	63
India	1	2	6	454	136	21	8	2,974	55	4	3	282	840.0	37	21	57
Pakistan	2	2	5	120	38	16	6	779	26	3	5	148	115.0	27	25	54
Burma	3	3	6	17	3	6	1	658	15	2	3	62	41.0	78	19	55
Bangladesh	4	1	4	13	1	8	1	134	67	5	7	866	116.0	29	9	53
Nepal	5	1	9	8	2	14	1	137	17	1	2	139	19.0	20	5	50
Afghanistan	6	6	2	6	0	6	1	647	12	4	4	23	15.0	12	15	42
Sri Lanka	7	2	6	2	0	3	1	65	16	1	4	262	17.0	87	22	69
Bhutan	8	1	6	0	0	0	1	47	2	1	4	43	2.0	5	3	48
Maldives	9	1	6	0	0	0	1	0	10	2	8	500	.15	5	100	—
Mauritius	10	1	6	0	0	0	1	2	50	2	7	450	.90	60	44	—

Nations of the World: South Asian Nations

Country	Economic Profile				Military Capability							Army Profile			
	Industrialization Index	GDP (in billions)	Per Capita GDP (in billions)	Living Standard Index	Active Manpower (in thousands)	Military Budget (in millions)	Percent of GDP	Budget per Man (in thousands)	Reserve Forces (in thousands)	Paramilitary Forces (in thousands)	Mobilized Forces (in thousands)	Available Divisions	Armored Fighting Vehicles	Combat-Capable Aircraft	Tonnage of Ships (in thousands)
Averages & Totals	3	$40,613	$3.3	4	66,079	$1,501,009	3.7%	$23	64,559	59,035	89,567	3,363	742,878	96,049	30,747
India	5	$235.0	$0.3	2	1,400	$14,000	6.0	$10.0	250	400	1,400	40	4,800	780	220
Pakistan	4	40.0	0.3	1	485	2,800	7.0	6.0	510	160	900	22	2,600	440	95
Burma	2	10.0	0.2	2	180	300	3.0	2.0	26	75	190	15	110	22	7
Bangladesh	3	18.0	0.2	1	102	210	1.2	2.0	0	50	100	5	60	50	8
Nepal	0	3.2	0.2	2	40	40	1.3	1.0	0	30	40	3	30	0	0
Afghanistan	2	3.0	0.2	1	60	300	10.0	5.0	0	75	60	5	1,600	210	0
Sri Lanka	2	6.0	0.4	1	50	600	10.0	12.0	25	40	50	3	250	25	3
Bhutan	0	0.0	0.2	1	4	1	0.3	0.3	12	15	8	1	0	0	0
Maldives	0	0.0	0.2	1	1	1	3.3	1.0	0	0	1	0	0	0	2
Mauritius	2	0.7	0.8	2	1	1	0.1	1.0	0	0	1	0	0	0	0

NATIONS OF THE WORLD: MIDDLE EAST NATIONS

		Country Profile						Geographic Profile				Population Profile				
Rank	Country	War State	Government's Stability	War Power	Attack Power	Total Quality	Nukes	Area of Sq. Kilometers (in thousands)	Percent of Arable Land	Transportation Net	Military Environment Index	Population (per sq. kilometer)	Population Total (in millions)	Percent of Literacy	Percent of Urban Dwellers	Average Life Expectancy
	Averages & Totals	2	6	14,916	7,371	6	2	289,581	14	4	5	42	12,264	63	41	63
1	Israel	4	9	479	336	48	7	21	17	7	9	238	5	82	86	77
2	Iraq*	7	5	326	163	22	4	434	12	3	7	41	18	56	66	66
3	Iran	7	6	183	73	22	4	1,636	8	3	4	34	55	49	47	57
4	Egypt	1	6	150	47	22	4	995	3	3	7	56	56	45	44	59
5	Syria	2	6	61	18	10	3	184	28	4	6	65	12	47	48	68
6	Jordan	1	8	21	8	16	1	92	4	4	8	33	3	71	44	69
7	Saudi Arabia	1	6	18	7	11	4	2,150	1	2	6	8	17	52	28	66
8	Algeria	1	7	18	5	8	3	2,382	3	4	6	11	26	52	52	65
9	Morocco	3	6	12	5	4	2	466	18	3	6	58	27	28	38	64
10	Kuwait	1	6	7	1	16	3	18	0	5	9	111	2	72	99	74
11	Yemen	2	5	6	1	8	1	528	6	2	6	19	10	20	20	50
12	Sudan	3	4	5	1	4	1	2,376	5	1	7	11	26	30	20	53
13	Libya	4	5	4	1	4	3	1,760	1	3	7	2	4	55	52	66
14	Lebanon	4	1	3	0	8	1	10	21	5	7	300	3	74	60	67
15	Tunisia	1	6	2	1	4	1	155	20	5	7	52	8	63	49	69
16	Oman	2	6	1	0	3	1	212	0	1	8	5	1	20	10	56
17	United Arab Emirates	1	5	1	0	1	1	84	0	1	9	24	2	68	90	70
18	Qatar	1	6	0	0	2	1	11	0	6	9	45	1	40	71	70
19	Bahrain	1	5	0	0	4	1	1	2	9	9	500	1	40	78	72

*Before its defeat.

Nations of the World: Middle East Nations

Country	Economic Profile				Military Capability								Army Profile		
	Industrialization Index	GDP (in billions)	Per Capita GDP (in billions)	Living Standard Index	Active Manpower (in thousands)	Military Budget (in millions)	Percent of GDP	Budget per Man (in thousands)	Reserve Forces (in thousands)	Paramilitary Forces (in thousands)	Mobilized Forces (in thousands)	Available Divisions	Armored Fighting Vehicles	Combat-Capable Aircraft	Tonnage of Ships (in thousands)
Averages & Totals	3	$40,613	$3.3	4	66,079	$1,501,009	3.7%	$23	64,559	59,035	89,567	3,363	742,878	96,049	30,747
Israel	7	$37	$7.4	7	645	$6,000	16.2	$9	700	20	645	18	11,000	750	23
Iraq*	2	30	1.7	3	950	14,000	46.7	15	220	11	950	51	7,300	450	8
Iran	3	94	1.7	3	550	6,000	6.4	11	360	60	1,000	30	1,500	80	70
Egypt	2	26	0.5	2	450	5,500	21.2	12	600	380	400	16	6,600	530	65
Syria	3	21	1.8	2	410	1,700	8.1	4	270	20	400	14	6,900	590	7
Jordan	2	5	1.7	3	85	600	12.0	7	30	10	90	5	2,300	140	0
Saudi Arabia	2	77	4.5	6	110	18,000	23.4	164	55	24	140	5	2,400	220	17
Algeria	5	60	2.3	3	140	1,100	1.8	8	140	30	180	8	2,500	300	14
Morocco	3	19	0.7	2	202	1,000	5.3	5	400	34	200	8	1,500	130	13
Kuwait	3	20	10.0	8	30	3,000	15.0	100	50	4	50	2	1,100	70	6
Yemen	0	6	0.6	1	50	500	8.3	10	70	35	60	4	1,100	160	13
Sudan	1	9	0.3	1	70	500	5.6	7	0	4	60	5	600	50	2
Libya	2	20	5.0	6	70	1,000	5.0	14	40	20	90	6	3,800	500	45
Lebanon	3	2	0.7	3	20	70	3.5	4	100	60	40	2	500	12	1
Tunisia	3	10	1.3	4	36	500	5.0	14	100	8	50	3	400	30	7
Oman	1	8	8.0	4	26	1,800	22.5	69	2	5	24	1	100	50	8
United Arab Emirates	1	23	11.5	7	49	2,100	9.1	43	0	1	46	1	900	80	3
Qatar	3	6	12.0	6	8	300	5.0	38	4	2	8	1	300	45	3
Bahrain	2	4	8.0	6	3	220	5.5	81	1.1	3	3	0	200	24	2

*Before its defeat.

NATIONS OF THE WORLD: EUROPEAN NATIONS

Country	Rank	War State	Government's Stability	War Power	Attack Power	Total Quality	Nukes	Area of Sq. Kilometers (in thousands)	Percent of Arable Land	Transportation Net	Military Environment Index	Population (per sq. kilometer)	Population Total (in millions)	Percent of Literacy	Percent of Urban Dwellers	Average Life Expectancy
		Country Profile						Geographic Profile				Population Profile				
Averages & Totals		2	6	14,916	7,371	6	2	289,581	14	4	5	42	12,264	63	41	63
Russia	1	4	6	800	640	16	9	22,141	10	4	4	13	292	95	62	69
Germany	2	1	9	356	249	58	6	350	35	9	6	223	78	99	82	74
Britain	3	2	9	237	190	51	9	242	29	9	6	236	57	99	78	75
Switzerland	4	1	9	231	46	14	5	40	10	8	4	175	7	99	58	78
France	5	2	9	227	136	42	9	546	32	8	5	103	56	99	71	75
Sweden	6	1	9	211	42	15	5	412	7	9	5	22	9	99	83	77
Turkey	7	2	7	179	72	19	5	771	30	6	5	73	56	70	45	64
Poland	8	2	5	105	42	20	4	305	48	4	8	128	39	98	58	70
Italy	9	1	7	104	34	21	5	294	32	6	5	197	58	93	70	76
Spain	10	2	7	56	14	12	4	499	31	8	5	80	40	97	49	77
Yugoslavia	11	2	6	56	11	18	3	255	28	7	5	94	24	91	39	72
Greece	12	1	7	31	13	10	3	131	23	5	5	76	10	95	65	77

13 Czechoslovakia	1	7	30	14	13	4	125	40	8	6	128	16	99	67	71
14 Netherlands	2	8	28	18	18	4	34	25	9	7	441	15	99	77	77
15 Romania	1	6	22	4	9	4	230	43	5	6	104	24	98	49	70
16 Belgium	1	7	22	8	17	4	30	24	9	9	333	10	98	95	77
17 Bulgaria	1	7	16	6	9	3	111	34	5	7	81	9	94	59	71
18 Hungary	1	8	15	6	13	3	92	54	7	8	120	11	99	51	69
19 Finland	1	9	13	2	32	4	305	8	6	4	16	5	99	59	75
20 Austria	1	8	11	3	17	3	83	17	7	6	96	8	98	52	75
21 Portugal	2	7	8	4	11	3	92	32	6	7	120	11	84	37	74
22 Denmark	1	8	7	3	18	3	42	61	9	8	119	5	99	80	75
23 Norway	1	9	2	4	14	3	308	3	4	4	13	4	99	57	76
24 Albania	1	5	2	0	3	1	27	21	3	5	111	3	75	34	73
25 Ireland	1	8	1	1	7	2	69	14	7	5	58	4	99	52	76
26 Cyprus (Greek)	1	5	1	0	7	1	6	47	4	6	89	0.50	90	45	
27 Cyprus (Turkish)	1	6	0	0	9	1	4	1	4	6	54	0.20	85	40	
28 Luxembourg	1	9	0	0	7	1	3	24	9	8	133	0	99	68	74
29 Malta	1	7	0	0	2	1	0	38	6	6	1,333	0	84	94	75
30 Iceland	1	9	0	0	4	1	100	0	5	2	2	0	99	87	78

NATIONS OF THE WORLD: EUROPEAN NATIONS

Country	Economic Profile				Military Capability						Army Profile				
	Industrialization Index	GDP (in billions)	Per Capita GDP (in billions)	Living Standard Index	Active Manpower (in thousands)	Military Budget (in millions)	Percent of GDP	Budget per Man (in thousands)	Reserve Forces (in thousands)	Paramilitary Forces (in thousands)	Mobilized Forces (in thousands)	Available Divisions	Armored Fighting Vehicles	Combat-Capable Aircraft	Tonnage of Ships (in thousands)
Averages & Totals	3	$40,613	$3.3	4	66,079	$1,501,009	3.7%	$23	64,559	59,035	89,567	3,363	742,878	96,049	30,747
Russia	7	$1,200.0	$4.1	4	3,200	$150,000	12.5	$47	3,000	600	4,400	160	65,000	8,500	790
Germany	9	1,300.0	16.7	8	400	25,000	1.9	63	320	25	550	16	8,500	900	250
Britain	9	770.0	13.5	8	300	25,000	3.2	83	310	8	220	16	6,000	700	950
Switzerland	9	180.0	25.7	9	1,100	3,000	1.7	3	0	14	500	18	2,600	250	0
France	9	950.0	17.0	9	350	24,000	2.5	69	300	90	450	26	9,000	1,100	550
Sweden	9	120.0	13.3	9	900	4,000	3.3	4	0	500	700	15	1,400	450	90
Turkey	4	65.0	1.2	4	610	2,500	3.8	4	900	130	700	24	7,500	500	220
Poland	7	270.0	6.9	5	340	4,000	1.5	12	400	90	400	15	5,000	600	44
Italy	9	830.0	14.3	8	320	14,000	1.7	44	600	210	420	10	5,500	600	205
Spain	7	290.0	7.3	6	300	6,000	2.1	20	900	110	300	13	2,800	280	210
Yugoslavia	5	155.0	6.5	6	200	2,200	1.4	11	500	15	200	18	2,500	400	45

Greece	5	47.0	4.7	6	200	2,400	5.1	12	400	28	330	18	4,400	330	155
Czechoslovakia	9	158.0	9.9	7	150	3,500	2.2	23	250	12	180	9	4,000	400	0
Netherlands	9	230.0	15.3	9	100	5,000	2.2	50	160	8	220	5	2,800	220	135
Romania	5	155.0	6.5	5	160	1,100	0.7	7	500	30	250	9	3,800	320	65
Belgium	8	160.0	16.0	9	85	3,300	2.1	39	150	15	130	6	1,800	110	9
Bulgaria	5	68.0	7.6	5	155	2,100	3.1	14	220	23	230	10	2,500	270	34
Hungary	7	92.0	8.4	6	80	1,800	2.0	23	120	14	120	5	2,600	150	1
Finland	6	90.0	18.0	8	31	1,200	1.3	39	600	5	500	21	400	70	15
Austria	6	120.0	15.0	8	50	1,100	0.9	22	230	4	290	22	700	24	0
Portugal	4	35.0	3.2	6	66	900	2.6	14	160	42	60	5	400	80	52
Denmark	6	102.0	20.4	9	28	1,700	1.7	61	70	0	70	5	800	85	40
Norway	8	83.0	20.8	9	34	2,000	2.4	59	260	1	240	5	500	80	49
Albania	3	2.0	0.7	1	40	150	7.5	4	40	12	50	2	220	90	10
Ireland	4	31.0	7.8	7	14	420	1.4	30	22	0	15	1	130	15	10
Cyprus (Greek)	3	1.7	3.4	5	12	100	5.9	8	35	4	40	2	250	6	1
Cyprus (Turkish)	2	0.4	2.0	4	3	6	1.5	2	6	0	12	1	12	0	0
Luxembourg	8	5.0	12.5	9	1	60	1.2	86	1	1	2	0	5	0	0
Malta	5	2.0	5.0	6	1	25	1.3	25	1	1	2	0	0	0	1
Iceland	3	6.0	30.0	8	1.1	5	0.1	50	1	0	1	0	0	0	7

NATIONS OF THE WORLD: AMERICAN NATIONS

Country	Rank	War State	Government's Stability	War Power	Attack Power	Total Quality	Nukes	Area of Sq. Kilometers (in thousands)	Percent of Arable Land	Transportation Net	Military Environment Index	Population (per sq. kilometer)	Population Total (in millions)	Percent of Literacy	Percent of Urban Dwellers	Average Life Expectancy
Averages & Totals		2	6	14,916	7,371	6	2	289,581	14	4	5	42	12,264	63	41	63
United States	1	2	9	1,000	800	43	9	9,166	20	9	3	27	250	99	74	76
Canada	2	1	9	44	22	34	5	9,858	5	3	5	3	27	99	75	77
Brazil	3	2	7	41	7	8	4	8,456	7	2	3	18	152	76	61	66
Cuba	4	6	6	37	7	15	2	111	23	6	3	99	11	98	60	73
Argentina	5	1	7	20	5	14	6	2,736	9	5	7	12	33	94	81	70
Chile	6	1	6	12	5	8	3	749	7	5	7	17	13	94	79	72
Colombia	7	3	7	8	2	6	2	1,039	4	3	3	32	33	88	65	66
Peru	8	2	6	7	2	4	3	1,280	3	2	4	17	22	80	63	63
Nicaragua	9	4	7	7	2	11	1	120	9	3	4	33	4	87	50	62
El Salvador	10	7	4	6	1	8	1	21	27	5	7	238	5	65	42	62
Mexico	11	1	8	6	2	3	4	1,923	12	4	5	46	88	89	64	70
Venezuela	12	1	8	3	1	4	3	882	3	3	6	23	20	85	75	70
Bolivia	13	1	4	1	0	2	1	1,084	3	2	4	6	7	62	39	54
Ecuador	14	1	6	1	0	1	2	277	6	2	3	40	11	86	42	66
Uruguay	15	1	6	1	0	2	2	174	8	6	7	17	3	94	83	71
Paraguay	16	1	5	0	0	2	1	397	20	2	5	13	5	81	40	69
Guatemala	17	3	6	0	0	1	1	108	12	4	4	93	10	50	36	61
Costa Rica	18	1	8	0	0	3	1	51	6	4	3	59	3	93	41	76
Honduras	19	3	6	0	0	1	1	112	14	4	6	45	5	56	31	65
Dominican Republic	20	1	7	0	0	1	1	48	23	4	5	167	8	74	47	62
Jamaica	21	1	7	0	0	2	1	11	19	5	8	273	3	74	41	76
Panama	22	1	7	0	0	1	1	76	6	4	7	39	3	90	54	73
Guyana	23	1	6	0	0	0	1	197	3	2	4	5	1	85	40	66
Trinidad	24	1	7	0	0	1	1	5	14	6	8	200	1	98	50	70
Haiti	25	2	2	0	0	0	1	28	20	1	5	214	6	23	24	55
Belize	26	1	7	0	0	1	1	23	2	2	5	9	0	92	50	70
Suriname	27	1	2	0	0	0	1	161	0	1	4	2	0	65	60	68

NATIONS OF THE WORLD: AMERICAN NATIONS

Country	Economic Profile				Military Capability								Army Profile		
	Industrialization Index	GDP (in billions)	Per Capita GDP (in billions)	Living Standard Index	Active Manpower (in thousands)	Military Budget (in millions)	Percent of GDP	Budget per Man (in thousands)	Reserve Forces (in thousands)	Paramilitary Forces (in thousands)	Mobilized Forces (in thousands)	Available Divisions	Armored Fighting Vehicles	Combat-Capable Aircraft	Tonnage of Ships (in thousands)
Averages & Totals	3	$40,613	$3.3	4	66,079	$1,501,009	3.7%	$23	64,559	59,035	89,567	3,363	742,878	96,049	30,747
United States	9	$5,000	$20.0	9	1,500	$180,000	3.6	$120	1,200	110	900	38	31,000	8,000	9,200
Canada	9	480	17.8	9	85	7,000	1.5	82	25	6	35	2	1,400	200	210
Brazil	6	320	2.1	4	320	2,400	0.8	8	500	240	300	18	1,400	230	180
Cuba	5	4	0.4	3	160	900	22.5	6	120	20	250	21	1,500	210	21
Argentina	6	75	2.3	4	90	900	1.2	10	340	27	150	6	1,100	180	170
Chile	6	20	1.5	4	90	800	4.0	9	100	27	150	6	600	90	150
Colombia	5	35	1.1	3	85	300	0.9	4	100	100	110	4	300	70	35
Peru	4	19	0.9	3	120	700	3.7	6	180	70	200	8	900	1,130	210
Nicaragua	3	2	0.5	3	40	150	7.5	4	30	2	50	4	200	18	1
El Salvador	3	4	0.8	2	50	180	4.5	4	20	20	40	4	100	90	1
Mexico	5	136	1.5	4	130	600	0.4	5	250	100	150	10	220	130	82
Venezuela	7	48	2.4	5	45	800	1.7	18	30	20	50	4	400	140	48
Bolivia	3	5	0.7	3	28	180	3.6	7	25	5	25	3	150	50	10
Ecuador	3	10	0.9	3	40	160	1.6	4	20	0	45	4	300	60	22
Uruguay	5	8	2.7	6	22	110	1.4	5	30	2	25	3	160	20	10
Paraguay	2	8	1.6	2	16	70	0.9	4	20	7	20	2	80	20	5
Guatemala	3	11	1.1	3	40	250	2.3	6	20	12	42	3	60	25	1
Costa Rica	4	5	1.7	3	9	30	0.6	3	6	0	12	1	2	2	1
Honduras	2	5	1.0	2	18	70	1.4	4	3	5	24	1	90	30	1
Dominican Republic	4	6	0.8	3	21	60	1.0	3	30	1	13	1	45	10	15
Jamaica	3	3	1.0	4	3	30	1.0	9	0	0	3	0	16	0	0
Panama	3	4	1.3	4	4	40	1.0	10	0	2	4	0	12	0	4
Guyana	0	0	0.4	2	6	50	12.5	8	0	2	5	0	6	0	1
Trinidad	5	4	4.0	5	3	50	1.3	17	0	0	2	0	0	0	2
Haiti	1	2	0.3	1	7	20	1.0	3	0	1	6	0	18	10	2
Belize	0	0	1.0	2	1	10	5.0	10	0	0	1	0	15	0	0
Suriname	1	1	2.5	3	3	30	3.0	10	0	1	3	0	30	0	1

Country	Rank	War State	Government's Stability	War Power	Attack Power	Total Quality	Nukes	Area of Sq. Kilometers (in thousands)	Percent of Arable Land	Transportation Net	Military Environment Index	Population (per sq. kilometer)	Population Total (in millions)	Percent of Literacy	Percent of Urban Dwellers	Average Life Expectancy
Averages & Totals		2	6	14,916	7,371	6	2	289,581	14	4	5	42	12,264	63	41	63
South Africa	1	4	8	65	29	42	6	1,221	10	4	5	33	40	55	48	63
Ethiopia	2	3	3	28	4	6	2	1,101	12	2	4	45	50	34	15	51
Nigeria	3	2	5	22	12	15	2	911	31	2	3	130	118	28	23	48
Angola	4	5	4	9	1	6	1	1,247	2	2	4	7	9	20	21	43
Zimbabwe	5	3	4	4	1	6	1	387	7	3	4	28	11	47	20	61
Tanzania	6	1	5	2	0	4	1	886	5	3	3	29	26	79	7	51
Kenya	7	1	6	2	0	6	1	569	3	5	6	44	25	47	10	61
Somalia	8	2	3	2	0	2	2	627	2	1	5	14	9	60	9	53
Uganda	9	3	1	1	0	2	1	200	23	3	4	85	17	52	7	50
Senegambia	10	1	5	1	0	5	2	202	25	3	6	45	9	11	33	50
Chad	11	5	3	1	0	4	1	1,259	2	1	6	4	5	16	14	39
Mozambique	12	4	4	1	0	1	1	784	4	1	3	19	15	14	8	46
Zaire	13	2	3	0	0	1	1	2,268	3	4	2	15	35	42	30	52
Ghana	14	1	5	0	0	3	1	230	5	1	4	65	15	30	31	59
Cameroon	15	2	5	0	0	2	1	469	13	2	3	23	11	65	25	50
Madagascar	16	1	5	0	0	1	1	582	4	2	5	21	12	52	14	51
Guinea-Bissau	17	1	5	0	0	1	1	28	9	1	4	36	1	15	?	45
Gabon	18	1	6	0	0	4	1	258	1	2	5	4	1	65	32	52
Ivory Coast	19	1	6	0	0	1	2	318	9	3	4	38	12	24	32	53

#	Country														
20	Mali	1	4	0	1	1	1,220	2	1	5	7	9	10	17	45
21	Niger	1	4	0	2	1	1,267	3	1	4	6	8	8	6	49
22	Rwanda	1	4	0	1	1	26	43	1	7	231	6	30	?	51
23	Liberia	1	5	0	1	1	96	1	2	5	31	3	20	28	54
24	Guinea	1	5	0	0	1	246	6	2	5	28	7	48	9	42
25	Burkina Faso	1	2	0	0	1	274	10	1	7	33	9	7	11	47
26	Congo	1	3	0	0	1	342	2	2	4	9	3	80	40	56
27	Zambia	2	3	0	0	1	741	7	2	5	11	8	53	43	55
28	Sierra Leone	1	5	0	1	1	72	23	2	5	56	4	15	18	44
29	Burundi	1	4	0	0	1	25	29	5	4	280	7	38	5	51
30	Djibouti	1	6	0	1	1	22	0	2	7	18	0	20	65	47
31	Namibia	1	6	0	0	1	805	2	1	3	1	1	69	15	50
32	Botswana	1	7	0	1	1	585	2	1	6	2	1	33	12	59
33	Mauretania	1	3	0	0	1	1,030	1	3	5	2	2	17	23	45
34	Togo	1	5	0	0	1	54	25	1	4	74	4	18	15	55
35	Equatorial Guinea	1	5	0	1	1	28	5	3	2	14	0	55	15	46
36	Malawi	1	2	0	0	1	94	25	1	5	96	9	25	10	48
37	Central African Republic	1	2	0	0	1	623	3	1	7	5	3	20	20	46
38	Benin	1	5	0	0	1	111	12	4	6	45	5	11	14	49
39	Lesotho	2	7	0	1	1	30	10	3	9	67	2	66	6	60
40	Swaziland	1	6	0	0	1	17	8	3	7	59	1	69	15	50
41	Cape Verde Island	1	6	0	0	1	4	9	2	8	100	0	37	20	61
42	Seychelles	1	6	0	0	1	1	4	2	8	200	0	60	37	71
43	Comoro Island	1	2	0	0	0	2	35	2	8	250	1	15	?	56
44	São Tomé & Príncipe Island	1	6	0	1	1	1	1	2	5	100	0	55	?	68

Nations of the World: African Nations

Country	Economic Profile				Military Capability							Army Profile			
	Industrialization Index	GDP (in billions)	Per Capita GDP (in billions)	Living Standard Index	Active Manpower (in thousands)	Military Budget (in millions)	Percent of GDP	Budget per Man (in thousands)	Reserve Forces (in thousands)	Paramilitary Forces (in thousands)	Mobilized Forces (in thousands)	Available Divisions	Armored Fighting Vehicles	Combat-Capable Aircraft	Tonnage of Ships (in thousands)
Averages & Totals	3	$40,613	$3.3	4	66,079	$1,501,009	3.7%	$23	64,559	59,035	89,567	3,363	742,878	96,049	30,747
South Africa	7	$85	$2.1	4	100	$3,600	4.2	$36	450	130	300	18	5,000	340	38
Ethiopia	2	5	0.1	1	300	400	8.0	1	100	150	300	24	1,500	150	8
Nigeria	3	77	0.7	2	95	300	0.4	3	10	20	110	4	750	80	40
Angola	1	5	0.6	1	90	800	16.0	9	0	300	110	7	900	155	6
Zimbabwe	3	6	0.5	2	45	350	5.8	8	20	21	55	7	200	55	0
Tanzania	1	5	0.2	1	40	210	4.2	5	10	2	42	4	150	21	2
Kenya	3	9	0.4	1	22	220	2.4	10	0	2	19	2	160	60	1
Somalia	0	2	0.2	1	60	100	5.0	2	25	10	70	1	800	60	3
Uganda	0	4	0.2	1	32	120	3.0	4	0	0	32	7	50	0	0
Senegambia	3	2	0.2	1	10	100	5.0	10	0	4	11	2	100	12	2
Chad	0	1	0.2	1	12	40	4.0	3	8	5	15	1	60	4	0
Mozambique	1	1	0.1	1	35	110	11.0	3	12	24	36	1	450	60	2
Zaire	2	5	0.1	1	50	60	1.2	1	0	30	25	4	200	26	1
Ghana	3	6	0.4	2	10	60	1.0	6	0	3	11	4	80	10	3
Cameroon	1	12	1.1	1	8	150	1.3	19	10	4	8	1	80	14	2
Madagascar	1	2	0.2	1	21	35	1.8	2	5	7	20	1	60	12	3
Guinea-Bissau	0	0	0.2	1	9	15	7.5	2	0	2	7	0	90	0	0
Gabon	2	3	3.0	3	3	60	2.0	20	0	5	3	0	70	14	1
Ivory Coast	3	10	0.8	3	7	90	0.9	13	12	7	11	0	50	6	2

Country	C1	C2	C3	C4	C5	C6	C7	C8	C9	C10	C11	C12	C13	C14	C15
Mali	0	2	0.2	1	7.00	60	3.0	9	3	6	10	1	110	25	0
Niger	0	2	0.3	1	3.00	15	0.8	5	2	3	5	0	60	0	0
Rwanda	0	1	0.2	1	6.00	40	4.0	7	0	2	6	1	25	2	0
Liberia	2	1	0.3	1	5.00	30	3.0	6	12	3	7	1	12	0	2
Guinea	1	2	0.3	1	10.00	80	4.0	8	6	9	12	0	120	6	3
Burkina Faso	0	1	0.1	1	9.00	50	5.0	6	0	1	7	0	90	0	0
Congo	0	2	0.7	1	9.00	60	3.0	7	0	3	8	1	200	18	1
Zambia	1	2	0.3	1	16.00	65	3.3	4	0	1	15	0	120	50	0
Sierra Leone	1	1	0.3	1	3.00	8	0.8	3	0	1	3	0	12	0	1
Burundi	0	2	0.3	3	6.00	45	2.3	8	0	2	5	0	60	3	0
Djibouti	3	0	0.7	1	3.00	40	13.3	13	2	1	4	0	40	0	0
Namibia	1	1	0.8	2	6.00	15	1.5	3	0	2	2	0	40	0	0
Botswana	2	2	2.0	1	3.00	25	1.3	8	5	1	3	0	50	5	0
Mauretania	0	0	0.5	1	11.00	15	1.5	1	0	6	14	1	100	6	1
Togo	1	1	0.3	1	6.00	30	3.0	5	0	1	5	0	90	12	0
Equatorial Guinea	0	0	0.3	1	2.00	5	5.0	3	2	2	1	0	20	0	0
Malawi	1	1	0.1		5.00	22	2.2	5		1	6		40	0	0
Central African Republic	0	1	0.3	1	4.00	20	2.0	5	0	2	4	0	30	0	0
Benin	0	1	0.2	1	4.00	50	5.0	13	2	2	5	0	40	0	0
Lesotho	0	1	0.3	1	1.00	5	1.0	5	0	5	1	0	0	0	0
Swaziland	1	1	1.0	1	1.00	4	0.4	4	1	1	2	0	0	0	0
Cape Verde Island	1	0	0.5		1	5	2.5	5	0	0	1	0	8	0	1
Seychelles	0	0	2.0	3	1.00	11	5.5	11	1	1	2	0	15	0	2
Comoro Island	0	0	0.4	1	1.00	5	2.5	5	0	0	1	0	0	0	1
São Tomé & Principe Island	0	0	0.4	1	0.20	1	2.5	5	1	0	1	0	0	0	0

revolutionary. Yet if war is a matter of degree, than there are few nations in the world capable of getting a proper war going. For the remainder, any action is basically large-scale police work.

NOTES ON THE CONFLICTS

For those who are not keen on numerical analysis, what follows is a brief comment (in alphabetical order) on each nation covered in the chart.

Afghanistan—No ability to go much beyond its own borders because of the civil war left in the wake of the Russian withdrawal. Even after the civil war is settled, Afghanistan will continue to pose no major threat to its neighbors, except for unpredictable raids by one of the many continually warring factions. Alexander the Great encountered this 2,500 years ago, which goes to show you that there are some things that are consistent in history.

Albania—Too small, too obsessed with internal order, and surrounded by stronger powers. Major military threat beyond its borders is official or unofficial support to ethnic Albanian populations in neighboring countries.

Algeria—Islamic fundamentalists taking over, economy a mess, and the military in disarray.

Angola—Peace with South Africa still leaving the civil war unresolved. Cubans are gradually leaving, along with Russian aid.

Argentina—Still suffering the aftereffects (low morale and reduced budgets) of its 1982 defeat by Britain in the Falklands War. Slowly rebuilding.

Australia—Beset by economic problems, and the lack of any immediate threat, its armed forces slowly fading away.

Austria—Officially neutral since the 1950s, and now without a Warsaw Pact threat. Not likely to increase its forces.

Bahrain—Threatened by Iraq and Iran, friendly to U.S. forces and likely to increase its own.

Bangladesh—Poverty-stricken and without any armed threats except from within.

Belgium—Never quite able to meet all of its NATO commitments, now retrenching in the face of the nonexistent Warsaw Pact threat.

Belize—Long-standing tension with Guatemala (which claims Belize as a "lost province") producing avid attention to military matters and ties with Great Britain.

Benin—Poor African nation with no active external enemies.

Bhutan—Poverty-stricken monarchy on India's northern border. Nominal defense forces and no disputes with anyone.

Bolivia—Long-festering dispute with Chile over lost access to ocean. Too poor to create an armed force that can do anything about it. Military activity is largely against internal opposition.

Botswana—Poor, landlocked African nation with minor border disputes with neighbors. Insignificant armed forces.

Brazil—The major military power in South America. Minor border disputes with Paraguay and Uruguay.

Britain—Domestic economic problems and the disappearance of the Warsaw Pact have created a decline in force levels.

Brunei—Incredibly rich oil state surrounded by Malaysia. No disputes with larger neighbor, but protected by British Ghurka mercenaries.

Bulgaria—Fear of the Turks, and a weakening of its traditional Russian "protector," likely to keep the military in a strong bargaining position.

Burkina Faso—Landlocked and poor, has internal strife and not much military power.

Burma—Poor nation ruled by junta and beset by many internal disputes. No disputes with neighbors.

Burundi—Poor and landlocked, has no external disputes. Major conflict between majority Hutu people and militarily stronger minority Tutsi.

Cambodia—Fifteen-year-old civil war continuing with central government still supported by Vietnam.

Cameroon—Minor border disputes with neighbors, little internal unrest. Nominal armed forces.

Canada—With nominal armed forces, relying on U.S. fleet for protection from any potential threats.

Cape Verde Island—Nominal armed forces, no internal or external disputes.

Central African Republic—Poor and landlocked, has no external disputes but some internal ones. Nominal armed forces.

Chad—Has ongoing civil war, partially fomented by Libya, with some factions supported by France. Weak central government.

Chile—Strong economy, democratic government, efficient military tradition, but shrinking armed forces because of lack of internal or external threat.

China—Increasing unrest, but 1980s decision to shrink (and modernize) armed forces still under way. Priority still on economic development.

Colombia—Armed forces partially corrupted by drug traffickers. Paramilitary forces steadily increasing to fight drug lords. Endemic internal disorder for last forty years.

Comoro Island—Minor dispute with France, but otherwise a militarily insignificant ministate.

Congo—Minor dispute with Zaire over border, minor internal opposition. Nominal armed forces.

Costa Rica—No armed forces, only paramilitary troops. No internal or external disputes.

Cuba—Large armed forces, declining economy, no external threats (except the imagined U.S. one), and growing internal opposition.

Cyprus (Greek)—Heavily armed Greek portion of Cyprus, faces Turkish forces in other part of island.

Cyprus (Turkish)—Same as Greek Cyprus.

Czechoslovakia—No external threats. Internal dispute between Czechs and the third of the population that are Slovaks. Declining armed forces due to demise of Warsaw Pact.

Denmark—No external or internal threats. Declining armed forces due to demise of Warsaw Pact.

Djibouti—Dispute with Somalia over border and Somali nomads. Strong ties with France and basically under French protection.

Dominican Republic—No external disputes, low-level internal dissent. Weak armed forces.

Ecuador—Minor dispute with Peru, internal disorder. Lackluster armed forces.

Egypt—Long-standing disputes with Sudan and Libya, minor internal disorder. Militarily professional and good at getting the most out of a low budget.

El Salvador—Has ongoing civil war.

Equatorial Guinea—Minor dispute with Gabon, weak economy, and low-level internal disputes. Lackluster armed forces.

Ethiopia—Has ongoing civil war.

Finland—Neutral and well prepared to defend it.

France—Well-diversified armed forces, from strategic nuclear missiles to intervention forces.

Gabon—Minor dispute with Equatorial Guinea and some internal disputes.

Germany—Newly unified, military will be smaller than former West German armed forces. Most professional and effective armed forces in Europe.

Ghana—Ongoing internal disputes, above average (for Africa) armed forces.

Greece—Major military objective is preparation for a war with Turkey, which Greece has little chance of winning.

Guatemala—Claims Belize, but lacks the military force to take it. Much internal dissent.

Guinea—Very poor nation with equally poor armed forces.

Guinea-Bissau—Very poor nation with equally poor armed forces.

Guyana—Disputes with Venezuela and Suriname. Nominal armed forces.

Haiti—Very poor nation traditionally run by armed forces (which are good for little beyond oppressing Haitians).

Honduras—Some disputes with neighbors, quite a bit of internal dissent. Armed forces oriented toward suppressing insurgency.

Hungary—Downsizing and restructuring its armed forces in the face of the demise of the Warsaw Pact. Also, growing potential for war with Romania over a territorial dispute.

Iceland—Nominal armed forces, depends on United States.

India—Regional superpower, with lots of good infantry, some tanks, and a few nukes.

Indonesia—Sundry minor disputes with numerous island neighbors, plus some serious internal unrest. Armed forces largely paramilitary.

Iran—Demobilized after disastrous war with Iraq in the 1980s. Rebuilding forces on a more professional model. Still faces substantial internal problems and possible renewal of war with Iraq.

Iraq—So-so armed forces and lots of internal and external enemies.

Ireland—Nominal armed forces, no real foreign or internal threats.

Israel—Armed to the teeth and very good at combat. Forces lose their edge after many years of inaction, but not as quickly as hostile neighbors in the same situation. Biggest problem is internal, with Arab population.

Italy—Conscript-based forces, with many professional segments. Shrinking in the face of the end of the Cold War.

Ivory Coast—No local and few internal disputes. Somewhat above average armed forces for Africa.

Jamaica—Very small, but professional armed forces. No external, but a few internal, disputes.

Japan—Well-trained and lavishly equipped forces. Without nuclear weapons, not likely to cause neighboring China or Russia any trouble.

Jordan—Small, but professional armed forces. Not as good as they used to be, but still a cut above all the neighbors (except Israel).

Kenya—Increasing internal disputes putting the military's traditional professionalism to the test.

Korea, North—Armed forces well-trained and -equipped and likely to follow orders (at least initially). The country is in danger of political upheaval, which the military may not be able to handle.

Korea, South—Similar to North Korean forces, with somewhat more modern equipment. More politically reliable, if only because the South is a functioning democracy.

Kuwait—Forces crushed by Iraq in mid-1990, rebuilt in Saudi Arabia and slated for expansion in the future.

Laos—Landlocked backwater with lackluster armed forces and not much to fight over.

Lebanon—Has ongoing civil war.

Lesotho—Minimal armed forces, depends on South Africa for defense and its very existence.

Liberia—Has endemic civil war.

Libya—Lavishly equipped but ineptly trained and led armed forces. Continually interferes with neighbors.

Luxembourg—Minimal armed forces, depends on its neighbors.

Madagascar—Island nation disputing ownership of some nearby islands with France. Minimal armed forces.

Malawi—Landlocked and poor, not much military power.

Malaysia—Some disputes with its neighbors of several island groups.

Maldives—Island microstate without much to worry about. Minor dispute over some nearby islands.

Mali—Landlocked and poverty-stricken, not much for the military to do.

Malta—Small island state in strategic position, so theoretical threat from Libya.

Mauritania—Long-standing hostility with Senegal possibly serious, although neither side could really afford it.

Mauritius—Small island state without much need for armed forces.

Mexico—Too small to take on the United States up north and much larger than any neighbors to the south. Armed forces thus nominal.

Mongolia—Caught between China and Russia, thus only minimal armed forces.

Morocco—Ongoing war with separatists in the western Sahara. One of the better armed forces in the area.

Mozambique—Has ongoing civil war.

Nepal—Has ongoing internal unrest. Government reluctant to use too much force.

Netherlands—Small but professional military. Scheduled to become smaller with the end of the Warsaw Pact.

New Zealand—Steadily shrinking armed forces. No one in the area to use them on.

Nicaragua—Even with the settlement of the civil war, military remains relatively large but not terribly efficient. Primary objective is internal politics.

Niger—Landlocked and poor, has border dispute with Libya.

Nigeria—Military superpower in the region. Lots of quantity, some quality. Threat of another civil war (last one in the 1960s).

Norway—Small but efficient forces, backed by a large body of trained reserves.

Oman—Uses a lot of mercenaries, has the money to pay for it.

Pakistan—Has fairly large, fairly professional forces, faced with many internal threats and one major external one (India).

Panama—Civil disorder in the wake of the U.S. 1989 invasion. Only armed forces are primarily paramilitary.

Papua–New Guinea—Much of the population is Stone Age, nominal military.

Paraguay—Landlocked and caught between much larger nations. Low quantity and quality of forces result.

Peru—Beset by internal problems, armed forces organized to deal with them.

Philippines—No external enemies, but plenty of internal ones. Armed forces reflect this.

Poland—Breakup of the Warsaw Pact led to shrinking of the Army. Morale was low through the 1980s because of internal political strife. Still afraid of Germans and Russians.

Portugal—Big shrinkage after decolonialization of 1970s. Not much rebuilding since.

Qatar—Another Persian Gulf ministate trying to purchase the best defense that money can buy.

Romania—Never very efficient in the best of times, has gotten much worse since the fall of the Communist government in 1989. Still faces possible conflict with Hungary over Transylvania.

Russia—Massive arms reductions from 1990 treaties; major morale problems; and declines in defense industry efficiency and military budget. A shadow of what it was in the 1980s, but still formidable, and large.

Rwanda—Similar to Burundi, with constant violence between Hutus and Tutsis, except here the Hutus are in charge.

São Tomé and Príncipe—Island ministate, of no military significance.

Saudi Arabia—Has ancient warrior tradition, but still trying to master the skills of modern soldiering.

Senegambia—Senegalese troops had a good reputation in the French service during the colonial period. Armed forces a cut above neighboring forces.

Seychelles Island—Island ministate not much interested in military affairs.

Sierra Leone—Poor, no important internal or external threats. No military power.

Singapore—Small city-state, disproportionately large and efficient armed forces. Robust economy worth defending.

Somalia—Traditional warriors, have not yet mastered modern warfare. Disputes with all neighbors as well as internal strife. Never a dull moment.

South Africa—Regional superpower. Modern and efficient army, navy, air force, and paramilitary. Probably has nukes. Much internal strife, but no neighbors that are a threat.

Spain—Relatively small but gradually modernizing forces. No external threats, although some internal strife.

Sri Lanka—Has ongoing civil war.

Sudan—Has ongoing civil war.

Suriname—Has ongoing civil strife.

Swaziland—Poor, under the thumb of South Africa. Some internal strife.

Sweden—Small country, large economy, powerful reserve based armed forces. A longtime neutral and successful at it.

Switzerland—Same drill as Sweden.

Syria—Police state at odds with all its neighbors and full of internal strife. Military of questionable efficiency against competent opponent (as in Israel).

Taiwan—Losers in the 1940s Chinese civil war. Man for man, one of the best armed forces in the region. Some internal strife, still claims rule of mainland China, but unlikely to go to war over it.

Tanzania—Minor border disputes, otherwise undistinguished military power.

Thailand—Serious border problems with Cambodia, some internal strife. Armed forces tend toward corruption and lackadaisical performance.

Togo—No significant internal or external threats. Not much in the way of armed forces either.

Trinidad—Island ministate with nominal armed forces.

Tunisia—No internal or external threats. Reasonably efficient, but small armed forces.

Turkey—Some internal strife, some disputes with neighbors, but has sufficiently efficient armed forces to handle just about any situation. Probably still the strongest (potential) Muslim military power.

Uganda—Has ongoing civil strife.

United Arab Emirates—Collection of ministates in the Persian Gulf that buys the best defense it can.

United States—With the decline of Russia's military effectiveness, now the premier world military power.

Uruguay—Surrounded by larger nations, has basically token armed forces whose main task is keeping the population in line.

Venezuela—No serious internal or external threats, competent armed forces for the region.

Vietnam—Very poor, has internal strife and hostile neighbors (particularly China). Lots of combat experience in ill-equipped (but large) armed forces.

Yemen—Just finished one civil war, and may now be headed for another. Hostile to its large (but less populous) neighbor Saudi Arabia. Lots of warriors but not a lot of well-trained soldiers. Poor.

Yugoslavia—Large armed forces, good fighters, lurching into civil war.

Zaire—Poor and corrupt, has internal and external strife. Armed forces largely for keeping population in line.

Zambia—Poor, doesn't have many internal or external enemies. Nominal armed forces.

Zimbabwe—One of the better-run nations in Africa. Small armed forces have no chance against more efficient troops in neighboring South Africa.

DATA AND SOURCES

Analysts have to be better than their data. The authors and their researcher, Al Nofi, found five different GDPs for Zaire. That's all right—Zaire probably doesn't know what its GDP was. We used an averaged figure. In December 1983 we found published aggregate foreign-debt estimates for the Philippines that ranged from $17 billion to over $25 billion. That's a difference of more than 40 percent. The figures are suspect, but both indicate that the Philippines has a severe debt problem.

Many of the numbers have gone through the wash and come out scrubbed. They are not, however, squeaky clean. They are colored by the authors' interpretation. We have no doubt made some mistakes in interpretation, but the intent was always to try to penetrate the statistics. Governments, especially dictatorships, purposely lie to their people and the world. That is part of their survival strategy. Even governments in open societies regularly mislead their people. This is called politics or public relations.

Our sources of information are many. There are the obvious ones: *International Defense Review, Janes Defence Weekly, Aviation Week & Space Technology, International Security, Time* magazine, *U.S. News and World Report, The New York Times, The Washington Post, The Wall Street Journal, The Christian Science Monitor, The Economist, Oil and Gas Journal, Le Monde, Die Zeit, Stern,* and a half dozen others.

Some sources are not so obvious: *Focus, The Jerusalem Post, The Week in Germany,* and many other newsletters or international reports. We did not use a scrap of classified evidence or data, though no doubt censors would scream if they found out what a good library can provide. We have also used information provided by Afghan resistance groups, transcripts from *The MacNeil/Lehrer Report,* sources provided by dissidents, propaganda provided by governments. We made use of the U.S. State Department's *Background Notes* series, *Facts on File,* and *Fiche du Monde Arabe.*

The real sources of this book lie in what we'll call "deep background." Machiavelli's *The Prince* and Von Clausewitz's *On War* are vital to any adequate understanding of power politics. Both theorists have aged well. Their books are utilized by today's power politicians.

Other useful references include Hyams's *Soil and Civilization,* Tuchman's *A Distant Mirror,* Newbigin's *Geographical Aspects of Balkan Problems* (a work of genius and apparently out of print since 1915), Liddell Hart's *Strategy,* Thucydides's *The Peloponnesian War,* Fuller's *The Foundations of the Science of War,* White's *Metahistory,* Chomsky's *Language and Responsibility,* Said's *Orientalism,* and Fall's *Street Without Joy.*

INDEX